ISBN 978-1-331-07007-8
PIBN 10140855

This book is a reproduction of an important historical work. Forgotten Books uses
state-of-the-art technology to digitally reconstruct the work, preserving the original format
whilst repairing imperfections present in the aged copy. In rare cases, an imperfection in
the original, such as a blemish or missing page, may be replicated in our edition. We do,
however, repair the vast majority of imperfections successfully; any imperfections that
remain are intentionally left to preserve the state of such historical works.

1 MONTH OF FREE READING

at

www.ForgottenBooks.com

By purchasing this book you are eligible for one month membership to ForgottenBooks.com, giving you unlimited access to our entire collection of over 700,000 titles via our web site and mobile apps.

To claim your free month visit:

www.forgottenbooks.com/free140855

Similar Books Are Available from
www.forgottenbooks.com

COHELETH,

COMMONLY CALLED

THE BOOK OF ECCLESIASTES:

𝔗𝔯𝔞𝔫𝔰𝔩𝔞𝔱𝔢𝔡 𝔣𝔯𝔬𝔪 𝔱𝔥𝔢 𝔒𝔯𝔦𝔤𝔦𝔫𝔞𝔩 𝔥𝔢𝔟𝔯𝔢𝔴,

WITH A

COMMENTARY, HISTORICAL AND CRITICAL.

BY

CHRISTIAN D. GINSBURG.

Βλέπομεν γὰρ ἄρτι δι᾽ ἐςόπτρου ἐν αἰνίγματι,
τότε δὲ πρόςωπον πρὸς πρόςωπον. — 1 Cor. xiii. 12.

PRINTED BY D. MARPLES, LIVERPOOL.

TO

MY FATHER-IN-LAW,

WILLIAM CROSFIELD, ESQ.,

THIS WORK

IS AFFECTIONATELY INSCRIBED.

CONTENTS.

PREFACE.

THE present is another volume of the five Megiloth upon which I undertook to comment. The notes are more extensive than those upon the Song of Songs — 1. Because I have endeavoured to trace more fully the connection of Biblical Exegesis in its four great epochs — to shew what influence the Versions of antiquity, belonging to the first epoch, had upon the Mediæval Expositors of the second; how far, again, these ancient Versions and the Jewish Commentators of the Middle Ages of the first two epochs have influenced the Translations of the Reformers in the third epoch; and how much Modern Criticism, forming the fourth epoch, is indebted to the former epochs; and 2. Because, in tracing the historic connection, with the original sources before me, I have found that commentators of high rank have frequently both misquoted and mistranslated the ancients, and especially the Hebrew writers, to such an extent as might hardly have been credited had not the originals accompanied my translations.[1] I trust that the translation of the important Chaldee Paraphrase, the collation of the inestimable but neglected Syriac Version with the original, and the discovery

---

[1] Compare, for instance, the flagrant errors of Hugh Broughton, p. 118; Dr. Gill, p. 175; Hävernick, Keil, and Stuart, p. 12; Preston, Appendix III.

of the Version from which Coverdale made his translation, given in the Appendices, will be found acceptable contributions to Biblical Literature.

I embrace this opportunity of acknowledging my obligations to my friend, the Rev. W. C. STALLYBRASS, for kind assistance occasionally rendered; and to Mr. DAVID MARPLES, the printer, who has manifested more than a professional interest in this volume, and to whose care and good taste the correctness of the work is largely indebted.

If the Commentary now presented to the public should throw any light upon the acknowledged obscurities of the book, or if the exhibition of the various and conflicting views propounded by the pious and the learned should lower the offensive tone of dogmatisers, I shall esteem it a sufficient reward for the seven years' labour bestowed upon it.

10, RAKE LANE, LIVERPOOL,
        July, 1861.

INTRODUCTION.

SECTION I.—TITLE OF THE BOOK, AND ITS SIGNIFICATION.

THIS book is called in Hebrew קֹהֶלֶת *Coheleth*, the appellation which its hero gives himself. This term occurs seven times in the book; three times in the beginning (i. 1. 2. 12), three times at the end (xii. 8. 9. 10), and once in the middle (vii. 27) of it. That it is not a proper name, but *an appellative*, is evident from its having the article in xii. 8, and especially from its being construed with a feminine verb in vii. 27. It is generally agreed that *Solomon* is described by this designation, as David *had no other son* who was King of Israel in Jerusalem; *vide* i. 1. 12.

The precise signification of this appellation has, from time immemorial, been a matter of great contention, and the occasion of numerous and most conflicting opinions. According to its form קֹהֶלֶת is participle active feminine, Kal, from קָהַל, kindred with קוֹל, Greek καλέω, Latin *calo*, and our English word *call;* it signifies primarily *to call*, then *to call together, to assemble, to collect.* Like דִּבֵּר, כֹּזֵב, נֹגֵן, קֹוֶה, שֹׁחֵר, this participle is the only instance in which *the Kal* is used; but the sense is easily ascertained from the other conjugations. As the Niphal נִקְהַל, *i. e.* the passive of Kal, means *to be called, to be collected together* (Exod. xxxii. 1; Levit. viii. 4; Numb. xvi. 3; xvii. 7; Josh. xviii. 1; xxii. 12 *al.*), קֹהֶלֶת the Kal part. act. fem. means *congregatrix*, bie Verſammelnbe, bie Verſammlerin, *collectress, female gatherer.*

Now the difficulty consists in determining three questions,

B

viz., what did Solomon collect? why does he bear this name
here? and how came it to be in *the feminine gender?*

i. As to the first question, namely, *what* did Solomon collect?
we submit that a reference to the passages where the verb קָהַל
occurs, either in Niphal (Exod. xxxii. 1; Levit. viii. 4; Numb.
xvi. 3; xvii. 7; xx. 2; Josh. xviii. 1; xxii. 12; Judg. xx. 1;
2 Sam. xx. 14; 1 Kings viii. 2; 2 Chron. v. 3; xx. 26; Esth.
viii. 11, ix. 2. 15. 16. 18; Jerem. xxvi. 9; Ezek. xxxviii. 7); or
Hiphil (Exod. xxxv. 1; Levit. viii. 3; Numb. i. 18; viii. 9;
x. 7; xvi. 19; xx. 8. 10; Deut. iv. 10; xxxi. 12. 28;
1 Kings viii. 1; xii. 21; 1 Chron. xiii. 5; xv. 3; xxviii. 1;
2 Chron. v. 2; xi. 1; Ezek. xxxviii. 13; Job xi. 10); shews
beyond a doubt that it is *invariably* used for collecting or
gathering *persons*, especially for religious purposes. So also its
derivatives, קָהָל ,קְהִלָּה, מַקְהֵלִים and מַקְהֵלוֹת, *without exception* denote assemblies or gatherings *of people.* The natural
signification of קֹהֶלֶת therefore is, *an assembler of scattered
people into the more immediate presence of God; a gatherer of
those afar off unto God;* and we retain the literal meaning of
assembler, gatherer.[1]

ii. From this definition of *Coheleth,* the second question, viz.,
why Solomon bears this title here? is easily answered. He
has it *because it is descriptive of the design of the book,* and
because it connects his labours here with his work recorded in
1 Kings viii. Solomon, who is there described *as gathering*
(יַקְהֵל) the people to hold communion with the Most High in
the place which he erected for this purpose, is here again represented as *the gatherer* (קֹהֶלֶת) of the same people, who, through
inexplicable difficulties and perplexities in the moral government of God, loosened their ties, and were in danger of becoming
totally detached from that community.

---

[1] So also Aquila, συναθροιστής; Symmachus παριμιαστής; Midrash Yalkut, Eccles.
i. 1; Rambach, Notæ uberiores in Ecclesiasten, contained in the second volume
of Michaelis, Notæ uberiores, p. 828; Van der Palm, Ecclesiastes philologice et
critice illustratus, Lugd. Batav., 1784, p. 50, &c.; Wangemann, Der Prediger
Salomonis, Berlin, 1856, p. 44.

Before we proceed to the examination of the third question, we shall review the different modes in which these two questions have been propounded.

1. One of the traditional opinions given in the Midrash Rabba is that קֹהֶלֶת means *preacher*, and that Solomon obtained this name *because his discourses were delivered before* (קָהָל) *the congregation.*[1] But—1. The verb קָהַל does not at all include the idea of *preaching*; 2. The explanation *preacher* ascribes an office to Solomon which is nowhere mentioned in the Scriptures. The appeal to xii. 9, where we are told that Coheleth "*taught the people wisdom*," no more proves Solomon to have been a preacher, than a reference to Deut. iv. 5, where we are told that Moses *taught the people* the divine institutions, or to Deut. xi. 19, where the Israelites are commanded *to teach their children*, would prove *that they were preachers*. The phrase לִמֵּד דַּעַת simply means *to impart knowledge, to inform*, irrespective of the way in which it is done (comp. Is. xl. 14); and the passage in xii. 9 would never have been forced into that far-fetched sense, if it had not been for want of proof that *Coheleth* means *preacher*. 3. The title *preacher* is too modern, and quite inconsistent with the book itself; since iv. 17, and almost all the succeeding appeals, which are in *the singular number*, "Keep *thy* foot when *thou* goest," &c., shew that these discourses *were not delivered before an assembly of people*, as the Midrash and others will have it. 4. This explanation entirely destroys the connection between the design of the book and the import of the symbolic name Coheleth, which, according to our interpretation, is very obvious.

2. We are told that *Coheleth* means *gatherer* or *acquirer of wisdom*, and Solomon is called by this name *because he gathered or acquired much wisdom*, just as he is called elsewhere

---

[1] Midrash Rabba, שהיו דבריו נאמרין בקהל, Eccles. i. 1; hence the Sept. ἐκκλησιαστής; the Vulg. *ecclesiastes*; and St. Jerome's explanation, ἐκκλησιαστής *Græco sermone appellatur qui coetum, i. e., ecclesiam congregat.*, Comment. *in loco ;* Luther, Coverdale, the Geneva Version, the Authorised Version, and many modern commentators.

" gatherer son of Jakeh " (Prov. xxx. 1), *because he gathered or acquired all* the wisdom, and gave it out again.[1] As offshoots of this must be regarded the two following interpretations: —

3. *Collector, compiler*, and that Solomon is so called *because he collected together in this book diversified experience and various views and maxims for the good of mankind.*[2]

4. *Eclectic*, ἐκλεκτικός, a name given to Solomon by his father or teacher, *because of his skill in selecting and purifying, from the systems of different philosophers, the accumulation of sentiments contained in this book;* just as the great philosopher, whose original name was Aristocles, was by his teacher called Plato, in consequence of the fluency of his speech or the comeliness of his person.[3]

5. Coheleth means *accumulated wisdom*, and this appellation was given to Solomon *because wisdom was accumulated in him.*[4] But all these interpretations are alike contrary to the signification of קָהֵל, which never means *to gather* THINGS, or *to compile*, but invariably denotes *to gather* PEOPLE, *to convene an assembly.* The view mentioned in No. 3 incurs the additional censure of regarding this book as *a compilation* of different sayings and maxims, whereas it is a regular treatise upon a definite subject, and each part of it gradually develops the design of the author; and the view given in No. 5 is contrary to the grammatical form of קהלת which is *the active* participle, and can therefore not be taken in *a passive* sense.

6. It means *the reunited, the gathered soul*, and *it describes Solomon's re-admission into the Church, in consequence of his*

---

[1] Rashi על שקיהל חכמות הרבה וכן במקום אחר קוראו אגור בן יקה שאגר כל החכמה והקיאה ; and also Rashbam *in loco.*

[2] Grotius, Annot. ad Ecclesiat. i. 1; Mayer, A Commentary upon the holy writings of Job, David, and Solomon, p. 771; Mendelssohn, Commentary on Ecclesiastes, translated by Theod. Preston, London, 1845, p. 130; Friedländer, Der Prediger, Berlin, 1788, p. 91; Heinemann, Uebersetzung des Koheleth, Berlin, 1831, p. 3.

[3] Rosenthal, Koheleth, übersetzt nebst einem ebräischen Commentar, Prag., 1858, p. 17.

[4] Ibn Ezra, נקרא כן על לשון החכמה שנקהלה בו.

repentance; and the first verse we are told ought to be translated, " The words of the soul, or person congregated or gathered unto the church or congregation of saints, viz. of the son of David, King in Jerusalem." [1] This explanation owes its origin to the last-mentioned view, and is guilty of the same violation of grammar, viz., assigning to the *active* participle קֹהֶלֶת *a passive* sense.

7. It means *the penitent,*[2] and describes the contrite state of Solomon's heart for his apostacy. But, apart from the fact that even the Arabic word קהל, which is appealed to for this meaning of the Hebrew קֹהֶלֶת, cannot be made to bear this sense ; recourse to a cognate language, in order to assign an anomalous signification to a frequently occurring and well defined expression, must always be deprecated. Besides, this interpretation is utterly at variance with the book itself, since there is not a single passage in it which, according to its plain sense, can be construed into *a confession of sin,* or taken as the language of *a repenting and contrite heart,* denouncing sin as *a heinous crime.*

8. It signifies *concessus, an assembly, an academy;* and the first verse is either to be translated, " The sayings of the academy of the son of David," חֲכָמִים *wise men* being supplied after קֹהֶלֶת,[3] or " The sayings of a member of the academy," &c., בַּעַל being supplied before קֹהֶלֶת.[4] To say nothing of its intolerant harshness, chap. i. 12 shews the utter inconsistency

---

[1] Cartwright, Metaphrasis et Homiliæ in Librum Salomonis qui scribitur Ecclesiastes, Amstelodami, 1647, fol. 1; Bishop Reynolds, Annotations on the Book of Ecclesiastes, vol. iv. of his works, London, 1826, p. 38; Granger, Exposition on Ecclesiastes, London, 1621.

[2] Coecejus, Comm. in i. 1, and Heb. Lex. *in voc.;* Schultens, Diss. de Utilitate dialectorum Orient. ad tuendam integritatem cod. Heb., c. 2, § 24; Schröder, Instit. Ling. Hebr., p. 236, quoted by Van der Palm, p. 48; Holden, p. xxxiv.; Knobel, p. 5.

[3] Döderlein, Scholia in Libros Vet. Test. Poet., p. 170, &c.; and his Salomo's Prediger und Hohes Lied, Jena, 1784, p. xv., &c.; Nachtigal, Koheleth oder die Versammlung der Weisen, Halle, 1798, p. 20, &c.

[4] Gaab, Beiträge zur Erklärung des sogenannten Hohenlieds, Koheleth, &c.; Tübingen, 1795, p. 48.

of this interpretation, for, according to it, Solomon addresses his literary society, " I, O academy! was King in Jerusalem," thus making Solomon inform the members of the society over which he was president *who* and *what* he was, as if they did not know it.

9. It means *an old man*, and Solomon indicates by the name Coheleth his weakness of mind, when, yielding to his wives, he worshipped idols.[1] Here, again, recourse is had to the Arabic to obtain this sense, which must be repudiated, for the reason given in No. 7. Besides the Hebrew has several terms for *old man* (שִׂיבָה, זָקֵן), and if the sacred writer had intended to convey this idea, he would assuredly have chosen one of them, and not have felt obliged to assign a foreign signification to a well-known Hebrew word.

10. It means *exclaiming voice*, and the words of the inscription ought to be rendered, " The words of the voice of one exclaiming," being analogous to the title assumed by John the Baptist (John i. 23).[2] But as this far-fetched explanation is also obtained by appealing to a cognate language, we must reject it, for the reason already given.

11. It means *Sophist*, according to the primitive signification of the word, which implied a combination of philosophy and rhetoric, קֹהֶלֶת being the same as σοφιστής in Greek, with this difference, that the Hebrew sage was so denominated, from his being the occasion of a great concourse of people who came to hear him, whilst the Greek speaker obtained his name from the wisdom he professed to teach.[3]

12. It means *philosopher*, or *moralist*.[4]

---

[1] Simonis Lex. Heb. *in voc.;* Schmidt, Salomo's Prediger, oder Koheleth Lehren, Giessen, 1794, p. 80, &c.

[2] Lud. de Dieu, as quoted by Desvoeux, p. 477, and Holden, p. xxxi.

[3] Desvoeux, A Philosophical and Critical Essay on Ecclesiastes, London, 1760, p. 479, &c.

[4] Spohn, Der Prediger Salomo, Leipzig, 1785, p. 3; Gaab, Beiträge, &c., p. 48; Auerbach, Das Buch Koheleth neu übersetzt mit einem Hebräischen Commentar, Breslau, 1837, p. 28, &c.

13. It means *the departed spirit* of Solomon, which is introduced as speaking throughout this book in the form of a shadow.[1]

These interpretations are so far-fetched, and so unnatural, that they require no refutation, and the enumeration of them will tend to shew the soundness of the explanation we defend.

iii. With regard to the third question, viz., *How* came this title to be in the feminine gender? we reply, Because *Solomon personifies Wisdom*, who appears herself, in Prov. i. 10, and viii. 1, &c., as Coheleth, or *the gatherer* of the people.[2] Such a personification of wisdom also occurs in the New Testament, as will be seen from a comparison of Luke xi. 49, 50, with Matt. xxiii. 34, and is in perfect harmony with the notions which were current about Solomon, who is regarded as wisdom incarnate, and is represented as teaching in this capacity (Book of Wisdom, vii. 7 — ix.). Moreover, this explanation is both substantiated by and explanatory of the otherwise inexplicable construction of *Coheleth* with a *feminine* verb (אָמְרָה קֹהֶלֶת) in vii. 27, which already Rashi (אמרה קבוצת החכמה) and Ibn Ezra (ומלת אמרה קהלת על לשון החכמה), though giving a different interpretation of Coheleth, were obliged to admit that *it is owing to wisdom being spoken of.* The assertion, therefore, that this incarnation of wisdom is not indicated by the sacred writer, utterly ignores this passage. The objection that such expressions as, *I gave my heart to know wisdom; I acquired wisdom* (i. 16. 17; ii. 12); *wisdom stood by me* (ii. 9); *wisdom was far from me* (vii. 23), &c.,

---

[1] Augusti, Einleitung in das Alte Testament, p. 240, &c.

[2] So also St. Augustine, *Sapientia semel per Salomonem cecinit*, quoted by Knobel, p. 6, and by Hengstenberg in Kitto, Cyclop. Bib. Lit., art. Ecclesiastes, vol. i., p. 594; Geier, in Salomonis Regis Israel Ecclesiasten Comment. ed. quartua, Leipsiæ, 1711, p. 10; Le Clerc, Comment. Concio. Salom. i. 1; Rambach, Notæ uberiores in Ecclesiasten Salomonis, contained in vol. ii. of Michaelis, Notæ uberiores, p. 835; Carpzov. Int. ad Lib., p. 201; Holden, p. xlvi.; Ewald, Krit. Gramm., p. 569; and his Sprüche Salomo's und Koheleth, Göttingen, 1837, p. 189; Köster, Das Buch Hiob und der Prediger Salomo's, Schleswig, 1831, p. 102; Hitzig, Die Sprüche und der Prediger Salomo's, Leipzig, 1847, p. 128; Wangemann, Der Prediger Salomonis, Berlin, 1856, p. 43; Hengstenberg, Der Prediger Salomo, Berlin, 1859, p. 39, &c.

are incompatible with it,[1] arises from a confusion of wisdom animating a person with a personified idea; the wisdom which is concrete in Solomon with absolute wisdom. It must be borne in mind that Solomon, though animated by and representing wisdom, does not lose his individuality; and hence he speaks sometimes of his own experience, and sometimes utters the words of wisdom, whose organ he is, just as the Apostles are sometimes the organs of the Holy Ghost. Comp. Acts xv. 28.

This question, too, viz., How came this title to be in the feminine gender? has been variously answered

1. It is in the feminine gender, because קֹהֶלֶת, *Coheleth*, refers to נֶפֶשׁ, *the intellectual soul* understood.[2] But this explanation, though virtually the same as that which we have given, is very indistinct, in consequence of the views of its propounders respecting *the signification* of Coheleth.

2. It is in the feminine form, *to shew the great excellency of the preacher*, or *his charming style*, which this gender indicates.[3]

3. It is in the feminine, *because a preacher travails, as it were, like a mother, in the spiritual birth of his children*, just as the Apostle Paul says, "My little children, of whom I travail again in birth till Christ be formed in you" (Gal. iv. 19), *and has tender and motherly affection for his people.*[4]

4. It is in the feminine, *to describe the infirmity of Solomon, who appears here as worn out by old age.*[5]

5. The feminine is used in a *neuter sense*, because the departed spirits have no specific gender (comp. Matt. xxii. 30),[6] in accord-

---

[1] Knobel, p. 7.

[2] Rashi, אמר הקהלת מי שבו קבוצת החכמה: אמרה קבוצת החכמה; ואמרה נפשו המשכלת המקבצת החכמה, on xii. 8, and vii. 27; Rashbam, on vii. 27; Ben Melech, on vii. 27, which has been followed by many Christian commentators.

[3] Lorinus, Comment. in Ecclesiasten, Moguntiæ, 1607, p. 12; Zirkel, Untersuchung über den Prediger mit Philologischen und Kritischen Bemerkungen, Würzburg, 1792.

[4] Pineda, Comment. in Ecclesiasten, Antw., 1620, *in loco;* Mayer, Comment., p. 771.

[5] Mercer, Comment. *in loc.;* Simonis, Lex. Heb. *in voc.*

[6] Augusti, p. 242, &c.

ance with the explanation given in ii. 13. These views require no refutation.

6. The termination ת, is not at all feminine, but, as in Arabic, is used as *an auxesis* to the force of the word, so that קֹהֶלֶת means *a pre-eminent preacher*.[1] But, apart from the fact that such a usage of the feminine termination has no parallel in Hebrew, and that recourse to a foreign language is to be deprecated, this αὔξησις means *much;* accordingly, קֹהֶלֶת would signify *much preaching*, and not *pre-eminent preacher*.

7. The feminine gender is to be explained, from the custom in Hebrew and other languages of designating by *feminine* and *abstract* names persons holding certain *ranks* and *offices*.[2] Against this explanation we urge — 1. That Coheleth is neither a name of *rank* nor of *office*, but simply *describes the act of gathering the people together;* 2. That the construction of the feminine verb with it in vii. 27, is utterly irreconcileable with this view; 3. That abstracts, though sometimes expressed by feminine forms, are never formed from *the active participle;* and 4. That there is not a single instance to be found where *a concrete is first made an abstract, then again taken in a personal sense*.

SECTION II. — CANONICITY OF THE BOOK.

In inquiring into the canonicity of any book of the Old Testament, it must always be borne in mind that no inspired writer gives a catalogue of the books regarded as canonical up to his time, and that even the earliest uninspired notice taken of the entire canon is a simple reference to its threefold division, viz., *the Law, the Prophets, and the other writings*, i. e., *Hagiography*.[3] The reason of this categorical designation is obvious.

---

[1] Jahn, Einleitung in das Alte Testament, p. 828, &c.

[2] Desvoeux, p. 477; Gesenius, Lehrgeb., p. 468, and 878; Knobel, p. 8, &c.; Herzfeld, Coheleth übersetzt und erläutert, Braunschweig, 1838, p. 25; Stuart, A Commentary on Ecclesiastes, New York, 1851, p. 107; Plumptre, in Smith's Dictionary of the Bible, art. Ecclesiastes.

[3] Comp. the Prologue to Jesus son of Sirach, ὁ νόμος καὶ οἱ προφῆται καὶ τὰ ἄλλα πάτρια βιβλία, and farther on, ὁ νόμος καὶ αἱ προφητεῖαι καὶ τὰ λοιπὰ τῶν βιβλίων. And see also Luke xxiv. 44.

The sacred books were too well known to every Israelite to require a more specific account of them. It was only when the superiority of the inspired books had to be defended before *a heathen, who was ignorant of their number and import,* that Josephus felt himself obliged *to enumerate* and *describe them* more particularly. "We have not," he submits, "a countless number of books opposing and contradicting each other, but only *two-and-twenty,* containing the records of every age, which are justly believed to be Divine, and of these *five* belong to Moses, *thirteen* to the Prophets, and the remaining *four* contain hymns to God and maxims of life for men."[1] But even this vindication being necessarily confined to *the certainty of the number, the publicity, and veracity* of the Hebrew records, as contrasted with *the countless number of the concealed writings* of the Hellenists, rendered it superfluous to give the names of books which were well known to every Jew, and which would have been utterly useless to Apion, the heathen. It is, however, generally admitted that these twenty-two books are: 1—5, the Books of Moses ; 6, Joshua ; 7, Judges and Ruth, which belongs to that period; 8, first and second Samuel; 9, first and second Kings ; 10, first and second Chronicles ; 11, Ezra and Nehemiah, because Ezra appears in Nehemiah, and because both were ascribed to one author (comp. Baba Bathra, 15, a; Sanedrin, 93, b) ; 12, Esther; 13, Isaiah ; 14, Jeremiah and Lamentations, by the same author; 15, Ezekiel; 16, Daniel ; 17, the Minor Prophets, put together because of their smallness, and also to obtain the number 22 ; 18, Job; 19, the Psalms ; 20, the Proverbs ; 21, Ecclesiastes ; 22, the Song of Songs.

---

[1] Comp. Joseph. cont. Apion. i. 8, with Eusebius, Hist. Eccles. iii. 10. Josephus' division of the Scriptures into twenty two books is owing to an ancient custom to obtain the number of the Hebrew alphabet, or some other significant or sacred number, when divisions were made. The division into *four-and-twenty* books, עֶשְׂרִים וְאַרְבָּעָה, which is adopted by the Massorites, and is become a technical name among the Jews for the Old Testament, is from the Greek-speaking Jews, who made it according to the Greek alpbabet, containing *twenty-four letters.* For the same reason, the Iliad and the Odyssey are respectively divided into *twenty-four books.*

The correctness of this admission is evident, from the catalogue of the inspired writings given in the Talmud. Here, again, we must remark that this formal account of the books is not given *to shew which are canonical*, as this would have been superfluous in the eyes of the Talmudists and of the Jews, since every Israelite *well knew from of old* the canonical books; but is incidentally brought forward to point out the order in which they are to follow each other — a circumstance which greatly increases its importance and value. Three subjects are discussed in Baba Bathra, pp. 13 and 14, viz., 1. The agglutination or joining together of the canonical scrolls or books; 2. The order in which they are to follow each other; and 3. Their respective authors or compilers. The first discussion, viz., about the agglutination of the scrolls, throws no direct light upon the point under consideration. The gross misunderstanding, however, of the passage in the Talmud which contains it will be seen in the foot-note.[1] The third discussion will be

[1] The passage is, ת״ר מדביק אדם תורה נביא׳ כתובים כא׳ דברי ר׳ מאיר ר׳ יהודה אומר תורה בפני עצמה נביא׳ בפני עצמן וכתובי׳ בפני עצמן וחכמים אומרים כל אחד ואחד בפני עצמו ואמר רבי יהודה מעשה בביתוס בן זונין שהיו לו שמונה נביאים מדובקין כאחד על פי ר״א בן עזריה ויש אומרים לא היו אלא א׳ א׳ בפני עצמו אמר ר׳ מעש׳ והביאו לפנינו תורה נביאים וכתובים מדובקים כאחד והכשרנום׳ : *Our Rabbins teach that one may join the Pentateuch, the Prophets, and the Hagiography together in one, so said R. Mayer; R. Jehudah said the Pentateuch by itself, the Prophets by themselves, and the Hagiography by themselves; and the Sages said, each book by itself. Then R. Jehudah said it happened that Bayithos, the natural son, had the eight Prophets joined together in one, according to the advice of R. Eliezer bèn Azariah; but others said that it was not so, but that each one was by itself. Then Rab said, it happened that the Law, the Prophets, and the Hagiography were brought before us joined together in one, and we pronounced them lawful.* And this decided the question. The whole discussion is so plain that it requires no comment, and we are amazed that Hävernick (Allgemeine Einleitung in das Alte Test. erster Theil, erste Abth. 1854, p. 40) should have taken it to treat upon the *division* of the canon, and then have disconnected and so wofully mistranslated the words, וחכמים אומרים כל אחד ואחד בפני עצמו, die Weisen sagen: alles ist eines und jeder Theil bestehet wieder für sich, d. h. bildet wieder ein für sich abgeschlossenes Ganze: *The wise men say, the whole is one, and each part forms one again for itself,* i. e., *forms again for itself a complete whole:* and that he should also have disconnected the decision of the discussion, omitted the last and most important word, and translated והביאו לפנינו תורה נביאים וכתובים מדובקים כאחד, "und sie haben uns hinterlassen die Thorah, Propheten und Hagiographen verbunden zu einem Ganzen," *and they (i.e., the*

examined in the section appropriated to the authorship of this book. It is the second, viz., the discussion about the order of the sacred books, which is of the utmost importance to the identity of Josephus' canon, inasmuch as in it all the inspired books are mentioned *by name*. Here, then, we have it beyond the shadow of a doubt that the books which, according to Josephus (*l. c.*), formed the sacred canon long before his time; which no Jew, as he tells us, dared to alter in any way; upon which all the Jews are taught from their very infancy to look as the decrees of God; and for which every Jew, if necessary, would gladly die, are, according to the order of this discussion, *the Pentateuch, Joshua, Judges, Samuel, Kings, Jeremiah, Ezekiel, Isaiah, and the Minor Prophets; Ruth, Psalms, Job, Proverbs, Coheleth, Song of Songs, Lamentations, Daniel, Esther, Ezra, and Chronicles.*[1] The Old Testament canon

same wise men) have bequeathed to us the Law, the Prophets, and the Hagiography, united in one whole, connecting it with the preceding quotation. Keil, who almost rewrote this part of Hävernick's work, has espoused this extraordinary blunder; so also Professor Stuart, who gravely tells us (Critical History and Defence of the Old Testament Canon, Davidson's ed., London, 1849, p. 233, &c.), " In the Gemara Tract, Babba Bathra, fol. 13, c. 2, we find the following declaration : Our wise men say that the whole is one, and each part is one by itself; and they have transmitted to us the Law, the Prophets, and the Kethubim, united together in one." The works of Hävernick, Keil, and Stuart occupy too high a position, both here and on the Continent, to leave so flagrant an error unnoticed.

[1] תנו רבנן סדרן של נביאים יהושע ושופטים שמואל ומלכים ירמיה ויחזקאל ישעיה ושנים עשר מכדי הושע קדים דכתיב תחלת דבר ה' בהושע וכי עם הושע דבר תחלה והלא ממשה ועד הושע כמה נביאים היו אמר רבי יוחנן שהיה תחלה לארבעה נביאים שנתנבאו באותו הפרק ואלו הן הושע וישעי' עמוס ומיכה וליקדמיה להושע ברישא כיון דכתיב נבואתיה גבי חגי זכריה ומלאכי סוף נביאים הוו חשיב ליה בהדהו וליכתביה לחודיה וליקדמיה איידי דזוטר מירכס מכדי ישעיה קדים מירמיה ויחזקאל ליקדמיה לישעיה ברי' כיון דמלכים סופיה חורבנא וירמיה כוליה חורבנא ויחזקאל רישיה חורבנא וסופיה נחמתא וישעיה כוליה נחמתא סמכינן חורבנא לחורבנא ונחמתא לנחמתא *The Rabbins teach that the order of the Prophets is—Joshua and Judges, Samuel and Kings, Jeremiah and Ezekiel, Isaiah and the Minor Prophets, of which Hosea is the first, as it is written, " The Lord spake to Hosea first." (Hos. i.) But has Hosea really spoken first? and were there not many prophets between Moses and Hosea? R. Jochanan replied, because he was the first of the four prophets who prophesied at that time, viz., Hosea, Isaiah, Amos, and Micah. Then Isaiah ought to be put at the head of these? Since his prophecy was written upon Haggai, Zechariah, and Malachi, the last of the prophets, it was considered as separate, and written down separately, and was put at the head because it is little and might easily be*

therefore, which we now possess, is the canon which the Jews had long before the time of Christ, and *Coheleth* composed one of the sacred books which our Lord called τὰς γραφὰς, *the Scriptures* (Matt. xxii. 29). Hence the Septuagint version, which was made before the Christian era, the translations of Aquila, Symmachus, and Theodotion, which belong to the first two centuries of Christianity, and the Catalogue of Melito, bishop of Sardis (fl. 170 A. D.), which he brought from Palestine — all these include *Coheleth*.

As reference is frequently made to the discussions in the Talmud, &c., where it is affirmed objections have been made at a very early period against the canonicity of Coheleth, we believe that the real force of these passages will best be seen by giving them entire. Upon the declaration in the Mishna, that all the books in the Bible *pollute the hands*, (i. e., *are inspired*, or *canonical*, see my Commentary on the Song of Songs, p. 3,) including the Song of Songs and Coheleth,[1] *R. Jehudah said the Song of Songs does pollute the hands, but about Coheleth there is a difference of opinion: R. Josi said Coheleth does not pollute the hands, and the difference of opinion is about the Song of Songs. R. Simeon said Coheleth is one of those points upon which the decision of Beth-Shammai is more lenient and Beth-Hillel more rigid. Then R. Shimeon Ben-Azzai said, I have*

lost. Since Isaiah was before Jeremiah and Ezekiel, ought not Isaiah to be at the head? As the book of Kings ends with tribulation, and Jeremiah is all tribulation, and Ezekiel begins with tribulation and ends in consolation, whereas Isaiah is all consolation, tribulation is joined to tribulation (i. e., Jeremiah to the end of Kings), and consolation to consolation (i. e., Isaiah to the end of Ezekiel.)
The order of the Hagiography is Ruth, Psalms, Job, Proverbs, Coheleth, the Song of Songs, Lamentations, Daniel, Esther, Ezra, and Chronicles. To him who says that as Job lived in the days of Moses, the book of Job ought to be put first, as the beginning, we reply, we must not begin with punishment. Ruth, too, contains chastisements? But such chastisements as have a happy issue.

1 כל כתבי הקדש מטמאין את הידים שיר השירים וקהלת מטמאין את הידים ר' יהודה אומר שיר השירים מטמא את הידים וקהלת מחלוקת ר' יוסי אומר קהלת אינה מטמא את הידים ושיר השירים מחלוקת רש"א קהלת מקולי ב"ש ומחומרי ב"ה אמר ר"ש בן עזאי מקובל אני מפי שבעים וזקנים ביום שהושיבו את ר' אליעזר בן עזריה בישיבה ששיר השירים וקהלת מטמאים את הידים (ידים פ"ג ה')י'

*received it from the mouth of the seventy-two elders, at the time
when R. Eliezer Ben-Azzai was appointed elder, that the Song
of Songs and Coheleth pollute the hands.*—Yadayim, v. 3.

In the Talmud, where the same discussion is given, we are
told :[1] *R. Mayer said Coheleth does not pollute the hands, but
there is a difference of opinion about the Song of Songs ; R. Josi
said the Song of Songs does pollute the hands, and the difference
of opinion is about Coheleth ; whereas R. Simeon said Coheleth
is one of those points upon which the decision of Beth-Shammai
is more lenient and Beth-Hillel more rigid ; but Ruth, the Song
of Songs, and Esther pollute the hands ; this is according to what
R. Joshua had said.   R. Simeon ben Menasia submitted that
Coheleth does not pollute the hands, because it contains Solomon's own
wisdom.   Whereupon they said unto him, and has he (Solomon) only
indited this (Coheleth), and has it not long been said that he also
spoke three thousand proverbs (1 Kings v. 12), and said, too, Do
not add to his words? (Prov. xxx. 6).   What means this* (ואומר)
*" and he said "?   If thou (R. Simeon) wilt say he (Solomon)
said it appropriately, having written down what he wished and
kept back what he wished, then come. and hear, Do not add to His
words (i. e., to God's words).* — Megila, 7, a.

In another tract of the Talmud it is recorded:[2] *R. Jehuda,
son of R. Samuel, son of Shilath, said in the name of Rab, the
sages wanted to declare Coheleth apocryphal, because its statements
contradict each other.   And why have they not declared it
apocryphal?   Because it begins with words of the Law and ends
with the words of the Law: it begins with the words of the Law,*

¹ ר' מאיר אומר קהלת אינו מטמא את הידים ומחלוקת בשיר השירים ר' יוסי אומר שיר השירים מטמא
את הידים ומחלוקת בקהלת ר' שמעון אומר קהלת מקולי ב"ש ומחומרי ב"ה אבל רות ושיר השירים
ואסתר מטמאין את הידים הוא דאמר כר' יהושע תניא ר' שמעון בן מנסיא אומר קהלת אינו מטמא
את הידים מפני שחכמתו של שלכה היא אמרו לו וכי זו בלבד אמר והלא כבר נאמר וידבר שלשת
אלפים משל ואומר אל תוסף על דבריו מאי ואומר וכי תימא מימר טובא אמר דאיבעי איכתיב ודאיבעי
לא איכתיב תא שמע אל תוסף על דבריו (מגילה ז' ע"א)׳

² אמר רב יהודה בריה דר' שילת משמיה דרב בקשו חכמים לגנוז ספר קהלת מפני שדבריו סותרין זה
את זה ומפני כה לא גנזוהו מפני שחחילתו דברי תורה וסופו דברי תורה תחילתו דברי תורה דכתיב
מה יתרון לאדם בכל עמלו שיעמול תחת השמש ואמרי דבי ר' ינאי תחת השמש הוא דאין לו קודם
השמש יש לו סופו דברי תורה דכתיב סוף דבר הכל נשמע את האלהים ירא ואת מצותיו שמור כי זה
כל האדם (שבת ל' ב')׳

for it opens with the words, " What advantage has man in all his labour wherewith he labours under the sun ? " (i. 3) and it is said in the school of R. Jannai that " under the sun" means that which is unprofitable for him ; just as " above the sun" denotes that which is profitable for him: it ends with the words of the Law, for it concludes with the words, " In conclusion, all is heard ; fear the Lord, and keep his commandments," &c. (xii. 13.) — Shabbath, 30, b.

In the Midrash we read,[1] *" the sages wanted to declare Coheleth apocryphal, because they found sentiments in it tending to infidelity."*—Vayikra Rabba, 161, b.

Thus also St. Jerome tells us :[2] *the Hebrews say that, among other writings of Solomon which are obsolete and forgotten, this book ought to be obliterated, because it asserts that all the creatures of God are vain, and regards the whole as nothing, and prefers eating and drinking and transient pleasures before all things. From this one paragraph it deserves the dignity that it should be placed among the number of the divine volumes, in which it condenses the whole of its discussion, summing up the whole enumeration, as it were, and says that the end of its discourse is very easily heard, having nothing difficult in it, namely, that we should fear God and keep his commandments* (xii. 13, 14).

But we submit that these discussions, so far from impairing, confirm the canonicity of Coheleth, since they shew beyond a doubt — 1. That these objections, which were by no means confined to the book in question, were urged by the school of Shammai, which exercised a supercilious rigour in the interpre-

---

[1] בקשו חכמים לגנוז ספר קהלת מפני שמצאו בו דברים מטים לצד מינות (ויקרא רבה. קסא. ע״ב׳)

[2] Aiunt Hebraci, cum inter cetera scripta Salomonis, quæ antiquata sunt, nec in memoria duraverunt, et hic liber obliterandus videretur, eo quod vanas assereret Dei creaturas et totum putaret esse pro nihilo et cibum et potum et delicias transeuntes præferret omnibus : ea hoc uno capitulo meruisse auctoritatem, ut in divinorum voluminum numero poneretur, quod totam disputationem suam et omnem catalogum hac quasi ἀνακεφαλαιώσει coarctaverit et dixerit finem sermonum suorum auditu esse promptissimum, nec aliquid in se habere difficile, ut scilicet Deum timeamus et ejus præcepta faciamus.—*Hieron. Comment.* xii. 13.

tation of Scripture;[1] 2. That they were overruled by the positive declaration from the seventy-two elders, which is to us of the utmost importance, being a testimony anterior to the Christian era, that Coheleth is canonical; 3. That the objections against it were based upon apparent contradictions and difficulties ; and 4. That these difficulties had been so satisfactorily explained by the Rabbins themselves, that when the apparent contradictions of the book of Proverbs were urged against its canonicity, the satisfactory solution of Coheleth was adduced as an instance to caution against accepting contradictions too rashly.[2]

Coheleth is the fourth of the (חָמֵשׁ מְגִילוֹת) *five Megiloth,* or books, which are read annually in the synagogue at five appointed seasons. The reason for its occupying *the fourth* position in the present arrangement of the Hebrew canon is, that the feast of Tabernacles, on which it is read, is *the fourth* of these occasions.

SECTION III. — DESIGN AND METHOD OF THE BOOK.

The design of this book, as has already been intimated (*vide supra,* p. 2), is *to gather together the desponding people of God from the various expediencies to which they have resorted, in consequence of the inexplicable difficulties and perplexities in the moral government of God, into the community of the Lord, by shewing them the utter insufficiency of all human efforts to obtain real happiness, which cannot be secured by wisdom, pleasure, industry,*

---

[1] Comp. Graetz, Geschichte der Juden iv., p. 40, &c.; Jost, Geschichte des Judenthums und seiner Secten, i., p. 61, &c.

[2] The passage alluded to is as follows : ואף ספר משלי בקשו לגנוז שהיו דבריו סותרין זה את זה ומפני מה לא גנוזוהו אמרי ספר קהלת לאו עיינינו ואשכחינן טעמא הכא נמי ליעיינין; *and also the book of Proverbs, they* [the wise men] *wanted to declare apocryphal, because there are statements in it contradicting each other. And why did they not declare it apocryphal? They said, the book of Coheleth was not* [declared apocryphal], *because we have examined it and found its meaning; let us therefore here* [the Book of Proverbs] *also examine more closely,* Shabbath 30, b. Preston (Comment. on Eccles., p. 75), in citing this passage, has omitted the word לאו, and therefore mistranslated the whole; he has also given a wrong reference to it, viz., Mishna, Shabbas, ch. x. Plumptre (in Smith's Dictionary of the Bible, art. Ecclesiastes, p. 473) quotes it from Preston, with these errors uncorrected.

wealth, &c., but consists in the calm enjoyment of life, in the resig-
nation to the dealings of Providence, in the service of God, and in
the belief in a future state of retribution, when all the mysteries
in the present course of the world shall be solved.

The method which the sacred writer adopts to carry out this
design is most striking and effective. Instead of writing an
elaborate metaphysical disquisition, logically analysing and
refuting, or denouncing, *ex cathedra*, the various systems of
happiness which the different orders of minds and temperaments
had constructed for themselves, Solomon is introduced as recount-
ing his painful experience in all these attempts. Thus by laying
open, as it were, to the gaze of the people the struggles of a man
of like feelings with themselves, who could fully sympathise with
all their difficulties, having passed through them himself, and
found the true clue to their solution, the sacred writer carries out
his design far more touchingly and effectively than an Aristotelian treatise, or the Mount Ebal curses upon the heads of the
people, would have done.

The book consists of *a Prologue, four sections,* and *an Epilogue·*
the Prologue and Epilogue are distinguished by their beginning
with the same phrase (i. 1; xii. 8), ending with two marked
sentences (i. 11; xii. 14), and embodying *the grand problem* and
solution proposed by Coheleth; whilst the four sections are indicated by the recurrence of the same formula, giving the result of
each experiment or examination of particular efforts to obtain
real happiness for the craving soul (ii. 26; v. 19; and viii. 15).

The PROLOGUE — i. 2 – 11 — gives the theme or problem of
the disquisition. Assuming that there is *no hereafter*, that the
longing soul is to be satisfied with the things *here*, Coheleth
declares that all human efforts to this effect are utterly vain (2)
and fruitless (3); that conscious man is more deplorable than
unconscious nature: he must speedily quit this life, whilst the
earth abides for ever (4); the objects of nature depart and retrace
their course again, but man vanishes and is for ever forgotten
(5 – 11).

The FIRST SECTION—i. 11–ii. 26—records the failure of different experiments to satisfy the cravings of the soul with temporal things, thus corroborating the allegation in the Prologue, and also shewing what their disappointment from this point of view led to. Coheleth, with all the resources of a monarch at his command (12), applied himself assiduously to discover, by *the aid of wisdom*, the nature of earthly pursuits (13), and found that they were all fruitless (14), since they could not rectify destinies (15). Reflecting, therefore, upon the large amount of wisdom he had acquired (16), he came to the conclusion that it is all useless (17), as the accumulation of it only increased his sorrow and pain (18). He then resolved to try *pleasure*, to see whether it would yield the desired happiness, but found that this too was vain (ii. 1), and hence denounced it (2); for, having procured every imaginable pleasure (3–10), he found that it was utterly insufficient to impart lasting good (11). Whereupon he compared wisdom with pleasure (12), and though he saw the former had a decided advantage over the latter (13, 14, a.), yet he also saw that it does not exempt its possessor from death and oblivion, but that the wise and the fool must both alike die and be forgotten (14, b.–16). This made him hate both life and the possessions which, though acquired by industry and wisdom, he must leave to another, who may be a reckless fool (17–21), convincing him that man has nothing from his toil but wearisome days and sleepless nights (22, 23); that there is, therefore, nothing left for man but to enjoy himself (24, a); yet this, too, he found was not in the power of man (24, b. 25), God gives this power to the righteous and withholds it from the wicked, and that it is, after all, transitory (26).

The SECOND SECTION—iii. 1.–v. 19.—Having shewn in the preceding section that neither *wisdom* nor *pleasure* can ensure lasting good for man, Coheleth now shews that *industry* is also unable to secure it.

All the events of life are permanently fixed (iii. 1–8), and hence the fruitlessness of human labour (9). God has indeed prescribed bounds to man's employment, in harmony with this fixed order of things, but man through his ignorance often mistakes it (10, 11), thus again shewing that there is nothing left for man but the enjoyment of the things of this world in his possession, being the gift of God to the righteous (12, 13). The cause of this immutable arrangement in the events of life is, that man may fear God, and feel that it is He who orders all things (14, 15). The apparent success of wickedness (16) does not militate against this conclusion, since there is a fixed day for righteous retribution (17); but even if, as is affirmed, all terminates *here*, and man and beast have the same destiny (18–21), this shows all the more clearly that there is nothing left for man but to enjoy life, since this is his only portion (22). The state of suffering (iv. 1), however, according to this view, becomes desperate, and death, and not to have been born at all, are preferable to life (2, 3). The exertions made, in spite of the prescribed order of things, either arise from jealousy (4), and fail in their end (5, 6), or are prompted by avarice (7, 8), and defeat themselves (9–16). Since all things are thus under the control of an Omnipotent God, we ought to serve him acceptably (17 – v. 6), trust to his protection under oppression (7, 8), remember that the rich oppressor, after all, has not even the comfort of the poor labourer (9 – 11), and that he often brings misery upon his children and himself (12–16). These considerations, therefore, again shew that there is nothing left for man but to enjoy life the few years of his existence, being the gift of God (17 – 19).

The THIRD SECTION — vi. 1 – viii. 15. — *Riches* comes now under review, and it, too, is shewn to be utterly unable to secure real happiness (vi. 1 – 9), since the rich man can neither overrule the order of Providence (10), nor know what will conduce to his well-being (11, 12). And lastly, *prudence*, or what is generally called *common sense*, is examined and shewn to be as unsatisfactory as all the preceding experiments. Coheleth thought that to live so as to leave a good name (vi. 1 – 4); to listen to merited rebuke (5 – 9); not to indulge in a repining spirit, but to submit to God's Providence (10–14); to be temperate in religious matters (15–20); not to pry into everybody's opinions (21, 22)— lessons of prudence or common sense, higher wisdom being unattainable (23, 24); to submit to the powers that be, even under oppression, believing that the mightiest tyrant will ultimately be punished (viii. 1–9), and that, though righteous retribution is sometimes withheld (10), which, indeed, is the cause of increased wickedness (11), yet that God will eventually administer rewards and punishments (12, 13), that this would satisfy him during the few years of his life. But as this did not account for the melancholy fact that the fortunes of the righteous and the wicked *are often reversed all their life-time*, this common sense view of life too proved vain (14); and Coheleth therefore recurs to his repeated conclusion, that there is nothing left for man but to enjoy the things of this life (15).

The FOURTH SECTION — viii. 15–xii. 7.—To shew more strikingly the force of his final conclusion, submitted at the end of this section, Coheleth gives first a *résumé* of the investigations contained in the preceding sections. Having found that it is impossible to fathom the work of God by wisdom (viii. 16, 17); that even the righteous and the wise are subject to this inscrutable Providence, just as the wicked (ix. 1, 2); that all must alike die and be forgotten (3–5), and that they have no more participation in what takes place here (6); that we are therefore to indulge in pleasures here while we can, since there is no hereafter (7–10); that success does not always attend the strong and the skilful (11, 12); and that wisdom, though decidedly advantageous in many respects, is often despised and counteracted by folly (13–x. 3); that we are to be patient under sufferings from rulers (4), who by virtue of their power frequently pervert the order of things (5–7), since violent opposition may only tend to increase our sufferings (8–11); that the exercise of prudence in the affairs of life will be more advantageous than folly (12–20); that we are to be charitable, though the recipients of our benevolence appear ungrateful, since they may after all requite us

(xi. 1, 2); that we are always to be at our work, and not be deterred by imaginary failures, since we know not which of our efforts may prove successful (3 – 6), and thus make life as agree able as we can (7), for we must always bear in mind that this is the only scene of enjoyment; that the future is all vanity (8) · but as this too did not satisfy the craving of the soul, Coheleth at last came to the conclusion, *that enjoyment of this life, together with a belief in a future judgment, will secure real happiness for man* (9, 10), *and that we are therefore to live from our early youth in the fear of God and of a final judgment*, when all that is perplexing now shall be rectified (xii. 1 – 7).

The EPILOGUE — xii. 8–12. — Thus all human efforts to obtain real happiness are vain (xii. 8); this is the experience of the wisest and most painstaking Coheleth (9, 10) ; the Sacred Writings alone are the way to it (11, 12); there is a righteous Judge, who marks, and will in the great day of judgment judge, everything we do ; we must therefore fear Him, and keep His commandments (13, 14).

SECTION IV. — IMPORTANCE OF THE BOOK.

To understand more clearly the importance of this book, and the gap it fills up in the Old Testament lessons, it will be necessary briefly to examine the state of things to which the doctrine of temporal retribution had in the course of time given rise. Only those who have a special cause to plead will deny that the principle of virtue and vice being visibly rewarded on earth is enunciated, wherever the subject of righteousness and wickedness is spoken of in the Old Testament. God declares, at the very giving of the Law, that he will shew mercy to thousands of those who love Him and keep His commandments, and visit the iniquity of those who hate Him to the third and fourth generation (Exod. xx. 5, 6); that they who honour their parents shall be blessed with long life (*Ibid.* 12). The whole of the twenty-sixth chapter of Leviticus and the twenty-eighth chapter of Deuteronomy are replete with promises of earthly blessings to those who will walk in the way of the Lord, and threatenings of temporal afflictions upon those who shall transgress His law. The faithful fulfilment of these promises and threatenings, in the early stages of the Jewish history, convinced every Israelite that "God judgeth the righteous, and God is angry with the wicked *every day*," and afforded a source of consolation to which the righteous resorted when the power of the wicked threatened destruction (1 Sam. xxiv. 13 – 16 ; xxvi. 23 ; Ps. vii. ; ix.). When David, therefore, received the calamitous tidings that Saul in a malicious freak had caused eighty-five priests to be killed, and that his own life was in imminent danger, he addressed the mighty tyrant in the full assurance of this righteous retribution :

> " Why gloriest thou, hero, in wickedness ?
> The favour of God endureth for ever.
> Thy tongue deviseth mischief
> Like a sharp razor, thou mischief-maker !
> Thou lovest evil more than good,
> Lying more than speaking uprightly.
> Thou lovest all sorts of destruction, deceitful tongue !
> God shall therefore smite thee down for ever,
> He will seize thee, and snatch thee out of the tent,
> And root thee out of the living land.
> The righteous shall see it and fear,
> And they shall laugh over him —
> ' See there the man who made not God his bulwark,
> And trusted in the multitude of his riches, strengthened himself
>   in his wickedness ;'
> But I am as a green olive-tree in the house of God ;
> I trust in the favour of God for ever and ever ;
> I will praise Thee, because thou hast executed it,
> And hope in Thy name, because it is good before thy saints."
>
>   Ps. lii.

Like a net of fine threads is this doctrine spread over the entire Old Testament (compare Psalms xvii. 1, 2 ; xxvi. 1, 2 ; xxviii. 1 – 3; xxxv.; liv. 7 – 9 ; lv. 20 – 24 ; xc.; cxii.; cxxv. 3 ; cxxvii.; cxl.; cxli. 10 ; Prov. x. 6 ; xi. 5 – 8. 19 ; xii. 7 ; Hag. ii. 15 – 20 ; Zech. i. 2 – 6 ; viii. 9 – 17 ; Malachi ii. 17). It is also propounded in the New Testament. Thus our Saviour says, in his sermon

on the Mount, " Blessed are the meek, for they shall inherit the
earth " (Matt. v. 5) ; and declares that " every one that hath
forsaken houses, or brethren, or sisters, or father, or mother, or
wife, or children, or lands, for my name's sake, shall " not only
" inherit everlasting life," but shall receive " *an hundredfold here
in this life* " (comp. Matt. xix. 29, with Mark x. 29, 30 ; Luke
xviii. 29, 30)

But whilst provision was made in the New Testament against
the difficulties arising from the mysterious inequalities in the
distribution of the fortunes of man by the removal of the
boundary line between the world that is now and the world that
is to come, and the extension of the sphere of retribution, thus
affording transcendent consolation to the suffering saint, in the
face of the prosperous sinner, and enabling him to say, " Sorrowful, yet alway rejoicing; poor, yet making many rich; having
nothing, yet possessing all things " (2 Cor. vi. 10) ; " I have
learned, in whatsoever state I am, therewith to be content " (Phil.
iv. 11) ; " for the sufferings of this present time are not worthy
to be compared with the glory which shall be revealed in us "
(Rom. viii. 18): the Old Testament, by limiting the bar of
judgment to this side of the grave, yielded no explanation of, or
succour under, the distracting sight of the righteous suffering
all their life, and then dying for their righteousness, and *the
wicked prospering and prolonging their days through their
wickedness.*

Such a bewildering state of things, as permitted by an
inscrutable Providence, frequently engendered jealousy, anger,
malice, and revenge on the part of the righteous, who, in despair,
were alternately ready to join issue with, or to rise against, the
wicked. It was under such circumstances that Psalm xxxvii.
was written —

" Be not inflamed against the wicked,
Be not envious at the evil-doers,
For soon shall they be cut down as the grass,
And wither as the green herbage.
Trust in Jehovah and do good,

Rest quietly in the land, and cherish truth,
And delight in Jehovah,
And He shall grant thee thy heart's desire.
Roll thy cause upon Jehovah,
And trust in Him, He will accomplish it,
And shall display thy righteousness as the light,
And thy justice as the noon-day.
Be silent before Jehovah, and wait on Him,
Be not inflamed against the successful in his course,
Against the man who practiseth deceit.
Abstain from anger, and leave wrath,
Be not inflamed, so that thou also dost evil;
For evil-doers shall be cut off,
And they that wait on Jehovah, they shall possess the land.
Only a little longer, and the wicked is no more,
And thou shalt search in his place, but he will be gone;
While the meek shall possess the land,
And delight in great peace.
Let the wicked plot against the righteous,
And gnash upon him with his teeth;
The Lord shall laugh at him,
For he seeth that his day is coming
Let the wicked draw the sword, and stretch their bow,
To cut down the poor and the needy,
To murder the upright in conduct;
Their sword shall enter into their own hearts,
And their bows shall be broken.
Better the little of a righteous man,
Than the abundance of many wicked.
For the arms of the wicked shall be broken,
But Jehovah upholdeth the righteous.
Jehovah knoweth the days of the pious,
And their inheritance shall be for ever;
They shall not be ashamed in the time of distress,
And in the days of famine they shall be satisfied.
But the wicked shall perish,
And the enemies of Jehovah shall vanish like the excellency
    of pastures;
They shall vanish in smoke.
The wicked borroweth and repayeth not,
But the righteous is merciful and giveth;
For the blessed of Him shall inherit the land,
And the cursed of Him shall be cut off.
By Jehovah are the steps of this man fixed,

And He delighteth in his way;
Though he stumble, he shall not fall,
For Jehovah supporteth his hand.
I have been young and am grown old,
And never have I seen the righteous forsaken,
Or his seed begging bread;
Every day he is merciful and lendeth,
And his seed must be blessed.

" Depart from evil and do good,
And ever rest quietly;
For Jehovah loveth righteousness
And forsaketh not his saints,
They are always preserved;
But the seed of the wicked are cut off.
The righteous shall possess the land,
And shall dwell therein for ever.
The mouth of the righteous speaketh wisdom,
And his tongue uttereth justice,
The law of his God is in his heart,
His steps shall not totter.
The wicked lurketh for the righteous,
And seeketh to slay him;
Jehovah leaveth him not in his hand,
Condemneth him not when he is judged.
Wait upon Jehovah, and heed His way,
And He shall raise thee to the heritage of the land.
Thou shalt see the destruction of the wicked;
I, too, saw a wicked man, overbearing,
And spreading as a green, deep-rooted tree,
Yet he disappeared, and lo! he was no more,
And I searched for him but he could not be found.
Mark the pious, and behold the upright,
For there is a future for the man of peace.
While the impious are destroyed together,
The future of the wicked is cut off.
And the salvation of the righteous is from Jehovah,
Their strength in time of distress;
And Jehovah helpeth them and delivereth them,
He delivereth them from the wicked, and saveth them,
For they trust in him."

Since, however, this Psalm, as well as Psalms xlix. and lxxiii.,
called forth by similar circumstances, endeavour to console the

E

distressed, and allay the prevailing scepticism in the moral government of God, by assuring the people that this contrariety of fortunes is only *temporary*, and that the righteous shall ultimately prosper and prolong their days *upon the earth*, and the wicked shall suddenly be cut off in great misery, thus keeping within the narrow limits of present reward and punishment; they leave the main difficulty unsolved. Hence the recurrence of this perplexity passing over almost into despair, when these reassurances and consolations were not realised by experience, and when, moreover, the sufferers, however conscious of their innocence, were looked upon as rejected of God, in consequence of some secret guilt. The book of Job, which has so successfully combated the latter notion, shewing that the afflictions of the righteous are not always a proper test of sin committed, only confirmed the old opinion that the righteous are visibly rewarded here, inasmuch as it represents their calamities as transitory, and Job himself as restored to double his original happiness *in this life*.

After the Babylonian captivity, when the political affairs of the nation were such as to render the disparity of the destinies of men and their moral life still more striking, the people began to arraign the character of God —

> " Every one that doeth evil
> Is good in the sight of Jehovah, and he delighteth in them,
> Or where is the God of justice ? " — Mal. ii. 17.

> " It is vain to serve God,
> And what profit is it that we keep his ordinance,
> And that we walk mournfully before Jehovah of Hosts ?
> For now we pronounce the proud happy ;
> They also that work wickedness are built up;
> They even tempt God, yet they are delivered." — *Ibid.* iii. 17. 18.

Awful as this language appears, it had by no means reached its climax. The inheritance of the Lord, which was to be the praise and the ruler of all the earth, was now reduced and degraded to the rank of a mere province by the Persians; her inhabitants, to whom the idea of bondage was most revolting (comp. Matt. xxii. 17, with John viii. 33), were groaning under the extortions and tyranny of satraps; her seats of justice were filled with most unprincipled and wicked men (Coheleth iii. 16); might became right, and the impunity and success with which wickedness was practised swelled most alarmingly the ranks of the wicked (*Ibid.* viii. 10, 11).

Under these circumstances, when the old cherished faith in temporal retribution was utterly subverted by the melancholy experience of the reversion of destinies; when the diversified minds of the desponding people, released from the terrors of the Law, began to import as well as to construct philosophic systems to satisfy the cravings of their minds (*Ibid.* xii. 12), and to resort to various other experiments to obtain happiness, the paramount importance of a book which opens a new bar of judgment in the world to come, when all present irregularities shall be rectified by the Judge of the quick and dead, will at once be obvious.

SECTION V. — HISTORICAL SKETCH OF THE EXEGESIS OF THE BOOK.

Few books in the Bible have given rise to greater diversities of opinion than Coheleth. So conflicting were the views about it up to his time, that Luther remarked, " difficult as this book is, it is almost more difficult to clear the author of the visionary fancies palmed upon him by his numerous commentators, than to develop his meaning." What would this sagacious reformer have said, if he could have forseen the countless speculations of which it has been the subject for the last three hundred years? A complete history of the interpretation of this book would of itself form a large folio. Our object, therefore, in this *sketch*, is simply to give the leading and most striking views which Jews and Christians, in different ages, have formed of Coheleth.

A. JEWISH EXPOSITIONS.

217, B.C. — 50, A.D. — The Apocryphal book called " the Wisdom of Solomon"[1] may, in a certain sense, be regarded as

---

[1] The age of this book is a point of great contention; the above figures shew

the first comment upon Coheleth, inasmuch as it imitatively combats the same errors. The evils which were occasioned by the absence of retributive justice, and which had called forth Coheleth, became more general and formidable with the prolonged and increased sufferings of the people, and hence gave rise also to the book of Wisdom. To invest its solemn warnings and salutary lessons with greater weight, the author of the book of Wisdom personates Solomon, and both imitates and quotes the very language of Coheleth, which for similar reasons was also ascribed to this wise monarch.

Having shewn, in the first chapter, that sin separates man from God, and renders him unfit for the acquisition of wisdom, the author of the book of Wisdom introduces, in the second chapter, the wicked as declaring their own views of the life and destiny of man (1 – 9).

THE BOOK OF WISDOM.	COHELETH.
ii. 1. For those who do not judge aright speak among themselves thus: Short and gloomy is our life, and there is no remedy in the death of a man; and no one is known to have returned from Hades.	Not many are the days of his life (v. 19); all his days he eats in darkness, and has much trouble and grief and anger (v. 16); no one has power over the day of death (viii. 8); no one can release from Hades (iii. 22).
2. For we are born by chance, and after it we shall be as if we had never existed; for the breath in our nostrils is smoke, and thought is a spark in the beating of our heart.	For man is chance (iii. 19), and after it he goes to the dead, i.e., to oblivion (ix. 8); the death of man and beast is the same, and both have the same breath or spirit (iii. 19).

the two extremes of the hypotheses about it. As it is beyond our range to enter into a discussion upon this subject, we refer to Calmet's Preface to this book, given by Arnold in his commentary upon the apocryphal books, being a continuation of Patrick and Lowth's commentary on the Bible; Kitto, Cyclop. Bib. Lit., art. Wisdom of Solomon; De Wette, Einleitung in das Alte Test., § 314; Ewald, Geschichte des Volkes Israel, iv., p. 554; Graetz, Geschichte der Juden, iii., pp. 315, 493; Jost, Geschichte des Judenthums, i., p. 376, &c.; Herzfeld, Geschichte des Volkes Israel, ii., p. 75; Grimm, Das Buch der Weisheit, Kurzgefasstes Exegetisches Handbuch zu den Apocryphen des Alten Test. sechste Lieferung, p. 32, &c.

THE BOOK OF WISDOM.	COHELETH.
3. When extinguished, the body turns into dust, and the spirit vanishes like the subtle air.	Man, like beast, is of the dust, and turns into dust; his spirit vanishes away like the beast's (iii. 20, 21).
4. And our name is forgotten in time, and no one remembers our works; and our life passes away like the residue of a cloud, and is dispersed like a mist driven away by the beams of the sun, and crushed by the heat thereof.	Their name is forgotten (ix. 5), there is no remembrance of those who passed away (i. 11).
5. For our life is a passing shadow, and there is no returning of our end; for it is closed, and no one returns.	When man departs he returns no more (see comment. on i. 11).
6. Come, then, let us enjoy present pleasures, and diligently use the world while young.	Go eat thy bread with joy, and drink thy wine with a cheerful heart (ix. 16); rejoice, young man, while young, and let thy heart cheer thee in the days of thine early life (xi. 9)
7. Let us fill ourselves with costly wine and perfumes, let no flower of the spring escape us.	Let thy garments at all times be white, and let no perfume be lacking upon thy head (ix. 8).
8. Let us crown ourselves with rose buds before they wither.	
9. Let none of us be without his share of voluptuousness; let us leave everywhere tokens of our joyfulness, for this is our portion, and this our lot.	I did not keep back my heart from any pleasure, this was to be my portion from all my toil (ii. 10); there is nothing better for man than to rejoice in his works, for this is his portion (iii. 22; comp. also ix. 17, and ix. 9).

Those who assert that the book of Wisdom was written either to oppose the erroneous sentiments expressed in Coheleth, or to supplement and vindicate its misunderstood passages,[1] have failed to see that both books owe their origin to the same circumstances, and combat the same errors.[2]

[1] Augusti, Einleitung in das Alte Test., p. 249; Schmidt, Salomo's Prediger oder Koheleths Lehren, p. 71, note.

[2] Comp. Grimm, Introduction to his Comment. on the Book of Wisdom, p. 29, &c.

300, B.C. — 550, A.D. — The exact age of the Midrashic literature upon Coheleth cannot now be ascertained.   When the
prophetic fire began to be extinguished, and the voice of the
prophets was gradually dying away, a number of God-fearing
teachers arose, who, by their instruction, encouragement, and
solemn admonitions, rooted and builded up the people in their
most holy faith.   As the Bible formed the central point, around
which their legends, sermons, lectures, discussions, investigations, &c., clustered, a homiletico-exegetical literature was, in the
course of time, developed, called *Midrash* (מדרש[1]), which became
as mysterious in its gigantic dimensions, as it is in its origin.
Starting with the conviction that all sciences, as well as the
requirements of man for time and eternity, are contained in the
Scriptures, and that every repetition, figure, parallelism, synonym,
word, letter, nay the very shape and ornaments of the letter, or
titles, must have some recondite meaning, "just as every fibre of
a fly's wing, or an ant's foot, has its peculiar significance," the
text was explained in a fourfold manner, viz., 1. פשט, in *a
simple, primary,* or *literal; 2.* דרש, *secondary, homiletic,* or *spiritual; 3.* רמז, *allegorical; 4.* סוד, *recondite* or *mysterious sense,*
which was afterwards designated by the acrostic *Pardes,* פרדס,
transposing the ר and the ד.

The rules for this exegesis afforded as great a facility for
introducing into the text, as for deducing from it, any and every
imaginable conceit.   A few of them will suffice as a specimen.

1. A word is to be explained both with the preceding and
following words (מקרא נדרש לפניו ולאחריו).   Thus, וְשָׂרַי אֵשֶׁת
אַבְרָם לֹא יָלְדָה לוֹ וְלָהּ שִׁפְחָה מִצְרִית וּשְׁמָהּ הָגָר, *and Sarai,*

---

[1] מדרש (from דרש, *to investigate*) properly denotes *the investigation* or *study* of
the Bible, which, in accordance with the above-mentioned manner in which it
was pursued, developed itself in the הלכה (from הלך, *to go*), *current law, fixed rule
of life,* also called שמעתא (from שמע, *to hear*), *what was heard* or *accepted,* and
הגדה, Chaldee, אגדה, *what was said,* without having the authority of a law, *i.e.,
free exposition, homilies, moral sayings and legends.*   It is the collection of the
latter development (*i.e.,* of the homilies and legends) which is now called מדרש,
or מדרש הגדה.

Abraham's wife, bare him no children; and she had an handmaid, an Egyptian, whose name was Hagar (Gen. xvi. 1), is explained first, *and Sarai, Abraham's wife, bare no children to him and to herself* (לוֹ וְלָהּ); and then again, *to him* (*i. e.*, Abraham) *and to her* (*i. e.*, Sarai) *there was an handmaid* (לוֹ וְלָהּ שִׁפְחָה).

2. Letters are to be taken from one word and joined to another, or formed into a new word (גוֹרְעִין וּמוֹסִיפִין וְדוֹרְשִׁין); thus וּנְתַתֶּם אֶת־נַחֲלָתוֹ לִשְׁאֵרוֹ, *then ye shall give his inheritance unto his kinsman* (Numb. xxvii. 11), is explained, *and ye shall give the inheritance of his wife to him, i. e.*, the husband, taking away the ו from נַחֲלָתוֹ, and the ל from לִשְׁאֵרוֹ, and forming the word לוֹ, *i. e.*, וּנְתַתֶּם אֶת־נַחֲלַת שְׁאֵר לוֹ, deducing therefrom that a man inherits the property of his wife, (שְׁאֵר) (Baba Bathra, iii. 6.)

3. Words containing the same letters are exchanged for one another. Comp. my Commentary on the Song of Songs, p. 27.

4. The letters of a word are transposed; thus עֲמָלֵנוּ, *our labour* (Deut. xxv. 7), is made to mean *our children*, עֹלָמֵנוּ, by transposing the מ and the ל.

5. Letters resembling each other in sound or appearance, or belonging to the same organ, are interchanged; accordingly תּוֹרָה צִוָּה־לָנוּ מֹשֶׁה מוֹרָשָׁה קְהִלַּת יַעֲקֹב is explained, *the Law which Moses has given us is* (מְאָרָשָׂה) THE BETROTHED or WIFE *of the congregation of Jacob* (Deut. xxx. 4), by changing the ו in מוֹרָשָׁה for the א, and the שׁ for the שׂ.

6. Every letter of a word is reduced to its numerical value, and the word is explained by another of the same quantity; thus, from the passage, *And all the inhabitants of the earth were of one language* (Gen. xi. 1), is deduced that they all spoke *Hebrew*, שָׂפָה being changed for its synonym לָשׁוֹן,[1] and הַקֹּדֶשׁ $5 + 100 + 4 + 300 = 409$, is substituted for its equivalent אחת $1 + 8 + 400 = 409$. This rule is called גרמטיא = גימטריא = γραμματεία, from γράμμα, *letter*, from its bearing upon the letters.

7. Every letter of a word is taken as an initial or abbreviation

[1] Preston, not perceiving this, could not comprehend how the Rabbins make these two numbers the same. Comment. on Eccles., p. 69.

of a word. Accordingly the long and costly tunic which Jacob
made for his beloved Joseph, as an expression of peculiar fondness, indicated the troubles into which the Patriarch plunged his
favoured son, inasmuch as פַּסִים (Gen. xxxiii. 13), by this rule of
interpretation, called נוֹטְרִיקוֹן = *notaricun*, from *notarius*, a short-
hand-writer, one who writes with abbreviations, is פּוֹטִיפַר סוֹחֲרִים
יִשְׁמְעֵאלִים מִדְיָנִים *Potiphar*, who imprisoned Joseph, and the
merchants, who bought and sold him again as a slave.

8. The letters of the alphabet are taken in their inverse order,
א, the first letter, is expressed by ת, the last letter of the
alphabet; ב, the second letter, by שׁ, the last but one; ג by ר;
ד by ק; ה by צ, and so on. Accordingly שֵׁשַׁךְ, *Sheshach*, is
explained by בָּבֶל, *Babel* (Jer. xxv. 26; li. 41); לֵב קָמָי by כַּשְׂדִּים
(ibid. li. 1). This mode of interpretation is called אתבשׁ *Athbash*,
thereby indicating this inversion.[1]

Strange and arbitrary as these rules may appear, it will be
seen in the sequel that they have been followed by the ancient
translators of the Bible, and in some of the Patristic commentaries. We shall also see that the overlooking of this fact has
caused many modern critics to regard the apparent discrepancies
between the ancient versions and the Hebrew original, as owing
to different readings or wilful corruptions of the text on the part
of the Jews, when, in truth, these deviations are simply the
result of the application of one or the other of these exegetical
rules.

The Midrashic view is, that Solomon wrote this book *to expose
the emptiness and vanity of all worldly pursuits and carnal gratifications, and to shew that the happiness of man consists in fearing*

---

[1] When the reference is omitted in the illustrations of the exegetical rules,
the cited explanations will be found in the Midrash Rabba, or Midrash Jalkut,
upon the respective passages. For fuller information on this ancient mode of
interpretation, we must refer to the excellent treatises of Frankel, Ueber den
Einfluss der Palästinischen Exegese auf die Alexandrinische Hermeneutik,
Leipzig, 1851; Programm zur Eröffnung des jüdisch — theologischen Seminars
zu Breslau, Breslau, 1854; Hirschfeld, Die hagadische Exegese, Berlin, 1847;
Ben-Chananja, Jahrgang, i., pp. 116 and 227, &c.

God and obeying his commands. When young and joyful, the inspired monarch composed songs; when middle-aged and sober, he wrote wise proverbs and prudential maxims; and when old and weary of life, he described every earthly pleasure as vain and empty.[1] As is frequently the case, these much misunderstood Rabbins have given the proper view of the design of the book, though the nature of the Midrash precluded a regular commentary upon Coheleth in the historico-critical sense of the word.

1 A.D. — It now remained to be shewn how Solomon, who in his old age was seduced by his foreign wives to idolatry, also became a preacher of righteousness in his old age. The elastic rules of interpretation, aided by an oriental imagination, soon contrived to deduce it from the text. In chap. i., verse 12, Coheleth says, "I was king over Israel," *i.e.,* "*and am no more.*" Taking Solomon to be the author of Coheleth, this strange and remarkable assertion legitimately leads to one conclusion only, viz., that there was a period in his life when *he was dethroned.* Hence arose the legend, that when Solomon, elated with riches and wisdom, departed from the ways of the Lord, he was dethroned by Ashmodai, the king of the demons, and expelled from his capital as an example of the effects of sin. It was then that this ex-monarch went about the provinces and towns of the land of Israel mourning over his guilt, and saying, "I am Coheleth, whose name was formerly Solomon, who was king over Israel in Jerusalem, but through my sins have been driven from my throne and residence." Having thus confessed his sins, and denounced the folly of attempting to find satisfaction in earthly pleasures, the penitent Solomon was in his old age reinstated in the possession of his kingdom, where he died, at peace with God and man. There can be no doubt that ·this view is, *at least,* as old as the Christian era, being found in the earliest Jewish traditions.[2]

---

[1] רבי יונתן אמר שיר השירים כתב תחלה ואחר כך משלי ואחר כך קהלת ומייתי לה רבי יונתן
מדרך ארץ כשאדם נער אומר דברי זמר הגדיל אומר דברי משל הזקין אומר דברי הבלים רבי חוני
חמוי דרבי אמי אמר הכל מודים קהלת בסוף : ילקוט חלק שני קפבי

[2] See Midrash Yalkut on Coheleth i. 12.

100 – 250 A.D. — But though the homiletic (דרש), the allegorical (רמז), and the mysterious (סוד) modes of treating the
Bible were adopted by a large majority of the Rabbins, being
more suited to the practical and spiritual requirements of their
congregations, it must not be supposed that *the literal sense*
(פשט) was excluded, or even neglected.   Free enquiry into the
text and context of the Bible, and free expression of doubts
about the inspiration of any portion of Scripture which was
transmitted as canonical, were far more tolerated and encouraged
by these Rabbins, who are so often accused of bigotry and persecution (mostly by those who do not understand them), than
even in our free England.   Thus we find, in the Mishna, that
some, after a critical examination of its context, came to the conclusion that this book was not inspired.   Others went farther
still, and maintained that it contains *heretical sentiments.*[1]   Yet
these Rabbins were not put out of the synagogue as unfit
teachers of those committed to their care.

300 – 400 A.D. — From the passage in St. Jerome's commentary upon this book, given in the foot-note to p. 15, it will be
seen that the doubts with regard to the inspiration of Coheleth
had been entirely removed from the minds of the Jews in his
days, and that they allegorised it very largely.   Thus he tells
us that they interpret iii. 2–8 as referring to their past and
future history.

" The time for being born and for planting" refer to God's choosing and
making Israel his people; " the time for dying and plucking up that which
is planted," to their being carried away into captivity; " the time for
killing," to their bondage in Egypt; " the time for healing," to their
deliverance from it; " the time for breaking down," to the destruction of
the temple; " the time for building up," to their building the temple again;
"the time for weeping," to the taking of Jerusalem; "the time for laughing,"
to its restoration a second time; " the time for casting away stones," to
the dispersion and casting away of the Jews; " the time for gathering
stones," to their being gathered in again from among all nations; " the
time for embracing," to the love of God which compassed them about as a
girdle (Jer. xiii. 7, &c.); " the time for refraining," to the removing of God's

---

[1] *Vide supra,* p. 13, &c.

love, and their misery in the captivity, which God shewed to Jeremiah by a girdle hid in a rock and marred; "the time for getting and keeping," to the time of blessing and preserving them ; " the time for loosing and casting away," to the time of their rejection ; " the time for sowing," to the time of sowing them again ; "the time for keeping silence," to the present silence of the prophets ; " the time for speaking," to the time when God shall again speak unto them and comfort them in the land of their enemies; " the time for hatred," to the time when they crucified Christ; "the time for love," to the time of the patriarchs, when God loved them ; " the time for war," to the time of their impenitence ; " the time for peace," to the time when the fulness of the Gentiles shall come in, and all Israel be saved.[1]

400–500 A.D.—The old view and the allegorising of this book became more and more general.   It is related in the Talmud[2] (Gittin. 68, b), that the fugitive Solomon came before the Sanhedrin, declaring that it was he who had been king over Israel, that they tested the truthfulness of his assertion, and found it to be correct.   The indelicate means, however, adopted for this test, as there recorded, shew the vitiated taste of the age in polluting a legend otherwise so attractive and instructive.[3] An anecdote, however, related in another part of the Talmud (Abodah Sarah iii.), in connection with Coheleth x. 20, will shew that the strictly literal explanation was not ignored.

The Emperor Antoninus complained once to Rabbi that the great men of Rome annoyed him much.   Rabbi made no reply, but took the Emperor into his garden several successive davs, and each day pulled a radish out of the ground.   Whereupon the Emperor answered, You are right; you shew me thereby that I am to remove these great ones singly, and not all at the same time, lest they rise against me.   Why did Rabbi convey his advice in this manner? why did he not *say* what the Emperor should do?   He feared lest it should reach the ears of these great ones, and thereby cause persecution of the Jews.   But could he not tell it secretly to the Emperor? He remembered the passage, " The birds of heaven convey the report." Coheleth x. 20.

[1] Hieron. Com. in loco.
[2] For the development and completion of the Talmud, see my Commentary on the Song of Songs, p. 24, &c.
[3] אני קהלת הייתי מלך על ישראל בירושלים כי מטא גבי סנהדרין אמרו רבנן מכדי שוטה בחדא מילתא לא סריך מאי האי אמרו ליה לבניהו קא בעי לך מלכא לגביה אמר להו לא שלחו להו למלבווה ' קאתי מלכא לגבייכו שלחו להו אין קאתי שלחו להו בידקו בכרעי' שלחו להו במוקי' קאתי וקא תבע להו בניוותיהו וקא תבע לה נמי לבת שבע אימיה אתייה לשלמ' והכו ליה עוקתא ושושילתא דחקוק עליה שם כי טייל חזייה פרח ואפי' הכי' הוה ליה ביעתותא מיני : גיטין סח ב

600 A.D. — The Chaldee paraphrase,[1] which is the first entire commentary upon this book, based its explanations upon this view. Chap. i. 12 is thus paraphrased : —

When King Solomon was sitting upon the throne of his kingdom, his heart became elated with riches, and he transgressed the word of God; and he gathered many horses and chariots and riders, and he amassed much gold and silver, and he married wives from foreign nations. Whereupon the anger of the Lord was kindled against him, and he sent to him Ashmodai, the king of the demons, and he drove him from the throne of his kingdom, and took away the ring from his hand, in order that he should roam and wander about in the world to reprove it; and he went about the provincial towns and cities of the land of Israel, weeping and lamenting, and saying, " I am Coheleth, whose name was formerly Solomon, who was King over Israel in Jerusalem."

Those passages which are most perplexing to the historico-critical commentator form no difficulty whatever to the Chaldee paraphrast. Chap. ii. 24, where hilarity is recommended as the best thing for the disappointed sons of toil, is referred to the gathering of strength for the service and glory of God :

There is nothing comely for man but that he eat and drink and make his soul see good before the sons of man, to perform the commandments, to walk in the straight path before Him, so that it may be well with him from his labour.

Chap. iii. 17 – 22, which has been so frequently quoted to shew that Coheleth denies the immortality of the soul, is made to describe *the awful condition of the wicked in the great day of judgment*, and to set forth the necessity of fearing the Lord —

17. I said in my heart, the righteous God will judge in the great day of judgment, because a time is appointed for every thing; and for every work done in this world they will be judged.

18. I said in my heart concerning the children of men, that as for the chastisements and evil events which come upon them, it is God's doing, to

---

[1] The very inferior style of this paraphrase, as well as *some* of its legends and allusions, shew most unquestionably that it was written at the end of the fifth, or the beginning of the sixth century. But though committed to writing at this period, when the late portions of it were introduced, any one acquainted with the Midrashic literature will at once perceive that it contains legends and Hagadic interpretations as old as, and even older than, the Christian era.

try and to prove them, and to see whether they will return in repentance; He leaves them in rest, and they are healed. But the wicked, who are like cattle, do not repent, therefore they are unalterably convicted by it to do them evil.

19. For the destiny of the wicked and the destiny of the beast of the field there is one destiny for both of them, and as the beast of the field dies, so he dies who does not return in repentance before his death, and the breath of life of both is judged alike in every respect; and the advantage of a sinner over the beast of the field is nothing but the burial-place, for all is vanity.

20. All go to one place; all the inhabitants of the earth are made of dust, and when they die all return to the dust.

21. Who is wise to know the breathing spirit of the children of men, whether it goes upwards to heaven, and the breathing spirit of the beast, whether it goes downwards to the earth?

22. Therefore I saw that there was no good in this world but that a man should rejoice in his good works, and eat and drink and do good to his heart, for this is his good part in this world, to acquire thereby the world to come, so that no man should say in his heart, Why am I giving away money to do charity? I had better leave it to my son after me, or be nursed for it in my old age; because who can bring him to see what will be after him?

With all the allegorising and spiritualising of this paraphrast, he yet anticipated modern criticism, inasmuch as he saw that the deplorable state of things delineated in this book could not possibly refer to the prosperous reign of Solomon, and that it therefore describes the time *when Jerusalem was trodden down under the foot of the Gentiles, and the Jews carried into captivity.* But as he adhered to the traditional opinion that Solomon was the author of the book, the paraphrast was obliged to resort to the expedient that Solomon was transported by the spirit of prophecy into the distant future, whose history he depicts. Hence i. 12 is thus paraphrased: —

The words of prophecy which Coheleth, that is, the son of David the King, who was in Jerusalem, prophesied. When Solomon, the King of Israel, saw by the spirit of prophecy the kingdom of Rehoboam his son, that it will be divided with Jeroboam the son of Nebat, and that Jerusalem and the holy temple will be destroyed, and that the people of Israel will be carried away into captivity, he said, by His word, Vanity of vanities is this world, vanity of vanities is all for which I and my father David have laboured, all is vanity!

800 – 1040 A.D. — This view of Solomon's career became so
popular that it gave rise to a beautiful and entertaining Midrash
or Romance, in which the monarch's exile is said to have been
three years.   During this time he came into the country of
Ammon, was met and taken up by the royal cook, whom he soon
excelled, and succeeded, by the command of the king.   Whilst
in this position, the king's daughter was enamoured of him.
The king, grieved at it, drove them both away; they however
married, and she, by finding the ring which Solomon lost, and
which was the cause of Ashmodai being able to dethrone him, was
the means of restoring him to his throne in Jerusalem.   Being
reinstated into his glorious possession, " Solomon sent for his
wife's father, the king of the children of Ammon, and said to him,
Why hast thou unlawfully destroyed two souls?   Tremblingly
he replied, Far be it from me! I have not killed them, I only
expelled them into the desert, and know not what has become
of them.   Whereupon Solomon, of blessed memory, said, If thou
shouldst see them, wilt thou be able to recognise them?   Know
then that I am the cook, and thy daughter is my wife.   And
Solomon sent for her, and she came and kissed her father's hand,
who went back to his land in exceeding great joy."[1]   Rapoport,
who ingeniously tries to shew the psychological and ethical ideas
of this legend, aptly compares it to the German " Faust."[2]

1040 – 1105. — Rashi,[3] the celebrated commentator and
founder of the Germano-French Rabbinical literature, though
somewhat affected by the reaction in favour of the literal and
grammatical exegesis, which took place at, and progressed ever
since, the beginning of the seventh century, in consequence of the
extravagant length to which the allegorisers had gone, still

[1] This Midrash is printed by the indefatigable Jellinek, in his Bet ha-Midrash,
vol. ii., pp. 86, 87.

[2] See the very elaborate article, *Ashmodai*, in his Erech Millin.

[3] *Rashi*, רש״י, is an abbreviation for רבי שלמה יצחקי, *Rabbi Solomon Yitzchaki*,
erroneously explained by Buxtorf, *Rabbi Solomon Jarchi*.   He was born at
Troyes, in Champagne, in 1040, where also he died, about 1105.   Interesting
sketches of him are given in Zunz Zeitschrift für die Wissenschaft des Judenthums, p. 277, &c.

adheres to the traditional view of this book. He, too, maintains that *Solomon was dethroned by Ashmodai for his sins, and when brought to repentance wrote this book, to reprove the worldly minded of their folly, and to admonish · them by his sad expe rience to return to the Lord.*

As the commentary of Rashi abounds in grammatical and traditional lore, we give the following specimen of the first chapter : —

Chap. i. 1. *The words, &c.* — Wherever דברי is used at the beginning of a book, it shews that it is full of reproof ; thus, at the beginning of Deuteronomy, " These are the words (דברים) which Moses spake " (Deut. i. 1), which is seen from the words, and " Jeshurun got fat and kicked " (*Ibid* xxxii. 15). So also Amos, beginning with " The words of Amos," and continuing, " hear this word, ye kine of Bashan " (iv. 1) ; the book of Jeremiah, commencing with " The words of Jeremiah," and going on, " ask ye now, and see whether a man doth travail with child " (xxx. 6) ; and, " The last words of David " (2 Sam. xxiii. 1), which are followed by " but the sons of Belial shall be all of them as the thorns thrust away " (*Ibid.* ver. 6). So here, " The words of Coheleth," are followed by, " and the sun rises " (ver. 5), and " all the rivers flow into the sea " (ver. 7), comparing the wicked to the sun, moon, and sea ; so it is interpreted in the book Siphri, from which I gather that the context here speaks of the wicked, who are like the brightness of the sun, which ultimately goes down. There is also another interpretation there, viz., " All the rivers flow into the sea ; " what is meant thereby ? " It refers to the idolaters, those fools who worship the waters, believing that there is something in them, because they see the ocean, that all the streams flow into it, and yet it is never full ; and they do not understand that the same waters which flow into it come back again, for the waters of the streams which run into the sea are the same waters which have run before, for they return by a submarine passage, and go again upon the earth into the sea, and come back again under the sea ; therefore the rivers never cease running, and the sea is never full ; but there is no reality in the water." Thus far the Siphri. קהלת, *collector*, because he gathered much wisdom. And so we find that he is called Agur : " The word of Agur (*i.e.*, gatherer) the son of Jakeh " (Prov. xxx. 1), because he gathered wisdom and brought it up again. Others, however, interpret קהלת *preacher*, because he spoke all his words in an assembly. " King in Jerusalem," *i. e*, the city of wisdom.

2. *Vanity of vanities, &c.* — Coheleth complains, saying, respecting the creation effected in seven days, that it is altogether vanity of vanities. הֶבֶל has a Chatuph Pattach, because it is *construct*, i. e., *The utmost of all vanities.* הבל is mentioned seven times in this verse, referring to the work of the seven days of the creation.

3. *What advantage, &c.* — יחרון is *reward, advantage.* תחת *in exchange for.* 'שמש *sun, i. e.*, law, so it is called in Prov. vi. 23, " the law is light." Every labour for which he gives up the study of the law, what advantage is there in it?

4. *Generation goes, &c.* — However the wicked man may labour and exert himself to oppress and rob, he does not destroy his works, for when this generation is gone, another generation comes, and takes all away from his children, as it is written, " the poor will rob his children " (Job xx. 10).

But the earth abideth for ever. — And who are those that continue? The meek and the humble, who are bowed down to the earth, as it is written, " the meek shall inherit the earth " (Ps. xxxvii. 11). And the Midrash Tanchumah says that all Israel is called *land*, as it is written, " ye shall be a delightsome land " (Mal. iii. 12).

5. *And the sun, &c.* — When the sun rises in the morning, and sets in the evening, and travels all the night, then he pants to return to the same place where he rose yesterday, that he may rise there again.

6. *He goes to the, &c.* — הרוח is the *spirit, tendency* of the sun, called in French *talent*, comp. " whither the spirit was to go " (Ezek. i. 12).

And upon his, &c. — So it will also be to-morrow; the course or circuit which he ran yesterday he goes round to-day. He goes to the south always in the daytime, and comes round by the north in the night. He turns round alternately east and west; sometimes his course is in the day, and sometimes comes round in the night; in the summer solstice he walks, and in the winter solstice the sun turns round. So are the wicked; however the sun may shine, it will ultimately go down; however much that which appertains to them may go on and increase, their end is to return to the place of their defilement. From an unholy place they come, and to an unholy source they return.

7. *All the streams, &c.* — All the streams flow into the sea; and the sea is not full, because they do not remain therein, for the great ocean is higher than any part of the earth, as it is written, " he that calleth for the waters of the sea, and poureth them out upon the face of the earth " (Amos ix. 6). And how can one pour out, if not from a higher place to a lower? And the streams flow in channels under the mountains from the ocean, and return again; and this is the meaning of the words, " from the place to which the streams go, there they return again;" so is the wicked man, " in all points, as he came, so shall he go " (v. 16).

8. *All, &c.* — This refers to the third verse. If a man gives up the study of the law to employ himself in idle things, he will find them wearisome and unattainable; and if he is occupied with sight-seeing, his eye will not be satisfied; and if with the hearing of the ear, his ear will not be filled.

9. *What was, &c.* — Nothing is new that a man learns apart from the law; he will find nothing but what had already been in existence since the six days of the creation. But he who studies the law will constantly find in it new things, as it is written, " Let her breasts satisfy thee " (Prov

v. 19); just as the breast, wherein substance is found as long as the infant uses it; and so we find in the Talmud (Tract Chagiga), that R. Eliezer ben Harkanus propounded things which no one ever heard before, not even in the mysterious vision of Ezekiel.

10. *There is, &c.* — If you meet anything apart from the law respecting which it is said, Behold, this is new! whereas indeed it is not new, for it has been in existence in days bygone, only there is no remembrance of the former things, therefore they appear to be new. So also things which will happen in the future, will not be remembered by the generation that will follow them. The Midrash Agadah expounds the words, " there is no remembrance of the former," of the Amalekites, whose remembrance has been destroyed, and the latter part of this verse, viz., " and to the latter," &c., of the Edomites, whose remembrance will be destroyed, as it is written, " And there shall not be any remaining of the house of Esau" (Obad. i. 18).

12. *I, the preacher, &c.* — I was king of the whole world, afterwards only over Israel, afterwards only over Jerusalem, and afterwards only over my staff, because it is said, *I was* king in Jerusalem, but am no more now.

13. *And I gave my heart to know*, inquire in the law, which is wisdom, and to understand thereby all the evil work which was done under the sun, mentioned above. And I understood thereby that it is an evil occupation which the blessed God gave to the children of men, namely, " life and death, good and evil" (Deut. xxx. 15). ענין רע is *an evil conduct, occupation.* לענות בו *to occupy themselves.* ענין may, however, be taken in the sense of *dwelling*, or it may signify *meditation, thought*, so also לענות בו. The word נתן means *having it before them.*

14. רעות רוח *breaking of the spirit*, as " be crushed (רֹעוּ), ye people, and be broken" (Is. viii. 9). רוח *talent.* The end of every work terminates in pain of heart.

15. *The crooked, &c.* — He who is perverted when alive, cannot correct himself when dead; he who prepares in the day of preparation, eats on the Sabbath. And our Rabbins refer it to one who committed incest and had a bastard, or to a follower of the law who deserted it, being once right and afterwards became wrong.

And he who separated himself cannot be numbered. — That is, he who separates himself from the number of the righteous cannot be numbered with them when they receive their reward.

16. *I spoke, &c.* — Now, having come down from my greatness, I set my heart to say, Who would have said of me that I should come to this position?

17. *And I have* set my heart now to know the nature of wisdom, and to what it leads, and the nature of madness and folly. הללות *madness, confusion*, comp. mixed (מָהוּל) with water (Is. i. 21). שכלות *folly.*

I *know* now that there is a crushing of the spirit even in wisdom, for though a man relies much on his wisdom, and does not keep himself from forbidden things, the result is that he brings anger upon anger. I said I will multiply horses, and not cause the people to go down into Egypt, but at the end I made them go down. I said I will multiply wives, and they will not turn my heart; and yet it is said of me that " his wives turned away his heart" (1 Kings xi. 4). And it is also said that he relied much on his wisdom, and did many things; as it is written, "The man spake unto Ithiel, even unto Ithiel and Ucal" (Prov. xxx. 1).

How much this eminent commentator has contributed to Biblical exegesis, and how far he has anticipated and influenced modern expositions, will be seen in the sequel; though, to form a proper estimate of what exegesis owes to him, a thorough perusal of all his writings is necessary. The painstaking and honest Gesenius recognised, though not fully, the merits of Rashi, and other Jewish expositors,[1] which bolder and more pre-judiced critics deny, mostly without reading their writings.

1085–1155. — To Rashbam[2] belongs the honour of first eluci-dating the true design of this book. This distinguished Rabbi, possessed of a highly cultivated and classical mind, clearly saw that i. 2–11 *contains the burden of the argument; that it con-trasts the speedy passage of human life with the permanent existence of nature, thus shewing the advantage of the latter over the former; that all the ensuing experiments recounted in this book to dispel the melancholy effect of this contemplation were useless, and that com-fort could alone be found in the calm enjoyment of life, in resigna-tion to the dealings of Providence, in the belief in a future state, when all that is perplexing in the present state of things shall be rectified.*

Rashbam moreover saw that the first two verses and epilogue of Coheleth were subversive of the Solomonic authorship of the book. But instead of adhering to this alternative, which could hardly be expected from an expositor living in a period when

[1] See the Dissertation prefixed to his Manual, Hebrew and German Lexicon, 3rd ed., Leipzig, 1828, and the translation of it by Dr. Robinson, in the American Biblical Repository for 1833.

[2] Rashbam, רשב"ם, is the acrostic of רבי שמואל בן מאיר, Rabbi Samuel ben Meier; he was the grandson of Rashi, and was born about 1085, and died about 1155. See Zunz, zur Literatur und Geschichte, i., p. 70, &c.

historical exegesis was struggling hard to emerge from the abyss of allegory, he contented himself with the admission that these portions were added by others. The marvel is, that he has said and done so much. His style is simple and beautiful; and the commentary, which has only recently been published, by the praiseworthy Jellinek,[1] besides evolving the design of the book, also contains valuable criticisms. Yet all that Ewald said in noticing the book was, "Although we cannot expect any very great profit from the learned Rabbins of the middle ages for the Old Testament hermeneutics of the present day, and especially from their writings upon such books as Coheleth and the Song of Songs, yet they deserve publication for the history of interpretation."[2] We cannot say that if Ewald had perused this commentary he would have formed a different estimate of it. Every one acquainted with the writings of this very learned but very crotchety and prejudiced writer knows that he runs down every book which he has not written himself, or which does not repeat or does not eulogise what he has said. How different from Gesenius!

The following is a specimen of Rashbam's commentary:—

1. *The words of Coheleth, &c.*—Solomon is called Coheleth, because he gathered wisdom from all the children of the East, and was wiser than any man, as he is also called in another place, "Agur (gatherer), the son of Jakeh" (Prov. xxx. 1), *King*, because he was king in Jerusalem.

2. *Vanity of vanities, said Coheleth.*—He has not as yet said it, except in these words, where he repeats them in order to shew, in general and in particular, that all is vanity. Parallel passages to this are found in Ps. cxv. 1, "Not unto us, O Lord, not unto us;" Ps. xciii. 3, "The floods have lifted up, O Lord, the floods have lifted up;" and Ps. xcii. 10, "For lo, thy enemies, O Lord, for lo, thy enemies," beginning first with the predicate, and then mentioning the subject. Because he is anxious to give the subject, therefore he brings it in the middle of the sentence, and then begins his remarks again. So it is here; he mentions the name of Coheleth in the first part of the sentence, and then resumes the subject and proceeds.

[1] Commentar zu Koheleth und dem Hohen Liede von R. Samuel ben Meier, herausgegeben von Adolph Jellinek, Leipzig, 1855.
[2] Jahrbücher der Biblischen Wissenschaft von Heinrich Ewald, Jahrb. vii., p. 155.

These two verses were not written by Coheleth, but by him who compiled these words as they are at present. What he means by " vanity of vanities" is, that he gave his heart to search and to investigate the affairs of this world, and found all vanity.

3. *What advantage, &c.* — All these words refer to what is said below, " Nothing is good for man but that he should eat and drink," &c. (*infra,* ii. 4.) That is to say, all these works of man are vanity, and there is no work so good for man as that he should eat and drink, and rejoice with his portion. מַה־יִּתְרוֹן, *What reward and advantage has a man from all his labour that he labours under the sun?* for his end is to pass away and vanish from the world, and return no more. According to this explanation, there is a connection between this sentence and the sequel. " *Under the sun,*" because there is no hiding-place from its heat, therefore he mentions it; and it is the same as the phrase " under heaven."

4. *One generation goes and another comes,* for all die and return to the dust, but the earth remains for ever, that is to say *abides,* for it does not move from its place.

5. *And the sun rises.* — In the morning he rises in his place in the east, and in the evening he goes down and sets in the west, and then travels all night, because he pants and hastens to reach his place by the time of the morning, where he rose to-day. And also to-morrow he will rise there, and travel under the sea from the east towards the south, and then go through the south and west until he turns and goes to the north till he reaches his place in the east. When the sun is in the north, and gradually approaches the east, the word סוֹבֵב is properly used for it.

6. *Round, &c.* — This clause is a repetition of the words, " he goes to the south and returns to the north," that is to say, he returns and goes round all the quarters of the world. " And on its circuits the wind returns," so it always goes round again on its movements and courses, and goes round all the quarters of the world; but man is to-day here and to-morrow in the grave, and his works cease, so that he is remembered no more; therefore it is said, What advantage has man?

7. *And the sea, &c* — For if it were full, the streams would no longer flow into it. " To the place where the rivers go, there they go again." So to-morrow they will go again into the sea, for they do not leave off their habit and course; but man leaves his course and habit, he vanishes away from the world. All this refers to " What advantage hath man?"

8. " *All things, &c.* — All the works of this world are wearisome, for no man can enumerate them all. " The eye is not satisfied with seeing," for man looks out constantly, and hopes for new things. " The ear is not full with hearing." The ear constantly hears, and desires to hear, the works which are done in the world. Because the ear is hollow, therefore the word מָלֵא, *to fill,* is used. יְגֵעִים is *intransitive, weary, faint.* Comp. Deut. xxv. 18.

9. *What was, &c.* — And what advantage has man in all this, since what

has been long ago that will be in the future, and what has been done long ago will be done again, for there is nothing new under the sun.

10. *Is there anything, &c.* — If there be anything of which it is said, Behold there is something new, it is not true, for such a thing has happened long before us.

11. *There is no remembrance, &c.* — This refers to the question, What advantage has man? לָרִאשׁוֹנִים, *i.e.*, the *children of men who were born before us in this world* have no remembrance, since they have been dead long ago, and their memory is lost. And also succeeding men (לָאַחֲרוֹנִים), those who will come after us, will not be remembered by those who will follow them, for all die, and will be remembered no more. For if a man dies to-day, there will not be born another man like him, since men are not like each other; but other defunct creatures are remembered, for when one of them dies to-day, another is born like unto it; therefore those who see it say, "This creature is like unto the one which died;" hence there is a difference in this respect between rational and irrational creatures. For this cause it is said, What advantage has man?

12. *I, Coheleth, &c.* — Because I was king, and had leisure on account of my greatness.

13. *And I gave it, &c.* — To enquire in the works of the world, and I found that it is an evil employment which God has given to man to occupy himself therewith עִנְיָן is from ל״ה, changing the ה into a ו, and לַעֲנוֹת is from the same root (עָנָה), therefore the repetition is idiomatic, just as we find לִקְנוֹת קִנְיָן from קָנָה and לִבְנוֹת בִּנְיָן from בָּנָה, both having the same signification.

14. רְעוּת רוּחַ, *The inclination of the spirit.* רְעוּת is from רָעָה, *to desire*, just as דְמוּת is from דָמָה *to liken*, and עֲנוּת from עָנָה, *to humble, to afflict.* רוּחַ is *talent* in French.

15. *The crooked, &c.* — If a man has perverted his works, he can never be right in his works before God. And he who has omitted anything, the omission can never be counted among the other things which he has dutifully discharged.

16. *I said in my heart, &c.*, i.e., פינשיימי = *pensai moi* in French. לֵאמֹר, *thus I said.* עַל כָּל *more* than all the wise men who were before me in Jerusalem before I was born.

17. *And I gave my heart, &c.* — וָדַעַת, *i. e.*, לָדַעַת comp. דעת יעשה ישראל. The word הוֹלֵלוֹת has the same meaning as in chap. ii. 2. שִׂכְלוּת, *wisdom.* The words are repeated, because of the former phrase, *to know wisdom*, which is repeated. רַעְיוֹן, *gratification, inclination*, like רְעוּת רוּחַ; and as צִבְיוֹן, from צָבָה, *to desire;* אֶבְיוֹן, from אָבָה, *to want;* עֶלְיוֹן, from עָלָה, *to be above;* הֶגְיוֹן, from הָגָה, *to meditate;* so רַעְיוֹן, is from רָעָה, *to desire.*

18. *For in much, &c.* — Because of much wisdom a man thinks deeply about everything which the eyes see, and therefore he is much irritated. יֹסִיף is a repetition of the same sentence; because he increases much wisdom

and much knowledge, he meditates and pries into the works which God has done in the world, desiring to know why he made them thus; because he does not understand them, hence he is irritated, and increases his pain through the multitude of his thoughts.

The difference between Rashbam and Rashi is remarkable, and shews the striking progress Biblical exegesis has made. Whilst the grandfather constantly refers to the Midrash Tanchuma, the Midrash Agadah, and the Rabbins whose allegories he adopts, the grandson has not a single allusion to the Midrash, but firmly adheres to the text and context, tracing the logical sequence of every verse, and explaining the difficult grammatical forms and words.

1092 – 1167. — It cannot be said that Ibn Ezra or *Rabe*,[1] as he is sometimes called, did as much for *evolving* the design of this book in the Spanish school of exegesis, in which he deservedly occupies so distinguished a position, as Rashbam has done for it in the Germano-French school.

Ibn Ezra, too, maintains that Solomon wrote this book in his *old age,* to give the new and rising generation the benefit of his past experience.[2] As to the design of Coheleth, Ibn Ezra believes *that since the works of God, though good in themselves, do not produce a good effect upon all men, owing to the various dispositions, modes of thinking, &c., &c., of the recipients, — just as the same sun which bleaches the garment tans the face of the fuller, — the Lord inspired Solomon to explain these things, and to teach the right way, to shew that all the devices of man are vanity, that the fear of God can alone make him happy, and that this fear can only be obtained by the study of wisdom.*

The following is Ibn Ezra's introduction to Coheleth, and the first chapter of his commentary : —

---

[1] *Rabe,* רא״בע, is an abbreviation for *Rabbi Abraham ben Ezra,* רבי אברהם בן עזרא He was born in Toledo, in 1092, and died in Rome, in 1167. See Reland, Analecta Rabbinica; Vitæ celeberrimorum Rabbinorum, pp. 69 -80; Ersch und Gruber, Encyclop. i., pp. 79–84; Fürst, Biblioth. Judaica i., pp. 251–257.

[2] עניני הספר יורו כי באחרית ימיו חיברו כאילו יאמר לדורות הבאים כך וכך נסיתי בימי חיי See his commentary on i. 12.

PREFACE TO ECCLESIASTES.

The way of life is above to the wise, that he may depart from hell beneath. As a captured stranger longs to return to his own country, and be with his own people, so the intellectual spirit pants to get up to the highest stages, until it reaches the abode of the spirits, which dwell not in houses of clay. For bodies are compared to houses, whose foundations are in the dust, hence we find "angels, whose dwelling is not with flesh." — (Dan. ii. 11.) This is the case when the spirit — washed and purified from the impure lusts of the flesh, which are despicable, and defile holiness, lowering it into the depths of hell — determines to know its origin, and to see its own mystery with the unclouded eye of wisdom, so that that which is afar off is brought near, and the night becomes like the day; then it will be prepared to know truths comprised in faithful words, which will be indelibly engraved upon it in its separation from the body, for the writing is the writing of God, therefore the spirit sent into this world is confined in the body until death. All this is for its own benefit, and although it suffers for some years, yet it will rest and rejoice world without end.

All works are divisible into four classes : — 1. Altogether good. 2. Good for the most part, but having also some evil. 3. Altogether evil. 4. Evil for the most part, but having also some good. The first class is the portion of the sons of God, the second belongs to men on earth, and the two remaining have no existence, for the Lord God could not create anything but what is good. Everything being good, as a whole, as it is written, "And God saw everything that He had made, and behold it was very good" (Gen. i 31). And if there was some evil amongst it, it was slight, for it is not compatible with divine wisdom to withhold much good because of a little evil. The cause of the evil, however, lies in the imperfection of the recipient, and we cannot compare the works of God to any other work but his own, since all are his own works. Thus we find that the sun makes the spread out cloth white, at the same time that he makes the face of the fuller brown. Here, then, the same operation comes from the same operator, and yet there are different results, because the recipients are different.

The thoughts of men differ in proportion to the difference of the nature of their bodies; and their different natures again arise from the various conditions of the heavenly bodies, and the place of the sun, and those which are influenced by him, and by various climates, religions, and food, and many other innumerable things; and yet every one thinks himself right.

Therefore the Lord God of Israel has stirred up the spirit of Solomon, his friend, to explain desirable things, and teach the right way.

For no work made by a creature can stand, as in fact no creature is able to create any substance, nor to annihilate any; all the works of the creature being only imitations and non-essentials; as, to separate that which is united, and unite that which is separated, to set in motion that which is at rest, and to set at rest that which is in motion. The works of man are therefore altogether nothing and vanity, except to fear the Lord.

No man can attain the fear of the Lord, unless he ascends the ladder of wisdom, and is built and established on understanding.

COMMENTARY.

Chap. i. 1. *The words, &c.* — It is written that Solomon " spake three thousand parables, and that his songs were a thousand and five" (1 Kings iv. 32). Now, a parable is a thing with which another is compared, as we find, " Put forth a riddle, and speak a parable unto the house of Israel" (Ezek. xvii. 2). Here the parable is the great eagle, and the thing compared with it is Nebuchadnezzar. But the expression (שִׁיר) *song* is generally placed at the beginning, and (דָּבָר) *word* in the middle; but because Solomon was desirous to indite words which should impress the heart, he *began* with the expression (דִּבְרֵי) *words.* דִּבְרֵי, *words,* has not, however, always the same importance, as may be seen either from the following verse, or from this verse itself. Here the following verse also shews the impressiveness designed in the first verse. *Coheleth* is Solomon, for there was no other king of the sons of David, the anointed of the Lord, besides Solomon; he was called *Coheleth* (קֹהֶלֶת), *because wisdom was gathered in him.* He mentions *the residence* of his dominion, because it was his glory, as we find the king of Jerusalem was called Melchisedec; for Jerusalem was called Salem, as is evident from Ps. lxxvi. 2.

2. *Vanity of vanities, &c.* — By *vanity* (הֶבֶל) Coheleth describes the empty things of this world, and הֶבֶל is *construct* to הֲבָלִים, although there are no *Segoleth nouns* which change in the construct, except חֲדַר מִשְׁכָּבֶךָ (Exod. vii. 28), סְגוֹר דַּלְתֶּךָ (Isa. xxvi. 20), מְסַפֵּחַ חֲמָתְךָ (Hab. ii. 15), and even these have a Patach, and the word in question has Tzere. The repetition of the same noun in the genitive plural is used either for *superlatively good,* as מֶלֶךְ מְלָכִים, *King of Kings,* i. e, *the highest king;* or for *superlatively bad,* as עֶבֶד עֲבָדִים, *servant of servants,* i. e., *most abject servant;* hence הֲבֵל הֲבָלִים *vanity of vanities,* denotes *utmost vanity;* so also אַךְ הֶבֶל בְּנֵי אָדָם כָּזָב בְּנֵי אִישׁ בְּמֹאזְנַיִם לַעֲלוֹת הֵמָּה מֵהֶבֶל יַחַד, *surely men of low degree are vanity, and men of high degree are a lie; to be laid in the balance, they are altogether lighter than vanity* (Ps. lxii. 10), the מ in מֵהֶבֶל being *the comparative,* as the מ in מִכֹּל שֶׁהָיָה לְפָנַי בִּירוּשָׁלָיִם, *more than all who were before in Jerusalem* (Eccles. ii. 9), and in מִכֹּל מְלַמְּדַי הִשְׂכַּלְתִּי, *I have more understanding than all my teachers* (Ps. cxix. 99), meaning, if men were to be put in a balance with vanity, they would be lighter than vanity. The repetition, " vanity of vanities," indicates *perpetuity,* as " the floods have lifted up, O Lord, the floods have lifted up their voice" (Ps xciii. 3), and " they compassed me about, yea, they compassed me about" (*Ibid.* cxviii. 11). That it should not be said, Granted that there is vanity in the things of this world, but there is solidity as well, he therefore adds, *all is vanity.*

3. *What advantage, &c.* — יִתְרוֹן is according to the analogy of וִכָּרוֹן, and is derived from the verb, the נ of which is defective (*i. e.* פ״נ), as is evident from the Hiphil. The meaning is, since all is vanity, what profit has man from all his work. The sense of the phrase, *under the sun*, is *revolving time*; for the sun alone is the cause of time, since the day depends upon the sun, from its rising to the setting thereof; the night, too, is from sunset to sunrising, whether the moon and the stars are seen or not; so also seedtime and harvest, cold and heat, summer and winter depend upon the inclination of the sun, whether northward or southward. Although the moon has strong influences upon rivers and aqueous plants, and upon the human brain; although Pleiades has binding influences, and Orion loosing influences;[1] yet all their influences put together, when compared with those of the sun, are like one of its many parts. Although the sun is one, yet its influences differ, both according to the changes of the hundred and twenty *planets* which form the seven planets, and according to the change of the course of all of them, caused by the motion of the greatest sphere which projects. Therefore the position of the heavenly bodies will never be found alike, even for one moment. Hence it is written in the book Yetzirah, cap. i. § 4, " Two letters build two houses, three build six, &c., &c., till the mouth cannot tell, nor the ear hear, this endless transposition and multiplication."[2] But the labour of searching after wisdom, in order to enlighten the mind, has an advantage; for the spirit of man is not subject to the sun.

4. *One generation, &c.* — Because everything under the sun is composed of four elements, from which they proceed and to which they return, viz., fire, air, water, and earth, these four are adduced; and the earth is mentioned first, because she is as it were the mother; then the sun is mentioned, the abode of fire, because of its great heat, and this is the generating fire; then the air and the water. Respecting the earth, Coheleth says that all things created out of it will return to it, just as we find, " Dust thou art, and unto dust thou shalt return" (Gen. iii. 19); and that the

---

[1] According to Ibn Ezra on Job xxxviii. 31, Pleiades has the power of consolidating vegetation, and Orion of dissolving it.

[2] What the book Yetzirah — which Ibn Ezra quotes — means by " two letters form two houses," is, that two letters yield to combinations or transpositions, *e. g.*, אב and בא; three yield six, *e. g.*, אמש, אשם, מאש, משא, שאם, and שמא; four yield twenty-four, and so on. In order to ascertain how often a certain number of letters can be transposed, the product of the preceding number must be multiplied with it. Thus

$$
\begin{array}{rrr}
\text{Letter } 2 \times & 1 = & 2 \\
3 \times & 2 = & 6 \\
4 \times & 6 = & 24 \\
5 \times & 24 = & 120 \\
6 \times & 120 = & 720 \\
7 \times & 720 = & 5040, \text{ and so on.}
\end{array}
$$

H

earth will continue undiminished as long as one generation comes from it
and another returns to it. It may be that the word דור means *sojourners*,
thus we find "to dwell in the tents of wickedness" (Ps. lxxxiv. 10).[1]

5. *The sun rises, &c.* — Mathematicians have long since propounded, that
all visible creatures are divisible into ten parts, and the sun is the greatest
of all, and there is none like it; it is the root in the universe, just as the
point is in geometry, and the number one in mathematics; and the sense
is, although the sun has a motion rising and setting, it returns back to its
former place, and the place in which the sun rises to-day is nearer than the
one in which it will rise to-morrow; and because its motion is to the north
and south, therefore it rises twice a-year in one place, and once from the
extremity of the south, and once from the extremity of the north, thus
completing a year. But though this is also the case with the moon, the
five planets, and all the heavenly bodies, yet is the sun alone mentioned,
because of its being the greatest, as we find, "in them has he set a
tabernacle for the sun" (Ps. xix. 4), not mentioning the stars. שואף means
panting, comp. בְּאַוַּת נַפְשָׁהּ שָׁאֲפָה רוּחַ, *at her pleasure she snuffs up the wind*
(Jer. ii. 24), thus, as it were, panting after air in her desire to return to
the place.

6. *It goes, &c.* — Some say that this verse also refers to the sun, which
goes to the north and to the south, and explain רוּחַ to mean *the side;*
but this is incorrect, as is evident from the words, וְעַל סְבִיבֹתָיו שָׁב הָרוּחַ, *and
the wind returns upon its circuits;* the whole verse therefore refers to the
wind, which moves to the north and to the south, when it goes round from
the south to the north by the east, and when it goes from the north to the
south it goes by the west, therefore Coheleth says, סוֹבֵב סֹבֵב הוֹלֵךְ הָרוּחַ, *round
round goes the wind;* and at the end of the year it turns again on its
circuits, when the sun turns, which is the cause of all the motions of the
wind; and the navigators know these things, for these motions vary in the
same manner every day in the year.

7. *All the rivers, &c.* — Although all the streams flow into the sea, yet it
does not overflow, so as to transgress the law and cover the earth, because
the waters which flow into it return constantly to their own place, for there
is evaporation constantly rising from the sea to the sky, which forms the
clouds; the sweet waters only ascending because of their lightness, and the
vapour is converted into rain, as it is written, "He calleth for the waters of
the sea, and poureth them out upon the face of the earth" (Amos v. 8); and
the waters of the springs are from the rain, and the streams are from the
springs, as we see in the time of drought that most of the springs are dried
up; and again we find it written, "The brook dried up, because there had

[1] Ibn Ezra means thereby all living beings which have their temporal abode
upon this earth, including all animal and vegetable life. This explanation of
דור, *everything that sojourns, that moves about upon the earth*, is also followed by
Mendelssohn and Preston.

been no rain in the land" (1 Kings xvii. 7); and this explains how the streams return again from the place whither they went. And Solomon has not explained the cause of the waters returning to their place, just as he did not explain the cause of the sun returning from the west to the east; whether it is above the sky, or from the sides, or it is below the earth, being an orb, and placed in the midst of the highest sphere; for all these things require proofs, or such an explanation of everything seen by the eyes as not to require proof. And the object in mentioning these four, viz., the sun, which is the element of fire, the air, the water, and the earth, is because all things existing under the sun — plants, beasts, men, the fowls, and the fish of the sea — are all formed of them. And if the elements return back to their own place, where they formerly were, how can those abide which were formed of them ? and as the creatures are vanity at their beginning, so they will be at their end; and if man is vanity, much more so is his work, which is accidental, and still more his thought, which is an accident of an accident, as it is written, "The Lord knoweth the thoughts of men that they are vanity" (Ps. xciv. 11).

8. *All, &c.* — Some interpret יְגֵעִים *transitively, wearying others*, according to the analogy of מְלֵאִים, but this is incorrect, for יְגֵעִים is *neuter*, as the other instance, עָיֵף וְיָגֵעַ, *faint and weary*, in Deut. xxv. 18, shows: and if it were as they interpret it, it ought to have been מְיַגְּעִים, the Piel, comp. אַל תִּיגַע שָׁמָּה, *do not weary these* (Josh. vii. 3); but יְגֵעִים is *intransitive*, meaning that the things themselves are faint and defective, there is no strength in them, therefore man cannot describe them. Having described the four elements, which continue in the same position, and if they are set in motion they return again at the end to their former position; knowing the general principle and the particulars ensuing therefrom, that they do not continue one moment in the same position, therefore, no man is able to describe them.

And the eye is not satisfied with seeing them; for the cause of the eye seeing objects is that they are reflected in the pure air. And they do not abide even one moment. The ear is not filled with hearing the particulars, for the cause of hearing is also the entrance of the air containing the forms of the sounds, and these two cannot abide; therefore the eye cannot master them in their particulars, nor can the ear hear all their numbers, because they are innumerable to man, for the Creator alone knows both generals and particulars, for they are all the works of His hands.

9. *That which was, &c.* — The singer (David) said of the heavenly Being, that "He commanded, and they were created; He hath also established them for ever and ever" (Psalm cxlviii. 5); and of the earthly beings he said, that "His name alone is excellent" (*Ibid.* v. 13). That is to say, they are altogether vanity. The words "what was will be" refer to the spheres and their hosts, for they are like wheels continually turning round, and their beginning is like their end, and their end like their beginning.

What was done will be done. — This refers to the different kinds of beings, viz., man, horses, every species of animal and vegetable life, the propagation of which depends upon the motions of the heavenly bodies. As long, therefore, as these heavenly bodies abide, these kinds will also continue in the same way, being formed according to these heavenly bodies. And the meaning is, "Although 1 cannot enumerate the particulars, the generals are observed, known, and described; and in this way it is seen that the upper and lower worlds continue in the same manner, and there is nothing new."

10. *Is there, &c.* — יֵשׁ is frequently found to denote *something* RARELY *met with;* comp. וְיֵשׁ אֲשֶׁר יִהְיֶה הֶעָנָן, *and when it rarely happened that the cloud rested, &c.* (Numb. ix. 20); יֵשׁ מְפַזֵּר וְנוֹסָף, *it sometimes happens that one scatters and yet increases* (Prov. xi. 24); יֵשׁ רָשָׁע מַאֲרִיךְ, *it sometimes happens that a wicked man is prolonged in his wickedness* (Eccl. vii. 15), for, generally speaking, "the years of the wicked are shortened" (Prov. x. 27). If any thing should seem new to one, the same has already happened before. עֹלָמִים means *times, ages;* thus, צוּר עֹלָמִים, *rock of ages* (Is. xxvi. 4); מַלְכוּתְךָ מַלְכוּת כָּל־עֹלָמִים, *thy kingdom is a kingdom of all ages* (Psalm cxlv. 13); תְּשׁוּעַת עֹלָמִים, *a salvation for all ages,* i. e., *everlasting* (Is. xlv. 17).

11. *There is no remembrance, &c.* — If it is questioned whether such a novel thing has actually happened in former days, it is because there is no remembrance of former things; which will also be the case with the things that will take place in days to come, they too will be forgotten at a later period. Hitherto Solomon spoke in general, and now he begins to take up specifically those things which occurred to him.

12. *I, Coheleth, &c.* — The contents of this book shew that Solomon wrote it in his advanced days, and appeals as it were to the new and rising generation, and tells them, 'such and such things I have tried in my lifetime, and forsooth I could try everything because of my being king.' *Over Israel* is mentioned, because there was always among them prophets and wise men, such as the children of Zerach,[1] and not as the sons of Kedar who dwelled in tents, and thereby shewing that he was king over a wise and intelligent people. *Jerusalem* is mentioned, because its situation is advantageous for the reception of wisdom. It is known that the habitable world is divided into seven parts, and there are no men with proper faculties to acquire wisdom except in the three central parts, for the foremost and the hindmost parts, being either too hot or too cold, interfere with the nature of man. It is, moreover, known that the latitude of Jerusalem is 33 degrees, and this is the centre of the habitable world, for habitation is impossible except beyond the degrees where the sun inclines either in the north or south.

13. *And I gave my heart, &c.* — It is better to connect this verse with

[1] Ethan, Heman, Chalcol, and Darda, the celebrated sages, who were contemporaries with Solomon. Comp. 1 Kings v. 11; 1 Chron. ii. 6.

what follows; and the meaning is that he searched after knowledge. This is the sense of לָתוּר. Comp. כְּתוּר הָאָרֶץ, *from searching out the land* (Numb. xiii. 25), i. e., *to see desirable things*, and the source of all things, though this is an unpleasant task, since men are often employed in unprofitable things. לַעֲנוֹת, *to be employed*, is from the same root as עִנְיָן, *employment*. Some, however, maintain that it is from the same root as עָנִי, *afflicted*, and say that the verb has here the same signification as in אֲנִי עָנִיתִי מְאֹד, *I was greatly afflicted* (Ps. cxvi. 10), and עָנָה גְאוֹן יִשְׂרָאֵל, *he humbled the pride of Israel* (Hos. v. 5). But it is more likely that it denotes *to testify*, as לֹא־תַעֲנֶה בְרֵעֶךָ, *thou shalt not testify against thy neighbour* (Exod. xx. 16); and even עָנִיתִי, in Ps. cxvi. 10, is to be taken in the same sense, just as we find וַיַּעַן אִיוֹב, *and Job declared* (Job iii. 2), and this is evident from the immediately following words, אֲנִי אָמַרְתִּי בְחָפְזִי, *I have said in my haste;* compare also יִשְׁמַע אֵל וַיַעֲנֵם, *the Lord will hear them* (Ps. lv. 20), i. e., he will testify against them. And when Coheleth had employed himself with discovering the nature of things, he found that they were vanity and striving after the wind. The meaning of the phrase *under heaven* is the same as *under the sun*. It may be that in the words *under heaven*, as in *under the sun*, Coheleth alludes to the upper sphere, where all the heavenly hosts are. Now the knowledge of astrology is connected with the forty-eight forms of the sphere, and after Coheleth had employed himself to learn by this science the nature of all things which are produced by the power of heaven, he saw that it was a sore and difficult employment, because of the limited knowledge which man has, to enumerate the causes and effects, as there is no number to the heavenly hosts, and the ancients knew no more than 1022. This is moreover proved by the connection of *under heaven* with *there is an appointed time for everything* in iii. 1. So also is the phrase to be understood in ii. 3.

14. *I saw all the, &c.* — The meaning of רְעוּת רוּחַ may be the same as אֶפְרַיִם רֹעֶה רוּחַ וְרֹדֵף קָדִים, *Ephraim feeds on wind, and follows after the east wind* (Hos. xii. 2), i. e., *feeds upon that which neither profits nor satisfies;* רוּחַ, *wind*, means *emptiness*, because the wind escapes in various directions, so that no man can lay hold on it; thus we find *they sow wind* (Hos. viii. 7), and *the wind passes over it* (Ps. ciii. 16). It is, however, more likely that רְעוּת, as רַעְיוֹן, signifies *thought*, just as דְמוּת and דִמְיוֹן, two different forms of לׁ"ה, have the same meaning.

15. *The crooked, &c.* — מְעֻוָת is participle *passive*, according to the analogy of מְדוּבָּר, and may be derived from two different roots, one regular (עָוַת), and the other irregular (עָוָה), signifying the same thing. The word לִתְקֹן is *intransitive*, and, according to the first interpretation of the two preceding verses, the meaning is, having seen that everything is vanity, this vanity cannot be rendered solid, for that which is defective cannot be rectified, because its nature is radically defective; and he who is defective cannot be numbered with the perfect. This interpretation implies an omission of

בַּעַל, *man*, before חֶסְרוֹן, or takes חֶסְרוֹן as an *adjective;* as רָאשׁוֹן. *the first*, and אַחֲרוֹן, *the last.* חֶסְרוֹן may also be regarded as referring to מְעֻוָּת; so that מְעֻוָּת by itself would denote *naturally defective*, and מְעֻוָּת חֶסְרוֹן, *accidentally defective.* If we, however, adopt the second interpretation, viz., that man is born in defective circumstances, then man has no power to perfect himself, and it is found that he who occupies himself with the investigation of the nature of things by the operation of the heavenly bodies, occupies himself uselessly; and this is the case with most men and most of their works.

16. *I said, &c.* — Because the heart is the habitation of the spirit, and is created first in the body — for it is like a king, and the intellect like its minister — therefore it is used for wisdom, and knowledge, and taste, and the operation of thought being the first receptacle of the heavenly soul; just as lips are used for language, because words proceed out of them. Hence it is said, " A wise prudent heart" (1 Kings iii. 12), " He who buys a heart loves his soul" (Prov. xix. 8).

I have increased and added wisdom, i.e., he compiled and learned the wisdom of the ancients, and added to it.

And my heart saw much wisdom, i.e., which he did not compile. The *adverb* הַרְבֵּה, like רֵיקָם, is construed both with the singular and with the plural, comp. כִּי־הִרְבּוּ יִהְיוּ, *for they shall be many (infra,* xi. 8), *the infinitive absolute* has a quametz; comp. הַרְבָּה אַרְבֶּה, *multiplying, I will multiply* (Gen. xxii. 17).

17. *And I gave, &c.* — Having learned wisdom, and added to it, I gave my heart to know the nature of folly (comp. וַיִּתְהֹלֵל בְּיָדָם, *and he feigned himself mad in their hand* (1 Sam. xxi. 14), and the nature of wisdom, which is the opposite of folly, although this also is a vain striving).

18. *For in much, &c.* — Because when he sought to know wisdom, he found that the wise man, who understands the affairs of the world through his great knowledge, has constant provocation and pain, and has no pleasure in his children, because he knows that their end is to die, either in his lifetime or afterwards; nor does he rejoice in riches, which fly away like a bird, and cannot help or save in the day of trouble; and the day of death stares into his eyes.

It will be seen from this specimen, and still more from other parts of the commentary, that the peculiar philosophical and astrological notions which Ibn Ezra entertained greatly interfered with his tracing the logical sequence of the text, inasmuch as he constantly introduces his favourite theories into the declarations of Coheleth. Still, the commentary is a masterpiece, and a storehouse of varied learning. It contains more grammatical and lexicographical lore than any modern exposition of

Coheleth we have yet seen, and some of his ingenious criticisms deserve the greatest attention of grammarians.

Thus, in trying to explain why the superior power of wisdom is characterised as excelling the strength of *ten* mighty men (chap. vii. 19), Ibn Ezra remarks —

The number *ten* is mentioned, because it is the arithmetical completion, as this decade is the highest of all, for all above it are merely units. Moreover, since the main strength of a thing lies in its beginning, middle, and end, the א (*one*) being in Hebrew the first or beginning, the י (*ten*) the end, and the ה (*five*), together with ו (*six*), form the middle [of this number ten]; hence these four letters אהוי constitute the original vowels: and no word or syllable can be pronounced without one or the other of these letters.[1]

On xii. 5, Ibn Ezra disputes the existence of *diminutives* in Hebrew. He says —

R. Adonim ben Temim, the Babylonian (who flourished at the end of the 10th century), whose soul is in Paradise, maintains that אֶבְיוֹנָה is an epithet for the human spirit; and he thus analyses it—אֶבְיוֹן is *adjective mas.* and אֶבְיוֹנָה the *fem.*; and if thou wantest to make it *diminutive*, it will be אֶבְיוֹנָה, the proper names אֲמִינוֹן, *Aminon* (2 Sam. xiii. 20), and גַּשְׁמוּ, *Gashmu* (Nehem. vi. 6), he says are also diminutives. But this is poor grammar, since there is no word in Hebrew which can be made into a diminutive; and if the genius of the Hebrew languages had admitted of making diminutives, we should have found hundreds and thousands of them in the Scriptures. Now אַמְנוֹן, *Amnon*, and אֲמִינוֹן, *Aminon*, are two names of the same individual, just as שְׁלֹמֹה, *Shelomo*, and שַׁלְמוֹן, *Shalmon*, אַבְשִׁי, *Abshai*, and אֲבִישַׁי, *Abishai*, אַבְנֵר, *Abner*, and אֲבִינֵר, *Abiner*. As for the ו in גַּשְׁמוּ, *Gashmu*, it is redundant, as in יִתְרוֹ, *Jethro*, i. q., יֶתֶר, *Jether*.[2]

Ewald, who sneers at the Rabbins of the middle ages, will be surprised to find his theory about אמינון (Hebrew Grammar,

---

[1] ומנין עשרה בעבור היותו סך חשבון והוא ראש הכלל כי כל מה שיש למעלה ממנו הם אחדים בעבור היות עיקר כל דבר הראש ואמצעיתו וסופו היה הא"לף בלשון הקדש בתחלה והי"וד בסוף יהג' היו הה"א והו"ו אמצעיים ואלה הארבעה אותיות הם למשך ולא יתכן שימצא אות או תנועה ־ק שיהיה אחד מהם נמשך עמו

[2] אמר ר' אדונים בן תמי' המזרחי נ"ע כי אביונה כנוי לרוח בני האדם וכן דקדוקו אביון אדם השם לזכר ואביונה לשון נקבה ואם תצטירנה תהיה אביונה וכן מלת אמינון וגשמו אומר וזהו דקדוק עניית כי אין בלשון הקדש מלה שהתקשינו כלל ואילו היה זה ה ביסוד הלשון להקטין יהיו נמצאים במקרא למאות ולאלף' ואולם אמנון ואמינון שני שמות לאיש אח' כמו שלמה ושלמון אבשי ואכישי אבנר ואבינר יהוסף וי'ו גשמו כמו יתר ויתרו

§ 167), propounded by a Rabbi of the tenth century, and so ably opposed by another Rabbi of the twelfth century.

1100. — From the constant remarks of Ibn Ezra, — *some say* (יש אומרים, ii. 12 ; iii. 1. 18 ; iv. 12. 17 ; v. 19 ; ix. 17 ; x. 4, al.), *some interpret it* (יש מפרשים, iii. 11 ; iv. 19 ; v. 1. 2. 5 ; vii. 1. 19 ; viii. 5. 8. 10 ; x. 1, al.), *most interpreters* (רוב המפרשים, iv. 17 ; x. 6, 9), *one of the interpreters says* (אחד מן המפרשים, ii. 16 ; x. 17), &c., — it is evident that numerous commentaries, which are now lost, have been written on this book in the tenth, eleventh, and twelfth centuries. Would that we at least had a history of the various views which those forgotten commentators entertained concerning Coheleth ! It would no doubt have formed a curious and valuable addition to the literature of Biblical interpretation. However, one of these views is preserved by Ibn Ezra, who tells us in his commentary, chap. vii. 3, that[1] —

In consequence of the difficulties and apparent contradictions of this book, as, for instance —

In one place he says —		In another he says the reverse —	
Anger is better than laughter	vii. 3	Anger rests in the bosom of fools	vii. 9
In much wisdom is much anger	i. 18	Remove anger from thy heart	xi. 10
It is good and comely to eat and drink	v. 17	It is good to go to the house of mourning	vii. 2
I praised mirth	viii. 15	To mirth I said, What avails she?	ii. 2
What advantage has the wise man over the fool ?	vi. 8	There is an advantage to wisdom over folly	ii. 13
I praised the dead	iv. 2	A living dog is better than a dead lion	ix. 4
There is no work, nor account, nor knowledge, nor wisdom in the grave	ix. 10	There is an appointed time for every thing there	iii. 17

1 שיראו בדברי שלמה בספר הזה דברים קשים מהם שיאמר במקומות רבים דבר ויאמר הפך הדבר ובעבור זה אמרו חכמי ישראל ז״ל בקשו חכמים לגנוז ספרקהלת מפני דבריו סותרין זה את זה אמר טוב כעס משחוק והפך זה כי כעס בחק כסילים ינוח וכן כי ברוב חכמה רוב כעס והפך זה והסר כעס מלבד וכן טוב אשר יפה לאכול ולשתות והפך זה טוב ללכת אל בית האבל וכן ושבחתי אני את השמחה והפך זה ולשמ' מה זה עושה וכן כי מה יותר לחכם מן הכסיל והפך שיש יתרון לחכמה וכן ושבח אני את המתים והפך זה כי לכלב חי הוא טוב מי האריה המת וכי כי אין מעשה וחשבון ודעת וחכמה בשאול והפך

In one place he says —	In another place the reverse —
It shall not be well with the wicked, and he shall not prolong his days . . vii. 13	There is a wicked man who prolongs his days in his wickedness vii. 15
It shall be well with those who fear God viii. 12	There are wicked to whom it happens according to the. doings of the righteous . viii. 14

And many more like these will be found by an attentive reader, for which, as the wise men of Israel of blessed memory tell us, the sages wanted to make this book apocryphal, though it is well known that the least among the wise will not write a book and contradict himself in it. WHEREFORE, ONE OF THE COMMENTATORS EXPLAINED *Coheleth* (קְהֵלֶת) BY ASSEMBLY, AND MAINTAINED THAT THIS BOOK WAS COMPOSED BY THE DISCIPLES OF SOLOMON, AND CONTAINS THE DIFFERENT OPINIONS OF EACH OF THEM. But this opinion is utterly inadmissible, because the words " Coheleth *was a wise man*" (xii. 9), shew that it refers to a single individual. So also " Coheleth *was desirous* to find acceptable words" (xii. 10), and especially " I, Coheleth, *was king*" (i. 12), are most conclusively against it.

It will be seen, from this view of Coheleth, that as literal and grammatical interpretation progressed, the sceptical passages in this book, which were so easily converted into orthodoxy by the allegorisers of former days, became more and more perplexing.

1135 – 1204. — The great philosophers of the twelfth and thirteenth centuries, who created a new epoch in Jewish literature, now began to grapple with these hard sayings of Coheleth, which they occasionally quote and explain in their respective works. Thus Maimonides,[1] in his More Nebochim, ii. 28,

כי עת לכל חפץ וכן וטוב לא יהיה לרשע ולא יאריך ימים והפך יש רשע מאריך ברעתו וכן אשר
יהיה טוב ליראי האלהים והפך יש רשעים שמגיע אליהם כמעשה הצדיקים והמחפש היטב ימצא עוד
כאלה בספר הזה וידוע כי הקל שבחכמים לא יחבר ספר ויסתיר דבריו בספרו והוצרך אחד סן המפרשים
לפרש מלת קהלת כמו קהלת יעקב ואמר כי תלמידיו חברו הספר וכל אחד אמר כפי מחשבתו וזה אינני
נכון כלל בעבור ויותר שהיה קהלת הכם והנה הוא אחד ועוד בקש קהלת למצא דברי חפץ והראיה
הגמורה אני קהלת הייתי מלך

1 Maimonides, or *Rambam*, רמב"ם, as he is also called, from the initials of רבי משה בן מימון, *Rabbi Moses ben Maimon*, was born on the 30th of March, 1135,

defends Solomon from the heretical opinion, as deduced from Coheleth, i. 4, *that this world has existed from all eternity.* As the Rev. Theodore Preston, who gives this part of Maimonides' work,[1] has so wofully mistranslated it, we have been obliged to make a new translation, which is given in Appendix III., together with his version and the Hebrew.

1142. — Nathaniel, called in Arabic Abul-Barcat Hibat Allah b. Malka, who was the medical Coryphæus of the Mahommedan dominions in the twelfth century, as well as a distinguished philosopher and Hebraist, and who was designated "the only one of his time," *Wachid-al Zeman,* because of his extraordinary services, now tried his skill on this difficult book. His commentary, which is written in Arabic, has never been published, but the MS. is in the Bodleian Library, Oxford. Isaac Ibn Ezra, son of the immortal commentator, celebrated Abul-Barcat's commentary on Coheleth in a poem, in which he declares that this Solomonic book will henceforth (1143 A. D.) go by the name of him who has so successfully unlocked its meaning.[2] Some idea, however, may be formed of the merits of this commentary from the following specimen, quoted by the learned Pocock in his *Notæ Miscellaneæ ad Portam Mosis* ·[3]—

פקאל מי יודע וג' עלי רסם אלתוביך ואלנכרה עליהם פקאל אן מן הו צאורף מתחקק רוח
בני האדם עולה למעלה ואנדא מחפוטׁה ענד אלכׁאלק אלי יום אלנשר פירדהא אלי גסדהא ואן
רוח הבהמה ליס להא רגׁעה בל הי נאזלה אלי ספל אלאריץ מהׁל אלגסם אלרי יתלאשא ויצׁמהל פארא
עלם דלך ותחקקה פינׁב עליה אן לא יקים נפסה כאלבהאים וירכב שהותה והו יעלם אן אללה טׁאלבה

Dixit, Quis noit, &c., viâ increpationis et aversationis ipsorum, quasi diceret, Quisquis noverit, ac pro certo habuerit, Spiritum hominum ascendere sursum, ac servari ipsum apud Creatorem usque ad diem resurrectionis, qui tum in

in Cordova, and died 13th December, 1204. An instructive sketch of the life and labours of this most illustrious philosopher is given by Jost, in Herzog's Real-Encyclopädie für Protestantische Theologie und Kirche, vol. viii., p. 691–697; Graetz, Geschichte der Juden vi., p. 310.

[1] The Hebrew Text, and a Latin version of the Book of Solomon called Ecclesiastes; with original Notes, philological and exegetical. London, 1845, p. 18.

[2] Comp. Zeitschrift der Deutschen Morgenländischen Gesellschaft, Jahrgang, 1859, p. 711; Graetz, Geschichte der Juden, vi., p. 303.

[3] The theological works of Dr. Pocock, London, 1740, vol. i. p. 196.

corpus suum ipsum remittet, spiritum autem jumenti non iterum reverti,
sed descendere in imum terræ instar corporis quod tabescit et dissolvitur;
hæc cùm certò noverit, oportet illum non se jumentorum more gerere, et
cupiditatibus suis indulgere, cùm sciat Deum de ipso rationem sumpturum.

1270.—The celebrated Zohar, or the Talmud of the Kabbala,
as it is aptly called, which, as is now critically certain, was
compiled in the second half of the thirteenth century,[1] also refers
to the hard sayings and apparent contradictions of Coheleth, and
attempts to overcome the difficulty by resorting to the hypothesis, *that Solomon quotes the language of ignorant unbelievers to
expose their folly.*   Chap. iii. 19, is thus commented upon: —

> Solomon did not say this for himself, as the other words, but he repeats
> here the words of the worldly fool, who says so. And what do they say?
> That " the destiny of man and the destiny of beasts," &c. They are fools,
> because they know not, nor do they enquire into wisdom; they say that this
> world goes on by chance, and the Holy One, blessed be He, takes no cog-
> nisance of it; but that " the destiny of man and the destiny of the beast is
> the same, and the same destiny happens to all." And as Solomon knew
> these fools who spoke in this manner, he called them beasts, for they
> degraded themselves into mere beasts by uttering such sentiments.[2]

This attempt to explain away the obnoxious passages, is substantially the same as the one mentioned by Ibn Ezra (*vide*

---

[1] For the development of the Zohar see Jost, Geschichte des Judenthums, &c.,
vol. iii., p. 74 - 81. Preston's remark on Mendelssohn's Introduction (p. 76), that
" the Zohar is *a most ancient* Jewish commentary on the Pentateuch," is a mere
repetition of an impudent assertion of the Kabbalists, who palmed it upon *Simeon
ben Jochai*, which is now entirely exploded. Compare also Steinschneider's very
able work on Jewish Literature, London, Longman, &c., 1857, p. 11,1 &c.; and
Die Religionsphilosophie des Sohar und ihr Verhältniss zur allgemeinen jüdischen
Theologie, von D. H. Joël, Leipzig, 1849.

[2] לא אמר שלמה דאי קרא מגרמי' כשאר אינון מלין אלא אהדר אינן מלוי דטפשאי דאלמא
דאמרו כך ומאי אמרי כי מקרה האדם ומקרה הבחמה וגו' מפשאי דלא ידעין ולא מסתכלין
בחכמתא אמרי דהאי עלמא אזיל במקרה וקב"ה לא אשגח עלייהו אלא מקרה האדם ומקרה
הבהמה ומקרה אחד וגו' וכר שלמה אסתכיל באינין מפשאי דקארי דא קרי להון בהמה דאינון
עבדי גרמייהו בהמה ממש בגין דאמרין מלין אלין   This passage is quoted by Mendelssohn
in his very elaborate Introduction to his Commentary on the Book of Ecclesiastes.
The biblical student will find a great mass of valuable information in this
Introduction, which has been translated by Preston in the work quoted in Note 2
of the preceding page, and in the foregoing note in this page.

supra, p. 57), only that there the heretical sentiments are ascribed to the different disciples of Solomon, whereas here they are put into the mouth of unbelievers generally.

To the period of the Zohar we must ascribe the Midrash Themurah, which is based upon Coheleth. The design of this Midrash is *to shew that all the opposites which exist upon this earth, e. g., riches and poverty, beauty and deformity, &c., contribute to the harmony of the whole, and speak of the wisdom of the Creator; and they must respectively be received with thankfulness and resignation.* To enforce this lesson, the Midrash especially expatiates upon chap. iii. 1 – 8, in connection with Ps. cxxxvi.[1]

1280 – 1350. — Joseph Ibn Caspi, a celebrated expositor and philosopher, who flourished in the beginning of the fourteenth century, wrote a commentary on this book, propounding, according to his own assertion, quite a new theory of its import. He maintains that *the design of Coheleth is to teach man that his occupations with the affairs of this world are to be as little as possible, since they are all vain, and that he is to give himself up to the study of the law and science.* This Coheleth sets forth in twenty-one arguments, which are first treated according to the ten הבלים in connection with the passages of Scripture, and then according to their logical sequence. Whereupon he gives some hints on the perfection of the soul, and on prophecy, as connected with the *active mind*, and quotes ten verses from this book, which, according to him, recommend the Aristotelian medium between the two extremes. Caspi wrote this commentary when he was fifty years old, and called it *The Seal of Life;* it has never been printed, but the MS. is at Oxford. Our notice of it is taken from Steinschneider's very elaborate and excellent article on Joseph Caspi, in Ersch and Gruber's Encyclopedia, the remarks of which on this commentary we

---

[1] This Midrash is comprised in the collection of small Midrashim edited by Jellinek, to which reference has already been made, p. 38, note i.

subjoin in the foot-note.[1] Ibn Caspi's extremely scarce commentary on the Song of Songs we published in our " Introduction to the Song of Songs," pp. 47–49, where the reader
will find the theory of active and passive mind largely
developed.

1298 – 1370. — Though the celebrated *Bechinoth Olam* (Trial
of the World), does not profess to be an exposition of our book,
yet there can be no doubt that the design of its author was to
propound, in a popular and attractive style, the doctrine of
Coheleth. Jedajah Penini, *the Jewish Cicero*, as he is called by
Christians, like Coheleth, *shews, in the most striking manner, the
utter vanity of all earthly pursuits and pleasures, apart from a
future life and judgment.* Like Coheleth, he finishes his intro
ductory part — which forms the basis of the succeeding contem
plations — with the appalling fact that man is a prey to death;
whereupon he shews the unsatisfactory nature and vanity of all
human pursuits, and then, like Coheleth, concludes with setting
before man the fear of God and a future world. A few specimens
will shew the resemblance of the Bechinoth Olam to Coheleth.
After describing the transcendent powers of the human mind,
and the heavenly endowments of man (§ 1), and yet the evil to

---

[1] Der Commentar zu Kohelet befindet sich in Parma und in Oxford. Im
Epigraph rühmt Josef von sich vom Knaben=bis zum Greisenalter (Ps. xxxvii.
25) Bücher verfaßt zu haben, im Alter von 50 Jahren diesen Commentar, dessen
Text die Aufgabe des Menschen dahin bestimme, die Beschäftigung mit den Angele=
genheiten dieser Welt, da sie eitel seien, auf ein Minimum zu beschränken,
und sich dem Studium des Gesetzes und der Wissenschaft hinzugeben, was
Kohelet durch 21 Beweise dargethan habe. Er nennt diesen Commentar ein
Siegel des Lebens (חתימה לחיים) für alle seine Sorgen und Gedanken. Die
angeblichen 21 Beweise Salomon's werden Zusammenhange der Bibelstellen
nach den 10 הבלים ausgeführt, dann in logischer Ordnung kurz zusammengefaßt.
In dieser allgemeinen Erläuterung behauptet er etwas Neues geleistet zu haben,
und specielle, bereits vor ihm gegebene Erklärungen übergehen zu dürfen. Nach
diesem gewissermaßen polemischen Theile fügt er einige Andeutungen über
Vollkommenheit der Seele, Prophetie mit Rücksicht auf die " active Intelligenz"
bei, führt zehn Verse aus Kohelet an, welche die (Aristotelische) Mitte zwischen
den Extremen empfehlen. Auf diesen " Commentar Kohelet's" verweist Johanan
Allemanno in der Einleitung zu seinem Commentar über das Hohelied. Ersch
und Gruber, Allgemeine Encyclopädie, Zweite Section, vol. xxxi. p. 64.

which this highly gifted man is exposed (§ 2), Jedajah says, in § 3 —

For a man of such capacities I am filled with sorrow and grief; this Saphir masterpiece is exposed to chance and misfortune, like a target to the arrows; he is the object of disgrace and contempt, like the lower brutes; he is weighed down with oppression and contumely, from his youth to his hoary age. He who ought to sit in the counsels of wisdom, pines away in solitude; he who is like a son of God, is doomed to silence. The shepherd of truth must feed upon the wind; the bearer of wisdom and morality must succumb under his burden. Wisdom denies help to him who trusted to his intelligence for deliverance; the hands are weakened of him who holds fast to his integrity; or if calamities befall man, he dies and is no more, as the brute of the field and the beast of the forest; the sacred temple is mixed up with clods, and thrown down under trees; the body formed by compass of God, is consigned by God to rest in darkness. This contemplation heavily afflicts me, and I cannot be comforted. The masterwork of God loath-somely disappears, and is no more! Cedars planted by God's own hand are felled down! I studied man, I carefully examined his nature, and I found no imperfection in him, except that he is a prey to death.

This is also the burden of the prologue in Coheleth, and in both forms the basis of the argument. Having shewn that this is the deplorable condition of man, R. Jedajah, like Coheleth, goes on to shew that no human effort can pacify the disturbed mind, apart from the fear of God and the belief in a future existence; that it is the prospect of travelling on to a life beyond the grave, which reconciles us to the afflictions we have to pass through on our way to it. Imitating Coheleth, Jedajah there-fore counsels us, towards the end of his treatise —

Remember thy Creator, who has entrusted thee with a noble soul! thou hast taken her in as a stranger upon this earth; thou givest her shelter as a guest. As long, therefore, as she sojourns in thy dark abode, she looks to the place whence she came; she thinks in her low estate of her former glory, how she stood high in the holy place, and mourns! Pity her, and speak comfortably to her, for none but thou canst save her. As long as she is with thee, she is like a bird caught and imprisoned by a careless child; she sees many birds freely fly over her, right and left, about their nests, but has no power to overcome the youth who holds her; and she is afflicted. If thou dost not wish to lay violent hands on this thy trust, cultivate and guard her. Why stir up evil? why lose thyself in a maze of devices, and thus multiply thy wearisome labour and toil? Thou knowest how immense is the work of cultivating the soul, and how short are the days of our life to do it; and had we to live a thousand years twice told, it would be too short, for the desired object is far off; but the days of our sojourn here are few and evil, and do not suffice to accomplish even little things. Attend, therefore, my ears, I will teach you help; see, my heart, see that thou forsake the besotting things of time; enjoy from earthly things as much as is necessary for the sustenance of life, which cannot be neglected without suffering; take of the best fruits of the land, of its spices for the preservation of thy health, of its sweetness for thy enjoyment; but shun all excess, let that be for the beasts of the field, and the men who are like them; leave consuming pleasures, and ants' treasures, that vanish like a dream, the interpretation of which is, "the body will soon decay before its time, and the spirit goes down like the spirit of the beast after death." My heart, may this be the dream of thy persecutors, and its interpretation for thy enemies! Take my counsel, whilst thy branches are still green, whilst thy sun is not clouded, and thou art young and cheerful, and hast strength to run the race with the swiftness of the hart, to obtain the prize, and to rouse others from their lethargy and earthly pleasures by thy sweet savour, and by the brightness of thy light. Why, then, sleepest thou? why delay to tear off the delusive mask, and escape from infatuations? Arise, invoke wisdom, before the days of evil come, before the many infirmities of old age draw nigh, and strength is changed into weakness, and hope into despair.

We need hardly remind the reader of the relationship which this paragraph sustains to the twelfth chapter of Coheleth. It will be seen that Jedajah, like the sacred writer, whilst setting before us the bright prospect of the life to come, also recommends the cheerful but moderate enjoyment of the blessings of the life that now is. This imitation is still more striking when we compare the concluding remarks of the two books. Coheleth, towards the end, praises "the words of the wise," and admonishes that all heed should be paid to them (xii. 11, 12). Jedajah finishes by urging that all attention be given to the thirteen articles of belief written by Maimonides, who was greatly attacked in those days —

Finally, turn neither to the left nor right from all that the wise men have believed, the chief of whom was the distinguished teacher *Rambam*, of blessed memory, with whom no one can be compared from among all the wise men of Israel who lived since the conclusion of the Talmud; then I shall be sure that thou, enriched with all the knowledge of religion and philosophy, wilt fear the Lord thy God.

The *Bechinoth Olam* has always occupied a very high position among the Jews, and has been a source of comfort to many, who looked upon Coheleth as a sealed book.[1]

1399. — The Nitzachon of R. Jomtob Lipmann Mühlhausen has also taken up some of the hard sayings of Coheleth. This Nitzachon, or *Victory*, is a polemical work against Christianity, written in Cracow about 1399, according to a MS. note. It consists of seven parts, according to the seven days of the week, and three hundred and fifty-four sections, ten of which are devoted to what the author regards the most difficult passages of Coheleth. The following are the first three sections: —

§ 311. Chap. i. 1, 2, *Vanity of vanities, &c.* — Forbid it that such a thought should ever enter into the heart, that the works of the blessed God in the creation of the world are vanity! for he has created all things for his glory (comp. my Comment. § 3). The meaning is, that all the labour wherewith one labours to acquire and enjoy the things which are under the sun is utterly vain and profitless; all the exertions which man makes in this world which is under the rotation of the sun, for his aggrandisement, gratification, and enjoyment, and which are not for the glory of God. The "under the sun" is mentioned, because most of the pursuits of man in this lower world consist in growing fruit and other things which depend upon the sun; whereas, all the work ought to be for the glory of God, who is above the sun. Comp. § 68. And thus King Solomon, peace be upon him, concludes this book by saying, "Finally, all is heard, fear God and keep his commandments, for for this all is man" (xii. 13), *i.e.*, for this was man created. And in this sense the Rabbins, of blessed memory, have explained it, viz., Man has no advantage from that wherein he labours *under* the sun, but he has an advantage from his labours in the law which is *before* the sun.

§ 312. iii. 19, *For the destiny of man, &c.* — Let not thy heart lead thee astray to think that Coheleth speaks here of the soul, since he says himself that "the spirit shall return to God" (xii. 7), see § 120. Now, the end of this verse shews his meaning, where he says, "As the one dies, so dies the other," *i.e.*, it is with regard to the dying of the animal's spirit that he says

---

[1] A sketch of R. Jedajah's life will be found in Stern's beautiful edition of the *Bechinoth Olam*, Wien, 1847. See also Jost, Geschichte des Judenthums und seiner Sekten, vol. iii., p. 28, &c.

all have the same spirit," for this spirit does die, since it is of the wind which is upon the waters (comp. § 1) ; but of the upper spirit which returns to God it is impossible to say so, for this continues to live, as I shall shew in § 320.

§ 313, *And the advantage of man, &c.* — I have already explained, in § 312, that the spirit returns to God, and that it has an essential and great advantage. The advantage, therefore, which is here denied, refers to that which is earthly and carnal, for the word אָדָם, *man,* is derived from אֲדָמָה. *earth,* and it is for this reason that Coheleth does not here use the word אֱנוֹשׁ, *man,* as I explained in § 5. And the meaning is, that as regards the body, there is no advantage in it over the body of the beast, for all came from the earth and return to the earth again ; but as regards the intellect, there is an advantage in it. Comp. §§ 76 and 312.

20. *Who knows, &c.* — מי יודע means he who is worthy to know. Comp. Joel ii. 14, *i. e.,* he who is worthy, let him take these words to heart, that the spirit of man goes up, for this is its nature (comp. my Comment. § 76), and must give an account ; and the spirit of the beast goes naturally down, for the spirit of the beast is from the elements, from the wind which blows upon the earth, and has no reward or punishment.[1]

R. Lipmann has been *quite as successful* in refuting Christianity, as he has here shewn himself to be in removing the difficulties from Coheleth. In justice, however, to this Rabbi, it must be said that he always makes a distinction in his polemics between Christianity and Christians ; and whilst he attacks the former, he endeavours to prove, from Isa. lxvi. 23 and the concluding words of Psalm cxlv., *that all conscientious and pious non-Israelites will be saved.*[2] When we bear in mind the state of Christianity in his days, the bitter sufferings which were then inflicted upon the Jews in the name of Christ, and the awful curses pronounced by the heads of the Church against all those who were out of its pale, instead of being surprised that R. Lipmann wrote against such a system, we wonder at his charity.

[1] Liber Nizachon Rabbi Lipmanni, &c., curant. Theod. Hackspan, Norinberg, 1644.

[2] Comp. נם צדיקי אומות העולם יש להם חלק לעולם הבא : וכתב רמ״בם גוי המקיים שבע מצות, § 265. See also § 333, בני נח מסברת לבו אע״פכ אינ׳ נקרא מצדיקי אומות העולם ויברך כל בשר שם קדשו לעולם ועד אין זה מורה לקיום העולם אלא מורה על נשמת צדיקי אומות העולם שהזמה בכלל כל בשר

1490. — It is difficult to gather from the *Michlal Yophi* (Perfection of Beauty) what the author took the design of this book to be. As far as it can be stated with any definiteness, it seems to be that *Solomon examined in this book the various conflicting opinions which he gathered together (hence the name* קֹהֶלֶת) *respecting the affairs of this world, and the destiny of man, and came to the conclusion that the best thing for man is to fear God, and to remember that there is a future judgment.*[1]

The Biblical student will always feel grateful to R. Solomon ben Melech for this very useful manual, which is a compilation of grammatical and critical notes on the whole Old Testament from the best Jewish commentators, such as Rashi, Ibn Ezra, Kimchi, &c.

1475 – 1530. — So numerous and conflicting were the opinions about this book in the fifteenth century, that R. Isaac Aramah, who was desirous of making himself master of the subject, was perfectly astonished to find that both the ancient and more modern commentators were so greatly divided. *Some forcing upon it a strange and far-fetched literal sense; others, a philosophical meaning, too mysterious and profound to be understood; and others, again, interpreting it according to the Midrash, find in it laws and statutes full of piety. The point in which all of them have erred alike is, that they alter the sense of the book into palatable sentiment; and yet not one of them has put such sense into it as to be able to boast, with reason, that they have drawn from this rock wholesome food, or elicited sweetness from this flint* (*i.e.,* from this difficult book). Rejecting, therefore, all these different views, R. Aramah came to the conclusion, *that every statement in this book is perfectly plain and consistent with orthodoxy, that it contains the sublimest of all contemplations, and teaches the highest order of heavenly wisdom.* Rabbi A. was therefore amazed how it could ever enter into the minds of commentators to think that the sages, of blessed memory, wanted to put such a book among the apocrypha, and that the only reason

[1] מכלל יופי with the לקט שכחה of Abendana, Amsterdam, 1661, p. 47.

why they left it in the canon was, that *the first* and *last words* of it were consistent with the law.

" Now, it was not because thinking men found it difficult to discover the good sense of it that the sages wanted to hide this book, but for fear of the multitude, who waste the riches of the law. But as it is the habit of these ignorant people to look merely at the beginning and the end of a book, and these portions unmistakeably contain the fear of God, therefore the wise men at last determined not to hide it from these people."

Such, then, is the forced interpretation which this Rabbi gives of the plain words of the sages, entirely ignoring what they distinctly say, that " the book contains sentiments tending to infidelity;" that " it utters Solomon's own wisdom," &c. (*vide supra*, pp. 14–16). Yet Aramah exclaims against the far-fetched explanations of others.

1548. — As grammatical exegesis was comparatively little pursued in the sixteenth century, the difficulties of Coheleth occasioned no trouble, and the book was regarded by its commentators as surpassing all other books of Scripture in heavenly lessons. Thus Elisha Galicho, or Galiko, who flourished in the second half of the sixteenth century,[1] tells us, in the preface to his commentary on Coheleth —

Since all the pursuits of this world and its lusts cling to the creature in consequence of his earthliness and desire, and the soul of man covets these things, and is in danger of being inextricably ensnared by them, many lessons are given in the Law, Prophets, and Hagiographa, to point out the way to the tree of life. Hence both the earlier and latter sages carefully composed encouragement and admonitions, parables and proverbs, to teach man wisdom by moral sayings, the fear of God, and the fear of sin, making hedges and fences for the benefit of the multitude. And Solomon excelled all in his moral Proverbs, which are as numerous as the advantages which accrue to man when he inclines his ears to them. Now, to surpass even these, he wrote Coheleth, the whole of which, from beginning to end, is perpetually turning round the same point, and that is, to expose the

[1] The first edition of this Commentary, said to have been published in Venice, 1548, is extremely scarce. I have never seen it; the one I possess was published in Venice, 1578, 4to, Giov. di Gara.

vanity of all earthly pursuits, and to teach man to know that his happiness is no happiness at all, and that his wishes and desires are vain and delusive, and will not bear examination; that the great object of life in this world is to attain to the perfection of the soul, and its immortality; to acquire that light which will shine in the light of the countenance of the Eternal King in the world to come. This is the design of this holy book, which is a guide whereunto all must look.

Having thus given the design of the book, R. Galicho divides it into *twenty-seven* sections, according to the number of letters in the Hebrew alphabet, including the five final letters, and gives a minute analysis of the contents of each section.

The first section (chap. i. 1–11) speaks in general terms of the affairs of this world, and of the dignity of the human soul, shewing that it is in the nature of the soul to cling to things which tend to its perfection.

The second section (chap. i. 12 – ii. 11) speaks more particularly of the pursuits of this world, such as wisdom, pleasure, mirth, riches, covetousness, &c., and sets forth their respective dangers.

The third section (chap. ii. 12–24) gives the distinction between wisdom and folly, shewing that man ought to despise the pursuit after mammon, and lay hold of that which will elevate the soul.

The fourth section (chap. iii. 1–9) speaks of the allotted times of adversity and prosperity, being intimately connected with what precedes, thereby shewing either that Israel is not subjected to chance, or that we are not to relinquish our hope, when in adverse circumstances, for the coming of better days, or that there is certainty in times or seasons, or that an apparently bad time may really be good, and *vice versa.*

The fifth section (chap. iii. 10–17) speaks of the design and use of our afflictions; of the fact that the righteous sometimes suffer, whilst the wicked prosper; and shews why man is created in a state of depravity, and what human nature was before its fall.

The sixth section (chap. iii. 18–22) refutes the opinion of the

wicked respecting their prosperity and the sufferings of the
righteous, as well as the opinion of those who believe that the
world is under chance, and not Providence, and deny the immortality of the soul; and then dwells upon the happiness of the
soul in a future state.

The seventh section (chap. iv. 1–8) takes up again the existence of Providence; the good of sufferings, which are sent to
awaken to repentance, to make one active who has the power of
diminishing crime, but does not exercise it in consequence of
being unscrupulously engrossed in the affairs of this life out of
jealousy; speaks of those who, despite all sufferings, continue in
sin; of a pious and God-serving man, but withal not too self-
confident, whose example ought to be imitated, yet is shunned
and despised; of the punishment of him who refuses to get
married, and dies without issue; of the evil of sin, and the
advantage of holiness; and of the responsibility of man to choose
the service of God.

The eighth section (chap. iv. 9–16) praises the connection
with the pious as helping one in the service of God; blames
those who associate with the impious, and speaks of the union of
the good disposition with the soul.

The ninth section (chap. iv. 17 – v. 7) enters minutely into
the subject of divine worship, viz., prayer, and its necessary
concomitants, almsgiving and vows, setting forth the evil consequences of violating these; it speaks of the necessity of
departing from evil, which is the essential cleansing of ourselves
and preparation to enter the house of God, the world of spirits;
of the strict performance of vows, and of shunning pleasure.

The tenth section (chap. v. 8–19) continues to speak of the
advantage of benevolence and almsgiving, even in rendering
wealth more durable, thus shewing the folly of acquiring money,
and not contributing to the cause of God, and the evils to which
unhallowed riches will lead, and the necessity of working for
that which elevates the soul; and then passes on to the fact that
some benevolent and almsgiving men lose their fortunes, whilst

misers and lewd men multiply their wealth; or it may be that
the particulars still speak of the purifying of the body and soul
for going into the house of God, which is the land of Israel, and
not to run after the pleasures of riches, as purification is a
blessing to the man who practises it, and to his issue, and in
the hour of death; mammon, however, is the ruin of a man both
here and hereafter.

The eleventh section (chap. vi. 1–6) speaks of the blindness
of the worldly men who, notwithstanding all the indications
that their prosperity is not a matter of chance, but from Provi
dence, wantonly squander the bounties of God, as if their own
strength had acquired them; thus neither enjoying these gifts
themselves, nor devoting them to the glory of God — better an
untimely birth than such men.

The twelfth section (chap. vi. 7–12) speaks of the infatuation of
the worldly rich, who do not see that the study of the law surpasses
all, and that there is no advantage to a wise man above a fool,
except that he investigate things, to be confirmed in the service
of God; shews that, by possessing knowledge, one who has been
an old sinner may yet amend his ways; and then goes on to
vindicate the creation of passions, &c. Or it may speak of the
many warnings man requires to abstain from carnal pleasures,
&c.; of what the penitent must undergo, and of the superiority
of a penitent over a righteous man, since the former has not only
to labour for the future, but also to amend the past.

The thirteenth section (chap. vii. 1–12) speaks of the superiority of the enjoyment of the soul in the world of spirits, to
bodily happiness in this world; of the excellency of a good
name, which is to be acquired by remembering the day of death,
by visiting the houses of mourners, by listening to the corrections
of teachers, by hating evil inclinations, by listening to the
teaching of the law and refusing to hear the mockery of fools,
and not to despair of getting a good name even in old age.
There are, however, other means whereby to get a good name,
viz., to consider the end of a thing from the beginning; to be

cheerful under sufferings, and not murmur against God; to help the needy; not to trust to one's-self, but to be watchful over one's besetting sins, and to study the word of God.

The fourteenth section (chap. vii. 13 – 24) mentions things which, when observed, will prevent a man losing his good name, namely, keeping of God's wonderful works constantly before his eyes; not to be over wise so as to attempt to take away from or add to the word of God; to examine his conduct daily, not to slip either in prosperity or adversity. Or it tells us to preach repentance in the days of calamity; to beware of a little knowledge; to add to theory practice, as each is beautiful in its season; not to be over wicked or over righteous in our own estimation; to set a good example; to be always occupied with the study of God, which will keep from the innumerable sins by which we are surrounded; and above all to be meek.

The fifteenth section (chap. vii. 25 – viii. 1) mentions the weapons wherewith we are to conquer the evil heart, viz., studying the word of God, wisdom, bearing in mind a future judgment, comparing a good with an evil act, and their respective consequences, not to have too much intercourse with women, whose cunning the wise alone can elude, &c., &c.

The sixteenth section (chap. viii. 2 – 10) advises to obey God rather than man, even at the peril of life, since the loss of it in the service of God here will secure us everlasting life hereafter; tells us that the tyrant who compels us to transgress the word of God will bé severely punished in the world to come, cautions us not to judge the things which take place by their outward appearance, &c.

The seventeenth section (chap. viii. 11 – 15) speaks of the marvellous forbearance of God with the wicked, of the righteous sharing in the punishment of the wicked, and that they are joyfully to submit to sufferings or death.

The eighteenth section (viii. 16 – ix. 3) speaks of the inscrutableness of God's dealings, of the folly of trying to find them out, of the wickedness of making God the author of evil, &c., &c.

The nineteenth section (chap. ix. 4 – 6) speaks of the power of sin, and of the still greater power of meekness; or shews that man must combine both his component parts, *i. e.*, matter and form, for the service of God, and the sinner may yet experience the power of repentance.

The twentieth section (chap. ix. 7 – 12) expatiates upon the penitent, declares that it is never too late to repent, and shews the reward reserved for those who repent, &c., &c.

The twenty-first section (chap. ix. 13 – x. 4) speaks of the advantage of wisdom over strength, and of the infatuation of worldly men, who do not see this.

The twenty-second section (chap. x. 5 – 15) speaks of the fact that men prefer folly to wisdom, and though they discover their error, they will not leave it; advises men to enter deeply into the wisdom of the law, shews how to pursue it, cautions against yielding to the evil heart, &c., &c.

The twenty-third section (chap. x. 16 – 20) advises leaders of communities and kings to set a good example to those under them, not to indulge in pleasures which may lead them to commit violence and oppression, then God will withdraw his protection and blessing, &c., &c.

The twenty-fourth section (chap. xii. 8) recommends alms-giving, which, like good conduct, is a pillar of the world; or recommends kindness to those who are engaged in the study of the law, for though we may have no return for it here, we shall be blessed for it hereafter, &c.

The twenty-fifth section (chap. xi. 9 – xii. 1) recommends that we should enlist in the service of God from early youth, or perhaps suggests that we should neither be dejected nor too buoyant, remembering that we shall be brought into judgment for all we do, &c., &c.

The twenty-sixth section (chap xii. 2 – 7) describes the weakness of our bodily frame in old age, in consequence of which we are unable to do much good, hence the admonition to remember the Creator whilst we are young.

The twenty-seventh section (chap. xii. 8 – 14) repeats the assertion made in the beginning, namely, that all worldly pursuits are vanity; describes the wisdom of Coheleth, and the claim he has to our attention; and concludes by telling us that all depends upon fearing God and obeying his commandments.

We have given a copious extract of this analysis, if such it may be called, because Galicho is the first expositor who gives a summary of the contents of Coheleth. The commentary is chiefly allegorical, very extensive, and abounds in quotations from the Midrashim, and other Rabbinical writings.

1580. — Though we now find all commentators agreeing in the traditional view that Solomon wrote this book in his old age, when he repented, and was restored to God and his earthly kingdom, yet their opinions as to the design and plan of Coheleth are as divergent as ever. Every fresh commentator either actually or virtually regards all his predecessors as having misunderstood Coheleth. Accordingly, the distinguished Moses Alshech[1] submits that Solomon wrote this treatise *to teach that man has been sent into this world to gain the world to come.*

As one goes from a palace to the town, to trade in various articles, in order to bring good things to his house, to satisfy his soul from all the transactions he has made in the city whither he went, so that he may rejoice in the palace whence he came, as this is his home, and this the place where he rests from all his labours wherewith he laboured in the city to which he went; — but he who does not labour in the city, to gather good things, will return to his palace whence he came just as he left it, and, instead of pleasure, he will have sorrow and distress; — so will it be with every man of Israel who leaves the mansions of the upper world, the enjoyments and pleasures in the palace of the King of the Universe, and comes into the houses of clay of this world to engage in the law and commandments, that he may bring into the treasury of the Holy King, in the upper world, wherewith to satisfy his soul from his labours in this world. But if he

---

[1] Moses Alshech was born in Safet, Upper Galilee, about 1520. He was the pupil of the famous Jos. Karo, and made such astonishing progress in the acquisition of varied learning, that he became one of the most distinguished commentators of the sixteenth century, and occupied the office of chief Rabbi in his native place, where he died about 1595.

chooses his way in this world to sit down, and not do anything in the law and commandments, and indulges in eating the fat and drinking the sweet things of this world, and throws the work of the law and the commandments behind his back, then an untimely birth is better than he. For the spirit shall return to God without any good, and full of after-growths of the miry clay, and scabs of sins and transgressions; and will have brought all this evil upon him by his own lusts. For the delusive good things of this world he gradually forsakes the Lord, till he despises the good and chooses the evil. Wherefore Solomon, in his great wisdom, here teaches man to know the vanity of earthly pursuits, so that the righteous may lay hold of the way of the Lord to perfect his heart, since there is nothing good but the service and fear of the Lord all the day. And this it is with which he concludes: " The end of the matter is, All is heard, fear God," &c., &c.[1]

As it is to be expected from this celebrated Rabbi and preacher, his commentary contains many beautiful thoughts and attractive parables, which might be serviceable to homilists, but does not contribute much to the exegesis of the book.

1631. — Far less interesting, but much more recondite, than Alshech, is the commentary of El. Loanz,[2] who, like Solomon, according to tradition, betook himself in his old age to write upon the vanity of all earthly things. " *When Solomon began in his latter days*," says this Kabbalist, " *to learn Mishna Thorah, he found it his duty to speak publicly to the people words of wisdom and instruction.*"

This Baal-Shem also grapples with the difficulties and hard sayings of Coheleth, and the manner in which he attempts to explain them does no credit to the Kabbalah, of which he had such a wonderful knowledge, as will be seen from the following specimen of the introduction to his commentary : —

As to the words, " Rejoice, O young man, in thy youth," &c. (xi. 9), we find in the Midrash Rabba that R. Samuel, the son of Isaac, says that the wise men wanted to hide Coheleth, because there are in it sentiments which lean to infidelity; they said that it contains Solomon's own wisdom,

---

[1] Commentary on the Five Megilloth, Offenbach, 1721, p. 48, &c.

[2] Eliah Loanz, also called Baal-Shem (the renowned or wonder-working man), from his marvellous knowledge of the Kabbala and El. Ashkenasi, was born in Frankfort-on-the-Maine about 1550, and died in Worms, 1636.

because he uttered the above words. Moses said, " Ye shall not follow the ways of your hearts," &c. (Numb. xv. 39), and Solomon says, "Walk in the ways of thy heart" (xi. 9), doing away, as it were, with judge and judgment; but when he said, " for all this, God will bring thee into judgment (*Ibid.*), they said that " Solomon, honour be upon him, said well." Now, this proceeding is a matter of great astonishment to every intelligent man ; 1. How could our sages, of blessed memory, pass judgment upon the beginning of the verse, without at once seeing the orthodox end of it, and thus try to hide the book ; especially as we so frequently find the saying in the writings of our Rabbins, of blessed memory, "Fool! always look to the end of a sentence !" ? 2. Why were our sages going to contradict themselves ? Have they not already declared (Perek Hasholeach, p. 45), in the name of R. Nachman — and there was no difference of opinion about this — that a scroll of the law copied by an infidel must be burned ? and has not Yoreh Deah (§ 281) explained this declaration, " Even if there is no flaw or mistake in such a copy, it must be burnt, from the very fact that an infidel made it ?" yet this book, which tends to infidelity, the sages wanted to hide, when they, according to their own teaching, ought to have burnt it. 3. If the beginning of the verse is heresy, how can the end be so orthodox as to merit the approbation, " Solomon has said well," &c. ? 4. The passage begins with, " Rejoice, O young man," and against this they exclaim, " It is Solomon's own wisdom," as if this were the great difficulty in their eyes ; when in fact the words, " and walk in the ways of thy heart," are the difficulty, inasmuch as they contradict the injunction of our Rabbi Moses, peace be upon him. 5. Why did they not say that Solomon also contradicts Moses in the following clause of the same verse ? — Comp. " Walk in the sight of thine eyes" (xi. 9) with " and ye shall not walk after your eyes" (Numb. xv. 39). 6. Why were they going to conceal it ? why had they not the courage to explain the difficulties as R. Hanah did, or R. Levi, which is recorded in the Talmud (Shabbath, 30, 2), *e.g.*, R. Hanah said, What is the meaning of " Rejoice, O young man, in thy youth, &c., &c. . . . God will bring thee into judgment" ? The former, the evil spirit (היצ׳ר) in man, cries, the latter is the language of the good spirit (היצ׳׳ט). R. Levi said, the former refers to the joy in the words of the law, the latter to good works ; and Rashi, the great luminary of blessed memory, explains " Rejoice, O young man" in the study of the law, " and walk in the ways of thy heart," *i.e.*, understand, as far as thou canst see, what is in thy heart, what good works thou canst do ; " and know that for all this," &c., *i.e.*, know that for all thou hast learned thou wilt be judged, if thou dost not keep it. 7. Why did they regard the first part of this verse as heretical, and not other passages, such as " Whatsoever thine hand findeth to do," &c. (ix. 10) giving liberty to anything one likes, because " there is no work nor account in the grave" (*Ibid.*), thus doing away with all future judgment, and making the grave a place of refuge ? I therefore wonder that they did not give this

passage as a reason for wanting to conceal the book, rathe .nan the verse,
" Rejoice, O young man," especially as it occurs first.   They would have
liked to take this too in the sense of R. Hanah and R. Levi, viz., to regard
the bad passages as being from the evil spirit, and the good passages from
the good spirit; and to say that the reason why they wanted to conceal the
book was because they feared lest one wickedly inclined should take it up,
and prefer to be guided by the beginning of the verse, which is heretical,
and not look to the end, or, if he saw it, would say the former part is the
true one.   But when they saw that it concludes with, "and know that for
all this," &c.—which shews that R. Hanah's explanation is untenable, for,
according to his meaning, " all this" ought to be omitted — they come to
the conclusion that עַל־כָּל־אֵלֶּה must be explained by *nevertheless*, as Resh
Lakish interpreted it, *i. e.*, " Rejoice in thy learning, and do good to thy
heart, to understand what is in thy heart, according to the sight of thine eyes,
for thou canst not judge except what thine eye sees, and know that, notwithstanding this, God will bring thee into judgment."   The other difficulties
still require a solution; let us therefore inquire into the seventh question,
viz., why the sages did not think of hiding the book for the assertion,
" Whatsoever thine hand finds to do," &c. (ix. 10); and the cause of it is,
either it is to be explained as we have stated it in the commentary, or that
the word חשבון refers to מעשה; and Coheleth says, because thou canst not do
any good work in the grave, which might be balanced against thy sins, since
the dead are free from all the commandments; and that it is preceded by
the passage, " and enjoy life with thy wife," wherein Coheleth incites to the
observance of the law and its commandments, as it is explained below, so
that it does not belong to the heretical passages.   But when they saw this
verse they were astounded and dismayed at its foolish sentiments, since
even a fool would be led thereby to heresy; and they at first thought
that Solomon talked foolishness in saying, " Rejoice, O young man," and
therefore they said that this is Solomon's own wisdom, *i. e.*, it is nothing
but nonsense; it does not become one of the common people to talk so,
much less a wise man like Solomon, for how can the term ילדותי be applied
to *a young man* בחור? it ought to be שמח בחור בבחרותך בחרותך; but more than this,
it is heretical, since Moses said, " Ye shall not walk in the way of your
heart" (Numb. xv. 39), and Solomon here says, " Walk in the way of your
heart," &c.   Now, why the sages did not burn it, but intended to hide the
book, is because Solomon was no infidel; on the contrary, if his words are
properly examined, it will be seen that they are perfectly true, and becoming
such a wise man as he was.   That an empty-headed man may shelter
himself under the literal meaning of the words, is no reason why the
wise men should have burned a book of such sublime sentiments.   For
we find in the Pentateuch, " *let us make* (נעשה) *man* (the plural), yet there
is no fear of its leading to infidelity [or polytheism], for the answer is
close by it, in the singular, וַיִּבְרָא, *and he* created (Gen. i. 26, 27), so it is with

the sentiments of Solomon. The reason, however, why the wise men wanted to hide the book is, that there were in those days some popular philosophers among the Gentiles who were greatly followed, and our sages were afraid lest one of them should come forward, and say, Behold, he whose wisdom spread all over the world says, "Rejoice, O, young man," &c., and not understanding his meaning, he may be led thereby into infidelity; it therefore occurred to our sages to hide the book. But when they saw his remark, "And know that for all this he will bring thee into judgment," &c., they saw that the beginning of the verse was no nonsense, and the middle was not heretical; for the law of interpretation compelled them to take the first part of the verse also in a good sense; and they explained, "Rejoice, O young man," as referring to the mind, which attains to its highest stage by studying the wisdom of the law; i.e., till thou art called a young man; whilst thou art still a boy of tender years, occupy thyself to such an extent with the law that thou mayest be called young man; and although thou dost not study it for its own sake, yet thou wilt do thy heart good, for when thou shalt become a young man thy heart will draw thee to that which is good, to study the law for its own sake; for, as the sages of blessed memory said, "begin from motive, and you will end in doing a thing from being purely interested in it;" and mark that, notwithstanding all thy studies in the law, God will bring thee into judgment, for thou mayest not have studied, or acted, or thought as thou oughtest to have done."

This curious defence of the sages in retaining Coheleth in the canon is very important, inasmuch as it shews that even the Kabbalists, with all their contempt for literal interpretation, were greatly staggered at the difficulties adduced by these wise men for their first intention to conceal the book; and that their reasons for setting aside this intention are beset with greater difficulties than the book itself.

1724.—In the commentary of Moses Landsberger, Kabbalistic interpretation seems to have reached its climax. He does not assign any design to the book, or admit any literal meaning, but explains every verse according to the rules *Grammatia* and *Notaricun*.[1] The redeeming part of Landsberger's work is, that it is extremely short. Thus all he tells us on chap. i. 15, " *The crooked cannot be made straight*," is, *that it means Cain, Korah, Balaam, Ahithophel, Gehazi, and Doeg, the six wicked ones who,*

[1] For these rules of interpretation, see p. 31, &c.

according to Aboth de Rabbi Nathan, have no portion in the world to come.[1]

1770. — A new era now commenced in Biblical exegesis, and in Hebrew literature generally. The immortal Mendelssohn was now directing the mispent Jewish intellect and zeal to the proper study of the Word of God, in accordance with the literal and grammatical sense. His first effort to this effect was the publication of a Hebrew commentary on Coheleth, which appeared, according to the Jewish chronology, in 5530, *i. e.*, 1770 of the Christian era.[2]

Mendelssohn, too, complains that "nearly all the commentators who have preceded me have almost entirely failed in doing justice to their task of interpretation . . . . I have not found in one of them an interpretation adequate to the correct explanation of the connection of the verses of the book; but, according to their method, nearly every verse is spoken separately and unconnectedly; and this would not be right in a private and insignificant author, and much less in a wise king" (p. 73). As to the design of the book, Mendelssohn thinks *that Solomon wrote it to propound the doctrine of the immortality of the soul, and the necessity of leading a cheerful and contented life; and interspersed these cardinal points with lessons of minor importance, such as worship, politics, domestic economy, &c.*

Mendelssohn divides the book into thirteen sections. The *first* section, which is a sort of introduction, is from chap. i. 1 to verse 11; the *second*, from chap. i. 12 to ii. 11; the *third* is from chap. ii. 12 to 26; the *fourth*, from chap. iii. 1 to iv. 3; the *fifth*, from chap. iv. 4 to 16; the *sixth*, from chap. iv. 17 to v. 19·

[1] This precious document is contained in the שומר אמונים, *the guard of the faithful*, as he calls his commentary on the Pentateuch and five Megilloth, published in Offenbach, 1724, p. 40, &c.

[2] This commentary was so highly thought of, that it was almost immediately translated into German, by J. J. Rabe, the translator of the Mishnah, and published in Ansbach, 1771. A translation has also more recently been published by Theodor Preston, London, 1845, to which our references will be made, for the sake of the English reader.

the *seventh*, from chap. vi. 1 to vii. 14; the *eighth*, from chap. vii. 15 to viii. 9; the *ninth*, from chap. viii. 10 to ix. 12; the *tenth*, from chap. ix. 13 to x. 15; the *eleventh*, from chap. x. 16 to xi. 6; the *twelfth*, from chap. xi. 7 to xii. 7; the *thirteenth* section, which is, as it were, the conclusion and seal of the contents, is from chap. xii. 8 to the end of the book.

How much this distinguished philosopher and commentator has followed the criticisms, and sometimes even the peculiarities, of Ibn Ezra, will be seen in the course of our Commentary.

1788.—As the above commentary appeared with the Hebrew original which it purported to elucidate, David Friedländer, the worthy disciple of Mendelssohn, published, in 1788, a translation of Coheleth, according to the explanation of his master, with an introduction of his own, and a valuable " treatise upon the best use of Scripture."

We cannot do better than give Friedländer's own words, respecting what he thinks is the design, unity, style, &c., of this book.

The real import of the whole work is : " Contemplations upon the fruitless struggle after happiness and the vanity of human affairs." A tone of unity pervades the whole book from beginning to end, which puts it beyond a doubt that the varied experience and observations given therein have all been made by the august author, and that they are not observations made by others which he has simply collected or compiled. This is moreover evident from the interspersed wise maxims which, as is well known, are the oldest fruit of human sagacity; and are the result of real experience, contained in pithy sayings which memory easily retains. The remarks are made from a profound knowledge of the world and mankind, and are taken from common life ; they have mostly a tinge of melancholy, and sometimes the colour is even thickly laid on. This imparts to them a deep interest; we hear a powerful prince of the past, possessing all the greatest earthly happiness, philosophising upon the wrong use of life, and stirring us up to the fear of God, virtue, and morality. What a powerful reason to trust to his experience, and to listen to his advice ! The august author has adopted no definite plan. In his own fashion he goes through the whole of human life, and throws out his remarks upon its several positions. He contemplates, teaches, mourns, comforts, imparts counsel, contradicts, and corrects himself; and although the whole betrays the course of mere social ideas, yet the principal thread upon which all things are strung is never entirely lost.

From this point of view the apparent contradictions are easily solved. The author is no dogmatic and phlegmatic teacher, but a warm and animated examiner of truth. To a philosopher, it is essential to listen to the opposite opinions. He, without regarding his own system, listens to all objections which can be made, and does not fear the consequences of statements he admits. The difference, however, between the philosopher and our august author is, that in his book two voices, as it were, speak; or, in other words, that he candidly places before the eyes of the reader all the objections which he makes, and all that transpires in his inmost soul; HE IS NOT AFRAID TO THINK ALOUD. It would therefore be dishonest if we were to charge him with all the opinions which he adduces, and thus requite his openness; justice demands that we should adhere to that which this great man gives, at the end of his contemplations, as the result of his investigations, namely, THE CONCLUSION WHICH CONTAINS ALL IS, FEAR GOD, KEEP HIS COMMANDMENTS, THIS IS THE DESTINY OF MAN.

The best commentaries agree that Coheleth must be judged in this way, and no careful reader can refuse his assent to this opinion.

It will be seen from the above that the import and plan of this book differ from the import and plan of all other books of the Bible. The same is the case with its language; it is unmistakably different from the language of older or contemporary writings. Single words and phrases, compounds and idioms, as well as certain repetitions and favourite expressions, are peculiar to this book. It may therefore rightly be asserted, that with respect to expression and style, as well as import and tone, Coheleth has no companion in the whole Bible. Whether this is merely to be ascribed to the author's manner of philosophising, or to some other causes, I dare not decide. But this much is certain, that the great obscurity which rests upon the whole is very much increased through the want of parallels; it is this which increases the difficulty of interpreting it.[1]

In addition to this very comprehensive introduction, Friedländer gives a summary of the contents of every paragraph, which Mendelssohn has not done. As we have therein not only the disciple's opinion of the plan of Coheleth, but also the idea of the great master, we give it entire.

The first section (chap. i. 1–11) is an introduction, wherein the preacher speaks generally: all earthly things, all the work and industry of man, are utterly vain and useless. All things in nature will always continue as they now are, for everything has been predetermined; all things move in a per-

[1] Der Prediger, aus dem Hebräischen von David Friedländer, Berlin, 1788, pp. 82–86.

petual round; man cannot create anything new, he can only separate or join in a different way that which is created.

The second section (chap. i. 12 – ii. 11). — Searching does not make us happy; the more knowledge, the more suffering. The impossibiliy of accomplishing our desire to make the imperfect perfect, and correct the crooked, is a source of grief. The enjoyment of sensual pleasures, so far from making us happy, terminates in disgust; neither does the combination of intellectual enjoyment and sensual pleasures make one happy: all is vanity and emptiness.

The third section (chap ii. 12–26). — Wisdom has indeed an essential advantage over folly. To be occupied in researches and study, is a far nobler employment than to pursue sensual pleasures; still, the wise and the fool have the same destiny, the name of both is soon forgotten. This makes life hateful; the thought that I may leave my hard-earned goods to an unworthy heir is also grievous. Nay, even one's own enjoyment of the present is not in the power of man, for all is fixed beforehand.

The fourth section (chap. iii. 1 – iv. 3). — A further development of the same idea. Everything seems to have its root in eternal predestination; everything in the moral and physical world is subject to an iron necessity; man can make no alteration in the course of things. Nothing, however, is absolutely evil; things are apparently evil, but result in good. God's ultimate design is always effected; when men choose they act arbitrarily, but after all the will of God is done. There must be a future when good and evil will be rewarded, else the injustice so frequently practised here would be incompatible with the justice and mercy of the Creator. A future would necessarily presuppose immortality, still this cannot be demonstrated from the nature of the soul; man and beast seem to be accidental and perishing beings; but the violence perpetrated under the sun, the tears of the oppressed, speak loudly for a future and immortality.

The fifth section (chap. iv. 4–16) is on matters of social happiness. Many find a source of happiness in the exertion of industry, but the mainspring is jealousy, every one being desirous to be above his neighbour. Verse 5 gives the remark of the industrious, and verse 6 the reply of the lazy. The royal preacher recommends social and matrimonial life; married people have a good reward; children make the bond of union still tighter. The wise ought to rule; birth has no claim to the throne. The populace are always for new governments; the worthlessness of popular favour.

The sixth section (chap. iv. 17 – v. 19). — True piety consists in fearing God, and not in costly sacrifices, or in much unintelligible prayer; sin not, and sacrifice not. Human government is imperfect; one man cannot superintend all the government, and the prince is easily deceived by the necessary multitude of state officials. Even a farmer-king must have subordinates whom he trusts, how much more requires a great potentate? Riches do not make happy; they often make one unhappy. Man departs

M

naked from this world, and many a one does not even take with him
good actions as a sign of his conduct; many a one wastes away this life by
niggardliness; a rational use of one's possessions is happiness and the
will of God.

The seventh section (chap. vi. 1 – vii. 14). — Repeated complaints against
Providence, that many want the sense to enjoy their possessions. The
advantage of wisdom is nothing, if the wise must suffer. The doctrine of
predestination is repeated in answer to these complaints; we cannot contend
with a mighty one; murmuring is therefore useless, especially as that which
the wise must do without is worthless and vanity. The idea of earthly
happiness is very vague, which is shewn by several examples; then follow
detached lessons and wise sayings. The whole universe is intimately connected, and bears the impress of the sublimity, goodness, and wisdom of the
Author; it is therefore reasonable that we should not murmur against God,
but bear our fate with patience and resignation.

The eighth section (chap. vii. 15 – viii. 9). — Rules for governing and
admonitions to princes. Absolute justice is impracticable for the transactions of government; experience, too, teaches that it is not for man. It is
now impossible to ascertain whether man was originally perfect; at present
he is not. Folly and ignorance are the source of vice; sensuality, which
goes by the name of folly, is here personified as a harlot, and, by the way,
an attack is made upon the whole female sex. Another cause of evil in the
world is man's daily increasing wants; naturally he has few wants, but they
are multiplied in social connections. Rules for subjects. Admonitions not
to enter into any conspiracy against rulers. A faithful servant of state will
suffer and be quiet; a tyrant does not last long; he can, as little as other
earthborn children, escape plagues, natural death, and being killed in war —
experience shews this.

The ninth section (chap. viii. 10 – ix. 12). Further contemplations on
the apparent prosperity of the wicked and adversity of the good. Because
punishment does not always follow immediately upon transgression, the
wicked are inclined to believe that there is no retribution; but it is certain
that the righteous will be happy in a future life; the prosperity of the wicked
is but momentary, and will pass away like a shadow. If the virtuous were
always prosperous and the vicious unfortunate, there would be no merit in
virtue. We cannot judge the whole, and from the little we see taking
place upon earth, no conclusion can be formed; but this much is certain,
that without another world and immortality, future punishment and reward,
the whole would be inexplicable. To judge from what takes place here
below, sensual pleasure would seem the highest good; and this too brings
care and trouble, and at last causes disgust and vexation. If all terminated
with this life, everything would contradict our moral nature, for the same
things happen alike to all. It cannot be reconciled with the justice of the
Creator, that so many sinners, without repenting in the least, depart into

the realms of the dead; their existence becomes for them a positive curse. Moreover, without a future, earthly life would be the highest good; and life, however miserable, would be preferable to annihilation, from which the soul recoils. The living dog would be better than a dead lion. What keeps us from breaking all laws, to accomplish all for which we have power, to break through all bonds which are in the way of our gratifications? But all this is contrary to the moral sense of man. Moreover, this happiness is not always the portion of the able and wise. The swift does not always win the race. This is another source of pain to him who denies a future life. The conviction of immortality, and reward and punishment in another life, can alone remove the doubt and reconcile these contradictions. Here below we are not able to survey the whole, to distinguish apparent good and apparent evil, and hence are also not able to judge of the way of Providence; but the future will throw light upon all these obscurities, and solve all these apparent contradictions into the most beautiful harmony.

The tenth section (chap. ix. 13 - x. 15) Observations on the value of intellectual powers with respect to political matters, illustrated by an example — the smallest error of a wise man may involve the most serious consequences. Fools do not rule long; if they attain to important offices, through the rashness of the prince, their honour is of short duration. Flatterers and slanderers cannot go on long; being always obliged to contrive new ways to advance, they consume their powers. Wisdom goes only one way, the straight one, and thereby always overthrows her enemies.

The eleventh section (chap. x. 16 - xi. 6). Description of a bad government; caution in judging it is recommended. Encouragements to commerce and alliance with other nations; rules to be observed thereby. As the preacher recommends attention to misfortunes which may happen in the course of nature, so he also warns against all superstitious sooth-saying, forebodings, watching the clouds, and other offsprings of an unbridled imagination.

The twelfth section (chap. xi. 7 - xii. 7). Rest is desirable after labour, and enjoyment of what one has acquired. But the enjoyment must be moderate, and in keeping with the laws prescribed by the fear of God and the regulations of man. Hereupon follows an allegorical description of old age, and the decay of the mind and body, which is extremely difficult to explain. (Many words in this section are foreign, and can only be explained and translated by conjecture.)

The thirteenth section (chap. xii. 8 - 14). The conclusion. The preacher says that his object in this treatise was to teach man the truth which is useful for them, and that he has endeavoured to express himself attractively, to make a deeper impression on them. The conclusion of the whole enquiry is, that all the doings of man will be brought before the judgment of God, and that we are therefore to fear Him and keep His commandments.

This sensible introduction and analysis of Coheleth shew how creditably Friedländer responded to the appeal of his master in defence of rational exegesis.

1831. — In 1831 Moses Heinemann published a translation of Coheleth, with brief but comprehensive notes. He too thinks that this book *contains a collection of diverse experience, observations, opinions, truths, and lessons of wisdom, which Solomon collected together* (hence the name קֹהֶלֶת, *collector* or *compiler*), *to shew that everlasting life is the sole end of our existence here, and that everything earthly and sensual is vain, foolish, and transitory*.[1] This view of regarding the book as a collection of different opinions, &c., has its origin in an anxiety to remove from Solomon every obnoxious sentiment.   Hence Heinemann's very forced explanation of

Chap. iii. 18-21. *I thought in my heart, &c.* — Among the different sections of faith, egotism often produces so-called libertines, who ridicule all Divine revelation and reject every religious ordinance; whilst, touching freedom of will, they consider the giving of law to emanate from their peculiar intellect, and form rules of life according to their arbitrary inclinations.   Respecting such arrogant individuals Coheleth remarks that they consider themselves the chosen of God by virtue of their reason, making the greatest dignity of man and his prerogatives above all other creatures to consist in being the cause of their actions.   Coheleth, whilst characterising such a mode of thinking as recommends acts contrary to the Divine will as sceptical, places the latter on a par with the use of intuitive actions in irrational creatures, and regards the works of both, like all earthly things, as perishable and aimless, as vain and empty.   And though it is certain that the human spirit, by virtue of its power of development and capacities, rises higher and higher to the uppermost intellectual spheres, yet are we as unable to say whether such a misguided spirit as has departed from the way of the law will reach that uppermost height, where the obedient may approach the Deity to enjoy its bliss in the voice of the Divine favour, as we are unable to define the low point of the animal spirit.[2]

1837. — This mode of forcing upon the sacred writer philosophic sentiments, which are alike contrary to the scope of the

---

[1] Uebersetzung des Koheleth, nebst grammatisch exegetischem Commentar von Moses Heinemann, Berlin, 1831, p. 3, and p. 129.

[2] Commentary, p. 38, &c.

passage and the simple meaning of the text, in order to overcome difficulties which are insurmountable without the true clue to the design of the book, is adopted to a still larger extent by S. H. Auerbach. In 1837 he published a German translation of this book, with the original text, and a Hebrew commentary, maintaining quite a new theory, that Solomon wrote Coheleth (which signifies *philosophy*) *to shew the relation of man both to himself and to his fellow men, or society.*

The sacred writer (Auerbach tells us) starts with the idea that all things in nature are ordained by the Creator for a certain end, unknown to us, whereunto all creation must follow, according to the inwardly working powers of the Deity. And as man, though individually possessing a free will in relation to the whole, is subject to these laws of nature with all his actions and will — so that he, like all other creatures, cannot and must not resist the power of the whole, or the great design of the Creator — he cannot calculate beforehand with certainty the result of his actions, or the success of his aims and efforts. If, therefore, his aims are to be successful, they must harmonise with those of the whole, or of God. But, as the purposes of God are unknown to man, nay are incomprehensible, a harmony and a right conduct on the part of man with regard to God must be purely accidental. Successful undertakings are therefore nothing else than accidentally right and proper catches of the design or will of God, inasmuch as those undertakings have been subservient to the aim of the whole.

The creative will of the divine powers — אֱלֹהִים, synonymous with the expression *nature, i. e.,* the producing power — which, united in the one Being (יְהוָֹה), unremittingly work on in such a diversity of ways, that the power of the human soul, being borne along, only passes a subjective judgment, dependent upon the present moment. The soul can comprehend and grasp things only as they are momentarily brought before her by the sensible world. All depends upon this external, momentary, and accidental impression. Even to will and not to will, or love and hatred, are not in the positive intellectual powers of man, but in the positive representation of things; and on this, again, time and space, by which man is swayed, have an important influence, so that one and the same thing, which received in one moment our affirmative, will in the next moment have a negative.

Man has indeed the power of adding to or taking from existing things, or to hate and love; but this power is circumscribed by time and circumstances, namely, can be exercised only in the position in which the things are before him (לְפָנָיו, Coheleth ix. 1), in the outer and sensible world. Hence the fate of a man very often depends upon a single accident or judgment; and hence also the defects which he sees are frequently not objective, but subjective. Thus, for instance, the most moral, just, pious, and wise man may suffer throughout the whole of his life for a single error, because he has not rightly comprehended and judged a thing *there* (שָׁם, *Ibid.* iii. 17), where it then was in time and space; and the unrestrainable consequence, which is always only in accordance with the Divine purpose as regards the whole, will stamp his act, then performed, as a failure and misdemeanor.[1]

Having given us this philosophic disquisition, which we are to take as the main idea of the sacred writer, Auerbach submits that the book consists of two parts, comprising two treatises or discourses; the first, as we gather from his Commentary, extends from chap. ii. to vii. 24; and the second, from chap. vii. 25 to xii. 8, and that each of these parts has two sections, viz., i. 1 – iii. 22, and iv. 1 – vii. 24, form the two sections of the first part; and vii. 25 – ix. 10, and ix. 11 – xii. 8, are the two sections of the second part. The first section, in each case, we are told contains the enquiry, or is philosophical; and the second gives the application, or is practical.

PART I.

THE FIRST SECTION (chap. i. 1 – iii. 22) treats on the relation of man to himself with respect to the all-ruling order of God here below, in which man can neither effect a change nor produce anything new, and hence cannot of himself, with his physical or moral powers, be the author of his earthly happiness. And the section concludes with the lesson deduced therefrom, that, since man is as perishable and vain as all other creatures, it can hardly be defined with certainty whether his powers and capacities, when compared with those of animals, are to be regarded as superior, inasmuch as man and the animal are both passive instruments of Providence, the whole of man's earthly happiness would accordingly be to make the best of his fate and of the present, and submit resignedly to the fulfilment of his duties. Hereupon follows

THE SECOND SECTION (chap. iv. 1 – vii. 24), which is the application or practical part, wherein the author discloses to man his grossest defects and infirmities, warring in him and depriving him of the enjoyment of peace, *e. g.*, avarice, envy, &c., &c., in order to cure the evil.

PART II treats on the relation of man to his fellow man, or society, and in

THE FIRST SECTION (chap. vii. 25 – ix. 10) examines whether and how man can therein find happiness. His first thought on social life leads to woman, the natural and inseparable companion of man, who fatally affects the destiny of man. He is then forced, as it were, by her to the consideration

---

[1] See the introductory Epistle to the Commentary, pp. 8 and 9.

of the pomp and gaiety of the world, the varieties of fame, wealth, and ambition, since that which man desires under these circumstances, he, even with his innate capacities, cannot obtain, if he is not favoured by special circumstances. As in the former part, the author shews us the vanity of man's exertion and toil, and then concludes with the lesson that man, knowing his frailty, should enjoy life with the woman he loves, and try to derive as much pleasure as possible from all his toil. Whereupon again follows —

THE SECOND SECTION (chap. ix. 11 – xii. 8) which is again the application, or the practical one. The sacred writer gives some of the most important rules of life to the man who is to enter into social life, e. g., to have social feelings, to be dauntless, cautious, diligent, forbearing, &c., and concludes with the admonition to enjoy life, before the weakness of old age comes on, and death terminates our existence.

At the conclusion (chap. xii. 8-14) a few verses are appended, which con· tain a summary view of the whole work, telling us that the sacred writer wanted to find out something new, and, instead of it, felt himself constrained to write down the old truth; that all the words of the wise tend to one thing; that therefore all book-making, and prying into things, are super- fluous; and that we are to fear God and keep His commandments, because by this only will the good or bad of every action be determined.[1]

To make the sacred writer propound this philosophic theory, Auerbach proceeds to translate many passages in a most unna- tural and unjustifiable way. The rendering of chap. iii. 18–22 will suffice as a specimen.[2]

I thus thought with respect to men: May God make it clear to them, that they may see how that, with respect to their existence, they are like beasts. For whether it be the destiny of man, or that of a beast, it is always only one destiny; the one dies like the other, the capacities of both terminate alike, and the superiority of man is without influence, because all is vain. Both make the same way, they come from the earth, and return to it. Who can therefore determine whether man's higher strivings be higher, and the animals' lower strivings be lower? I, on the contrary,

---

[1] See the introductory Epistle to the Commentary, pp. 12 and 13.

[2] Ich dachte also in Betreff der Menschen: möge es ihnen Gott erläutern, daß sie einsehen, wie sie in Rücksicht ihres Daseins gleich dem Viehe sind. Denn, es sei das Schicksal des Menschen oder das des Viehes, es ist immer nur Ein Schicksal; jener stirbt wie dieses, beider Fähigkeiten laufen auf Eins hinaus und auch des Menschen Vorzug ist ohne Einfluß, weil Alles eitel ist. Sie machen beide einen gleichen Weg; sie entstehen von der Erde und kehren dahin zurück. Wer kann also nun bestimmen, daß des Menschen höheres Streben das Höhere sei, und des Viehes niedriges Streben das Niedrige sei; ich beschließe

conclude that man has no other advantage than to rejoice in the discharge of his duties, for this alone is his portion, because no one can shew him the future and its consequences.

1838.—No commentator, since Rashbam, has so strictly adhered to the literal and grammatical meaning of Coheleth as Herzfeld, now chief Rabbi of Brunswick, and so well known by his very elaborate history of the Jews. He, however, advances a new theory, viz., that *the design of Coheleth is to demonstrate the vanity of all things; and, by thus shewing up the exertions of* ALL *men to be alike vain, the sacred writer tries to comfort his unhappy nation, who imagined that* THEY ALONE *are given up to misfortunes.* Thus Herzfeld tells us —

The sole tendency of the book is to teach the vanity of human efforts. And now, since xii. 9, and the whole colouring of the book, shew that it was intended for the people, the question is, what effect did the writer think to produce thereby upon the people? It could surely not have been the intention of our old Jewish sage to make philosophers of the people; and just as little could it have entered into his mind to temper the pride of his fellow-citizens with such a *memento mori,* since this nation had, for thousands of years, not been out of the school of sufferings for a single decade of years. There is, however, another object left: the demonstrations in our book of the vanity of all that is human, are so entirely free from all peculiarly national colouring — so much so, that the peculiarly national term יהוה, to designate the Deity, is dropped, and אלהים is invariably used — that the writer evidently did not intend to confine his demonstrations to the circumstances under which this people lived, but extended them to the circumstances of mankind generally. Now, by shewing that the exertions of *all* men are alike vain, he tries to comfort his unhappy people, and take away their belief, that they alone were given up to misery.[1]

The chief Rabbi of Brunswick divides the book into *nineteen* sections. The *first* section is from chap. i. 1 to 11; the *second,* from chap. i. 12 to 18; the *third,* from chap. ii. 1 to 11; the

vielmehr, daß bem Menschen nichts mehr frommt, als sich seiner Pflichterfüllung zu erfreuen, denn nur dieses ist sein Theil, weil ihm Niemand die Zukunft und ihre Folgen zeigen kann.

[1] Coheleth übersetzt und erläutert von Dr. L. Herzfeld, Braunschweig, 1838, p. 10, &c.

fourth, from chap. ii. 12 to 23; the *fifth*, from chap. ii. 24 to
iii. 15; the *sixth*, from chap. iii. 16 to iv. 3; the *seventh*, from
chap. iv. 4 to 12; the *eighth*, from chap. iv. 13 to 16; the *ninth*,
from chap. iv. 17 to v. 6; the *tenth*, from chap v. 7 to vii. 9;
the *eleventh*, from chap. vii. 10 to 22; the *twelfth*, from chap
vii. 23 to 24; the *thirteenth*, from chap. vii. 25 to viii. 13; the
fourteenth, from chap. viii. 14 to 15; the *fifteenth*, from chap.
viii. 16 to ix. 12; the *sixteenth*, from chap. ix. 13 to x. 3; the
seventeenth, from chap. x. 4 to 20; the *eighteenth*, from chap. xi. 1
to xii. 8; the *nineteenth* section is from chap. xii. 9 to 14.

The commentary is preceded by an introduction of three
chapters, treating respectively on the *contents*, *tendency*, and
character of Coheleth. The third chapter, viz., the one treating
on the character of the book, is directed against Knobel, who, in
his then recent commentary, entered very minutely into the
later Hebrew words and phrases of Coheleth, shewing up a prodigious number of them, and Herzfeld reduces " the expressions
and constructions foreign to the old literature," to about eleven
or fifteen, and " the Chaldaisms " to about eight or ten. This
has been hailed by the defenders of the antiquity of Coheleth,
who to this day quote the chief Rabbi of Brunswick, in opposition to those who maintain that the diction of this book belongs
to the time when the Hebrew language was extremely vitiated
and rapidly dying away. But the chronological order we have
adopted will soon bring us back to Herzfeld, and his view upon
this subject.

1848. — The sixteenth volume of Cahen's celebrated edition
of the Hebrew Bible, with a French translation, and philological
and explanatory notes, contains a commentary on Coheleth,
which, as Cahen informs us,[1] is chiefly made up from a communication of Leopold Dukes, to whom Hebrew literati are so

---

[1] La plus grande partie de ce que nous allons dire sur *L'Ecclesiaste* est de
M. Dukes; il en est de même des notes. Ce savant a bien voulu nous donner
sur ce livre intéressant un travail que nous avons tantôt modifié, tantôt abrégé.
Nous avons aussi puisé à quelques autres sources. La Bible, par S. Cahen,
tome seizième, à Paris, 1848, Avant-propos., p. xxv.

largely indebted for his numerous literary productions. ¯ We must therefore regard that which Dukes and Cahen conjointly propound about this book as the Duko-Cahen view.

The design of the book, we are here told, *is to propound the philosophy of life, which the author*, who is a sceptic, *does, by treating upon the following questions: What is the world? What is its destiny? Is it governed by a superior intelligence, or is it the toy of chance? Is the soul mortal or immortal?* To give the reader a proper idea of this novel view, we must let these learned men speak for themselves. Cahen says that —

M. Dukes compares the course of the reflections of Ecclesiastes to the veil which, among the Egyptians, covered the statue of Isis. No mortal was permitted to raise this veil, but every one was allowed to give his opinion as to what was behind it. Heraclites and Democrites, placed before this veil, commented on it each in his own way, the one weeping, the other laughing; our book holds the middle course between these two ways. Doubt resembles a cloud which appears on the horizon, grows imperceptibly, and announces tempest, which the power of man knows not how to appease. Doubt begins with the individual, and finishes with the world; the solution begins with the world, and finishes with the individual. Doubt is the fruit of contemplation, but it is like children who instruct their mothers, or like spices which give a good flavour to food. Doubt by itself is of no use; its value consists in the service which it renders to reflection; one is not to stop at doubt, it must serve him as a vehicle. Doubt is as old as reflection. Before Descartes, a Spanish proverb said, *El que no duda, no sabe alcun res* — He who doubts nothing knows nothing; and before the Spanish, a Greek philosopher had already propounded this principle as the foundation of all knowledge.

The sacred writer was a philosopher, who wished to view life from an elevated stand-point; he would not content himself with the limited horizon of those men who, taking life as it is, do not complain, except when fortune is against them. He speaks for humanity, and his words have always found an echo. His book is a great monologue, which presents life to us in energetic traits, and its laconic style shews the profoundness of the thinker. It is scepticism softened by maxims. The object which the writer has most prominently before him is the future destiny of man.

It is doubt, the vanity of the things of this world, which forms the thread of the entire book. The writer begins with "*All is vanity*" (i. 2), and repeats it at the end of the book (xii. 9). To prove this, he accumulates different observations on human life and its vicissitudes. He weighs all, business and leisure, pleasure and pain, joy and sorrow, and determines what is true and what is false; what is lasting, and what is perishable; what is real, and what is apparent. He adopts no methodical arrangement, but simply the association of ideas. He asks himself, What is the world? What is its destiny? Is it governed by a superior intelligence, or is it the toy of chance? Is the soul mortal or immortal? These are the questions on which our author treats.[1]

1854. — Whilst Cahen was editing his gigantic Bible work in France — where Rashi, Rashbam, and many other eminent Jews had laboured to explain the Word of God, at a period when the so-called Christians were engrossed with the Crusade and the extermination of heretics — Philippson was at the same time busy with the publication of a similar work in Germany. This splendid edition of the Bible, besides giving the Hebrew original with a German translation in parallel columns, and a critical and exegetical commentary, is illustrated with upwards of five hundred English woodcuts.

The Rabbi of Magdeburg also could not acquiesce in any of the multifarious theories propounded by the long succession of commentators, as to the design of Coheleth, and therefore advanced a new view. He maintains that *the object of the book is to shew that a belief in the vanity of human life is not only compatible with a belief in God and moral efforts, but that by combining the two together the sole end and value of life is manifested.*[2] According to Philippson, Coheleth consists of *three parts and an epilogue.*

THE FIRST PART (chap. i. 2 – iii. 22), which is the general one, has *three sections.* After giving the main observation as if it were the motto, that all is vanity (chap. i. 2), the sacred writer shews that this applies to all things in general (sect. i , chap. i. 3–11), and to the affairs of life in particular (sect. ii., chap. i. 12 – ii. 23), and then deduces therefrom a rule of life, and shews its soundness (sect. iii., chap. ii. 24 – iii. 22).

---

[1] See Introduction, pp. xxv., xxvii. We wish our space had permitted us to give the whole of this very instructive Introduction.

[2] Die Israelitische Bibel, von Ludwig Philippson, Dritter Theil, 1854, pp. 746, 747.

THE SECOND PART (chap. iv. 1 – xi. 8), which is the special one, has *two sections.* Coheleth considers the more important events of human life from the point of view attained (sect. i., chap. iv. 1 – vii. 12), and describes the conduct of a wise man according to his opinion, following the given rule of life (sect. ii., chap. vii. 1 – xi. 8).

THE THIRD PART (chap. xi. 9 – xii. 8) gives the result of the whole investigation, a close application of his established rule of life, and concludes with the main observation, namely, that all is vanity.

THE EPILOGUE (chap. xii 9–14) having been added by the author shortly after the completion of the book, in consequence of some scruples which arose among a small circle of friends to whom he first read it, warns that the book is not to be read with levity of mind, and shews, in a brief and striking manner, its religious stand-point.[1]

This is the design, and this the division of the book, according to the chief Rabbi of Magdeburg, Dr. Philippson.

1855. — We now return to the chief Rabbi of Brunswick, Dr. Herzfeld. In the first volume of his " History of the people of Israel " (of which the first number appeared in 1855), Herzfeld, after the lapse of seventeen years, takes up again his old favourite, Coheleth. As so much has been said about his defence of the book, we shall give his more matured view of its design and age entire.

The design of Coheleth is *to shew that all is vanity, and that man cannot secure even the vain happiness of this earth.* The author puts his observations into the mouth of Solomon, because in him were united royal power and great wisdom, the fame of which would invest his words with authority ; and because he only who possessed all this, and by means of it secured all kinds of pleasures, is entitled to such a general declaration that all is vanity. Accordingly, Solomon shews that all his splendour could not yield him happiness; nor could all human wisdom do it, because of its being very limited, and because it is utterly impossible by its aid to turn to our

¹ Die Israelitische Bibel, von Ludwig Philippson, Dritter Theil, 1854, pp. 750, 751.

advantage sublunary things, for all things, even the "transactions, love, and hatred" of man, are under a divine fatality; nor, lastly, was virtue capable of making him happy, since earthly happiness is not always bestowed according to moral worth, but is purely a gift of God. This will not appear awful to one who believes in a future life, where virtue, unrewarded here, will be rewarded; but this belief, which was then still novel, had to struggle with such great doubts in the mind of the author, that it often was overcome. When looking in such hopeless moments at the distribution of happiness and misery, without any regard to the worth of the recipient, he would have regarded God as unjust, but for the pious feelings which strove against it; he therefore preferred to conclude that God governs the world by a higher and inscrutable method, according to which he distributes unmerited lots in single instances, without however being unjust, when that higher method does not require it. Man can receive good from God in two ways — as a reward for virtue, whenever that method permits it; and as a free gift, most likely in order to further that method; but man may also lose it in two ways — first by his vicious conduct, and then through a wrong adjustment of his circumstances. Hence, although we cannot with certainty secure happiness by our industry, there are instances, nevertheless, where our conduct may influence our happiness or misery. It does not contradict his theme when the author, in treating upon it, especially towards the end, intersperses a number of peculiar moral and wise rules, recommending the enjoyment of every lawful pleasure which presents itself, manly self-denial in misfortune, quiet endurance of all that cannot be averted, in which the epicurean and stoical views are thoroughly blended together. Still these interspersed rules are a secondary matter with the author, and are often involuntary digressions; his main object is to preach the vanity of all things human. By keeping his illustration free from all national colouring, the author, who probably wrote about the end of the Persian dominion, wanted to shew his oppressed nation that no other nation is much better off than they are; the Messianic hopes must have nearly disappeared at that time. As to the importance of the book, we submit that the very fact of its entering upon new ground, *i. e.*, philosophy, is in itself of no small importance. There are single questions in the Prophets and Psalms of higher importance, but they are not explained, not dialectically pursued; they are either left unanswered, or answered not logically, but in a lyrically or prophetically peremptory declaration. A more expansive course has indeed been pursued in the book of Job; the enquiry *why* and *whether* (not whether and why) the righteous often suffer and the wicked prosper, receives many phases; but here again the discourses turn throughout into the lyric, and with the lyric the argument is lost; and God, who appears at the conclusion, does not answer the proposed question, but cuts it off, and bids the sophists be silent. It is only in Coheleth that it appears in prose, which is the only adequate form for philosophic disquisition; and it is not the author's fault that the way which

he opened has been left untrodden by his successors. Moreover, the indepen-
dence and openness of his sentiments are highly to be praised; in these he
has not only surpassed all the canonical and apocryphal writers, but also
Philo and the philosophers of our Arabian school.   He has also, from his
point of view, satisfactorily solved the proposed question.   It is only to be
regretted that he has not conceded a value to virtue independent of reward,
as his investigations brought him so closely to it.   The treatise is unequal.
That the author drops Solomon almost entirely, as soon as he has made him
explain that all his grandeur could not make him happy, is owing to
the fact that a royal mouth was not requisite for the other declarations,
and. as has already been remarked, that he never seriously intended to
ascribe it to Solomon.   There is a plan in the arrangement of it, which
however is not always preserved, and we must frequently be satisfied with
the unity of the theme, which is far better observed.   The style of the
composition is for the most part simple in the discursive portions, but
sometimes diffuse and clumsy, because the author had to create a philosophical language. The words newly made or newly applied for this purpose
indicate skill; the observations and admonitions interspersed are in a
gnomological form, but are no great performance; finally, the description
of old age and approaching death, at the end of the book, though suffering
from an oriental redundancy of figure, has a great charm in its vacillation
between lyric and elegy.[1]

To this exposition of the design, importance, plan, and diction
of the book, which is given in the text of the history, Herzfeld
adds, in the twentieth Excursus, a disquisition on the authorship
of Coheleth.   As this must be especially interesting to those who
have so frequently appealed to him upon this subject, we shall
also give it entire.

All that I have to say upon Coheleth will be found dispersed through the
introduction of my Commentary, published in 1838, except the much
disputed Solomonic authorship, about which I promised to explain myself
another time.   Some greatly blamed me for this caution, and others again
charged me with taking Solomon to be the author, although the very reverse
is to be deduced from numerous passages in the introduction and commentary.
The cause of my silence was simply owing to the fact that seventeen years
ago a Jewish theologian could not handle Biblical criticism without serious
danger.   However, the point then passed by must now be retrieved.

The book itself states (i. 1. 12) that a son of David, king in Israel, i e.,
Solomon, is the author; and hence the origin of the unanimous popular

[1] Geschichte des Volkes Iisrael, von Dr. L. Herzfeld, Nordhausen, 1857;
Zweiter Band, pp. 28–31.

tradition, which is by no means contradicted by the assertion that King
Hezekiah and his associates wrote Coheleth (Baba Bathra, 15, a), as this
simply refers to the final editorship. But Solomon, whose father first elevated Jerusalem to a royal residence, could not say " more than all (kings)
who were before me in Jerusalem" (i. 16; ii. 7), nor recommend to wait
cautiously for an opportunity to rise against a tyrant (viii. 5, 6), nor give a
description of a royal spendthrift (x. 16–19), nor were the people so unhappy
in his time, as iv. 1, v. 7 presuppose. The complaints about unrighteous
judges (iii. 17), about violence (iv. 1; v. 7), about unworthy filling of places
of honour (x. 5-7)—it might be urged, are not so very strange, for a king who
has once placed himself in the position of a popular teacher. But still, this
objection against the Solomonic authorship has some weight when added to
the former. Moreover, the belief in the return of the soul to God, though
questioned in iii. 21, being nevertheless so common as to be discussed in a
popular work, and even obtain the victory, cannot be ascribed to Solomon, for
there is no trace of it to be found from his days till after the exile. Finally,
I have shewn in my commentary (p. 13–22), that although many words and
phrases in Coheleth are wrongly explained as later Hebrew or Chaldee,
there yet remains a considerable number of both in the book. All these
arguments combined are perfectly sufficient to shew that Solomon is not the
author of this book. This done, we can now give some clues for ascertaining
the date of its composition, which we were obliged to omit before. The
Chaldaisms in it would not oblige us to put it later than the Chaldee
invasion; but the state in which the doctrine of the immortality of the soul
appears therein, and its eleven to fifteen later Hebrew expressions, speak
for its being written a century at least after the exile. But it appears to me
to be of a still later date, from the two following reasons:— 1. The word
קהלת, as I have already shewn in the commentary (p. 25), denotes such a
speaker in congregations, as the *Sopherim* (סֹפְרִים) were. The author could
not have newly formed this word in order to apply it to Solomon, as this
designation is not at all applicable to him; it must already have existed, and
obtained the secondary signification of *teacher of wisdom*, before it could be
applied to Solomon. Now, the *Sopherim* (סֹפְרִים) did not appear in Judea
till the time of Ezra, and the expression *Coheleth* (קֹהֶלֶת), to designate them,
must have originated after it; and its transition from the primary to a
secondary sense must have taken place later still. 2. The בַּעֲלֵי אֲסֻפּוֹת (xii. 11)
are evidently the same as the סֹפְרִים. On the other hand, the political horizon
of the author (iv. 13-16, comp. the commentary) does not tally with the
dominion of the Ptolemies extending to the Maccabean period, or with the
Seleucean to a date nearly as late, but perfectly corresponds with the last
century of the Persian dominion. I therefore believe that this book was
written shortly before the era of Alexander the Great. The fear, that every
sigh about the rulers may be betrayed (x. 20), perfectly harmonises with
this time. This view does not, indeed, agree with the remark that Coheleth

was locked up because of its questionable contents, till the men of the great synagogue liberated it (Aboth R. Nathan, c. 1) ; but this modern note cannot subvert a well weighed result of criticism, and is also contradicted by Shabbath, 30, b, where it is related that " the sages " wanted to hide it from the people, but ultimately abstained from it.[1]

We think that Rabbi Herzfeld will henceforth be no authority with those who have hitherto appealed to him in corroboration of the pure Hebrew diction and Solomonic authorship of Coheleth.

1858. — There is, however, another Jewish commentator, though not a chief Rabbi, yet of some considerable ability, who still maintains the Solomonic authorship, and might henceforth have been quoted as an authority upon this subject instead of Herzfeld, were it not for the extravagant and eccentric theories which he propounds. The individual is Nathan Rosenthal, who published, in 1858, the text of Coheleth, with a German translation, and an extensive Hebrew commentary, in which he advances an entirely new view as to the design of this book. According to him, Solomon, who was an *Eclectic* (קֹהֶלֶת, *vide supra*, p. 4, No. 4), wrote this book, *both to shew that wisdom is useful only in proportion as it is combined with the fear of God and the keeping of his commands, and to remove from us the pernicious opinion of the philosophers, who believed that everlasting happiness, and the immortality of the soul, depend upon the cultivation of the intellect, and not upon our conduct and works ; thus making no distinction between those who serve God and those who serve him not, by teaching us the very reverse, namely, that it is through the law and fear of God that man can attain to spiritual and everlasting happiness.*[2]

As to the question, " How could Solomon collect different philosophic systems which were foreign to the Jews, and did not appear among the Gentiles till many centuries after, since

---

[1] Geschichte des Volkes Israel, vol. ii., pp. 66, 67.

[2] Koheleth von Salomo, übersetzt nebst einem ebräischen Commentar von Nathan Rosenthal, Prag., 1858, p. 11.

Thales, the first philosopher, lived about four hundred years after Solomon?" Rosenthal submits that philosophic systems existed from time immemorial; that Plato got his wisdom from the Prophets; Socrates learned his from Ahithophel and Asaph the Korahite; Aristotle stole his from the writings of Solomon, which he seized when at Jerusalem with Alexander,[1] &c., there being nothing new under the sun, since even the *Telegraph* is referred to in Ps. xix. 4.[2] Chap. iii. 18 will suffice as a specimen of some of his renderings.

> I thought within myself about the talk of the children of men that they enjoy the food of the gods, and give themselves the appearance that they are their favourite animals.[3]

Rosenthal maintains that Solomon refers in this passage to the food of the gods, and the nectar which the ancients said the soul enjoyed when reposing from her labours.

1860.—The last, and the most remarkable, Jewish production on Coheleth, is by Professor S. D. Luzzatto. It is printed in the third annual volume of Hebrew Essays and Reviews,[4] and purports to be the Introduction to an unpublished commentary upon our book, written thirty-six years ago. After bitterly complaining that all commentators have misunderstood and outraged the sense of Coheleth, Luzzatto maintains that *the book totally denies the immortality of the soul, and recommends the enjoyment of carnal pleasures, as the only thing left for man;* that it was written after the Babylonish captivity by a man of the name of Coheleth, who, to invest it with authority, ascribed it to Solomon,

---

[1] Koheleth von Salomo, übersetzt nebst einem ebräischen Commentar von Nathan Rosenthal, Prag., 1858, pp. 12, 13.

[2] על ההמצאה החדשה של חקות חוט היוצא בכל מרחקי ארץ ונושא אומר ודברים עד קצה תבל הנקרא טעלעגראף אף שהיא אחת מן ההמצאות היותר חדשות ואינו נמצא כדומה לו בעולם הישן שמעתי מחכם אחד שיש רמז עליה בכתוב : אין אמר ואין דברים בלי נשמע קולם בכל הארץ יצא קום ובקצה תבל מלהם p. 22

[3] Ich dachte nach auf die Reden der Menschen in meinem Innern, daß sie Götterspeisen genießen, und geben sich das Ansehen, daß sie seine Lieblings=thiere sind.

[4] Ozar Nechmad: Briefe und Abhandlungen jüdischer Literatur betreffend; herausgegeben von Ignaz Blumenfeld: Dritter Jahrgang, Wien, 1860, pp. 15–25.

whose name did originally appear in the book; that the contemporary sages, recognising this trick, and knowing the real
author, erased the name Solomon, put in the proper name,
Coheleth, and left the words " son of David, king in Jerusalem "
to brand the impostor; for every one knew the mean position of
Coheleth, and by declaring himself to be king, and son of David,
he would be denounced as a madman.   All this, however, was
forgotten in the course of time.   And when the later sages
found this book, purporting to be the composition of the royal
son of David, and saw that it contained infidel sentiments,
being unable to prevail with the majority of their colleagues to
exclude it from the canon, they, in their anxiety to redeem the
character of Solomon, and the sacred Scripture, from the charge
of heresy, added three half verses thoroughly orthodox, viz.,
וְדַע עַל־כָּל־אֵלֶּה יְבִיאֲךָ הָאֱלֹהִים בַּמִּשְׁפָּט, and know that for all
this God will bring thee into judgment (xi. 6, b); וּזְכֹר אֶת־בּוֹרְאֶיךָ
בִּימֵי בְּחוּרֹתֶיךָ, and remember thy Creator in the days of thy
youth (xii. 1, a); and וְהָרוּחַ תָּשׁוּב אֶל־הָאֱלֹהִים אֲשֶׁר נְתָנָהּ, and
the spirit shall return to God who gave it (xii. 8, b); the first
addition of eight words, the second of five, and the third of six,
making in all nineteen words; as הָאֱלֹהִים, however, occurs twice,
it must only be taken for one word, hence eighteen only remain;
and these are י"ח מלין תקון סופרים, mentioned in the Talmud
(Shabbath, 97, a), of which no one ever knew the meaning
till Professor Luzzatto thus identified them with the interpola-
tions before us!

   This is an epitome of a somewhat extensive Introduction,
written in Hebrew by this master of the Hebrew language.
The Professor, however, tells us, in a letter to the editor of this
Annual, that he thinks better of Coheleth in his advanced
years; but what his better thoughts are he does not condescend
to say.[1]

---

[1] ואתה דע לך וידעו כל קוראי אוצרך ,כי לא ככל מחשבותי או מחשבותי עתה ,ויש בפירושי זה
כמה דברים שאינם עוד נכונים בעיני ,ויש בו גם כן דברים שאני מסופק בהם ;ודרך כלל מעלת ספר
קהלת גדלה בעיני אחרי בואי בימים ·הרבי יותר מכה שהיתה בימי חרפי

Other Jewish commentaries, not mentioned in this sketch, will be found in the Appendix. We now proceed to —

B. CHRISTIAN EXPOSITIONS.

In the early part of the Christian era Coheleth seems not to have been in great favour with the Fathers of the Church, judging from the general silence which prevails about it in the first, second, and a part of the third centuries. This is rather ominous, as we should have expected that, from its shewing the emptiness of all earthly things, this book would be welcomed by the suffering followers of Christ, who had to lose all for their Master's sake, and to take up their cross and follow Him. Whether this silence is owing to the fact that Coheleth is nowhere quoted in the New Testament, or to the doubts which existed in the minds of some respecting its canonicity, or to some other cause, it is not easy to divine.

210 – 270. — However, in the first half of the third century, the wonder-working Gregory (Thaumaturgus), who was born at Neocæsareia, in Cappadocia, at the beginning of the third century, and died in 270, wrote a short metaphrase of Coheleth.[1] Considering that he was the pupil and convert of Origen, the father of allegorical interpretation in the Greek Church, we are astonished to find such a comparatively simple paraphrase. According to Thaumaturgus, *the design of the Preacher is to shew that all the affairs and pursuits of man which are undertaken in human things are vain and useless, in order to lead us to the contemplation of heavenly things.* Like the Midrash,[2] Thaumaturgus regards the book as prophetic: " Solomon," says he, " son of David, king and prophet, also the most distinguished of all men, and the wisest prophet." The following is a specimen of his mode of paraphrasing : —

Chap. i. 8. *All things, &c.* — The things which man contemplates, his pursuits as well as his words, have neither measure nor end. There is

[1] Metaphrasis in Ecclesiast., in his works edited by Gerardus Vossius, Leipzig, 1604, 4to; or in Gallandii Biblioth. Patrum, Paris, 1788, tom. iii.

[2] *Vide supra*, p. 37.

indeed a large supply of their words, but there is no fruit from their endless talk, which is replete with error.

9, 10. *What, &c.* — What is it that is new which has not already been found by experience, provided it were remarkable and worthy of record? and there is nothing new and fresh, and unknown to the ancients.

11. *There is no remembrance, &c.* — As the past is buried in oblivion, so the present things will in the process of time sink into oblivion to a future generation.

12. *I, the Preacher, &c.* — Nor do I now, speaking as Preacher, utter these words without consideration; but I, to whose honour has been entrusted the sovereignty of the Jews, have diligently and accurately examined and weighed these things.

14. *I have seen all, &c.* — All these inferior things here below are full of a prodigious and execrable spirit, so much so that no man is able to enumerate them, nay rather to contemplate them, so excessive is the absurdity which has taken possession of human affairs.

331 – 396. — The first attempt to explain this book was made by Gregory, bishop of Nyssa, in Cappadocia, who was born about 331, and died about 396. He wrote a number of homilies on Coheleth, eight of which are extant, comprising the first three chapters, and it need hardly be said that his explanation is allegorical. He maintains that the design of this book is *to elevate the mind above every material object, and to quiet it, so that it may soar above all which seems great and sublime in this world, to that which the perceptions of the senses cannot reach, and to excite in it a longing after the super-sensible.*[1]

The following is a specimen of Gregory's exposition : —

Chap. i. 1. *The words of the Preacher, &c.* — Why is this book more than any other called " the words of the Preacher," seeing that Moses and the Prophets were also read in the church and congregation ? Because in other books there are many things about wars, cities, countries, and marriages, which are not so profitable to the Church of God, but the doctrine of this book relates to the only canon of ecclesiastical life, for it sets forth those things whereby one may lead an upright and virtuous life.

9. *What is that, &c.* — He refers to the resurrection and the reunion of the body with the soul. Taking, as the basis of his comment, the Septuagint interrogative rendering of this verse viz., *What is that which has been ?*

[1] Homil. 1 init. in his works edited by Morell and Grester, 2 vols., Paris, 1615–1618, reprinted in 1638.

reply, *That which is to be, and What is that which has been done?* reply, *That which shall be done,* Gregory remarks: Now, what does this interrogation mean when from what we have been told, viz., that all things are vanity, we might object, if all things be vanity, it is evident that there could never have been any of those things which have existed, for that which is vain cannot exist at all; moreover, what cannot exist, no one would speak about, when considering those things which have existed? Accordingly, if these things do not exist, tell me what is that which has been, or how does it continue to exist? To this question I reply, briefly, Do you wish to know "what is that which has been?" consider what is that which shall be and you will know it; reflect what you shall be who have elevated yourself by a life of virtue, if you have moulded your life in all good impressions; if you have been removed from all the pollutions of vice; if you have purged your nature from natural impurities, consider, I repeat, what you shall be when you have thus been adorned, and with what beauty you shall invest yourself if you can comprehend these things by reason. You see then the meaning of "what is that which has been?" namely from the first, that which has been formed after the image and likeness of God. And where now (I speak to him who teaches these things) is that which has existed in times past, and will again exist in the future, but does not exist now? He who teaches these sublime things replies that the present things have been called vanity, because these sublime things are not among them.

What is that which has been done? reply, *That which shall be done.* Let no one suppose that there is here a senseless repetition in the words, *has been* (הָיָה), and *has been done* (וְנַעֲשָׂה), as the former refers to *the soul,* and the latter to *the body;* the soul which has always existed (הָיָה) without sin shall be purged and be so again, and the body which was made at first (נַעֲשָׂה) shall be made again.

And there is no new, &c. — Since the resurrection is nothing but a restoration of the pristine state and condition.

10. *Behold this is new, &c.* — What has been said he endeavours to confirm by the words immediately following; if anything really exists now, it is that which has existed in the ages before us, as the passage declares it; but wonder not if the things which have existed are forgotten, for the things which are now will one day also be buried in oblivion.

11. *There is no remembrance, &c.* — Just as we have now no remembrance of the happiness in which man was created, so in the resurrection there will be no remembrance of the misery which man now suffers; for when our nature turned to sin, a forgetfulness of good things came upon us, but when we shall return to goodness, evils shall be buried in oblivion.

338. — Shortly after the appearance of Gregory's Homilies in the Greek Church, St. Jerome, the father of allegorical interpretation in the Latin Church, wrote an elaborate commentary

upon this book, with the express purpose of inducing St. Blesilla, a Roman young lady, to lead a monastic life. Accordingly, he maintains that the design of Coheleth is, *to shew the utter vanity of every sublunary enjoyment, and hence the necessity of betaking oneself to an ascetic life, devoted entirely to the service of God.* It is almost superfluous to say that St. Jerome explained the book allegorically. The following is a specimen of his mode of interpretation.

Chap. iv. 8. *There is one, &c.* — This is Christ, for he is one, and there is not a second, for he came to save the world without any companion ; and though there be many sons of God, many who, by adoption, are called the brethren of Christ, yet there was none so worthy as to be joined with him in this work. Of his labour for our sins and sufferings for us there is no end; man's understanding cannot comprehend the greatness thereof.

The eye is not satisfied, &c. — Christ is always desiring and seeking our salvation, nor does he say, " For whom do I labour ? " for though we despise his love, and refuse his mercies, he still labours to bring us to repentance, in order to win us to himself.

9. *Better two than one, &c.* — For it is better to have Christ dwelling in us than to be alone, open to the snares of the enemy.

10. *If one falls, &c.* — Christ raises him up who is a partaker of Him; but woe to him who when he falls has not Christ in him to raise him up again.

But one alone, &c. — Unless Christ sleeps and rests with us in death, we shall never be able to receive the glow of everlasting life.

11. *If two lie together, &c.* — If any one should be dissolved by death and lie in the grave, yet if he has Christ with him he shall be warmed, and, being quickened, shall quickly live again.

12. *And if one, &c.* — If the devil, assaulting man as a stronger, shall prevail against him, he shall stand, when Christ shall stand for him as his fellow.

Before such a mode of interpretation all difficulties disappear, and the most heterodox sentiments are easily converted into thoroughly orthodox admonitions. In most instances this Rabbi of the Christian Church had nothing to do but to Christianise the allegories of the Rabbins of the Jewish Church. Thus the commendation of eating and drinking, which the Midrash refers to the service of God,[1] St. Jerome explains of THE SACRAMENT

[1] *Vide supra*, p. 36.

OF THE LORD'S SUPPER; *bonum est veros cibos et veram sumere potionem, quos de agni carne et sanguine in divinis voluminibus invenimus.* He also tried to get over the inconvenient passages, by putting them into the mouths of sceptics and opponents to the truth, whom he introduces as speaking [1] — a scheme which has been adopted by subsequent expositors.

380. — It is not to be wondered at that some who adopted the view propounded by St. Jerome, viz., that this book teaches the utter vanity and worthlessness of every earthly pleasure, refused to deduce from it the necessity of leading an ascetic and monastic life, regarding such a doctrine as contrary to the goodness and beneficence of the Creator, and rejected the book as Epicurean and uncanonical. Hence we find that Philastrius, bishop of Brescia, who wrote a catalogue of heretics and heresies about the year 380, refers to those *who reject many things in the Old Testament, and among these the book of Ecclesiastes, because they read in it that everything under heaven is vanity of vanities, and because Ecclesiastes advises every one to eat and drink, and indulge in pleasures.*

The prelate's reply to these two objections is rather remarkable, and shews how easily heretics were disposed of in those days. To the charge, that this book denounces all the creatures of God as vain and worthless, Philastrius replies that they are here so described, *in comparison with the future glory of believers in Christ.* As to the second objection, namely, that we are here recommended to indulge in eating and drinking, the bishop submits that Solomon *speaks of spiritual food,* of the sacrament of the Lord's Supper, as St. Jerome explained it, respecting which the Prophet said, "Taste and see that the Lord is good."[2]

---

[1] *Et hace inquit aliquis loquentur Epicurus, et Aritippus, et Cyrenaici,* ix. 7, 8.

[2] Si dixit, vanitas vanitatis est, quæ in sæculo sunt, hæc utique transeuntia prædicavit propter futuram illam gloriam eminentem et perpetuam, ut ait apostolus; transit enim figura hujus mundi et gloria. Si autem figura et vita et honor et dignitas mundi istius cessabunt et destruentur, illa quippe erit desideranda cœlestis et angelica dignitas, quæ incorporatione ac passione et resurrec-

333 or 40 – 397 — The comparatively few heretics who urged their reasons against the inspiration of Coheleth, made no impression upon such a man as the eloquent St. Ambrose, bishop of Milan, who was born in 333 or 340 at Augusta Trevirorum (Treves), and died in his bishopric in 397. From his great fondness of celibacy and monasticism, in commendation of which he wrote several treatises, and from the ascetic mode of his life, we are quite prepared to find that this book formed St. Ambrose's armoury, supplying him with abundant weapons to defend the nothingness of all earthly enjoyments. Coheleth is therefore largely quoted by our ascetic Father in his various productions. The following is a specimen of his exposition : —

Chap. iv. 8. *There is one, &c.* — Who is this but He of whom it is said, Your Master is one in heaven ? (Matt. xxiii. 8). He is not the second, because He is the first ; He has not a second, because He alone is without sin ; He alone is without a helper.[1]

9. *Better two, &c.* — Does Christ labour ? He does labour, but it is in us ; He labours by making us labour, by supporting us in our labour ; and He that labours in us gives us a reward for our labours.

10. *If one falls, &c.* — Christ did not fall, but cast Himself down ; He humbled himself that He might make us his followers. He will raise us up, because when He was down he raised Himself up.

11. *If two lie together, &c.* — We are dead with Christ, and therefore live with Him ; Christ is dead with us that He may heat us ; and he who dies in Christ, being warmed by Christ, receives the vapour of life and resurrection.

12. *Two are better than one.* — That thou mayest know that this is spoken in mystery, and not of *the number two* being better than one, he added a mystical thing, namely, a threefold cord is not easily broken ; for three which are not compounded are not broken, and the Trinity which is of an uncompounded nature cannot be divided, because God who is one and simple, is whatsoever is.[2]

15. *I saw all the living, &c.* — Christ is the second young man ; he is the first according to his dignity, none being before him ; but the second

tione quippe est Christi credentibus adventura, quæ non temporalis, carnalis ac caduca. . . . Non de hac esca solum carnali dicebat . . . . sed diversam escam gloriamque sanctorum hominem nuntiabat. . . . . De qua esca ait et Propheta: Gustate et videte, quia suavis est Dominus. Bibl. Patr., tom. iv., p. 42.

[1] De Virgin., c. 10.　　　　　[2] Cohorta ad Clericos.

according to the flesh, because the second Adam. Moreover, I say I not only read that he is the second, but that he is the last; he is both the first and the last : he is the first, because through him are all things; the last, because through him shall be the resurrection.[1]

354 – 430. — St. Augustine, bishop of Hippo, who was born in 354, at Tagaste, an inland town in Numidia, like his tutor and father in God, St. Ambrose, explains this book allegorically. " *Having discovered the vanity of this world, the wisest of men wrote the whole of this book for nothing else but that we might discern that life which is not vanity under the sun, but real under Him who made the sun.*"[2]

The following is a specimen of St. Augustine's exposition : —

ii. 24. *There is nothing better for man but to eat, &c.* — We cannot understand this better than as referring to the partaking of that table, which our Priest after the order of Melchizedeck has instituted for us in the New Testament. For this sacrifice succeeded all the Old Testament sacrifices, which were only shadows of good things to come ; as we hear our Saviour speaking prophetically in the fortieth Psalm, " Sacrifice and offering thou didst not desire, but a body hast thou prepared me." For his body is offered and sacrificed now, instead of all other offerings and sacrifices. That Ecclesiastes cannot mean by eating and drinking, which he so often recommends, carnal pleasure, is sufficiently evident from the passage, where he says, " it is better to go to the house of mourning than to the house of feasting."

x. 16. *Woe to thee, O land, &c.* — Ecclesiastes calls the devil a child, because of his foolishness, and pride, temerity, and petulance, and other vices incident to childhood; but Christ he calls the son of the great, of the holy patriarchs belonging to the free city, because he descended from them according to the flesh.[3]

550. — It is quite a relief to the monotony of patristic exposition to find Olympiodorus, surnamed Diaconus, or Monachus, who lived in the middle of the sixth century, and sustained the office of Diaconus in Alexandria, advance a new theory, viz., *that Solomon treats in this book upon natural things, and thus designs it to be a treatise on natural philosophy, which would*

[1] De Virgin., c. 12. [2] De civit. Dei, xx., c. 3.
[3] De civit. Dei, xvii., c. 20.

P

*otherwise be wanting in the Sacred Scriptures, and intersperses
this treatise with a few moral sentences and maxims.* As to the
objectionable passages, Olympiodorus maintains that Solomon
does not speak his own mind, but *acts the part of one who is
astonished at seeing what transpires in the world.*[1]

787. — Elias of Crete, supposed to have been the metropolitan
of Crete who took part in the second General Council of Nicæa,
A. D. 787, treats of Ecclesiastes in his commentaries on the
Orations of Gregory Nazianzen. He entirely espouses the view
of Gregory, bishop of Nyssa, whose very words he repeats, viz.,
that " *this book is emphatically called Ecclesiastes, because its
doctrine relates to the only canon of ecclesiastical life, truly setting
forth those things through which we may be able to realise a life
combined with virtue. For the things which are here set forth
tend to make the mind live above the senses, and raise itself to those
things which are nobler than sense and desire,*" &c. To this Elias
adds, that —

Ecclesiastes advises us not to waste our admiration on any of the things
here below, since all things in nature end in vanity; no remains are
left of them when they go. Just as they who write upon the water,
though they labour to form signs of letters upon the aqueous element, leave
no impression behind, so is every earthly pleasure, for no sooner is the act
over than the pleasure is gone, and leaves no trace behind. Ecclesiastes
again and again recurs to this subject, that, by repeatedly speaking upon
the same things, he may more effectually place before our eyes the vanity
of the things of human life, and shew that this vanity is not confined
to the visible part of these things, but is altogether inherent in them.
Having shewn the vanity of all things, Ecclesiastes adds that this condition
of things, and the misery of life, are not to be ascribed to God, but to
man's wilful violation of God's commandments.[2]

This view was adopted by all the writers of the middle ages,
and received a freshness from the mystical and metaphysical
treatment of the scholastics, worthy of their hair-splitting
intellects.

---

[1] Bibl. Patr., tom. xiii., p. 602.
[2] Opera Gregory Nazianzen, Paris, 1630, p. 575.

1096 – 1140. — Thus Hugo of St. Victor[1] says, that *the design of this book is to persuade us to despise the world, by shewing us the vanity of all earthly things.* The vain things discussed by Ecclesiastes are reduced to three classes : — 1. Things made *for* man ; 2. Things made *by* man ; and 3. Things made *in* man. In the things made for man, there is the vanity of mutability ; in the things made by man, there is the vanity of curiosity ; and in the things made in man, there is the vanity of mortality.[2]

Having given the three titles of the author (viz., Preacher, Son of David, and King,) in the first verse, Hugo maintains that Solomon gives the sum of these three parts of his book in verses 2, 3, and 4. In verse 2, the vanity of mutability is maintained, which is discussed in the first part of the book, viz., chap. i. 5–11 ; verse 3 mentions the vanity of curiosity, which is discussed in the second part, viz., chap. i. 12 – xi. 10 ; and verse 4 mentions the vanity of mortality, which is discussed in the third part of the book, viz., chap. xii. 1–14.

The first vanity is natural, and becoming the nature of worldly things ; the second is sinful, because perverse and froward ; the third is penal and miserable. The first is the occasion of sin, the second is sin, and the third is the punishment of sin.[3]

The following is a specimen of his mode of exposition : —

Chap. iii. 5. *There is a time to cast away stones.* — If we regard stones as the brave deeds of virtue, the casting away of stones is the multiplication of

[1] Hugo of St. Victor was born in 1096, either at Ypres, in the Netherlands, or in Lower Saxony, and became an Augustinian canon in the monastery of St. Victor, at Paris, where he died in 1140, aged forty-four. His works were printed in 3 vols. fol., Rouen, 1648. An interesting sketch of his life is given in Herzog, Real-Encyklopädie für Protestantische Theologie und Kirche, vol. vi., pp. 307–315.

[2] Ostendit secundum triplicem vanitatem, omnia esse vanitati subjecta, id est caduca, transitoria, videlicet et quæ propter homines facta sunt et quæ ab hominibus facta sunt et quæ in hominibus facta sunt. In his, quæ propter homines facta sunt, vanitas est mutabilitatis. In his, quæ ab hominibus facta sunt, vanitas est curiositatis. In his, quæ in hominibus facta sunt, vanitas mortalitatis.

[3] Prima vanitas naturalis est, et apta sive congrua ; secunda vanitas culpabilis est, quia perversa : tertia vanitas pœnalis et misera. Prima causa est peccati secunda peccatum : tertia pœna peccati.

good works. *To gather stones* is, after laborious effort, to gain the fruit of good works. There is a time therefore for both casting away and gathering stones, because a man ought first to discipline himself in the anxieties of active life, that he may afterwards discern the fruit of his works in the pleasure of contemplation.

1096 – 1164. — The celebrated Peter Lombard[1] is by no means behind his contemporary, Hugo of St. Victor, in the allegorising of this book, as will be seen from the following specimen : —

Chap. xii. 5. *The almond, &c.* — Following the Vulgate's rendering of this verse, viz., *The almond tree shall flourish, the grasshopper shall be made fat, and the caper shall be destroyed*, this scholastic remarks, The almond tree is Christ. There are three things in the almond, viz., the rind, the shell, and the kernel ; and Christ consists of three substances — the flesh corresponding with the rind, the mind with the shell, the divinity with the kernel. The rind is bitter, the shell is strong, the kernel is sweet. But *when* shall the almond flower ? In the resurrection, for it seemed dead and dry in His passion and death. As the almond flowered, so the grasshopper fattens, *i. e.*, the Gentiles, and the caper bush is scattered, *i. e.*, the Jewish people. By the grasshopper, not without cause, are the Gentiles indicated ; for, as the grasshopper moves by leaps, nor can it move without leaping, so the Gentiles moved after Zion by leaps. But the caper bush is scattered, because the barren brought forth most, &c. — Isa, liv. 1.

1100 – 1173. — Richard of St. Victor,[2] the *Coryphœus of the mystics*, fully sustains this reputation by his treatment of this book. The following is a specimen of it : —

Chap. i. 7. — *All the rivers flow into the sea, &c.* — We know that the water of rivers is sweet, and that of the sea is bitter. What, then, is it for rivers to run into the sea, but for all fleshly passions to end in bitterness ? *Therefore* all rivers run into the sea, because the issue of joy is sorrow. All sweet waters are changed into bitter in the sea, because laughter is mingled with grief.

[1] Peter Lombard was born about 1096, at a village near Novaria, in Lombardy, hence his surname Lombard ; went to France to study theology, was made Professor of Divinity in 1141, and Bishop of Paris in 1150, where he died in 1164. For a sketch of his Life see Herzog, vol. viii., pp. 466-476.

[2] Richard of St. Victor was born about 1100, in Scotland, went to Paris to prosecute his studies, became first a canon and then prior of St. Victor, near the walls of Paris, where he died in 1173. His works were published in 2 vols. fol., Rouen, 1650. Comp. Herzog, vol. xiii., pp. 19-22.

Galfrid, another scholastic of this period, thus expatiates upon—

i. 5.— *The sun also ariseth, &c.*—This indicates mystically the Divine Saviour. The true Sun of Righteousness " arose" on the night of his nativity, and " set" in his passion, and " hastened to the place whence he arose" on the day of his ascension, &c.[1]

1221–1274.—Bonaventura,[2] who also maintains that *this book describes the vanity of earthly things, to teach thereby contempt for the world*, propounds this view in a far more speculative manner than any of the schoolmen. As to the objection, that the creatures of God, which he himself pronounced " very good " (Gen. i. 31), and designed for a certain end, cannot be characterised as vain, Bonaventura replies that they are not called vain because they are deficient in goodness or order, but because they are wanting in unchangeableness. Therefore, although everything is vanity, yet it is not so vain but it has some reality and good. Now, as the world is vain because it yields no permanent support, and God alone possesses intransmutable repose (*intransmutabilitatis quietem*), therefore true life and happiness can be found in God only.[3]

1270–1340.—With Nicholas de Lyra, forerunner of the Reformation, a new era begins in Biblical exegesis. Unlike the rest of the schoolmen, who knew little of Greek and nothing of

---

[1] The above specimens of scholastic interpretation are selected from *Badius Ascensius, Allegoriarum Bibliorum*, 1520, which contains expositions of thirty of the most distinguished schoolmen, arranged in the order of the books of the Bible. It is to be regretted that this comprehensive and most interesting manual of mediæval exposition has become so very scarce.

[2] Bonaventura is the ecclesiastical name of the celebrated Franciscan, Fidenza, who was born at Bognarea, in Tuscany, in 1221, and died Bishop of Albano, in 1274. He was seized with a dangerous illness when four years old, from which he recovered through the intercession of St. Francis, to whose prayers his mother recommended him. This great saint, on beholding the convalescent Fidenza, exclaimed, *O buona ventura*, hence his name *Bonaventura*. See the sketch of his life in Herzog, vol. ii., pp. 290-294.

[3] Quod objicitur, quod creaturæ non sunt vanæ, quia valde bonæ et in finem ordinatæ, solvendum, quod non dicuntur vanæ per defectum boni, vel ordinis, sed per defectum esse incommutabilis et sic omnis creatura est vana nec ita vana, quin habeat veritatem et bonitatem. Expositio in librum Ecclesiast. Opp., tom. i., p. 294, *seq.*, Mogunt., 1609.

Hebrew, De Lyra, who was born a Jew, brought to his work a refined mind, well stored, both with his vernacular Hebrew and a large acquaintance with Greek. He could therefore no more follow the frivolities and cavilings of his fellow-expositors; but, whilst admitting the four modes of interpretation beautifully expressed in the rule —

> Litera gesta docet, quid credas allegoria,
> Moralis quid agàs, quo tendas anagogia:

> *The literal teaches the bearing, the allegorical what to believe;*
> *The moral what to do, the anagogic where to go,*

he maintains that the literal meaning must be thoroughly understood before we can comprehend the spiritual, *inasmuch as all mystical exposition presupposes a literal sense as its foundation. To those who are desirous of advancing in the study of the Sacred Scriptures, it is therefore necessary to begin with the understanding of the literal meaning, especially as from the literal sense only, and not from the mystical, can we derive arguments or clear up difficulties.*[1] Acting upon such a rational rule of interpretation, and availing himself of all that was valuable in the Jewish expositors, we do not wonder that he produced such a beautiful commentary upon the Bible,[2] for which he obtained the title, *Doctor planus et utilis*, and gave a new tone to Biblical exegesis.

As to his view on Coheleth, though he has not fully hit upon its design, yet he has come nearer to it than any of his predecessors, inasmuch as he maintains *that as mankind look for happiness in different directions, — wealth, pleasure, honour, knowledge, &c., — Solomon, whose wisdom was formed in different ways, sets himself to shew that felicity consists in none of these, but in the fear of God.*

[1] Omnes expositiones mysticæ præsupponunt sensum literalem tanquam fundamentum   . ideo volentibus proficere in studio Sacræ Scripturæ necéssarium est incipere ab intellectu sensus literalis, maxime cum ex solo sensu literali et non ex mysticis possit argumentum fieri ad probationem vel declarationem alicuius dubii.

[2] Biblia sacra latina, cum postillis, Venice, 1480, 4 vols. folio; the edition we have used.

He divides the book into two parts: in the first part (chap. i. 2 – vii. 12), Solomon descants *on the false sources of happiness;* and in the second part (chap. vii. 1 – xii. 14), which has two sections, he treats *upon true happiness,* shewing that it consists *objectively* in God alone; *formally* (formaliter) in the clear vision and enjoyment of God in meritorious works; to which Solomon urges us, on to the end of chap. xi., and persuades us to *promptitude* in chap. xii.

How much the Reformation and the Reformers owe to this converted Jew, may be seen from the well-known Roman Catholic saying —

> Si Lyra non lyrasset,
> Lutheris non saltasset.

> *If Lyra had not played profanation,*
> *Luther would not have danced the Reformation.*

1528. — The new path thus opened by De Lyra was at last crowded by a host of Reformers, who, though discarding all the metaphysical conceits of the schoolmen, were too absorbed in the doctrines of our utter inability to do anything good, of the insufficiency of the law, and justification by faith alone, to see anything else in this book. Thus John Brentius, the Suabian Reformer, who wrote the first Protestant commentary on Coheleth,[1] maintains *that this book is, so to speak, an appendix to the Law of Moses. Now the Law teaches that man of himself is utterly unable to act virtuously, and that the more he exerts himself to acquire righteousness by his own works and thoughts, the more he fails in the attempt.* WITH THIS DOCTRINE THIS LITTLE BOOK PERFECTLY AGREES, AND TEACHES THAT ALL THE POWER OF MEN, THEIR WISDOM, REASONING, AND DESIGNS, GRIEVOUSLY DEVIATE FROM THE NATURAL EMPLOYMENT OF CREATED BEINGS; FORSOOTH THERE IS NOT ONE WHO, IF LEFT TO HIMSELF, COULD BOAST OF BEING ABLE, IN THE SMALLEST DEGREE, EITHER TO ACQUIRE

---

[1] Ecclesiastes Salomonis, cum commentariis, juxta piis adque eruditis Johannis Brentii, Haganoæ, 1528.

There is, however, a striking feature introduced by Brentius
into the practical bearing of this book, which has been entirely
overlooked by his predecessors.   Whilst all the Fathers and
Schoolmen maintain that the tendency of Coheleth is to make us
despise every earthly pleasure, the Suabian Reformer submits
that it teaches man piously and cheerfully to *enjoy* the good
creatures of God.

1532. — This idea is still more fully developed by Luther,
who declares *that Solomon condemns the evil lust, and not the
creatures themselves;* since he says himself, respecting the use of
the creatures, that —

There is nothing better than to be cheerful, and enjoy one's life; to eat,
drink, and delight in one's employment; he would therefore contradict himself, if he also condemned the things themselves, and not rather the abuse of
them, which consists in the human passions.   Some foolish persons, not
understanding these things, have absurdly taught contempt for and flight from
the world, and have committed many foolish things themselves; as we read
in the lives of the Fathers that there were some who even shut themselves
up from ever seeing the sun; *reminding us of the passage where Solomon
condemns him who eats all his days in darkness* (well they deserve to have
their eyes put out), and for the sake of religion lived in the most sordid
plight; whereas, living above the world is not living out of the world.[2]

Luther maintains that *the design of this book is to teach us to
use with grateful hearts the things present, and the creatures of
God which are bountifully bestowed upon us by the blessing of
God, without anxiety about future temporal blessings; to have a
quiet and tranquil heart, and a mind full of cheerfulness and
contentment with the will and dealings of God.*[3]

[1] Ad hanc rationem libellus iste accedit et docet, omnium hominum vires,
sapientiam, rationem atque consilia a genuino creaturarum usu fæde aberrare ac
retrocedere, nimirum, ne quisque sit, qui glorietur ac cristas erigat, se posse vel
quidque sibi relictus coram Deo sive ad justitiam parandam sive ad creaturas
felici atque prospero exitu tractandas.   Prœmion, p. 11, b.

[2] Ecclesiastes Salomonis cum annotationibus Martin. Lutherus, Vitemberg,
1532. See the Preface.

[3] Est status et consilium hujus libelli erudire nos, ut cum gratiarum actione

The sagacious Reformer has not only done much towards the better understanding of the *true design* of Coheleth, but has also discovered, by sheer penetration, without possessing any critical knowledge of the original, that Solomon could not have been the author of this book. He says, in his Table Talk, *This book wants more completeness; it is too abrupt. . . . . Solomon himself has not written the book of Ecclesiastes, it was compiled by Sirach at the time of the Maccabees. . . . . It is like the Talmud, made up of many books, which perhaps belonged to the library of King Ptolemy Euergetes in Egypt.*[1]

1556. — Melancthon succeeded still more in shewing the true scope of Coheleth. According to him, *the design of the book is to propound the doctrine of an overruling Providence, the necessity of obedience and submission, the doctrine of a future judgment, and the importance of attending to our calling.*[2]

As to the utility of the book, he remarks that —

It confirms us in the belief of an overruling Providence, and shews us that we are to be submissive in every station of life, and perform the duties of our calling; that we should cling to the consolations he propounded, notwithstanding the many difficulties we have to encounter; that we should know that to follow our calling is pleasing to God; that He is the Ruler of his Church; that He wishes us to invoke his aid; that He will assuredly help those who faithfully serve Him in their calling; and that His Church will finally pass into eternal intercourse with the Deity, when God will be all in all. If we believe this, we shall submit to God, and act in accordance with His will; we shall neither repine at nor despise the duties of our calling, nor fall blindly into contempt of God, after the manner of the Epicureans.

utamur rebus præsentibus et creaturis Dei, quæ nobis Dei benedicatione largiter dantur et donata sunt, sine solicitudine futurorum, tantum ut tranquillum et quietum cor habeamus et animum gaudii plenum contenti scilicet verbo et opere Dei.

[1] Dies Buch sollte völliger sein, ihm ist zu viel abgebrochen. . . . . So hat Salomo selbst das Buch, den Prediger, nicht geschrieben, sondern es ist zur Zeit der Maccabäer von Sirach gemacht . . . . Dazu so ist's wie ein Talmud aus vielen Büchern zusammengezogen, vielleicht aus der Liberey des Königs Ptolemäus Euergetes in Aegypten. Table Talk, p. 400 and 401, Förstermann and Birdseil's edition.

[2] Enarratio concionum libri Salomonis cui titulus est Ecclesiastes, secunda editio, Vitemberg, 1556.

1580. — Thomas Cartwright is, to my knowledge, the first English Protestant who wrote on Coheleth.[1] This celebrated Puritan maintains that Solomon — who was called Coheleth (i. e., *the reunited* or *gathered one*), because he was reunited with the Church from whence he had been expelled, in consequence of his grievous sins — wrote this book *to give a divine solution of the problem respecting the greatest good for man.* "What in many books of the Sacred Scriptures is referred to occasionally and incidentally, the Preacher discusses through an entire book, and, discussing, settles it definitely. The method which this Prophet pursues in his enquiry is to refute the unsubstantial happiness— the mark of the foolish, of the besotted, and of the ignorant— and then vividly to describe the true and genuine happiness, as identified with piety towards God, and with the fruits of rectitude towards man."[2] "The prophets of God imitate the thrifty and skilful farmer, who first weeds out the thorns, and uproots other baneful growths, before he commits the good seed to the ground."[3]

1588. — The learned Whitaker, in defending this book, espoused the patristic view, viz., that Solomon exhorts men, with a divine eloquence, to despise and contemn the world.[4]

1597. — The next English production is a poetical paraphrase of Ecclesiastes, written by Henry Lock, and dedicated to Queen Elizabeth.[5] Lock, like Cartwright, regards the book as *a treatise on the highest good.* SOLOMON, *the King of Peace,*

---

[1] Metaphrasis et Homiliæ in Librum Solomonis, quis inscribitur Ecclesiastes. He wrote this commentary towards the end of his life, and it was published after his death in Amsterdam, 1647.

[2] Lectori. [3] Homiliæ, p. 452.

[4] A Disputation on Holy Scripture against Papists, by William Whitaker, D.D. The Parker Society's edition, pp. 31, 32.

[5] Ecclesiastes, otherwise called the Preacher, containing Solomon's sermons, or commentaries (as it may probably be called), upon the forty-ninth Psalm of David his father, compendiously abridged, and also paraphrastically dilated in English Poesie, according to the analogy of Scripture and consent of the most approved writers thereof, by H. L., Gentleman. London, printed by Richard Field, dwelling in the Blackfriars, near Ludgate, 1597.

YEDIDA, *the Beloved of God;* ECCLESIASTES, *the Preacher, who in his Proverbs instructed thee as a child to a civil and honest life, in this work instructeth thy manly thoughts to the inquisition of the highest good, to the end that by his last song of heavenly love thy ripened thoughts might be inflamed with that glorious bridegroom, Christ Jesus.*

As this paraphrase is one of the scarcest books in our language, we give the whole introduction of this great curiosity, and a specimen of the paraphrase.

To the Christian Reader,

It is the most fit subject for the nobility of man's spirit to meditate of felicity, and a true saying of Aristotle, that *omnia appetunt bonum.* Yea, the common practice of our high-minded age is to strive for the same in the superlative degree. But so foolish and new-fangled are our desires, that, wishing we wot not what, and seeking it we know not how nor where, we come all far short of the same, and some run headlong to the despised contrary (looking for it on earth), and, thereby groping for it to their graves, they are there cut off of their hopes, and die discontented with their haps. Whereas, if they acknowledged it to be the tree of life, planted in the heavenly paradise, they would less labour their bodies for attaining these transitory shadows of pleasures, and more exercise the faculties of the soul for achieving the same, so much the more despising these instable and imperfect happinesses of this life, as they found their foolish affections of the flesh (doting on thee) to work neglect of the nutriment of their soul, and slackens in the constant travail in religion and virtue (which is requisite for the long journey we have to pass through life and death thereunto). But this having been the sickness of all ages, and specially of the Jews in Solomon's time, (which induced him, as it should appear, to take so great pains in removing them from that error,) I the less marvel that our age, flourishing in the pride of like long peace and plenty, under her Majesty's most happy reign, be also sorted with the world as they were, dreaming of that perfection and perpetuity here, which God by nature hath denied unto us, and but by her Highness' reign we could hope for. And since it is the duty of every part and member of the body to join in the assistance and care of the whole, if any particular of it should suffer, I have in a dutiful compassion of this common calamity endeavoured to seek forth some mithridate for this poison, by which so many perish, and have here brought thee a dose of the wisest Physician's composition that ever had practice of that case—who did not (for the experiment of his potion's quality) first kill many patients in trial thereof, but, applying it to his own wound first, dares confidently write *probatum est*, and, by the seal of the Holy Spirit and consent of the Church, doth warrant thee to taste of the same. It is a receipt so oldly composed, perhaps, that thou respectest it the less, or of so small price that thou shamest to take it; or, perhaps, knowing the bitterness of the taste, thou hast as lieve continue sick as to try it. But deceive not thyself, it is not the nature of the perfectest drugs, which with age increase in strength, of the kind of *Sibillæs'* works, which, refused, grow higher prized; and of the herb called woodrose, which, only handled, had an evil smell, but, more forcibly rubbed, yieldeth sweet savour. Receive it therefore as confidently as he assured it, and as kindly as I intend it — who, in respect that the obscurity of many places, the contrariety (as at first would appear) of some points, and strange dependency of the whole together, have done my careful and studious endeavour (by consideration and imitation of the best interpreters thereof) to explain the sense, accord the different plans, to join by probable connecion the whole discourse together; which (as well to distinguish the several arguments as to vary the verse, and please the reader) I have not altogether unfitly distributed into three sermons, each one containing four chapters a-piece. The first especially shewing the vain opinion of felicity, which is not in earth to be found. The second pointing more directly (by the lawful use of this life) the true way unto her. The last teaching her residence to be in heaven, and persuading the speedy pursuit of her favour. And that you might truly consider of the carriage of the matter, according to the scope of the text, I have caused the same to be quoted in the margin, reducing for memory's sake into two abstract lines of verse, set in the top of every leaf, the substance of every page's contents, which afterwards as thou seest is paraphrastically dilated page by page, in the plainest form I can devise. Who, in respect of the gravity of the argument, did restrain my pen from the helps of much profane learning, and in consideration of the antiquity of the work, and majesty of the author, could not (without great indecency) have used the authorities of men, or of so late times (as since the learnings flourished, whence we now receive our common light). Like naked truth, therefore, . I pray thee receive it, for its own if not my sake, and in anything I seem to swerve from thy conceit of many points, I pray thee confer further therein with *D. Gregorius, Neocesariensis Epist. Olimpiodorus; D. Salonius Epist.; Viennesis; Theod. Beza; John Serranus; Anth. Corranus; Tremelius;* all interpreters and paraphrasers in prose upon this work; and *J. Lectius; Ro. Lemmannus; J. Viniames;* reducers thereof into Latin poesie; or any other thou likest better of; so shall my errors be covered or excused; whilst their different forms, distributions of methode and interpretations, will leave thee (I am persuaded) in some points as little satisfied as this my labour shall do — who in some things was forced to digress from them all, when, either too much in one place or too little in another, they followed the form of a paraphrase which they undertook; into which error also it is not unlike but that I have sometimes falled myself, and I doubt not but many things more might have been said, and perhaps to more purpose than I have done, but *non omnia possumus omnes*. According to my sufficiency I have discharged myself faithfully unto thee, and therefore I trust (in these days wherein some pernicious, many uncivil, and a swarm of superfluous and unprofitable books pass from the press) it shall not be needful for me to use great insinuation for thy favour, since it lieth not in the bounds of a Preface to prepare a perverse mind, or in the nature of such a work to go a-begging for a grace. I will therefore cut off that labour, and only signify unto thee the excellency of this work, compiled by the wisest man and mightiest king of Israel, even *Solomon*, the King of Peace; *Yedida*, the Beloved of God; *Ecclesiastes*, the Preacher, who in his Proverbs instructed thee as a child to a civil and honest life, in this work instructeth thy manly thoughts to the inquisition of the highest good. To the end that by his last song of heavenly love thy ripened thoughts might be inflamed with that glorious bridegroom, Christ Jesus, to whose holy direction I heartily commend thee.

1. *These sacred words King David's son did preach, who Israel taught,*
2. *All vanity of vanities, he calls, more light than thought.*

1. The words of the Preacher, &c.

   1. The heavenly words of Holy David's son,
      Who over Israel's race sometimes did reign,
      Wherewith to virtue he his subjects wone,
      Whilst in Jerusalem he did remain,
      And to instruct them thus did not disdain.
         Those words, no vain discourse it is I write,
         Pen'd by a Prince, as God did them indite.

      Strange doctrines, which some paradoxes call,
      But yet the quintessence of holy creed,
      Lives pure Elixer, which is sought of all,
      T' assuage care's corrosives, in heart that breed,
      Of happiness the generative feed;
         Of moral speculation practice found;
         Of constant faith the quiet fruit he found.

      The fairest happiness which some propound,
      In minds, in bodies, and in fortune's gifts,
      (Which all conjoined seldome times are found)
      But to a vain conceit the fancy lifts,
      And their best sectaries do lose their drifts;
         The crown it is of heaven's most glorious state,
         Earth's fruits all vain ; care, folly, and debate.

2. Vanity of vanities, saith the, &c.

Yea vain, all vain (saith he), man's soul well proves,
Whoever on earth's spacious orb below
Hath breath, life, being, sense, or what so moves
By vegetative kind; or which doth owe
To nature a declining state to grow.
　　　Vain in the root, in bud, in flower all vain;
　　　Vain fruit, whose offsprings vainly vades again.

1605. — "The far-famed Hebraist," Hugh Broughton, published. "a Commentary on Coheleth or Ecclesiastes," in 1605, which he "framed for the instruction of Prince Henry our hope."[1] Broughton maintains that " all this book of Coheleth, or Solomon, tendeth to open Nathan's speech (1 Chron. xvii.) touching the eternal throne of David ; and all this syllogism ariseth hence by the Jews' grant, in the Chaldee upon this place.

If all things under the sun be subject to extreme vanity, the eternal throne promised unto David must be of another world :
But all things under the sun be subject to extreme vanity
Therefore this is all the man, to look unto the judgment of God for another world, and unto the throne of the better stay!

The proposition is omitted, as lapped in the prophecy of Nathan closely, and not to be opened directly to the profane, who would contemn all speech of the world to come. And the humble would conceive it."[2]

It is most unaccountable that this great Hebraist, who boasted that a learned Rabbi, with whom he conversed in Hebrew, said to him —

" Oh that you would set over all your new Testament into such Hebrew as you speak to me ! you should turn all our nation,"

should so wofully mistranslate the only quotation he makes from Ibn Ezra, viz., נקרא קהלת משם החכמה הנקהלה בו, which he renders he is called Koheleth, BY THE TERM OF wisdom, which

[1] A Commentary upon Coheleth or Ecclesiastes, framed for the instruction of Prince Henry our hope, by Hugh Broughton, 1605.
[2] Ibid., pp. 13, 14.

was gathered in him, not knowing that מֵשֶׁם is a common idiomatic term for *an account of,* i.e., *he is called Coheleth* ON ACCOUNT
OF *the wisdom which was gathered in him.* For the merits of
Broughton's translation of Coheleth, we must refer to the commentary, where different renderings are discussed.

About this time Greenham's "brief sum of Ecclesiastes"
appeared, which occupies less than a page in the folio editions of
his works. Keeping to the old traditional view, this celebrated
Puritan maintains that *Solomon became sorrowful of his folly,
and being desirous to leave to the world a testimony of his sorrow,
he taketh upon him in this book the person of a public penitentair,
professing it to be a monument of his unwise dealing, and therefore
it may be called Solomon's recantations. . . . . Solomon
sheweth in this book that he proved all, and yet this is his conclusion, that to fear God, in reverent regard to keep his commandments, is all a man can come to, the only way to find peace of
conscience, and to assure us of the favour of God.*[1]

1606. — Roused by the zeal for Biblical studies which the
Reformation had kindled in the Protestant Church, the Jesuits
were now determined that they would not be behind their
opponents. And it is only justice to say, that, as a repository of
patristic and mediæval lore, the commentary of Lorinus[2] surpasses all that had hitherto been published on Coheleth by
Protestants. But though this work, like all others of the same
school, is very useful for historical purposes, it contributes little
or nothing to critical exposition, as will be seen from the
following specimen.

According to Lorinus, *this book lays down a natural discipline,
but, at the same time, things empty and vain are therein distinguished from things which are profitable, and admonitions are
given to relinquish the one and to pursue the other, that God may*

[1] The works of Richard Greenham, fifth edition, London, 1612, p. 628.
[2] Joannis Lorini Avenionensis Societatis Jesu, Commentarii in Ecclesiasten.
Moguntiæ, 1607. The edition which I possess is the second edition; the first
appeared in Lugd., 1606.

be feared and the commandments obeyed.[1]   Therefore devotion to the sciences is expressly repudiated in chap. i.; the craving for luxuries, in chap. ii.; the desire of long life, in chap. iii.; the lust of rule, in chap. iv. and part of chap. v.; the greediness after riches, in the latter part of chap. v. and chap. vi.; the art of divination, in chap. vii.; the chase after praise and fame, in the former part of chap. viii.; the hunt after fortune, in the latter part of chap. viii. and beginning of chap. ix.; vigour of body, in the latter part of chap. ix. and chap. x.; a certain kind of youthful indulgence, in chap. xi. and chap. xii

The following is a specimen of his commentary: —

Chap. iii. 20. *All go, &c.* — The Royal Bible leaves out the word πορεύεται. It is retained in all the editions of the Septuagint, and in the Sixtine Manuscripts; also in an old translation, where it is rendered *vadunt.* By the word *place* may be understood *state* and *condition,* and not merely the space containing it. As in Job (vii. 10), "And his own place will know him no more." Sometimes the word seems even to denote *time,* compare " Up to that time (loci) I had told nothing" (Neh. ii. 16).

All are of the dust, &c. — The Chaldee restricts this to *man.* (All the inhabitants of the world have been created of dust, and when dead they shall be turned into dust) ; but though the Hebrew word הכל may be rendered in the masculine gender, and thus be understood of men only, yet mention has also been made of beasts. The earth is called by Lucretius and others *the mother of all things ;* hence words implying maternal relation are fittingly applied to it. As παμμήτωρ, *mother of all ;* παντρόφος, *nourisher of all ;* πανδῶρα, *giver of all gifts ;* δημήτηρ, *great mother ;* 'Εκ γὰρ δὴ πάντα καὶ εἰς γῆν πάντα τελευτᾶ, *for of the earth all things are, and to the earth all things in the end return.* Indeed, all things made, being compounds, consist for the most part of earth, and are resolved into it especially; to man, however, the term is peculiarly adapted, for he was formed directly by God from the earth. Comp. also xii. 7 of this book, "And the dust return to its own earth, whence it came;" and Genesis iii. 19, "Till thou return to the ground, for out of it wast thou taken, for dust thou art, and unto dust shalt thou return." There is a similar expression, *infra* chap. v. 14. Job evidently speaks of the earth as mother; and this idea is sanctioned by Chrysostom, by St. Thomas, and Gregory on Job ; also by Jerome, Cyprian, Gaudentius of Brixa, and Prosper. Job is speaking either of Adam or of the human

[1] Naturalem disciplinam hic tradi, simul tamen inania ac vana ab utilibus necessariisque secerni, monendo relinquendam vanitatem, et utilia honestaque sectanda, ut timeatur Deus, ejusque mandatis pareatur. Prolegomena, cap. v.

race universally, which descends from the same original. The story of
Brutus is well known, how he obtained the supreme authority in the
city, because he kissed his mother the ground; having thus interpreted
the oracle from the cave. Similar to this is the answer of the soothsayers
respecting the dream of Julius Cæsar. It was customary with the ancients,
according to the testimony of Varro, to place the new-born babe instantly on
the ground, and to invoke the goddess Ops, who is the earth itself. The
same deity was named Levana, from lifting up out of the earth, *a levando;*
Fauna, from favouring, *a favendo;* Fatua, from speaking, *a fando;* as if it
were not lawful to speak before touching it (viz., the earth), Maia too,
and Bona, and Magna Mater. Ecclesiasticus seems to have used this same
term in the passage, " There is a heavy yoke on the sons of Adam, from the
day of their leaving their mother's womb until the day of their burial in
the mother of all " (xi. 1). But the author of the Book of Wisdom also
states of himself, " And when I was born I breathed the common air and
fell upon the earth, which is of like nature " (vii. 3). Upon this consult our
commentary. Hence the Latins speak of the new-born babe falling on the
ground, and by lifting up a son denote educating him and adopting him as
one's own. Augustine, in addition to many profane writers, mentions a
ceremony, in which the infant, after being discharged from the womb, was
lifted up naked from the ground. On this point Macrobius is preeminently
deserving of perusal; lastly, also, our own Pontanus and Pineda. That
same author of the Book of Wisdom calls the first man (γηνενέα καὶ πρωτόπλαστον),
earth-born and first framed; Paul uses the expression *of the earth, earthy;*
and the Greek profane writers also use the first epithet, especially the poets;
just as the Latins use the terms *earth-born and progeny of earth,* when
describing the formation of man from the earth. Hear how these have
expressed what Ecclesiastes here gives as an apophthegm, Phocylides
says:

Σῶμα γὰρ ἐκ γαίης ἔχομεν καὶ πάντες ἐς αὐτὴν
Λυόμενοι κόνις ἐσμὲν.-

*Our body we derive from the earth, and we all
are resolved into it, and become dust.*

Earth must be restored to earth, says Cicero (Tuso. 3), when repeating the
words of Euripides. They commit a very grave error who think that men
can spring from the earth without the intercourse of male and female, in
the same manner that things spring from putrid matter. This opinion
seems to have been held by Plato, and by the poet Stesicorus, Empedocles,
and Parmenides, the Egyptians and Athenians, Avicenna and other Arabians,
Anaximander, Archelaus, Zeno, Cardan, whom Scaliger ridicules and refutes,
inasmuch as the thing was never known to occur. It is also contrary to
Aristotle, who scouts this very theory; as also Tychiades. As if, says the
latter, men could spring from the earth like vegetables. Read on this
Christopher Vega. The thought is sometimes indulged, that all other things

R

are to be resolved into earth, and are nothing but earth. So says Arnobius of those magnificent temples of idols, and Chrysostom and Bernard of gold and silver, calling them red and white earth.

The earth.—In Hebrew and Chaldee it is עָפָר, or עַפְרָא, in Greek χοῦς, words which properly mean *dust*. They are so found in Genesis ii. 7, where the formation of the body of Adam is described; although in the sentence of his death, and his return to earth, whence he was taken (*ibid.* iii. 19), the term τῆς γῆς, *earth*, is found, which the translator renders *dust*, and in the former passage, *the mud of earth;* and an older translation, which Augustine adopts, has *the dust of the earth*, though sometimes he employs the rendering of the two former. Job puts God in mind, *Remember, I beseech Thee, that as* MIRE *hast Thou made me, and* INTO DUST *Thou wilt make me return* (x. 9). Man, no doubt, was made of earth mixed with water; of this water watering the earth, Moses immediately after makes mention, when describing the *creation;* hence, with propriety, has the translator substituted the term *mud* for *dust:* by this *mud*, or *clay*, or *mire*, he designates the body as distinguished from the soul, an opinion which Pineda approves, following Gregory of Valentia (though Toletus thinks otherwise, being rather of opinion that the entire man is meant, so that the earth may be taken for the body, and the water for the soul); and because the earth is the larger ingredient, for that reason it is sometimes called *dust*, sometimes *earth*, instead of *clay*, *mire*, and *slime*. Josephus has happily said, that man was formed of fermented earth, using the word φυροῦσθαι, which means *earth mixing with water, and kneading it as it were into dough*. Symmachus, however, in this passage uses the word τῆς γῆς, *earth*, and the old Latin translator uses HUMI, *the ground*. These words are sometimes confounded, and are differently used, according to the words with which they are joined. Some by earth understand chaos, as if allusion were made to the oblique case, χοός. Their notion is, that in the beginning matter was made without any form at all, and that to this allusion is made in the Book of Wisdom (xi. 18), by the expression, *invisible matter;* and in the Epistle to the Hebrews, *that things visible were made of things invisible;* but consult what we have said in our work on Wisdom. Man, in his relation to God, is compared to the potter's clay, that he may learn humility, and to submit himself entirely to the Divine counsels, and to implore the Divine assistance.

Return.—Whilst men are formed of all that is corruptible, nay rather whilst they are constantly flowing by, there is a perpetual onward movement on our passage to the goal of corruption, and to the point of circulation. As we have seen in the first chapter, one generation passes away and another succeeds; by our birth we enter as it were by one gate, at death we depart through another. There is no standing still, because the fashion of this world passeth away. Like snakes we move round and round, and complete our τὸν ἐνιαυτὸν, *circular year of life*. We glide away like waters that return not, and we walk on a path that we shall never retrace.

1612. — Though Piscator also regards Ecclesiastes *as the production of Solomon's old age, in attestation to his people of his repudiation of idolatry*, yet he, like Brentius and Luther, maintains, in opposition to the patristic and mediæval view, that this book recommends *a cheerful and grateful enjoyment of earthly blessings.*[1] He divides the book into two parts : —

I. DOCTRINAL, concerning the nature of true happiness, on which the sacred writer exhibits —

    a. Negatively, that it does not exist in the bare possession of earthly good ;.

    b. Positively, in a natural serenity arising from a filial fear of God, and the legitimate enjoyment of earthly good bestowed by Providence.

II. ADMONITORY, which, like the preceding part, also consists of two sections.

    a. A dissuasion from undue anxiety for the acquisition of earthly good ;

    b. A persuasion to fear God, to good works, and the cheerful enjoyment of earthly good bestowed by Providence.

Piscator's commentary contains judicious critical notes, and has deservedly occupied a distinguished position with the authors of the Assembly's annotations, who used it greatly to their advantage, as may be seen by a comparison of the two works.

1620. — Pineda was determined not only to outdo all Protestant expositors, but even to surpass his fellow-Jesuit commentator Lorinus, and therefore produced a folio volume on Coheleth, of one thousand and seventy-nine pages. As far as *the design* of the book is concerned, this bulky volume contributes nothing towards its elucidation, inasmuch as Pineda simply repeats what the Fathers have said, viz., that the object of *Ecclesiastes is to teach us the vanity of all that is earthly, and to direct our minds*

---

[1] Johannis Piscatoris Commentariorum in omnes libros veteris Testamenti Tomus Tertius, p. 403.

to that which is heavenly. Its chief merit consists in supplying us with a thorough digest — more thorough even than that of Lorinus — of all that the Fathers and others have said upon each verse. In addition to this, Pineda gives, in nine parallel columns, at the end of each chapter, the Vulgate, the Venice version, that of R. Shirwode,[1] variations of the Hebrew, translations of the Septuagint, Syriac, Arabic, the Brylinger edition of the Bible (1582), and variations of other interpreters; and then gives, in four lower columns, two versions of the Chaldee paraphrase (viz., that of Zamara from the Complutentian Bible, and of Peter Costus, ·published 1554), and a‾ catena of the Greek Fathers.

The following specimen will give an idea of this most elaborate commentary ·—

Cap. iii. 21. *Who knoweth, &c.*

1. The difficulty of the meaning, beasts figurative.
2. The question, in the relative *Who.* The proof of the immortality of the soul by the wise.
3. To know or to be ignorant, of experience. *To know,* for to reflect, illustration from Paul.
4. The sign of the interrogative in Hebrew. The *spirit.* What?
5. Whether Limbus is described as the place *beneath.* Before Christ all souls descended beneath. The two expositions identical.
6. Where will the souls released from the body be judged ?
7. Periphrasis for immortality and corruption. Examples from Moses, Judges, and Ezekiel.

---

[1] " Robert Shirwode," says Wood, " received his first education in the city of Coventry, whence, being translated to the University of Oxon, made a conside-rable progress in logicals, but more by far in the Hebrew and Greek languages. Thence, in his mature years, he went to Lovaine, in Brabant, where, about the year 1519, he succeeded Robert Wakfel, an Englishman, in the reading the Hebrew lecture to the academicians of the place."—Athenæ Oxonienses, vol. i. column 58. He published a commentary on Ecclesiastes, under the title, *Liber Hebræorum Concionatoris, seu Ecclesiasten, nuper ad verita-tem Hebraicam recognitus, cum nonnulis annotationibus Chaldaicis et quon-rundam Rabbinorum sententiis, textus obscuros aliquos literaliter explanantibus.* Antwerp. 1523, *qu.* This I am sorry I could not obtain, in consequence of its extreme rarity, and hence was obliged to omit it in the chronological order of the history.

1. That this passage is somewhat obscure is shown by Olympiodorus, who describes it as enigmatic. " Everywhere," he says, "the Preacher, teaching us by enigmas, directs our thoughts to a future life." Therefore many think, as we have shown before, that these words are among those which recognise slightly the immortality of the human soul, as Olympiodorus, " in secunda exponendi ratione," Nicolaus, Cajet. Bonav. Arbor., have deduced. But we have said, and affirm again, that these are the proper, actual, real sentiments of Solomon. And I now add, that so far from this passage affecting the solid and firm truth of the immortality of the soul, it strikingly confirms it. For common error and popular ignorance (if this is possible on a matter so clear and true) does not enfeeble the truth which it rejects or ignores, nor can it strengthen the falsehood which it sanctions. Olympiodorus, however, when he mooted the whole difficulty of the passage, notes the first and literal sense of the phrase, " *spirit of beasts*," as the name applied to those men " who, not improving the gift of reason, are compared to senseless brutes," or who appear to be deficient of sense. Of whom it might be questioned, he says, as it seems very doubtful to us, whether those who are reckoned worthy of the name of wisdom be so reckoned in the Divine judgment, and those who are now placed in the rank of beasts and of the ignorant be not placed in a better and loftier position by the supreme judgment. But soberly, both the antecedents and the course of the present passage require that the word " beast" should be taken in a literal, and not a figurative sense, as all interpreters agree.

2. Jerome says that by this question is indicated the difficulty of the matter, as it appears to be blasphemous. " Who knows, if the spirit," &c. Not that he makes no distinction between animals and the dignity of the human soul; but by asking *who*, he wishes to shew the difficulty of the matter. For the pronoun *who* in the Bible denotes difficulty, and not impossibility; for example, Isa. liii. 8, " Who shall declare ?" Ps. xv. 1, " Who shall abide ?" Jerem. xvii. 9, " Who can know it ?" These words of Jerome have been copied by Salonius and Hugo Carensis ; Kaldæus also seems to have glanced back at the same thing, when he says that the knowledge of the immortality of the soul belongs not to every one, but to the wise only. "Who being wise," he says, "who knows ?" &c. And verily, if the subject be of certain knowledge, and demonstrative by reasoning, it belongs to none but to philosophers and ·the wise; nor did Olympiodorus adopt this opinion when he said, " This is plainly discovered by every one who has the least share of reason." Just as, referring to the *natural light of reason*, unless eclipsed by the density of the body, says Chrysostom (Homil. 4, De Provid.), those who doubt the immortality of the soul might doubt also whether it is daylight at the meridian. Cajetan is offended from an entirely opposite extreme, when he affirms, that " who knoweth " is the same as if he had said, " none knoweth." " For no philosopher," he says, has hitherto proved the immortality of the soul, and no reasoning seems to be conclusive ; but we receive it on faith, and it

harmonises with rational probability." He has taught this in chap. ix. Epist. to Rom. And, in truth, Scotus concurs in the same opinion (iv. distinct. 43, quest 2). Before either of these, Hugo Victor has, in his way, written admirably; "It cannot be known by man with the same certainty as those things which it is impossible to doubt, and which are proved to the sceptical or doubtful by demonstrative evidence." These were followed by Vatab., who remarks on this verse, that the immortality of the soul "can only be ascertained by the Word of God." And in like manner, Campensis John Ferus, then Julius Scaliger (De Subtil. contra Cardanum. Exercit. 307, c. 20). But having touched on this point, as in duty bound, so to this Physician we leave the questions connected with the demonstration of the immortality of the soul, and, concurring with the most sagacious philosophers, let us quit the books concerning the soul. And perchance Ecclesiastes has this matter little in view.

3. "*Who knoweth*."—The word Jadagh, by which we often denote the knowledge and opinion of the intellect, is also connected with practice and sense. A hundred instances might be adduced which are familiar to the inquirer. From this root are the expressions in Gen. iii. 7, "They knew" (felt, it was palpable to them) "themselves to be naked," and Gen. xxii. 12, "Now know I that thou fearest God." It is therefore possible to construe the word in this sense, when everything common to the man and the beast may be perceived by the senses, who verily can say that he has with his senses felt, seen, discovered the immortality of the soul! Hugo Victor smelt out this meaning; "No one," he says, "knows this of men as those things are known which are seen, and heard, and touched, and perceived with the other senses; for they think that nothing is known which is not discerned by the bodily eye, and felt by the touch!" In this way, R. Salom. thinks, the word *to know* may be taken for reflecting or pondering on the soul; *q. d.*, "Who ponders that his soul is immortal? that it will stand at the Divine bar before the supreme Judge; and that, both in immortality and responsibility, it exceeds the brute? For the bulk of men so live, that they neither think nor ponder, but rather openly profess self-ignorance."

The original word in Psalm xxxv. 8, has this force, "Let destruction come on him which he knoweth not." Chaldæus elegantly renders it, "Let the calamity which he neither knows nor considers come on him." And so, Ps. cxxxix. 1, "Thou knowest my downsitting and uprising." Therefore, Solomon says, the man is hardly to be found who ponders in his heart, who considers the dignity of his nature, who regards himself as more important and better than the brutes. With this the phrase of the Apostle appears to correspond, 2 Cor. v. 1; "We know" (we know well, we forget not, it falls not away from our recollection or thought) "that if our earthly house of this tabernacle," &c. It thus appears that the Apostle answers the query of Solomon, Who is it that understands, *i.e.*, considers, this? We, replies Paul; we know, *i.e.*, consider, fix the attention of heart and mind, we understand well, are skilled by habit to contemplate earnestly, as the rude and undisciplined are incapable of the thought. If you suggest to a carnal man any lofty and spiritual reflection, he might reply, I surely know it to be so, but I know it not in the sense of reflecting it and revolving it in my mind? Therefore it is designedly that the Preacher asks, "Who knoweth?" who hath by repeated thought and discourse discovered the truth of the immortality of the soul and of the future judgment?

4. *If the spirit of the children of Adam.* — The interrogation is correct, being also found in the Septuagint and the ancient version of Jerome. There is this distinction, however, that whereas these subjoin the particle of interrogation to the verb (if it ascends, if it descends), in the Hebrew it is affixed to the verb itself; for ה (He) is customarily affixed to the word as a note of interrogation. "Spirit" here does not stand, as above, for breathing, but for the living soul, although in the original it is the same word, Ruach, as before.

Ascends above, and the spirit of beasts descends below. — It is very easy to understand what Solomon wished to signify by the words. Jerome explains the words "ascend above" to mean "ascend to heaven." Olympiodorus says more explicitly, "*above*" is used for the "kingdom of heaven," "*beneath*," for the lower abyss; and Kaldæus appears to follow this principle of interpretation, "And who understands whether the souls of men ascend above the firmament; or the spirit of beasts, below the earth?" In almost the same way Complut.; but Costa has, "Who, I ask, so excels in wisdom that he can discover whether the spirits of men fly into heaven, and the spirit of brutes lies fixed in the ground?" Both the Chald. and Septuag., the Syriac and Arabic versions retain the second part from the Hebrew, which reads, "Whether the spirit of beasts descends beneath the earth."

A briefer Dissertation on the signification of the words "Above and beneath," "Ascend and descend."

5. It seems too much to demand that the "descending" as well as "ascending" and "above" should have reference to heaven — an interpretation which many later writers, after the Chaldee and Jerome, too readily admit. If you object to this, that this sentiment is brought out by Solomon at a period when yet the souls of the righteous had not risen to heaven, but had gone down to the deep, *i. e.*, to the place which was limbus, and the abode of the holy fathers; they reply, that by "above" is meant the state and place of reward, which was possibly meanwhile under the earth, but afterwards in the higher heaven, whither the souls of the righteous were transplanted when their first retreat was opened by the King of Glory. Yet hardly ever will you find this mode of speaking in the Scriptures, that, before the advent of the Lord Christ, "the spirit of men ascended," but rather that it "descended" to the deep, or at most was carried to Abraham's bosom, which was a part of the deep, a vast chaos separating the place of the damned from the repose of the just. Besides, it seems forced and harsh

that the abode of the fathers and of the just should be called heaven. Lastly, as " the Preacher " speaks generally of immortality and the last judgment, it did not behove him to look back on the souls of the righteous, for they are only a few who rise " above " to the place of holy rest.

Therefore Arboreus, wishing this to be the idea of Solomon, contends that when he said this, all were conducted to the deep equally, although with a different design and issue ; *i. e.*, the human souls were borne to the lower regions, but not all to the same place ; as Jacob has said, Genesis xxxvii. 35, " I shall go down to my son in sorrow." Therefore no human spirit then "ascended above" to the heavenly joys. Hence we deny that Solomon, in the distinction he made between the spirit of men and of brutes, meant that the immortal spirit, released from the chains of the body, would fly to the higher regions. But, says he, who understands absolutely ? who, through only human authority ? Who can know by himself whether his hope is true or false ? Who, on his own proof, can instil faith into us on this matter ? This principle of interpretation is rare, although it but little deviates from that view of the immortality of the soul, and of Divine judgment, which other expositors recognise here.

In the third place, the exposition of the Greeks in the Catena is not very dissimilar. " Because," says it, " it is impossible before the judgment to determine clearly what renders the righteous unrighteous. For many unrighteous pass into unrighteousness, &c., yet are raised above ; and, on the other hand, many righteous fall into unrighteousness, and are plunged into evil." You see here what Didymus, the author of the Catena, would understand by the terms " above," " beneath," " ascend," and " descend," and of the state of lofty virtue and of vice, and of infamous and flagrant sin.

6. In the fourth place, Cajet. Nicolaus, Bonavent. Dionys., and several more recently, call the place "above" the scene of Divine judgment and recompense. But the reason for which the place " above" comes to represent the Divine judgment is not explained. Whether the judgment of souls departed from the body will be conducted in some higher sphere is uncertain. Although, from the passage resembling this in Cohel. xii. 7, " and the spirit shall return to Him who made it," it appears that the judged souls, loosed from the body, stand before the Supreme Judge, and are revealed at His bar ; because at the last judgment day, when the Judge comes in clouds, and the righteous are caught together with Christ in the air, they appear placed in the air, or in the upper sphere, but below heaven, as the form of speech current among the holy Fathers not obscurely points out For so Chrysostom (Homil. xiv. in Matt.) says, " All souls, when they depart hence, are carried to the awful tribunal." And in the same strain, Augustine (Lib. de Vanitate Sæculi, cap. i.) wrote, " When the soul is severed from the body, the angels come and conduct it before the bar of the Judge." This view, expressed in similar words, is common to other Fathers, viz. that souls are conducted to a certain place, whither, as they are not admitted to

heaven before the judgment, the Judge comes, his presence being attested by a special manifestation, and the sentence is passed. This point, I think, is uncertain, and not determined by the wiser theologians, whether in the instant of death it is carried to any other place than heaven, or to the abode of the lost, or into purgatory. Therefore no special place " above " is assigned for the judgment of souls. If a sphere " above " is spoken of for the judgment, it is because God the Judge dwells in heaven. Albeit the high and the lofty is regarded as removed from none. It becomes us therefore to say, that the immortal soul ascends "*above*," or returns to its Maker, because it " falls into the hand of the living God." But truly the " souls of beasts descend beneath," *i. e.*, because there is no judgment for them, or aught worthy of recompense.

7. But, fourthly, according to the use and hidden meaning of the scriptural term, this seems to be a periphrasis for the immortality of souls; of the natural extinction of the souls of brutes, and of the natural immortality of the souls of men, as well as of the eternal future. For this reason, to " *ascend above* " signifies the same as to save the surviving, not to suffer it to be reduced with the body to dust. To " *descend beneath* " is equivalent to being entirely dissolved with the body. Hence Hugo Victor wisely explains these words, " The spirit of the children of Adam rises above, because, in the dissolution of the body by death, the survivor continues in life ; and the spirit of beasts descends beneath, since it melts away with the body into corruption." So Job laments, chap. xvii. 16, " Into the deepest pit my all have gone down," *q. d.*, it is all over with his interests, his wealth, and life, and the universe is gone into a terrible condition. So it is usual to call incurable death and inevitable ruin " the lowest hell " (Deut. xxxii. 22), " the lowest pit " (Ps. lxxxviii. 6), " the stones of the pit " (Isa. xiv. 19); for, being swallowed up by the earth, or departing and being reduced to the earth, they speedily vanish. And from the opposite idea is derived the phrase to " rise from the earth," which is equivalent to the words, to be saved, to survive, to live. An instance occurs in Ps. xxx. 3, " Thou hast brought up my life from the grave," properly, in Hebrew, " made to ascend " or " exalted," as Vatab. renders it. The Psalmist immediately explains himself, " Thou hast kept me alive, that I should not go down to the pit," *i. e.*, " beneath " to the sepulchre. And in Prov. xxiii. 14, " and shalt deliver his soul from hell." To this class belongs the expression, " the low parts of the earth " (Ezek. xxvi. 20). The word " descend " frequently refers to death and the grave; Gen. xlii. 38 ; xliv. 29, 31 ; Ezek. xxvi. 20. Hence it is apparent that the term " beneath " has reference to corruption and death ; " above," to life and preservation ; and as the phrase " ascend above " signifies to be saved, so to " descend beneath " means to perish, and the earth into which the descent is made is the state of corruption. Thus, also, to " return to God," who is the Author of all life, implies that the soul does not perish, but is united to the Original of life. So " the spirit returns unto Him who made it " (chap. xii. 7).

s

VULGAT.	VENETA.	SHIRW.	VARIETAS EX HEBRÆO.
21. *Quis no-uit si spiritus filiorum Adá as-cendat sursum: & si spiritus iu-mentorum desce-dat deorsum?*	21. Quis co-gnoscit spiritú filiorum homi-nú nú ille ascé-dat sursum, & spiritú iuméto-rú num ille de-scendat deorsú in terram?	21. *Quis scit, an ille spiritus filiorú hominis ascendit sur-sum? spiritus iumenti an ille descédit deor-sum in ter-ram?*	¶ 21. *Hier.* G. P. T. Quis sciens. *Camp.* quotusquis-que interim nouit. T. G. an spiritus. *Camp.* An hominis anima ascensura sit sursum. G. An spi-ritus filiorum hominum sit is qui ascendat sursum. R. Spiritus filiorum homi-num ascendens ipse sur-sum. *Hieron.* T. Spiritus pecotis. P. R. Spiritus iumenti. G. S. An spiri-tus animalis. *Camp.* An anima reliquorum ani-mantium. *Cor.* Spiritus bestiæ. G. S. sit is qui descendit subtus terram. R. descendens ipse sub terram. T. deorsum in terram. *Camp.* cum cor-poribus interitura sit.

CATENA GRÆCORUM.

21. *Et quid abundauit homo a peccatore,* &c. Quid igitur inter hos discriminis este deprehendi quidve præstantius inueni? Nihil (inquit) cum vniuersa sint vanitas, prætar rationalem, spiritalemque lætitiam, quæ ex honestis hominum, virtu-tisque operibus apta nata est com-parari. Nam qui ab hac lætitia semel exciderit, ad illam rursus huius tantum præsentis vitæ admi-niculis, nullo se modo restituet, quantumuis ea probet, appetatque, qu ɜ ad illius recuperationem apprime faciunt.

ineda's gigantic commentary has no equal, and is indispen-le to the historico-critical expositor.

1621. — Within twelve months of the appearance of Pineda's rk, John Ferdinand, another Roman Catholic, also published immense folio of five hundred and seventy pages upon heleth,[1] which is a little more critical than those of his Catho-predecessors, Lorinus and Pineda. Like several Protestant

Commentarius in Librum Ecclesiastes, Auctore Tr. Joanne Ferdinando, gistro Vilillensi. Romæ, 1621.

SEPTUAG.	SYRIAC.	ARAB.	BRYLIN.	VARIETAS EX ALIIS INTERP.
21. Et quis nouit spiritus filiorú hominis, si ascédat ipse sursú? & spirit. pecoris si descendat ipse deorsum in terram?	21. *Et quis cognoscit spiritum filiorum hominum ascendere sursum, & spiritum iumétorum descendat deorsum in terram?*	21. Et quis cognouerit omné spiritú filij hominis, anima eius ascendet sursum, & si spiritus animalis animus descenderit ad profundum terræ?	21. *Et quis nouit spiritum filiorum hominis si ascendit ipse sursum? & spiritum bestiæ si descendit ipse deorsum in terram?*	21. *Hier.* quis scit *Thaum.* incertum. *Compl.* quis nouit spiritu, *Thaum.* incertum de animabus humanis. *Compl.* si ascendit. *Thaum.* in altum subuolaturæ. *Compl.* & spiritum bestiæ. *Olymp.* spiritus iumenti. *Compl.* si descendit ipse. *Thaum.* an deorsum sint defluxura.

CHALD. COMPLUT. ZAM.

Et quis est sapiens, qui sciat, si spiritus omnis filiorum hominis, ascendat supra firmamentum, & spiritus omnis iumenti descendat sub terram.

CHALD. PETR. COSTI.

21. *Quis quæso tantum sapientia excellit, vt ei exploratum esse possit num animi hominum in cælum peruolent, spiritus vero brutorum animantium desixus humi iaceat.*

commentators, Ferdinand regards this book as *a treatise u the highest good, which, according to* him, *consists in despis every earthly good, and in adhering to the service of G Solomon, being raised above men, and enlightened with the Diu light, condemns all earthly things, all the desires of men, and the opinions of the philosophers, who make human happiness consist in created good and perishing things, and not in th things which make us truly happy.*[1]

[1] Supra hominem elevatus, divinoque illustratus lumine damnat cuncta terr

The specimens we have given from the commentaries of
Lorinus and Pineda will give a fair idea of Ferdinand's mode of
interpretation.

1621. — Whilst the chief leaders of the Reformation on the
Continent were issuing expositions upon this book on the one
hand, and Roman Catholics, in emulation, were plying us with
their bulky folios on the other, no commentary on Coheleth,
written in English, was published till 1621, when the small
quarto of Thomas Granger made its appearance.[1] Granger, too,
regards Coheleth as *a treatise upon the highest good. It is*
Solomon's Ethics, *his tract* DE SUMMO BONO, *of the chief and
complete felicity, and the world's vanity, and therefore the very
root, seed, or kernel of all happy knowledge, both of good and evil,
in all things, natural, political, ecclesiastical.*[2]

The main purpose of Solomon in this book is to shew wherein the blessed
estate and happy condition of man in this vale of misery consisteth. Which,
seeing that it is not to be found in the world, I mean out of the Church,
the wise men of the world are of so different, yea contrary opinions among
themselves, and all aberr from the truth, because, being in darkness,
they neither know God nor themselves, neither what is good nor what is
ill for man in this vain life. Again, they lay down this for a ground or
principle, that there is a *summum bonum*, or felicity, by the wisdom and
endeavour of man to be found in the things of the world; but, this ground

hominum desideria, et omnes opiniones Philosophorum, qui in bono creato, et in
his rebus perituris constituunt fælicitatem hominis, pro re quæ nos beatificat.
P. 7.

[1] J. Serranus' "godly and learned commentary upon Ecclesiastes," which
appeared, 1585, is *a translation* from the Latin; Cartwright's Homilies are in
Latin, and were not published till 1648; Henry Lock's is *a poetical paraphrase;*
and H. Broughton's is simply a translation of Coheleth, with a general introduction, but without a commentary. As to Mr. Barham's quoting Pilkington (see
the Bible Revised, part i., p. viii. Intr.) as one of those commentators on
Ecclesiastes who deserve special mention, we can only say, that if he had perused
the biographical notice prefixed to the Parker Society's edition of this prelate's
works, he would never have fallen into this error. The author of this biographical notice (the Rev. James Scholefield) shews, beyond a doubt (p. ii.), that
Pilkington's lectures on Ecclesiastes were never published.

[2] A familiar exposition or commentary on Ecclesiastes, wherein the world's
vanity and the true felicity are plainly deciphered, by Thomas Granger, London,
1621. See the beginning of the *third* Dedicatory Epistle.

being false, all their buildings must needs fall down to the ground. But Solomon here, by the special instruction and direction of the Spirit of God, layeth down such a felicity as the world by their wisdom could not comprehend. The brief sum whereof is this, *Fear God and keep his commandments;* or, in a word, *faithful obedience is the chief good.* This is the theme, or question, as appears by the conclusion of all, chapter xii. 13. Now the argument of confirmation is thus framed : —

PROP. — *Either is the fear of God and obedience to His laws the chief good, or else it is to be found in and by the things of this world, which we call the goods of the body, the goods of the mind, the goods of fortune, or outward goods.*

Principal Syllogism.

ASSUM.—*But it is not to be found in and by these things.*
CONCL.— *Therefore is the fear of God, and obedience to His laws, the chief good.*

The proposition is evident, the assumption is to be proved.

PROP. — *If all be most vain, then there is no felicity or chief good to be found in the things of the world.*

prosyllogism, *i.e.,* a reason confirming the principal.

ASSUM.—*But all things are vanity, most vain.*
CONCL.— *Therefore, &c.*[1]

Granger labours to establish syllogisms, prosyllogisms, epi syllogisms, throughout the book.

1627. — Though the enormous Roman Catholic commentaries chiefly consist of the same copious extracts from the Fathers and the mediæval writers, we should be sorry to miss the large folio of Cornelius a Lapide on Ecclesiastes. Not that this Jesuit contributed much towards developing *the true design* of Coheleth, for he simply repeats the opinion of St. Augustine and St. Jerome upon this subject, and says that *the scope of the book is to teach us true wisdom, enabling us to discern vanity from truth, and to see that all the things which present themselves upon this earth, alluring and enticing us, are utterly vain, and that those things in heaven are really true and solid, so that by learning this lesson we may rise to a contempt of this vain world, and be*

[1] Commentary, pp. 2, 3.

possessed with a love for and longing after heaven and God, the true and the solid.[1]

Neither has Lapide improved upon the division of the book; for, like De Lyra and others, he divides it into *two parts:* —

Part I. (chap. i. 1 – vi. 12) shews that all earthly things which are highly esteemed by vain man, are empty and vain, and that consequently the happiness said to exist in them is vain.

Part II. (chap. vii. 1 – xii. 14) explodes this vanity, and shews that truth and true happiness are centred in virtue, and in the fear and service of God.

Accordingly, Ecclesiastes refutes those who consider supreme happiness to consist in knowledge, in chap. i.; reproves those who, like the Epicureans, place it in pleasure, in chaps. ii. and iii.; those who place it in honour, in chap. iv.; and those who consider it to consist in riches, in chaps. v. and vi.; the former part of these chapters being occupied with refuting the opinions of others, and the latter part, with establishing his own. He then speaks in chap. vii. of three kinds of good, of the *soul, body,* and *fortune,* and the opposite evils; then, shewing the ·use of all things, &c., that all our affairs are controlled by Divine Providence. And recommends, in chap. viii. to the end of the book, that we should lead a godly life, shewing how we shall at last be united with God, and enjoy eternal happiness.[2]

---

[1] Finis et scopus hujus libri est, docere veram sapientiam; scilicet qua secernamus vanitatem à veritate; nimirum ut cognoscamus vana esse omnia quæ in terris se ostentant, alliciunt et abblandiuntur; vera verò et solida esse, quæ in cœlis sunt, ut ex hac dispari cognitione assurgamus ad mundi, utpote vani, contemptum, ac ad cœli Deique, utpote veri solidique amorem et desiderium.—R. P. Cornelii a Lapide, e Societate Jesu, Commentarius in Ecclesiasten. Antverpiæ, 1694, p. 4.

[2] Verùm dico duas primarias Ecclesiastis esse partes. Prior est à c. i. usque ad cap. vii. quâ ostendit omnes res mundi sublunares, quas homines vani magnas æstimant, inanes esse et vanos, ac proinde vanam esse felicitatem quæ in ijs collocatur. Posterior à c. vii. porrigitur usque ad finem, qua depulsa vanitate, demonstrat veritatem veramque felicitatem sitam esse in virtute, ac Dei timore et cultu. Igitur primo statim capite eos refellit, qui scientiâ summum bonum metiebantur, secundo item ac tertio capitibus eos redarguit, qui in voluptate finem bonorum, ut Epicurei collocarunt; quarto capite eos, qui in honoribus;

But the chief utility of this book is its lengthy quotations from the Fathers and schoolmen. It must also be added that Lapides' commentary is more critical than those of his fellow-Jesuit expositors, Lorinus, Pineda, and Ferdinand.

1628. — The highly gifted William Pemble, who died in his thirty-second year (April 14, 1623), while on a visit to his tutor, Richard Capel, minister of Eastington, in Gloucestershire, wrote an analytical exposition of Ecclesiastes, which was published in 1628, and is embodied in the several folio editions of his entire works.[1] Capel, who published the commentary of his pupil, prefixed a dedicatory epistle to it, giving therein his own opinion of the design of the book, which entirely agrees with that of Pemble.

" As we in our sickness," says the teacher, " complain of what occasioned our sickness, rather than of the disease itself; so Solomon, when he came to himself, made this book, wherein his drift is, not to stand so much upon his fall, as the means of his fall ; I mean the vanity not of some but of all worldly matters, which were the means and occasion that first drew him from the Lord; such sweet things did deaden his taste, and made him that he could not relish the things of heaven."

This is rather an ingenious attempt to account for the remarkable fact, that there is not *a single recantation* in the book, which is described as *Solomon's Recantation*.

"Coheleth," says the pupil, "a preacher, or reconciled penitent, or both, this being his penitential sermon, or writing delivered to the church or assembly of the faithful Jews,"

---

quinto et sexto eos confutat, qui in divitiis et opibus felicitatem posuère. Prior itaque hæc capitum sex portio in refellendis alienis occupatur; altera verò totidem capitum pars in confirmanda sua sententia versatur. Igitur c. vii. de tribus bonorum generibus disserit: *Animi*, inquam, *corporis* et *fortunæ*, deque contrariis malis. Quis horum omnium sit usus, utque res omnes nostræ à divina pendeant providentia, luculenter ostendit. Hinc ad finem usque libri de vita piè ac justè transigenda, quo tandem Deo conjungamur, et felicitate perfruamur æternâ, concionatur, p. 5.

[1] Solomon's Recantation and Repentance, or the Book of Ecclesiastes briefly and fully explained. Works, p. 273, &c.

institutes an inquiry "*wherein man's chiefest good and blessedness consisteth.*" He proceeds in the first part (i. 1 – vi. 12) " NEGA- TIVELY, *disabling the virtue of such things as might seem to make us happy;* and declares, in the second part, (vii. 1 – xii. 14) AFFIRMATIVELY and POSITIVELY, *wherein man's blessedness stands, and whereby it is obtained. This he doth —*

" 1. Particularly, in the several degrees and means of true happiness, so far as in this life we may attain unto it, in chaps. vii., viii., ix., x., xi., and part of chap. xii.

" 2. Summarily, in the conclusion of this whole discourse, chapter xii. 8."

As this is the first entirely analytical commentary, and as it shews how the Scriptures were reduced to the logic and mathematical precision of the time, we give a specimen of Pemble's Analysis of chap. i. 1–7.

Inscription, verse 1, describing the author of the book —
1. By the person he now takes on him, *Coheleth,* a Preacher, or recon- ciled penitent, or both, this being his penitential sermon, or writing, delivered to the Church or assembly of the faithful Jews.
2. By his parentage, son of David.
3. By his dignity and office, a king, amplified by the place, in Jerusalem.
Doctrine, enquiring wherein man's chiefest good and blessedness con- sisteth, wherein he proceedeth —
1. Negatively, disabling the virtue of such things as might seem to make us happy, which is done —
   1. Generally, in one main proposition, That there is nothing within the compass and power of created nature that can make a man happy. This negative proposition is —
      1. Delivered (verse 2), concluding all under vanity, and that most vain vanity, weakness, inconstancy, fruitlessness, &c., and that repeated, to make it seem the more vain.
      2. Confirmed by four general reasons.
2. Affirmatively. See chap. vii.
      Verse 3. 1. From the *fruitlessness* of all human actions, endea- vours, counsels, and projects, wherein he busieth himself under the sun, *i. e.*, in matters of this world, whose uttermost extent is confined within the possibilities of the creature, and the circuit of this life. All the happiness that man may propose or procure to himself by those means, if it be resolved into its sinful issue and

conclusion, ends in nothing, and leaves unto a man no profit, יתרון, *i.e.*, residue, and remaining fruit to abide with him; when all that account is subducted, there resteth nothing but ciphers.

2. From the *mutability* and changeable condition of man himself. Eternity is an inseparable accident of perfect felicity; nor can those things make us truly happy, which cannot establish us in the perpetual enjoyment of our bliss. And thus are the things of our world, whose greatest strength cannot alter the frail and perishing estate of man. But (verse 4) generation cometh, and generation passeth away, both fathers and children, all are at last thrust out of possession of the earth's felicity. In which only complement of true felicity, man is so far from being happy as his condition is worse than that of other creatures, yea, of those that seem most inconstant. Instances are four —

1. The *earth* abiding for ever, seeing the rise and fall of all ages, the stage of all actions, the womb that giveth and receiveth all, viler than the worst man for its nature, better than the most happy for its continuance in that being that it hath (verse 4).

2. The *sun* (verse 5) which, as a champion, runs his course from one end of heaven to the other; and with an even and unaltered motion observes the time of rising and setting; so setting in the evening, as it ariseth with equal glory and brightness in the morning (not so in man). *Sotes occidere*, &c.

3. The *winds* (verse 6), which seem most unsteady and changeable in their motion, yet so pass over the quarters and coasts of the world, as they observe their circuits, סביבתיו, wherein they run their compass yearly, monthly, and daily (in some places) as God ordains, who brings them out of his treasury.

4. The *waters*, a shuttle and running substance, yet more durable and lasting than man and his felicity. The sea still holding the same quantity since the creation for depth and wideness, notwithstanding the infinite access of all rivers emptying themselves into it; and as the sea is never full, so are rivers never empty, the waters still running, but still renewed by supply from the clouds and their fountains (verse 7).

1636.—This opinion is also espoused by Cocceius, the founder of the Theological school bearing his name.[1] The following is his analysis of the book : —

A. Thesis (i. 2).
B. Demonstration. Because —
I. Labour is unprofitable (3), from 1. *The nature of things* (4–7). 2.

1 Cocceji Opera, Editio Tertia, Amstelodami, vol. ii., p. 520, *seq.*

Imperfection of things (8–12). 3. *The kinds of labour,* where there is,
(1.) Examination (13). (2.) Attestation (14). (3.) Declaration (15). (4.)
Demonstration. *a.* In proof of wisdom and folly (16). A §. Absolute
(18, &c.) B. §. Comparative (chap. ii. 12, &c.) *b.* The result of the proof.
A. §. Hatred of life (17). B. §. Hatred of work (18). C. §. Despair of
work (20). 4. *The reasons,* I. placed (1.) generically ; (2.) specifically
(iii. 2). II. Reference to the thesis (9). III. Illustrates (1.) The government of God (11). (2.) Invocation of good (12). (3.) Its confirmation
(13, &c.) Because—
II. Labour oppresses. 1. The injustice and violence of men (chap. iv. 1).
2. The effect of these on (1.) Society. *a.* Emulation (4). *b.* Envy (5).
(2.) Individuals, avarice (6, &c.) 3. The vanity of overmuch help (13, &c.).
Because—
III. There is danger in well doing, in 1. Approach to God's house (chap.
v. 1). 2. Prayer (2). 3. Vows (4, &c.). 4. Recognition of the Divine
government (8). Because—
IV. The common hope of good is vain. 1. Honour. 2. Money (10).
3. Abundant increase (11). 4. Satisfaction (12). 5. Treasures (13, &c.)
6. A large family (chap. vi. 3). Because —
V. The fruit of labour is transient (7, 8). Because—
VI. Eager desire is vain (9). 1. Τὸ παρόν, is better. 2. Men remain
within their own rank (10). 3. Hope and gladness heap up vanity (11).
4. Uncertainty of human good (12). (1.) Overshadowed good. (2.) Unknown future. (3.) Good not subjected to sensible test. Hence, better is
(*a.*) Name to ointment (chap. vii. 1). (*b.*) Day of death to day of birth.
(*c.*) Society of the mourning than of the merry (2). (*d.*) Sorrow to
laughter (3). (*e.*) The end than the beginning (8). (*f.*) Patience (9).
(*g.*) Wisdom with inheritance (11). (*h*) Justice and wisdom, with the
excess of each (16, &c.). (*i.*) Pleasure than wisdom, wherein 1 §. Thesis,
extolling wisdom (chap. viii. 1). 2 §. Confirmation, from the fruits of
wisdom. (1.) In public life (3). (2.) Private (5). 3 §. Antithesis
(1.) Defects of wisdom in (1.) Public life. (2.) Private (9, 10, &c.)
(2). Pleasures of good, which includes in it
i. Proposition (15).
ii. Confirmation, from the inconvenience of wisdom (16).
A. Useless labours (17).
B. Utter emptiness, from 1. Common appointment of God (chap. ix. 1).
2. Common uncertainty (2). 3. Common lot (3, &c.). 4. Obstructions to
wisdom (13).
(*b.*) Impertinence of those to whom it is necessary (16). (*c.*) Their
guilt (18). (*d.*) Mixture of folly in the wise (chap. x. 1). (*e.*) Unjust
distribution of honour (5, &c.). (*f.*) Επανορθωσις, concerning vain and baneful
pleasure (15). (1.) The state from the throat (17). (2.) Constitution
from care (18). (1.) In an example of evil (19). (2.) Of good (20).
(3.) Evils following.

a. Envy (20). *b.* Neglect of the needy (chap. xi. 1). *c.* The Pretext
(4). (*d.*) Advice given (6).
  (3.) In life itself (7). (4.) In better portions of life (9, &c.).
  C. Epilogue, in which the author
    1. Concludes his thesis (chap. xii. 8).
    2. Delivers its use (9).
      1. Προσοχη (10).
      2. Rei colophon (13).

1637.—The states of the Netherlands, where our persecuted
Puritans and other eminent divines found an hospitable
asylum, and where many of their elaborate works were first
published, now obtained a vernacular authorised version, with
large annotations, by the advice and authority of the States-
General given to the Synod of Dort. "The Dutch Annotations," as they are called, were so highly esteemed, that they
were translated into English by Theodor Haak, in 1657,[1] and
were recommended by Parliament, along with Diodati, to the
authors of the Assembly's Annotations. The Dutch Annotators
agree, with "many of the learned," that *Solomon wrote this book
in his old age, after that he had for many years together turned
away from the right path of true godliness, but was now again
converted unto God. Wherein he, by inspiration of the Holy Ghost,
before the whole congregation of God, testifieth his earnest sorrow
and repentance for the former part of his life, loathing and
abhorring it, as being vanity of vanities, whereby a man is not
able to attain unto temporal rest, and satisfaction or contentment
of mind, much less unto the highest and chiefest good, which is
everlasting salvation. In like manner his intent and purpose is,
by his own example and pattern, to lead all men to virtue and
piety.*

To this end and purpose he doth in *the first place* make a short recital of
the whole course of his life, and wherein he had chiefly taken his delight
and recreation. Then, in *the second place*, he relateth also that he heeded
and observed the practice and course, about which many men did most

[1] The Dutch Annotations upon the whole Bible, translated by Theodor Haak,
2 vols. fol., 1657.

busy and trouble themselves in this life, being, for the most part, vanities, yea also wicked and ungodly devices, he testifying that the All-wise and Almighty God directeth and governeth all things according to His will and pleasure, and that things do not fall out in the world by fortune or chance, as many men do imagine. *Lastly*, Solomon exhorteth all men to fear and serve God uprightly, and to practise and perform all good works and duties, rejoicing in an honest and godly manner in the things which they do enjoy, and have received at the bountiful hand of God, especially while they are yet young, strong, and of perfect memory and understanding, having at all times the severe and righteous judgment of God before their eyes.[1]

It will be seen that these Dutch divines, like the early Reformers, recognise that this book *recommends a grateful enjoyment of the good creatures of God.*

1639. — Determined that the Roman Catholics should no longer have the monopoly of the large folio commentaries, Michael Jermin, "Doctor in Divinity, and Rector of St. Martin's, Ludgate," now produced a folio upon Ecclesiastes.[2] The mode of commenting on the text which our Protestant divine adopted is similar to that pursued by the Catholics, whom he evidently imitates; and we are sorry to say that the copy is infinitely inferior to the original, as will be seen from the following specimen. With many of his predecessors, Jermin thinks that *the scope of the Royal Philosopher, the Ecclesiastical King of Israel, in this book, is to shew where the greatest good of man is, by shewing it not to be in the things of this world; he declareth what it is, by declaring what we must be, in the fear of the Lord, and in keeping his commandments.*

A specimen of his commentary —

Chap. vi. 4. *For he cometh in with vanity, &c.* — Saint Bernard, speaking unto man, saith, *Cogita unde veneris, et erubesce, ubi sis et ingemisce, quo vadis et contremisce,* Think from whence thou camest, and be ashamed, where thou art, and sigh for sorrow, whither thou goest, and tremble with

---

[1] Vol. i., not paged.

[2] A Commentary upon the whole book of Ecclesiastes, or the Preacher, by Michael Jermin, Doctor in Divinity, and Rector of St Martin's, Ludgate, London. 1639.

anguish (Ser. de. Primord. Med. et Noviss.) Saint Austin, also, speaking unto man, saith, *Intelligas ergo in quantum sit ingressus tuus flebilis, progressus tuus debilis, et egressus tuus horribilis*, Understand, therefore, how lamentable thy coming is, how feeble thy going on is, how terrible thy going out is (l. cui tit. Speculum Peccato). It is the like manner of expressing himself, and of setting out man's misery and condition, which here the Preacher useth. *He cometh in with vanity*, with the vanity of original corruption, *and departeth in darkness*, in the darkness of his actual transgressions. For these are darkness, indeed, by which the light of God's favour is darkened and kept from us, the light of knowledge is darkened and shut up in us, by which the darkness of eternal misery is brought upon us. Saint Austin noteth (Ps. viii.), *Non dicit Deus, fiant tenebræ, et factæ sunt, et tamen tenebras ordinavit, et divisit à luce tenebras*, God did not say, Let there be darkness, and there was darkness; but yet God ordered the darkness, and divided the darkness from the light: it is so with the transgressions of men; God never said, Let them be; but, having their being from man, he ordereth them, and by his justice divideth them from the light of happiness. But here is nothing said of the covetous wretch's life; his vain coming in, his dark going out mentioned; we read nothing of his wretched life, as if that were not worthy to be remembered. And indeed it follows, *His name shall be covered with darkness;* whereby is not meant only that his name shall be forgotten, for then it had been enough to have said, *his name shall be covered.* But, seeing it is added that *his name shall be covered with darkness*, it is meant that the foulness and blackness of his actions shall make his name to be as a thing abhorred to be thought upon. And surely when vanity lets him in, and darkness shuts him out, what could it be but wretchedness that kept him company in the meanwhile? But it seemeth to me that the original here may not amiss be translated, *he cometh into vanity, and goeth into darkness.* First, he cometh into vanity: Saint Ambrose, shewing the vanity of man's life, and that it is but a shadow, telleth us (Ps. cxviii.), that when the Son of God was born of the Virgin, it is said that the power of the highest overshadowed her; *Quia in umbram descendit, ab umbra incipiens operari salutem hominis, et consummaturus claritate solis æterni*, Because he descended into a shadow, from a shadow beginning to work the salvation of man, which he will finish in the brightness of the Eternal Sun. And the same Father, considering the words of David, *I will live and keep thy words*, thereupon noteth (*ibid.*), *Vivam ait, quasi nondum vivens; hic enim in umbra vivimus. Ergo vita ista in corpore, umbra est vitæ, et imago, non veritas*, He saith, I will live, as not living yet, for here we live in a shadow. This life therefore in the body is a shadow and au image of life, not the truth of it. Secondly, *He goeth into darkness; sed forte tales esse putet homo, quales patiuntur in carceribus inclusi. Utinam tales essent, tamen in tabilus nemo vult esse. In his autem carcerum tenebris possint includi et innocentes. In talibus enim tenebris sunt inclusi martyres*, But perhaps some one may think this darkness to be such as they suffer who are shut up in prison. I wish that it were such; but yet in this darkness no one would willingly be. But, in the darkness of prisons, innocents may be shut up, for in such darkness martyrs have been imprisoned, as Saint Austin speaketh (Homil. 40). This, therefore, is another *darkness*, this is that outer darkness of which the Scripture speaketh, and into which he is cast, *Qui extra Deum penitus est, quoniam dum tempus est corrigi noluerit*, Who is without God wholly, because, when there was time, he would not be corrected, as St. Austin speaketh, (Ps. v.) So doth St. Ambrose also expound the outer darkness, saying, *Quicunque extra sunt promissa cœlestium mandatorum, in tenebris exterioribus sunt; quia mandata Dei lumen sunt. Et quicunque sine Christo est, in tenebris est, quia lumen in tenebris est Christus*, Whosoever are without the promises of the heavenly commandments, they are in outer darkness, because the commandments of God are light. Whosoever is without Christ, he is darkness, because Christ is a light in darkness. And of this outer darkness St. Austin saith, *Penitus autem esse extra Deum, quid est nisi esse in summa cæcitate?* But to be wholly without God, what is it but to be in extreme darkness? Into this darkness, therefore, it is that the soul of a covetous wretch goeth, when the life into which he came is vanished away. And when his soul thus lieth in the darkness of horror, when his body lieth in the darkness of the grave, then is his name also covered, either with the darkness of silence, abhorring to mention it, or, if it be mentioned, with the darkness of reproaches that are cast upon it.

1643. — It is remarkable that, notwithstanding all the oriental celebrities and Biblical scholars who lived in England at the period, the first commentary upon the entire Bible in English is a translation from the Italian of Diodati, the history of which is as follows. John Diodati or Deodati, who was born at Geneva (not at Lucca), on June 6, 1575, where he also died on October 3, 1649,[1] published the first edition of his Italian version of the Bible at Geneva, 1603, fol., issued a second edition with notes in 1607, 4to, and a third improved edition in 1641, fol. He also began publishing a French translation of the Bible, with many additional notes, in 1644, which he

[1] Orme's remark, that Diodati was "born 1576, died 1638" (Bibliotheca Biblica, p. 150), is a most unaccountable blunder. Even the English-translator of Diodati, R. G., as he signs himself, is inaccurate in the biographical and bibliographical remarks which he makes in his address to the reader, as will be seen from the excellent article on Diodati in Ersch and Gruber's Encyclop., sect. v.

finished in 1646. The annotations of the second edition were published by R. G. in 1643, and thus supplied the English reading public with a commentary on the whole Bible. R. G. also published a second edition in 1648, inserting additional notes, which Diodati made in his French Bible, and a third edition in 1651. Diodati's annotations were so highly esteemed that they were recommended, along with the Dutch annotations, to the author of the Assembly's annotations. But, whatever may be the merits of these notes on other portions of Scripture, they throw no additional light upon Coheleth, since Diodati simply repeats what many of his predecessors have said, viz., *Solomon, towards the latter end of his life, after he had seen so many trials, and committed so many errors, makes here a solemn kind of speech for a public confession, and the instruction of the Church upon two very weighty and necessary points. The first is, how a faithful man ought and may wisely govern his life in this world, to live happily therein. The other, how he should direct it towards the sovereign end of eternal happiness.*

The following is a specimen of his analysis : —

Solomon's design in this book (excellent
1. For its *principal author, one Shepherd*, chap. xii. 11.
2. For its *instru-mental* author, Solomon, com-mended for his
 1. *Wisdom.*
 2. *Assiduity* in teaching words of
  1. *Truth*, chap. xii. 10.
  2. *Delight.*
  3. *Power* to
   1. Quicken as *goads.*
   2. Fasten as *nails*, chap. xii. 11)

doth shew wherein the *summum bonum* or *true happiness* of man doth consist; a thing eagerly sought after by the heathen philosophers, but never found out by them, they in this argument being as men destitute of *light*, and wandering in *darkness*. This *happiness* doth Solomon the Preacher define—

1. *Negatively*, in the six first chapters, shewing wherein it *doth not* consist, therein confuting the vain opinions and con-jectures of the philosophers.
2. *Affirmatively*, in the six last chapters, shewing wherein this *happiness doth* consist, therein rectifying the judgment of all that seek after it.

1644. — As a literary curiosity must be mentioned, Quarles'
poetical paraphrase of Ecclesiastes, published by his widow in
1644.[1] The title of the book, viz., *Solomon's Recantation*, shews
that Quarles follows the opinion that this is a penitential dirge.
The following is a specimen of this curious paraphrase, which
consists of twelve sections, according to the number of the
chapters, each section being followed by a soliloquy of similar
length.

Chap. i. 1–11 · —

1. Thus says the best of preachers and of kings,
   Thus Solomon, the son of David sings,
2. The greatest happiness that earth can prize
   Is all most vain, and vainest vanities.
3. What profit can accrue to man ? what gains
   Can crown his actions, or reward his pains ?
   Beneath the orb of heaven's surrounding sun,
   What, worth his labour, hath his labour done ?
4. One generation gives another way,
   But earth abides in one perpetual stay ;
5. The prince of light puts on his morning crown,
   And in the evening lays his glory down,
   Where, leaving earth to take a short repose,
   He soon returns, and rises where he rose.
6. The troubled air provokes the southern states,
   And then it blusters at the Borean gates ;
   It whirls about in his uncertain sphere,
   And rides his unknown circuit everywhere.
7. All rivers to the seas their tribute yield,
   And yet th' hydropic seas are never filled,
   Their sliding streams pursue their passage home,
   And drive their hasty tides from whence they come.
8. The world is all composed of change, nor can
   Her vanity be charactered by man ;
   The eye's not satisfied, and what we hear
   Fills not the concave of th' insatiate ear :
9. The thing that heretofore hath been, we see
   Is but the same that is, and is to be ·
   And what is done, is what is to be done ;
   There's nothing that is new beneath the sun.
10. What novelty can earth proclaim, and say
    It had no precedent before this day ?

[1] Solomon's Recantation, &c., by John Quarles, London, 1644.

No, no; there's nothing modern times can own,
The which precedent ages have not known ;
11. The deeds of former days expire their date
In our collapsed memories, and what
Time's early sunshine hath not ripened yet,
Succeeding generations shall forget

1644. — The appearance of Grotius' Commentary on the Old
Testament in 1644, a year before his death, gave a new tone to
the interpretation of the Hebrew Scriptures in general, and to
that of Coheleth in particular, through the profound scholarship
and great liberality displayed therein. This acute critic takes
Coheleth to mean *collector*, *compiler*, and regards the book as[1]
*a collection of different opinions concerning happiness, as pro-
pounded by those who were reputed sages by their own people, just
as the book of Job discusses the different opinions respecting the
Divine government of human affairs.* We are therefore not to
wonder if we find things in it which we cannot approve, since
all the different opinions are necessarily *mixed up with his argument, just as Aristotle does, before giving his final opinion ;* but
the beginning and end sufficiently *shew the drift of the book, for
which, as the Hebrews say, it deserves a place in the canon.*

The main service, however, which Grotius has rendered with
regard to this book, is his shrewd discovery that Solomon is not
its author, which no commentator had made since the days of

---

[1] Melius fortè vertetur συναθροιστής (*coacervator*), quomodo verbum קהל per
συναθροίζειν verti solet, ut intelligamus redactas in hunc librum varias hominum,
qui sapientes apud suos quisque habebantur, opiniones περὶ τῆς εὐδαιμονίας (*de
beatitudine*), planè sicut liber Jobi omnes ferme quæ fuerunt aut esse possunt de
divina rerum humanarum gubernatione, aut contra eam, sententias complectitur. Quare mirari non debemus, si quædam hìc legimus non probanda; omnes
enim sententias cum suis argumentis recitanti, ut Aristoteles facere solet prius-
quam quid definiat, necesse erat id accidere ; sed cùm et initium et finis satìs
monstrent quod sit scriptoris propositum, ob eas causas (ut aiunt Hebræi),
meritò in canonem receptus est. Ego tamen Solomonis esse non puto, sed
scriptum seriùs sub illius Regis, tanquam pœnitentiâ ducti, nomine. Argumentum
ejus rei habeo multa vocabula, quæ non alibi quàm in Daniele, Esdrâ et
Chaldæis interpretibus reperias. Hugonis Grotii Opera, 4 vols. Londini, 1679,
vol. i., p. 258.

Luther   "*I believe,*" says he, "*that the book is not the production of Solomon, but was written in the name of this king, as being
led by repentance to do it.   For it contains many words which
cannot be found except in Ezra, Daniel, and the Chaldee para-
phrasts.*

Grotius' notes are very brief, but always very instructive, and
abound with parallels from the Classics.

1645. — Stimulated by the annotations on the Bible, which
the Germans, the Dutch, the Italians, and the French Protestants possessed, English Protestants were at last determined
to have something similar.   To this end a committee of Parliament nominated some of the most learned divines of the day,
supplying them with books, and recommending to them the
Dutch and Diodati's Annotations, to produce a similar work.
Hence the commentary upon the Scriptures, known by the
erroneous name of " The *Assembly's* Annotations,"[1] which was
first published in 1645; then, with improvements, in 1651; and
a third edition, 1657.   Dr. Reynolds, bishop of Norwich, is the
author of the Commentary on Ecclesiastes.   Reynolds follows
the opinion of many of his predecessors, that *Solomon makes
known his repentance to all the Church, that thereby he might*

---

[1] "The Annotations on the Bible," says Neal, "which go under their [the
Assembly's] name, were neither undertaken nor revised by them, but by a Committee of Parliament, who named the commentators, and furnished them with
books; nor were they all members of the Assembly, as appears by the following
list.   Those with asterisks were not of the Assembly.

The Commentary on	Written by
The five books of Moses........	Rev. Mr. Ley, Sub-Dean of Chester.
The two books of Kings	
The two books of Chronicles	
Ezra	Dr. Gouge.
Nehemiah ....·	
Esther	
The Psalms	*Mr. Meric Casaubon.
Proverbs	Mr. Francis Taylor.
Ecclesiastes	Dr. Reynolds.
Solomon's Song	*Mr. Smalwood, recommended by Arch-bishop Usher.

glorify God, and strengthen his brethren, thus imitating his father David; he therefore translates chap. i. 1, *The words of the soul, or person congregated or gathered unto the church or congregation of saints,* &c.[1] He also divides the book into two principal parts, in the first of which (chap. ii. – vi. 12) the penitent king shews, from his own experience, that happiness can neither be found in wisdom, knowledge, pleasures, honour, greatness, power, nor in an outward form of religion, it all being vanity; but in the excellent means which he prescribes in the second part (chap. vii. – xii. 12), viz. : —

Contentation of heart in the sweet and free enjoyment of all outward blessings, with thanksgiving, and in the fear of God; quiet and humble acquiescency under the holy and powerful providence of God, in all the events which befall us in the world; sincerity of heart in his worship, and prudent piety in our vows, prayers, and addresses unto him; patience of spirit under all the oppressions we meet with in the world; a composed preparedness of mind to undergo sorrows and afflictions; prudent and pious moderation of spirit in our behaviour towards all men, that so we may preserve our names from calumny, and our persons from danger; meekness, charity, patience towards such as offend, considering common frailty and our own weakness; sobriety of mind, contenting ourselves with a measure of wisdom and knowledge, and not busying ourselves with things too high for us; practical prudence, which may render us beautiful in the eyes of others; loyalty and obedience towards magistrates, that our lives may not

The Commentary on	Written by
Isaiah	
Jeremiah	Mr. Gataker.
Lamentations	
Ezekiel	*Mr. Pemberton, in the first edition,
Daniel, and the smaller Prophets	*Bishop Richardson, in the second.
Matthew	
Mark	Mr. Ley.
Luke	
John	
St. Paul's Epistles	Dr. D. Featly; but his notes are broken and imperfect, the author dying before he had revised them.

There were two other persons concerned in this work, who might probably have the other parts of Scripture allotted them, not here mentioned, viz., Mr. Downham, and Mr. Reading." History of the Puritans, part iii., chap. x.

[1] Annotations upon all the books of the Old and New Testament, third edition, 2 vols. London, 1657., vol. i. not paged.

be made uncomfortable by their displeasure; wisdom to discern of time and
judgment; preparedness of heart against inevitable evils; submission to
the holy and invincible providence of God, admiring his works, adoring his
judgments; joyful fruition of comforts; conscionable and industrious walking
in our particular callings; wisdom so to carry ourselves amidst the many
casualties which meet us in the world, as that we may by our loyalty
towards superiors decline the danger of displeasure from them, and by
our charity to inferiors lay up a good foundation for ourselves against the
time to come; lastly, moderation in the use of comforts here, and preparation, by the fear of God and keeping of his commandments, for death and
judgment hereafter.   That by these means, as our life is sweet, so our death
may be welcome.   That the piety of our youth may help us to bear the
infirmities of our age, and to lift up our heads in the day of redemption.

Reynolds' commentary, though homiletic, contains many
critical remarks, explanations of idioms, &c., and not only surpasses all English expositions on Ecclesiastes which preceded it,
but will bear comparison with those which have succeeded it.

1647. — Whilst homiletic commentaries were now being
multiplied in England, Germany continued to furnish us with
critical expositions ; and the elaborate work of Geier on
Coheleth will always be an honour to its age.[1] Geier, however,
is satisfied with the old opinion that *Solomon's design in this book
is partly to confess the vanity of those things which he had formerly
been so fond of, to his utter ruin, and partly to deter others from
the like fondness of vanities, and to lead them to the true sovereign
good, which is the fear of God.*[2] He also divides the book into
two principal parts, though he differs from his predecessors in
making the first part, which shews wherein happiness does not
consist, to extend from i. 1 to ix. 18; and the second part,
shewing wherein true happiness does consist, to extend from
x. to xii. 14.

---

[1] In Salomonis Regis Israel Ecclesiasten Commentarius Martini Geïeri,
Lipsiæ, 1647; editio quarta, Lipsiæ, 1791, is the one we have used.

[2] SCOPUS denique, Salomoni in hoc librô præfixus, fuit, partim confessionem
edere vanitatum cum damnô hactenus tractatarum, partim alios omnes simili vanitatum sectatione deterrere, atque ad verum summum bonum adducere, nempe ad
Timorem Dei, p. 5, vi.

The following is the tabular view which Geier gives of the argument of Ecclesiastes ·[1] —

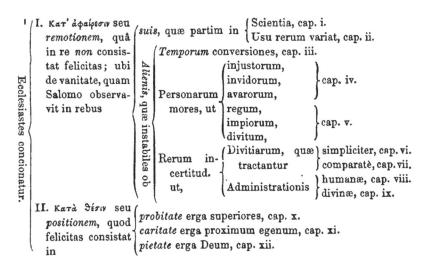

Ecclesiastes the Preacher

I. Κατ' ἀφαίρεσιν, or the remonstration. The things in which happiness does *not* consist because of the vanity which Solomon observed.

from the experience of others, because of the instability of

from his own experience, — not in knowledge, chap. i. / nor in pleasure, chap. ii.

Time, being changeable, chap. iii.

Persons, because their character — being unjust, invidious, and avaricious, } chap. iv. / king impious, and rich, } chap. v.

Things, being uncertain, viz., — Riches which are contracted } absolutely, chap. vi. / comparatively, chap. vii. / Administration — human, chap. viii. / divine, chap. ix.

II. Κατὰ θέσιν, or the position wherein happiness *does* consist.

in *uprightness* towards superiors, chap. x. ·
in *benevolence* towards the poor, chap. xi.
in *piety* towards God, chap. xii.

Geier's commentary contains much that is critically valuable.

1647. — It is not surprising that Lightfoot, who declared himself a mere child in Hebrew and Rabbinical learning, in

[1]

Ecclesiastes concionatur.

I. Κατ' ἀφαίρεσιν seu *remotionem,* quâ in re *non* consistat felicitas; ubi de vanitate, quam Salomo observavit in rebus

Alienis, quæ instabiles ob

suis, quæ partim in — Scientia, cap. i. / Usu rerum variat, cap. ii.

Temporum conversiones, cap. iii.

Personarum mores, ut — injustorum, invidorum, avarorum, } cap. iv. / regum, impiorum, divitum, } cap. v.

Rerum incertitud. ut, — Divitiarum, quæ tractantur } simpliciter, cap. vi. / comparatè, cap. vii. / Administrationis — humanæ, cap. viii. / divinæ, cap. ix.

II. Κατὰ θέσιν seu *positionem,* quod felicitas consistat in

probitate erga superiores, cap. x.
caritate erga proximum egenum, cap. xi.
pietate erga Deum, cap. xii.

cómparisóṅ with Hügh Broughton, adopted the singular view of the latter, that *the design of Coheleth is to shew that the king-dom promised to David is not of this world.* In his " Chronicle of the Times, and the Order of the Texts of the Old Testament," which appeared in 1647, Lightfoot says, upon —

THE BOOK OF ECCLESIASTES.

After his great fall, Solomon recovereth again by repentance, and writeth this book of Ecclesiastes, as his penitential dirge for that his folly. He calleth himself in it *Koheleth*, or *the gathering soul ;* either *recollecting itself*, or, *by admonition, gathering others*, that go astray after vanity. He sheweth in it, that all things on this side heaven are but vanity ; and he had found it so by sad experience ; and so the kingdom promised to David, which was to be everlasting, must not be expected to be of this world, as John xviii. 36.[1]

1651. — Far superior, in a critical point of view, to every-thing which has hitherto been published on Ecclesiastes, is the scholarly commentary of Mercer. Like Luther and others, he maintains that *the design of this book is to shew the vanity of human affairs, studies, projects, and dispositions, and to condemn the restless anxiety and fickleness of man ; and, having drawn us away from these, to invite us to the contemplation of lofty realities, to the fear of God, and to the keeping of his commandments.* It moreover teaches us *to enjoy present things with a calm and grateful heart, without anxiety and solicitude, which Christ also teaches.*[2]

Without being tedious in detailing the various opinions of others, Mercer's commentary is a storehouse of Rabbinical and other varied learning, which this learned expositor does not

[1] Comp. his Works, vol. ii., p. 205, Pitman's edition.

[2] Scopus hujus libri et institutum est rerum humanarum, studiorum, consili-órum et affectuum vanitatem ostendere, ac irrequietam humanorum animorum curiositatem et inconstantiam damnare ; deinde nos ab ea subvehere ad rerum sublimium considerationem, ad timorem et judicium Domini ac observationem ejus mandatorum, ut ad extremum libri concludit סוף דבר, *finis verbi*, &c. Interim etiam docet rebus praesentibus pacatè et tranquillè frui cùm gratiarum actione sine anxietate et solicitudine ; ut Christus etiam docuit.—Joannis Merceri Commen-tarii in Jobum, et Salomonis Proverbia, Ecclesiasten, Canticum Canticorum. Amsterodami, 1651, p. 518.

quote to parade his learning, but thoroughly examines, and shews what is feasible and what is not. Mercer's commentary is as much a repository of Rabbinical lore, as the commentaries of the Jesuits Lorinus, Pineda, and A. Lapide are of Patristic and mediæval literature, without the prolixity of the latter.

1653. — The second English commentary on the entire Bible is that of "John Mayer, Doctor in Divinity." Though our English divine espouses the old view of the design of this book, yet he puts it into a somewhat different shape. *Here*, he says, *are observations touching the vanities of this world, and sentences uttered hereupon, partly as the author hereof, Solomon, thought in the time of his vanity, and partly after that, by repentance, he rose up again, persuading to the fear of God, and to the keeping of his commandments.*[1]

Mayer's commentary is brief, but terse and lucid, and by no means deserves to be so very scarce.

1654. — The ecclesiastical administration, directed by the tyrannical William Laud, archbishop of Canterbury, had driven some of the most pious and learned divines to seek an asylum in the American wilderness. "There, a few resolute Puritans — who, in the cause of their religion, feared neither the rage of the ocean nor the hardship of uncivilised life; neither the fangs of savage beasts nor the tomahawks of more savage men — had built, amidst the primeval forests, villages which are now great and opulent cities, but which have, through every change, retained some trace of the character derived from their founders."[2] There, too, these uncompromising Puritans have raised to themselves monuments of piety and learning, which neither the corroding power of time nor the mighty deeds of valour could destroy or overtop. Among the number of those who sought a refuge in New England, in 1633, was the eminent John Cotton, who, besides many other works, wrote an exposition

[1] A Commentary upon the Holy Writings of Job, David, and Solomon, &c., by John Mayer, Doctor in Divinity, London, 1653, p. 771.

[2] Macaulay, History of England, vol. i., p. 92.

on Ecclesiastes, which was published in London, 1654, two
years after the death of the author, by his fellow minister,
Dr. Tuckney.[1] Cotton maintains that *the design of this book is
to describe the corruption of all things, in order to bring us to
Christ, as pourtrayed in the Canticles.* This learned divine
submits that—

> The way to stir us up to seek after Christ is to behold and be convinced
> of the vanity of all things here below. When Eve brought forth Cain, she
> hoped she had got the promised seed (Gen. iv. 1 with iii. 15). But when
> she saw by his spirit and carriage that she was deceived in him, she called
> her next son Abel (Gen. iv. 2), which signifieth *vanity.* And *so* she must
> see all things to be before she bring forth Seth, the father of the promised
> seed. Now Abel, or *vanity,* expresseth the state of all the creatures by the
> fall. And Solomon taketh up Eve's word, and amplifieth it; *Vanity, yea
> vanity of vanities.* So this whole book is a commentary upon the state of cor-
> ruption (Rom. viii. 20). A fit introduction to Christ in the Canticles.

He, too, divides the book into two parts; the first part shews,
" that the chief good of the sons of men is not to be found in
all the creatures under the sun, nor in man's labours and ways
about them, for they are all vanity and vexation of spirit; and
the second part shews, that it is to be found in the fear of God
and the keeping of his commandments." Cotton's remarks upon
chap. i. 2, which contains the argument of the first part of the
book, is a literary curiosity, and shews how successfully the
hair-splitting logic of the old country was transplanted into the
New World.

> Chap. i. 2, *Vanity of vanities, &c.*—Here is set forth—
>
> i. The condition of all things, by the adjunct of *vanity, all is vanity;* and
> this is amplified by many ornaments of rhetoric.
> 1. *An hyperbole,* VANITY ITSELF; for, Vain.
> 2. *Polyptoton,* VANITY OF VANITIES.
> 3. *Epizeuxis,* (the like sound continued in the same sentence,) VANITY
> OF VANITIES.

[1] A brief exposition, with practical observations, upon the whole book of
Ecclesiastes, by John Cotton. Published by Anthony Tuckney, D.D., Master of
St. John's College in Cambridge, London, 1654. Second impression, corrected,
London, 1657, is the edition we have used.

4. *Anadiplosis*, (the same sound repeated in the end of one sentence, and the beginning of the other,) VANITY OF VANITIES, VANITY, &c.

5. *Epanalepsis*, (the same sound repeated in the beginning of the sentence, and in the end,) VANITY, &c., ALL IS VANITY.

6. *Anaphora*, (the same sound repeated in the beginning of the sentences,) VANITY, &c., VANITY, &c.

7. *Epistrophe*, (the same sound repeated in the end of the sentences,) OF VANITIES, &c., OF VANITIES.

8. *Epanodos*, (the same sound repeated in the beginning and midst, in the midst and end,) VANITY, VANITY, VANITY.

9. *Numerus oratorious*, (the same number of syllables repeated in both sentences,) VANITY OF VANITIES, VANITY OF VANITIES.

10. *Climax*, (the same sound continued and increased by degrees,) VANITY OF VANITIES, VANITY OF VANITIES, &c.

11. *Paranomasia*, (the repeating of like sounds, yet somewhat different.)

ii. This confirmed by the testimony of Coheleth, saith the Preacher.

1655. — John Richardson, bishop of Ardagh, who furnished the notes on Ezekiel, Daniel, and the Minor Prophets, for *the second* edition of the Assembly's Annotations,[1] published in 1655 a volume of " Choice Observations and Explanations " upon the entire Old Testament, " containing in them," as he modestly tells us, " many remarkable matters, either not taken notice of or mistaken by most," which he intended as " Additionals to the large Annotations made by some of the Assembly of Divines."[2]   But, notwithstanding the promises made on the title-page, as far as Ecclesiastes is concerned, this prelate simply repeats what Bishop Reynolds has said in the Assembly's Annotations, which it pretends to supplement.

1657. — Twelve months after the appearance of the preceding works, Sir Edward Leigh, the well-known author of the Critica Sacra, and Annotations on the New Testament, issued a thin folio of annotations on the five poetical books of the Old Testament, viz., Job, Psalms, Proverbs, Ecclesiastes, and

[1] *Vide supra*, p. 144, note 1.
[2] Choice Observations and Explanations upon the Old Testament, &c. London, 1655.

Canticles, " being encouraged in the publication thereof by the
epistle of a grave and reverend divine (John Trapp), who hath
honoured him with the patronage of a late learned work of his
that way." The baronet thinks that *the subject of this book is to
set forth the vanity of the creature in reference to the satisfaction
of the souls of men.* " God set up two great lights in Solomon's
heart, one shewing the excellency of Christ, in the Canticles,
the other, the vanity of the creature, as in Ecclesiastes."[1] It
will be remembered that Cotton propounds the same view.
Leigh's commentary only occupies twelve pages of the work,
and is necessarily very meagre.

1658. — Less pretentious, but more lucid, than Leigh's, is the
commentary of Arthur Jackson on Ecclesiastes, contained in his
annotations upon the same five books.[2] This Nonconformist
divine thoroughly espouses the view propounded by his predecessors, that *the book is Solomon's penitential dirge.* Though
Jackson has been anticipated by several English commentators,—
for he truly remarks, in his epistle to the reader, " When I first
undertook this work of writing these Annotations upon the
Scriptures, there was not, as I remember, any piece of this
kind extant in English, save only the Geneva marginal notes,"—
his commentary could not have been well spared at that
period, since it possesses several excellencies ; it is brief, and
generally very much to the purpose.

1659. — Dissatisfied with the method, hitherto adopted, of
vindicating Solomon from the heterodox sentiments contained in
this book, by either putting them into the mouth of infidels, or
by affirming that he entertained them prior to his repentance,
Dr. Gell saw no other alternative but to allegorise the difficult
passages. Hence, in his elaborate essay toward the emendation

[1] Annotations on the five poetical books of the Old Testament, &c., by Edward
Leigh. London, 1657, p. 157.
[2] Annotations upon the five books immediately following the historical part of
the Old Testament, commonly called the five doctrinal or poetical books, to wit,
the book of Job, the Psalms, the Proverbs, Ecclesiastes, and the Song of
Solomon, by Arthur Jackson. London, 1658.

of the authorised version, a folio of eight hundred and five pages, he thus explains —

Chap. ix. 9. — *Enjoy life with the wife which thou hast loved, &c.* — The wife here means our *memory and thoughts.* And an excellent portion it is *in this vain life,* that with our *wife,* our *memory and thoughts,* we may *see* and *enjoy* the *divine life,* and the *words of life,* and *keep the words of life in our heart and in our soul* all the days of our *vain life.* For unless thus, or in the like manner, the advice of Solomon be understood, a sensual Epicurean might make notable use of it, to confirm himself in his voluptuousness.[1]

Yet this essay displays great learning on the part of the author, and was so highly esteemed, that it was translated into German shortly after its appearance in England.

1660. — " The grave and reverend divine," Trapp, who encouraged Sir Edward Leigh to publish his volume on the poetical books, now issued a commentary on the same books himself. According to this Puritan divine, this book contains *Solomon's sapiential sermon of the sovereign good, and how to obtain to it.* " How many several opinions there were amongst them concerning *the chief good* in Solomon's days is uncertain; divers of these he confuteth in this book, and that from his own experience, the best school-dame."[2] This shews that Trapp resorted to the old expedient of putting the objectionable passages into the mouth of heretics, with which Gell was displeased. Both Trapp and Mayer published commentaries on the entire Bible; the former illustrates the meaning of Scripture by numerous anecdotes and parallels from profane history, whilst the latter gives a lucid digest of the opinions of those who have preceded him, in addition to his own judicious remarks. We could never understand why these commentaries have been allowed to become so extremely scarce, and modern expositions of a much inferior character to usurp their place.

---

[1] An Essay toward the Amendment of the last English translation of the Bible, by Robert Gell, D.D. London, 1659, pp. 642, 643.

[2] A Commentary upon the books of Proverbs, Ecclesiastes, and the Song of Songs, by John Trapp. London, 1660, p. 217.

1664.—The celebrated Cornelius Jansenius, bishop of Ypres,— whose immortal work, called *Augustinus,* inflicted such a wound on the Romish Church as neither the power nor wisdom of its pontiffs will ever be able to heal, — wrote a commentary on Ecclesiastes, which was published, together with his annotations on other portions of the Bible, in 1664, six years after the death of the author.[1]   After finding fault with Luther for denying the Solomonic authorship, the prelate maintains that *the design of the book is* as St. Gregory of Nyssa and St. Jerome have declared it, viz., *to incite us to contemn the world, and to raise our minds to the super-sensible.*[2]

1666. — Dr. John Smith, a member of the Royal College of Physicians, published in 1666[3] a very curious critico-anatomical treatise upon the six former verses of the twelfth chapter of Coheleth, in which he endeavours to shew that Solomon was thoroughly conversant with all the modern discoveries of anatomy, as well as with the circulation of the blood.   After describing the Harveian theory of the circulation, the Doctor remarks : —

This is the true doctrine of the excellency and motion of the blood, and of the use of the heart and the parts appertaining thereunto; all which were perfectly known to Solomon, as will abundantly appear anon, in the explication of the symptoms we are now about.   Yet it pleased the Lord that this knowledge should, with the possessor of it, sink into dust and darkness, where it lay buried for the space of two thousand five hundred years at the least, till it was retrieved thencefrom by the wisdom and industry of that incomparable and for ever to be renowned Dr. William Harvey, the greatest honour of our nation, and of all societies of which he was a member.[4]

The following is his analysis of the six verses : —

[1] Cornelii Jansenii Episcopi quondam Iprensis Analecta in Proverbia, Ecclesiasten Sapientiam, Habacuc, Sophoniam.   Lovanii, 1644, editio secunda, 1673.

[2] Scopus et argumentum totius libri est, ut breviter expressit S. Gregorius Nyssenus Serm. i. in Ecclesiasten, mentem suprà sensum attollere, hoc est, ut inquit Hieronymus ad contemptum mundi homines provocare, p. 117.

[3] The Portrait of Old Age, wherein is contained a sacred anatomy both of soul and body, and a perfect account of the infirmities of age incident to them both, by John Smith, of the College of Physicians.   London, 1666, third edition, 1752.

[4] Page 206.

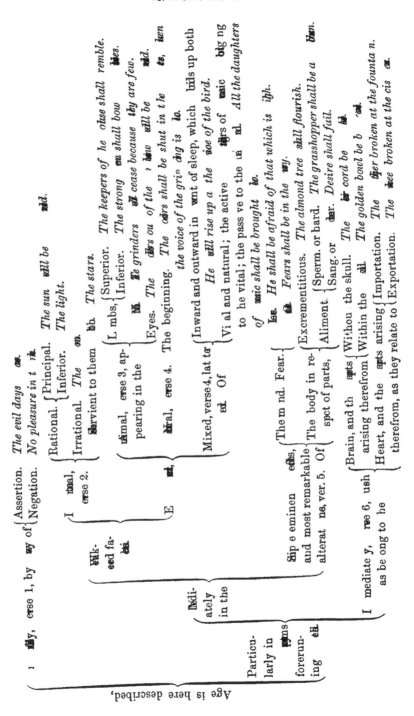

Pool, in whose house Dr. Smith died, thought so highly of this production that he introduced the substance of it into his Synopsis.

1680. — An anonymous commentary appeared in 1680, in London, which is unquestionably the most extraordinary production on Coheleth. *Solomon, we are told, in the all-penetrating spirit of true prophecy, discloses here the deep things of God's divinity, and the natural and spiritual things of the first and second creation, what each amounted to. He, like other awakened spiritual saints, infallibly prophesies or foretells what will become of any men or angels to eternity (as found rebelliously fixing in their first-creation life and state of vanity, or obediently surrendering it for the second) in eternal life or death.*

The following is a specimen of this commentary upon chapter iv. : —

VERSE 9. — *Two are better than one ; because they have a good reward for their labour.*

The birth of new creature life, in the true saint, makes, with his natural man, *the two that are better than one;* or than the natural man, single and alone, however perfect, *wise, strong, honourable, and glorious.* The natural man of the saint, is by his spiritual man (under and with the fountain-spirit of life in Christ) fetched up, by way of death and resurrection, into the everlasting life of the spiritual, in lieu of its fading natural. This completed, the whole person is spiritual. *I live, yet not I, but Christ in me,* says Paul (Gal. ii. 20). He had *the two, better than one;* he, and the Spirit of Christ. By the death of nature, as to its own law-life, and quickening of it up into Christ's gospel-life, the Spirit of Christ lives in the whole saint, and he in it, as his Ruler, Lord, and King. But man alone, in his own nature, however wise and righteous, will find himself at length not only destitute of, but in unchangeable enmity to, that spirit of Christ, in which alone any can be saved. The natural man, in his own uncrucified will and self-chosen course therein, remains single and alone, to his final ruin. The reason why the said *two are better than one* is, *because they have a good reward for their labour.* Man, fixed in his own life and way, and so in enmity to God; what reward can he expect but final wrath, as *the meet recompense of his error?* On the obedient death of nature (in which *it is impossible to please God* in anything) is man raised into that life of grace, in which it is as impossible not to please him in everything. *The reward* of this will be the full enjoyment and clear vision of God for ever.

VERSE 10. — *For if they fall, the one will lift up his fellow ; but woe to him that is alone when he falleth : for he hath not another to help him up.*

The gospel-spirit of Christ, in the saint, takes his whole natural man (partly crucified and partly not) into its care and protection. And so the fountain, gospel-spirit, in Christ himself, takes the whole man of the saint into its protection, under the covering shadow and cherishing influence of its *twofold cherubim-wings*, as also under the joint regard and care of his infinite and almighty Divinity. The saint is deeply concerned, in this case, when Christ has committed to him (set up in him, and entrusted him with, his unspeakable spiritual gift, or life) that unchangeable good thing, to recommit that and himself back again to Christ, for the nourishing, strengthening, and encouraging it, against all the counterworkings of his rebellious, and (in part) uncrucified natural mind or man, which will, to its last gasp, without any interruption, fight against God, and his spiritual mind. Till all the mystical nerves and bones thereof be cut asunder and broken, all the life and strength thereof utterly extinguished and abolished, is it a perpetual warrior against the spirit of Christ, in himself and saints. *Paul* found *this fleshly foe of his own house, this carnal mind of enmity,* about him, long after his gospel-conversion and true spiritual saintship (Rom. vii. 17, 23). On this he cries out, *O wretched man that I am, who shall deliver me from this body of death?* (v. 24.) This enemy within the saint, till fully run down into death, exposes him to frequent slips and sore miscarriages, as in *Solomon* and other saints has been evident. But, *that that is born of God,* in them, *and never sins, recovers their falling,* miscarrying *natural man,* or spirit (by a gradual and at length total death-work thereof, upon it) into harmony with itself, Christ, and God most high, in *a newness of life,* for evermore. *This war of spirit against flesh* (Gal. v. 17), is not finished but by the total death of *the fleshly mind.* *Flesh* will not leave off fighting till dead, and therefore ought not spirit (or the spiritual man in the saint) to leave off fighting while anything of life is left in it. The continually sinning natural spirit, till fully crucified, will, in the course of its own will, need *daily forgiveness, as well as an offending brother,* even to *seventy times seven* (Matt. xviii. 21, 22). Through the *propitiatory, covering mercy-seat,* which spiritual life brings the saints under, God so looks on his obedient spiritual man, as not to impute to him the daily sins of his natural man (Rom. iv. 7, 8). Thus is the spiritual man also under Christ *as a covering shadow* to the natural, in the same person, and qualified *to help up* or recover it *out of all its* failings and *backsliding steps.* The spiritual man, under the holy anointing, is to the, decayed, *old, grey-headed,* crucified natural, *the fresh oil* David *prayed for* (Ps. lxxi. 9, 18), that gives a new verdure and fresh lustre to the whole person of the saint — *a glory that excels and remains* for ever. Thus, on all accounts, to wit, the sins of the guilty natural spirit (or the mystical *grey hairs,* decays, *old age* and death, brought upon it by the demolishing, crucifying-work of Christ and the spiritual, as its only cure) the spiritual is ready at hand *to help it up* out of all falls in his lifetime, and out of that grave or death that extinguishes all power of sinning or falling in him. Christ and the spiritual man fetch him up into an everlasting harmony with them, in their *newness of life.*

T. — *But woe to him that is alone when he falleth ; for he hath not another to help him up.*

Here is the deplorable condition of all fixed in the life of nature, and so in unchangeable enmity to the spirit of grace, that is the only meet helper and lifter up of the natural spirit out of all its falls. Submitting to the death of the natural man is the only way by which the saint receives that spiritual life that can help it at all dead lifts out of its falls, and out of that death (that is the only cure of all evil in it) into its never-sinning life. When man chooses his fading creature-life before God's, and God, in judgment on him, gives him his choice, or *chooses his delusions* (Isa. lxvi. 4), who can help him up? *If God be against him, who can be for him?* Himself he cannot help. He is gone, then, on all hands. All that finally refuse the terms of receiving the spirit of grace reject it. And all that wilfully reject it *God will reject*, with all *their false confidences in their own. He will swear in wrath, they shall never enter into his rest.* What then can they say or do? or any other for them? who will or can help them up, when fallen under the final wrath of God?

VERSE 11. — *Again, if two lie together, then they have heat ; but how can one be warm alone ?*

The natural man of the saint receives light and warmth from the spiritual, as fast as baptised, transformed, and raised into a marriage-union with it in its life, and so made an equal yoke-fellow to it, under Christ's most easy and delightful yoke or government over both. As fast as the natural and spiritual man of the saint come to a right conjugal union, as *of twain made one new man*, the whole saint and Christ do lie in the intimate embraces of conjugal love, with mutual delight and satisfaction in one another, for ever. A most comfortable spiritual *warmth* and cherishing influence from Christ does the saint find in this mystical marriage-union with him, figured by the literal marriage-union (Eph. v. 22. 32). Christ and the saint are *one spirit; as man and wife, one flesh* (1 Cor. vi. 16, 17). *Christ is head to all saints,* and every saint; they *members of his mystical body, flesh, and bones.* So is Christ's spiritual state of life and headship, and saints' relation to him therein, expressed in the very words of the figurative literal headship and relation of the man to the woman. The marriage-union of the saint with Christ, and their mutual love therein, is indissoluble and everlasting, because founded in a spirit of everlasting righteousness and love. Saints are everlastingly subject, and most delightfully obedient to him; and he most delightfully kind to them beyond all words for ever.

1683. — Matthew Pool, however, returned to the old view, that *Solomon wrote this book in his old age, as a public testimony of his repentance and detestation of all those vain and wicked courses to which he had addicted himself, wherein he followed the example of his father David, who after his fall penned the fifty-first Psalm.* He also divides the book into two parts, viz., *negative* and *positive,* and accounts for the heterodox sentiments by saying "that Solomon speaks some and most things in his own name, but some other things in the name and according to the opinion of worldly and ungodly men."[1]

1691. — According to Sebastian Schmidt,[2] *the design of Coheleth, which is given in the twelfth chapter, is,* 1. *To call man away from the vain things of this life, wherein he centres his*

[1] Annotations upon the Holy Bible, &c., 2 vols. fol. London, 1683-1685, vol. i. Introduction to Ecclesiastes. These annotations, however, were not all written by this eminent Nonconformist; he died when he reached the fifty-ninth chapter of Isaiah. The following is a list of the several portions of the Bible, and the names of those who commented upon them :—

Genesis to Isaiah, i.-lviii.	} Matthew Pool.	
Isaiah lix. and lx.	} Mr. Jackson of Mousley, son of Arthur Jackson, and corrector of the first edition of Pool's Synopsis.	
Isaiah lxi.-lxvi. Jeremiah Lamentations	} Dr. Collins.	
Ezekiel Minor Prophets	} Mr. Hurst.	
Daniel	Mr. Cooper.	
Matthew Mark Luke John	} Dr. Collins.	
Acts	Mr. Vinke.	
Romans	Mr. Mayo.	
The Epistles to Corinthians Galatians	} Dr. Collins.	
Ephesians	Mr. Veal.	
Philippians Colossians	} Mr. Adams.	
Thessalonians	Mr. Barker.	
Timothy Titus Philemon	} Dr. Collins.	
Hebrews	} Mr. Obadiah Hughes.	
Of James Peter Jude	} Mr. Veal.	
John	Mr. Howe.	
Revelation	Dr. Collins.	

[2] *Scopus* hujus *libri* manifestè habetur in fine cap. xii. scilicet (1) avocare à vanitatibus quibuscunque hujus mundi, in quibus aliqua hominis beatitudo collocatur: cap. xii. 8 et (2) à variis autoribus profanis, qui ad vanam mundi beatitudinem deducunt extra scripturam sacram. ver. 12, tandem vero (3) adducere ad timorem Dei, observationem præceptorum ejus nominatim etiam in pio hujus mundi cum lætâ conscientia usu, judicii extremi meditationem, præmiumque sanctorum in altera vita, vers. pen. et ult. Commentarius in librum Solomonis regis, hebr. Koheleth, græc. et lat. Ecclesiastes dictum. Argentor. 1691. My edition is 1704.

happiness (xii. 8); 2. *From those profane teachers who lead him to indulge in the vain happiness of this world, contrary to the Sacred Scriptures* (verse 12); *and* 3. *To lead him to the fear of God and the keeping of his commandments* (13, 14).

Schmidt divides the book into *five* parts or sections ·[1]—

i. (Chap. i. 1), The title of the book, which, being so very short, can hardly be called a division.

ii. (Chap. i. 2 – iii. 12), wherein Solomon gives his exposition of true happiness; a. *negative*, by refuting that which is false, and centred in the things of this world without God (i. 2 – iii. 11), and b. *positive*, by shewing that it consists in the fear of God, and in the hope of a future life (iii. 12–14).

iii. (Chap. iii. 15 – iv. 16), wherein six examples are given from human life, through which man may be prevented from securing this highest good.

iv. (Chap. iv. 17 – xii. 8) gives lessons respecting the true service of God and a happy life, in fourteen rules of life.

v. (Chap. xii. 9 – 14), this last section gives the epilogue.

---

[1] *Partes Libri Ecclesiastæ* sunt *quinque.* i. *Titulus :* qui quidem adeo brevis, ut vix possit pars dici, cap. i. 1.·

ii. *Summi boni expositio :* per *summi boni falsi*, in rebus hujus mundi positi, extra Deum, *remotionem* à ver. 2, cap. i. ad cap. iii. 12, et *veri* simul in Deo et pietate alteram vitam sperante positi *insinuationem*, cap. iii. 12-14. Removetur falsum, *tum* asserendo falsitatem : *tum* probando, quia omnia in mundo vana sunt. Ubi I. Salomonis de vanitate totius mundi *propositio* sive *assertio*, cap. i. 2. II. *Ejusdem probatio* [sumta (1.) Ex conscientiæ humanæ compellatæ testimonio, ver. 3. (2.) À vanitatis rerum demonstratione : *tum* perpetuarum, ver. 4-7, *tum* transeuntium, laborisque omnis rerum, ver. 8-11, *tum* actionum atque laborum hominum, quæ *probatur* (1.) Autoritate Salomonis, ver. 12, 13. (2.) Explicatione vanitatis ipsius earum, quæ *duplex* est : *prior*, imperfectæ in se bonitatis, ver. 14, et prolixè exponitur à ver. 16, inclus. cap. i. usque ad cap. iii. 1, exclus. *posterior*, impossibilis sine Deo operationis, ver. 15, deduciturque à ver. 1, cap. iii. usque ad ver. 12 exclus.] à ver. 7, cap. i. usque ad cap. iii. 12 exclus.

iii. (Pars) *Monstratio sani Judicii* de variis in vita humana casibus, quibus offendi homo et ab amplexu expositi veri summi boni absterreri potest : quorum imprimis vi. sunt à ver. 15, inclus. cap. iii. usque ad cap. iv. 17 exclus.

iv. De *cultu Dei et beata* hoc in mundo *vita informatio :* constans doctrinis xiv. à ver. 17, inclus. cap. iv. usque ad cap. xii. 9 exclus.

v. *Ultima* est *Epilogus* à ver. 9 cap. xii. usque ad finem libri. — *Commentarius in librum Salomonis regis, &c.*, p. 11.

1694. — In 1694, more than forty years after the death of the author, appeared Alexander Nisbet's exposition on Ecclesiastes.[1] Nisbet was one of those Scotch divines who felt the want of a national commentary to represent the doctrines of their Church, and formed a plan to this effect with Mr. Robert Douglas, Mr. Rutherford, Mr. Robert Blair, Mr G. Hutcheson, Mr. James Ferguson, Mr. James Durham, Mr. John Smith, &c., all of whom had particular books allotted to them.[2] But the work was never completed. Mr. Warner, in his Epistle to the Reader, prefixed to Nisbet's commentary, accounts for its being published so long after the author's death. " It was perfected," says he, " and made ready for the press before his death, and had long since come abroad into the world, if it had not been for some assertions the author had upon chap. viii. 4, concerning obedience to supreme powers, which did not relish with the late times, wherein supremacy and absolute power were screwed up to the greatest height."

However, Biblical exegesis did not sustain any very great loss in consequence of this commentary being hid from the public for so many years, as will be seen from the view which Nisbet takes of Coheleth. *Solomon*, according to this Scotch divine, *being restored again, is Ecclesiastes, a penitent soul, preaching his repentance to the Church;* THE MESSIAH, *the true Solomon, who was known by the title,* SON OF DAVID, *is now speaking to the same by his type* " The scope of the Spirit of God, by this divine preacher, being to point out to miserable fallen man the way to recover his lost happiness, he doth *first* proceed *negatively*, to convince him wherein it cannot be found " (chap. i. 2 – iv. 12), and *second*, " gives directions for attaining to that true peace and quietness which is attainable in this life " (chap. vi. – xii. 14).

1700. — Bishop Patrick restricts the design of the book to

---

[1] An Exposition, with practical observations upon the book of Ecclesiastes. Edinburgh, 1694.

[2] Comp. Gillies, Hist., col. 1, 296.

what is said in chap. xii. 13, viz., *fear God, and keep his commandments*, this is the happiness of man, or the chief good. "The sense of the whole sermon, as we may call it," says this excellent prelate, "seems to be comprehended in this syllogism—

Whatsoever is vain and perishing cannot make man happy;
But all men's designs here in this world are vain and perishing;
Therefore they cannot, prosecuting such designs, make themselves happy."

The bishop, though agreeing with most of his predecessors that the book is to be divided into two parts, makes each part to consist of *six* chapters. He also maintains "that those words which seem to countenance men in the neglect of religion, and to open a gap to licentiousness, are only opinions which he intends to confute according to the method he had propounded to himself in this book. Wherein he first represents the various ends men drive at, which in the very entrance of it (that men might not mistake his meaning) he pronounces to be so vain, that he had no words significant enough to express their vanity; and then their different opinions about God and His providence, and their own souls." [1]

1701. — Maintaining that this book is a treatise upon the highest good, F. Yeard, dean of Achonry, was dissatisfied with the method hitherto pursued of making *Solomon* repeat the heterodox sentiments, and hence endeavoured to prove, in his paraphrase upon Ecclesiastes,[2] that *the preacher introduces a refined sensualist, or a sensual worldling, who interrupts him, in order to attack and ridicule his doctrine.* Of course, these impertinent interruptions and impudent mockeries, in which this sensualist indulges at the expense of no less a personage than King Solomon, are introduced and cut short whenever and wherever the Dean thinks it proper.

---

[1] A Critical Commentary and Paraphrase on the Old and New Testament, by Patrick, Lowth, Oswald, Whitby, and Lowman. 4 vols., London, 1848, vol. iii., pp. 112, 113.

[2] A paraphrase upon Ecclesiastes, &c., by F. Yeard, Dean of Achonry. London, 1701.

1703. — A decided approach towards developing the true design of Coheleth is to be seen in the treatise of Du Hamel. *The design of Ecclesiastes is,*[1] he says, *to collect the different opinions of men, and the different reflections whereby the mind is wont to be agitated concerning the end of the righteous and the wicked, and to set forth, at the conclusion of the book, what we ought to think respecting it. He says we should also hear the end of his discourse, viz., fear God and keep His commandments, for in this consists the whole duty of man, in this is every blessing, in this is happiness. This is the main object of the book; the other things are introduced, as it is generally done in a dissertation or disquisition, and are for the most part the opinions of the great mass of the people. He sometimes seems to assent to the opinions of others, but instantly refutes them, being fully convinced of this one thing, that happiness must be sought in God alone, that created things cannot render us happy, that they are vain and full of instability.*

1710. — As might be expected, Matthew Henry adheres to the old traditional view, which he expresses in his own quaint manner. *Ecclesiastes,* he tells us, *is a penitential and practical sermon, the text or doctrine is,* VANITY OF VANITIES, ALL IS VANITY (chap. i. 1); and the use and *application of it by way of exhortation is, that we are to* REMEMBER OUR CREATOR, TO FEAR HIM, AND TO KEEP HIS COMMANDMENTS. *The scope of the book is to shew that our happiness consists not in being as gods to ourselves, to* HAVE *what we will, and* DO *what we will, but in having him*

---

[1] Hoc Ecclesiastæ fuit propositum, ut varias hominum opiniones et varias quibus animus agitari solet cogitationes circa fines bonorum et malorum colligeret ac tandem quid sentiendum sit in calce libri proponeret. Finem, inquit, loquendi pariter audiamus, Deum time et mandata ejus observa, hoc est enim omnis homo, hoc est omne hominis bonum, hæc ejus felicitas. Ea est summa libri, reliqua instar dissertationis aut disquisitionis ac plerumque juxta vulgi sententiam proferuntur. Interdum aliorum opinionibus videtur assentiri, sed statim eas refellit; id unum omnino persuasus, felicitatem in Deo uno quæri oportere, res creatas nos beare non posse, vanas esse et inconstantiæ plenas. Salomon, ii., iii., cum annott. Rotomagi, 1703.

that made us to be a God to us.[1]   Like his predecessors, he divides this sermon into two parts, viz., a *negative* and *positive*, and puts the objectionable passages into the mouth of atheists and epicures.

1718. — Having experienced the vanity of all things, by being suddenly hurled from a high position of honour and trust to a state of degradation, the celebrated Matthew Prior betook himself, from a fellow-feeling, to write upon the adventures of the royal preacher, and produced the admirable poem, *Solomon on the Vanity of the World.*   With the poetic and literary merits of this production we have nothing to do.   That question has long since been decided by a far more competent and appropriate tribunal.   Our object is to give the author's idea of the design of the book.   Prior's opinion is, that *Solomon teaches us not to repine at the miseries of life, which are ordained by Omnipotence, and from which the richest, the wisest, and the greatest of men was not exempt, but to submit to God's providence, and cheerfully to look forward to death as a release from a life replete with vanities and miseries.*

The pleasures of life, says he, do not compensate for the miseries; age steals upon us unawares, and death, as the only cure of our ills, ought to be expected, but not feared.   This instruction is to be illustrated by the action of some great person.   Who, therefore, more proper for the business than Solomon himself? and why may he not be supposed now to repeat, what, we take for granted, he acted almost three thousand years since?   If, in the fair situation where this prince was placed, he was acquainted with sorrow; if, endowed with the greatest perfections of nature, and possessed of all the advantages of external condition, he could not find happiness; the rest of mankind may safely take the monarch's word for the truth of what he asserts.

Prior makes the whole poem a soliloquy, divided into three books; the first shewing the insufficiency of knowledge, the second of pleasure, and the third of power.   "Solomon is the person that speaks; he is at once the hero and the author; but

---

[1] An Exposition of the Old and New Testament, &c., by Matthew Henry, 3 vols.   London, 1828, vol. ii., p. 582.

he tells us very often what others say to him. Those chiefly introduced are his rabbis and philosophers in the first book, and his women with their attendants in the second ; with these sacred history mentions him to have conversed, as likewise with the angel brought down in the third book to help him out of his difficulties, or at least to teach him how to overcome them."

The following is the concluding advice given by the angel, and embodies the lesson of the whole : —

> Now, Solomon, remembering who thou art,
> Act through the remnant life a decent part ;
> Go forth, be strong; with patience and with care
> Perform and suffer ; to thyself severe,
> Gracious to others, thy desires suppressed,
> Diffused thy virtues, first of men, be best.
> Thy sum of duty let two words contain,
> O, may they graven in thy heart remain !
> Be humble, and be just.   The angel said :
> With upward speed his agile wings he spread,
> Whilst on the holy ground I prostrate lay,
> By various doubts impelled, or to obey
> Or to object ; at length (my mournful look
> Heavenward erect) determined thus I spoke ·
>   Supreme, all-wise, eternal Potentate !
> Sole Author, sole Disposer of our fate !
> Enthroned in light and immortality,
> Whom no man fully sees, and none can see '
> Original of Beings, Power Divine !
> Since that I live, and that I think, is thine ;
> Benign Creator ! let'thy plastic hand
> Dispose its own effect ; let thy command
> Restore, great Father, thy instructed son,
> And in my act may Thy great will be done.[1]

Thus Prior makes the remedy which this book yields for the ills and woes of this life, to consist in entire resignation to the will of God, and not in a future life, when all things shall be shewn to have worked together for our good. The poet, moreover, thinks that Ecclesiastes is not a regular and perfect treatise,

---

[1] See Prior's Poems, in Bohn's Cabinet Edition of the British Poets, vol. iii., pp. 62. 79.

but that in it great treasures are " heaped up together *in a confused magnificence.*"

1720. — More sober than the above production, and more consistent with the subject, is the commentary of Rambach, contained in the second volume of comments published by D. J. H. Michaelis.[1] As Rambach adopted the view and even the divisions of Sebastian Schmidt, we refer the reader to page 157, where we have given an analysis of his commentary.

1723. — The idea started by Luther, that Ecclesiastes is a sort of patch-work, has been espoused by Wachter, who, however, went far beyond the great Reformer, maintaining that *it consists of a medley of extracts from the different writings of Solomon, and that it is a hopeless task to search for any connection in translating it.* Accordingly, he remarks upon[2] —

Chap. i. 4. *One generation passeth away, &c.* — How this verse, as well as the three following, come here, is difficult to say ; I leave it to those to think about it who try to shew a most beautiful connection between all the sayings in this book. They believe that these furnish a few illustrations of vanity taken from nature, and that here is the first, namely, the perishing of generations   Now that a generation passes away, and is destroyed, may indeed be called vanity. But Solomon not only speaks of passing away, but also of *coming on,* of generations, and contemplates the *perpetuam successionem,* or the perpetual succession and constant continuation of the human race. That this continuance (since one generation is always joined to the other, as if they were all one generation which departs and returns,

[1] Uberiorum Adnotationum Philologico-exegeticarum in Hagiographos Vet. Testamenti Libros, vol. ii.   Halae, 1720.

[2] Wie dieser Vers samt den 3 folgenden hieher gehöre, ist schwer zu sagen, ich lasse die nachdencken, die die schönste Connexion aller Aussprüche in diesem Buche zeigen wollen.   Sie meynen, daß dieses einige Exempel der Eitelkeit in der Natur seyn, und zwar hier das erste, nehmlich der Untergang der Geschlechter. Allein, daß ein Geschlecht dahin und untergehet, ist wohl Eitelkeit zu nennen. Salomo aber redet nicht nur vom Hingehen, sondern auch vom Kommen des Geschlechtes, und siehet eigentlich auf die perpetuam successionem oder stete Folg und immerwährende Fortsetzung des Geschlechtes der Menschen.   Ob diese Beständigkeit, da immer ein Geschlechte am andern hanget, als wären sie ein Geschlechte, das weggehet und herkommet, wie die Sonne, Wind und Flüsse immerdar wiederkommen, eine Eitelkeit sey, kan ich mir nicht einbilden, und eben so wenig die Beständigkeit der Erden.—Der Prediger Salomo neu übersetzt mit Kurzen Anmerkungen von G(eorg) W(achter) Memmingen, 1723, pp. 3. 6. 10. 14.

just as the sun, wind, and rivers always return) should be vanity, I cannot imagine, and just as little can I imagine it of the continuance of the earth.

1726. — Calmet, like Bishop Patrick and others, restricts the design of the book to what is said in chap. xii. 13, 14. *This book,*[1] says this learned Benedictine monk, *may be considered as a discourse or harangue, wherein Solomon wishes to shew that everything in this world is only vanity and vexation of spirit, and that there is but one thing solid, one on which man may safely build, viz., the fear of God, the keeping of His commandments, and the expectation of a judgment.*

1727. — Dr. Edward Wells, so well known by his Sacred Geography, published the third volume of his paraphrase of the Old Testament, containing Ecclesiastes,[2] in 1727. He adopts Bishop Patrick's view, as well as his division of the book. Dr. Wells' production is a simple paraphrase of the bishop's commentary, as the former tells us himself in the introduction to the first volume. " Bishop Patrick's commentary being large, and consequently chargeable to be procured, I judged I might be of service to young students in divinity, who have not much to lay out in books, if what made the chief substance of the said bishop's commentary was reduced 'into a paraphrase." Dr. Wells has by no means improved upon the bishop's commentary ; we do not therefore wonder that, whilst his Sacred Geography has undergone several editions, and was even translated into German, his paraphrase is little known, and scarce.

1729. — More correct, though not entirely so, is the view

---

[1] On peut considérer cet ouvrage comme un discours ou une harangue, dans laquelle Salomon veut prouver, que tout ce qui est dans le monde n'est que vanité et qu'affliction d'esprit, qu'il n'y a qu'une seule chose de solide et sur laquelle l'homme puisse faire quelque fond : c'est sur la crainte de Dieu, sur l'observation de ses loix, sur l'attente de ses jugemens. — Commentaire literale sur la Bible, tom. v., Paris, 1726, p. 2.

[2] An Help for the more easy and clear understanding of the Holy Scriptures, being the books of Job, Psalms, Proverbs, Ecclesiastes, and Canticles. Oxford, 1727.

propounded by J. Hardouin, that *what Ecclesiastes inculcates from time to time, and to which all his maxims tend, is that the best,*[1] *the most quieting, the most innocent, the most happy thing for a man in this life is to enjoy himself with his family in his repasts; to be contented with the good he may have acquired by legitimate labour, and to recognise that to be able to do this is a gift of God, which must therefore be used with thankfulness; that in this as well as in all other things he might not forget that we shall be called to the judgment bar of God.*

1731.—The learned Le Clerc advances a new theory that[2] *Wisdom, who is the speaker in this, having gathered from the grave contemplations of human life, what is shunned and what is accomplished, pronounces by the mouth of Solomon what of this is vain.*

He makes no attempt to analyse the book, but prefixes to each chapter a brief summary of its contents. Thus he says that—

Chap. i. speaks of the emptiness of human wisdom.

ii. The emptiness of pleasure, wealth, wisdom, joy.

iii. The uncertainty of all things, the weakness of the human mind in things divine, the venality of human tribunals, the external resemblance between men and brutes.

iv. Solomon's view of oppression, of the envious, of the avaricious, and of senseless things.

v. Admonitions on the worship of God, vows, magistrates, riches.

vi. Accessory disadvantages of riches and the miseries of human life arising from disquietude; infirmities and ignorance of the human mind.

[1] Que le meilleur, c'est à dire, le plus tranquille, le plus innocent, le plus heureux, en cette vie, est de jouir soi-même avec sa famille dans ses repas, du bien qu'un travail légitime peut avoir acquis, et de reconnaître, que de le pouvoir faire, c'est un don de Dieu, dont il faut par conséquent user avec action de grâces. Qu'en cela enfin et en toutes autres choses, il ne faut point oublier que nous serons tous cités au jugement de Dieu. C'est ce que l'Ecclesiaste inculque de temps en temps et à quoi rendent toutes ses maximes.—Paraphrase de l'Ecclesiaste avec des remarques. Paris, 1729, Préface, p. 12.

[2] Eadem, nempe, sapientia quæ, è vitæ humanæ seria contemplatione, quid vitandum, quid faciendum sit colligit; eadem, inquam, sapientia omnibus pensitatis, rerum quarumvis hujus vitæ inanitatem, ore Salomonis, prædicat.—Veteris Testamenti libri Hagiographi, &c. Amstelædami, 1731, p. 677.

vii A good name, excessive joy, injustice, patience, the guise of evil
speakers, the corruption of men and especially of women.
viii. On reverence towards superiors, and Divine Providence.
ix. The innocent and the wicked are subjected to the same fate on
earth; death evaded by neither, whereby all hope is extinguished; events not in the power of men; the praise of wisdom.
x. The inconvenience of folly in all; in those who govern, in
works, in vain attempts, in sovereignties.
xi. Liberality in almsgiving, and the use of life.
xii. Remembrance of God in youth, the advancing disadvantages of
old age figuratively described, and death; all things empty
except the fear of God, who brings all to judgment.

1732. — Bauer, in his elaborate commentary,[1] assures us that
Coheleth has hitherto been entirely mistaken by those who
pretended to elucidate it; that *it contains Solomon's last and
solemn address, which he wrote down and delivered to the congregation of Israel after the flight of Jeroboam into Egypt, as
is evident from 1 Kings xi. 41,[2] that its purport is to exhibit the
doings of men here upon earth, and the infirmities and sins mixed
up therewith, and to shew how they may improve their works
under the sun,* and that it therefore treats upon the *summum
hominis officium,* GOOD WORKS, and not upon the *summum bonum,*
GOOD DAYS.[3] To this end Solomon, after the introduction

---

[1] Erläuterter Grund-Text vom Prediger Salomo. M. Christian Friedrich
Bauer. Leipzig, 1732.

[2] This proof he derives from *his* translation of the passage, which is — Und
weiter die Rede Salomonis, und alles, was er gethan hat, und seine Weißheit,
sind nicht diese geschrieben im Buche die Rede Salomonis. — *Ibid.*, p. 3.

[3] Sie handelt von Eitelkeiten, das ist von eitlen und üblen Verrichtungen der
Menschen, wobey er der Eitelkeit immer entgegen stellet, was gut, oder was
besser wäre, und die Menschen thun solten unter dem Himmel, die Zeit ihrer
Lebens-Tage über. Es ist dannenhero ein grosser Fehler, daß die Ausleger vom
Prediger Salomo nicht sorgfältig genug haben attendiren und bemercken wollen,
daß Salomo durch das Wort Eitelkeit verstehe das vereitelte Welt-Leben und die
menschlichen Fehler und Schwachheiten, nebst denen dahin gehörigen Vorur-
theilen; und daß er denen Eitelkeiten entgegen stelle אֲשֶׁר יִרְאֶה טוֹב ein solches
Gut, das sie thun sollen. Man hat nicht eingesehen, daß Salomo der Eitelkeit
entgegen stelle cap. ii. 3, summum hominum officium, so etwas gutes, das die
Menschen-Kinder thun und vor ihre vornehmste und beste That hatten solten, als
bey deren Ubung und Verrichtung es dem Menschen wohl und glücklich gehen
würde. Weil nun, nach der heydnischen Philosophie, summum bonum und

(i. 1 – 11), enumerates first his own doings, stating their faults and how he corrected them (i. 12 – iii. 15) ; he then proceeds to the various doings of others, shewing also their faults, and how they ought to be corrected (iii. 16 – xii. 8), and concludes by addressing himself to his son Rehoboam (xii. 9, &c.)

1734. — However, to the great annoyance of Bauer, which he had not even the power to conceal, all his protests against the wrong interpretations of others, and all his confident assertions about the correctness of his views, were of no use. Peter Hanssen, in spite of all, published a commentary shortly after, in opposition to Bauer, in which he gives the following analysis of the design of the book. 1. King Solomon made the basis of his contemplation the intrinsic value of human life, which he calls יתרון. 2. But he does not find it in human life as enjoyed in this world. 3. Hence he teaches that life in this world, when looked upon apart from eternity, has no value whatever, that it derives it entirely from the future (chap. iii. 11).[1] 4. To this end he puts הבל, or *vanity*,[2] everything which does

---

summum hominis officium lange nicht so nahe miteinander verwandt sind, als nach des Salomonis seiner weisen Einsicht, so ist man dahero auf die Meynung gerathen, wenn Salomo von Eitelkeiten rede, so verstehe er dadurch Unglücks= Fälle und Fatalitäten, durch welche man unglücklich würde, und das gute, so er den Eitelkeiten entgegen stelle, sey nicht summum hominis officium, sondern summum bonum, nicht was gut und löblich ist, daß man es thue, sondern was in diesem Leben nur zu geniessen gut wäre. Kurz, Salomo handele nicht von guten Wercken, sondern nur von guten Tagen, und denenselben stelle er Unglücks= Fälle und böse Tage als Eitelkeiten entegen. Da doch Salomo in diesem ganzen Prediger handelt von dem Thun der Menschen hier auf Erden, was bey solchem Thun sich vor Eitelkeiten finden, und was dargegen gut und besser wäre vor den Menschen und er thun solte unter der Sonnen, cap. i. 3. Wie denn wohl zu mercken, daß das Wort eitel, ingleichen Eitelkeit nach der Hebräischen Mund=Art von ganz besonderer Bedeutung ist, und sich bloß dem eitlen Leben und Wandel der Menschen beylegen lässet. —Erläuterter Grund=Text vom Prediger Salomo. M. Christian Friedrich Bauer. Leipzig, 1732, pp. 5, 6.

[1] Betrachtungen über den Prediger Salomo, &c., von Peter Hanssen. Lübeck, 1734. Zweite Auflage, 1744.

[2] 1. Der König hat den innerlichen Werth des menschlichen Lebens, welchen er Zithron nennet, zum Grund seiner Betrachtung gelegt. 2. Er findet ihn aber nicht in dem menschlichen Leben, wie es in dieser Welt genossen wird. 3. Daher lehret er, daß das Leben in dieser Welt, wenn man es ausser der Ewigkeit

not further our real happiness, in contrast with יתרון, and submits that, if there is no other life, all the inward and outward aspirations belong to the dominion of vanity. And whilst he demonstrates this by various arguments, he also teaches, 5. That although human life, apart from eternity, has no יתרון, it nevertheless has a טוב, or a certain kind of good; 6. This good man must seek to enjoy, but in such a way as not to interfere with the acquisition of the יתרון. 7. His first and last argument must be employed in behalf of the eternity in question, and the judgment through which we enter therein, and immediately obtain the יתרון. 8. And indeed man must prepare for it from his youth, that he may not miss this peculiar end of the present life. This constitutes the main import, which Solomon has interspersed with diverse salutary lessons, which are specially useful to rulers, and which he appears to have written chiefly for the use and admonition of his son and heir-apparent.

1748. — " The learned Dr. Gill" adopts the Rabbinical view, that *Solomon wrote this book in his old age, after his fall and recovery out of it, and when he was brought to true repentance for*

anfiehet, gar keinen Werth habe, sondern denselbigen allein aus dem Zukünftigen herleiten müsse, C. 3, 11. 4. Er sezt zu dem Ende dem Jithron das Hefel oder Eitele, so nichts zu unserer wahren Vollkommenheit beyträgt, entgegen, und behauptet, daß, wenn kein ander Leben nach diesem wäre, alle innerliche und äusserliche Empfindungen in dieses Reich der Eitelkeit gehören. Wie er nun dieses mit verschiedenen Gründen beweißt, so lehret er 5. Obgleich das menschliche Leben von der Ewigkeit abgesondert, kein Jithron hat, so komme ihm doch ein Tof oder eine gewisse Güte zu. 6. Diese Güte muß der Mensch zu geniessen suchen. Doch so, daß es an Erlangung des Jithron nicht hinderlich sey. 7. Sein erstes und leztes Augenmerk muß immer auf die bevorstehende Ewigkeit, und auf das Gericht, dadurch wir in selbige eingehen, und folglich das Jithron erlangen, gerichtet seyn. 8. Und zwar muß der Mensch sich von Jugend auf dazu anschicken, damit er dieses eigentlichen Endzwecks des gegenwärtigen Lebens nicht verfehlen möge. Wie nun dieses den Haupt-Inhalt aufmacht, so streuet Salomo allerley heilsame Lehren mit ein, die insonderheit den Regenten nüzlich sind, und welche er vornehmlich seinem Sohn und Cron-Erben zum Nuzen und zur Erinnerung scheint geschrieben zu haben. This quotation is made from Rabe's translation of Mendelssohn's commentary on Ecclesiastes, where the learned translator has reprinted Bauer's, Hanssen's, Desvoeux', and J. D. Michaelis' versions in four parallel columns, and has also given an analysis of their respective views of Coheleth.

it ; and that the general scope and design of it is to expose the
vanity of all worldly enjoyments, to shew that a man's happiness
does not lie in natural wisdom and knowledge, nor in worldly
wealth, nor in civil honour, power, and authority, nor in the mere
externals of religion ; but in the fear of God and the worship of
Him. It encourages men to a free use of the good things of life*
in a moderate way, with thankfulness to God ; to submit with
cheerfulness to adverse dispensations of Providence ; to fear and
honour the king, to be dutiful to civil magistrates, and kind to the
poor ; to expect a future state and an awful judgment ; with many
other useful things.

It must not be supposed, however, that Gill deduces this design
from logically tracing the proper position which each verse
occupies with regard to the whole argument, and a rational
explanation of the text. His commentary chiefly consists of
heterogeneous spiritual explanations, and a medley of Rabbinical
quotations, which he frequently misunderstood. The following
specimens of his mode of interpretation and mistranslations of
the Rabbins will shew the correctness of these remarks : —

Chap. vii. 28. *One man among a thousand have I found.* — It is a great
rarity to find a good man, truly wise and gracious ; there are many that
walk in the broad way, and but few that find the strait gate and narrow
way, and are saved ; they are but as one to a thousand (see Jer. v. 1 ;
Matt. vii. 13, 14). Or rather, by this one of a thousand is meant the
Messiah, the Wisdom of God he sought for (verse 25), and now says he
found ; to whom he looked for peace, pardon, and atonement, under a sense
of his sins ; who is the messenger, an interpreter, one among a thousand ;
yea, who is the chiefest among ten thousands (Job xxxiii. 23 ; Cant. v. 10),
who is superior to angels and men, in the dignity of his person ; in the
perfection, purity, and holiness of his nature ; in the excellency of his
names ; in his offices and relations ; and in his concern in the affairs of
grace and salvation ; and who is to be found by every truly wise and
gracious soul that seeks him early and earnestly, in the word and ordinances,
under the illumination and direction of the blessed Spirit. ˙ If it is to be
understood of a mere man, I should think the sense was this : of all the
men that have been ensnared and taken by an adulterous woman, but one of
a thousand have I observed,—and perhaps Solomon has respect to himself,—
that was ever recovered out of her hands. *But a woman among all those*
have I not found : that is, among all the harlots and adulterous women I

ever knew or heard of, I never knew nor heard of one that was ever reclaimed from her evil ways, and reformed or became a chaste and virtuous woman ; he may have respect to the thousand women that were either his wives and concubines, and, among all these, he found not one that deserved the above character ; for this is not to be understood of women in general, for Solomon must have known that there have been good women in all ages, and perhaps more than men ; and that there were many in his days, though those with whom his more intimate acquaintance was were not such, which was his unhappiness ; and his criminal conversation with them is what he lamented and repented of. It may be interpreted thus, *One man, the Messiah, among all the sons of men have I found free from original sin ; but one woman among all the daughters of Eve I have not found clear of it.*

How revolting to our feelings, to say nothing of the gross violation of the laws of language, to make the one man be either " *a penitent that has been ensnared and taken by an adulterous woman,*" or " *the Messiah, among all the sons of men, free from original sin.*" We shall now give a few instances of his mistranslation of the Rabbins.

Chap. v. 8. *And there be higher than they.* — Gill here remarks, " Aben Ezra interprets it of the secret of the name of God, which he says is inexplicable." The following are Ibn Ezra's words :— דע כי יש שומר שרואה זה החמס ואיננו אחד רק הם רבים וכל אחד גבוה מעל גבוה ושומרים רבים לא ידע איש מספרם כי הם גבוהים על אלה שמעלתם איננו שוה והיודע סוד השם ידע כי גבוה מעל גבוה הם חמשים וחמשה ולא אוכל לפרש, *know that there is a watch who sees this oppression, and not one only, but there are many, and every one of them is higher than the other ; there are so many watches, that no man can know their number, for they rise higher than those whose degrees differ or vary ; and he who is acquainted with the mystery of the sacred name,* i. e., *with divinity, knows that the words* " *higher than the high*" *refer to the fifty-five angels, and I cannot explain it.*

V. 20. *For he shall not much remember the days of his life, &c.* — " Be they more or fewer as Jarchi," adds Gill. Now Jarchi, as he is erroneously called, says nothing of the sort; his words are כי לא הרבה ׳ שאין אורך ימים בעולם הזה ׳ יזכור את ימי חייו ׳ כי מעט הם ולא הרב׳ ולמה יטרח לאסוף הון יטרח בדבר העומד לו לעולם הבא בחייו:, " *for not many,*" *for life here is not long ;* or LITERALLY, *for there is no length of this in this world.* " *He shall remember the days of his life,*" *for they are few, and not many ; and why shall he toil to gather wealth ? let him rather labour in his life for that which will stand by him in the world to come.*

Gill's remark is evidently owing to his mistaking מעט ולא הרבה for *be they more or fewer.*

Upon the same verse Gill says, —

"Some, as Aben Ezra observes, and which he approves of, and is agreeably to the accents, render the words *if he* has *not much, he remembers the
days of his life*, if he has but little of the good things of this life, he
remembers how few his days are he has to live." Ibn Ezra's words are

כי לא יש מפרש אם לא יעמוד לו הטוב הרבה יכור את ימי חייו שדהתענג בהם ויש לו בזכירתם
שמחת לבב והנכון בעיני שהוא כן יכור כי לא הרבה ימי חייו ואת נוסף כמו ובא הארי ואת הדוב

" *If not.*" Some interpret it, *if happiness does not remain long with one, he
should remember the days of his life wherein he enjoyed himself, and he will
have joy of heart in the remembrance thereof. I, however, think that the
proper meaning is this, Let him remember that the days of his life are not
many, and that* את *is redundant, as in* " *And there came a lion and* (ואת) *a
bear*" (1 Sam. xvii. 34).

This misrepresentation of Ibn Ezra is all the more serious,
since it deprives this learned Rabbi of the honour of being the
first who gave the right construction of the text, and makes him
talk nonsense. These few specimens must suffice here.

Other errors quite as flagrant, or even more so, will be found
dispersed throughout the commentary, and are noticed in their
proper places. We have felt it a disagreeable duty to expose
these blunders, because Gill is regarded, along with Lightfoot,
as the oracle upon Rabbinical literature; and because many a
divine, who prefers devoting his time to the acquisition of some
profane language, rather than to the study of the original of the
Old Testament, from which he professes to teach the will of God,
looks up to Dr. Gill as his guide in Jewish matters.

1749. — The learned and eccentric William Whiston tells us [1]
that he wrote " *a very small dissertation on the book of Ecclesiastes,
to shew that it is a collection of Solomon's reflections about points
of the greatest consequence ; the most of them when he was a
religious man, in his first and last days ; but several of them
when he was irreligious and sceptical, during his amours and
idolatry. This book is not printed.*"

1751. — Grotius' criticisms on Ecclesiastes began at last to
produce their effect upon the Continent. We now find the

[1] Memoirs of the Life and Writings of William Whiston. London, 1749, p. 347.

learned John David Michaelis, so well known as the editor of and annotator on Lowth's Prælections on Hebrew Poetry, boldly maintaining that a prophet who lived after the Babylonish captivity wrote this book in the name of Solomon, in order that he might be able, in the person of so happy and wise a king, to philosophise all the more touchingly about the vanity of human happiness; and that the *design of Coheleth is to shew, in the first place, the great imperfections of the happiness of a man who is left to himself, and is separated from God* (chap. i. 1 – iv. 16), *and, secondly, to point out the means to a true and lasting enjoyment of this life* (chap. iv. 17 – xii. 14)

i. Solomon substantiates his main proposition (chap. i. 2), by shewing the transitoriness of pleasure sought in knowledge (3 – 14), the grief we experience at the discovery of imperfections which we cannot rectify (15 – 18), the insufficiency and fleetness of sensual pleasures (ii. 1 – 11), and our inability, with all our wisdom, to avoid meeting with the same fate as the brute (12 – 26), because of the unavoidable destinies which issue from the fixed course of the world (iii. 1 – 15), and from unavoidable misfortunes (iii. 16 - iv. 3), and because man uses his work, which ought to be a pastime, as a means to obtain fame and riches, and engages therein chiefly out of envy and jealousy (iv. 4 – 16).

ii. Whereupon he gives the directions for happiness: to be religious (iv. 17 – v. 6), not to be too uneasy through the evils which befall others (7, 8), to abstain from too great a love for money (9 – 12), to be cheerful and patient at the wickedness which the wisdom of God permits to take place, remembering our own sinfulness (vii.), to endure the injustice of government without rebellion (viii. - ix. 10), to use labour as a means for maintaining contentment, since it is mostly rewarded, as is evident from the example of a wise and foolish mode of government (11 – 18), continuing to encourage us to work (xi. 1 – 6),

---

[1] Poetischer Entwurf der Gedanken des Prediger=Buchs Salomons. Göttingen, 1751. Zweite Auflage, 1762.

with this restriction, however, that we are to enjoy the lawful
pleasures of life (7, 8), yet not to forget the changeableness of
all earthly things, or the fear of God (xi. 9 – xii. 7); then follows
the conclusion (8 – 14).

1753. — In England, too, the writings of Grotius aided the
progress of liberal criticism, as may be seen from the almost
unparalleled remarks of Bishop Lowth on Ecclesiastes. The
learned prelate says [1] —

> There is another didactic work of Solomon, entitled *Kohelet* (Eccle-
> siastes), or the Preacher; or rather, perhaps, Wisdom, the Preacher; the
> general tenor and style of which is very different from the book of
> Proverbs, though there are many detached sentiments and proverbs
> interspersed; for the whole work is uniform, and confined to one subject,
> namely, the vanity of the world exemplified by the experience of Solomon,
> who is introduced in the character of a person investigating a very difficult
> question — examining the arguments on either side, and at length disen-
> gaging himself from an anxious and doubtful disputation. It would be very
> difficult to distinguish the parts and arrangement of this production; the
> order of the subject and the connection of the arguments are involved in so
> much obscurity, that scarcely any two commentators have agreed concerning
> the plan of the work, and the accurate division of it into parts or sections.
> The truth is, the laws of methodical composition and arrangement were
> neither known by the Hebrews nor regarded in their didactic writings.
> They uniformly retained the old sententious manner; nor did they submit
> to method, even where the occasion appeared to demand it. The style of
> this work is, however, singular; the language is generally low, I might
> almost call it mean or vulgar; it is frequently loose, unconnected, approaching
> to the incorrectness of conversation; and possesses very little of the poetical
> character, even in the composition and structure of the periods — which
> peculiarity may possibly be accounted for from the nature of the subject.

Thus this refined scholar and acute critic believed that
Solomon was simply *introduced* or *personated* in this treatise,
and that *the language is low*, of course too low for the golden
age of Solomonic Hebrew, though the wary prelate chose not
to express it so.

1760. — As if to corroborate at once the remark of the foregoing

---

[1] Lectures on the Sacred Poetry of the Hebrews. Lecture xxiv., Gregory's
translation, third edition. London, 1835, pp. 270, 271.

writer, "that scarcely any two commentators have agreed concerning the plan of the book," the first exposition which appeared after the publication of that statement is a protest against all its predecessors. Thus Desvoeux maintains that *the author's design is to prove the immortality of the soul, or rather the necessity of another state after this life, from such arguments as may be afforded by reason and experience*,[1] and that it is upon this principle alone that this book can be understood and explained. He says —

The whole discourse may be reduced to three propositions, every one of which, when properly reflected upon, yields a strong proof of a future state of rewards and punishments. But it must be observed that, though in all reasonings two propositions must be apprehended by the mind in order to form any conclusion, yet it is not always necessary both should be expressed. When the second is so obvious, that it does in a manner obtrude itself upon the mind, as soon as the first is mentioned, or so certainly true that no man in his right senses can well question it, then a philosopher may, according to the strictest rules, and an orator generally does, leave it to be understood and supplied by the attentive reader or hearer; and this is what the logicians call an enthymeme. Now I hope this proposition, *human affairs are under the inspection and government of a wise, powerful, and infinitely perfect Being, who can never be supposed to act but agreeably to his attributes*, shall be easily granted to be one of those, which may be left unexpressed in a religious argument. Then let it be considered as the *minor* or second proposition of a syllogism, whereof any of the three we are going to mention is the *major* or first proposition; and I am much mistaken if the doctrine I look upon as being chiefly taught in this book, does not appear to be the regular consequence of such a syllogism. These three propositions, every one of which is attended with its proper apparatus of proofs and special observations, are the following: —

I. No labour or trouble of men in this world can ever be so profitable as to produce in them a lasting contentment, and thorough satisfaction of mind.

II. Earthly goods, and whatever we can acquire by our utmost trouble and labour in this world, are so far from making us lastingly happy, that they may be even looked on as real obstacles to our ease, quiet, and tranquillity.

---

[1] A Philosophical and Critical Essay on Ecclesiastes; wherein the author's design is stated; his doctrine vindicated; his method explained in an analytical paraphrase, annexed to a new version of the text from the Hebrew, &c., by A. V. Desvoeux. London, 1760, p. 79.

III. Men know not what is or is not truly advantageous to them, because they are either ignorant, or unmindful, of that which must come to pass after they are dead.

Therefore any one may conclude that there must be a state of true and solid happiness for men out of this world.

PROPOSITION I. — Chap. i. 2, 3.

Chap. Ver.

I. 4 – 11. First proof. — The course of nature.

12, &c. Second proof. — Men's occupations.

16 – 18. First Head. — Wisdom or philosophy.

II. 1, 2. Second Head. — Pleasure.

3 – 10. Both jointly.

11. General conclusion of the second proof.

A review of the second proof, with special conclusions relating to every particular therein mentioned, viz.,

12 – 17. I. Wisdom.

18 – 23. II. Riches.

24 – 26. III. Pleasure.

III. 1, &c. Third proof. — Inconstancy of men's will.

9. Conclusion of the third proof.

A review of the second and third proofs considered jointly, with special observations and corollaries.

10, 11. First observation. — God is inculpable.

12 – 15. Second observation. — God is the Author of whatever befalls us in this world.

16, 17. First corollary. — God shall redress all grievances.

18, 21. Second corollary. — God must be exalted, and man humbled.

22. Third corollary. — God alloweth men to enjoy the present.

IV. 1. Fourth proof. — Men's neglect of proper opportunities, evidenced in several instances, viz.,

1 – 3. I. Oppression.

4. II. Envy.

5, 6. III. Idleness.

7 – 12. IV. Avarice.

V. 13 – 9. V. Misapplication of esteem and regard.

N. B. — V. 1 – 9 is a digression, containing several admonitions, in order to prevent any misconstruction of the foregoing remarks.

10 – 12. VI. Expensive living.

PROPOSITION II. — Chap. v. 13.

V. 14 – 17. First proof. — Instability of riches.

Desvoeux's commentary is one of the most curious and elaborate productions on Ecclesiastes; it contains much valuable criticism, but the author is too rash in his emendations of the text, and too fond of forcing upon the sacred writer the most far-fetched interpretation, in order to establish his preconceived notions. The philological notes are distributed under different heads, without any regard to the order of chapters and verses; hence it is very difficult to find the comments upon the respective verses in this ill-arranged mass of singular learning.

1768. — A similar fate to that which induced Prior to write his poem on the vanity of the world, gave rise to another poetical paraphrase of Coheleth, which was published anonymously in 1768.[1] "The author (a Turkey merchant)," whose name is said to be Mr. Brodick, "was at Lisbon during the great earthquake, just then sitting in his night-gown and slippers. Before he could dress himself, part of the house he was in fell, and blocked him up. By this means his life was saved, for all who had run out were dashed to pieces by the falling houses "[2] He saw all his property swallowed up. Some time after his arrival in England, he lost his eyesight, when her Majesty was pleased to make him pensioner in the Charter House, where he died, January, 1795.

Brodick entirely espouses the traditional view that Solomon wrote this book in his old age, after having openly violated the laws of God. "The only atonement he could now make was to point out the rock on which he had split, to the end that future

---

[1] Coheleth, or the Royal Preacher, a Poetical Paraphrase of the Book of Ecclesiastes. Most humbly inscribed to the King. Printed for J. Wallis, at Yorick's Head, Ludgate Street, 1768. Reprinted, with supplementary notes, by Nathaniel Higgins, at Whitchurch, Salop, 1824. This is the edition to which we refer.

[2] Wesley's Journals, Monday, Feb. 8, 1768, as quoted by Dr. Adam Clarke in his introduction to Ecclesiastes.

princes might take warning by his example. He therefore
thought it a duty incumbent on him to make his repentance as
public as his crimes, and to leave an eternal monument to
posterity that the wisest of men, when left to their own conduct,
are liable to the greatest failings; that a contempt of religion,
especially when princes set the example, always introduces a
general corruption of manners, and that those in the most
exalted stations, no less than those in the meanest, have occasion
enough to be reminded of their duty — in a word, that the
welfare or ruin of a nation depends, in great measure, on the
virtuous or vicious deportment of those who hold the reins of
government."[1] The subject of the book is *the chief or sovereign
good, which man, as a rational and accountable being, should here
propose to himself.* Brodick also, both in the division of the
book and in accounting for the difficult passages, follows his
predecessors. " Solomon," says he, " shews in the first place
what is *not* happiness, and then what it really is. He frequently
speaks, not according to his own sentiments, though he proposes
the thing in a naked and simple manner, designedly making
use of such terms as might set the picture in a fuller and clearer
light. . . . . We must therefore take particular care to
distinguish the doubts and objections of others from Solomon's
answers."

That Wesley should have seen such great originality in this
production as to lead him to say that " the author of it understands both the difficult expressions and the connection of the
whole better than any other either ancient or modern writer
whom I have seen," and that Adam Clarke should have
" *cordially subscribed* to Mr. Wesley's opinion," we must ascribe
to the peculiar warm-heartedness of our Wesleyan brethren,
which often manifests itself in hyperboles.

1770. — As the unfortunate Dr. Dodd, in his valuable commentary upon the Bible, adopts Desvoeux's view, we must refer
to page 179, where we have given an analysis of it.

[1] Introduction, p. xii.

1777. — Kleuker[1] maintains that the design of this book is neither *to teach the fear of God*,[2] as some affirm, nor *to set forth the vanity* of all earthly things,[3] as others will have it, but *to shew that the object, value, and cardinal duty of life are, that man should quietly pursue his course, do good as his hand finds it, and, instead of embittering his days under the sun, cheerfully eat and drink, and be contented with his labours during his transitory life, for this is his portion for all the trouble and toil which he has.*[4]

1778. — The interruption theory advanced by Dean Yeard found at last an eminent defender in the person of Herder. This refined poet and scholar says[5] —

There are two voices to be distinguished in this book; the one is of a subtle inquirer who searches after truth, and, in the tone of I, mostly concludes with, "All is vanity;" whilst the other, in the tone of Thou, frequently interrupts him, upbraids him with the temerity of his inquiry, and mostly concludes with, What will be the ultimate result of the whole life? There are indeed no proper questions and answers, doubts and solutions; but still a something proceeds out of one and the same mouth which resembles both, and is to be distinguished by interruptions and continuations. Hence the book may be divided into two columns,

[1] Salomonische Schriften: Erster Theil, welcher den Prediger enthält. Leipzig, 1777.

[2] Das „Fürchte Gott" ist nicht Hauptzweck des Buches, sondern bloß eine Schlußsumme und gleichsam ein Orakelspruch für die Praxis des Herzens, p. 9.

[3] Es ist nicht Endabsicht der Rede, dieses (die Eitelkeit alles Irdischen) und weiter Nichts zu lehren, sondern diese Empfindung ist nur Grundannahme zu höherem Ziel, chap. i. 2.

[4] Der Zweck, Werth und Cardinalpflicht des Lebens bestehet darin, daß der Mensch ruhig seinen Gang fortgeht, das Gute thut, wie seine Hand es findet, und statt sich seine Tage unter der Sonne zu verbittern, mit Freude isset und trinket und seiner Arbeit froh wird, in den Tagen seiner Vergänglichkeit, denn das ist sein Theil für alle Müh' und Arbeit, die er hat, p. 22. Elster's Commentar über den Prediger, p. 24.

[5] Es sind zwei Stimmen zu unterscheiden, die eine eines Grüblers, der Wahrheit sucht und in dem Ton seines Ichs meistens damit „ daß Alles eitel sei" endet, während eine andere Stimme, im Tone des Du, ihn oft unterbricht, ihm das Verwegene seiner Untersuchungen vorhält, und meistens damit endet: was zuletzt das Resultat des ganzen Lebens bleibe? Es ist nicht völlig Frage und Antwort, Zweifel und Auflösung, aber doch aus einem und demselben Munde Etwas, das beiden gleichet und sich durch Abbrüche und Fortsetzungen unterscheidet. Man kann das Buch also gleichsam in zwei Kolumnen theilen, davon die eine dem ermatteten Sucher, die zweite dem warnenden Lehrer gehöret.

the one belonging to the exhausted enquirer, and the other to the warning teacher—

THE ENQUIRER.	THE TEACHER.	THE ENQUIRER.	THE TEACHER.
i. 1 – 11.		vii. 1.	vii. 2 – 15.
i. 12 – 18.		vii. 16.	vii. 17 – 23.
ii. 1 – 11.		vii. 24 – 29.	
ii. 12 – 26.		viii. 1.	viii. 2 – 13.
iii. 1 – 15.		viii. 14 – 17.	
iii. 16 – 22.		ix. 1 – 3.	ix. 4 – 10.
iv. 1 – 16.		ix. 11 – 18.	
	iv. 17.	x. 1 – 3.	x. 4.
	v. 1 – 8.	x. 5 – 7.	x. 8 – 19.
v. 9 – 19.			x. 20.
vi. 1 – 11.			xi. 1 – 12.

As to the import of the book, Herder remarks [1] *I know no book of antiquity which describes the sum of human life, the vicissitudes and vanities in its occupations, projects, speculations, and pleasures, as well as that which is alone real, lasting, progressive, changeable, profitable therein, more fully, more impressively, and more concisely than Coheleth.*

1779.—It is rather remarkable that Eichhorn should have arrived at the same conclusion, independently of Herder. He regards this book *as a dialogue between a passionate inquirer and a calm teacher.*

There is evidently, says he,[2] an interchange of two different persons in the book. There is an observer or inquirer, who looks gloomily upon the life and destiny of man, and in his youthful warmth draws exaggerating conclusions from his observations, and seldom does justice to the good of

---

[1] Mir ist kein Buch aus dem Alterthume bekannt, welches die Summe des menschlichen Lebens, feine Abwechfelungen und Nichtigkeiten in Geschäften, Entwürfen, Speculationem und Vergnügen, zugleich mit dem, was einzig in ihm wahr, dauernd, fortgehend, wechselnd, lohnend ist, reicher, eindringlicher, kürzer beschriebe, als diefes.—Briefe über das theologische Studium; Elster's Commentar, pp. 18, 19.

[2] Es wechseln ganz offenbar zweierlei Personen in dem Buche ab, ein Betrachter, Beobachter, Forscher, der mit finsteren Blicken Leben und Schicksal der Menschen umfaßt und in jugendlicher Hitze die Folgerungen aus feinen Bemerkungen überspannt und dem Guten dieser Erde felten Gerechtigkeit wider= fahren läßt. Ihm zur Seite steht ein alter Weifer, der das Feuer des rafchen

this earth. By his side stands an aged sage, who assuages the fire of the hasty youth, leads him back to the path of truth which he has overstepped in the warmth of his temper, and shews him that evil has a good side. The former always concludes with the complaint that all is vanity, and the latter, with the inference which a sage will deduce from the course of the world.

THE ENQUIRER.	THE TEACHER.
Chap. i. – iv. 16.	Chap. iv. 17 – v. 11.
v. 12 – vi. 12.	vii. 1 – 14.
vii. 15.	vii. 16 – 22.
vii. 23 – 29.	viii. 1 – 8.
viii. 9 – ix. 6.	ix. 7 – 10.
ix. 11 – 18.	x. 1 – 4.
x. 5 – 7.	x. 8 – xii. 7.
The conclusion of the book	xii. 8 – 14.

1779. — Jacobi maintains that this book is intended to be *exclusively a guide for courtiers;* a fact which, he greatly deplores, has hitherto been overlooked. He says [1] —

The chief object of the writer is not to depict the life of men generally, although some features of it are alluded to, but to describe the life of those courtiers who do not find it their vocation to be idle and lazy, but to think, think profoundly, labour zealously, wearisomely, and anxiously, and deprive themselves of their best pleasures, and rarely obtain the object of their desire. The life of such persons, being that which he had experienced himself, he depicts with a master-hand, and gives the wisest and most wholesome lessons how such persons, who make their own life wearisome, may obtain peace of mind, and greatly enjoy the pleasures of life, which the benign Creator and Ruler of the world has bestowed upon them.

Jünglings mäßigt, ihn auf den Pfad der Wahrheit, über den er in der Hitze weggeschossen war, zurückführt und zeigt, wie auch das Böse seine gute Seite habe. Jener endigt immer mit der Klage, das Alles eitel sei und dieser mit den Folgerungen, die ein Weiser aus dem Lauf der Welt ziehen wird. Einleitung in das Alte Testament, iii., p. 648, &c.; Elster's Commentar, pp. 19, 20.

[1] Die Haupt-Absicht des Verfassers dieser Schrift ist nicht das allgemeine Leben der Menschen zu beschreiben, obgleich auch von selbigem ein und anderer Zug angebracht wird, sondern er schildert das Leben derjenigen Hofleute, welche ihren Beruf nicht im Müßiggange und Tändeln finden, sondern denken, weit hinaus denken, eifrig, mühsam, ängstlich wirken, sich des mehresten Vergnügens berauben, und den vorgesetzten Zweck ihrer Wünsche selten erreichen. Das Leben solcher Personen, welches er an sich und andern erfahren, schildert er mit

1784.—None of these views, however, could satisfy Döder·lein,[1] who submits that the author, who probably lived about the time of the Babylonish captivity, started the notion that this book was a prælection or treatise delivered by Solomon to his literary academy,[2] as *Coheleth* signifies such an academy; and that the *theme and main import of it is given in* chap. i. 2, 3, *and is repeated again in* xii. 8, *as the result of all the observations and discourses, namely, the vanity of all earthly things, which men prize so highly and labour for so arduously.*

It shews[3] the nothingness, or, as Luther puts it, the vanity, the perishableness, the instability, the defectiveness, the unsatisfactoriness found in the earthly things which man seeks, values, and toilsomely seizes; it proves that man does not find here below that which he strives after; that he cannot find it however much he may toil in the world, exert both mind and body, and spare neither trouble nor pain, because every earthly good is transitory, and the enjoyment of it is mingled with anxiety and uneasiness; that if earthly good, of whatever kind it be, is the end of man, and wearisome striving after it the means to obtain it, his trouble is thankless, useless, and profitless.

der Hand eines Meisters, und giebet die weisesten und heilsamsten Lehren, wie solche, sich selber das mühseeligste Leben schaffende Personen zur Ruhe des Geistes gelangen und die Vergnügungen des Lebens geniessen, weit besser geniessen könnten, die ihnen der gütige Schöpfer und Regierer der Welt gönnet.—Das von seinen Vorwürfen gerettete Prediger=Buch des Salomos. Zelle, 1779, pp. 10, 11.

[1] Salomons Prediger und hohes Lied neu übersetzt mit kurzen erläuternden Anmerkungen von D. Johann Christoph Döderlein. Jena, 1784.

[2] Wie es scheint, so erdichtet der Verfasser des Buches, daß dieß eine Vorlesung, oder eine Abhandlung sey, welche Salomo seiner gelehrten Akademie vorgelegt habe. Denn diese Akademie möchte ich unter dem Namen Koheleth, verstehen, pp. xv., xvi.

[3] Thema und Hauptinnhalt des Buches wird hier (K. i. 2, 3) angezeigt und K. xii. 8 als Resultat aller Betrachtungen und Discurse wiederhohlt. Es ist die Nichtigkeit oder, wie Luther sezt, die Eitelkeit, d. i. die Hinfälligkeit, der Unbestand, das Mangelhafte, das Nichtbefriedigende, das in den irrdischen Dingen, die der Mensch sucht, schäzt, mit Mühe hascht, angetroffen wird; es ist der Beweiß daß er hier das nicht finde, wornach er strebt, nicht finden könne, so sehr er sich auf der Welt plagt, beschäftigt, Geist und Körper anstrengt, und weder Mühe noch Schmerz scheut, weil jedes Erdengut flüchtig, der Genuß von jedem mit Gram und Unruh vermischt ist; daß wenn Erdengut, von welcher Art es auch sey, Endzweck, und mühsames Streben darnach Mittel ist, seine Mühe undankbar, vergebens, und unbelohnt seye, pp. 1, 2.

Döderlein divides the book into five sections, with a prologue and epilogue.   The following are his divisions : —

Prologue ... chap.	i.	1 _ 11	Section iv.	vi.	9 _ x. 1
Section i. chap.	i.	12 - 18	v.	x.	2 - xi. 6
ii.	ii.	1 - v. 8	vi.	xi.	7 - xii. 8
iii.	v.	9 - vi. 8	Conclusion ..	xii.	8 - 14.

1785. — Spohn, again, maintains that Coheleth is neither a continuous discourse nor a dialogue, but adopts the view of Grotius, that it is *a compilation of moral sentences*.   He says [1]—

As to the order and disposition according to which the author of Ecclesiastes arranged his thoughts, I affirm that he who seeks in it a logical disposition will not find it, in spite of all art.   It consists of moral maxims, which directly or indirectly promote true fear of God — maxims which call our attention to the wise government of God, to lead us thereby to repose firm confidence in God — maxims which draw our thoughts away from the world, and direct them to virtue.   In this way we can be cheerful, and enjoy the pleasures which the Creator offers us on all sides, in the midst of our wearisome labours and the perishableness of all earthly things.

The chief value of this elaborate commentary consists in the copious collation which it gives of the various readings of the Greek versions.   Spohn was, however, too fond of emendations, and frequently adopted other readings, simply because they differed from the received text.

1787. The confused commentary of Greenway, in England, forms a lamentable contrast to the last-mentioned scholarly production on the Continent.   Greenway's eccentric commentary

---

[1] Was die Einrichtung und Anlage, nach welcher der Verfasser des Predigers seine Ideen geordnet habe, betrift, so halte ich dafür, daß derjenige, der eine logikalische Disposition darinne suchet, bey aller Kunst, sie nicht finden wird. Es sind moralische Sätze, die näher oder entfernter wahre Gottes Verehrung befördern; Sätze, welche auf die weise Weltregierung Gottes aufmerksam machen, um dadurch zu einem festen Vertrauen gegen Gott geleitet zu werden; Sätze, die den Sinn von der Welt abziehen und auf Tugend hinlenken.   Auf dieser Weise können wir frölich seyn und Freuden, die der Schöpfer von allen Seiten darreicht, bey unsern Mühseligkeiten, bey der Hinfälligkeit aller irdischen Dinge genießen.   Der Prediger Salomo aus dem hebräischen aufs neue übersetzt und mit kritischen Anmerkungen, von M. Gottlieb Leberecht Spohn.   Leipzig, 1785, p. xxxvi.

consists of three parts, and was published at different times
the first part, containing chaps. ii., vii. 23 – 29, xi. 7 – 10, and
xii. 1 – 13, was published in 1781 ; the second part, containing
chaps. iii., iv., v., vi., and vii., has gone through three editions,
none of which bears a date ; the third part, containing chaps.
i., viii., ix., x., xi. 1 – 6, and xii. 14, with some desultory
" reflections and notes " on different portions of Scripture,
appeared in 1787. As to the design of the book, Greenway
adopts the patristic opinion, that " *it is a discourse, and that the
sum and substance of the observations and instructions delivered
therein is, that the present world, and everything belonging to it, is
mere vanity.*"

Some idea may be formed of the manner in which our author
has acquitted himself in this " New Translation, with a Paraphrase," from the following remarks, which he subjoined to the
first part : —

The translator considers the Hebrew text, as it appears in our printed
Bibles, merely as a translation ; the original text being the letters without
vowel points, without pauses, and even without any division into words.
He therefore thinks himself at liberty, whenever the context requires it,
either to read with different points, or to divide the letters differently into
words or sentences. He supposes himself, too, at liberty to read some sorts
of words either with or without a *Vau*, with or without a *Yod ;* for all
readers have seen and allowed the necessity of doing this in many instances,
and therefore it may be necessary in others, which they have not been
aware of. He has, too, now and then taken the liberty of applying that
common rule, *Literæ homogeneæ, sive unius organi facile inter se permutantur,*
where no application of it perhaps has been made before. And these are
all the liberties he has presumed to take, except he has in a single instance
supposed a word should be read with an *Aleph epentheticum,* as is done in
the present way of reading the text in many places.[1]

After this specimen, the reader will not be surprised to hear
that this commentary is rarely to be met with complete.

1790. — A more scholarly performance than Greenway's, is
the translation of Ecclesiastes which Dr. Hodgson, principal of

[1] Ecclesiastes, in three parts. A new Translation, with a Paraphrase. To
which is added a new Translation of other passages of Scripture, with notes and
reflections. Part i., p. 14.

Hereford College, Oxford, published in 1790.[1] It is to be regretted that the Doctor has studiously avoided any expression, in his critical notes, which might lead the reader to discover what his view was on the design of the book. The merits of his renderings and notes will be found discussed in the course of the commentary.

1793. — Biblical criticism had now made such progress on the Continent, that even the Roman Catholic Jahn found the sound laws of interpretation far more powerful than the teachings of the infallible Church. Hence, contrary to all tradition, he, like many Protestant commentators, affirmed that the language and import of Ecclesiastes *preclude the Solomonic authorship*,[2] and joined issue with Luther, in maintaining that the design of the book is *to teach men to repress their restless and eager efforts, which hurry them on in heaping up wealth, in securing pleasures, and acquiring honours ; and, at the same time, to instruct them not to increase the troubles of life, by denying themselves the enjoyment of harmless, though uncertain and fleeting pleasures.*

1794. — Similar to this is the view of Pfannkuche,[3] who says that *the design of the sacred writer is to recommend to the mind*

---

[1] Ecclesiastes; a new Translation from the original Hebrew, by Bernard Hodgson, LL.D., Principal of Hereford College, Oxford, 1790.

[2] Salomo spricht im ganzen Buche, da aber die Sprache und Schreibart dieses Weisen, wie sie in den Sprüchwörtern vorliegt, in unserm Buche nicht zu finden ist, sondern viele Chaldaismen und jüngere Worte vorkommen, so kann man schliessen, daß es von Salomo nicht herrühre. Dieses wird noch dadurch bestätigt, daß Salomo schwerlich so bitter über Unterdrückung, Ungerechtigkeit bei Gerichtsstellen, Erhebung der Thoren zu hohen Würden, &c., klagen konnte, wenn er nicht eine Satyre auf sich selbst machen wollte; auch bei Lebzeiten konnte er wohl nicht schreiben, ich war König in Jerusalem, noch bin König in Jerusalem, da dieses Jeder wußte. Der Verfasser muß also in jüngerer Zeit gelebt haben, nur hat er seine Beobachtungen dem weisen Könige in den Mund gelegt. Einleitung in die göttliche Bücher des Alten Bundes, § 214.

[3] Scriptorem totum in eo esse, ut animum de futuro securum, sorte quacunque contentum lætitiæque patentem tamquam bonorum in hac rerum inconstantia et fragilitate extremum, malorumque, quibus vita undique septa sit, lenimen præsentissimum prædicet atque commendet.—Exercitatt. in Ecclesiasten. Gotting., 1794, pp. 7, 8.

contentment with its lot, without anxiety for the future; and to be open to pleasure, as if it were the extreme of happiness, in the midst of the prevailing inconstancy and frailty of things; shewing the most efficacious means of mitigating the evils whereby life is surrounded on every side.

1794. — Simultaneous with Pfannkuche's commentary, appeared the small but elaborate work of John Ernest Christian Schmidt on Coheleth, wherein the learned author maintains, that *the design of this book is to prescribe laws to all human exertions, no matter what the object for which they are made, in order to keep them within proper limits, so that it may be regarded as the most beautiful commentary on the figure of the Greek Nemesis;* that Solomon was not its author; that it consists of twelve essays, written under different states of mind, and at different periods, and was not finished for publication; but is simply a sketch of a work which the author intended to work out at some future period. The following are the twelve essays : —

Essay i. chap. i. and ii.	Essay vii. chap. vi. 7 - vii. 10.
ii. iii.	viii. vii. 11 - 29.
iii. iv. 1 - 16.	ix. viii. 1 - 13.
iv. iv. 17 – v. 6.	x. viii. 14 - ix. 10.
v. v. 7 - 19.	xi. ix. 11 - x. 20,
vi. vi. 1 - 6.	xii. xi. 1 - xii. 7.

Epilogue, by a later hand, chap. xii. 8 - 14.[1]

1795. — Gaab thinks that *the design of this book is to teach us how to live cheerfully and contentedly, in the midst of all the imperfection and instability of our fate.*

This art, he says,[2] is not shewn to us in a strictly connected whole, but in a collection of single observations and sentences. Just as Canticles is a

---

1 Salomo's Prediger oder Koheleth's Lehren, von Johann Ernst Christian Schmidt. Gießen, 1794, pp. 23, 82, 100.

2 Der Zwek dieses Buchs ist, zu lehren, wie man bei aller Unvollkommenheit und Unbeständigkeit seiner Schiksaale dennoch froh und zufrieden leben könne. Diese Kunst wird aber nicht in einem streng zusammenhängenden Ganzen, sondern in einer Sammlung einzelner Betrachtungen und Sentenzen gezeigt;—so wie das Kantikum eine Kolleftion kleiner Gedichte, so ist der Prediger eine

collection of small poems, so Ecclesiastes is a collection of larger or smaller moral essays and admonitions. It is the production of some later writer, who perhaps lived after the Babylonish captivity, and had either no perfect command of the language, or wrote it in this book very incorrectly and negligently, and in the assumed person of Solomon ; just as Cicero, in his *De senectute*, spoke in the name of Cato, *ut majorem rem auctoritatem haberet oratio.*

1798. — The various theories hitherto advanced about the import and division of Coheleth sink into utter insignificance before the discoveries made by the learned and lynx-eyed Nachtigal. *This book*, he tells us,[1] *contains the investigations of several associations of literary men among the Israelites ; it contains propositions which at that time formed the limits of philosophic speculation, and which seem to have been proposed intentionally, to agitate and to explain doubts, and thus to develop the intellectual faculties.*

The book consists of the following parts, although not indicated by the Massorites : —

I. PROSAIC PARTS, or later additions and remarks, made by several classifiers, collators, and readers of this book. These are —

1. The superscription, i. 1.
2. The words, אָמְרָה קֹהֶלֶת, i. 2 ; vii. 27 ; xii. 8.
3. The additions at the end, xii. 8 _ 14.

II. POETICAL PARTS, constituting the chief portions of the book, and consisting of three kinds of poetry.

Kollektion größerer oder kleinerer moralischer Aufsätze und Ermahnungen. Er ist das Werk irgend eines späteren Schriftstellers, der vielleicht gar nach dem babylonischen Exil lebte, die Sprache entweder nicht ganz in seiner Gewalt hatte, oder sie wenigstens in dieser Schrift sehr inkorrekt und nachläßig schrieb, und in der angenommenen Person Salomos, wie Cicero bei seinem Schriftchen : de senectute in Catos sprach, ut majorem auctoritatem haberet oratio.—Beiträge zur Erklärung des sogenannten Hohenliebs, Koheleths und der Klaglieder von Professor Gaab.   Tübingen, 1795, pp. 48, 49.

1 Dieses Buch enthält die Forschungen mehrerer Versammlungen denkender Männer unter den Israeliten ; es enthält Sätze, die damals die Gränze der philosophischen Speculation waren, und die zum Theil absichtlich vorgelegt zu seyn scheinen, um Zweifel und Beleuchtung der Zweifel anzuregen, und so die Geisteskräfte zu entwickeln — Koheleth oder die Versammlung der Weisen, gewöhnlich genannt der Prediger Salomo's. Bearbeitet von J. C. C. Nachtigal. Halle, 1798, p. 67.

1. *Antiphonies*, *i. e.*, a poetical treatise upon one subject, made by different singers, who partly define more minutely the idea which constitutes the subject of conversation ; sometimes correcting the expressions of other singers, but mostly corroborating the main proposition in question, and exhibiting its different sides without intending to contradict.

The way in which these songs originated was perhaps this: the President of the society of the Israelitish sages rose and sang, "*Vanity, vanity, all is vanity!*" The assembly repeated this verse as a chorus. Thereby the key-note was struck which determined the subject of conversation for this session, and gave an impetus to further investigation. The president now sang the fleetness and changeableness in human life, and in nature generally ; and the assembly joined in at every pause with, *Vanity, vanity, all is vanity!* Another singer rose after the president, and sang in the name of Solomon, the most admired Jewish king, and who was considered as having had most of the enjoyments of this life, the vanity of all that is looked upon as happiness upon the earth, and of all human plans, and the assembly of singers, at appropriate places, animated the song with their accords. When this singer left off, or the ideas of the sentences belonging to him were exhausted, a third singer arose, then a fourth, then a fifth, &c., &c., &c. Each endeavoured to corroborate the same idea by some illustrations, to exhibit it in some different shade, and also to correct here and there the remarks of the other singers.

A careful comparison of these single sections will, it is to be hoped, convince every unprejudiced person that the different spirit which breathes in them, as well as the difference in the mode of treating the subject, *indicate different singers*, Compare, for instance, chap. i. 12 - ii. 26, with chap. iii. 1 - 8, 9 - 15, 16 - 22 ; chap. iv. 1 - 6, 7 - 9. The other antiphonies (viz., chap. v. 9 - vi. 9, and viii. 8 - x. 1), which are separated from the first (viz., chap. i. 2 - iv. 16) by proverbs, &c., &c., were most probably sung at other sittings of the same assembly of sages, or perhaps in similar assemblies of other Jewish sages, formed immediately after the first. The last group of antiphonies (chap. xi. 7 - xii. 7) is, in its main parts, treated differently from the others, and can hardly be ascribed, in its present form, to the same assembly of sages to whom the first three groups most probably belong.

Two things connected with these songs, and influencing their explanations and mode of treatment, still deserve to be noticed — 1. *Most of the singers in this book appear in the person of a philosopher of antiquity ;* compare, for example, i. 12 ; iii. 16 ; iv. 1. 7 ; v. 12 ; vi. 1 ; vii. 15 ; viii. 9. 16 ; ix. 11. Solomon, who is one of the sages here introduced, and who also appears in the Book of Wisdom, is easily recognised. The other sages we shall perhaps never know, owing to the want of historical identifications. 2. In many of these antiphonies, we notice a singular interweaving of ideas, which to us occidentals appear to be widely separated; comp. ii. 3, with ver. 1 ; ii. 9 with i. 16 ; ii. 18, 19, with 12, 13 ; iii. 11 - 14 with ii. 24 - 26.

2. *Maxims of the sages,* of which there are three collections in our book

1. chap. iv. 17 – v. 8.   2. chap. vi. 10 – vii. 2.   3. chap. x. 2 – xi. 6.

Some of these maxims are evidently connected together (only they are sometimes separated in the present recension of the original, *e. g.,* vii. 14, 18, 16, 17, 20) ; some even seem to have such a bearing to each other as the antiphonies, *i. e.,* are occasioned by the same idea, but expressed by different minds, and we may describe these as anti-maxims (Gegensprüche); as, for example, vii. 1 – 9 ; x. 16 – 19. Most of the maxims, however, are now so separated and isolated that all the exertions of commentators have failed to connect them with the other portions of the book. Several questions suggest themselves upon this point, *e. g.,* How did these maxims originate? What connection have they with the assembly of sages? What connection with the antiphonies? To what periods are they to be ascribed? or Do they belong to one period? &c., &c. We may perhaps assume that the making of such gnomes was assigned to a special sitting of the assembly of sages ; or that a few singers appeared with some maxims, after a group of antiphonies, as a relief ; or that the collator who collected and compiled the antiphonies sung in the assembly of Jewish sages, also found collections of maxims which partly belonged to the same sages, and connected with the others as one whole, because they indicated a similarity in composition and spirit. The second hypothesis will appear the most probable one, to one who regards the present arrangement of this book ; and the third, to one who has no regard for it.

3. *Hidden questions,* or *propositions and their solutions.* Of this mode of treatment, so common among the sages of the East, we have in this book only a small collection, namely, vii. 23 – viii. 7, where we find two hidden questions and their solution.

The following is Nachtigal's view of Coheleth : —

Superscription, chap. i. 1.

I. Antiphonies, chap. i. 2 - iv. 16

Chorus, chap. i. 2

1. (I. 1.) chap. i. 3 - 7	8. (II. 6.) chap. ii. 16,17	15. (V.) chap. iii. 16 - 22
2. (I. 2.) 8 - 11	9. (II. 7.) 18, 19	16. (VI) iv. 1 - 6
3. (II. I.) 12 - 15	10. (II. 8.) 20, 21	17. (VII.) 7 - 9
4. (II. 2.) 16 - 18	11. (II. 9.) 22, 23	18. (VIII.) 10 - 12
5. (II. 3.) ii. 1, 2	12. (II. 10.) 24 - 26	19. (IX.) 13 - 16
6. (II. 4.) 3 - 11	13. (III.) iii. 1 - 8	
7. (II 5.) 12 - 15	14. (IV.) 9 - 15	

II. Maxims of the sages, chap. iv. 17 - v. 8

1. chap. iv. 17   2 chap. v. 1 - 6   3. chap. v. 7, 8

III. Antiphonies, chap. v. 9 - vi. 9

1. chap. v. 9 - 11	3. chap. v. 17 - 19	5. chap. vi. 7 - 9
2. 12 - 16	4. vi. 1 - 6	

IV. Maxims of the sages, chap. vi. 10 - vii. 22

1. chap. vi. 10	8. chap. vii. 3, 4	15. chap. vii. 14
2. 10	9. 5, 6	16. 18
3. 11	10. 7, 8	17. 15
4. 11	11. 9	18. 16, 17
. 12	12. 10	19. 19
12	13. 11, 12	20. 20
5. vii. 1, 2	14. 13	21. 21, 22

V Obscure questions, and their solutions, chap. vii. 23 - viii. 7

    1. First Question, with six answers, chap. vii. 23 - viii. 1

    2. Second question, with two solutions, chap. viii. 1 - 7

VI. Antiphonies, chap. viii. 8 - x. 1.

1. chap. viii. 8 - 10	5. chap. ix. 1	9. chap. ix. 11, 12
2. 11 - 13	6. 2 - 4	10. 13 - x. 1
3. 14, 15	7. 4 - 6	
4. 16, 17	8. 7 - 10	

VII. Maxims of the sages, chap. x. 2 - xi. 6

1. chap. x. 2	8. chap. x. 11	15. chap. xi. 1
2. 3	9. 12 - 14	16. 2
3. 4	10. 14	17. 3
4. 5	11. 15	18. 4
5. 6, 7	12. 16, 17	19. 5
6. 8, 9	13. 18, 19	20. 6
7. 10	14. 20	

VIII. Antiphonies, chap. xi. 7 - xii. 7

1. chap. xi. 7 - 8	3. chap. xii. 1, 5
2. 9, 10	4. 6, 7

Prosaic additions, chap. xii. 8 - 14

1. chap. xii. 8	4. chap. xii 11	7. chap. xii. 12
2. 9	5. 12	8. 13, 14
3. 10	6. 12	

1802. — The third volume of Dr. Coke's commentary, containing Ecclesiastes, was published in 1802.[1] The commentary

---

[1] A Commentary on the Holy Bible. By Thomas Coke, LL. D., of the University of Oxford. London, 1802, vol. iii., p. 395, &c.

on this book, like that on all the other portions of the Bible, is
mostly a reprint of the unfortunate Dr. Dodd's work; and as
the latter adopted Desvoeux's view, that *the design of the book
is to prove the immortality of the soul, or rather the necessity of
another state after this life* (see p. 179), the former, of course,
also espoused it. We could never discover why Dr. Coke so
unceremoniously appropriated this work, except that he thought
it more to the glory of God that an exposition on the Bible
should have the name of a respectable Wesleyan doctor, rather
than that of a clergyman of the Church of England who had
died upon the scaffold.

1804. — The brief notes of Dr. Priestley on Ecclesiastes,
contained in the second volume of his notes on the Scriptures,
have the advantage of embodying in a little space the old view,
that *the object of the whole work is to shew the vanity of the
ordinary pursuits of mankind; in what the true enjoyment of life
consists; and the importance of having a constant respect to God,
and the laws that he has prescribed to us.*[1] We are, however,
surprised to find that this famous Unitarian doctor, who insisted
so much upon strictly literal and grammatical exposition and
criticism, should paraphrase —

Chap. iii. 21. *Who knoweth the spirit of man, &c.* — What difference is
there between the breath of life in man, and that which animates a beast,
except that the one breathes upwards, and the other downwards?

1813. — Though Adam Clarke has done nothing towards
elucidating the design of Coheleth, inasmuch as he adopts the
opinion of the Turkey merchant,[2] and of so many others besides,
that *the subject of the book is the chief or sovereign good, which
man, as a rational and accountable being, should here propose to
himself;* yet he has done good service in disputing two points
tenaciously held in England, viz., *the penitential character* of

---

[1] Notes on all the Books of Scripture, for the use of the pulpit and private
families, in four volumes. Northumberland, vol. ii., 1804, p. 279, &c.

[2] *Vide supra*, p. 183.

Solomon as described in this book, and *the purity of the diction.*
He says —

> I can by no means adopt the hypothesis, that the book was written by
> Solomon *after* he was restored from his grievous apostasy. This is an
> assumption that never was proved, and never can be. I must say, the
> *language* and *style* puzzle me not a little. *Chaldaisms* and *Syriasms* are
> certainly frequent in it, and not a few *Chaldee words* and terminations;
> and the style is such as may be seen in those writers who lived at or after
> the captivity. If these can be reconciled with the age of Solomon, I have
> no objection; but the attempts that have been made to deny this, and
> overthrow the evidence, are in my view often trifling, and generally
> ineffectual. That Solomon, son of David, might have been the *author* of the
> whole *matter* of this, and a *subsequent writer* put it in his own language, is a
> possible case; and, were this to be allowed, it would solve all difficulties.[1]

1818.—The view, that this book treats on *the sovereign good,* is
also entertained by Umbreit, in his commentary, which he characterises as *Coheleth, the wise king's struggles of the soul.*[2] The only
novelty about this production is the arbitrary way in which the
author transposes the text. According to him the order is this—

chap. i. 1 - v. 8	chap. x. 11	chap. ix.
viii. 2 - 19	vii. 7, 19	x. 1-3, 12-15,
vi. 1 - 12	viii. 1	4-7,16,19,18,
vii. 1 - 10, 13, 11	vii. 14, 15, 16, 20	8, 9, 17, 20
x. 10	17, 18, 21-29	xi.
vii. 12	viii. 14 - 17	xii.

Adopting this, he assures us we shall be all right.

1821. — We do not wonder that Dr. Ralph Wardlaw, in his
Lectures on the Book of Ecclesiastes, should still adhere to the
traditional opinion, that this book contains Solomon's repentance; that " *we behold him here, after a temporary apostasy
from the Lord God of Israel, ' confessing, and forsaking, and
finding mercy ;' we behold him returning from the broken and*

---

[1] The Holy Bible, with a commentary and critical notes. By Adam Clarke,
LL.D., F.S.A., &c. London, 1836, vol. iii., p. 2524.

[2] Das Buch welches in der Reihe der alttestamentlichen Schriften ben Namen
„Worte Koheleth's" trägt, behandelt kein andres Thema, als dieses: Was ist
des Menschen höchstes Gut? Koheleth's des weisen Königs Seelenkampf ober
philosophische Betrachtungen über das höchste Gut, von Friedrich Wilhelm Carl
Umbreit. Gotha, 1818, p. 10.

empty cisterns of the world to the Fountain of living water."[1]
Dr. Wardlaw does not pretend to be critical; and when he
does go out of his homiletic province, to correct the authorised
version, he is generally wrong.

1822. — But we are astonished that Mr. Holden, in his
elaborate work, should have altogether ignored the remark of
Dr. Adam Clarke, that *it never was and never can be proved*
that Solomon wrote this book *after* he was restored from his
grievous apostasy; and should still maintain, that " *when, by the
grace of that Almighty Being whom he had offended, Solomon was
made sensible of his transgression, he became a sincere penitent,
and published to the world the evidence of a broken and contrite
heart in the book of Ecclesiastes.*" [2]   He says —

The leading object of the Ecclesiastes is an inquiry into the Sovereign
Good, which the author conducts upon the plan of first proving what does
not constitute it, though too often regarded in that light by the folly of mankind; and, in the next place, shewing that it consists in Wisdom, or Religion,
which, for that reason, is highly extolled.   The book, in fact, may be
considered as designed to praise and recommend True Wisdom to the
observance of men, as the only real and permanent good.[3]

Mr. Holden, moreover, tells us, that Solomon has divided the
book *into two parts* and *thirty-three sections.*

PART I., which extends from i. 2 to vi. 9, is taken up in
demonstrating the vanity of all earthly conditions, occupations,
and pleasures, and consists of the following nineteen sections —

Sec. 1. The vanity of all earthly things   chap. i. 2
     2. The unprofitableness of human labour, and the
         transitoriness of human life   .   .   . i. 3 - 11
     3. The vanity of laborious inquiries into the ways and
         works of man   .   .   .   .   . i. 12 - 18
     4. Luxury and pleasure are only vanity and vexation
         of spirit .   .   .   .   .   . ii. 1 - 11

[1] Lectures on the Book of Ecclesiastes, by Ralph Wardlaw D.D., 2 vols.
Glasgow, 1821. Second edition, 1838, vol. i., p. 7.
[2] An Attempt to illustrate the Book of Ecclesiastes. By the Rev. George
Holden, M.A. London, 1822, p. lxxiv.
[3] *Ibid.*, p. lxxii.

PART II., which extends from vi. 10 to xii. 14, is occupied in eulogising wisdom; in describing its nature, its excellence, and its beneficial effects; and consists of the following fourteen sections : —

Mr. Holden's commentary is one of the best productions on
Ecclesiastes in our language.

1823. — The ordinary divergency of opinion is again relieved
by an extraordinary discovery of D. Gottlieb Philipp Christian
Kaiser, Professor in Erlangen.   He assures us that[1] *the lives of
the kings of the house of David, from Solomon down to Zedekiah,
are positively and plainly chronicled in this book in strict order,
a fact which not one of all the translators or commentators for
two thousand years has even as much as faintly dreamt of; that
the overthrow of the Jewish state is pragmatically balanced in it;
and that, through this historic key alone, is every chief difficulty
removed from the way of interpreting this book.*   Kaiser says[2] —

We have here an unknown kind of oriental poetry, an allegorico-
historico-didactic poem, which connects, in a veiled and collective manner,
the spirit of historic pragmatism of the Hebrews and Jews, and which

---

[1] Keiner der auf uns gekommenen Ueberseher und Ausleger, als solcher, seit
2,000 Jahren ahndete, daß in dem Buche das Leben der Davidischen Könige von
Salomo bis Zedekia in strenger Ordnung sehr klar und bestimmt gezeichnet,
der Umsturz des jüdischen Staates darin pragmatisch erwogen und durch diesen
historischen Schlüssel jede Haupt-Schwierigkeit der Auslegung beseitiget wird.—
Koheleth, das Collectivum der Davidischen Könige in Jerusalem, ein histo-
risches Lehrgedicht über den Umsturz des jüdischen Staates, von D. Gottlieb
Philipp Christian Kaiser.   Erlangen, 1823, p. v.

[2] Wir lernen vielmehr hier eine noch unbekannte Dichtungsart des Orients
kennen, ein allegorisch-historisches Lehrgedicht, welches verschleiert und collec-

gives us occasionally really important solutions of the secret history of the Jewish kings, *e.g.*, the conduct of Josiah towards the Egyptian king Necho. Moreover, through this key we also gain something in a dogmatic point of view, inasmuch as every stumbling-block disappears, and the author of Coheleth appears throughout consistently to attack unbelief and luxury; some of his remarks being ironical and satirical, as is evident from his calling the poem a satire in xii. 11.

Kaiser divides the book into sixteen sections —

Sec. 1. Contains the prologue . chap. i. 1 - 11
    2. The life of Solomon . . . . i. 12 - ii. 11
    3. Contains the complaint about Solomon's successors, Jeroboam, king of Israel, and Rehoboam and Abijam, kings of Judah . . . ii. 12 - 26
    4. The life of King Asa . . . . iii. 1 - 15
    5. The life of Jehoshaphat . . . . iii. 16 - 22
    6. The life of Jehoram . . . . iv. 1 - 6
    7. King Ahaziah and Queen Athaliah iv. 7 - 12
    8. Kings Joash and Amaziah . . . . iv. 13 - 16
    9. The life of Uzziah . . . . . iv. 17 - v. 19
    10. Contrast between Jotham and Ahaz, to the advantage of the former . . . . vi. 1 - 12
    11. Hezekiah, Manasseh, and Ammon . vii. 1 - 14
    12. Reflections on Josiah . . . . vii. 15 - viii. 13
    13. Gives the collective expression of the assembly with regard to the above-named sovereigns, especially with regard to Josiah and his successors, as well as the end of Jehoahaz viii. 14 - ix. 10
    14. The life and end of Jehoiakim . . . ix. 11 - x. 4
    15. Reign of Jehoiachin and Zedekiah . x. 5 - xi. 8
    16. Conclusion . . . . . . xi. 9 - xii. 14

The following specimen of Kaiser's interpretation of chap. iii. 16 – iv. 12, comprising the lives of three kings, will shew how he overcame the most difficult portion of this book : —

tivifch ben Geift bes hiftorifchen Pragmatismus ber Hebräer unb Juben concentrirt, unb hie unb ba wirflich wichtige auffchlüffe über bie geheime Gefchichte ber jübifchen Könige ertheilt, z. E. über bas Benehmen bes Jofia gegen ben egpptifchen König Necho. Dogmatifch fällt burch ben hiftorifchen Schlüffel auch aller Anftoß weg unb ber Verfaffer bes Koheleths bleibt fich in ber moralifchen Bekämpfung bes Unglaubens unb bes Luxus burch unb burch gleich; manche feiner Aeufferungen finb Jronie unb Perfiflage, wie er benn felbft fein Gebicht K. xii. 11 ein Spottgebicht nennt. Pp. xiii., xiv.

THE LIFE OF JEHOSHAPHAT, chap. iii. 16 - 22.

iii. 16. *And, moreover, I saw, &c.* — עוֹד is primarily *the infinitive*, and means *in returning, turning back, moreover.* It is here equivalent to שַׁבְתִּי, *I turned, I became a successor,* or *the kingdom turned, underwent a change in government,* vide infra, iv. 1, and the explanation thereupon. Jehoshaphat succeeded Asa in Judah.

Under the sun, i.e., in a kingdom; here it means in the dominion of the ten tribes, or of Israel, as Jehoshaphat lived at the time when Abab was king over Israel. Jezebel, Abab's idolatrous wife from Sidon, wrote false letters in the name of Abab, and got unprincipled boys, who gave false witness against Naboth, that he blasphemed God and the king. Whereupon Naboth was stoned, and Abab confiscated his vineyard (1 Kings xvi. 29, &c., xxi.) Then Elijah prophesied of Abab: "In the place where dogs licked the blood of Naboth, shall dogs lick thy blood, even thine;" and of Jezebel: "The dogs shall eat Jezebel by the wall of Jezreel." Both these were fulfilled. Jehoshaphat lived to see the tragical end of Abab, and took part in the war which the latter waged against the Syrians, and in which he perished, and Jehoshaphat escaped with great difficulty. Immediately after this war, in which Abab received the reward of unrighteous judgment and of unjust possessions, Jehoshaphat set up righteous judgment and judges in Israel, and said to the judges, "Take heed what ye do, for ye judge not for man, but for the Lord" (2 Chron. xix. 1 - 6).

17. *God shall judge, &c.* — This refers to the name Jehoshaphat, יְהוֹשָׁפָט, which signifies *Jehovah judges.* His name itself may also have reminded him of his duty to institute righteous judgment. NOMEN ET OMEN HABUIT. שָׁם, *there, i.e.,* in the place of judgment. There is no necessity, with Houbigant and Döderlein, to alter the reading.

18. *I said in my heart, &c.* — Are the sons of men (the rulers) beasts to themselves? do they make themselves beasts? The corpse of Jezebel, which was thrown down from the window and eaten by the dogs, became a נְבֵלָה, *carcase, a beast,* though she was the daughter of a king (2 Kings ix. 34). According to verse 37 of the same chapter, her carcase became "as dung upon the face of the field in the portion of Jezreel," referring to אִיזֶבֶל, which signifies *no dung.* Isaiah speaks with fearful earnestness of this circumstance (v. 23 - 25), and probably Ps. xlix., in which the word בְּהֵמָה is used of man (ver. 14), was composed on this event. Comp. also ver. 5; Ezra, viii. 29; Sirach xl. 3 - 8. The forty-ninth Psalm was copied for the sons of Korah; and at the time of Jehoshaphat they sang songs, according to 2 Chron. xx. 19. The eighty-fifth Psalm, too, was composed with reference to Jehoshaphat's upholding justice; comp. ver. 11 - 14.

19. מוֹתַר הָאָדָם מִן הַבְּהֵמָה אָיִן has rightly been rendered by Van der Palm, *neque de homine plus reliquum est (erat), quam de bestia.* It refers to the fact, that of the body of Jezebel, only the skull, hands, and feet were left. This historical reference does away with the dispute, whether the author could

have uttered in vexation anything which is dogmatically not true. He has simply narrated a historical event. In verses 21 and 22, however, he speaks ironically, in the name of a collective king, whose principles were not firm.

20, *All go to one place.* — Here, too, many have thought that it is asserted that everything is of dust, whereas it still refers to the history of Ahab and Jezebel, to which allusion is also made in Isa. v. 23 - 25, " which justify the wicked . . . . and their blossom shall-go up as *dust* . . . . their carcases are as dung in the midst of the streets." In this sense the word *dust* also occurs in the sequel, chap. xii. 7 (*i.e.*, as the extinction of the royal dignity); compare also 1 Kings xxi. 21, where the destruction of Ahab is spoken of.

21. *Who knoweth.* — Some have endeavoured to find epicurean sentiments in this verse, whereas the very reverse is what he taught The sense is: I (collective-king, not the author of this book) thought it sometimes uncertain, especially at this awful event, whether the spirit of man goes upwards (*i. e.*, to God), and has an advantage over the spirit of beasts. The author himself says the very reverse, in xii. 7.

22. *Wherefore I perceive.* — Therefore I thought that sensual pleasure is good, because no one could know what shall be after this life. This is again ironically spoken, respecting the unbelief of leaders who are the source of luxury.

THE LIFE OF JEHORAM, chap. iv. 1 - 6.

Chap. iv. 1. *And I turned.* — וְשַׁבְתִּי means, my dominion got another ruler (comp. 1 Kings ii. 15), the kingdom has changed hands (1 Chron. xi. 14. 23; and *supra*, ii. 20). Commentators incorrectly render it *adverbially*, i. e., *I considered again*, &c.

Oppression, &c. — Jehoram commenced his reign by killing his six brothers, to whom their father Jehoshaphat.had given fortified cities, 2 Chron. xxi. 1, &c.; 2 Kings, viii. 16, &c.

2. *And I praised, &c.* — שַׁבֵּחַ is a *verbal adjective*, construed with מִן, and denotes *esteemed happier;* the Sept. ἐπῄνεσα, better Symmachus ἐμακάρισα. Thus Crœsus exclaimed upon the stake, in the words of Solomon, " No one is to be esteemed happy before his death!" Plut. vit. Sol.

4. *Again I considered.* — קִנְאַת, *jealousy*, is fear for the rule of his brothers.

5. *The fool* (הַכְּסִיל) Jehoram also served idols. Besides, he was a fool because he entangled his own hands, that is, did not unite himself with his brethren. Comp. חָפַק iii. 5.

He ate his own flesh, that is, executed his own brothers. Compare Judges ix. 2, where a brother is called the *flesh* (בְּשָׂר) of his brother; and also the phrase, *to eat the flesh of a people*, Micah iii. 3. Relations by blood are called in Scripture the same flesh, because of their kindred stock.

6. *Better a handful, &c.* — Jehoram had nothing but travail and vexation of spirit and conscience by his bad earthly gain. The Edomites and Libnah

revolted against him ; the Philistines and the Bedouin Arabs took away all
his substance, his wives, and his sons, except Ahaziah ; and he died of a
loathsome and sore disease in his bowels, probably dysentery, and was not
buried in the sepulchre of the kings.

KING AHAZIAH AND QUEEN ATHALIAH, chap. iv. 7 – 12.

7. *And I turned, &c.* — A new vanity! a new misfortune in the kingdom!

8. *There is one, &c.* (אֶחָד וְאֵין שֵׁנִי). — Ahaziah was the only remaining son
of Jehoram ; Jehu raised himself to the throne of Israel, and not only killed
the King of Israel, but Ahaziah, also, who reigned only one year; and we
are told, in 2 Chron. xxii. 9, that none of the house of Ahaziah could again
become king ; comp. 2 Kings viii. 25.

He hath neither son nor brother (גַּם בֵּן וָאָח אֵין לוֹ). — Athaliah, the mother of
Ahaziah, destroyed all the seed-royal which remained in Judah ; no son, no
brother of Ahaziah could immediately succeed him ; his mother, Athaliah,
undertook the government.   However, a son of Ahaziah, twelve years old,
was secretly obtained.   But Ahaziah had no advantage from his restlessness,
wherewith he betook himself to the covenant with Israel, and the war with
the Syrians.

9. *Two are better than one.* — To preserve the royal family, a covenant
was made in the meantime.   Jehoiada, the high priest, took Jehoshabeath,
the sister of King Ahaziah, to wife; the same hid the child Joash, and
her husband made a covenant with — 1. The captains ; 2. The Levites
and priests, as well as the guards; 3. The heads of the families.   After
the ambitious woman, Athaliah, had reigned six years, the plan to put
Joash upon the throne was carried out.   The high priest received for it "*a
good reward*" throughout his life ; he was already ninety years old when he
carried out this plan, and reached the age of a hundred and thirty years,
and, out of gratitude, was buried among the kings (2 Chron. xxiv. 15, 16).

10. *For if they fall, &c.* — יָקִים, *to raise up*, is also used in the sense of
preserving, a ruler or generation (2 Sam. vii. 12).   וְאִילוֹ must be taken for
וְאִלּוּ, *and when ;* comp. 8 Codd. Kenn. and Buxtorf, Lex. Chald. Talm. et
Rabb., and *infra*, vi. 6 ; in this case the ה in הָאֶחָד will appear more appropriate, *i. e.*, *but if it should happen that the solitary one falls.*

11. *Again, if two lie together.* — This refers to the marriage of the aged
Jehoiada with the king's sister.   Commentators, not knowing this historical
sense, and in keeping with their finding general lessons throughout this
book, regard this as a commendation of married life, with which, however,
the following proverb does not at all agree.

12. *And if one prevail.* — A third portion of those who committed perjury
posted themselves in the Temple, another third beset the royal palace, and
another stood at the gate ; and the people were only allowed to be in the outer
courts.   Joash, who was hid in the Temple, was anointed; Athaliah, the
idolatrous Israelitish princess, was slain ; and the prince was led to the
palace and to the throne amidst the rejoicings of the people (2 Chron. xxiii.

2 Kings xi.) The throne was preserved for the rightful sovereign by the efforts of the high priest; but never did a high priest seat himself upon the throne in the time of the kings.

Notwithstanding the ingenuity and learning displayed by Kaiser, we do not think that he has ever succeeded in inducing any one to adopt his theory.

1826. — After tracing these ingenious conceits, it is cheering to come to Ewald, whose *four pages* on Coheleth, subjoined to his work on the Song of Solomon, contain more critical acumen, and a clearer view of the true design of this book, than many a bulky volume noticed in this sketch. He says[1] —

The author, who is utterly unknown to us, was a pious Israelite — as is evident from traces in this book — whose heart was greatly touched with the sufferings of his brethren, and who felt himself compelled to impart unto them his well-meant written counsel under these oppressions. But he had no practice in writing, and it seems as if this book was his first production, the style being so little developed and compressed, and there being so little connection in the flow of his thoughts. The words are never strictly measured; the author frequently expresses himself too strongly, in the heat of his discourse; he frequently does not carry through his thought, and only hints at what is in his mind, and thus continually struggles with his thoughts and words. Hence the first and greatest obscurity, which, however, disappears when we become thoroughly acquainted with the mind of the venerated author. The author lived after the exile (I suppose about

---

[1] Der uns völlig unbekannte Verfasser war, nach den Spuren seines Buchs zu schließen, ein frommer Israelit, dessen Herz bei den Leiden seiner Mitbrüder bewegt ward und der ihnen schriftlich seinen wohlmeinenden Rath für die Drangsale der Gegenwart mitzutheilen sich gedrungen fühlte. Aber im Schreiben war er wenig geübt; fast scheint er diese Schrift zuerst geschrieben zu haben: so wenig gebildet und gedrängt ist die Sprache und so wenig zusammenhängend der Fluß der Gedanken. Die Worte sind nie streng abgemessen; oft drückt der Verfasser eine Sentenz im Feuer der Rede zu stark aus, oft führt er den Gedanken nicht vollständig durch und deutet nur an, was in seinem Innern ist; und so kämpft er beständig mit seinen Gedanken und Worten. Daher die erste und größte Dunkelheit, die sich indeß hebt, wenn man sich mit dem Geiste des ehrwürdigen Verfassers ganz vertraut gemacht hat. Und dieser Verfasser lebte nach dem Exil (Nach meiner Vermuthung etwa 100 Jahr von Alexander), in einer kummervollen, Geist und Körper niederdrückenden Zeit, unter der Tyrannei übermüthiger Herrscher, umgeben von Verzweifelnden und Irrenden. Unter solchen Umständen lebte der fromme Verfasser. Er wollte das Unglück wenn nicht heben, doch lindern, indem er seinen Mitbrüdern heilsame Vorsichtsregeln für die gegenwärtige Schreckenszeit bietet. Er räth zur Geduld

a hundred years before Alexander), in a time of mental and bodily oppression, under the tyranny of overbearing rulers, and was surrounded by
desponding and erring people. He was therefore anxious, if not to remove,
at least *to mitigate their misfortunes, by offering salutary precautions to his
brethren for those fearful times. He recommends them patience and endurance,
caution and wisdom; he denounces rebellion and the expression of too liberal
sentiments; but, above all, he directs his readers to a sincere fear of God, and
to the thought that God will one day judge everything, and rectify that which
is perplexing here upon earth; he finally advises them not to despond over
their misfortunes, but to enjoy life with a cheerful heart and gratitude to
God, before old age approaches with all its infirmities.*

1827.—Henzius maintains that[1] *the sacred writer shews in this
book that course which weak man, who is unable to see through
the intricacies of human life, ought to pursue, that he may be
happy, in the midst of so much inconstancy and vanity as are
attached to all things. Being persuaded that God is supreme
ruler of the world, and that he provides with supreme wisdom for
the affairs of man, and hoping for the immortality of the soul, he
submits that we should enjoy and endure, with a pious resolution,
whatever blessings and evils this present life brings with it, as
ordained by God; and that we should endeavour, with every
effort, to keep the laws of God in our various conditions of life.*

und zum Ausharren, zur Vorsicht und Klugheit; er tadelt die Empörung und
zu freien Reden; vor allem aber leitet er seine Leser zu einer echten Furcht
Gottes und zu dem Gedanken, daß Gott einst alles richten und das auf Erden
Ungleiche ebnen werde; er empfiehlt endlich, sich der zu großen Bekümmerniß
über das gegenwärtige Unglück zu entschlagen, und lieber die Zeit des Lebens,
bevor das hohe Alter mit seinen Schwächen komme, froh und mit Dank gegen
Gott zu genießen.—Das Hohelied Salomo's übersetzt mit Einleitung, Anmerkungen nnd einem Anhang über den Prediger von Dr. Georg Heinrich August
Ewald, pp. 152, 153, 154. Göttingen, 1826.

[1] Agit auctor in hoc libro de ratione, quam homo debilis, qui vitæ humanæ
implicitas difficultates clare perspicere minime possit, sequi debeat, ut in omnium
rerum tanta inconstantia atque vanitate felix evadat. Persuasum sibi habens,
Deum O. M. summum esse mundi rectorem summaque sapientia humanis rebus
providere, animæ vero immortalitatem sperans tantum et verisimilem potius
ducens quam certam in hanc abit sententiam; pia mente fruenda esse atque
toleranda quæ præsens vita afferat bona et mala, tanquam a Deo immissa, sum-
meque contendendum, ut in omnibus vitæ conditionibus leges divinæ obser-
ventur.—Progr. quo libri Ecclesiastæ argumenti brevis adumbratio continetur.
Dorpat., 1827.

1830.—According to Rosenmüller,[1] the design of the book is *to propound the sovereign good, which consists in enjoying the present life with a tranquil mind, and in leading a virtuous and pious life, so as to please God.* Like many others, he divides the book into two parts; the first part (i. 2 – iv. 6) depicts *the vanity of all earthly things,* and the second (iv. 7 – xii. 7) shews *what man ought to do by this vanity,* to which is added an epilogue (xii. 8–14), giving a summary of the whole doctrine.

1831.—Köster submits that this book is[2] *an oriental lecture to young men on that which is permanent in the vanity of earthly things.*

He divides the book into four sections, with a prologue and epilogue:—

PROLOGUE (chap. i. 2-11).—Looking at the general vanity of earthly things, the question arises, What abiding thing has man? (ver. 2, 3) since generations come and go like the sun, wind, and rivers (4-7), and nothing really new takes place upon the earth (8-11).

SECTION I. (chap. i. 12-iii. 22) treats upon the question, What is best, considering the vanity of that which is earthly? Or, What is *absolute* good?

SECTION II. (iv. 1-vi. 12).—Which is the better of two opposite things? Or, What is *relative* good?

SECTION III. (vii. 1-ix. 16).—The true wisdom of life in general.

SECTION IV. (ix. 17-xii. 8).—The true wisdom of life in the particular conditions of life.

[1] Tum vero docet, summum bonum homini in eo ponendum esse, cum ut vitâ præsente animo tranquilo suaque sorte contento fruatur, tum, ut pietati et virtuti studeat, quo propitium sibi reddat summum numem.

Ecclesiastæ liber *duabus* potissimum partibus absolvitur, quarum *prior* (cap. i.-iv. 16) in demonstranda vanitate rerum mundanarum et humanæ inprimis vitæ versatur, atque pleraque quæ homines moliuntur studia inania et fluxa esse ostendit; *posterior* (cap. iv. 17-xii. 7) quidnam hominibus in hac vita inprimis spectandum studendumque sit docet, regulasque vitæ recte instituendæ vitiorumque cavendorum ex vitæ humanæ observatione tradit. Additur Epilogus (cap. xii. 8-14) qui et hujus libri usum commendat, et omnis in illo traditæ doctrinæ summam brevi complectitur.—Ern. Frid. Car. Rosenmülleri Scholia in Vetus Testamentum, Partis nonæ, volumen secundum. Lipsiæ, 1830, pp. 9. 10. 18.

[2] Eine morgenländische Rede an die Jugend, über das Bleibende in der Nichtigkeit der irdischen Dinge.—Das Buch Hiob und der Prediger Salomo's von Dr. Friedrich Burchard Köster. Schleswig, 1831, p. 113.

EPILOGUE (xii. 9 - 14). — The strivings of the Preacher to compile syste-
matically wise maxims both for himself and others (9 - 11). The young man
is therefore to follow these maxims only, and learn their main import
(12 - 14).

1836. — According to Knobel,[1] *the design of Coheleth is to
shew the nothingness of human life and efforts, and to impart and
inculcate directions relative to it.* He divides the book into
two parts, one *partial*, and the other *theoretical;* and, with the
caution that we must not be too strict in tracing a logical
sequence and plan, as the author was not very particular about
it, he gives the following analysis of its contents : —

PART I. THEORETICAL (i. 2 - iv. 16). — Coheleth begins with the theme
of the whole book, that all is vanity (i. 2), and then proposes the question,
What is the value of human efforts (3) ? But, instead of giving a direct
answer, he describes the permanent, fixed, unchangeable, and ever-returning
course of things, to shew that the efforts of man to affect the course of
things ordered and governed from above are ineffectual and vain (4 - 11).
He also expresses this view about things generally (14), and illustrates it
by two examples from his own experience, viz., striving after wisdom
(12 - 18), and exertion for pleasure, pronouncing both these kinds of human
efforts vain, because they cannot secure lasting good (chap. ii.) Whereupon
he explains himself further about the cause of this state of things : all
efforts are vain, because man is dependent upon time and circumstances,
which God has powerfully and unalterably ordered in a fixed course
(iii. 1 - 15). But perhaps moral and immoral efforts may have a certain
effect, and therefore they are not altogether vain, and if the effect is not in
this world, perhaps in that which is to come ? This, however, is doubtful
(iii. 16 - iv. 3). The main principle deduced from this fruitlessnes of human
efforts, thus established and traced to its origin, is, that we are not to be too
zealous in our efforts, nor be guilty of the contrary (4 - 12), since even our
best exertions are temporary in their result, and are soon forgotten, which
shews their vanity (iv. 13 - 16).
PART II. is PRACTICAL (iv. 17 - xii. 7), and shews how the conduct of
man ought to be regulated according to the above theory of life. It opens
with directions about the practice of religion, visiting the temple, sacrifice,
prayer, vows (iv. 17 - v. 6). To this are joined directions about gain,

[1] Demnach wollte Koheleth die Nichtigkeit des menschlichen Lebens und Strebens
nachweisen und eine darauf bezügliche Lebens-anweisung ertheilen und ein-
schärfen. — Commentar über das Buch Koheleth von August Knobel. Leipzig,
1836, p. 39.

enjoyment of earthly goods; he then speaks of covetousness and avarice; the advantage and disadvantage of earthly goods; the misfortunes which come upon man in consequence of wealth, wherewith he has not even been satisfied, or of which he can take away nothing when he dies, &c., &c. In short, earthly goods are the theme (v. 7–vi. 12). Hereupon follow directions about true wisdom and morality, contrasting therewith their opposites; moderate zeal, patience, contentment, and a conduct void of any impropriety whatsoever, are recommended; whilst sensual enjoyment, revelry, impatience, discontentment, and every sort of improper dealing, are repudiated. And lastly, he shews where immorality mostly abounds (vii. 1–29). To this are joined further directions about political conduct; every enterprise against the ruler is censured, because, if he is bad, he will be punished from above (viii. 1–15). Coheleth adheres for the present to the last thought, and treats, in a digression, upon the incomprehensible and unchangeable government of God, who lets the same thing happen to all men alike, so that no human efforts have those results which are calculated upon and expected (viii. 16–x. 3). Whereupon he returns to rulers, gives his opinion of them and their dealings, and proposes rules by which to regulate our conduct towards them (x. 4–20). The last practical directions are about benevolence, which is recommended (xi. 1–6). Having thus given us rules for all the exigencies of life, Coheleth inculcates once more very impressively the main principle, that we are cheerfully to enjoy life, but not without the fear of God (xi. 7–xii. 7), and repeats his theme (8).

Knobel's commentary is one of the most elaborate and thorough productions on Coheleth.

1837. — In his translation of Coheleth, Ewald had now an opportunity of developing somewhat more fully the opinion about the origin and design of this book, which he briefly had propounded in the appendix to the Song of Songs eleven years before, already noticed, p. 205. *The object of Coheleth*, according to him,[1] *is to admit cordially all that is true about the condition of his own times, and the limitedness of man generally, be it ever so bitter or sad; and also to discover that which is good, furthering, imperishable, as well as acceptable to the will of God, in the midst*

---

[1] Die Aufgabe war, alles Wahre über den Zustand jener Zeit und die Beschränktheit des Menschen überhaupt, und wäre es auch noch so bitter und schiene es noch so traurig, ganz der Wahrheit nach zugebend, dennoch das mitten im irdischen Wechsel, Unverlierbare so wie dem göttlichen Willen Angemessene zu erforschen und als das Wahre Gut des menschlichen Lebens klar zu bezeich=nen. — Sprüche Salomo's, Kohelet von Heinrich Ewald. Göttingen, 1837, p. 183.

*of earthly changeableness, instability, and suffering, and set it
clearly before us as the real good of human life.* He says —

As a new truth is here to be established in opposition to so many vain
views and efforts, Coheleth is introduced as seeking and discovering the
permanent good for man.   He advances certain truths respecting the
relation of things to God, and then compares therewith the different views
and efforts of men, and finds much that is vain and empty.   Though he
tries and investigates all things, turning indefatigably to every side of the
examination and perception, he does not the less strictly observe the great
deficiencies and faults of his own times, and causes the voice of dissatisfaction
and despair loudly to be heard about them.   But, dissatisfied therewith, and
seeking above all to impart peace and consolation, he quickly changes from
an observing inquirer into an instructing and counseling senior friend, and
to our great surprise advances the most beautiful maxims about caution
and patience, fidelity and thoughtful industry.   Not perfectly satisfied and
satisfying, however, even with these detached wise maxims and admonitions,
he at last concludes, from his observations, experiments, and researches,
that there is no other lasting good for man than serene joy in God,
comprising as it does everything else.

Ewald, like Köster, divides the book into four parts, or
discourses —

Discourse I. (i. 2 - ii. 26). — The speaker starts here simply with the
vanity of all worldly things, and glances at the historical experience of
Solomon.   This is the most sad and melancholy portion of the whole work.

Discourse II. (iii. 1 - vi. 9). — Here, too, he starts with the order of
worldly things, and establishes the main theme from the disturbances in the
then world, and begins already to intersperse it with soothing maxims.

Discourse III. (vi. 10 - viii. 15). — He also establishes the main theme,
from the inability of wisdom to solve the problems of life.

Discourse IV. (viii. 16 - xii. 8). — The main theme is now completely
finished, amidst references to the frequently despised wisdom, whereupon
follows immediately the undisturbed admonition to lay hold of this as the
demonstrated supreme and lasting good.

A Postscript (xii. 9 - 14) gives some explanations about the author and
the book.

Ewald's masterly translation and analysis of this book are
accompanied by a few meagre and comparatively unimportant
notes.

1838. — A very elaborate article on " The Philosophy of
Ecclesiastes," appeared in the American Biblical Repository for

1838, by Dr. Isaac Nordheimer, the well-known author of the critical grammar of the Hebrew language. He entertains a similar view of the book to that of Piscator (*vide supra*, p. 123), viz., that its *design is to ascertain and exhibit the obligations of man to himself, to his fellow-man, and to God.*[1] The Hebrew grammarian thus philosophises upon the object of the book : —

When the mind, intent on investigating all the relations of life, goes onwards in its activity, without first examining into and ascertaining its. own powers, in order thereby to regulate its demands and decisions, it is liable to fall into a scepticism whose effects on practical life are exceedingly hurtful. Thus, the man who has resolved to subject life to a rigid scrutiny; to ascertain with precision the obligations of man to himself, to his fellow-man, and to God; and to institute a minute inquiry into his future fate, with the view of adjusting his life and actions accordingly, may easily, in forming his conclusions, strike into a wrong path, which, instead of conducting him to the haven of contentment, may lead to his eternal destruction : unless he first resolves to ascertain the extent of the powers of his mind, that he may know what, as man, he may expect to attain, and then set bounds to his endeavours by selecting some definite object of pursuit. For, by entering thus unprepared on his examination of nature and life, whenever he met with the reverse of that which he had hoped to find true, or whenever he came to the knowledge of the many unaccountable contradictions and apparently inexplicable enigmas which exist in nature, in the fate of man, and in the relations of man to his Creator, he would either be induced to regard the world as a vale of misery, and consequently drag out his useless life in hopeless discontent ; or, disheartened by the constantly recurring obstacles to his progress presented by the revolving course of events, he would deny the existence of everything exalted in nature, and thus degrade himself to a level with the brutes. To set bounds to this sinful endeavour, and to warn mankind of the danger attendant upon it, appear to have been the principal aim of the author of this book. In order to execute his arduous undertaking in the most effectual manner possible, he adopted, and with great propriety, the Socratic, or sceptical method of induction. The main feature of this method consists in a suspension of the final decision until the truth has been rendered perfectly evident, and the writer has it in his power to make assertions that shall be incontrovertible; hence it is the most perfect mode of attaining absolute certainty that can be conceived. In this manner it is that the author of Ecclesiastes institutes his examination into the powers of the human mind, which he carries to such fearful lengths that reason itself threatens to totter from its throne. All this is done in order to test its strength, and to bound

---

[1] Biblical Repository, vol. xii., 1838, p. 197, *seq*.

its sphere of action accordingly, to the end that it may not run in danger, from the impossibility of comprehending the highest phenomena in nature, of introducing into practical life the errors which are the result of such imperfect conceptions. And at last he arrives at the conclusion, that as reason can know itself in the form of human reason alone, it is utterly unable to penetrate the ultimate designs of the Deity, or even all the secrets of his works in nature, viz., that it can never succeed in discovering all the hidden powers which are constantly at work in the world ; and that, consequently, man has no right to complain of the apparent contradictions he meets with, much less to suffer himself to be led by them into error?

Nordheimer intended this article to be an introduction to a new translation of Ecclesiastes, which, however, was never published.

1840. — More simple than the last-mentioned article, and more to the point, is the view which Steudel propounded, in the fourth supplement to his Prælections on the Theology of the Old Testament. He says [1] —

The design of the book is to shew that everything earthly is unstable and uncertain, and that we can therefore find no satisfaction in anything, or in any exertion which is exclusively regarded as the end of life ; that nothing earthly will shew to us the Supreme Ruler of all, as such, distributing the blessings of life according to a fixed plan perceptible to the human eye, so that man might thereby be guided what to do and what to leave, in order to secure something that is satisfactory and enduring ; that no striving after earthly good or enjoyment, the accomplishment of great works, or the acquisition of a good name, will lead him to that end ; and that the rule for

[1] Der Zweck des Buchs ist nach der gegebenen Inhaltsübersicht dieser. Es soll gezeigt werden: alles Irdische ist unstet und unsicher; eben darum kann in Nichts, in keinem Streben, das ausschließlich als Lebensziel festgehalten würde, Befriedigung gefunden werden. Durchaus nichts Irdisches ist, was uns den höchsten Lenker aller Dinge als einen solchen nachwiese, der nach festem, dem Menschen erkennbaren Plane des Lebens Glück vertheilt, so daß der Mensch hiernach sein Thun und Lassen einrichten könnte, um etwas Befriedigendes und Standhaltendes für sich zu gewinnen. Nicht Ringen nach irdischem Gut und Genuß, nicht Ringen nach dem Zustandebringen großer Werke, nicht Ringen nach gutem Namen führt ihn zum Ziele; es hat wohl jedes seinen Werth, und wer das eine oder das andere besitzt, ist je nach dessen innerem Werthe mehr oder minder besser daran, als der, welcher es entbehrt. Aber theils findet er doch nicht das Vollkommene darin; theils mag ein Anderer, der nicht so ängstlich darnach trachtet, es auch davon tragen; theils endlich kann es ihm auch unter den Händen entschwinden, und den gehofften Erfolg nicht für ihn haben. So ergibt sich als Regel für das Erdenleben, zu genießen, -- doch vorwurfsfrei zu

our earthly life is to enjoy, without contracting any blame, what God gives us to enjoy; to be active in the sphere of activity which God indicates, till enjoyment and activity gradually diminish by themselves, and terminate with death; that we are to look forward to a future judgment, where good and evil will be rewarded and punished, and regulate our conduct here accordingly.

1844. — De Wette's matured view of Coheleth is given in his last edition of the historical and critical introduction to the Old Testament. The doctrine of wisdom, he says, which Coheleth here propounds, is *the nothingness and uselessness of all things, and the reality of enjoyment alone.*[1]

The following is his analysis of the contents of the book : —

The main theme is, *All is vain and fruitless*	chap. i. 2, 3
Reasons for it —	
1. The aimless course of things	i. 4 - 11
2. The vanity of striving after wisdom	i. 12 - 18
3. The vanity of earthly enjoyment, and all the efforts to have it in connection with wisdom, although the gratification of desire has the highest value	ii. 1 - 26
4. The transitoriness and changeableness of all things, whereby gratification is again commended as the best thing	iii. 1 - 15
5. The prevalence of injustice and violence among men, since, without a future retribution, the end of man is like that of the beast; for this reason death is more to be desired than life, which, however, is to be enjoyed cheerfully	iii. 16 – iv. 3
6. The vain efforts and strivings of men, commendation of quietness, and society	iv. 4 - 12

genießen, was Gott zum Genusse darbietet, und thätig zu seyn, wie Gott den Kreis der Thätigkeit zuweist, bis Genuß und Thätigkeit sich mehr und mehr von selbst verbietet, und durch den Tod sich schließt. Uebrigens darf und soll hier der Blick auf ein Leben der Vergeltung gerichtet bleiben, wo Gott als den Gerechten sich rechtfertigen wird, auf welchen deßwegen unser ganzes Thun und Lassen stets gerichtet seyn muß. — Mithin empfiehlt das Buch in Bezug auf die Gegenwart die Kunst, mit weiser Resignation das Leben als ein dem Wechsel unterworfenes mit seinen Freuden und Leiden hinzunehmen und nach Kräften zu befruchten, die Vergeltung aber der Zukunft anheimzustellen, übrigens so zu leben daß man ihrer nicht mit Furcht gedenken müße. — Vorlesungen über die Theologie des Alten Testamentes von Dr. Joh. Christian Friedr. Steudel. Berlin, 1840, Beilage iv., pp. 524, 525.

[1] Lehrbuch der historisch-kritischen Einleitung in das Alte Testament. Berlin, 1852, § 283.

This, according to De Wette, is all that Coheleth teaches; he gives *no hope of a future existence*, and the view which he propounds of the present life inclines to fatalism, scepticism, and epicureanism, as may be seen from the following passage:—

The doctrine of retribution on earth, elevated by no hope of a future state, which constitutes its religious principle, had to contend with power-ful doubts, which the sad experience of life afforded, and which shew them-selves already in Proverbs (xxiv. 19), and more plainly in the Psalms (xxxvii., lxxiii.) Now, the more unhappy and hopeless the times became, the more faith and inspiration grew cold, the more powerful these doubts became, and thus they formed themselves at last into the view of life as propounded by Coheleth, which inclines to fatalism, scepticism, and epicureanism.[1]

[1] Die irdische, durch keine Hoffnung auf das Jenseits gehobene Vergel-tungslehre, welche das religiöse Princip derselben ausmachte, hatte mit mächtigen Zweifeln zu kämpfen, welche die unglückliche Erfahrung an die Hand gab, und die sich schon in den Sprüchwörtern (xxiv. 19), deutlicher Ps. xxxvii., lxxiii., regen. Je unglücklicher und trostloser nun die Zeiten wurden, je mehr der Glaube und die Begeisterung erkalteten, desto mächtiger wurden jene Zweifel; und so gestalteten sie sich zuletzt zu einer Lebensansicht, wie sie Koheleth vorträgt, die sich zum Fatalismus, Skepticismus und Epikureismus hinneigt (§ 282), which Steuart most grossly mistranslates: " The doctrine of *retribution*, which

1844. — Undeterred by the positive declarations of De Wette respecting the lowering character of this book, Lisco published the same year the second volume of his commentary on the Bible, containing Ecclesiastes, in which he maintains that the design of Coheleth is *to shew that a contented and cheerful enjoyment of life is the sum of human happiness upon earth, and that this is impossible without truly fearing God.*[1]

He divides the book into *eleven* parts —

Part 1. declares, *All is vanity* . chap. i. 1-11
2. proves it from the Preacher's own experience . i. 12-ii. 26
3. The vanity of all things recommends a cheerful enjoyment of life . . . . iii. 1-22
4. Further description of the vanity of earthly things iv. 1-16
5. Different lessons, All is vanity . . . iv. 17-vii. 1
    a. Man before God. iv. 17-v. 6.
    b. The folly of covetousness, v. 7-16.
    c. Hence cheerful enjoyment of life is best, v. 17-19.
    d. Unhappy is the discontented rich man, vi. 1-vii. 1.
6. That which is good and that which is better vii. 2-29
7. The wise conduct in various relations of life viii. 1-17
8. The incomprehensible government of God ix. 1-x. 3
9. Different admonitions how to conduct oneself x. 4-xi. 6
10. Enjoy life wisely . . . . . xi. 7-xii. 8
11. Concluding remark . . . . xii. 9-14

1845. — In 1845 appeared Mr. Preston's translation of Mendelssohn's commentary on Ecclesiastes, with additional

constitutes the religious element of the book, has many strong doubts to contend with, and these his own experience of misfortunes helped to supply. . . . . The more unhappy the times were, and the more they led to despair, the more also that belief and animation grew cold, the stronger did those doubts become; so that they finally shaped themselves into the ordinary system of *Epicureanism* joined with *Fatalism.* This the author of the book professes." Commentary on Ecclesiastes, p. 25.

[1] Zweck ist ihm die feste Begründung der Ansicht nud Ueberzeugung: Ein froher, heiterer Genuß des Lebens ist die Summe des menschlichen Glückes auf Erden, er ist aber ohne wahre Gottesfurcht nicht möglich.—Das Alte Testament mit Erklärungen, Einleitungen, Aufsätzen und Registern, von Friedrich Lisco. Zweiter Bund. Berlin, 1844, p. 267.

notes by the translator.[1] As Mr. Preston adopts the view of
that distinguished philosopher, we refer to p. 78, &c., for the
analysis of his exposition.   Preston, however, differs from his
" guide " in the division of the book, inasmuch as he makes it to
consist of *seventeen* sections.

§ 1. chap. i. 2 - 11	§ 7. chap. iv. 4 - 16	§ 13. chap. x. 16 - 20
2. i. 12 - 18	8. v. 1 - 20	14. xi. 1 - 6
3. ii. 1 - 2	9. vi. 1 - vii. 14	15. xi. 7 - xii. 8
4. ii. 3 - 12	10. vii. 15 - viii. 1	16. xii. 9 - 12
5. ii. 13 - 26	11. viii. 2 - ix. 12	17. xii. 13 - 14
6. iii. 1 - iv. 3	12. ix. 13 - x. 15	

Mr. Preston's " original notes, philological and exegetical,"
contain a great deal of valuable matter, and are very superior
to those of Mr. Holden.

1845. — The valuable article on Ecclesiastes, in Kitto's
Cyclopædia of Biblical Literature, has done more towards
elucidating the true character of this book than any previous
production in the English language.   Though written by a
foreigner (Hengstenberg), yet it must be looked upon as the
first voice raised against the Salomonic authorship of Coheleth
by an English orthodox cyclopædia.   According to Hengstenberg, the book was written about the time of Malachi, when
" the author had received the mission to treat professedly,
and in a concentrated manner, the highly important sentence,
Vanitas vanitatum, omniaque vanitas," in order to deduce
therefrom some practical results.   The practical application,
says Hengstenberg, is placed before us in the following
manner :[2] —

What is incumbent upon man, since everything else is naught?   What
real good remains for us, after the appearance in every seeming good has

---

[1] קהלת, the Hebrew text and a Latin version of the book of Solomon, called
Ecclesiastes; with original notes, philological and exegetical, and a translation
of the commentary of Mendelssohn from the Rabbinic Hebrew, &c., &c., by
Theodore Preston, M.A., Fellow of Trinity College. London, 1845.

[2] A Cyclopædia of Biblical Literature, edited by John Kitto, D.D., F.S.A., vol. i.,
p. 596.

been deauroyed ? The answer is, Man shall not gain by cunning and grasping; shall not consume himself in vain meditations, nor in a hurried activity; he shall not murmur about the loss of that which is naught; he shall not, by means of a self-made righteousness, constrain God to grant him salvation; but instead he shall fear God (xii. 13; v. 6, 7), and be mindful of his Creator (xii. 1); he shall do good as much as he is able (iii. 12; and in other passages). And all this, as it is constantly inculcated by the author, with a contented and grateful heart, freed from care and avarice; living for the present moment, joyfully taking from the hand of the Lord what he offers, in a friendly manner. Man shall not be of a sorrowful countenance, but enjoy the gifts of God in quiet serenity. What would avail him all his cares and all his avarice? By them he cannot turn anything aside from him, or obtain anything, since everything happens as it shall happen.

1846. — In America, too, the progress of Biblical criticism gave a new tone to the interpretation of this book. Thus Dr. Noyes, in the introduction to his excellent version of Ecclesiastes, is of opinion that Coheleth was written about three hundred and thirty years before the Christian era, and, like Hengstenberg, maintains that *the main doctrine, or speculative view, of the author is the vanity of human things, that is, of human striving, and of human fortunes and experiences; and his most prominent practical precept is, that men should enjoy the present blessings of life as they come, without anxiety and over-strenuous exertions, relating to distant and future good.*[1]

Dr. Noyes gives the following analysis of the book, consisting of *twelve* sections, to shew the correctness of his opinion about its design :—

The principal thought is first laid down, that all is vain and unprofitable (chap. i. 1, 2). This view the Preacher illustrates—
1. By the wearisome, ever-recurring changes which are taking place, without bringing to pass anything new, or leading to any new result, adapted to give satisfaction to the mind of man . . . chap. i. 4-11

[1] A new translation of the Proverbs, Ecclesiastes, and the Canticles, with Introductions and Notes, chiefly explanatory. By George R. Noyes, D.D., Hancock Professor of Hebrew, &c., &c., in Harvard University. Boston and London, 1846, p. 78.

2 F

11. A new illustration of the vanity of human life, drawn
from the circumstances, that success does not always
answer to a man's strength, wisdom, or other advantages, and that wisdom, with all its benefits to the
public, often brings but little consideration to its
possessor. Then follow various proverbial maxims,
shewing the advantages of wisdom and prudence, and
the evil of rulers unfit for their station, and designed
to regulate their conduct in private and public.
This section closes with a recommendation of liberality to the poor, and of diligent exertion in our
appropriate pursuits, without an over-anxious solicitude respecting the issue of our labours . ix. 11 xi. 6
12. The Preacher now exhorts to a cheerful enjoyment of
life as it passes, and the putting away of care and
sorrow, in view of that portion of life's vanity which
consists in the evil days of old age, and of the long
period of darkness in prospect (xi. 7 – xii. 8). Then
follows a repetition of the chief truth which has been
illustrated in the work, namely, the vanity of human
things; and the final recommendation of the Preacher,
as the conclusion of the whole matter, and the whole
business of man, namely, " to fear God and keep his
commandments " . . . . . xii. 9 - 14

1847. — Germany continued to furnish us with increasingly-
important works on Ecclesiastes. The brief commentary by
Hitzig, contained in the seventh part of " The condensed Exegetical Manual to the Old Testament," penetrates as much into
the design of the book, and the circumstances of the time which
gave rise to it, as any of its more bulky predecessors. The
author, says this learned critic,[1] was induced to write this book
by the circumstances of his times. He wrote it not from mere
inclination, but compelled by bitter necessity and for a practical
end, *being desirous to teach how men are to adapt themselves to life*

[1] Zur Abfassung des Buches Koheleth bewogen den Verf. die Verhältnisse
seiner Gegenwart. Nicht nach Willkühr, sondern unter dem Zwange bitterer
Nothwendigkeit schrieb er, zu einem praktischen Zwecke. Er wollte lehren, wie
man sich überhaupt zum Leben stellen, wie man namentlich in einer Zeit, di
also beschaffen, sich verhalten solle. — Der Prediger Salomo's. Erklärt von
Dr. F. Hitzig; Kurzgefaßtes exegetisches Handbuch zum Alten Testament.
Siebente Lieferung. Leipzig, 1847, p. 124.

generally, and how to act in a peculiar time like his. He divides
the book into *three parts*, each consisting of four sections —

Part I. describes the vanity of all things, shewn in   chap. i. 2 - iv. 16
  Sec. 1. The vanity of all things, as well as of thinking
    about it   .   .   .   .   .   .   i. 2 - 18
    2. The vanity of wisdom exerting itself to secure
    happiness; conclusion deduced therefrom   ii. 1 - 26
    3. That all things, and even man himself, have a
    time appointed by God   .   .   .   .   iii. 1 22
    4. That life is full of sufferings, painful exertions,
    and disappointments   .   .   .   .   iv. 1 - 16
Part II. shews how we are to act under a state of vanity,
  being himself as yet uncertain what rule of life to
  adopt; adduces conflicting maxims   .   iv. 17 - viii. 17
  Sec. 5. How we are to regulate our life in the face of
    God's order   .   .   .   .   .   iv. 17 - v. 19
    6. The unhappiness of not enjoying enjoyments   vi. 1 - 12
    7. Turning the loud disapprobations against the
    sinfulness of man   .   .   .   .   vii. 1 - 29
    8. The incomprehensible absence of just retribution
    leads to the folly of sin   .   .   .   viii. 1 - 17
Part III. prescribes our conduct in life more definitely, as
  the author himself had by this time arrived at more
  certain conclusions about it   .   .   .   ix. 1 - xii. 8
  Sec. 9. Since annihilation follows this vain life, we must
    gain its cheerful side   .   .   .   .   ix. 1 - 10
    10. Wisdom is often of no use to the wise, but to others.
    The fool makes mischief, and brings misfortune
    upon himself   .   .   .   .   .   ix. 11 - x. 20
    11. How we are to act, having an uncertain future,
    old age, and approaching death before us   xi. 1 - xii. 8
    12. Epilogue, giving some information about the
    author, and the design of the book   .   xii. 9 - 14

Hitzig was closely followed by Moses Stuart, who has,
however, not always understood his guide. Compare *infra*,
p. 226, and especially the Commentary.

1848. — Whilst Hitzig, with his mastery of the genius of the
Hebrew language, has thus supplied the scholar with a help to
the understanding of this book, Heiligstedt aimed to furnish
the student with a *grammatical* analysis of the text. As to
the design of Coheleth, Heiligstedt maintains a similar view to

that of Rosenmüller, namely, *that it teaches that, in the midst of
the prevailing vanity of all things worldly and human, supreme
happiness consists in man's enjoying gladly and cheerfully the
blessings and pleasures of this life ; that the power of cheerfully
enjoying the good things of life is a gift which God imparts to
man ; that it is not lawful for man, whilst thus enjoying the good
things of life, to conduct himself immoderately and impiously, but
that he should live uprightly, and be always mindful of God, the
Supreme Judge and Creator.*[1]

1848.—Simultaneous with Heiligstedt's commentary, appeared,
in the *Studien und Kritiken*, a very masterly article on Coheleth,
written by J. G. Vaihinger. He submits that *the design of the
Preacher is to propound the immortality of the soul, wherein alone
the solution of the otherwise inexplicable problems of life are
happily to be found ; and to encourage us to look forward to a
future judgment, amid the discrepancies between the moral nature
and fate of man.*[2] He tells us —

The book consists of four interwoven poetico-dialectic discourses, all
treating upon the same theme, viz , the vanity of human life, as well as the
object and aim of it. Each discourse consists of three parts, which are
again subdivided into strophes and half strophes; the discourses resemble
those contained in the first part of Proverbs, and especially those found in
the Book of Job, only that they are much more complicated in the progress
of their ideas.

[1] In omnium rerum mundanarum humanarumque vanitate bonum vitæ
humanæ summum, verum et stabile nonnisi in eo constare, ut homo vitæ præsentis bonis et jucunditatibus læte et hilare fruatur; vitæ bonis læte fruendi
facultatem esse donum, quod Deus homini impertiatur ; tamen in illis vitæ bonis
læte fruendis homini non licere immoderatum et impium se gerere, sed eum
oportere in probitate manere et semper Dei, judicis sui summi et creatoris,
memorem esse. — Franc. Jos. Valent. Dominic. Maureri Commentarius Gram-
maticus Historicus Criticus in Vetus Testamentum, vol. iv., sec. ii. Lipsiæ,
1848, pp. xii., xiii.

[2] Hieraus ergab fich mir als letter Gedanke des Predigers die Abficht auf
die Unfterblichkeit des Geiftes hinzuweifen, in welcher allein die Löfung des
fonft unentwirrbaren Räthfels des Menfchenlebens fich glücklicherweife findet,
und bei dem unbefriedigenden Verhältniß zwifchen fittlicher Befchaffenheit und
menfchlichem Schickfal auf das jenfeitige Gericht Gottes zu warten. —Theolo=
gifche Studien und Kritiken. 1848, pp. 443, 444.

Discourse I. (chap. i. 2 – ii. 26) shews that by the eternal, unalterably fixed course of all earthly things, and the experience of the vain and unsatisfactory strivings after earthly wisdom and selfish gratifications, a God-fearing enjoyment of life, and accepting gratefully the present good, can alone constitute the end of our earthly existence.

Discourse II. (chap. iii. 1 – v. 19) shews that by the experience that all our efforts in the world depend upon time and circumstances, and that the success of human labour is altogether controlled by circumstances, the cheerful enjoyment of life, connected with the fear of God and humility, is to be recommended as the highest good.

Discourse III. (chap. vi. 1 – viii. 15) shews that by the observation that man is frequently deprived of the enjoyment of riches, acquired through the favour of God, either from the fault of others or his own, we must try in a nobler way to procure the real and cheerful enjoyment of life, by joyfully using earthly blessings, following higher wisdom, and avoiding folly.

Discourse IV. (chap. viii. 16 – xii. 8), considering the melancholy experience of the inscrutable government of God in the distribution of human destinies, nothing remains to us, besides the exercise of wisdom and the fear of God, for the quieting of our minds, but in looking forward to a retributive eternity, and to an otherwise cheerless old age, cheerfully and gratefully to enjoy the good and the beautiful in life, especially in our youth and in the vigour of our manhood.

The four discourses treat upon one main theme, namely, that human life and strivings are in themselves vain and unsatisfactory; prosperity and adversity, success and disappointment, depend entirely upon time and chance, or, in other words, upon the inscrutable government of God; and that the only end of existence would seem to be, to live a life of resignation, to enjoy cheerfully the good things it affords, forgetting all its evils, in connection with benevolence, wisdom, and the fear of God. But as man cannot of himself secure this, and, even if secured, it would in reality not be satisfactory, there must be, in spite of all doubt, a future judgment, where that adjustment will take place which is here sought in vain.

It is to be regretted that this excellent treatise is so much occupied with the needless investigation of strophes and half-strophes.

1848. — The strange version of Ecclesiastes by Francis Barham forms a lamentable contrast to these masterly productions on the Continent. In the preface of this translation we are told that *the main purpose of this book appears to be to describe the* summum bonum, *or chief good, and to delineate the best form of character and conduct which is most conducive to joyfulness or happiness.*[1]

This, Solomon represents to be inseparably connected with piety towards God, and philanthropy towards man. Like the divine Messiah to whom he refers, and who often confirmed his words, he teaches us to evidence our religion by our conduct. He recommends useful industry or profitable labour, and a cheerful, thankful, temperate. enjoyment of all temporal blessings, which are the proper rewards of persevering rectitude. He advocates a wholesome, generous, and genial system of divine philosophy, in which faith and adoration are blended with wisdom and virtue, usefulness and charity, peace and liberty. All these are represented to us in relation to the immortality of man, and the future judgment of the righteous and the wicked ; and we are continually warned against the vanity and vexation of spirit by which the foolish and profligate are deceived and tormented. Such appears to me a true statement of certain facts, which render the Book of Ecclesiastes a most valuable epitome of theoretical and practical divinity.

The following is a specimen of this version · —

Chap. i. 2. — In vain are vanities,
      In vain are· vanities — all is vain.
    3. Some profit should man have ;
      As all have their labour,
      Which they should execute under the sun.
    4. Therewith one generation advances,
      And another generation departs,
      And the earth fulfils its periods.

Yet we are told in the preface, " In a translation of the Holy Scriptures, beyond comparison with any other work, *the most exact fidelity to the original is of* SUPREME *importance ;* because, just in proportion as we deviate from the true meaning, we lose its peculiar, its *unique* value, as the expression of the mind of the Divine Spirit."

Not the least striking features about this production are the

---

[1] The Bible Revised, Part I. The Book of Ecclesiastes, by Francis Barham. London, 1848, pp. iv. vii.

flagrant literary blunders of which Mr. Barham is guilty.
" Among the translators or explainers of Ecclesiastes," he
says, " I would especially mention the names of the Jewish
Targumists and Cabbalists, with Philo, Maimonides . . . .
Pilkington, &c., &c." A tyro in Hebrew literature must know
that there is *only one* Targum on Ecclesiastes extant, and that
Maimonides never wrote a commentary on this book. As for
Philo, so far from having expounded it, there is not even a
single quotation from Ecclesiastes to be found in his works.
That Pilkington never published a commentary on it, has been
shewn in the foot note, p. 132. We have given more space and
prominence to Mr. Barham's work than it deserves, because he
published it as *the first part* of " The Bible Revised," which we
trust he will discontinue.

1849. — As Keil, in his continuation of Hävernick's Introduction to the Old Testament,[1] adopted Vaihinger's view, we
must refer to page 221, &c., for the analysis of it.

1850. — The American Biblical Repository contains another
article on Ecclesiastes, which was delivered as a lecture by
Professor Stowe, of Cincinnati.[2] The Professor's view of the
book will be seen from the following extract : —

Solomon . . . seeking happiness in the things of earth . . . is disappointed
and disgusted ; and, instead of repenting of his errors, he becomes dissatisfied
with the arrangements of Providence, misanthropic, and sceptical. His
conscience, however, is not entirely asleep, but occasionally interposes to
check his murmurings and reprove him for his follies. In this state of
mind he is introduced, and in the character of Koheleth gives full and
strong utterance to all his feelings. Hence, inconsistent statements and
wrong sentiments are to be expected in the progress of the discourse ; and
it is not till the close of the book that all his errors are corrected, and he
comes to " the conclusion of the whole matter," a humbled, penitent,
believing. religious man.

1851. — Dr. James Hamilton found the Professor's view so

---

[1] Hävernick's Handbuch der historisch-kritischen Einleitung in das Alte Testament. Dritter Theil ausgearbeitet von Dr. Carl Friedrich Keil. Erlangen,
1849, pp. 434–464.

[2] Biblical Repository for April, 1850.

nearly akin to his own, that he copied it in the preface to his Lectures on Ecclesiastes,[1] from which we made the preceding extract. There is therefore no necessity for recapitulating the Doctor's view.

1851. — Professor Stuart, as has already been remarked, closely follows the opinion of Hitzig, both as to the design and division of the book, " bating the strong *neological* tendencies " of his guide. Thus he tells us, that the design of Coheleth is *to shew the vanity and utter insufficiency of all earthly pursuits and objects to confer solid and lasting happiness, and also to instruct his readers how to demean thmselves accordingly.*[2] Like Hitzig, he divides the book into three parts, each part consisting of four chapters.

PART I. (chap. i. 2 - iv. 16.) — Coheleth shews the vanity of human efforts, and of all earthly things in which men seek satisfaction. He begins with the unchangeable order of things in the natural world. Over this, man can acquire no influence, and have no control (i. 4 - 11). He then proceeds, in various ways, to illustrate and establish the position, that all human efforts to obtain abiding good in the present world are vain and fruitless. The acquisition of wisdom, or riches, or honours, and also indulgence in sensual pleasure, fail of their end. The most to which one can attain, is to enjoy the fruits of his toil in the sober gratification of the natural appetites. Providence has so arranged the vicissitudes of things, that they all have their regular course; and all that we can do is merely to submit to this, having no power to change or arrest it. After all the strivings of men, all go down to the grave, and perish in common with other living creatures around them. In fact, so multiplied are the sorrows of life, resulting from man's weakness, and springing from oppression, and from vain strife for wealth and defeated objects of ambition, that it is better to die than to live (i. 12 - iv. 16).

PART II. (chap. iv. 17 – viii. 17.) — Having thus established the general theory, he now gives practical instruction, beginning with religion. Frequenting the place of worship, prayer, offerings, and vows are here brought to view, and instructions are given. Thence he proceeds to descant on a variety of topics, with which the happiness and comfort of men are deeply

[1] The Royal Preacher; Lectures on Ecclesiastes, by James Hamilton, D.D., F.L.S. London, 1851, pp. ix., x.

[2] A Commentary on Ecclesiastes, by Moses Stuart, lately Professor of Sacred Literature in the theological seminary at Andover, Mass. New York, 1851, p. 23.

concerned. Several of these topics, *e.g.*, riches, wisdom, the oppression of rulers, &c., are introduced again and again, as occasion prompts, and in order to present them in all their important aspects. In the course of this part of his work divers objections are presented, some of which are answered forthwith, and some after intervening matter, which pressed upon his mind, has been thrown in.

PART III. (chap. ix. 1 - xii. 8.) All doubts now disappear. The ultimate conclusions to which Coheleth has come, after examining into the whole matter before him, are now brought before us. God is supreme, and all things and all men are in his hands. He has made, and intends to make, no distinction between men as to their mortality and exposedness to suffering. This, although it is a source of much concern and sorrow, must be borne, as having been appointed by him. Rational and cheerful enjoyment, so far as practicable, he permits, and even enjoins. Moreover, wisdom may alleviate some evils, and prevent some others ; so that, although it is not itself the chief good, and cannot of itself secure solid and lasting happiness, it may be of much use even in the common affairs of life. In the midst of exposure to oppression and misfortune, it may help to direct our conduct, so far as to avoid as much evil and secure as much good as is possible. A diligent observance of active duty, and a thankful enjoyment of what can be enjoyed, are the sum of what we can do to mitigate the sorrows and trials of life. Through all, and in all, with which we are concerned, and at all seasons of life, God is to be remembered, and also his judicial power to be recognised. Then comes a description of old age, and its preparation for and approach to the tomb, when the soul returns to God, to appear before his tribunal.

CONCLUSION (chap. xii. 9 - 14), wherein Coheleth gives a brief account of himself, and of his object in writing the book.

We have said before (p. 220) that Stuart does not always fairly represent Hitzig. Let the following specimen suffice. Referring to Hitzig's remarks on chap. vii. 26, Stuart says —

Hitzig seems to represent him [Coheleth] as expecting to find at least some of a good character among women, and as being disappointed in not finding them. Says he, *more suo :* Er denkt zu fischen und krebst, *i.e., he designs to catch fish, and catches crabs.* But. levity apart, his disappointment could not be great at not finding them among the class of women whom he describes. He was *grieved*, rather than disappointed.

Now Hitzig says nothing about *being disappointed* in the character of woman. What he says is, that to alight all at once upon the woman, in ver. 26, when he has declared, in ver. 25, that he was determined to find *wisdom, &c., &c.,* seems at first

sight as if he *caught crabs when he intended to fish.* The following are Hitzig's own words in their connection [1] —

Chap. vii. 25. *I turned, &c.* — The counsels given in ver. 16 – 24 have
likewise displeased him, because, according to them, moderate sinning would
be wisdom, and he knows, *à priori,* that sin is folly. Hence he now strives
to find that it (sin) is really folly (*b*); in which case, that which is wisdom
will soon be apparent, namely, the forsaking of sin. — ולבי is subordinate
= *with my heart,* i. e., *understanding.*

To know and to search. — The two accusatives belong to בקש, before which
the ל is not repeated, in order to separate it externally from the preceding
infinitive. For חשבון, see ver. 27.

26. *And I found, &c.* — On his way, Coheleth finds woman; *he intends
to fish, and catches crabs:* how is that? Intending to find that sin is folly,
he fixed upon a certain object; and we see that (בקש חכמה וגו), *his search
after wisdom, &c.,* is directed, in the first place, to comprehend sin in its
nature and consequences. Pursuing this object (comp. ver. 27, *b*), Coheleth
finds that which he brings before us in this verse, namely, that he must
search for sin where it grows, in man (Job v. 6, 7); and he looks for it at its
very source (comp. Sirach xxv. 24), where it appears most marked; he goes
to the woman, who was regarded in the East as morally weaker than man.
Thus, she is brought forward as the representative of sin, as incarnate
מרשעת, wickedness.

We have thought it a duty to Sacred literature to clear
Hitzig from this misrepresentation and charge of " levity,"
made by one who is more indebted to this scholar for his

---

[1] Die Rathschläge aber V. 16 ff. haben ihn ebendeßhalb nicht befriedigt,
weil ihnen zufolge ein mässiges Sündigen Weisheit wäre, ihm aber *a priori*
fest steht, daß die Sünde Thorheit seyn sollte. Also bestrebt er sich nun zu
finden, daß sie auch wirklich Thorheit sey (b); in welchem Falle, was Weisheit
sey, sich bald ergeben würde, nemlich die Sünde zu lassen. — ולבי ordnet sich
unter = mit meinem Herzen d. i. Verstande. Zu erkennen und zu forschen]
Die beiden Affus. gehören nur zu בקש, vor welchem, um es äusserlich von den
vorhergehenden Infin. zu trennen, ל nicht wiederholt wird. — Ueber חשבון s.
zu V. 27. — V. 26. Auf seinem Wege findet Koh. das Weib; er denkt zu
fischen und krebst, — wie geht Das zu? Wenn er daß die Sünde Thorheit sey
finden will, so hat er sich ein bestimmtes Ziel gesteckt; und wir merken, daß
sein בקש חכמה וגו zunächst darauf ausgeht, die Sünde in ihrem Wesen und ihren
Folgen zu begreifen. Dieses Ziel verfolgend (vgl. V. 27b) findet Koh., was
er V. 26. vorbringt. Nemlich er muß die Sünde da aufsuchen wo sie wächst,
im Menschen (Hi. v. 6. 7), und sucht sie an ihrer Quelle (vgl. Sir. xxv. 24) wo
sie zugleich am markirtesten hervortritt: beim Weibe, das im Orient überhaupt
für moralisch schwächer denn der Mann gilt. Also wird dasselbe als Reprä-
sentant der Sünde, als eingefleischte מרשעת, vorgeführt.

criticisms on Ecclesiastes than any one else. We must add, that the charge frequently preferred against the Germans of indistinctness and confusion of thought often arises from a misunderstanding of their meaning.

Stuart's commentary, with all its defects, is incomparably the best work on Ecclesiastes in the English language. He has endeavoured to give a grammatical analysis of the text, as well as to trace the logical sequence of the context, and has shewn the untenableness of the opinion that Solomon was the author of the book.

1854. — Kitto would neither be moved by the article on Ecclesiastes in his own Cyclopædia, nor take notice of the more elaborate refutation of the Solomonic authorship by Professor Stuart. He looked upon all the arguments advanced against Solomon having written the book as forming "a monument of microscopic ingenuity in criticism,"[1] and as having been satisfactorily disposed of by Mr. Holden and others. As to the design of the book, he tells us that he was formerly inclined to acquiescence in the conclusion that it is an inquiry after the *summum bonum*, THE CHIEF GOOD ; but, upon more deliberate consideration, he thinks that *the object of it is, by shewing the emptiness of all things earthly, to force those who follow its general argument to deduce the absolute necessity of a future and better existence, as the only solution of the otherwise inscrutable phenomena which the course of men's life presents.*

1855. — In Germany, however, Biblical criticism has by this time made such progress that there are but few who can muster courage to defend the Solomonic authorship. The only question of dispute with them is whether it is to be assigned to the earlier or latter part of the Persian dominion, or to a post-Persian period. Elster, in his valuable commentary published in 1855, is of opinion that Coheleth lived at the latter end of the unhappy Persian dominion, about three hundred and fifty

---

[1] Daily Bible Illustrations, &c. By John Kitto, D. D., F. S. A. Job and the Poetical Books. 1854, p. 365.

years before Christ, and that *the design of the book is to exhort the suffering and desponding Israelites to retain their pristine joy in life, the true nature and import of which are to rejoice in good, and to be happy in God.*[1]

Elster's commentary, comprising one hundred and thirty-three pages, does honour to the author, and will always afford a source of information and pleasure to every reader.

1856. — The interest which we find now manifested in Ecclesiastes is almost unparalleled. In England, Scotland, America, and Germany, scholars of different grades and of various opinions tried their skill to elucidate it; and we have to notice no less than six several productions in this single year. At home we have a very thorough article of Dr. Samuel Davidson on Coheleth, in "The Text of the Old Testament Considered."[2] This excellent Hebrew scholar, like the preceding writer, is of opinion that the author of the book lived in the later part of the Persian government, not long after the time of Malachi, *i. e.*, 350 – 340 B. C., and that *his design is to institute the inquiry after the* SUMMUM BONUM. Though adopting substantially Vaihinger's division of the book, and mode of tracing the gradual development of the sacred writer's thoughts, Dr. Davidson has succeeded in giving to this part of the work all the appearance of originality, by purging it from Vaihinger's hair-splitting speculations about strophes and half-strophes, and by infusing into it some independent thoughts. The following is his analysis : —

The contents are comprehended in four discourses.

DISCOURSE I. (chap. i. 2 – ii. 26.) — After proposing the general theme in

---

[1] Er wendet sich an die einzelnen Individuen, und an diese richtet er seine Mahnung, deren Kern die Lehre bildet: die ursprüngliche, unmittelbare Freude am Leben sich zu bewahren, welche Freude aber ihr wahres Wesen, ihren wahren Inhalt hat in der Freude am Guten, in der Freude in Gott. — Commentar über den Prediger Salomo, von Ernst Elster. Göttingen, 1855, p. 28.

[2] The Text of the Old Testament Considered; or, The Second Volume of Horne's Introduction to the Bible, by Samuel Davidson, D. D., LL. D. London, 1856, pp. 781 – 790.

the second and third verses, that all is vanity, Koheleth shews the vanity of
theoretical wisdom applied to the investigation of things, and then of
practical wisdom directed to the enjoyment of life, arriving at the result,
that man by his efforts cannot obtain abiding good.

DISCOURSE II. (chap. iii. 1 - v. 19.) — The second discourse begins with
a description of the absolute dependence of man on a higher, immutable
Providence, succeeded by an answer to the inquiry after the *summum bonum*,
that there is no higher good for man than to enjoy himself; but that
such good cannot easily be attained amid the many disappointments which
are observable on earth.   Under these circumstances, however, a man
should strive after happiness, through the fear of God and a conscientious
fulfilment of duty, trusting in the providence of the Most High, and setting
a proper value on earthly possessions, by means of contentedness with the
share bestowed by God, and cheerful enjoyment of the benefits received.

DISCOURSE III. (chap. vi. 1 - viii. 15.) — In the third discourse the
writer sets forth the vanity of striving after riches, develops the true
practical wisdom of life, and shews how it is to be gained, notwithstanding
all the incongruities of earthly life.

DISCOURSE IV. (chap. viii. 16 - xii. 8.) — In the fourth discourse these
incongruities are more particularly examined, maxims being laid down, at
the same time, for the true enjoyment of life; after which, the whole is
summed up in the enunciation of the same sentiment which stands at the
beginning, viz., that solid, unchanging happiness is not to be found in
earthly things.

1856. — In Scotland there appeared a " New Translation and
Exposition of the Book of Ecclesiastes ; with Critical Notes on
the Hebrew Text. By Benjamin Weiss." This zealous
missionary is very wroth with " the torturers of Sacred Writ,
who have maintained that (according to their lexicon) they
discovered in this book many passportless Chaldaisms, and
therefore they have denied its Solomonic authorship." Mr.
Weiss meets all the lingual difficulties with the assertion that
the rich and wise Solomon knew the post-exile *patois*, and, in
corroboration of it, asks these critics, " What language did
Solomon employ in courting, or in obtaining his foreign women
from their parents?"[1]   After this specimen of his mode of
arguing, we are not at all surprised to hear Mr. Weiss repeat

[1] New Translation and Exposition of the Book of Ecclesiastes; with critical
notes on the Hebrew text.   By Benjamin Weiss, missionary to the Jews, &c., &c.
Dundee, 1856, p. 10.

the old story, that *this book contains Solomon's penitential dirge and lamentation over his sins.*

1856. — In America, we have this year " The Book of Eccle siastes explained, by James M. Macdonald, D. D." And though the Doctor pretends to give us " the *results* of criticisms on the Hebrew without the process by which it has been reached," yet, contrary to the results of the best critical investigations, he maintains that Solomon wrote this book, and that " *we undoubtedly have the proof and monument of his repentance in the book of Ecclesiastes.*"[1] It is rather strange that one of Dr. Macdonald's reasons for not intending to prepare a gram- matical praxis for students in Hebrew is, that " this has been so ably and fully done by such scholars as Van der Palm, Desvoeux, Rosenmüller, *Gesenius, &c.*" Any one, even slightly acquainted with the history of exegesis, knows that Gesenius never wrote a commentary on Ecclesiastes. But the identifica- tion of authorship is evidently not among Dr. Macdonald's gifts.

1856. — Dr. Ludwig von Essen is one of the several Germans who commented on Coheleth in 1856. As a priest of the Roman Catholic Church, he is quite enraged with the Protestant heretics for denying the Solomonic authorship of this book, and grieved to find Jahn and Herbst, members of the true Church, infected with this heresy. Von Essen's work, however, is not a regular exposition of Ecclesiastes, but simply *a contribution*[2] towards it, consisting of four sections : —

Section I. discusses the superscription, and II. the authorship of the book ; III. the period of life in which Solomon wrote it, whether before or after his fall; and IV. gives an explanation of the difficult portion of it, viz., chap. iii. 18 – 22. As to the design of the book, Dr. Von Essen thinks that *Solomon wrote it*

[1] The Book of Ecclesiastes explained. By James M. Macdonald, D.D. New York, 1856, p. 69.

[2] Der Prediger Salomo's. Ein Beitrag zur Erklärung des alten Testa- mentes. Von Ludwig von Essen, Doctor der Theologie, &c. Schaffhausen, 1856.

*after his fall and recovery, and designed it to be a monument of
his conversion.*[1]

1856. — The next German work on Ecclesiastes, issued from
the press this year, which we have to notice, is that of
Dr. Wangemann. He is the only Protestant commentator in
Germany, as far as we know, who has the courage still to
maintain *that Solomon was the author of this book, and that it
contains the monarch's confession of sin.* He says[2] —

The book contains the confessions of a richly-gifted and much experienced
soul; it is the outflowing of the fulness of a sinful heart, condensing the
manifold results of an excited life into one sum. This sum has described
its starting point in the first verse, namely, that all things under the sun
are vanity; and its terminus in the words, "Fear God, and keep his
commandments, for he shall demand an account of this life." Between
these two poles the confessions move about in great fulness, with a geniality
peculiar to the richly endowed Solomonic spirit which cannot be fathomed
by the measures of our intellectual comprehension and scheming.

Wangemann, also, divides the book into two parts, with an
introduction and conclusion. The following is his analysis · —

I. INTRODUCTION, i. 1–11.
    A. Superscription and table of the principal contents, i. 1–3.
        a. The author stated (1).
        b. The starting point (2).
        c. The theme (3).
    B. The starting point established, i. 4-7.
        The vanity and fruitlessness of all earthly things.

[1] Unserer Meinung nach hat Salomo das Buch Koheleth nach seinem Falle
geschrieben, d. h. mit andern Worten, wir glauben, daß Salomo sich von seinem
Falle wieder erholt und sich von seinen Sünden wieder bekehrt hat, und daß
unser Buch ein Denkmal dieser Bekehrung sei. *Ibid.*, p. 70.

[2] Das Buch enthält Bekentnisse einer reich begabten und vielerfahrenen Seele,
es ist ein Ausfluß aus einem vollen Sündenherzen, welches die mannichfachen
Ergebnisse eines bewegten Lebens unter eine Summa zusammenfaßt. Diese
Summa hat ihren Ausgangspunct im ersten Verse selbst angegeben, daß nämlich
Alles unter der Sonne eitel sei — und ihren Endpunct in dem Worte: Fürchte
Gott und halte seine Gebote, denn er wird Rechenschaft fordern von deinem
Leben. Zwischen diesen beiden Polen bewegen sich die Bekenntnisse in großer
Fülle, mit der einem salomonisch reich begabten Geiste eigenen Genialität,
welche sich nicht unter das Maß verstandesmäßiger Begriffe und Schematisirungen
befassen läßt. — Der Prediger Salomonis nach Inhalt und Zusammenhang
praktisch ausgelegt von Dr. Wangemann. Berlin, 1856, p. 20.

C. The theme established, i. 8 – 11

Man's labour in itself is without result.

II. Principal portion of the book, i. 12 - xii. 7.

    A. Introduction, i. 12 – 15.

        Solomon describes his personal connection with the question mooted.

    B. First Part, i. 16 – vii. 14.

        Observations on the strivings of men under the sun, and description of the relation in which man, as creature, stands to God, his Creator.

        1. Solomon's observations from his own life, i. 16 – iii. 15.

            a. First attempt — striving after wisdom, i. 16 - 18.

            b. Second attempt — sensual enjoyment, ii. 1, 2.

            c. Third attempt — all kinds of work, ii. 3 – 10.

            The practical application of the foregoing, ii. 12 – 19.

            d. Fourth attempt — ceasing from work, ii. 20 – 23.

            e. The practical conclusion that follows from this course, ii. 24 - 26.

            f. The theoretical conclusion that Solomon draws from the observations of his life, iii. 1 – 8.

            God fixes time and measure; man's own doings divide themselves in opposites, and in themselves give no satisfaction.

            g. Close of the first section, iii. 9 – 15.

            Man's goal is not in time, but in eternity.

        2. Solomon's observations in reference to other men, and their dealings with each other, iii. 16 – iv. 12.

            a. The scene of this intercourse resembles a tribunal, iii. 16 - 17.

            b. Man's foolish thoughts concerning himself, iii. 18 – 22.

            c. The dealings of men with each other, iv. 1 – 8.

            d. The practical conclusion, drawn from the observation of men's intercourse, iv. 9 – 12.

        3. The conclusions at which Solomon arrived, from his observations of his own life, as well as from the dealings of men in general, iv. 13 – vii. 14.

            a. His own life is a failure, iv. 13 - 16.

            b. Reasons why Solomon fell under such severe chastisement from God, iv. 17 – v. 9.

                aa. First reason — he did not keep the vows of his youth, iv. 17 – v. 6.

                bb Second reason — Solomon's multifarious undertakings involved a complicated administration, and, in consequence, much injustice was brought about in the land, v. 7, 8.

2 H

1856. — The last treatise on Ecclesiastes of this year, which we intend to mention, is contained in Dr. Ernst Meier's "History of the Poetical-National Literature of the Hebrews." He submits that Coheleth, — who lived at the beginning of the unhappy Macedonian dominion, when the national feeling of the Jews was dead, and his suffering brethren were tired of existence, — *thoughtfully seeks to elevate himself above the confusion and misery of his time, and for this purpose has written down in this book, not only the result of his observations, but also the whole process by which he arrived at it. The result, however, is the thought that* ALL IS VANITY.[1] In other words, the design of Coheleth is to shew that there is, in reality, no *summum bonum*. He says —

The whole human life and striving appear to Coheleth fruitless and vain; there is, in reality, no true highest good for man. Hence, nothing remains for him but to enjoy life as cheerfully as possible, before joyless death terminates all his misery. Two main thoughts underlie the whole of his observations.

1. The human spirit cannot perceive, either in nature or in the moral world, a rational design and final object of development. Everything moves in a perpetual round; there is nothing abiding in the change of appearances, no satisfactory result, no real good. A righteous moral government of the world is indeed not to be denied, but it is equally certain that man can nowhere perceive it.

2. As man, with all his trouble and skill, can find no absolute object, no truly real good in life, he may at least achieve objects and advantages which have a relative value. The best thing for him, under these circumstances, is not to dive into the inscrutable plan of the Divine government of the world, according to which the righteous frequently suffer, whilst the wicked prosper. On the contrary, since man's life is apparently a prey to chance, we must use wisely time and circumstances, enjoy thankfully the pleasures of the fleeting moment which we can seize, but thereby not relinquish our belief in the Divine government of the world, and in a righteous retribution. These are the main thoughts which the author seeks to carry through, and to prove in various ways.

[1] Der Verfaßer selbst hat unstreitig viel erfahren und erlebt. Er sucht denkend sich über die Zerwürfniße und das Elend der Zeit zu erheben, und hat zu dem Ende nicht bloß das Resultat seiner Betrachtung, sondern auch den ganzen Weg, wie er zu demselben gelangte, in dieser Schrift niedergelegt. Dieß Resultat aber ist der Gedanke, daß Alles eitel sei. — Geschichte der poetischen National-Literatur der Hebräer, von Dr. Ernst Meier. Leipzig, 1856, p. 551.

1857. — After a lapse of nine years, the *Studien und Kritiken*
bring us again a very lengthy and elaborate article on Coheleth,
this time written by Umbreit.   As the purport of the article is
to shew *the unity* of Ecclesiastes, the author has not *formally*
stated his view of the design and object of the book.   It is,
however, evident, from the two passages which we subjoin in the
foot note, that Umbreit thinks *the design of Coheleth is to shew
the vanity of striving to secure something unchangeable or imperishable, amidst the changeable or perishing nature of all things
under the sun ; and that the sacred writer therefore recommends it
as the best thing for man, under these circumstances, not uselessly
to complain, but to enjoy the present with a calm resignation, and
to be conscientiously active and trustful in God, whilst looking
forward to the development of the future.*[1]

1858. — Ten years after the appearance of his article on
Coheleth in the *Studien und Kritiken*, Vaihinger published the
fourth volume of his commentary on the Poetical Books of the
Old Testament, containing " the Preacher, and the Song of
Songs."   As this exposition is based upon the author's view of
the design and plan of the book already described, we must
refer to page 221, *et seq.*, for this description.

1859. — Hengstenberg maintains that it is quite misleading

[1] Nach vorausgehender Ueberschrift (V. 1) vernehmen wir V. 2–3 den
Grundton des Predigers, der seine folgende Rede durchdringt und unter den
mannichfaltigsten Bewegungen und Beruhigungen seiner im unmittelbar uns
vorgehaltenen Streben nach einem Bleibenden im Vergänglichen lebendig
erregten Seele immer von neuem durchschlägt; wir haben das Thema und auch
das Ergebniß seiner Forschung und seiner philosophisch-poetischen Darlegung.
Er stellt die Behauptung an die Spitze, daß Alles ganz eitel und schnell ver=
gänglich sey, und daß es für den Menschen bei aller seiner Mühe, womit er
sich abmühet unter der Sonne, nichts Bleibendes gebe. — Indem der Prediger
bei der nicht zu verändernden Veränderlichkeit aller Dinge unter der Sonne,
wo ein Bleibendes zu erringen, eine vergebliche Mühe und die Klage darüber
eine nichtige ist, alle Weisheit des Lebens in die freie, stille Entsagung und
eine gewissenhaft thätige, in gottvertrauendem Hinblick auf die entwickelnde
Zukunft frommgenügsame Benützung der Gegenwart zum eigenen und zum Heile
Anderer gesetzt, richtet er in ergreifender Erhöhung des Geistes das letzte Wort
der Ermahnung [cap. xi., xii.] noch besonders an die Jugend. — Theologische
Studien und Kritiken.   Jahrgang, 1857, pp. 8, 9. 54.

to represent Coheleth as occupied with any single narrow theme; that *the book has no plan, its object being to inculcate various lessons, all of which are designed to make us fear God and live in him; hence the description of the vanity of all that is earthly, since he only knows what he has in God, to whom " Vanity of vanities, all is vanity!" has become a living consciousness.*[1]

Entering more minutely into the contents of the book, Hengstenberg says —

Coheleth appeared under those distressing circumstances of the time (*i.e.*, under the tyranny of the Persians), partly *consoling*, partly *admonishing* and *reproving*, so that " the rebuke of the wise ".is perceptible in it (chap. vii. 5). It is not accidental that the author begins with discharging his first mission, and that he does it with special zeal, his object being, above all, to encourage the heart of the people, — which, despite of its great infirmities, was still the people of his heritage, the people amongst whom God dwelled, — to return to their God. Only when this object had been attained could admonition and reproof be effectual. The writer begins his consolatory mission in a way which may appear at first sight somewhat striking. The people complain on all sides that everything is vanity of vanities; that their times are evil compared with the past, and especially with the glorious day of Solomon. But the writer breaks in with the proclamation that human life generally is vanity; that this world is a vale of tears; and that the difference between happy and unhappy times is much less real than it appears to superficial observation (chap. i. 2 - 11). The cross is borne more easily when we know that it is the universal destiny of man.

It will be remembered that Herzfeld also maintained that the declaration of the vanity of all things was intended as a comfort for the unhappy Israelites, *vide supra*, p. 88.

The great service, however, which Hengstenberg has rendered, consists in the fact that he, though *decidedly orthodox*, is

<hr/>

[1] Ein flüchtiger Blick auf den Inhalt zeigt, daß derselbe viel zu reich ist, um unter ein solches vereinzeltes Thema subsummirt zu werden. Will man einmal ein Thema aufstellen, so muß man es so allgemein fassen wie der Verf. selbst dieß thut in C. xii. 13: fürchte Gott. Die Furcht Gottes und das Leben in ihm zu fördern, darauf gehet zuletzt alles in dem Buche hin, dem dient auch die Darlegung der Nichtigkeit alles Irdischen: was er an Gott hat, weiß nur, wem das: „Eitelkeit der Eitelkeiten und alles Eitelkeit" zum lebendigen Bewußtseyn geworden ist.—Der Prediger Salomo ausgelegt von E. W. Hengstenberg. Berlin, 1859, pp. 15, 16.

compelled to declare that it is utterly impossible to reconcile the contents of this book with the Solomonic authorship, and that it is undoubtedly a post-exile production.

1859. — Keil, another unquestionably orthodox scholar, also asserts that "the language and import of the book shew that it originated in the times of Ezra and Nehemiah." His view of the design of the book has already been mentioned, page 224.

1859. — Dr Buchanan, however, abides by the old opinion, that Solomon wrote this book after Divine grace had raised him from his grievous fall, and that, guided by the Spirit of God, and taught by his own terrible experience, he has therein expounded *the chief good.* It is greatly to be regretted that the Doctor, who is evidently a total stranger to Biblical criticism, should yet dogmatise so offensively upon the subject, and quote those learned men who gave up a pre-conceived notion, as the result of scientific investigation, as an illustration of " *the perversity of the human mind.*" Speaking of the Solomonic authorship of Ecclesiastes,—which, as we have seen, has now been relinquished by such orthodox and learned scholars as Hengstenberg, Keil, Vaihinger, Elster, &c., — Dr. Buchanan says —

It certainly does seem strange that there should ever have been a question among critics or commentators as to the authorship of this portion of Scripture. Such, however, is the fact. There have been Rabbis and Talmudists among the Jews, and learned men in the Christian Church, who contrived to persuade themselves, and tried to persuade others, that not Solomon, but some one else, must have written this book. The circumstance seems only to prove that there is no point, however plain, about which the perversity of the human mind will not find means to raise a dispute.[2]

Nothing but ignorance could have indited the assertion that " there have been Rabbis and Talmudists among the Jews . . .

---

[1] Sprache und Inhalt verweisen die Entstehung des Buchs in die Zeiten Esra's und Nehemia's. — Lehrbuch der historisch=kritischen Einleitung in die Kanonischen und apokryphischen Schriften des Alten Testamentes von Karl Friedrich Keit, Zweite Auflage.   Frankfurt a. M., 1859, p. 383.

[2] The Book of Ecclesiastes; its meaning and its lessons, by Robert Buchanan, D.D. London, 1859, p. 12.

who contrived to persuade themselves, and tried to persuade others, that not Solomon, but some one else, must have written this book." *No Talmudist denied the Solomonic authorship of this book.* And had the Doctor been acquainted with Jewish literature or Biblical criticism, his homilies would have been less dogmatic and more profitable.. It is not to be expected that every preacher should have a critical knowledge of the Bible; but we have a right to expect that one who writes to shew the " *meaning* " of a portion of the Scriptures, who passes judgment upon Matthew Henry, that he is " not always *critically* accurate,"[1] and who ostentatiously quotes the Septuagint, the French and modern versions,[2] should know something about criticism. Let the following specimen suffice to shew how he is " *critically accurate* " : —

Chap. iii. 18. " I said in my heart," continues Solomon, " concerning the estate of the sons of men," &c. To remove the difficulty that hangs over this verse, it is only necessary to understand what he thus said in his heart as a prayer. The sons of men, to whose estate he refers, are evidently the worldly, the unspiritual, the carnal, as contradistinguished from those who are the sons or the children of God. In meditating upon their condition, and observing how completely they were engrossed with earthly things, the earnest desire arose within him, that God would shew them to themselves, to see that, living as they did, they were lowering themselves to a level with the beasts that perish.[3]

1860. — Though the Rev. Charles Bridges also follows the traditional view of this book in his exposition of Ecclesiastes,[4] yet the gentle spirit which he manifests towards those who entertain different opinions from his own, and the humility he displays in his work, form a striking contrast to the preceding writer, and therefore deprive criticism of its severity. How meekly he concludes the Preface · " He does not presume to have swept away all obscurities from the sky; but possibly a

[1] The Book of Ecclesiastes; its meaning and its lessons, by Robert Buchanan, D. D. London, 1859, p. 42.
[2] *Ibid.*, p. 111.   [3] *Ibid.*, pp. 128, 129.
[4] An Exposition of the Book of Ecclesiastes. By the Rev. Charles Bridges, M. A. London, 1860, pp. ix. xii.

few rays of light may have been cast upon the dark clouds. For instances of failure in interpretation, he would crave forbearance. For success, he would give the glory where alone it is due." No one who knows the writings of the excellent Mr. Bridges, will expect an exposition from his pen in harmony with the present results of Biblical criticism; and those who resort to his commentary for edification will be abundantly satisfied.

1860. — Mr. Plumptre, in his article on Ecclesiastes in Dr. Smith's Dictionary of the Bible, tries to temper the traditional view of this book with some of the results of modern criticism. He maintains that the book professes to be the confession of a man of wide experience, looking back upon his past life, and looking out upon the disorders and calamities which surround him; that the writer is a man who has sinned in giving way to selfishness and sensuality; who has paid the penalty of that sin in satiety and weariness of life; in whom the mood of spirit, over-reflective, indisposed to action, of which Shakspeare has given us in Hamlet, Jaques, Richard II., three distinct examples, has become dominant in its darkest form, but who has, through all this, been under the discipline of a divine education, and has learnt from it the lessons which God meant to teach him; and that the lesson which he has learnt, and which he teaches us, after reproducing the stages through which he has passed, is, that " *to fear God, and to keep his commandments, is the highest good attainable; that the righteous judgment of God will in the end fulfil itself, and set right all the seeming discords of the world.*"[1]

Mr. Plumptre tells us that " we may look on the whole book as falling into *five* divisions;" but in his analysis, however, he only gives us *four,* viz.: —

1. chap. i. 2 – ii. 26	3. chap. vi. 10 – viii. 15
2. iii. 1 – vi. 9	4. viii. 16 – xii. 8

We must therefore conclude that there is an error in printing.

---

[1] A Dictionary of the Bible. Edited by William Smith, LL. D., London, 1860, article Ecclesiastes.

As to the authorship of the book, though Mr. Plumptre apparently halts between the two opinions, his sympathies seem, however, to be with the anti-Solomonic side.

1860. — The irresistible force of modern criticism, as well as the insurmountableness of its results, may be seen in Mr. Ayre's edition of the second volume of "Horne's Introduction to the Critical Study and Knowledge of the Holy Scriptures." Supplementing Horne, who adopted Mr. Holden's view and division of Ecclesiastes (*vide supra*, p. 198, &c.), Mr. Ayre remarks:[1]—

Perhaps this book will be best understood if we consider it as divided into four different discourses.

DISCOURSE I. (chap. i. 2 – ii. 26) exhibits, in chap i., the vanity of theoretical wisdom directed to the knowledge of things; and, chap. ii., the nothingness of practical wisdom, which aims at enjoying life; whence the result is, that man, with all his striving, can attain no lasting good.

DISCOURSE II. (chap. iii. 1 – v. 19.) — Following the idea thrown out ii. 21 – 26, it begins with a description (iii. 1 – 8) of man's entire dependence on a higher, unchangeable Providence; and, in reply to the question of the chief good, shews that there can be no higher (iii. 9 – 22) than for a man to enjoy himself and do good; which, however (iv.), it is not easy to attain; still, a man must, in the fear of God, and a conscientious fulfilment of duty, seek trustingly and contentedly to use the earthly goods entrusted to him (v.).

DISCOURSE III. (chap. vi. 1 – viii. 15) shews the vanity of grasping at riches (vi.), then describes practical wisdom (vii. 1 – 22), and indicates the mode of its attainment, in spite of all the incongruities of earthly life (vii. 23 – viii. 15).

DISCOURSE IV. (chap. viii. 16 – xii. 7). — It further discusses these incongruities, and lays down rules for the conduct of a happy life which may please God, and conducts to the conclusion of the whole (xii. 8 – 14), that God's future judgment will clear up all present mysteries and irregularities.

This is the great object which the book intends to develop, but which is not disclosed till worldly reasonings are shewn to be insufficient. For, after each several discussion, a difficulty still remains, which has again to be taken up, till the reader's view is raised at last to that high judgment seat before which every wrong will be redressed.

---

[1] An Introduction to the Criticism of the Old Testament, &c. By the Rev. Thomas Hartwell Horne, B. D. Revised and edited by the Rev. John Ayre, M. A. London, 1860, pp. 744, 745.

As to the Solomonic authorship of Ecclesiastes, so far from quoting those who deny it as illustrating " *the perversity of the human mind*," Mr. Ayre says : —

It is not easy to decide upon the authorship ; different minds will arrive at different conclusions. The reasons which have been given make Hengstenberg and Keil, as well as other critics, believe that the book is not from Solomon. If this be conceded, the same proof will shew that the date of its composition must be placed not earlier than the exile. . . . It is fanciful to say that, as the Persian government, probably in its later administration, became oppressive, allusion is made to it; all that can fairly be supposed is, that the language might place it about the time of Nehemiah or Malachi, to which prophet's book Ewald considers Ecclesiastes to bear a marked resemblance.[1]

It will be seen that Mr. Ayre's view of the design, plan, authorship, and date of the book is the same as that of Vaihinger, Keil, and Dr. Davidson, and constituted one of the heresies imputed to the last writer, which helped to call for our author's revised and more orthodox edition of Horne's Introduction. Not that we object to this view; on the contrary, we hail it as a triumph of enlightened and liberal criticism in England. We are persuaded, that if those who repudiate the results of rational exegesis as " *the perversity of the human mind*," or heretical, were to bestow the labour upon Biblical criticism which every page almost of Mr. Ayre's revised volume indicates, they would manifest less ignorance and more charity.

What lessons of humility and forbearance ought we to learn from the sketch of what has befallen this book, when we see that *the pious* and *the learned*, both among Jews and Christians, have, with equal confidence, advanced the most opposite and contradictory theories about its meaning! We are positively assured, as we have seen, that the book contains the holy lamentations of Solomon, together with a prophetic vision of the splitting up of the royal house of David, the destruction of the temple, and the captivity; and we are also told that it is a discussion between a refined sensualist or hot-headed worldling,

[1] An Introduction to the Criticism of the Old Testament, &c., p. 471.

and a sober sage — That Solomon makes known in it his repentance to all the Church, that thereby he might glorify God, and strengthen his brethren, thus imitating his father David in the fifty-first Psalm; and that he wrote it " when he was irreligious and sceptical, during his amours and idolatry " — That " the Messiah, the true Solomon, who was known by the title, Son of David, addresses this book to the saints; " and that a profligate, who wanted to disseminate effectually his infamous sentiments, palmed it upon Solomon. It teaches us to despise the world, with all its pleasures, and flee to monasteries; it shews that sensual gratifications are man's greatest blessings upon earth — It is a philosophic lecture delivered to a literary society upon topics of the greatest moment; it is a medley of detached and heterogeneous fragments belonging to various authors and different ages — It describes the beautiful order of God's moral government, proving that all things work together for good to them that love the Lord; it proves that all is disorder and confusion, and that the world is the sport of chance — It is a treatise upon the *summum bonum;* it is " a chronicle of the lives of the kings of the house of David, from Solomon down to Zedekiah" — Its object is to prove the immortality of the soul; and to deny a future existence — It is designed to comfort the unhappy Jews in their misfortunes; it contains the gloomy imaginations of a melancholy misanthrope — It " is intended to open Nathan's speech (1 Chron. xvii.) touching the eternal throne of David; " it propounds the modern discoveries of anatomy, as well as the Harveian theory of the circulation of the blood — " It foretells what will become of men or angels to eternity (as found rebelliously fixing in their first-creation life and state of vanity, or obediently surrendering it for the second), in eternal life or death ; " it propounds a view of life inclining to fatalism, scepticism, and epicureanism ! What a solemn lesson for the pious and for the learned to abstain from dogmatism, and what an admonition not to urge one's own pious emotions or ingenious conceits as the meaning of the Word of God !

The title of the book ascribes the words therein contained to
Coheleth, or *female-gatherer* (*vide supra*, p. 1), *son of David,
King in Jerusalem.* In the twelfth verse of the first chapter
this enigmatic individual prefaces his autobiography by calling
himself by the same name; " I, *Coheleth*," says he, " was King
over Israel in Jerusalem." As Solomon was the only son of
David who was king over Israel, there can be no doubt that he
is meant by the appellation Coheleth. This is fully corroborated by the unequivocal allusions made throughout this book to
particular circumstances connected with the life of this great
monarch. Compare, for instance, Coheleth i. 16, &c., with
1 Kings iii. 12; Coheleth ii. 4 – 10, with 1 Kings v. 27 – 32,
vii. 1 – 8, ix. 17 – 19, x. 14 – 29 ; Coheleth vii. 20, with
1 Kings viii. 46; Coheleth vii. 28, with 1 Kings xi. 1 – 8 ·
Coheleth xii. 9, with 1 Kings iv. 32.

The question to be determined is, whether Solomon has really
said or written down the things contained in this book; or
whether some one else put these sentiments into his mouth as
peculiarly appropriate to him, in accordance with the well-
known form of personated authorship. In other words, Is
Solomon the *real author* of this book, or a *simple actor* in it ?

If we implicitly submit to the decision of tradition, we must
undoubtedly believe that Solomon is the *actual author* of this
book ; for this is beyond question the unanimous declaration
of both the Synagogue and the Church. The remark in the
Talmud (Baba-Bathra, 15, a) that King Hezekiah and his
associates wrote this book, as well as Isaiah, Proverbs, and the
Song of Songs,[1] does by no means contradict this traditional

---

[1] The whole passage is as follows : — מי כתבן משה כתב ספרו ופרשת בלעם ואיוב יהושע
כתב ספרו ושמונה פסוקין שבתורה שמואל כתב ספרו ושופטים ורות דוד כתב ספר תהלים על ידי
עשרה זקנים על ידי אדם הראשון על ידי מלכי צדק ועל ידי אברהם ועל ידי משה ועל ידי הימן ועל ידי
ידותון ועל ידי אסף ועל ידי שלש' בני קרח ירמיה כת' ספרו וספר מלכי' וקנות חזקי' וסיעתו כתבו
ימש'ק סימן : ישעיה משלי שיר השירי'וקהלת אנשי כנסת הגדול" כתבו קנד"ג סימן יחזקאל ושנים
עשר דניאל ומגילת אסתר עזר' כתב ספרו ויחס של דברי הימים עד לו, *who wrote them ?* [the

opinion, since this simply refers to *the final editorship*. But, if
we appeal to the internal evidence of the book itself, we must,
with equal certainty, conclude that Solomon is *the personated
author* of the sentiments ascribed to him, as will appear from
the following considerations · —

A. ARGUMENTS AGAINST THE SOLOMONIC AUTHORSHIP.

1. The book itself does not pretend to have been written by
Solomon. All the other reputed writings of this great monarch
have his name in the inscriptions. The book of Proverbs begins
with "The Proverbs *of Solomon*," so does the Song of Songs,
(*i.e., which is Solomon's*) Psalm lxxii. and lxxvii. And had this
book professed to be Solomon's, his name would surely have
appeared at least in the superscription.

2. The enigmatic and impersonal name Coheleth, *a female-
gatherer*, by which Solomon is designated in this book, shews
that he is simply introduced in an ideal sense, as the representative of wisdom.

3. The sacred writer himself clearly indicates, in chap. i. 12,
that he assumes Solomon as the speaker, for he represents him
as belonging to *the past*, making him say, " I *was* King over
Israel in Jerusalem." That the præterite *I was* (הָיִיתִי) shews
that, when this was said, Solomon was no longer king, is by no
means an invention of modern criticism ; it has been acknowledged from time immemorial, and has given rise to the legend

inspired book]. *Moses wrote his book, and the section of Balaam* (Numb.
xxii.-xxiv.), *and Job ; Joshua wrote his book, and the eight verses of the law*
(Deut. xxxiv. 5-12) ; *Samuel wrote his book, Judges and Ruth ; David wrote the
Psalms of the ten elders, viz., Adam, Melchizedek, Abraham, Moses, Heman,
Jeduthun, Asaph, and the three sons of Korah ; Jeremiah wrote his book, Kings
and Lamentations ; Hezekiah and his associates wrote Isaiah, Proverbs, the Song
of Songs, and Coheleth, designated* יִמְשֶׁ"ק [from their initials] ; *the man of the
Great Synagogue wrote Ezekiel, the twelve minor Prophets, Daniel, and Ezra,
designated by* קנ"ד ; *Ezra wrote his book, and the genealogies of the Book of
Chronicles, down to himself.* Nothing can be more plain than that the word כתב
is here used in the sense of *writing down, writing out, transcribing,* &c., for final
editorship, and has nothing to do with *authorship*.

that Solomon was dethroned by Ashmodai, king of the demons.
Hence the Chaldee paraphrase of this verse [1] —

> When King Solomon was sitting upon the throne of his kingdom, his
> heart became greatly elated with riches, and he transgressed the command-
> ment of the Word of God; and he gathered many horses, and chariots, and
> riders, and he amassed much gold and silver, and he married wives from
> foreign nations. Whereupon the anger of the Lord was kindled against
> him, and he sent to him Ashmodai, the king of the demons, and he drove
> him from the throne of his kingdom, and took away the ring from his hand,
> in order that he should roam and wander about in the world, to reprove it;
> and he went about the provincial towns and cities of the land of Israel,
> weeping and lamenting, and saying, "I am Coheleth, whose name was.
> formerly called Solomon, who was King over Israel in Jerusalem."

So also Midrash Yalkut, *in loco;* the Talmud, Gittin, 68, b;[2]
and Midrash Maase Bishlomo Hammelech.[3]   Nothing can be
more distinct than Rashi's explanation of the passage: " I was
at first," says he, " king over the whole world, then only over
Israel, then only over Jerusalem, and at last had only my
roaming stick; for it is written, I WAS king in Jerusalem, but
AM NOT KING NOW."[4]   Even Hugo of St. Victor could not get
over this præterite, and says that it is here used " because
Solomon had put off his kingly robes, abdicated his throne, and
was now lying in dust and ashes repenting over his sins, and not
deeming himself worthy to be king any longer."

Thus we have a long series of ancient witnesses confirming
the results of modern criticism, that the præterite, " *I was* king
(הָיִיתִי), represents Solomon as *being king no more.*"   But as
history forbids us to adopt their legend to account for this fact,

---

[1] כַּד הֲוָה שְׁלֹמֹה מַלְכָּא יָתִיב עַל כּוּרְסֵי מַלְכוּתֵיהּ אִיתְגְּנַבַה לִבֵּהּ לַחֲדָא עַל עָתְרֵיהּ וַעֲבַר עַל גְּזֵרַת
מֵימְרָא דַיָי וּכְנַשׁ סוּסָן וּרְתִיכִין וּפָרָשִׁין סַגִּיאִין וּצְבַר כַּסְפָּא וְדַהֲבָא לַחֲדָא וְאִתְחַתַּן בְּעַמְמִין נוּכְרָאִין מִן
יַד תְּקֵיף רוּגְזָא דַיָי עֲלֹוהִי וְשָׁדַר לְוָתֵיהּ אַשְׁמְדַאי מַלְכָּא דְשֵׁידֵי וּטְרַד יָתֵיהּ מִן כּוּרְסֵיהּ מַלְכוּתֵיהּ וּנְטַל
גוּשְׁפַּנְקֵיהּ מִן יְדֵיהּ בְּגִין דִיהַךְ מְטַלְטֵל וּגְלֵי בְּעַלְמָא וְלְאוֹכְחוּתֵיהּ וַהֲוָה מַחֲזַר עַל כְּרַכֵּי פִילְכֵי וּקִרְוֵי אַרְעָא
דִישְׂרָאֵל בָּבָא וּפְכַן וַאֲמַר אֲנָא קֹהֶלֶת דַהֲוֵי שְׁמֵיהּ שְׁלֹמֹה מִתְקְרֵי מִן קַדְמַת דְנָא הֲוֵיתִי מַלְכָּא עַל יִשְׂרָאֵל
בִּירוּשָׁלֵם

[2] *Vide supra,* p. 35.

[3] Jellinek, Baith Hammidrash, ii., p. 86, *et seq.*

[4] היתי מלך על כל העולם ולבסוף על ישראל ולבסוף על ירושלים לבדה ולבסוף אל מקלי שהרי נאמר
היתי מלך בָּירושלים אבל אכשיו אינו מלך

we have here most undeniable proof that the sacred writer describes Solomon as belonging to *the past*, and that he has assumed this great monarch as the speaker.

4. Various statements are made by Coheleth which are most incongruous, and are utterly irreconcileable with any other supposition than that Solomon is the assumed speaker.

a. In chap. i. 16 Coheleth says, " I have acquired far greater wisdom than any (king) who was before me in Jerusalem ; " so also, in ii. 7, " I bought me men-servants and maid-servants, and had house-born servants; I had also many herds of oxen and sheep, above all (the kings) who were before me in Jeru-salem." That Coheleth is here comparing himself with *kings* is evident from the nature of the case, as the comparison with individuals of a different rank to himself would fail to establish the point of greatness in question. Besides, the adjuncts בִּירוּשָׁלָםִ and עַל יְרוּשָׁלַםִ which are used with regard to both, and describe *the place of Coheleth's dominion* (i. 1. 12. 16; ii. 7. 9), shew, beyond the shadow of a doubt, that they also denote *the place of the sovereignty* of those with whom Coheleth compares himself. As Solomon, however, was only the second king over Israel, he could not therefore refer to a long succession of kings, and thus shews that he was assumed as the speaker at a very late period of the Jewish history. Hengstenberg, who admits that ii. 7 precludes the interpretations which take the comparison to consist between Solomon and non-royal personages, submits that, as Jerusalem was the seat of an ancient monarchy, which is evident from the fact that a noble member of it went forth to meet the patriarch Abraham, Solomon could therefore with propriety compare himself with the sovereigns who preceded him. But this explanation is simply gratuitous, as the Jewish history does not mention any line of kings who reigned *in Jerusalem*. The incidental and solitary mention of Melchizedek, king of *Salem*, is too mysterious and circumscribed to justify the comparison with a succession of kings in Jerusalem.

b. The addition *in Jerusalem* (i. 1. 12), which occurs in no other of the reputed writings of Solomon, shews that the book was written at a time when there was another kingship, the seat of which was *out* of Jerusalem, as this distinction became necessary only after the kingdom was divided into two, and when there was a royal residence in Samaria as well as in Jerusalem. The force of this argument may be seen from the feeble way in which it is opposed. " The addition, *in Jerusalem*," says Hengstenberg, " is to remind us that Coheleth gathered his experience in the very place whose complainings and sighings gave rise to the writing of this book." But have not all or most of the sacred writings been called forth by more immediate local circumstances? Why, then, does not some such reminder accompany the inscription of any other book?

c. Solomon speaks of his own wisdom, riches, and greatness as unparalleled (i. 16 ; ii. 7. 9). This is incompatible with modest wisdom and true greatness, and can only be accounted for on the supposition that the assumed Solomon is made to say it.

d. Coheleth declares, in ii. 18. 19, that he detested all his estates which he had toiled to acquire, because he must bequeath them to an utter stranger, who for aught he knows may foolishly waste all. Now, as this most unquestionably implies that he had no children of his own to inherit his possessions, it could not have been uttered by Solomon, who had an heir-apparent eagerly waiting to succeed him.

e. Coheleth recommends *individuals* patiently to submit to the decrees of the king, even when he abuses his authority, since the tyrant is sure to provoke the anger of *the mass* of his subjects, when condign punishment will inevitably be inflicted upon him by his people (viii. 2 – 9). The doctrine of such a relation of monarchs and their subjects could never have been propounded by Solomon, or by any other oriental sovereign, and we question whether we could even find a European monarch of the present enlightened age to endorse this view. Those who explain the whole passage as referring to God, and to the absolute obedience which creatures owe to the Creator, who is the King, are guilty of strange inconsistencies, as will be seen in the commentary.

f. The description given of a royal spendthrift, and of the misery which he inflicts upon his land (x. 16 – 19), could not proceed from the mouth of a king, and especially not from Solomon, who was himself a spendthrift, unless he intended to write a satire upon himself.

g. The state of violence and misery depicted with so much bitterness in this book — on the supposition that it could be made to harmonise with the reign of Solomon — must have been brought about by this monarch's own extravagances and sins. Is it possible that the author of these evils would speak of them in such terms? Mr. Plumptre meets this question by submitting that " there are forms of satiety and self-reproach of which this half-sad, half-scornful retrospect of a man's own life — this utterance of bitter words, by which he is condemned out of his own mouth — is the most natural expression." [1]   But we submit that it is impossible to shape the case in question into one of those forms. Here is a man, who has publicly abused God's mercies, who has violated God's law, abandoned himself to revelry with his harem of foreign and idolatrous women, for whose idols he at last built temples, and thereby caused others to be guilty of injustice and violence ; and yet all the confession he has to make before God and man is not to acknowledge his own crimes, and humble himself in dust and ashes, but simply *to complain of those whom he had made to sin.* The different things which Coheleth tells us he has tried in his lifetime, he does not in the slightest degree characterise as sinful, but simply as philosophic experiments which have failed to yield the contemplated result. And if this can be construed into an acceptable form of confession of sins and crimes, our notions of the holiness and justice of God and the moral laws of society must be radically wrong. No religious community in our days would accept such a document from an offender, as the proper expression of sin

[1] Smith's Dictionary of the Bible, art. Ecclesiastes, p. 474.

2 K

committed against God, and against its laws; and if we are in doubt as to what the Jews of old regarded as the proper "retrospect of a man's own life," laden with perhaps less guilt than that of Solomon, and what they deemed to be "the most natural expression" of such a retrospect, let us read the prayer of Daniel, and the prayer of Solomon himself at the dedication of the Temple, let us peruse the Penitential Psalms, but especially let us compare the fifty-first Psalm with the contents of "The Words of Coheleth," and we shall know whether the last can pass as such. We therefore submit that, supposing the description of the state of violence and misery given in this book could be made to harmonise with the days of Solomon, the bitter complaints of Solomon about others who simply acted a secondary part in bringing about this miserable state of things, without the slightest reference to himself, whose guilty conduct was the chief cause of it, would alone preclude the Solomonic authorship of the book.

5. But we submit that the state of oppression, violence, and misery depicted in this book cannot be reconciled with the reign of Solomon, and is therefore against the Solomonic authorship of it. Palestine, the inheritance of the Lord, was then groaning under the oppression of satraps, and presented such a scene of injustice and violence, that death was thought preferable to life, and not to have been born at all was deemed still better (iv. 1 – 4; v. 7); Asiatic despotism, which permits no will to its subjects, was rampant (viii. 1 – 4), filling "the holy places" with wicked officials (viii. 10), suddenly raising servants to posts of honour, and hurling the great from their lofty positions (x. 5 – 7); this tyranny, with its numerous spies, had penetrated into the privacy of families to such a fearful extent, that it actually became dangerous to give utterance to one's thoughts even in the secrecy of home (x. 20); wickedness and crime were perpetrated with perfect impunity, so much so, that people were thereby encouraged to commit heinous sins, and were led to deny the moral government of God (viii. 10, 11), and to neglect their duties

to the Creator (v. 1 – 5). The utter impossibility of attempting to reconcile this state of things with the age of Solomon is so manifest, that even Hengstenberg, after giving a summary of those sufferings, according to his analysis of the contents, affirms that, *this being the external and internal condition of God's people, the idea cannot for a moment be entertained that the book belongs to the time of Solomon, and that he was the author of it.*[1]

When Mr. Ayre declares, upon his own authority, that the argument derived from " the description of manners, and the complaints of oppression, misgovernment," &c., against the Solomonic authorship of this book " is of little weight," we have nothing to say; but when he adds that " Hengstenberg very properly rejects objections of this kind,"[2] evidently referring to his remark fifteen years ago in Kitto's Cyclopædia,[3] we question whether he has taken Hengstenberg's words in their legitimate sense; and maintain, that if he had been acquainted with Hengstenberg's commentary on Ecclesiastes, he would not have made such an assertion; for, besides the passage already quoted, Hengstenberg distinctly says that *the description given in the book of the oppression, misgovernment, &c., of God's people, fits solely and exclusively the Persian dominion.*[4]

6. The fact that Solomon is re e acquire wisdom, possessions, and renown, and as prosecuting his search after sensual enjoyments, *in order to ascertain what is good for the children of men* (ii. 3 – 9; iii. 12. 22, &c.), thus making philosophical experiments to discover *the summum bonum,* and to solve the problems of life, is both incompatible

---

[1] Sind nun das die äußeren und die inneren Zustände des Volkes Gottes, so wird nicht daran gedacht werden können, daß das Buch aus Salomos Zeit und von ihm verfaßt sey. Der Prediger Salomo, p. 6.

[2] An Introduction to the Criticism of the Old Testament, &c., p. 740.

[3] A Cyclopædia of Biblical Literature, art. Ecclesiastes, pp. 594, 595.

[4] Die dargelegten Züge nun passen einzig und allein auf die Zeit der Persischen Herrschaft über das Volk Gottes. . . . . Wie die äußeren, so passen auch die inneren Zustände des Volkes, wie sie sich in unserem Buche darstellen, auf die Zeit der Persischen Herrschaft. *Ibid.*, pp. 5, 6.

with the conduct of the historical Solomon, and is an idea
of a much later period than the age of this great monarch. It
was evidently introduced into Palestine by those Jews who
bestowed " much study " upon the " many books " (xii. 12) of
the Greek philosophers, and the speculations to which it gave
rise, as recorded in this book, contain the incipient forms of
Pharisaism and Sadduceeism.

7. The reference to a future bar of judgment, when all the
present irregularities in the moral government of God shall be
rectified by the Judge of the quick and the dead, whereby
Coheleth solves the grand problem of this book, shews, beyond
all doubt, that Solomon could not have been the author of it,
and that it must be a post-exile production.

With those who believe that the blessed Trinity is revealed
in the first verse of the first chapter of Genesis; that the doctrine
of justification by faith, the atonement, and all the other cardinal
truths of Christianity, are set forth in the chapters immediately
following, we do not intend to argue. We appeal to those whom
a rational and reverential study of Holy Writ, and a due regard
to the laws of language, have taught that God, who causes the
natural light at first to break feebly upon our eyes, and to increase
gradually in splendour till it attains to its meridian glory, also
caused the light of the Sun of Righteousness, at first beaming
faintly, to shine more and more unto the perfect day, and
we ask if *such an explicit declaration* about the return of the
soul to God, who shall hereafter judge not only every action
but every secret of man, whether it be good or evil, can be
assigned to the early dawn of Revelation? Let the dim
intimations respecting a future state, given under the types
and figures prior to the exile (Gen. i. 27, v. 24, xxxvii. 35,
xlix. 33; Deut. xviii. 10, 11; 1 Sam. xi. 6, xxviii. 7, &c.; Isa.
viii. 19; xxvi. 18, 19, xxix. 4; Ezek. xxxvii. 1–4), be compared with the naked truth, as declared after the exile by
Daniel (xii. 2, 3) in the Book of Wisdom (ii. 23, &c.; vi.
18, 19), Tobit (ii. 17), 2 Macabees (vii. 9. 36), and especially in

the New Testament; and we submit that the gradual development of this doctrine will be fully recognised; and hence it will also be conceded, that the distinct reference of Coheleth to a future judgment, precludes the idea of the Solomonic authorship of the book.

8. The strongest argument, however, against the Solomonic authorship of this book, is its vitiated language and style. We do not allude so much to the numerous Aramaic expressions, which have no parallel in any other portion of Scripture of equal size, and which would of itself be sufficient to shew that it is the last written work in the canon of the Old Testament, but we refer to the whole complexion of it. We could as easily believe that Chaucer is the author of Rasselas, as that Solomon wrote Coheleth.

B. — ARGUMENTS FOR THE SOLOMONIC AUTHORSHIP EXAMINED.

1. It is asserted that the book itself ascribes the words therein contained to Solomon, that it represents him as narrating his personal experience (I gave my heart to so and so; I did so and so; I saw; I concluded, &c.), and that to depart from the literal meaning of these statements is to call in question the truth of Scripture. But, as Mr. Plumptre rightly remarks, " this hypothesis, that every such statement in a canonical book must be received as literally true, is, in fact, an assumption that inspired writers were debarred from forms of composition which were open, without blame, to others. In the literature of every other nation, the form of personated authorship, where there is no *animus decipiendi*, has been recognised as a legitimate channel for the expression of opinion, or the quasi-dramatic representation of character. Why should we venture on the assertion that, if adopted by the writers of the Old Testament, it would have made them guilty of falsehood, and been inconsistent with their inspiration ?" [1] Other figures of speech, *involving the same principle*, are used both in the Old and New Testaments. Our

---

[1] Smith's Dictionary of the Bible, art. Ecclesiastes, p. 474.

Saviour, in his description of the poor and the rich man, not only gives the former a name, but puts statements into the mouth of the latter and of Abraham (the man *cried and said:* Father Abraham, and Abraham *said:* Son, remember, &c.), and is it urged, that to depart from the literal meaning here is to call in question the truth of Scripture? If it be admitted that the sacred writers used one figure of speech whereby they made people say things which in reality they did not say, there can be no difficulty in their using another figure which involved the same thing. No one ever thought that Plato, Cicero, &c., violated truth because they used it, and it never enters our minds to characterise the Book of Wisdom as an imposition, for personating Solomon. It is therefore unreasonable to urge that as an insurmountable difficulty here, which forms no difficulty at all elsewhere.

2. It is urged that the book has been handed down as Solomon's by the concurrent voice of tradition, and that it would be both " dangerous and irreligious to desert this combined testimony." But we submit that whatever may be the authority of tradition on other points, it has certainly no power to determine points of criticism, and that this is practically acknowledged by all modern expositors, as may be seen in every page of their works. Tradition has handed down the Book of Wisdom as the inspired work of Solomon. Clement of Alexandria, Origen, Tertullian, Cyprian, Athanasius, Cyril, Epiphanius, Eusebius, Augustine, Isidore, &c., quote it as such "To the testimony of those few among the ancients," says Calmet, "who have disputed its authority, we oppose a crowd of witnesses, in all ages of the Church, who have acknowledged and quoted it as divine Scripture. In short, to the scruples of those who, seeing antiquity wavering upon this point, have found some difficulty to persuade themselves to admit this book into the canon, we oppose the third council of Carthage, in 397; that of Sardica, in 347; that of Constantinople, in Trullo, in 692; the eleventh of Toledo, in

' See vol. ii. of Horne's Introduction, Davidson's cd., pp. 1323, 1324.

675; that of Florence, in 1438; and, lastly, the fourth session of the council of Trent, all of which expressly admitted this book into the class of holy scripture. And there is scarce any ancient father who has not quoted and commended it. Many of them attribute it to Solomon, others to some prophet, and all to an inspired writer."[1] Tradition has treated the parable of Dives and Lazarus as a real narrative, yet the most pious and learned Protestants deny the canonicity of the Book of Wisdom, and reject the interpretation of the passage in Luke, without regarding it as " dangerous and irreligious to desert this combined testimony." If we are at liberty to use our judgment in one case in defiance of tradition, surely we cannot be denounced for using it in another.

As the date of the book must be determined by internal evidence, it cannot be expected that it will ever be definitely settled. The Rabbinical Hebrew, in which it is written, leaves no doubt in our mind that it must have originated at least in the latter end of the Persian government (350 – 340 B.C.); and if it could be shewn that the Old Testament canon was not closed till after that time, the language and complexion of the book would fully justify us in assigning it to a much later period.

The form of the book is poetico-didactic, without the beautiful parallelisms and rhythm of the poetry written in the golden age of the Hebrew language. Even the grandest portion of the book (xi. 1 – 7), where the sacred writer rises infinitely above his regular level, is devoid of those charms which imparted such life and fascination to the older Hebrew poetry. The gnomes and maxims with which it abounds, and which have caused some erroneously to assign to it a *gnomological* character, are simply introduced to illustrate certain points in question, and only show that when the book was written, the proverbial sayings of the Solomonic age had already become household words, and were largely introduced in discussing the affairs of life.

[1] Preface to the Book of Wisdom, given in Patrick, Lowth, Arnald, Whitby, and Lowman's Commentary.

SECTION VII. — EXEGETICAL HELPS.

ANCIENT VERSIONS.

1. The Septuagint, } in Stier's and Theile's Polyglot.
2. The Vulgate,
3. St. Jerome, Translation and Comment., Opp. Tom. ii.
4. The Syriac, in Walton's Polyglot and Bible Society's ed.
5. The Chaldee Paraphrase, in Bomberg's and Buxtorf's Rabbinic Bible.

JEWISH COMMENTATORS.

6. Rashi, in the Rabbinic Bible.
7. Rashbam, edited by Jellinek.
8. Ibn Ezra, in the Rabbinic Bible.
9. Mendelssohn, translated by Mr. Preston.
10. Herzfeld, קֹהֶלֶת übersetzt und ausgelegt.
11. Cahen, La Bible. Tom. xvi.
12. Philippson, Die Israelitische Bibel, Dritter Theil.

CHRISTIAN COMMENTATORS.

13. Pineda, Comment. in Ecclesiasten.
14. Mercer, Comment. in Jobum, et Solomonis Proverbia, Ecclesiasten, &c.
15. Grotius, Opp. Tom. i.
16. Reynolds, Annotation on the Book of Ecclesiastes.
17. Le Clerc, Comment. in Vet. Test. Tom. iii.
18. Desvoeux, Philological and Critical Essay on Ecclesiastes.
19. Hodgson, Ecclesiastes, a new Translation.
20. Holden, An Attempt to illustrate the Book of Ecclesiastes.
21. Rosenmüller, Scholia in Vet. Test. P. ix , vol. ii.
22. Knobel, Commentar über das Buch Koheleth.
23. Ewald, Sprüche Salomo's Koheleth.
24. Noyes, A new Translation of the Proverbs, Ecclesiastes, &c.
25. Hitzig, Der Prediger Salomo.
26. Heiligstedt, in Maure's Comment. Vol. iv., sect. 11.
27. Stuart, A Commentary on Ecclesiastes.
28. Elster, Commentar über den Prediger.
29. Vaihinger, Der Prediger und das Hohelied.
30. Hengstenberg, Der Prediger Salomo, translated into English by D. W. Simon, in Clark's Foreign Theological Library.

For particulars about the dates and places of these commentaries, see the Historical Sketch.

THE

WORDS OF COHELETH,

SON OF DAVID, KING IN JERUSALEM.

WORDS OF COHELETH,

SON OF DAVID, KING IN JERUSALEM.

PROLOGUE.

CHAPTER I. 2 11.

Coheleth declares that all human efforts are utterly vain (2). Man has no
advantage from all his labour (3); he must speedily quit this life,
whilst the earth abides for ever (4). The objects of nature depart and
retrace their course again, but man vanishes and is for ever forgotten
(5 – 11).

2 Vanity of vanities, saith Coheleth, vanity of vanities, all is

1. *The words of Coheleth, &c.* For
the explanation of this verse, see
Introduction, sec. i.

2. *Vanity of vanities, &c.* Deeply
impressed with the brevity of man's
life, and with the conviction that no
human effort can protract man's
existence here, Coheleth denounces,
in the most intense language imaginable, all undue exertions to satisfy
the cravings of the soul. הֶבֶל (from
הָבַל, *to steam, to exhale, to breathe*),
prop. *steam, vapour, breath;* hence,
tropically, that which is unsubstantial and evaporates, *nothingness,
vanity,* is the *construct* of הֶבֶל, like
זֶרַע of זֶרַע, and חֲדַר of חֶדֶר, comp.
Ewald, Gram. § 213, a; Fürst, Lex.
s. v. The construction of the same
noun in the genitive expresses the
superlative degree, *vanity of vanities,* i. e., *utter* or *absolute vanity,*
comp. עֶבֶד עֲבָדִים, *servant of servants,*
i. e., *most abject servant* (Gen. ix. 25;
Numb. iii. 32 ; Song of Songs i. 1;
1 Tim. vi. 15 ; Gesen. § 119, 2 ;
Ewald, § 313 c.) The repetition of
the same phrase, *vanity of vanities,*
a second time, gives the highest
intensity to the statement; comp.
נָשְׂאוּ נְהָרוֹת יְהֹוָה נָשְׂאוּ נְהָרוֹת קוֹלָם, *the
floods have lifted up, O Eternal !
the floods have lifted up their voice*
(Ps. xciii. 3; cxv. 1). הֶבֶל here is
not to be taken as synonymous with
the Greek τὸ πᾶν, *the universe,* (Geier,
Rosenmüller, &c.), which contradicts
the sequel (iii. 11 – 14), and is contrary to the context, where the well-
regulated and permanent laws of

3 vanity: since man hath no advantage from all his toil
4 wherewith he toileth under the sun; for generation passeth
away and generation cometh on; while the earth abideth

nature are contrasted with the transitory existence of man, but refers to
כָּל עֲמָלוֹ וְגוֹ׳, all the undue human exertions, spoken of in the next verse.

3. Since man hath no advantage, &c.
The inspired writer gives here the
reason why he pronounced all human
efforts as useless, since, with all his
exertions, the rational man cannot
secure to himself any real and lasting
happiness. As this verse assigns a
reason for the statement made in the
preceding verse, Coverdale and the
Bishop's Bible rightly begin it with
for. Both in the Old and New
Testament, as well as in profane
writings, interrogations are frequently
used as emphatic denials; compare
הֲתַחַת אֱלֹהִים אָנֹכִי, am I instead of God?
i. e., surely I am not God, I am not
almighty (Gen. xxx. 2 ; l. 19 ; Zech.
i. 5; Matt. xvi. 26; Gesen. § 153, 2;
Ewald, § 324, b). This is especially
the case with מַה, which loses entirely
its interrogative force, and becomes
an emphatic negation; comp. מַה־לָּנוּ
חֵלֶק בְּדָוִד, we have no portion in David
(1 Kings xii. 16), and is parallel to
לֹא not, in the next clause; and וּמָה
אֶתְבּוֹנֵן עַל־בְּתוּלָה, and I should not look
upon a virgin (Job xxxi. 1), where the
Sept. has καὶ οὐ; the Vulg. ut ne, and
the Syriac, ܠܡܳܢ comp. also Job vi.
25; xvi. 6; and see Fürst, Lex., s.v 4.
The phrase מַה־יִּתְרוֹן לָאָדָם, therefore,
is tantamount to there is no ADVAN-
TAGE WHATEVER to man, &c. יִתְרוֹן
is from יָתַר. to extend, to run over, to
surpass, to leave behind, according to
the analogy of פִּתְרוֹן, interpretation,
and שִׁלְטוֹן power (infra, viii. 4; Gesen.
§ 84, 15; Ewald, § 163, d), and signifies that which is over, remainder,
gain, profit, benefit, remaining or
abiding benefit or happiness. This
word, which only occurs in this book,
(vide infra, ii. 11, 13; iii. 9; v. 8, 15;
vii. 12; x. 10), is frequently found
in later Hebrew writings. The ל in
לָאָדָם, the dative appurtenance, has
here taken the vowel of the article,
which is fallen away by contraction,
in consequence of the preposition
(Gesen. § 35, 2; Rem. 2). עָמָל signifies oppressive labour, toil, implying
wearisome effort, and is rendered
more energetic by the construction
עָמָל עָמֵל, the noun and the verb being
of the same root; compare the similar
construction in the New Testament,
ἐπιθυμία ἐπεθύμησα, with desire have
I desired, i. e., I have intensely or
greatly desired (Luke xxii. 15; John
iii. 29; Acts v. 28; Gesen. § 138, 1;
Rem. 1; Ewald, § 281). The phrase
is well rendered by the Sept., ἐν παντὶ
μόχθῳ αὐτοῦ ᾧ μοχθεῖ; and Chald., טָרְחֵיהּ
דְּהוּא טָרַח: the rendering of Luther,
Mühe die er hat; followed by Coverdale and the Auth. Ver., the labour
which he taketh, is too languid. The
שֶׁ in שֶׁיַּעֲמֹל is an abbreviation of אֲשֶׁר:
comp. Song of Songs i. 6; Gesen.
§ 36. The phrase תַּחַת הַשֶּׁמֶשׁ, under
the sun, which only occurs in this
book (i. 14; ii. 11. 17. 20. 22; iii. 16;
iv. 1. 3. 7. 15; v. 12. 17; vi. 1. 12;
viii. 9. 15. 17; ix. 3. 6. 9. 11. 13;
x. 5), and in later Hebrew writings,
is tantamount to עַל־הָאָרֶץ, which is
used in viii. 14. 16; xi. 2, and refers
to מַה־יִּתְרוֹן לָאָדָם בָּאָרֶץ, what
lasting benefit has man upon earth,
&c. The Chaldee curiously paraphrases this verse, what does man
bequeath to man after his death, of
all his toil which he toils, &c.

4. For generation passeth away, &c.
The utter failure and vanity of all
human effort is shewn by the fact
that man, with all his ploddings,
cannot protract his short continuance; generation after generation
drops off the tree of life, while the
earth abides for ever. What an awful
fact, that the world, and all the
objects around, are abiding, and

ס for ever.   The sun also riseth and the sun setteth, and,
though it pantingly goeth to its place, it riseth there again.

possess an immutable and ever-
returning course, but man has no
fixed abode here, and must rapidly
disappear from this scene of action.
Man's assiduity and perseverance
may secure for him affluence and
honours, yet the ruthless hand of
death violently shakes him off the
tree of life, scatters all his amassed
wealth, buries all his acquirements
in oblivion, while the earth, upon
which he displays his ingenuity,
abides for ever; and in this respect
the earth, man's workshop, has an
advantage over man.   Knobel and
Stuart, and, in fact, most commentators, make the sentiment of this verse
to be, " that as the earth is fixed
and immutable, admitting of no
change for the better, man has no
hope of lightening his misery by
vainly attempting to effect a change
in unchangeable nature; his condition in the world, and his relation to
it, must ever remain the same.   His
innate frailty, on the one hand, and,
on the other hand, the foreclosure
against any change in the things
without, concur to shew that he can
find no permanent happiness."   But
this is against the scope of the passage, which evidently contrasts the
transitory state (הֹלֵךְ) *of man*, with
the *permanently abiding condition*
(עֹמָדֶת) *of the earth*.   This is the
burden of the argument, that man,
who was made a little lower than the
angels, who is capable of developing
such intellectual life, should especially be so ephemeral, while inferior
nature abides permanently.   The
passage in Tacit. An. iii., c. 53, "All
human things go a certain round,
and there are revolutions in man
analogous to the vicissitudes of the
seasons," to which Knobel refers, is
inapposite.   More appropriate is the
remark of Ibn Ezra, בעבור היות כל נמצא
תחת השמש מורכב מארבעה מוסדים מהם יצאו
ואליהם ישובו והם האש והרוח הנך שהוא האויר
והמים והארץ זכר ארבעתם והחל בארץ שהיא

כמו היולדת ואחר כן זכר השמש מקום האש
בעבור רוב חומה והיא האש המולדת ואחר כן
הרוח והמים, *because all things that are
found under the sun are composed of
four elements, from which they proceed, and to which they return, and
these are fire, the quiet wind*, i. e., *the
air, and the water, and the earth,
these four are adduced; and the earth
is mentioned first, because she is, as it
were, the mother; then the sun is mentioned instead of fire, because of its
great heat, and this is the generative
fire; then the air and the water.*
הָלַךְ, *to go*, like words signifying *to
depart* in other languages, is euphe-
mistically used for *departing this
life, dying;* comp. *infra,* v. 14, 15;
viii. 10; Ps. xxxix. 14; Job x.
21; xiv. 20; and ὁ μὲν υἱὸς τοῦ ἀνθρώπου
ὑπάγει in Matt. xxvi. 24.   The ו in
וְהָאָרֶץ has, as frequently, an *adversative* meaning, *yet while* (Gesen.
§ 155, 1, b; § Ewald, 341, a).

5. *The sun also ariseth,* &c.   From
the firmly fixed earth, Coheleth proceeds to the perpetually coursing
sun, and here, again, he shews the
advantage of nature over man.   The
sun rises in brilliancy in the morning, and, though he, exhausted,
retires in the evening, and his
brightness is obscured by the darkness of night, yet he rises again
every morning in equal splendour,
rejoicing like a hero to run his
course again; but man, when he
goes, returns hither no more.   Thus
Job, when speaking of the same fact,
shewing the advantage of nature over
man, adduces a tree, which will grow
again after it has been cut down;
but man, when once cut off, appears
no more

There remaineth hope for the tree,
If it is cut down it striketh out again,
And its shoots do not fail;
If its roots moulder in the earth,
And its trunk decayeth in the dust,
It flourisheth again from the smell of water,
And, like young plants, groweth branches;
But man, he dieth and is destroyed,
Man, departing, is gone.   xiv. 7 - 9.

6 The wind goeth to the south, and turneth to the north; it
goeth round and round, yet the wind returneth to its course.

Still more striking is the parallel in
Catullus —

> Soles occidere, et redire possunt;
> Nobis cum semel occidit brevis lux,
> Nox est perpetua una dormienda.

> " Suns that set again may rise;
> We, when once our fleeting light,
> Once our day in darkness dies,
> Sleep in one eternal night."

CATULLUS, v.

Elster, therefore, has mistaken the
sense, in affirming that the sacred
writer adduces the course of the sun
to indicate " the gloomy impression
which the contemplation of it produces upon the human mind, because
this luminary appears tired of its
ever-restless motion, and annoyed at
the endless monotony of its course."
בּוֹא, *to go in, to enter,* is used of the
setting sun, because, according to the
Hebrews and other ancient nations,
it enters in the evening into the
ocean, its subterraneous dwelling
(Ps. xix. 5; Hab. iii. 11). The וְ in
וְאֶל is, as frequently, to be rendered
though. שָׁאַף, *to snuff, to breathe hard,*
to pant with running to its subterraneous dwelling (Job vii 2; xxxvi.
20). The rendering of the Septuagint, ἕλκει, *draws heavily,* and
Aquila, εἰσπνεῖ, *fetches breath, pants,*
faintly express the meaning of the
original, while that of Symm. Theod.
ἐπαναστρέφει, Vulg. *revertitur,* misses it
altogether. The Chaldee's, Rashi's,
and Rashbam's explanation of the
words וְאֶל מְקוֹמוֹ שׁוֹאֵף, " the sun, which
rises in the morning in the east,
and sets in the evening in the west,
goes pantingly all night through the
sea back to its place (i. e., the east),
where it rises again," yields substantially the same illustration which
we have deduced from this verse.
Ewald's rendering, die Sonne geht
unter (וְאֶל מְקוֹמוֹ) und zwar an ihren
Ort, wo sie keuchend aufgeht, *i. e.,*
the sun sets, and that in its place,
where it also rises pantingly, is both
forced in its construction and incongruous. Surely it is more natural

to expect that the sun would be described as exhausted at his setting,
after the long and swift course of the
day, than at his rising, when we are
expressly told that, refreshed, *he*
rejoices like a hero to run his race
(Ps. xix. 5). זרח is well rendered by
the Syriac ܢܕܢܚ ܬܘܒ שָׁב לזרח,
rises again, as is evident from the
context, where so much stress is laid
upon *the repetition* of the courses of
the objects adduced.

6. *The wind goeth to the south,* &c.
The howling and empty wind is
adduced as another proof that the
objects of nature have an advantage
over man. The apparently restless
and disorderly wind has its regular
course; it goes to the south, and
turns about to the north, and,
though it sometimes veers vehe-
mently round · the whole earth, it
always *returns* to its rounds; but
man, when he goes, returns hither
no more. The word רוּחַ, *wind,* is to
be supplied in the first clause from
the second. The repetition סוֹבֵב סוֹבֵב,
round, round, expresses *continuance*
(Gen. xiv. 10; Deut. ii. 27; Gesen.
§ 108, 4; Ewald, 313, a). The *south*
and *north* are mentioned, because
the *east* and *west* have already been
referred to in connection with the
rising and setting of the sun, and
thus all the four quarters of the
earth are divided between the sun
and the wind. The verb שׁוּב, *to*
return, is here construed with the
preposition עַל, *to,* as in Prov. xxvi.
11. כְּכֶלֶב שָׁב עַל־קֵאוֹ, *as a dog returns*
to his vomit (comp. also Mal. iii. 24).
The suffix in סְבִיבֹתָיו expresses *the*
well known, the regular rounds, or
course; the whole clause is well
rendered by the Vulg. *et in circulos*
suos revertitur. The Sept., Syriac,
Arabic, Vulg., Rashi, Rashbam,
who are followed by some modern commentators, refer the first
part of this verse to the sun, *i. e.,*

7 All the streams run into the sea, and the sea doth not
   overflow; the place where the streams go to, thence they
8 return again.   All words are feeble.   Men could never utter,

*the sun goeth towards the south, and
turneth about unto the north ;* but
this is against the symmetry of the
description, since it would predicate
too much of the sun and too little
of the wind.   Besides this would
break the thread of the argument;
since the sun, like the wind and the
streams, is evidently adduced to shew
that, notwithstanding his departure,
he returns again, which would be lost
according to this construction.   Still
more objectionable is the Chaldee
paraphrase, which refers *the whole*
of this verse to the sun.   When
Dr. Adam Clarke affirms that " our
Version alone has *mistaken* the meaning," as he calls it, I wonder that he
should have made such an assertion
in the face of Ibn Ezra, Luther,
Coverdale, the Bishop's Bible, &c.

7. *All the streams,* &c.   The flowing streams are the last instance
which the inspired writer points out
to illustrate his position.   These
streams, which apparently run off to ·
be absorbed in the bosom of the
mighty ocean, nevertheless return by
subterraneous passages and channels; but man, when he goes, returns
hither no more.   According to the
Hebrews, and other ancient nations,
the earth is surrounded by the great
ocean, with which the different seas
and rivers are connected by subterraneous passages and channels, and
it is through these that the streams
make their way backwards and for-
wards to their parent water (Gen.
vii. 11; Job xxxviii. 16; Prov. viii.
28; Sirach xl. 11); hence the Chaldee paraphrase of this verse, כָּל נַחֲלַיָּא
וּמַבּוּעֵי מַיָּא אָזְלִין וְנַגְדִּין לְמֵי אוֹקְיָנוֹס דְּמַסְחַר
לְעָלְמָא כְּגוּשְׁפַּנְקָא וְאוֹקְיָנוֹס לֵיתוֹהִי מִתְמַלֵּי וְלַאֲתַר
דְּנַחֲלַיָּא אָזְלִין וְנַגְדִּין תַּמָּן אִינִין תַּיְיבִין לְמֵיזַל מִבְּנוֹרֵי
תְהוֹמָא, *all the rivers and streams of
water run and flow into the ocean,
which surrounds the world like a ring,
and the ocean is not full; and to the
place where the rivers have run and*

*flowed, thither they return again
through the subterraneous channels*
(comp. also Hom. Il. xviii. 609 ; xxi.
196). נְחָלִים (from נָחַל, *to run, to flow*)
is better rendered *streams,* being of a
much wider meaning than the expression *rivers.* הַיָּם is *the great ocean*
which surrounds the earth, rendered
by the Chaldee, אוֹקְיָנוֹס, ὠκεᾶνός. אֵין,
not, prop. const. of אַיִן, *nothingness,* is
the negative of יֵשׁ, *is,* and includes
the verb *to be* in all its tenses (Gesen.,
§ 152; Ewald, § 321; Fürst, Lex. *s. v.*)
מְקוֹם, *place,* is the *const.* before
שֶׁ=אֲשֶׁר, to indicate that the relative
clause is to be regarded as one noun
(comp. *infra,* xi. 3; Gen. xl. 3; Lev.
iv. 24; Gesen. § 116,2; Ewald, § 332, c).
Ibn Ezra's explanation of the words,
וְהַיָּם אֵינֶנּוּ מָלֵא, *and the sea is not full,*
כי חמיד יעלה איד מהים אל הרקיע והם רוב
העננים והמים המתוקים יעלו בעבור קלוחם והאד
יֵשׁוּב גשם, *because there is evaporation
constantly rising from the sea to the
sky, which forms the clouds,—the sweet
waters only ascending because of their
lightness,—and the vapour is converted
into rain,* is too modern an idea,
and was unknown to the ancient
Hebrews, as is evident from the
passages quoted above, and from the
Chaldee paraphrase.   With Symmachus, the Vulgate, Chaldee, several MSS., Grotius, Umbreit, &c., שָׁם
is to be taken for מִשָּׁם, *thence,* as is
evident from verse 5, where the sun
is described as rising again (שָׁם) *in*
or *from* the place to which it went.
The words שָׁבִים לָלָכֶת, however, are
not to be rendered *they return to go
again,* but *they return again,* which is
evident from ver. 14, where the same
phrase occurs, and must be rendered
so ; the verb שׁוּב is frequently used
adverbially for *again ;* comp. לֹא תָשׁוּב
עֵינִי לִרְאוֹת טוֹב, *mine eyes shall not see
happiness again* (Job vii. 7; Gen. xxvi.
18 ; Gesen. § 142, 3 ; Ewald, § 285).

8. *All words are feeble,* &c.   Having shewn, in some · of the most

the eye could never be satisfied with seeing, and the ear
9 could never be filled with hearing all. What hath been still is,

prominent instances of nature, the permanency and uniformity of their existence and operations, contrasted with the transitoriness and instability of man, the sacred writer exclaims, that all human language is too feeble to enumerate all the objects in nature which possess the same properties, and might be adduced in illustration of his proposition — objects so numerous that the eye could never see, nor the ear hear of, them all. As דָּבָר in Hebrew, like the corresponding expressions in

other languages (comp. ܡܶܠܬܳܐ in Syriac, מִלָּה in Chaldee, from מְלַל, *to speak*, ῥῆμα in Greek, from ῥέω, *to speak*, whence also *res* in Latin, Sache in German, from fagen) is derived from a verb signifying *to speak* (דָּבַר), and, like its equivalents in other languages, denotes both *a word*, as uttered by the living voice, and *a thing* which a word is used to express; hence דְּבָרִים has here been rendered by some *words*, and by others *things*. The word יְגֵעִים, too, has been variously explained, as some took it in its *passive* signification, and others have assigned to it an *active* meaning. Thus the Vulg. has CUNCTÆ RES DIFFICILES, *all things are hard*, which Luther (es ift alles Thun so voll Mühe daß, &c.) and Coverdale (*all things are so hard*, &c.) follow. Desvoeux has, *all these considerations are tiresome*; Hodgson and Boothroyd have, *all things thus at their task*. But, against these renderings is to be urged, that though דָּבָר undoubtedly means also *a thing*, yet the context requires that it should be taken here in its primary sense, viz., *a word*, as is evident from the verb דִּבֶּר, with which it is connected, thus forming the well-known construction דִּבֶּר דָּבָר, (*vide infra*, vii. 21). As for יְגֵעִים, it is invariably used in *a passive* sense (comp. Deut. xxv. 18; 2 Sam. xii. 2), and can therefore

form no exception here. Moreover, the rendering we advocate is the one most compatible with the scope of the passage, as will be seen from the remarks upon the next clause.

The eye could never be satisfied, &c. The objects which might be adduced in illustration of this proposition are so numerous that the eye could never see them all, nor the ear hear all. As the eye is not only the inlet of thought, but is also the outlet of feelings and emotions, those inward conditions and actions are ascribed to it which it manifests.   Thus, because it *expresses* the hoping of the soul, the eye is represented *as hoping;* comp. עֵינֵי כֹּל אֵלֶיךָ יְשַׂבֵּרוּ, THE EYES *of all* HOPE *to thee* (Ps. cxlv. 15); hence, also, the phrase מַחְמַד עֵינַיִם, *the desire of the eyes* (1 Kings xx. 6); ἐπιθυμία τῶν ὀφθαλμῶν (1 John ii. 16), and the *insatiableness of the eye* in the text before us (comp. also *infra*, ii. 10; iv. 8; Prov. xxvii. 20). Reynolds, Gill, Holden, &c., explain the meaning of this clause, "the pleasure of these senses is so blunted by the same objects constantly presented, that they are pricked with further desire of new objects of delight." But this evidently arose from their mistaking the sense of the first clause. The sacred writer, having described the stability and regularity of several objects of nature, affirms, in this verse, that these are by no means all; that the objects which possess the same properties are too numerous to be described; and that the curious eye, which wishes to see them all, and the inquisitive ear that desires to hear all, could never be gratified, for the telling of them would require more words than man possesses; the human eye and ear, whose functions are of short duration, determined to compass all, would cease to exist long before all is told, and hence *could never be satisfied*.

9. *What hath been*, &c. The in-

and what hath been done is still done, and there is nothing
10　new under the sun.　　If there be anything of which it
is said, Behold this is new! it hath been long ago, in

ference is here drawn from the statement made in the preceding verse.
In all those objects of nature, therefore, we see that that which has
existed continues to exist, and the
motions which these existing objects
have made they make again ; the
earth, which has existed, still exists;
the sun is still the same, and runs
the same race ; the wind is still the
same, and returns to its well-known
course ; the streams are still the
same, and flow in the same manner
into the mighty ocean : it is the
same with numberless objects of
nature — their existence is permanent, their course regular and uniform, and there is no deviation.
מַה־שֶּׁהָיָה is rendered by the Sept.
interrogatively, τί τὸ γεγονός ; τί τὸ
πεποιημένον ; Vulg. *quid est quod fuit ?*
which is followed by the Arabic,
Luther, Grotius, Holden, Boothroyd,
&c.; but this is contrary to the usage
of the combination מַה־שֶּׁ in this book
(comp. *infra*, iii. 15 ; vi. 10 ; vii. 24;
viii. 7 ; x. 14; where it signifies *id
quod*, and where even the Sept., with
the exception of vii. 24, and the
Vulg., translate it so). As in other
languages, both interrogatives מִי,
who, for *persons*, and מָה, *what*, for
things, are used in Hebrew for *indefinite pronouns, whosoever, whatsoever*,
with the relative pronoun either expressed or implied (*infra*, v. 9 ; ix. 4;
Exod. xxiv. 14; Prov. ix. 4; Numb.
xxiii. 3 ; 1 Sam. xx 4; Gesen. § 37, 2;
Ewald, § 331, b ; § 357, c), so that
מַה־שֶּׁ exactly corresponds to מִי אֲשֶׁר in
Exod. xxxii. 33 ; 2 Sam. xx. 11.
The verb הָיָה, *to be*, refers to the
permanent existence of the objects
of nature, and עָשָׂה, *to do*, to their
uniform and regular operations. The
imperfect expresses the permanent
state, *it is now and ever shall be*
(Gen. xliii. 32; Prov. xv. 20; Gesen.
§ 127, 2 ; Ewald, § 136, b). אֵין כֹּל

nothing (Numb. xi. 6 ; Judg. xiii. 4;
2 Sam. xii. 13 ; 2 Kings iv. 2 ; Prov.
xiii. 7), corresponding to the Greek
οὐ πᾶς (Luke i. 37 ; Rev. xxi. 17;
Gesen. § 152, 1 ; Ewald, § 323, b).

10. *If there be anything*, &c. Having
affirmed that no innovation occurs
in the objects of nature, the sacred
writer states how, if anything should
seem new in the operations of nature,
it is to be accounted for; it is merely
owing to the individual who happens
not to be acquainted with the pheno-
menon which had taken place in
bygone years. The particle אִם, *if*,
is implied before יֵשׁ, *there is* ; comp.
Judg. xi. 36 ; Prov. xxiv. 10 ; Song
of Songs, viii. 1 ; Ewald, § 357, b.
דָּבָר, *a word* also *a thing*, vide supra,
verse 8. אֲשֶׁר in שֶׁיֹּאמַר, is not the
nominative, making it a *prosopopeia*
(Desv. p. 310), *a thing crying out to
the beholder, See this is new*, but is
the *accusative*; and יֹאמַר, the *third
person*, as frequently elsewhere, is
used for the *impersonal* or *passive ;*
compare exactly the same phrase
עַל־כָּל־אֲבֵדָה אֲשֶׁר יֹאמַר כִּי־הוּא זֶה, *for anything lost of which*, or *respecting
which, it is said that it is this*, i. e.,
דְּבַר־פֶּשַׁע, miserably rendered in the
Auth. Ver. (Exod. xxii. 8); and see
also *infra*, vii. 21 ; ix. 15; xii. 1. 5;
Gen. xi. 9 ; 1 Sam. xix. 22 ; Gesen.
§ 137, 3 ; Ewald, § 282, 2. The Sept.
renders the words יֵשׁ דָּבָר שֶׁיֹּאמַר, ὅς
λαλήσει καὶ ἐρεῖ, *whatsoever speaks and
says*, so also the Syriac ܟܠ ܢܡܠܠ
ܘܢܐܡܪ, as if the Hebrew were
כָּל שֶׁיְדַבֵּר וְשֶׁיֹּאמַר; the Vulg., again, has
NEC VALET QUISQUAM DICERE, *nor is
any man able to say*, as if the Hebrew
were לֹא יוּכַל אִישׁ לְדַבֵּר ; but we are
prepared for such deviations from
the Hebrew text, by the frequent
blunders which we meet in those
versions. The expression כְּבָר, from

11 the time of old, which was before us. But there is no

כָּבַר, *to plait, to bind,* or *tie strongly together,* hence *to be strong, great, long,* is used adverbially for *long ago, already, formerly;* אֵלֶּה, by which the Sept. renders it, and *jam* of the Vulg., are not exact equivalents, inasmuch as these refer to *both* time past and present, which has caused the translators of our Authorised Version and some commentators to ascribe the same signification to the Hebrew expression (*vide infra,* ii. 16), whereas כְּבָר is invariably used with reference to time *past;* it only occurs in this book (ii. 12, 16; iii. 15; iv. 2; vi. 10; ix. 6. 7), but is of frequent occurrence in later Hebrew writings. עוֹלָמִים, *the plur.,* is often used for *the ages of antiquity, the time that is past* (Is. li. 9), and the לְ before it expresses the time *when, in, within which* anything happens (Gen. vii. 4; Ps. xxx. 6; Ezra x. 8; Gesen. § 154, 3, e; Ewald, § 217, d). The words אֲשֶׁר הָיָה מִלְּפָנֵינוּ have occasioned some difficulty, owing to the verb הָיָה, which is *singular,* and refers to עוֹלָמִים, *plural.* Symmachus has ἐν τῷ αἰῶνι, לְעֹלָם אֲשֶׁר הָיָה both in the singular; several of Kennicott's and De Rossi's MSS. have אֲשֶׁר הָיוּ both in the plural; so also the Chaldee, דִּי הֲווּ לְקַדְמָנָא, *which* WERE *before.* Hitzig, Stuart, Elster, &c., try to account for the anomaly in the text, by regarding הָיָה as being used in a kind of *impersonal way* (compare Ewald, § 295, d). There is, however, no necessity for any of those alterations proposed by the ancient versions, or for the artificial explanation given by the modern commentators alluded to. The Hebrews, like other people, were not always very particular about making a verb, adjective, or pronoun agree with its subject in gender or number, especially in colloquial language; we have undeniable proof of this in chap. ix. 6; x. 15, 17; Jer. xlviii. 15; Dan ix. 24; Zech. xi. 5; Gesen. § 121, 6, Rem. 1; § 137, 1; Ewald, § 184, c. Hodgson's mode of eluding this

anomaly, by rendering the clause, *the same, which is now presented to us, happened ages ago;* or the similar one of Ewald, ſchon war vorlängſt, was geſchehn vor unſeren Augen, making it the subject of the sentence, which is followed by Heiligstedt, only increases the difficulty, by palming upon the words a very harsh and unnatural construction. Had the sacred writer intended to say what this rendering makes out, the original would have been הוּא אֲשֶׁר לְפָנֵינוּ I am therefore not a little surprised to see Philippson defend this forced construction.

11 *But there is no remembrance,* &c. Having shewn the permanent existence and uniform return of the objects of nature to the respective places from which they apparently vanished, as illustrated by the permanently abiding earth, the pantingly disappearing yet gloriously rising sun, the seemingly scattered but regularly returning wind, the engulfed and yet emerging streams, the sacred writer now contrasts these with the departing but never-returning and ever forgotten man, and thus establishes his proposition, that all human efforts to divert it are utter vanity, since "man has no advantage from all the toil wherewith he toileth under the sun." This verse, which contains the reason for the statement made in ver. 2 – 4, has been greatly misunderstood, through the rendering of אַחֲרֹנִים and רֵאשׁנִים by *former things,* and *things that are to come;* and by the affirmation that it accounts for the mistake that some commit in supposing certain things to be new which have merely been forgotten. A careful examination of the text and scope of the passage will, however, shew the incorrectness of this interpretation. The burden of the sacred writer — after having affirmed that all human effort is vain, as man's existence and activity here must for ever cease (ver. 2 – 4) — is to prove his position, which he

remembrance of former men, nor will there be any remembrance of future men among those who will live hereafter.

does by adducing, in the second clause of verse 4 and verses 5–10, instances of stability in objects of nature, and contrasting them with the instability of man. Then to take this verse (11) "as assigning a reason why some err in supposing that something new takes place," is to miss the whole force of the argument. It was to be expected, that after the inspired writer had enumerated his illustrations, he would recur to his main proposition, "the vanishing of man from this scene of action," which he does in our rendering. This is, moreover, corroborated both by the similar sentiment in ii. 16, 17; ix. 5, which is the burden of the sacred writer, and by the fact that the words ראשׁנים and אחרנים being *masculine forms*, are universally used for *men* (comp. Deut. xix. 14; Job xviii. 20; and *infra*, iv. 16), and never for *things*, which are expressed by the *feminine* (comp. ראשׁנות, Isa. xlii. 9;

xlvi. 9; xlviii. 3, &c.; Gesen. § 107, 3, b). The Chaldee has therefore rightly rendered it "לֵית דָּכְרָנָא לְדָרַיָּא קַדְמָאִין וגו׳, *there is no remembrance of the former* GENERATION; thus also Rashbam explains ראשׁנים by בני אדם שנבראו לפנינו בעולם, *the sons of men that were born before us in the world*, and אחרנים by ש, שיבאו אחרינו בעולם, *those men that will come after us in the world;* R. Bechai, Chobath Halvavoth; Alshech, &c. Knobel, Heiligstedt, Elster, &c., have also seen the inconsistency of rendering ראשׁנים and אחרנים by *former and future* THINGS, though they missed the sense of the passage. וְזִכְרוֹן is the *construct* of זִכָּרוֹן, *i. q.*, זֵכֶר, *vide infra*, ix. 5 (comp. Gesen. § 93, 3; Ewald, § 214, a), and, as is frequently the case, precedes a preposition (comp. Isa. lvi. 10; Ps. lviii. 5; Gesen. § 116, 1; Ewald, § 289, b). לָהֶם is used pleonastically. עִם, *with*, also *among*, like the Latin *apud* (comp. 2 Sam. xiii. 23; Isa. xxxviii. 11).

SECTION 1.

CHAPTER I. 12—II. 26.

Coheleth, with all the resources of a monarch at his command (12), applied himself assiduously to discover, by *the aid of wisdom*, the nature of earthly pursuits (13), and found that they were all fruitless (14), since they could not rectify destinies (15). Reflecting, therefore, upon the large amount of wisdom he had acquired (16), he came to the conclusion that it is all useless (17), as the accumulation of it only increased his sorrow and pain (18). He then resolved to try *pleasure*, to see whether it would yield the desired happiness, but found that this too was vain (ii. 1), and hence denounced it (2); for, having procured every imaginable pleasure (3–10), he found that it was utterly insufficient to impart lasting good (11). Whereupon he compared wisdom with pleasure (12); and, though he saw the former had a decided advantage over the latter (13–14, a), yet he also saw that it does not exempt its possessor from death and oblivion, but that the wise and the fool must both alike die and be forgotten (14 b - 16). This made him hate both life and the possessions which, though acquired by industry and wisdom, he must leave to another, who may be a reckless fool (17 - 21), convincing him that man has nothing from his toil but wearisome days and sleepless nights (22 - 23); that there is, therefore, nothing left for man but to enjoy himself (24 a); yet this, too, he found was not in the power of man (24 b - 25); God gives this power to the righteous, and withholds it from the wicked; and that it is, after all, transitory (26).

12, 13 I, Coheleth, was king over Israel in Jerusalem.   And

12 *I Coheleth,* &c. The sacred writer now proceeds to prove the burden of the argument stated in the prologue, and to shew the vanity of all human efforts to satisfy the craving of the immortal soul, by the failure of the many experiments which he has made to that effect. The first effort he made was WISDOM (13 - 18), an experiment so natural to an intellectual being, and which many cultivated minds have made since, in the absence of a belief in a future state. Coheleth states that he, having been a *king,* had ample means and opportunities of testing the best of the varied speculations of men. The præterite tense, הָיִיתִי, *I was* king, &c., shews that at the time when this was written Solomon was no longer king. The attempt of Ibn Ezra to account for this præterite, by insinuating עניני הסבר יורו כי באחרית ימיו חיברו כאילו יאמר לדורות הבאים כך וכך נסיתי בימי חיי, *that Solomon wrote it in his old age, and appeals, as it were, to the new or rising generations, and tells them such and such things I tried in my lifetime,* is an ingenious conceit, and does not remove the difficulty. The Chaldee fully felt this dilemma, and hence resorted to the traditional fable that Solomon, having departed from the words of the Law in the pride of his heart, was dethroned by Ashmodai, king of the demons, and thus said, "*I was* king but am not now;" comp. also Midrash Yalkut, *in loco;* Talmud, Gittin, 68, b; Midrash Maase Bishlomo Hammeleh, in Jellinek's

Baith Hammidrash ii., p. 86. Similarly Rashi, הייתי מלך על כל העולם ולבסוף על ישראל ולבסוף על ירושלים לבדה ולבסוף על מקלי שהרי נאמר היתי מלך בירושלים אבל אכשיו אינו מלך, *I was at first king over the whole world, then only over Israel, then only over Jerusalem, and then over my stick, for it is said, ' I* WAS *king in Jerusalem,' but I am not king now;* There is no doubt that the fable of Solomon's dethronement arose from an anxious desire to account for this difficulty, as the Rabbins evidently saw that הָיִיתִי means *I was,* and am *no more,* and to make Solomon die a penitent (see Steinschneider, Heb. Lit., p. 47). As far, however, as history is concerned, we know that Solomon was king till his death; and as he, therefore, could not write "*I was king,* and *am no more,*" which the Rabbins themselves admit is the meaning of הָיִיתִי, we, who do not believe the traditional fable, must conclude that some one later than Solomon was the author of this book. Moreover the expression (בִּירוּשָׁלַיִם), *in Jerusalem,* also shews that the book was written *after* Solomon, when the kingdom was divided into two, and when there was another royal residence besides *Jerusalem.* Ibn Ezra's attempt to elude this, by saying, ויאמר בירושלים בעבור היות מקומה נכון לקבל החכמה, *that Jerusalem is mentioned because it was the proper place for acquiring wisdom,* does not comport with an address of a king to his contemporaneous people.

13. *And I gave my heart,* &c. Thus circumstanced, Coheleth exa-

I gave my heart to enquire diligently into wisdom respecting all that is done under heaven ; this is an evil business which God hath given to the children of men to

mined, by the help of wisdom or philosophy, the nature of all human actions, in order to discover those sublunary gratifications and enjoyments which would remove the desponding impression made by the contemplation of the permanency and regularity in the objects and laws of nature, contrasted with the transitoriness and instability of man. But he soon found that the endeavour to seek human happiness in wisdom was a vain employment, which God has wisely imposed upon man, who, in the pride of his heart, looks to his own faculties for an infallible guide to happiness. As the heart is regarded among the Hebrews and other nations, not only as the seat of the passions, but also as possessing the faculty of thinking, judging, &c., &c. (Is. x. 7; Judg. xvi. 17; Job. xii. 3 ; 1 Chron. xxix. 18; comp. also cor in Latin ; Cicero, Tusc. i. 9 ; Plaut. Pers. iv. 4. 71) ; hence arose the phrases נָתַן לֵב, to give one's heart to something (vide infra, ver. 17; vii. 21; viii. 9. 16; Dan. x. 12; 1 Chron. xxii. 19); הֵכִין לֵב (2 Chron. xii. 14; xxx. 19); שִׂים לֵב (Is. xli. 22; Hag. ii. 15. 18) ; שִׁית לֵב (Job vii. 17 ; Ps. xlviii. 14 ; lxii. 11); and the Latin, animum applicare, attendere; hence, also, the phrases which apostrophise the heart, e.g., דִּבֶּר עַם לֵב, to speak to the heart (ver. 16) ; אָמַר בְּלֵב, to say to the heart (ii. 1). The rendering of Symmachus, προεθέμην, I sat before myself, or, I proposed to myself, is too languid. The Vulgate's rendering of this phrase is capricious and inconsistent. Thus, in the passage before us it is translated, PROPOSUI IN ANIMO MEO, I proposed in my mind; in ver. 17 of this chap , and viii. 9, DEDI COR MEUM, I have given my heart ; in vii. 21, NE ACCOMMODES COR TUUM, do not accommodate thine heart ; in viii. 16, APPOSUI COR

MEUM, I applied my heart. The synonymous expressions דָרַשׁ and חוּר, both primarily signifying to go, to go in search of anything, to seek, are here used not so much in any distinction of meaning, but, as two verbs of a similar import are frequently employed to give intensity to the statement (comp. infra, vii. 25; Song of Songs, v. 6 ; Matt. iv. 39). בָחָכְמָה, into wisdom, is wrongly rendered adverbially by the Vulgate (sapienter), which Luther (weislich), Holden (sagaciously and diligently), Preston (scientifically), &c., follow. The censure here uttered is not upon absolute wisdom, for this the sacred writer praises in the sequel ; but upon wisdom acquired for the purpose of guiding in the gratification of his desires, and for finding in it solid happiness. The sublunary works are the productions of men, as the Chaldee rightly paraphrases it (כָּל עוֹבָדֵי בְּנֵי אֱנָשָׁא), and not, as Ibn Ezra maintains, the operations of nature. עִנְיָן, from עָנָה to labour, to toil oppressively, to be oppressed, afflicted ; hence to cry out under it, then to cry aloud, in a more extensive sense ; to call out, to let one's voice be heard through joy or sorrow, thus אֵין קוֹל עֲנוֹת גְּבוּרָה וְאֵין קוֹל עֲנוֹת חֲלוּשָׁה קוֹל עֲנוֹת אָנֹכִי שֹׁמֵעַ, not the sound of the cry of victory, nor the sound of the cry of defeat, the sound of singing I hear (Exod. xxxii.18), hence to speak, according to the analogy of עִנְיָן, from קָנָה, בִּנְיָן, from בָּנָה, denotes work, business, employment, occupation. The word only occurs in this book (vide infra, ii. 23, 26 ; iii. 10 ; iv. 8 ; v. 2, 13 ; viii. 16) ; but is frequently used in later Hebrew writings in this sense, which is also given by the Sept. Aquila, Theodo. (περισπασμοί), Symm. (ἀσχολία), and many modern commentators, as, for instance, Knobel, De Wette, Preston, Philippson, &c.

14 busy themselves therewith. I considered all the works
that are done under the sun, and behold they are all

The renderings 𝔐üße (Luther), travail (Auth. Ver.), curiosity (Holden),
do not exactly express the sense.
עִנְיַן רָע, liter. an employment of sadness, i. e., a sad, an evil employment, or business. רָע, which is here,
as frequently elsewhere, a noun
(comp. Exod. xxxii. 22 ; Ps. lxxviii.
49), is placed in the genitive, after
עִנְיַן, to express its quality ; the same
construction occurs in iv. 8 and v. 13
(comp. Gesen. § 106, 1; Ewald, § 287,
f). The Sept. uniformly translates עִנְיַן
רָע, in the three places, περισπασμός
πονηρός, an evil occupation ; whilst the
Vulg. inconsistently renders it here,
OCCUPATIO PESSIMA, utterly bad occupation ; in iv. 8 and v. 13, AFFLICTIO
PESSIMA, utterly bad affliction. The
pronoun אֲשֶׁר is implied before נָתַן
(Gesen. § 123, 3 ; Ewald, § 332).
לַעֲנוֹת בּוֹ is not to give evidence of
himself (some quoted by Ibn Ezra,
Desvoeux, &c.), nor for their humiliation (another opinion quoted by
Ibn Ezra, Hodgson, &c.), nor that
they may weary themselves therein
(Luther, Boothroyd, &c.), for these
renderings are against the signification of עִנְיַן, by which the meaning of
עֲנוֹת must be determined, since the
phrase עֲנוֹת עִנְיָן is a construction of
very frequent occurrence (comp.
2 Sam. xvi. 23 ; 2 Kings xiii. 14 ;
Gesen. § 138, 1 ; Rem. 1 ; Ewald,
§ 281, a). The Sept., Vulg., Syriac,
Rashi, Rashbam, Ibn Ezra, Knobel,
De Wette, Preston, &c., rightly retain
the idiom.

14. I considered all the works, &c.
Having summarily stated, in the
preceding verses, that he was disappointed in the wisdom by which
he had hoped to remove the sad
impression which the contemplation
mentioned in 2 – 11 left upon his
mind, the sacred writer gives in this
and in the following verse the cause
of this disappointment. With all
the help that this so much coveted
wisdom could render, he found that

the efforts made, by her assistance,
to secure comfort and solid happiness, are mere vanity and striving
after the wind. רָאָה, to see, to view,
to consider. הַמַּעֲשִׂים, the works spoken
of in the preceding verse. The
phrase רְעוּת רוּחַ, which also occurs
in ii. 11. 17. 26 ; iv. 4. 6 ; vi. 9, has
produced a variety of renderings,
owing to the different etymologies
assigned to רְעוּת. Thus the Syriac

(ܪ̇ܘܥܝܢܐ ܕܪ̇ܘܚܐ), the Chaldee
(תְּבִירוּת רוּחָא), Vulg. (afflictis spiritus),
Rashi (שבר רוח), Alshech, Coverdale,
Authorised Version, &c., have breaking down or vexation of spirit, i. e.,
the contemplation of these things
breaks down or produces a crushing
effect on, or irritates, one's spirits,
deriving רְעוּת from רָצַץ=רָעַע, to
break, to depress. But as רְעוּת,
according to the analogy of שְׁחוּת,
from שָׁחָה, פְּדוּת, from פָּדָה, שְׁבִית, from
שָׁבָה, can grammatically only be
derived from רָעָה, which is moreover
corroborated by the parallel form,
רַעְיוֹן רוּחַ (infra, ver. 17 ; iv. 16), this
rendering is inadmissible. As the
only legitimate root, רָעָה, however,
signifies both to feed, and then spiritually to feed or feast upon anything,
to delight in anything, hence different
interpretations have been defended,
based upon one or the other shade
of meaning of the root. Thus Aquila,
Theod. (νομὴ ἀνέμου), Symmachus
(βόσκησις ἀνέμου), have feeding upon
the wind ; Rashbam, a pleasure for
the talented, (רְעוּת רְצוֹן רוּחַ מוּלָם בּלֵמוּ) ;
Desvoeux, company for the wind ;
but these interpretations are too
artificial. It is therefore better to
take the secondary meaning of the
word, viz., to desire, to strive after
anything, hence רְעוּת רוּחַ, a striving
after the wind ; so the Sept. (προαίρεσις
πνεύματος), Ibn Ezra (מחשבת רוח),
Gesenius, Rosenmüller, Knobel, De
Wette, Noyes, Heiligstedt, Stuart,
Elster, &c. This is corroborated by

15 vanity, and striving after the wind; for the depressed
cannot be set right, since he that is gone cannot be num-

Hos. xii. 2, where רָעָה רוּחַ, stands in
parallelism with רֹדֵף קָדִים.

15. *The depressed cannot be set
right,* &c. And the reason of this
is to be found in the fact, that no
cogitation of the human mind, no
amount of wisdom, however great,
can remove the depression produced
by the fact stated in 2 - 11, since it
cannot recall one who has departed
this life to be numbered among the
living. Thus the hope of finding
comfort in *wisdom,* terminates with
the same gloomy conclusion, as the
contemplation of nature in verse 11.
מְעֻוָּת, Pual part. of עָוַת *i. q.,* עָוָה, to
curve, to bend, passive *to be bent,
bowed down, depressed* (Ps. xxxviii. 7),
חֶסְרוֹן is masculine, and, according to
the analogy of אֶבְיוֹן, signifies HE *that
is wanting,* HE *that is gone.* לְהִמָּנוֹת,
to be numbered with (comp. Isa. liii.
12), *i. e.,* אֶת הַחַיִּים, *with the living.*
As the second clause assigns the
reason for the statement made in
the first, the ו in וְחֶסְרוֹן is therefore
to be rendered *for, since* (Gesen.
§ 155, l. e.) This we believe to be
the most natural interpretation of
the verse, which has called forth
such a variety of explanations from
time immemorial to the present
day. Thus the Talmud (Jebamoth,
22, b) explains the first clause of
illegitimate offspring זה הבא על הערוה
והוליד ממנה ממזר. The Vulgate has,
PERVERSI DIFFICILE CORRIGUNTUR,
ET STULTORUM INFINITUS EST NUME-
RUS, *the perverse are difficult to be
corrected, and the fools are infinite in
number.* The Chaldee refers it to
the sins of man, and his inability to
repent *after* death. *As a man who
has corrupted his ways in this world,
and dies in them without repentance,
cannot amend after his death; and a
man who departs from the Law and
the Prophets when alive, cannot be
numbered with the righteous in Paradise after his death.* This Midrashic
explanation is followed by St. Jerome

in his commentary: QUI PERVERSUS
NISI ANTE CORRIGATUR, NON POTEST
ADORNARI; RECTA ORNATUM RECIP-
TUNT, ET CURVA CORRECTIONEM, *he
that is perverse, unless he be first
corrected, cannot be adorned; right
things receive adorning, and crooked
things correction.* Similarly Rashi,
מעות בחייו לא יוכל לתקון משמח זה שחסר עצמו
ממנין הכשרים לא יוכל להמנות עמהם בקבול
שכרם, *he who is perverted when alive,
cannot correct himself when dead;
and he who absented himself from the
assembly of the righteous, cannot be
numbered with them when they receive
their reward.* Rashbam refers it to
the inability of man who has once
perverted his deeds, ever to appear
right in the presence of God as
before. שאם עוות אדם את מעשיו אינו
יכול להיות מתוקן במעשיו כבתחילה לפני הק״
ואם חסר שום דבר אותו חסרון אינו יכול להיות
נמנה. עיד מיני וסיפור עם המוחר שנשתיר Ibn
Ezra mentions two different interpretations. According to one, Coheleth
saw that everything is worthless;
that emptiness cannot be rendered
substantial, for *natural* defectiveness
(מְעֻוָּת) is irreparable or irremediable,
because that defectiveness is inborn,
and one who *becomes* imperfect
(וְחֶסְרוֹן) cannot be numbered among
the perfect ones. חֶסְרוֹן would accordingly stand for בעל חסרון, *one who has
failed,* בעל being omitted before
the word וְחֶסְרוֹן; or חסרון might be
taken as an adjective, like אַחֲרוֹן ראשׁוֹן,
or as a noun belonging to מְעֻוָּה, so
that מְעֻוָּת by itself would be *innate*
defectiveness, and מְעֻוָּת חֶסְרוֹן *contracted* defectiveness. " According
to the other interpretation, however,
man is not *naturally* defective, but
is, by birth, placed in imperfect
circumstances, and has no power to
perfect himself; and it is generally
found that those who strive to find
·out these sources by the help of
astrology or natural science, strive
to no purpose; and this is the case
with most men, and most of their

16 bered again. I therefore spake to my heart saying, " I, lo!
I have acquired far greater wisdom than any one who was

works." Thus, according to the first interpretation, the rendering of this verse would be, " The naturally defective is irreparable, and he who becomes imperfect can no more be numbered among the perfect ones;" and, according to the second, " The imperfect has no power to perfect himself, and the cause of the imperfection he cannot fathom," which Reynolds, Patrick, Gill, &c., nearly follow. Holden has, " That which is perverse is with difficulty corrected, and that which is defective is with difficulty supplied." These commentators apply this verse to the *moral* endeavours of man. Boothroyd and Philippson render it, "What is crooked cannot be made straight, nor can the defects of things be numbered," *i. e.*, all the efforts of man are vain, because the existing deficiencies cannot be improved, but must remain deficient, and these deficiencies are not to be met with here and there, but are innumerable. We will only remark here, on this interpretation, which refers it to man's *scientific* efforts, that it would require חֶסְרוֹנוֹת in the *plural*, and אֵין מִסְפָּר. Knobel and Stuart, who, taking the same view, refer the second clause to the inability of man to supply the things wanted to render human life happy, escape this censure. Noyes and others regard this verse as a proverbial phrase, introduced " to assign a reason why human striving should be vain, and human pursuits should be so incapable of affording satisfaction, namely, the perverseness of human nature, and the imperfections of human things. As that which is by nature crooked cannot by human endeavours be straightened — as the vine, for instance, cannot be made to grow up straight, like the poplar ; and as that which is naturally wanting to anything cannot be supplied by human exertion — for instance, a

man cannot be made to possess wings, like a bird, or more than two hands or feet — so there are irregularities, discords, imperfections, in human life and the course of human things, which are irremediable, and render it impossible for man to find complete satisfaction." Elster refers this verse to the imperfection of all human efforts both *moral* and *physical*, and their inability to obtain for man his highest aim ; the realities of life never coming up to one's conceptions, there being always something deficient which precludes the possibility of man's ever securing a complete harmony between them. But all these interpretations, apart from the other objections which might be urged against some of them separately, miss the thread of the argument. The design of the sacred writer is to shew that his resort to *practical wisdom*, for having the difficulty and sadness removed which the contemplation of nature has produced upon his mind, was " vanity and striving after the wind," since the fact stated in verse 11 cannot be obviated. To take, therefore, the verse before us as descriptive of the *moral state* of man, or of his *physical inabilities*, or of the *defects in nature*, is to overlook the very burden of the writer, as expressed in vv. 4 and 11, to which he evidently here returns, in shewing the inefficiency of wisdom, as is plain from our rendering, which is moreover corroborated by the fact that the Vulg., St. Jerome in his commentary, the Chaldee, Rashi, Rashbam, Ibn Ezra, &c., take מִסְפָּר and מֶעֻוָּת as referring to *persons*, and not to *things*.

16. *I therefore spake*, &c. Having described *to us* the inability of wisdom to remove that depression, the sacred writer makes a most pathetic appeal to *his heart*, being the seat of the intellectual faculties (*vide supra*,

before me over Jerusalem — my heart having seen much

ver. 13), before he summons it to try another experiment. .For the origin of the phrase דִּבֶּר עִם לֵב, *to speak to the heart*, and similar phrases (chap. ii. 1. 15; Gen. xxiv. 45; 1 Sam. i. 13; Ps. xiv. 1; xv. 2), see ver. 13. The pronoun אֲנִי before the verb, with the pronominal suffix, is not "designed to give special emphasis to the clause" (Stuart), but is used pleonastically, which is one of the characteristics of this book; comp. *infra*, ii. 1. 11. 14. 15. 18. 20. 24, &c. הִגְדַּלְתִּי וְהוֹסַפְתִּי, literally, *I made great and increased*, i. e., *I greatly increased, I became exceedingly great in wisdom;* the second verb, which is used as a complement, is subordinate to the first; *vide infra*, ii. 9; iv. 17; viii. 3; Song of Songs, ii. 3; Gesen. § 142. 3; Ewald, § 285. חָכְמָה is the accusative; comp. 1 Kings, x. 7; Gesen. § 138. The Vulg. erroneously renders this clause *magnus effectus sum, et præcessi omnes sapientia qui*, &c., which Luther, Coverdale, Authorised Version, &c, follow, but which is rightly rejected by Ibn Ezra and most modern commentators. The preposition עַל before כָּל, like *super* in Latin, and our words *over, above*, expresses the idea of *surpassing, going beyond anything;* comp. יָסַפְתָּ עַל הַשְּׁמוּעָה, *thou art greater than the report which I have heard* (2 Chron. ix. 6; Gen. lxix. 26; Ps. lxxxix. 8; Job xxiii. 2). The rendering, therefore, of Umbreit, "I have gathered much wisdom *respecting* all things," &c., is incorrect. כָּל, as frequently, is used *distributively, every one, any one*, which accounts for the verb הָיָה being in the singular. The reading כָּל אֲשֶׁר הָיוּ in the plural, which is found in one of De Rossi's MSS., and which is favoured by the Sept., Syriac, Chaldee, Vulg, &c., has evidently arisen from a desire of uniformity to ii. 7. The preposition עַל before יְרוּשָׁלַיִם is used in the sense of *power, dominion, rulership*, and refers to *all* the kings that sat upon the Jewish throne As, however, one king only reigned before Solomon

in Jerusalem, viz., his father David, we have here another proof that this book must have been written *after* Solomon, at a time when the writer could look back upon a whole succession of kings. Those who maintain the Solomonic authorship of this book have resorted to various expedients, in order to account for this incongruity. Thus the Chaldee has paraphrased it עַל כָּל חַכִּימַיָּא דִי הֲווֹ קֳדָמַי בִּירוּשְׁלֵם, *I have increased wisdom above all* THE SAGES *that were before me in Jerusalem*, which Rashi, Rashbam, Ibn Ezra, and many Christian commentators follow. Reynolds, Patrick, &c., refer it to *all men;* Gusselius restricts it to the princes, rulers, and civil magistrates in Jerusalem; and Gill refers it to the governors of Jerusalem, to the Jebusites, as well as to Saul and David. But see ver. 12, and ii. 7.

My heart having seen, &c. This clause gives the reason why the sacred writer appeals to the heart; because it was the *heart* that acquired that surpassing amount of wisdom and knowledge for the purpose of removing the sad impression, Coheleth therefore confers with it about the fruitless result of this experiment before trying another. As this clause is merely exegetical, it is better rendered participially. The *heart* is described as seeing wisdom, for the reason given in ver. 13. The phrase *to see wisdom* (see also *infra*, ii. 12, and Jer. ii. 31) is owing to the fact that the Jews did not view abstractions, but regarded the operations of the mind and feelings when they became objective and were visible in a concrete form. הַרְבֵּה, Hiphil, infin. abso., which has generally *Tsere*, with or without *Yod* (comp. הַקְדֵּשׁ, Judges xvii. 3; הַדְבֵּר, Exod. viii. 11; Gesen. § 53, 3, Rem. 2), meaning literally *multiplicando*, is used adverbially (*vide infra*, ii. 7; v. 6. 11, 16. 19; vii. 16, 17; ix. 18; xii. 9; Gesen. § 75, 5, Rem. 14, § 131, 2; Ewald, § 280, c). The Vulg., mis-

17 wisdom and knowledge, for I have given my heart to
  know wisdom and knowledge — I know that even this is
18 striving after the wind.   For, in much wisdom is much
  sadness, and multiplying knowledge is multiplying sorrow.

taking this usage of the infinitive, has wrongly rendered this clause : ET MENS MEA CONTEMPLATA EST MULTA SAPIENTER ET DIDICI, *and my mind has contemplated many things wisely, and I have learned.* Luther is equally wrong: Unb mein Herz hat viel gelernt unb erfahren.

17. *For I have given my heart, &c.* This is epexegetical of the last clause in the preceding verse : " My heart has seen much wisdom and knowledge, because I have applied it to acquire wisdom and knowledge ;" the participial rendering might therefore still be retained. The Authorised Version and Stuart's translation are confused; Coverdale's is far better: " My heart had great experience of wisdom and knowledge, for thereunto I applied my mind, that I might know what were wisdom and knowledge." The words לָדַעַת חָכְמָה וָדַעַת הֹלֵלוֹת וְשִׂכְלוּת are rendered by most modern commentators, *to know wisdom, and to know madness and folly;* but this is against the meaning of the words, as well as against the scope of the passage. וָדַעַת is not an *infinitive,* and can therefore not be rendered *to know,* like לָדַעַת; it is a *noun,* and must be translated *knowledge;* it is joined to the copula to חָכְמָה, *wisdom,* as שִׂכְלוּת is to הֹלֵלוֹת, and is regarded so by the Sept., Vulg., Syriac, Chaldee, &c. שִׂכְלוּת, again, is not *folly,* but, on the contrary, means *prudence;* it frequently occurs in Chaldee and later Hebrew writings, and has invariably this sense, which is also given here by the Sept., Syriac, Chaldee, Rashbam, Luther, &c. Moreover, this rendering is contrary to the context; the intention of the sacred writer is not to prove the inutility of *folly and madness,* but to shew the inefficiency of *wisdom* to remove that sad impression which the

contemplation of nature had produced upon his mind, and to secure lasting happiness. The introduction, therefore, of " folly and madness " breaks the whole thread of the argument. This objection is, of course, equally applicable to the expression הֹלֵלוֹת, *folly,* as it now stands in the text, which, in order to avoid this dilemma, has unwarrantably been rendered by Dathe, Desvoeux, &c., *splendid matters;* by Gill, *things boasted of;* by Boothroyd, *excellence.* I have, therefore, no hesitation in concluding that the words have crept into the text through the carelessness of a transcriber. This is placed beyond the shadow of a doubt by the immediately following verse, which concludes the argument, stating the result of acquiring חָכְמָה, *wisdom,* and דַעַת, *knowledge,*—the very words used in this verse,—but makes no mention whatever of " folly and madness." But if the clause is retained, not to obscure the argument, תְּבוּנוֹת, *intelligence,* must be substituted for הֹלֵלוֹת, *folly,* according to the Sept., Syriac, Chaldee, and Arabic. The perfect, יָדַעְתִּי, is used for the *present* (comp. Job ix. 2; x. 13; Gesen. § 126, 3; Ewald, § 135, b). הוּא, prop. pro., third pers., is used for the auxiliary verb *to be* (comp. Gesen. § 121, 2). רַעְיוֹן is the same as רְעוּת in verse 14, from רָעָה, just as רִמְיוֹן and דְּמוּת are merely different forms from the root דָּמָה, and have the same meaning (Gesen. § 84, 15, 16). The Vulg., mistaking the sense, translates the last clause: IN HIS QUOQUE ESSET LABOR ET AFFLICTIO SPIRITUS, *in this also there was labour and vexation of spirit.* Equally erroneous is Luther's rendering, Ich warb aber gewahr, baß folches auch Mühe ist.

18. *For in much wisdom, &c., i. e.,* since the acquisition of human know-

ii. 1 I then spake to my heart, Come, now, let me try thee
with mirth, and thou shalt see pleasure! And, lo! this

ledge, so far from being able to remove
the depression and secure solid happiness, causes only sorrow and disappointment. For the more knowledge
we acquire, the more clearly and
acutely we see and feel the fleetness
of life, the emptiness of our enjoyments, and the abortiveness of all
our efforts, *based upon this knowledge*,
to ameliorate our condition. It must
be borne in mind that the sacred
writer does not here depreciate the
acquisition of wisdom *in itself*, or
absolutely, for he eulogises it in this
very book (*vide infra*, ii. 13, 14, &c.)
It is the proud human wisdom which
dethrones God and deifies man, pre-
tending to give him laws and regulations whereby to make him happy;
it is this wisdom to which he resorted
in trouble; believing its pretensions,
he sought to be comforted by its
power, and found, as every one similarly circumstanced will find, that
the more he acquired of it, for the
purpose of finding comfort in it,
apart from God, the greater was his
sorrow and disappointment. A similar instance of *absolute* language
being used instead of *relative*, also
occurs in viii. 12, 13. For the
meaning of עֶרֶב, see *infra*, vii. 3 ;
Ps. vi. 8; x. 14. יוֹסִיף is taken by
some as the third person imp. Hiph.,
and the construction is regarded as
elliptical, וַאֲשֶׁר יוֹסִיף to stand for וְיוֹסִיף,
"*he* who increases" (Herzfeld, Hitzig,
Gesen. § 50, 3, Rem. 1); but the word
is better taken as the participle of
הוֹסִיף (comp. Is. xxix. 14; xxxviii. 5),
which, as is evident from other forms
of the Hiphil, returns to the Kal,
and forms its participle according to
this conjugation (Ewald, § 127, b).
The Chaldee paraphrase has rightly
rendered it by מוֹסִיף, so also Rashbam. The Sept., mistaking the
word עֶרֶב, *vexation*, for the assonant
דַּעַת, *knowledge*, renders the first
clause of this verse ὅτι ἐν πλήθει σοφίας
πλῆθος γνώσεως, " he who increases

wisdom increases *knowledge*." The
Chaldee refers the augmentation of
sorrow here spoken of, not to the man
who acquires wisdom, but to God,
and to his relatives, and curiously
paraphrases the verse. "For the
man who increases wisdom, when he
sins and does not repent, increases
the wrath of God; and the youth
who is multiplying knowledge, and
dies in his youth, is multiplying
pain in the heart of his relatives."
Equally erroneous is the Vulgate,
which, contrary to the signification
of the word מִכְאוֹב, and the scope of
the whole passage, renders the last
clause ET QUI ADDIT SCIENTIAM,
ADDIT ET LABOREM, *and he who adds*
knowledge adds also LABOUR, which
St. Jerome explains, SAPIENS DOLET,
TAM IN ABDITO QUAM IN PROFUNDO
LATERE SAPIENTIAM, NEC ITA SE
PRÆBERE MENTIBUS, SICUT LUMEN,
RISUI, SED PER TORMENTA QUÆDAM
ET INTOLERANDUM LABOREM JUGI
MEDITATIONE ET STUDIO AD EAM
PERVENIRE, *the wise man deplores that*
wisdom, which, lying hid in a depth of
secrecy, does not shew itself to the
mind as light does to the eyes, so
that a man cannot attain to it unless
it be by torments and intolerable
labour, by continual meditation and
study, applying it to the labour which
one has in acquiring knowledge.
Luther, though keeping more to the
meaning of מִכְאוֹב, has given it the
same erroneous explanation, Und wer
viel lehren muß, der muß viel leiden.

1. *I then spake to my heart*, &c.
Having found the acquisition of
wisdom unable to remove the depression and satisfy the longings of the
soul, Coheleth now appeals to his
heart to try another experiment; he
leaves the laboratory of knowledge,
and betakes himself to the bowers of
pleasure; but, alas! this, too, he
finds unable to divert his sorrow,
and allay the cravings of his mind.
The heart or soul, being the seat of

2 too is vanity. To mirth I said, Thou actest foolishly!

the intellect (*vide supra*, ver. 13), is constantly addressed in this book (see i. 16; ii. 1. 15; iii. 17); it is that in man which makes him dissatisfied with the things that are transient, and long for things which produce solid happiness. Similar instances occur, both in other parts of the Old Testament and in the New, where man, roused by difficult circumstances, apostrophises his mind (Ps. xlii. 6. 12; xliii. 5; Luke xii. 19). For the pleonastic use of the pron. אֲנִי after אָמַרְתִּי, which has already the pronoun, see i. 16. אָמַר בְּלֵב is the same as אָמַר אֶל לֵב (Gen. viii. 21); אָמַר לְלֵב (Hos. vii. 2); and דִּבֶּר עַם לֵב; and is well explained by Ibn Ezra ידבר עם נפשי. The rendering of the Sept. εἶπον ἐγὼ ἐν καρδίᾳ μου, which the Vulg. (*dixi ego in corde meo*), Luther (ich fprach in meinem Herzen), Authorised Version, and the modern commentators follow, is contrary to the immediately following apostrophe. לְכָה־נָּא is used for incitement (Numb. xxii. 6; Judg. xix. 11), the ה in the imper. לְכָה, is *paragogic* or *intensive*, and נָא is the particle of *incitement*; it is well rendered by the Chaldee כְּעַן, and explained by Ibn Ezra (Gen. xii. 11) מלה נא כמו עתה; *the expression* נָא *is like* Now, which we employ in the same sense. אֲנַסְּכָה is the Piel of נָכָה, to try, with the כ pronominal affix second person fem. (*vide infra*, vii. 23), referring to לֵב, *heart*, and ה paragogic (comp. יְדָעָה, Exod. xiii. 16); and is rightly rendered by the Sept. πειράσω σε ἐν εὐφρα-σύνη; Syriac and Chaldee, אֲבְחִין בְּחֶדְוָא, Desvoeux, Hodgson, Knobel, Booth-royd, Gesenius, Herzfeld, Ewald, Stuart, Philippson, Elster, Fürst, &c. The rendering of the Vulg. (*affluam deliciis*), which is paraphrased by Luther, ich will wohl leben; Coverdale, *I will take mine ease;* and Reynolds, *I will pour out plentifully wine with joy, I will pour out myself in delights*, is based upon a Rabbinic exposition, which is evident from Rashi (מסך יין לשתות), and Rashbam

(אתנהג עצמי בנסיכות של שמחה), who as usual transmit the traditional explanations. וּרְאֵה, *and thou shalt see*, i. e., *enjoy.* The ancients used the expression *to see* in a far more intense and comprehensive sense than we do. Personifying every passion and emotion, they spoke of seeing, when they were in the midst of them and shared in them. Hence the phrase רָאָה חַיִּים (*infra*, ix. 9), and the Greek ἰδεῖν ζωήν, *to see life;* ἰδεῖν θάνατον, *to see death.* The infinitive וּרְאֵה is used with reference to the future, because of the imperfect by which it is preceded, as indicated by the ו (Gesen. § 126, 6, a; Ewald, § 135, c), which is wrongly translated *therefore* by the Authorised Version. The preposition בּ before טוֹב, after רָאָה, a verb of sense, expresses the intensity and pertinacity with which the object is seized (comp. Gen. xxi. 16; Job iii. 9; Gesen. § 154, 3, 2; Ewald, § 217, f. 2, γ). The Vulgate's rendering of וּרְאֵה בְטוֹב, *et fruor bonis*, as well as Luther's ich will gute Tage haben, which is followed by Coverdale, *I will have good days*, are loose and tame paraphrases.

2. *To mirth I said*, &c. The indulgence in pleasure and merriment, so far from gratifying the cravings of the soul, is a mere temporary frenzy, and only causes man, when dethroned reason resumes the reins of her empire, to see and inveigh against the folly in which he had plunged. Coheleth does not denounce innocent cheerfulness and pleasure, for this he himself recommends in the sequel. What he repudiates is, that rational man, seeing the inability of wisdom to calm the mind saddened by the admonition of everything around that it has no abiding place here, and aching after solid happiness, should betake himself to pleasure and mirth, in the vain hope thereby to quiet the voice of reason. To denounce this in terms most emphatic, the sacred writer personifies pleasure and mirth, and then

3 and to pleasure, What doth she do? I resolved with my

tells the one that she acts madly, and ironically asks the other what *she* does? whether she acts differently? How, then, can rational man betake himself to those which act *so madly*, in hope of having his actions regulated by them in such a manner as to satisfy *reason?* שְׂחוֹק, *wanton pleasure, vide infra,* vii. 3. 6; x. 19. The preposition ל in לְשִׂמְחָה and לִשְׂחוֹק is not to be rendered *of* (Rashbam, Ibn Ezra, Authorised Version, Mendelssohn, Holden, Preston, Herzfeld, Philippson, &c.), nor *in respect to* (Knobel, Stuart, &c.), but is to be taken in its natural sense, *to;* so the Sept., Luther, Coverdale, Desvoeux, Hodgson, Rosenmüller, Boothroyd, Elster, &c. מְהוֹלָל Pual part. of הָלַל, *to shine, to glory, to boast, to vaunt, to be foolish, to be mad,* is the passive of הוֹלֵל, *to make foolish, to make mad* (*vide infra,* vii. 7; Is. xliv. 25; Job xii. 17), the causat. of Kal, and ought to be rendered as a neutral verb, *to act foolishly, to act madly,* as is evident from Ps. cii. 9, which is the only other passage where this participle occurs, and means *those who act madly against me;* and from the verb עָשָׂה, *to act,* which is used in parallelism with it in the text before us. The rendering of the Sept., Theodo., περιφόρα, *rambling about;* Symm. θόρυβος, *tumult;* Aquila, πλάνησις, *error;* do not express the sense. The paraphrase of the Vulgate (RISUM REPUTAVI ERROREM, *laughter I counted error*), and Ibn Ezra, (אמרתי כי הנושה לשחוק שהוא מהולל, *I said that he who inclines to mirth is mad*), are both languid, and against the text. In the Talmud (Sabbath 30, 2), מְהוֹלָל is taken for מְהֻלָּל, so also Rashi, who explains it משובח, *thou art praised,* and a contradiction is noticed between this passage, where mirth is praised, and vii. 3, where it is condemned. The interrogation מַה־זֹּה עֹשָׂה, *what does she do?* used as *an emphatic denial* (*vide supra,* i. 3) is exceedingly forcible. The sacred writer has declared that mirth acts the fool,

and now asks whether pleasure acts differently, or, in other words, denounces it as acting in the same manner. Following the example of the Chaldee paraphrase (מַה הֲנָאָה אִית לִגְבַר דִּי עָבְדִינָהּ, *what advantage does it yield to the man who indulges in it?*) Rashi (מַה טוּבה עושה, *what good does it produce?*) and Ibn Ezra, (מה טוב תעשה), modern commentators take the verb עָשָׂה in the sense of *yielding, producing,* and explain this clause, "what solid good does pleasure yield or produce?" But this requires an unnecessary departure from the usual meaning of עָשָׂה, *to do,* a harsh ellipsis of טוּב, *good,* and, above all, weakens the sense. The sacred writer has forcibly denounced mirth as acting the fool; and is it likely that he would treat pleasure, its parallel, with more leniency, simply ask what good it yields, and thus weaken the second hemistich? זה is an abbreviation of זֹאת, and is peculiar to later Hebrew writers (*vide infra,* ver. 24; v. 15, 18; vii. 23; ix. 13; 2 Kings vi. 19; Ezek. xl. 45; Fürst, Lexicon, *s. v.;* Ewald, § 183, a; Gesen. § 34). The Syriac rendering of מְהוֹלָל by ܡܟ݂ܢܐ ܗܘܬ݂, as if the original were מַה־יַּעֲל, which Houbigant has actually adopted, because it corresponds better to מַה־זֹּה עֹשָׂה in the next member; the Septuagint's version of מַה־זֹּה עֹשָׂה, τί τοῦτο ποιεῖς; *why doest thou thus?* as if the original were מַה עֹשָׂה אֶת זֶה, which is followed by Hodgson and Boothroyd; and the Vulgate's paraphrase, QUID FUSTRA DECIPERIS? *why art thou vainly deceived?* are to be rejected as unwarranted deviations from the text.

3. *I resolved,* &c. Having given us *summarily* the result of his experiment with pleasure, in verses 1 and 2, Coheleth now details some *particular* instances of the pleasures by which he vainly sought to remove the depression from his mind, and secure lasting happiness. He conferred and

heart to draw my body with pleasure, my mind guiding
with wisdom, and to lay hold on folly, till I should see
what is good for the sons of men which they should do

resolved with his heart — for the reason given in ver. 1 — to indulge in banqueting and pleasure, and thus try to satisfy the cravings of the soul. תַּרְתִּי בְלִבִּי, liter., *I thought with my heart*, i. e., *I and my mind came to the conclusion.* The sentence is *pregnant*, implying the result of the cogitation, and the determination to act in accordance with it. מָשַׁךְ, *to draw, to bring out, to cheer;* so the Syriac (ܠܡܸܡܬ݁ܟ݂ܰܫ), Rashi (לעדן), Rashbam (להתענג ולשמח עצמי), בי׳ן), Lee, &c. Others, however, render it *to lead* (Chaldee לְנַבְרָא בְּגִית מִשְׁתַּיָא דְּהַמְרָא יַת בִּסְרִי, TO LEAD *my body into the banqueting-house*), *to inure, to train* (Parchon לגדל ולהרבות), *to indulge* (Mendelssohn, Preston, &c.), *to make robust, to strengthen* (Reynolds, Patrick, Gill, Gesenius, Noyes, &c.), *to allure* (Herzfeld, Heiligstedt) *to hold on, to be constantly at it* (Knobel, De Wette, Elster, &c.), *to hold on*, i. e., *to cherish* (Fürst), which are far less suitable to the expression יַיִן, *wine.* The term יַיִן is frequently used by a synecdoche for all *delicacies* and *feasting* (comp. Prov. ix. 2 ; Song of Songs viii. 2), and is well explained by Rashi כל סעודת עונג קרויה על שם היין. Ibn Ezra appropriately renders בִּשָׂרִי by גופי, *body.* For the omission of the suffix after נֹהֵג, see Gesen. § 145, 2.

My mind guiding with wisdom, &c. Coheleth resolved to draw his body, as it were, with the alluring cords of pleasure, determined that his passions should not be wildly let loose, but that wisdom, by her prudent guidance in the selection of earthly gratifications, should hold the reins, and restrain the passions from running riot. This explanation is evident, from ver. 9. The words וְלִבִּי נֹהֵג בַּחָכְמָה, *my heart guiding with wisdom,* are parenthetical, as is evident from

לֶאֱחֹז, *to lay hold,* which, together with לִמְשׁוֹךְ, *to draw,* depends upon תַּרְתִּי, *I resolved.* The expression לֵב, *heart,* possessing the faculty of thinking, judging, &c. (*vide supra,* i. 13), is here more properly rendered *mind,* and stands in opposition to בָּשָׂר, *body.* נָהַג, *to guide,* is evidently designed to carry out the figure begun with, כָּשַׁךְ, *to draw.* It was not to be a blind drawing into every pleasure, but guided by vigilant prudence.

And to lay hold on, &c., *i. e.,* indulge himself in pleasure which he subsequently found to be mere folly, as stated in the preceding verse. This he did, not to revel in sensuality, but to see whether he, with all the vast resources at his command, could not discover how to sweeten the years of man's existence, few and bitter, contrasted with the everenduring objects of nature. To recount the almost countless explanations and observations palmed upon this verse, would be unprofitable. We must be satisfied with the leading renderings and expositions. Already the ancient versions are very discordant. Thus the Sept. has καὶ κατεσκεψάμην εἰ ἡ καρδία μου ἑλκύσει ὡς αἶνον τὴν σάρκα μου, καὶ καρδία μου ὡδήγησεν ἐν σοφίᾳ καὶ τοῦ κρατῆσαι ἐπ᾽ εὐφροσύνη, *and I examined whether my heart would draw out my flesh as wine, and my heart led in wisdom, and to lay hold on pleasure,* altering the text into תַּרְתִּי אִם לִבִּי תִמְשׁוֹךְ בַּיִן; the Vulg., COGITAVI IN CORDE MEO ABSTRAHERE A VINO CARNEM MEAM, UT ANIMUM MEUM TRANSFERREM AD SAPIENTIAM DEVITAREMQUE STULTITIAM, &c., which Luther (ba bachte ich in meinem Herzen, meinen Leib vom Wein zu ziehen, unb mein Herz zur Weisheit zu ziehen, baß ich ergriffe was Thorheit ist, &c.) ; and Coverdale (so I thought in my heart to withdraw my flesh from wine, to apply my mind unto wisdom,

4 under heaven, the numbered days of their lives ; I therefore

and to comprehend foolishness) follow, altering בְּיֵין into מְיֵין, בְּחָכְמָה into לְחָכְמָה, and וְלֶאֱחֹז בְּסִכְלוּת into וְלָסוּר מִסִּכְלוּת. Luther and Coverdale, not following the Vulgate in the last alteration, take the word אָחַז, *to lay hold of, to seize,* in the sense of *comprehending.* As these emendations are not supported by any MSS., we shall not pause to animadvert upon them, but pass on to the rendering given by St. Jerome in his commentary, in which he adheres to the text ; there he translates this verse, *Consideravi in corde meo, ut traherem in vino carnem meam, et cor meum deduxit me in sapientiam,* which he explains : VOLUI VITAM MEAM TRADERE DELICIIS, ET CARNEM MEAM AB OMNIBUS CURIS LIBERARE, ET QUASI VINO SIC VOLUPTATE SOPIRE ; SED COGITATIO MEA, ET RATIO NATU- RALIS RETRAXERUNT ME, ET DEDUX- ERUNT AD SAPIENTIAM REQUIRENDAM, *I desired to give my life to pleasures, and free my body from all cares, and put it to sleep, as it were, with wine and pleasure ; but my thoughts and natural reason drew me back, and led me to seek wisdom ;* so also Rashi, אַךְ אִם בְּשָׂרִי נִמְשָׁךְ בֵּין לִבִּי מִתְגַּלְגֵּל בְּחָכְמָה לְהַחֲזִיק בַּתּוֹרָה, *though my body inclined after pleasure, my mind urged by wisdom to lay hold on the Law ;* but this is contrary to verse 9, where we are told that wisdom, so far from repudiating, assisted in procuring pleasures. Ibn Ezra, who is followed by Mendelssohn, Reynolds, Patrick, Gill, Jermin, Desvoeux, Preston, Noyes, &c., maintains that Coheleth, seeing wisdom by itself produced pain, and pleasure by itself was of no use, resolves, in this verse, on a middle course — to unite the pursuits of wisdom with those of pleasure. But this is contrary to the scope of the passage, which obviously describes in detail (4 – 11) the pleasures categorically denounced as folly in ver. 2. But what is most subversive of this united indulgence in both wisdom and pleasure, is the fact that Coheleth,

having finished his description of wisdom, as given in i. 12 – 18, and of pleasure, as given in 4 – 11, discussed, in his *resumé,* ver. 12 – 14, the respective merits of wisdom and folly *separately,* and makes no mention whatever of this middle course, or *union* of both wisdom and pleasure. Hodgson's rendering, " I enquired of mine heart whether I should give myself unto wine, but mine heart inclined unto wisdom, or whether I should embrace folly," is contrary to the text. מִסְפַּר יְמֵי חַיֵּיהֶם is the *accusative of time;* the same phrase occurs in v. 17.

4. *I therefore increased my posses- sions.* Here, and in the following six verses, Coheleth enumerates some of the pleasures and enjoyments in which he indulged. The words הִגְדַּלְתִּי מַעֲשָׂי yield excellent sense in their literal translation, *I increased my works* or *possessions,* and do not refer to Solomon's costly and splendid ivory throne, overlaid with gold, as described in 1 Kings x. 18, but describe the undertakings of this monarch generally. David had built a cedar house (2 Chron. ii. 3), possessed vineyards, orchards, treasures of all kinds, and servants of all sorts (1 Chron. xxvii. 25-31); but Solomon, seeking happiness in grandeur, *increased* or *multiplied* (הִגְדַּלְתִּי) these *possessions* (מַעֲשָׂי) which he, as successor to the throne, inherited from his father. Hence " he builded houses ;" not satisfied with the royal residence already existing, he erected another, the completion of which occupied thirteen years; he built a mansion for his wife, and various other edifices (1 Kings vii. 1 – 8; ix. 17 – 19). מַעֲשֶׂה, *work,* like מְלָאכָה, is used metonomically for the effects of work, that which is gained by work, *wealth, riches, estates, possessions* (Exod. xxiii. 12 ; 1 Sam. xxv. 2 ; Isa. xxvi. 12). Ibn Ezra's explanation of הִגְדַּלְתִּי מַעֲשָׂי, viz., עָשִׂיתִי מַעֲשִׂים גְּדוֹלִים, which is followed by Luther, Autho- rised Version, and almost all modern

increased my possessions, I builded me houses, I planted
5 me vineyards, I made me gardens and pleasure-grounds,

commentators, is, to say the least, an
unnecessary paraphrase.

I planted me vineyards, &c. To
the in-door pleasures he added outdoor enjoyments. With all the pleasure that we derive from gardens
and parks, those who have not travelled in the East can form but
an inadequate idea how indispensable a part a garden forms of an
Eastern's luxury, and how great is
the enjoyment which he derives from
it. The burning heat of the Eastern
sun renders the interior of dwellings almost intolerable during the
day. Shady arched walks, therefore,
formed by vines planted in rows or
avenues, and trained above a trellis-
work, or airy and fragrant bowers
formed by the outspread branches of
trees in gardens, are retreats, the
delight of which an Eastern alone
can fully appreciate. It is this most
enviable, quiet, and shady retreat
that gave rise to the beautiful representation of happy and tranquil
Israel, as sitting under vines and fig-
trees (1 Kings iv. 25; Mich. iv. 4;
Zech. iii. 10). No wonder that the
Israelites selected such a charming
spot for serving their heavenly Father
(Gen. xxiv. 63; Matt. xxvi. 30; John
xviii. 1, 2); for entertaining their
earthly friends (Isa. li. 3); and for
burying those dear to them (Gen.
xxiii. 19, 20; 2 Kings xxi. 26; 2 Sam.
xxv. 1). Because one vineyard is
mentioned as belonging to Solomon
(Song of Songs, viii. 11), Knobel concludes that he had only that one, and
that "the author here exaggerates designedly, in order to shew that even
the best means of pleasure do not
yield any lasting satisfaction." But
surely the words, "Solomon had a
vineyard in Baal-Hammon," do not
affirm, or even remotely imply, that
he had none elsewhere. The one
there mentioned was for a particular
purpose (see my Commentary, *in loco*);
the passage describes the vineyard

in that locality. Besides, even if we
had not been told that Solomon had
planted himself vineyards, we should
naturally conclude that he had *many*,
since they form such an essential
part of Eastern enjoyment, and since
he came into possession of his father's
estates, which comprised vineyards
(1 Chron. xxvii. 27). The Chaldee
makes Solomon describe in this verse
the good works which he performed,
viz., the building of the Temple, and
the various edifices and courts belonging to it. Even the vineyards,
this paraphrase says, were planted
that the Sanhedrin might have wine
to refresh themselves during their
sittings and their religious exercises,
and for the purpose of offering obla-
tions upon the altar. The most
effectual refutation of this interpretation is to be found in verse 11,
where the works are characterised as
*mere vanity and striving after the
wind*, which could surely not be said
of such praiseworthy undertakings.

5. *I made me gardens, &c.* He
had not only vineyards, but also
gardens and pleasure-grounds, producing all kinds of delicious fruit,
and aromatics, which are most calculated to regale the senses, and are
so essential to Oriental luxury. The
Hebrew names for the different kinds
of gardens denote the occupation
assigned to Adam when the Lord
placed him in the garden of Eden.
We are told that the Lord God took
the man and put him in the garden
of Eden *to cultivate it* (לְעָבְדָהּ), and *to
guard it* (וּלְשָׁמְרָהּ); hence we find that
the expressions denoting gardens
signify one or the other of these two
offices. Thus גֵּן is derived from
גוּר = גָּנָה (for the termination ָ- see
Fürst, Lexicon, under מ 2, c), *to dig*,
hence *a garden* generally, cultivated
by means of spades and axes (Judg.
xv. 5; Job xxiv. 18), and afterwards
applied especially to a vineyard.
גַּן is from גָּנַן, *to guard*; hence that

6 and I planted in them trees of all sorts of fruit. I made
me pools of water, to water therefrom the grove shooting

which is guarded and protected
against every intrusion, *a guarden*;
the German, Garten, and the English, *garden*, denote the same thing.
פַּרְדֵּס, according to the analogy of the
quadriliteral פַּרְשֵׁז, is a compound of
פָּרַד and פָּרַם, *to break up, to separate*,
and denotes *a garden, a pleasure-
ground*, either from its being *separated, enclosed* (see my commentary
on the Song of Songs, iv. 13), or,
which is perhaps better, from its
being cultivated by *breaking up* the
ground with ploughs or other imple-
ments. The difference between גַּן
and פַּרְדֵּס cannot now be exactly
defined; the former, however, seems
to denote a garden containing smaller
plants, such as herbs, flowers, as
well as fruit-trees (Deut. xi. 10;
1 Kings xxi. 2), and the latter
pleasure-grounds or parks planted
with large trees, and containing different animals, in which sense it is
also used in other languages (comp.
Xenophon, Anab. i. 2. 4; Cyrop.
i. 4, &c.; Koran, xxxiii. 11). From
the delightful *regions* which it described, *Paradise* was afterwards used
for the blessed abode of saints in
glory (Luke xxiii. 43; 2 Cor. xii. 4;
Rev. ii. 7; comp. Wemyss, Clavis
Symb. 336; Kalisch, Gen. p. 108).
The distinction which Ibn Ezra
makes between these two expressions,
viz., that in גַּן trees of all kinds are
grown (יש בו אילנים רבים ממינים רבים),
while in פַּרְדֵּס only one kind is planted
(הוא ממין אחד), is not correct; * the
very passage to which he refers for
proof of his assertion (Song of Songs
iv. 13) contradicts it; for, not only
are there pomegranates described as
growing in this garden, but also
cypresses and nards, and, in fact,
" all sorts of frankincense trees."
Those who maintain that גַּן signifies
a place containing smaller plants
only, such as herbs, vegetables,
shrubs, flowers, &c., overlook the
fact that בָּהֶם, *in them*, refers to גַּן,

garden, as well as פַּרְדֵּס, *pleasure-
ground*. It may be that the Chaldee
paraphrase here is correct in taking
the royal garden mentioned in Neh.
iii. 15; 2 Kings xxv. 4, which was
situated at the pool of Siloam, that
is, at the mouth of Tyropæon (see
Robinson, Palestine, i. p. 333, &c.),
to be one of those which Solomon
planted. עֵץ, *sing.*, is used *collectively*
(comp. וַיִּתְחַבֵּא הָאָדָם וְאִשְׁתּוֹ בְּתוֹךְ עֵץ הַגָּן,
*and the man and his wife hid them-
selves among* THE TREES *of the garden*
Gen. iii. 8; Is. x. 19; Ps. lxxix. 5).

6. *I made me pools of water*, &c.
The intense heat in the East requires
that plants should be frequently irri-
gated to preserve them from being
parched up. As the streams which
were not dried up in the summer
were very few in Palestine, artificial
reservoirs were made to receive the
rain or collect the spring waters for
times of need. These tanks of water
constituted one of the most charming
features in gardens; rows of palms or
other trees, with outspread branches,
and studded with fruit, encircled
these rills, in whose waters the deep-
blue or grey dove was frequently
seen bathing, and reflecting upon its
golden breast the splendid colours of
the falling rays (Song of Songs v. 13).
Maundrell gives a beautiful description of the effect which these artificial
waters produced upon him, when
seeing the garden of the Emir of
Beyrout, anciently called Berytus
" The best sight that this place
affords, and the most worthy to be
remembered, is the orange garden.
It contains a large quadrangular
plot of ground, divided into sixteen
lesser squares, four in a row, with
walks between them. The walks are
shaded with orange trees of a large
spreading size. . . . Every one of these
sixteen lesser squares in the garden
was bordered with stone, and in the
stone-work were troughs, very artisti-
cally contrived, for conveying the

7 up trees; I bought me men-servants and maid-servants,

water all over the garden, there being little outlets cut at every tree, for the stream as it passed by to flow out and water it" (see Early Travels in Palestine, Bohu's edition, pp. 415, 416). This will give us some idea of what the gardens and reservoirs of the wisest and wealthiest Eastern monarch must have been. The pool of the king, mentioned in Nehem. ii. 14, is said to be one of those which Solomon made (Joseph. Bel. Jud. v. 4, c. 2). בְּרֵכוֹת is the *construct* of בְּרֵכָה, *a pool*, instead of בְּרֵכוֹת, perhaps to distinguish it from the plural construct of בְּרָכָה, *a blessing* (Ewald, § 212, c.), and is derived from the first meaning of בָּרַךְ, viz., *to kneel down*; hence a kneeling-place for cattle or men when drinking (comp. וַיַּבְרֵךְ הַגְּמַלִּים מִחוּץ לָעִיר אֶל בְּאֵר־הַמָּיִם, *and he made his camels* TO KNEEL *down without the city, by the well of water.* (Gen. xxiv. 11; Judg. vii. 5, 6, &c.) These passages are decidedly against those who derive the word in question from the secondary meaning of בָּרַךְ, *to bless;* hence *a pool*, which was accounted a special blessing in hot countries, or בָּרַךְ (Arabic), *to flow.* Instead of מֵהֶם, *masculine*, we should have expected מֵהֶן, feminine, since בְּרֵכוֹת, to which it refers, is feminine; but such disagreement in gender is of no uncommon occurrence (*vide infra*, x. 9; xi. 8; xii. 1). Although צוֹמֵחַ is a *neuter intransitive*, yet it is followed by an *accusative* עֵצִים; such instances are not unfrequent with verbs signifying *to grow, to flow*, &c, and imply abundance in the thing that stands in the accusative; comp. עָלָה כֻלּוֹ קִמְּשׂנִים, *the whole of it went up in nettles, i. e*, it entirely changed into them (Prov. xxiv. 31; Isa. v. 6; xxxiv. 13); just as it is said a burning house goes up in flames and smoke (Gesen. § 138, 1, Rem. 2; Ewald, § 281, b).

7. *I bought me man servants*, &c. An oriental potentate's happiness and luxury would be incomplete without a numerous retinue of ser-

vants of all kinds. To keep those magnificent edifices and pleasure-grounds in order, to provide for and serve his large and sumptuous table, to attend to his forty thousand stalls of horses (1 Kings iv. 26), Solomon must have required an enormous number of domestics, and it is therefore no wonder that when the Queen of Sheba beheld them "there was no more spirit in her" (1 Kings x. 5). The buying of servants here mentioned was practised among the Hebrews, in common with other nations, from time immemorial. Already Abraham, the father of the Hebrew nation, had an exceedingly large number of servants, which he bought (Gen. xvii. 12), and could muster three hundred and eighteen, *born in his house*, against the kings who had captured Lot and his household. (Gen. xiv.) Joseph was *sold* by his brothers as a slave to the Ishmaelites, who were traders both in costly spices and slaves (Gen. xxxvii. 28). Such slaves were called *the purchase of money* (מִקְנַת כֶּסֶף), ἀργυρώνητοι (Gen. xvii. 12. 23); their offspring, as well as the children of captives of war, who were made slaves (Numb. xxxi. 11. 26. 35; Deut. xx. 14, xxi. 10), born in bondage, belonged to the master, and are called *house-born* (יְלִידֵי בַיִת, οἰκογενεῖς, Gen. xiv. 14; xvii. 12), or *sons of a handmaid* (בְּנֵי אָמָה, Exod. xxiii. 12; Ps. cxvi. 16), or *sons of the house* (בְּנֵי בַיִת), as in the text before us and Gen. xv. 3. The usual value of a servant was fifty silver shekels for an Israelite (Levit. xxvii. 3) and thirty for a non-Israelite (Exod. xxi. 32). It must not, however, be supposed that Hebrew servitude bears any resemblance to that of the ancient Greeks and Romans, or to the modern slavery of the United States. The fact that the Hebrew language has no word for *slave*, considered as a mere *thing*, or *instrument*, under the absolute mercy of another—that the name עֶבֶד simply

and had house-born servants; I had also many herds of
oxen and sheep, above all who were before me in Jeru-

means *labourer*, and is the same
which God gave to his chosen people
Israel, to his favourite servant Moses,
to the prophets and kings, while the
Greek designation δοῦλος means *one
bound* or *chained*, the Latin *manci-
pium* denotes *captured goods*, which
seems also to be the meaning of the
modern expression *slave* — would
alone be sufficient to shew the dis-
similarity between the Jewish system
of servitude and the slavery of the
nations alluded to. We are, however, not left to prove the dissimi-
larity from the etymology of these
designations; the records of sacred
and profane history place it beyond
the shadow of a doubt. The Hebrew
servant, whether an Israelite or not,
had written upon his forehead by
the hand of the Creator, that he,
being a man, is, like his master,
created *in the image of God* (Gen. i.
27, comp. with ix. 5, 6); the natural
rights, therefore, of both master and
servant alike were regarded by God,
whose image they both bore, and
equal provisions were made for both
(2 Sam. xiv. 14; Prov. xxiv. 23,
xxviii. 21; Job xxxiv. 19, &c.); the
Greek slave was defined by Aristotle
to be *a living working tool* and possession (ὁ δοῦλος ἔμψυχον ὄργανον, Ethic.
Nicom. viii. 13; ὁ δοῦλος κτῆμά τι
ἔμψυχον, Polit. i. 4), and was regarded
as possessing fewer faculties than a
free man (Plato, Polit. ix. 1. 13), as
a being who had "nothing healthy
in his soul," which naturally differed
from other men, and as belonging
"to a race in which men possessing
any intellect ought never to trust."
This, Plato (Leg. vi. 19) tells us,
has the authority of the wisest of
poets, who, when speaking of Zeus,
says—

Ἥμισυ γάρ τ' ἀρετῆς ἀποαίνυται εὐρύοπα Ζεύς
Ἀνέρος, εὖτ' ἄν μιν κατὰ δούλιον ἧμαρ ἕλησιν.
"Half their mind wide-seeing Jove has ta'en
　From men, whose doom has slavery's day
　brought on." — ODYS. xvii. 832.

The Hebrew servant, working with
his master, who, like Saul or Elisha,
followed behind the plough (1 Sam.
xi. 5; 1 Kings xix. 19), or like Moses
and David tended the flock (Exod.
iii. 1; 1 Sam. xvi. 11, xvii. 20, 28,
34), also celebrated with his master,
when they both came home in the
evening, the Sabbath, and all the
numerous festivals, which released
him from labour nearly half the
time (Exod xx. 10; Deut. v. 14,
&c.), and was instructed in morals
and religion (Deut. xxxi. 10–13);
the Greek and Roman slave, being
regarded as belonging to a different
caste, "was not to be spoken to as a
free man" (Plato, Leg. vi. 19), and
his testimony in courts of law was
never taken unless extorted by torture (Demosth. c. Onetor. i. p. 874;
Cic. Partit. Orat. 34, pro Sall. 28).
The Hebrew servant, if he escaped
from his master, could not be delivered up to him by the inhabitants
of the place in which he sought
refuge (Deut. xxiii. 15,16); the Greek
and Roman slave, when he ran
away, was not allowed to take refuge
anywhere, the master pursued him
wherever he pleased (Xen. Mem. ii.
10, § 1, 2; Florus, iii. 19), and, when
caught, branded him with a red-hot
iron. The Hebrew servant had the
full protection of the law, if he lost
any member of his body through the
brutal treatment of his master, he
was immediately manumitted (Exod.
xxi. 26, 27), and, if killed, the master
was treated as a murderer (comp.
Exod. xxi. 12, with verse 20, and
Gen. ix. 5, 6), and, according to the
Talmud (Sanhedrin, 52, b), was
executed by the sword; the Roman
slave had no personal rights; he was
under the absolute power of his
master, who could brand, torture, or
put him to death at pleasure; if the
master was murdered by a slave, or
by an unknown assassin, all the
slaves on the premises were put to

8 salem; I amassed me also silver and gold, and the treasures

death (Tacit. Ann. xiii. 32), a brutal instance of which happened in the reign of Nero, when four hundred were executed for the murder committed by *one*, on the person of Pedanius Secundus, prefect of the city (Tacit. Ann. xiv. 42–46). A Hebrew servant — and be it remembered that we are speaking all along of servants who are non-Israelites — could marry the daughter of his master (1 Chron. ii. 35), the master himself frequently took a maid-servant (Gen. xxx. 3 ; Deut. xxi. 10–14), or gave her to his son for wife (Exod. xxi. 9). And if the servant was an Israelite, he could only serve six years (Exod. xxi. 2 ; Levit. xxv. 41; Deut. xv. 12), during which time he was to be considered as *a hireling*, and treated with the leniency of a citizen (Levit. xxv. 39–43); he could therefore acquire property, and redeem himself before the Sabbath-year (Levit. xxv. 40); if, however, he was released at the end of six years, his master was enjoined to supply him with every comfort (Deut. xv. 14). Such, then, was the humane treatment of Hebrew servants, and it stands out in bold relief when contrasted with the inhuman treatment of the Greek and Roman slaves, or with the legal position of slaves in the United States. The reader will do well to consult the following works on this subject:—Saalschütz, Archäologie der Hebräer, ii. p. 236–248; Mos. Recht., p. 702–708; Becker's Charicles, English edition; Parker, 1845, p. 270–280; Gallus, p. 212–234; Smith, Dictionary of Greek and Roman Antiquities, under *Servus;* Ramsay, Roman Antiquities, second edition, p. 94–101, and especially the very excellent treatise, Die Verhältnisse der Sklaven bei den alten Hebräern nach biblischen und talmudischen Quellen dargestellt, von Dr. M. Mielziner. Kopenhagen, 1859. קָנִיתִי is not POSSEDI, *I posssessed* (Vulg.), nor *I got* (Auth. Ver.), nor

ich hatte (Luther), but *I bought me* (Coverdale, Herzfeld, Hitzig, Stuart, Elster, &c.), as is evident from Gen. xvii. 12, 13. 23. 27, where *bought servants*, as here, are used in contradistinction to *home-born* ones. בְּנֵי בָיִת, *sons of the house, i. e.,* home-born servants, is well rendered by the Sept. οἰκογενεῖς; the Vulg. *multamque familiam habui*, which is followed by Luther (Gesinde), and Coverdale (*I had a great household*), is incorrect. For the *sing.* הָיָה construed with the *plural* noun בְּנֵי בָיִת, see i. 10; also Gen. xxvi. 14, xlvii. 17, 18 ; 2 Chron. xxxii. 29, the only passages where the construction מִקְנֶה צֹאן and מִקְנֵה בָקָר is to be found. It seems that מִקְנֶה here is the *construct*, instead of מִהְנָה. For the adverbial use of הַרְבֵּה, see i. 16, where also the usage of the phrase *above all, i. e.,* kings, is accounted for. מִכֹּל stands for מִלְכֹּל, the preposition לְ is omitted after מִן (*vide infra*, vi. 5. 8, vii. 2, ix. 4, xii. 12).

8. *I amassed me also,* &c. In addition to his numerous herds of cattle, in which the wealth of *people generally* for the most part consisted in ancient times, Coheleth also amassed riches in silver and gold, and treasures *peculiar to kings and kingdoms.* The fleet which Solomon sent to Ophir, manned by the skilful Tyrian mariners, brought him annually between four hundred and twenty and four hundred and fifty talents of gold (1 Kings ix. 26–28); his yearly revenue in gold was six hundred and sixty-six talents (£646,350), besides that which came in from vassal-kings and provinces (1 Kings x. 14, 15), and so great was the quantity of these precious metals which he had, that silver and gold were regarded in Jerusalem as stones (1 Kings x. 27 ; 2 Chron. i. 15). כָּנַס, *to heap up, to amass,* for the sake of keeping, and not for circulation. סְגֻלָּה (from סָגַל, kindred with סָגַר,, *to enclose, to shut up*), that which is shut up and taken care of,

of kings and kingdoms; I got me men-singers and women-singers, and the delights of men, a large number of wives;

a precious thing, a treasure (comp. my Commentary on the Song of Songs, v. 11). Herzfeld ingeniously accounts for the absence of the article in מְלָכִים, *kings*, and its presence before מְדִינָה, *kingdom*, because kings *constantly change*, while countries *fixedly abide.* מְדִינָה (from דּוּן, *to subjugate, to rule, to judge*), that which is governed, *a province, land* or *country* (Esth. i. 1, &c.; Ezra, ii. 1; Dan. xi. 24; Lam. i. 1), is a word belonging to later Hebrew. The phrase *treasures of kings and kingdoms* does not mean " the tribute paid to him by kings and kingdoms in treasures " (וְהַסְגֻרֵי מַלְכִין וּפַלְכִין אִתְיְהִיבוּ לִי לְכַרְגָּא, Chaldee, Reynolds, &c.), but denotes such costly things as are *peculiar to royalty*, in contradistinction to the wealth, consisting in *cattle*, which was *common to every opulent person*.

I got me men-singers, &c. To riches he added the charms and sensuous gratifications which constitute the great delight of men. The Hebrews, from the earliest periods, cultivated the art of music, which they seem to have pursued even in their Egyptian bondage, most probably to beguile many a weary hour, as is evident from Exod. xv. 20, where we find the presence of both vocal and instrumental music immediately after the exodus. How highly susceptible they were of its seductive power, is seen from the soothing effect it produced upon the disturbed mind of Saul (1 Sam. xvi. 16) and Elisha (2 Kings iii. 15), and from its general use in domestic life, at feasts and joyous meetings (Isa. v. 11, 12; Amos vi. 5; Sirach xxxii. 5, 6, xlix. 1). Professional singers of both sexes were employed by David (2 Sam. xix. 36; Sirach ix. 4), and at a later period even foreign women found maintenance among the Hebrews by singing (Isa. xxiii. 16). It was therefore to be expected

that Coheleth, in trying to indulge in all pleasures, would have singers of both sexes On music among the Hebrews, see Kitto, Cyclop. Bib. Lit.; Winer, Realwoerterbuch; Saalschütz, Archäologie der Hebräer, *s.v.*, עָשָׂה, *to do*, when used with regard to human beings, signifies *to get, to acquire, to procure* (comp. הַנֶּפֶשׁ אֲשֶׁר־עָשׂוּ בְחָרָן, *the men whom I acquired in Haran*, Gen. xii. 5). Respecting the etymology and signification of the words שִׁדָּה וְשִׁדּוֹת, an almost endless variety of opinions has obtained. The ancient versions, deriving it from שָׁדָה, *to pour out*, take שִׁדָּה in the sense of *out-pourers*, and refer it either to *persons* or *things*. Thus the Sept. (οἰνοχόους καὶ οἰνοχόας), and St. Jerome in his commentary (*ministros vini et ministras*), take these words as *men and women-pourers out of wine*, i. e., *cup-bearers*, evidently alluding to the מַשְׁקִים, *cup-bearers*, mentioned in 1 Kings x. 5; 2 Chron. ix. 4, whereas Aquila (κυλίκιον καὶ κυλίκια), Symm. (μέτρων σχήματα καὶ ἐπιθήματα), the Vulgate (*scyphos et urceos*), the Chaldee (מָדְנִין דִּשָׁרִין מַיָּא פָּשׁוֹר וּמַדְנִין דְּשָׁרִין מַיָּא חֲמִימִי), take it for *vessels* which are used for *pouring out* liquids. But against the first interpretation is to be urged, that *cup-bearers* are *only servants*, and as these have already been mentioned in the preceding verse, the repetition of them here would be mere tautology. The second is wholly inapposite, as the last clause of this verse describes *human beings*, and not *things*. What is, however, most subversive of both these renderings is the fact that the words in question are explanatory of the immediately preceding תַּעֲנוּגוֹת בְּנֵי הָאָדָם, which refers to *amorous* delight (comp. Song of Songs vii. 7). Equally forcible is this objection to the rendering of the Syriac by *musicians* (ܘܡܙܡ̈ܪܢܝܬܐ ܙܡ̈ܪ̈ܝܐ),

9 so that I greatly increased above all that were before me
10 in Jerusalem, my wisdom also standing me by; and nothing
that my eyes desired did I withhold from them; I did not

or *musical instruments*, (Ibn Melech כְּלֵי זָמָר, which is followed by Luther, Authorised Version, &c), deriving it from שָׁדַד, *to spoil, to ravish*, (hence שִׁדָּה, *a musician*, or musical instrument, that ravishes the heart), or *splendid and delightful coaches, palanquins* (מרכבות נוי עגלה צב לתענוג ולנוי), Rashi and Rashbam, who adduce, in corroboration of this explanation, the Talmudic usage of שִׁדָּה in Sabbath (שדה תיבה ומגדל), or *great abundance* (Paulus, Ewald, Elster, &c.) Ibn Ezra's opinion, therefore, is most natural, that שִׁדָּה signifies *a wife, a concubine*, and it may either be derived, as this learned commentator maintains, from שָׁדַד, *to violate, to spoil, to capture*, hence *a female captured in war*, a woman, as women formed the greatest treasures in the spoil of war, and are especially mentioned in the enumeration of the costly and highly prized articles which fell to the lot of the conquerors (Judg. v. 30); these fair captives became the wives or concubines of the warriors (Deut. xxi. 11), or of those to whom they were sold or presented. This derivation is followed by Mendelssohn, Desvoeux, Kleuker, Heinemann, Preston, &c. Or שִׁדָּה may be deduced from שָׁדַד, *impetum facere in aliquam, comprimere aliquam, concubere cum aliqua* (Prov. xix. 26, xxiv. 15), hence *a concubine*, so Herzfeld and Philippson. שִׁדָּה has a passive signification, according to the analogy of בִּזָּה, *spoil*, from בַּזַז, *to spoil*, זִמָּה, *a purpose*, from זָמַם, *to purpose*, &c. The repetition of the same noun in the plural, expresses multitude, (comp רַחַם רַחֲמָתָיִם, *a damsel, two damsels, i.e.*, many damsels, Judg. v. 30; דּוֹר דּוֹרִים, *generation, generations, i.e.*, many generations, Ps. lxxii. 5; Gesen. § 108, 4; Ewald, § 313, a). This rendering of שִׁדָּה by *woman, wife, concubine*, which is adopted by most modern commentators (Knobel,

Gesenius, De Wette, Noyes, Heiligstedt, Hitzig, Stuart, &c.), though defending various etymologies, is most compatible with the words תַּעֲנוּגוֹת בְּנֵי הָאָדָם, and is the one most naturally expected, since it would have been surpassing strange that Solomon, who was so enamoured of the fair sex, that he had a thousand wives and concubines (1 Kings xi. 1, &c.), should, as Ibn Ezra rightly remarks, so minutely enumerate his principal pleasures, and entirely omit, in this catalogue, his greatest delight.

9. *So that I greatly increased*, &c. In verse 4 Coheleth told us that he increased (הִגְדַּלְתִּי) his possessions, and now he tells us how *he greatly increased* (גָּדַלְתִּי וְהוֹסַפְתִּי) in riches and fame, through the amassing of such various and costly estates and treasures, effected by the help of wisdom. For the construction of גָּדַלְתִּי וְהוֹסַפְתִּי, see *supra*, i. 16. The words עָמְדָה לִּי are rendered by the Vulg. *perseveravit mecum*, which Luther, Coverdale, Authorised Version, &c., follow, and which Rashi, Reynolds, Patrick, Knobel, Hitzig, &c., explain, his wisdom was never smothered and suppressed, or undermined in the midst of all those pleasures, so that he always retained the full sense of his position and aim; but this interpretation is too far-fetched. The Chaldee explanation (סָיְּעָא יָתִי), *stood me by, assisted me*, which is also the second meaning given by Rashi, and followed by Mendelssohn, Herzfeld, Ewald, Elster, &c., is much more natural (comp. Dan. xii. 1; Esth. viii. 11; ix. 16).

10. *And nothing that my eyes desired*, &c. The object which he had in view in accumulating all these vast and multifarious estates is here given. It was not to gratify an avaricious propensity, which greedily seeks, grasps, and hoards up every-

keep back my heart from any pleasure, as my heart was to receive happiness from all my toil; and this was to be 11 my portion from all my toil. But when I looked at all my works which my hand worked, and at the toil which I toiled to accomplish them, behold all was vanity and striving after the wind, since there is no advantage under the

thing of value for the sake of the thing, but it was to enable him thereby to gratify every desire and indulge in every pleasure; it was this advantage that he sought to derive from all his toil. לֹּ expresses the Latin NULLUS, *nothing.* For the ascription of desire to the eye, see *supra*, i. 8. The *heart* is represented as freely indulging in pleasure, because it has been summoned to do so (i. 16), and because it has been described as having, in the first experiment, devoted itself to the acquisition of wisdom (i. 13). מֵהֶם is *masculine,* because עֵינַיִם, *eyes,* like all other members of the human body, although usually feminine, are occasionally employed as *masculine* (Job xxi. 20; Zech. iv. 10; Song of Songs, iv. 9; Gesen. § 107, 4, b; Ewald, § 174, d). The particle כִּי assigns a *reason* why Coheleth did not deny any pleasure to his heart, *since* he wanted to find that happiness in the pursuit after pleasure, which the pursuit after wisdom had failed to yield. The construction שָׂמֵחַ מִן, though rare, also occurs in Prov. v. 18; 2 Chron. xx. 27. מִן in such cases designates *the source out of which* the joy is derived. זֶה, *and this, i. e.,* ability to satisfy the desire of the eyes, and to grant the heart every pleasure, mentioned in the immediately preceding clause, was the portion which he obtained from all his toil. עָמָל, *labour,* is metonomically used for that which is acquired by labour, *the fruit of labour, abundance, wealth;* so vv. 18 and 19. This seems to be the natural meaning of this clause, though it has occasioned a variety of interpretations. The Vulg. has, *et hanc ratus sum partem meam, si uterer labore meo,* which Luther (unb baß hielt ich für mein Theil von aller meiner Arbeit) and Coverdale (*and this I took for the portion of all my trouble*) follow, and which Jermin, Gill, Preston, &c., explain to mean, this temporary enjoyment was all that Solomon desired to obtain, all that he had in view; but this is too harsh an ellipsis. The opinion of Rashi, Ibn Ezra, Reynolds, Patrick, Knobel, Noyes, Elster, &c., that Solomon describes here the inefficiency of all his toil, since it secured for him nothing more than temporary enjoyment, incurs the same objection, as well as anticipates the following verse.

11. *But when I looked at all my works,* &c. This verse states the conclusion at which Coheleth arrived respecting the power of pleasure, the second experiment by which he tried to remove depression from his mind, and supply the aching void,— and after the detailed description, substantiates the summary declaration made in verses 1 and 2. All the sumptuous banqueting, the magnificent edifices, the delightful vineyards, parks, and pleasure-grounds, the charming rills, the splendid retinue of servants, the numerous herds, the costly treasures, the enchanting music, the amorous delights, and the complete gratification of every desire, so minutely and forcibly described in 3 – 10, were utterly insufficient to quiet the mind craving after higher enjoyments, and to secure lasting happiness; and thus the pursuit after pleasure, like wisdom, proved mere vanity and striving after the wind. פָּנָה, *to turn,* in order to look, and *to look* (comp. וּפָנָה לְמָעְלָה, and he shall *look* upwards, Isa. viii.

12 sun.   I then turned to consider wisdom, and madness, and

21); it is used in its primary sense in the next verse; the preposition בְּ, by which it is followed, indicates that the looking is *minute inspection, examination* (Job vi. 28). The expression מַעֲשֶׂי describes the whole of the works, and is designedly chosen because it was used for the entire works at the beginning of this description (*vide supra*, ii. 2). עָמָל designates the *toil* which he had (לַעֲשׂוֹת) in *accomplishing* these works. For the phrase רְעוּת רוּחַ, *striving after the wind*, see i. 14; and for יִתְרוֹן, *advantage*, i. 3. לַעֲשׂוֹת, *to accomplish*, refers to כָּל מַעֲשַׂי, *all my works.* The Vulg. renders לַעֲשׂוֹת by *frustra*, mistaking it for לְהֶבֶל, *vanity.*

12. *I then turned to consider*, &c. Having shewn that both wisdom (i. 13 – 18) and pleasure (ii. 1 – 11) are *alike valueless*, as far as removing mental depression and securing permanent happiness are concerned; and being desirous that this *relative* estimate should not be taken for an *absolute* one, Coheleth now proceeds to shew their respective merits, independent of the use he had tried to make of them. The ability to inquire into and pass judgment upon the intrinsic value of wisdom and folly or pleasure, he claims, upon the ground that he, being so. mighty a potentate, had gained, through his extraordinary riches and wisdom, unparalleled experience, which his successors cannot be expected to surpass. That לִרְאוֹת here means *to see by comparing*, is evident from the following verse, where the advantage of wisdom over folly is given as *the result* of this *seeing* or *comparing*. The words הוֹלֵלוֹת וְסִכְלוּת, *madness and folly*, stand for שִׂמְחָה, *pleasure*, which is called מְהוֹלָל, *foolish actor*, and סִכְלוּת, *folly*, in ii. 1, 2, and are *coordinates* with חָכְמָה, *wisdom;* all these three nouns are objects of the action expressed by the verb רָאוֹת, *to see.* For the phrase *to see wisdom, vide supra*, i. 16. The particle כִּי is *causal*, assigning a *reason* for the preceding statement. The words מֶה הָאָדָם, *what is the man ?* as Ibn Ezra rightly remarks, imply a kind of undervaluing the person (comp. Ps. viii. 4). The accusative אֵת אֲשֶׁר, *whom*, depends upon עָשׂוּהוּ, *they have made*, i. e., *who has been made;* the third person plural, here with a pleonastic suffix, which is also found in vii. 13, like the third person singular, is as frequently used for the *impersonal* or the *passive* (comp. i. 10; Gen. xi. 9; Gesen. § 137, 3 ; Ewald, § 282). The interrogative is used for a strong negation (*i. e.*, " he will not be greater and have more experience than I," comp. i. 3; Gen. xxx. 2; Gesen. § 153, 2 ; Ewald, § 324, .b). Simple as this strictly grammatical explanation seems to be, yet few verses in this book have been more variously interpreted than the one before us; almost every word has been altered, or had some unnatural meaning forced upon it, either by the ancient versions or modern commentators. The first clause has only suffered from the Chaldee, which has הַלְחוּלְהָא דְמַלְכוּתָא וְסוּגִלְתָנוּ, *government of the kingdom and understanding*, instead of סִכְלוּת וְהוֹלֵלוּת, *madness and folly.* Jerome, in his commentary, takes the words הוֹלֵלוֹת וְסִכְלוּת, *madness and folly*, as a mere addition to חָכְמָה, *wisdom*, to shew that what man can attain has more madness and folly in it than true wisdom (*plus erroris stultitiæque habere quam veræ certæque prudentiæ*); somewhat similar, Hitzig and Stuart, *wisdom, even madness and folly;* and Mendelssohn, who explains it. " And I turned from looking for prosperity and happiness in all the works of madness and folly, though they be done scientifically." As the Chaldee is an unwarranted alteration, we shall pass it by, and notice the violent constructions of Jerome, and we submit — 1. That such an antithesis would require גַּם זֹאת, *even this*, or הִנֵּה, *behold*, before הוֹלֵלוֹת וְסִכְלוּת, *madness and folly*, and no brachyology or pathos could occa-

folly ; for what is the man that will come after the king,

sion the omissions. 2. That Coheleth nowhere calls absolute wisdom *folly*. 3. That it contradicts the immediately following verse. 4. That this violent construction is contrary to the scope of the passage, and has arisen from missing the thread of connection between this verse and the preceding statement, overlooking that Coheleth, having placed the *relative* value of wisdom and folly upon the same scale, is here evidently trying to shew their *absolute* worth. The ancient versions, the Jewish commentators, and the vast majority of modern expositors are therefore right in following the natural construction, and regarding all the three words as *objects* of the action expressed by the verb. Hitzig's argument, which is magnified by Stuart, that the common exegesis is a mere repetition of what was proposed in i. 17, falls to the ground, since it is based upon a misunderstanding of the design of this verse.

What is the man, &c. It is this part of the verse which has been so differently treated both by the ancient versions and modern expositors. The Sept , following a traditional explanation of הַמֶּלֶךְ, and altering some of the other words, has ὅτι τίς ἄνθρωπος ἐπελεύσεται ὀπίσω τῆς βουλῆς τὰ ὅσα ἐποίησαν αὐτήν, *for what man will follow after counsel as far as they use it ?* The Vulgate, adhering more closely to the Midrash, and omitting the words אֶת אֲשֶׁר כְּבָר, and altering עָשׂוּהוּ. the third person plural, into עָשָׂהוּ, *his maker*, has : QUID EST, INQUAM, HOMO, UT SEQUI POSSIT REGEM FAC-TOREM SUUM ? *what is man, said I, that he can follow the King his Maker?* Gussetius, however, who also espouses this Midrashic view, prefers retaining the verb עָשׂוּהוּ, in order to obtain an argument for the Trinity, since, according to him, this plural verb refers to הַמֶּלֶךְ, *the King of Kings*. The Chaldee paraphrase, of course, gives the tradition in full,

מַה הֲנָאָה אִית לִגְבַר לְצָלָאָה בָּתַר גְּזֵירַת מַלְכָּא וּבָתַר פּוּרְעָנוּתָא דְדָא כְבָר אתּנזרת עֲלוֹהִי וְאִתְעֲבִידַת לֵיהּ, *what use is it for a man to pray after the decree of the King, and after the sentence which has long been . passed concerning him, and has been executed upon him ?* which Rashi and Rashbam follow. Coverdale has, *for what is he among men that might be compared to me the king in such works ?* We must not pause to animadvert upon these traditional explanations and textual emendations, as they are contrary to the laws of exegesis ; we pass on to those who adhere to the received text, and base their various interpretations thereupon. Ibn Ezra explains it, כי מה יכולת תהיה באדם שיבא אחרי המלך וכל מה שיעשה ככר עשוהו אחרים, *for what power will the man have who will come after the king ? all that he will do, others have done long ago ;* so also Philippson. Or, which is substantially the same, *for what can the man do that cometh after the king ? even that which hath been already done ;* so the Auth. Version, Mendelssohn, Reynolds, Desvoeux, Knobel, De Wette, Noyes, Preston, Hitzig, Stuart, &c. (only that the last two, compelled by their misinterpretations of the first clause, alter עָשׂוּהוּ, *the third person plural*, into עֲשׂוֹהוּ, the *inf. const.* with the final ה omitted, thus obtaining the sense, *he shall do what long ago was his* (the king's) *doing*), and which H. Michaelis, Knobel, &c., explain, what will my successor to the throne do ? he will do that which others have done long before him. But against this is to be urged 1. That the supplying of the verb יַעֲשֶׂה in the second clause, or between מֶה and הָאָדָם is an exceedingly harsh ellipsis, and, even if it could be shewn that it ever takes place, which is very questionable, ought not to be resorted to unless absolutely necessary, which, however, is not the case here. 2. This objection becomes still more formidable, by making the accusative אֵת אֲשֶׁר־כְּבָר עָשׂוּהוּ depend upon this im-

13 who has been made long ago? and I saw that there is an
advantage to wisdom over folly, as is the advantage of light

plied verb.   3. It is evident from
אַחֲרֵי, *after*, which refers to the king's
successors to the throne (*vide infra*,
ver. 18), that כְּבָר is predicated of
royalty. The interpretation of Ibn
Ezra, referring אָדָם to *a private man*,
contrasted with *the king*, which most
modern commentators follow, incurs
the additional censure that it forces
upon the term אָדָם the sense *plebeian*
or *civilian*, in contradistinction to
מֶלֶךְ, *king*, which it never has, and
that, on the contrary, the article
before it shews that it refers to a
specific individual, the king's successor, *i. e.*, *he who comes after him.*
Greater still are the objections
against Jermin; *for what is that
man who shall attain after the king,
to that which they have already made
him?* which he explains, " to that
which wisdom, and the knowledge
of madness and folly have made
him;" and Holden, "*for what, O man,
shall come after the king?* anything
perfectly new? no; only *that which
hath been already done;* and there
fore I am well qualified to form a
correct judgment respecting them."
And what shall we say to Herzfeld's
explanation, who maintains that in
the words " wisdom, and madness,
and folly," Solomon contrasts himself
with the world at large; he is *wisdom
personified*, and the rest of the world
madness and folly; to justify this,
Solomon asks, *for what is the man
who comes after the king? i. e.*, who
surely is behind the royal sage? and
answers, *what has been done long ago,
i. e.*, acknowledged fruitless exertions,
folly; this is, as it were, the whole
man, and constitutes his being?
Could it have been believed that
so excellent a Hebrew scholar would
force such an obscuration upon the
text?   Ewald, Heiligstedt, and
Elster, feeling the objections against
supplying the verb יֵשׁעֶה, and the
harsh construction necessarily arising
from this proceeding, translate this

verse, *and I turned to see wisdom,
and madness, and folly, what the man
will be that shall follow the king,
compared with him who has been
chosen long ago.* But against this
is the particle כִּי, which by no means
admits of "מֶה וְגוֹ', being dependent
upon לִרְאוֹת, to say nothing of the
unnecessary and forced meaning
assigned to מֶה and אֶת, when the
legitimate signification yields good
sense.

   13. *And I saw that there is an ad-
tage to wisdom*, &c. The comparison
instituted in the last verse as to the
merits of absolute wisdom and folly
is here brought to an issue, and the
verdict is given in favour of the
former. However true that wisdom,
when acquired, to remove by *its*
power the depression caused by the
contemplation of the fact that, while
the world and natural objects abide
and constantly return to their wonted
actions, man has no abiding place
here, never returns when once gone;
that wisdom, when obtained to ameliorate by *its* laws the condition of man
and secure permanent happiness, only
increases our disappointment and
pain in proportion to the amount we
acquire for *that purpose* (*vide supra*,
i. 18); yet, considering it *absolutely*,
independent of the use Coheleth has
tried to make of it in the passage
alluded to, who, that has been constrained with the sacred writer to
denounce it as "striving after the
wind," as a canker growing in us
with the growth of wisdom, will not
also award the palm to wisdom *when
compared with folly?* Instead, therefore, of contradicting each other, as
some have vainly maintained, these
two statements are perfectly harmo-
nious. The cultivation of the mind
is far more exalting, delightful, and
exquisite to a rational being, than
the indulgence of the passions in degrading, enervating, and poignant
pleasures. Wisdom, therefore, like

14 over darkness.   The wise man, his eyes are in his head,
while the fool walks in ˙blindness, and yet I knew that the

splendid and genial light, illuminates
and quickens everything around it;
whilst folly, like brooding and lifeless
darkness, leaves gloom and depression in its train.   It is on this account that wise precepts are frequently called *light* (Ps. cxix. 105;
Prov. vi. 23), and ignorance is termed
darkness (Job xxxviii. 19).   For יִתְרוֹן
see *supra*, i. 3.   For מִן see Gesen.
§ 119, 1.   פִּיתְרוֹן in the last clause
stands for כְּיִתְרוֹן, the vowel *i* belonging to the feeble letter is not unfrequently transferred to the preceding
consonant (comp. וַיֵּלְךְ for וַיֵּלֶךְ, Jerm.
xxv. 36; Gesen. § 24, 1; Ewald,
§ 34, 10).   The Chaldee, desirous of
magnifying wisdom to the utmost,
has paraphrased it אִית מוֹתַר לְחוּכְמְתָא מִן
שָׁטוּתָא יַתִּיר כְּמוֹתַר נְהוֹר יוֹמָא מִן חֲשׁוֹךְ לֵילְיָא,
*the superiority of wisdom over folly,
is greater than the superiority of the
light of the day over the darkness of
the night.*
   14. *The wise man, his eyes, &c.*
Light and darkness, used in the preceding verse to shew the superiority of
wisdom over folly in *the abstract*, have
suggested in this verse the figurative
use of *open and closed eyes*, to illustrate these qualities as manifest in *the
concrete;* in the circumspect, reflecting, and heedful conduct of the wise
man, and the indiscreet, unreflect-
ing, and heedless dealings of the
fool.   הֶחָכָם stands *absolutely* for the
sake of prominence (comp. הָאֵל תָּמִים
דַּרְכּוֹ, *God, perfect is his way*, Ps. xviii.
30; Gesen. § 145, 2).   The words
עֵינָיו בְּרֹאשׁוֹ, *his eyes are in his head*,
i. e., has them in their useful place,
are tantamount to פְּקוּחוֹת, *are open*,
as is evident from the antithesis,
וְהַכְּסִיל בַּחֹשֶׁךְ הוֹלֵךְ, *and the fool walks in
blindness;* חָשַׁךְ, *to be dark, to be dim*,
is frequently used to denote the dimness of sight (*vide infra*, xii. 3; Ps.
lxix. 23; Lam. v. 17).   *To have one's
eyes open* is a well known phrase for
a *wise* and *watchful* man (comp.
שֹׁחַד יְעַוֵּר פִּקְחִים, *bribery blinds the open-*

eyed, Exod. xxiii. 8 with Deut. xvi.
19, where פִּקְחִים is exchanged for
עֵינֵי חֲכָמִים, *the eyes of the wise;* but
especially Prov. xx. 13, where open
eyes˙, as here, are contrasted with
sleep-closed ones).
   And yet I knew, &c.   But, nevertheless, this superiority cannot obviate
the fact stated in i. 3. 11. 18; the wise
man cannot devise anything to
exempt him from the fate common
to all, the contemplation of which
so much distresses Coheleth; the
wise man and the fool must die
alike.   The particle גַּם is frequently
used *adversatively*, for *yet, notwithstanding, nevertheless* (comp. *infra*,
vi. 7; Ps. cxxix. 2; Ezek. xvi. 28;
Gesen. Lex, *s. v.* 4; Ewald, § 354, a).
For the pleonastic use of אֲנִי. *I*, after
יָדַעְתִּי, with the pronominal suffix,
see i. 16.   מִקְרֶה (from קָרָה, *to meet,
to happen, to befall*), that which
befalls, *hap, fate, destiny, event*, and
refers here to *death*, which is the
burden of the sacred writer.   In
consequence of the poverty of the
Hebrew language, the cardinal אֶחָד
is used in this book in at least *six*
different significations, each of which
is expressed by a different word in
Latin — 1. In its primary sense as
cardinal, UNUS, *one* (vii. 28, ix. 18).
2. Indef. ALIQUIS, εἷς τις (iv. 8).
3. ALTER (iv. 10); 4. SOLUS (iv. 9.
10); 5. UNICUS (iv. 11); and 6. IDEM,
the same (ii. 14; iii. 19. 20; vi. 6;
ix. 2. 3; xii. 11, and in the passage
before us).   כֻּלָּם, *all of them*, denotes
also *both*, as is evident from *the two*
nouns, viz. חָכָם, *the wise man*, and
כְּסִיל, *the fool*, to which it refers.   It
is probably used instead of שְׁנֵיהֶם,
both, because these two classes constitute *all mankind*.   For the same
reason הַכֹּל, *all*, is often used for
both, (*vide infra*, iii. 19. 20; vi. 6;
vii. 15; ix. 1, 2; x. 19; and comp.
the well-known Talmudic phrase
דברי הכל, although referring to *two*
persons).   Hence the Vulg., though

15 same fate will meet both.   I therefore spake with my
heart, A fate like that of the fool must also meet me, even
me, and why am I then wiser? and I said to my heart

somewhat paraphrastic, has rightly
rendered this clause ET DIDICI, QUOD
UNUS UTRIUSQUE ESSET INTERITUS,
*and I learned that they were both
alike to die;* so also Rashi שניהם ימותו,
both die; and still better Rashbam,
וגם בכל זאת כוה כן זה שמתים שניהם כאחד,
*and nevertheless the one is like the
other, for both die alike.*

15. *I therefore spake with my heart,*
&c.   Seeing, then, that he as a
wise man, though *in other respects*
having unquestionable advantages
over the fool, cannot exempt himself
from death and oblivion, and that
wisdom, as far as the evil in question
is concerned, only makes him see
more clearly, and feel more acutely
the fleetness of life, the emptiness of
all earthly enjoyments, and the utter
inability of ameliorating his condition, Coheleth rightly characterises
the labour of acquiring wisdom more
than others as " striving after the
wind" (comp. *supra,* i. 13 – 18).   For
the use of אֲנִי, *I,* with the verb which
has the suffix of the same pronoun,
see i. 16, and for the phrase *to say*
or *to speak to the heart,* i. 13.   The
subject to יִקְרֵנִי, *will befall,* is the
implied מִקְרֶה, *fate,* before כְּמִקְרֵה, *i. e.,*
מִקְרֶה כְּמִקְרֵה הַכְּסִיל גַּם־אֲנִי יִקְרֵנִי, *a fate like
the fate of the fool will also befall me,*
as is evident from the כְּ in כְּמִקְרֵה,
which, when preceding a substantive,
denotes *something like itself* (comp.
וַיִּגַּע־בִּי כְּמַרְאֵה אָדָם, *an appearance like
the appearance of a man touched me*
Dan. x. 18; *infra,* viii. 14; Isa. v.
29; xxix. 4; Gesen. § 144; Ewald,
§ 221, a).   As our language has
the same ellipsis, we have imitated
it in the translation, which seems
preferable to the common rendering,
regarding יִקְרֵנִי as an *impersonal* verb.
The particle גַּם, *also,* used of accession, frequently denotes *even.*   The
repetition of the pronoun אֲנִי, the
nominative instead of אוֹתִי before the
verbal suffix נִי in יִקְרֵנִי, gives great

emphasis to the statement.   For similar instances, see 2 Chron. xxviii.
10.   הֲלֹא רַק־אַתֶּם עִמָּכֶם אֲשָׁמוֹת לַיהוָה
אֱלֹהֵיכֶם, *are not upon you, upon you the
sins against the Eternal your God?*
see also Gen. xlix. 8; Gesen. § 121, 3;
Ewald, § 311, a.   אָז, *then,* must
not be omitted (Vulg., a few MSS.,
some modern commentators); nor
changed into אָךְ (Houbigant), for
which there is no authority; nor
taken in the sense of *formerly,* (*i. e.,*
why have I been so wise *formerly?*
Knobel) ; nor as referring to *the
time when the fate of the fool also
meets him* (Herzfeld); nor *to the close
of life,* when all this experience has
been gained (Hitzig) ; nor *to the
point when his convictions are full*
(Stuart) ; but like כִּי, *then,* is a sign
of the apodosis: if it be so, if the
same fate befalls the wise and the
fool, why then, &c. — a sense which
our particle *then* also has (compare
Ewald, § 358, a).   יוֹתֵר is prop. part.
what is over, hence, as a substantive,
*surplus, residue, gain, profit (vide
infra,* vi. 8. 11; vii. 11), whence is
derived its *adverbial* signification,
more (infra, vii. 16; xii. 9).

This too is vanity, i. e., to acquire
wisdom above others, for the purpose
of removing by its power the depression of the mind, and to avert the
fate common to all (*vide supra,* i.
13 – 18).   זֶה, *this,* is therefore rightly
referred by Ibn Ezra to חָכְמָה, *wisdom.*
Knobel, Elster, &c., having missed
the logical sequence of this clause,
take it to refer to the destiny of
life, according to which the wise
man meets with the same fate as the
fool, which they say Coheleth pronounces " vanity."   The Septuagint,
anxious for the orthodoxy of the
sacred writer, inserts הַכְּסִיל, *the fool,*
between אָז, *then,* and יוֹתֵר, *more,* and
supplies דִּבֶּר from the immediately
following verb, and makes it διότι
ἄφρων ἐκ περισσεύματος λαλεῖ, *for this*

16 that this too is vanity; since there is no remembrance of the wise man as of the fool for ever, for, as in time past, both will be forgotten in days to come. And, alas!

reason, or perhaps *to this effect, the fool speaks abundantly;* putting the apparently heterodox sentiments into the mouth of a fool. So also the Syr.

ܩܢܠܐ ܕܗܡܕܠ ܗܼ ܠܐ ܡܩܠܐܠܠ

16. *Since there is no remembrance,* &c. The vanity of being wiser, in order to avert the fate that awaits all mankind, is shewn from the painful fact that both the wise man and the fool alike die, and are alike forgotten, which is the burden of the sacred writer (comp. i 11. 15). This verse fully corroborates our rendering of i. 11. For the construct זִכְרוֹן, comp. i. 16, where also is explained the use of the ל as a sign of the genitive. עִם, *with*, like עָמָּה (*infra*, v. 15), is from עָמַם, *to bind together, to unite, to connect.* Both expressions are properly *nouns*, signifying *a gathering, a union, a connection, close union of one with another, fellowship*, in nature or fate, of one with the other; hence the idea of *similarity, likeness, like, as*; (comp. חָלְפוּ עִם־אֳנִיּוֹת, *they pass away like ships*, Job ix. 26; Ps. lxxxviii. 5; and *infra*, vii. 11; Ewald, § 217, h). For עָמָּה, see *infra*, v. 15. בְּשֶׁכְּבָר is a compound of בְּ=בַּאֲשֶׁר (Gesen. § 36; Ewald, § 181, b), *inasmuch as, since* (*vide infra*, vii. 2, viii. 4; Gen. xxxix. 9. 23; Ewald, § 222, a; § 336, c), and כְּבָר, *formerly, time past* (comp. i. 10), and is used as anti- thesis to הַיָּמִים הַבָּאִים, *the coming days.* This explanation of the much dis- puted בְּשֶׁכְּבָר, which we believe to be most natural, and consonant with the sequel, seems also to have been entertained by the Chaldee, which paraphrases בְּשֶׁכְּבָר הַיָּמִים הַבָּאִים by מַה דַּהֲוָה כְּבָר בְּיוֹמוֹהִי כַּד יֵיתוּן יוֹמַיָּא דַעֲתִידִין לְמֶהֱוֵי בַּתְרוֹהִי, *that which was in his days long before, so will be the days that will come after him,* &c.; and Ibn Ezra, who interprets it הכל יהיה נשכח

בימים הבאים כמו בזמן שעבר, *all will be forgotten in the days to come, as in time past.* The rendering of the Sept. καθότι ἤδη, is ambiguous, inas- much as it may refer to time past or present, and has occasioned the ren- dering in the Auth. Ver., *seeing that which now is*, contrary to the signifi- cation of this word (*vide supra*, i. 10). This is one of the three instances (*vide infra*, ix. 6, 7), where our translators have shewn their incon- sistency in the translation of כְּבָר. The translation of Gesenius, Knobel, Elster, Fürst, &c., *since in the days to come all will have been long ago forgotten*, taking כְּבָר as qualifying the verb נִשְׁכָּח is very forced, inas- much as this adverb is too far removed from the verb. Herzfeld's version, wenn die kommenden Tage eine Zeitlang vorbei find, ist Alles vergessen, *when the coming days shall have passed some time, all will be forgotten*, resolving בְּשֶׁכְּבָר into בְּאֲשֶׁר כְּבָר, *when something*, כְּבָר *is past* (an opinion already mentioned by Ibn Ezra, אמר אחד מן המפרשים שהיא תורה על דבר עבר וכאשר עמד בפניו בשכבר הימים (הבאים אמר היה ראוי להיות בשכבר) is incon- gruous; since the coming days will always continue, and hence can never be characterised as *long past.* הַיָּמִים הַבָּאִים is the accusative of time, IN *the coming days* (Gesen. § 118, 2; Ewald, § 300, a). The Vulg., there- fore, ET FUTURA TEMPORA OBLIVIONE CUNCTA PARITER OPERIENT, *and the times to come shall cover all things with oblivion*, which is followed by Luther, und die künftigen Tagen ver- geffen alles, making הַיָּמִים הַבָּאִים the *nominative*, is an unwarrantable paraphrase. נִשְׁכָּח is the part. Niphal, used to denote *permanency* (comp. Isa. xxiii. 16). הַכֹּל, *all* for *both*, the wise man and the fool (*vide supra*, ver. 14). אֵיךְ, *how, alas*, apocopated from אֵיכָה, *i. q.*, אֵי and כֹּה, is an excla- mation of *pain* or *grief* (comp. Ps.

17 how dieth the wise, like the fool! Therefore I hated life,
for an evil pressure was upon me, the work which I worked
under the sun, as all is vanity and striving after the wind;

lxxiii. 19; Isa. xiv. 4), and is well explained by Rashbam, אֵיךְ הוּא דבר הַמִּתְקַיִּם; whereas the Auth. Version (*and how dieth the wise man? as the fool*), influenced by the traditional explanation of this clause, has departed from the simple meaning of the words. יָמוּת, the imperfect, like the participle in the preceding clause, denotes *continuance*. The Chaldee, anxious to make also this verse orthodox, paraphrases it, אֲרוּם לֵית דָּכְרָנָא לְחַכִּימָא עִם שַׁטְיָא לְעָלְמָא דְאָתֵי וּבָתַר מִיתַת גַּבְרָא מַה דַהֲוָה כְּבָר בְּיוֹמוֹהִי כַּד יֵיתוּן יוֹמַיָּא דַעֲתִידִין לְמֵיתֵי בַּתְרוֹהִי כּוֹלָא אִשְׁתְּכַח וְאֵיכְדֵין יֵימְרוּן בְּנֵי אֲנָשָׁא דְהִיא סוֹפָא דְצַדִּיקַיָּא כְּסוֹפָא דְחַיָּבָא, *because the remembrance of the wise man is not with the fool in the world to come; and after the death of a man, that which has been in his days long ago, so it will be in the days that will come after him, all will be disclosed; and how then say the sons of men that the end of the righteous is the same as the end of the wicked?* This Midrashic interpretation, which is given by Rashi, has as usual been adopted by Christian Fathers. Thus St. Gregory of Nyssa, who takes the statement in verses 14 and 15 as an objection urged by a sceptic, affirms that the sacred writer denounces it with the words, " *this, too, is vanity,*" and corroborates this denunciation by asserting, in the verse before us, that the remembrance of the wise man is not with the fool for ever; though they both die alike, their end is not alike; and by asking, " *How dieth the wise man? as the fool?*" which he explains, how therefore does any one say that the one dies like the other?

17. *Therefore I hated life,* &c. The fact that a life spent in toiling to acquire wisdom has no advantage whatever over a life wasted in frenzied folly, as far as the problem of Coheleth is concerned, produced in him

weariness of an existence pregnant with the consciousness of its certain, speedy, and gloomy dissolution, which became more poignant at every fruitless effort to avert it. Of course this refers to the state of life described in the preceding part of this treatise, when Coheleth sought to find by the aid of wisdom a satisfactory solution of the problems of life. We should have deemed it superfluous to make this remark, had not the Hagadic interpretation, in its anxiety to make the sentiment of this verse strictly orthodox, strangely perverted the meaning of the text, and had not that perverse exposition been adopted by the ancient versions and Fathers, and followed by some modern commentators. Thus the Chaldee paraphrases it וּסְנֵיתִי אֲנָא יַת כָּל חַיִּין בִּישִׁין אֲרוּם בִּישׁ עֲלֵי עוֹבָדָא בִישָׁא דִי אִתְעֲבִיד עַל בְּנֵי אֲנָשָׁא תְּחוֹת שִׁמְשָׁא בְּעָלְמָא הָדֵין, *and I hated all evil life, because evil was to me the evil work which is to the sons of men under the sun in this world,* making Coheleth express his disgust with sin. Hence the Sept., καὶ ἐμίσησα σὺν τὴν ζωήν ὅτι πονηρὸν ἐπ' ἐμὲ τὸ ποίημα τὸ πεποιημένον ὑπὸ τὸν ἥλιον; the Vulg., *et idcirco tæduit me vitæ meæ, videntem mala universa esse sub sole*; and the explanation of Gill, &c. Rashi, again, takes it as a prophecy respecting the wicked offspring of Rehoboam (מתנבא של דורו של רחבעם שהיו רשעים), whom Solomon hated. חַיִּים is not *the living* (Ibn Ezra, שם התואר לרבים), which is contrary to the context (comp. אֵיךְ יָמוּת in the preceding verse), but signifies *life* in *the abstract, i.e*, his own life. The preposition עַל, *upon,* when used with a noun, adjective, or verb, denoting *heaviness, burdensome, afflicting,* indicates *the pressure* or *weight* of the painful annoyance with which it lies *upon* the person (*vide infra,* vi. 1; viii. 6; Isa. i. 14; Job vii. 20; Gesen. § 154, 3, 6; Ewald, § 217, i). הַמַּעֲשֶׂה,

18 and I hated all my gain· which I gained under the sun,
as I must leave it to the man who shall come after me, and
19 no one knoweth whether he will be a wise man or a fool,
and yet he shall have power over all my gain which I have

the work, *i. e.*, the toil of men (*vide supra*, i. 14).

18. *And I hated all my gain*, &c. The weariness of life expressed in the preceding verse, is now followed by deploring all his works, which have not only utterly failed to satisfy the cravings of the soul, but which he cannot even bequeath to his own offspring, but must leave to a stranger. · For the pleonastic use of the pron. אֲנִי, *I*, after the verb, with the pronominal suffix, see i. 16. עָמָל, *labour, toil*, is, in this and in the two following verses, used metonymically for *the fruit of labour or toil, gain, riches, possessions*, which alone can be inherited; Rashbam, therefore, rightly remarks, את עמלי את עשרי. The verbal adjective, עָמֵל, obtains the force of a participle, by virtue of the pronoun added to it, and hence is followed by an accusative, and stands for the present tense (*vide infra*, 22; iii. 9; iv. 8; ix. 9). אַנִּיחֶנּוּ is not from יָנַח (Knobel) but from נוּחַ, like the forms הַזִּיל, *to despise* (Lam. i. 8), from הַלִּיז, זוּל, *to despise* (Prov. iv. 21), from הַסִּית, לוּז, *to incite* (Jer. xxxviii. 22), from סוּת; this Hiphil has a short vowel under the preformative, followed by *Dagesh forte* (Gesen. § 72, Rem. 9; Ewald, § 122, e). The phrase שֶׁיִּהְיֶה אַחֲרַי, *who shall be after me?* is the same as שֶׁיָּבוֹא אַחֲרֵי הַמֶּלֶךְ, *who shall come after the king?* in ver. 12, and precludes the possibility of referring it to Coheleth's *own son*, as is evident from the expression לְאָדָם, which could not be used to designate a child; and especially from the following verse, and verse 21. The strange rendering of the Vulgate, RURSUS DE-TESTATUS SUM OMNEM INDUSTRIAM MEAM, QUA SUB SOLE STUDIOSISSIME LABORAVI, HABITURUS HÆREDEM POST ME, *again I detested all my industry wherewith I most studiously laboured*

under the sun, being likely to have an heir after me, which has led some to regard this statement as expressing a querulous and mean selfishness, begrudging his heir the possession of the accumulated property; as well as the more softened paraphrase of the Chaldee, וּסְנֵיתִי אֲנָא יַת כָּל טַרְחוּתִי דִי טְרָחִית מְחוֹת שִׁמְשָׁא בְּעָלְמָא הָדֵין בְּגִין דְּאִישְׁבְּקִינֵיהּ לִרְחַבְעָם בְּרִי דְּאָתֵי בַתְרַי וְיֵיתֵי יָרָבְעָם עַבְדֵיהּ וְיֵסַב מִן יְדֵיהּ עֲשַׂרְתֵּי שִׁבְטַיָּא וְיַחְסִין פַּלְגוּת מַלְכוּתָא *and I hated all the labour which I laboured under the sun in this world, because I must leave it to Rehoboam my son, who will come after me, and Jeroboam his servant will come and take out of his hand the ten tribes, and possess half of the kingdom*, referring it to Rehoboam, which Rashi, Knobel, and many others follow, are both against the words of the text, and contrary to the character of Coheleth, who shews tender and fatherly feelings (iv. 8; v. 13). Orientals, to the present day, have the welfare of their children too much at heart to give vent to such mean selfishness. Jermin's explanation of this verse is really a curiosity: "It is commanded of God in the law of Moses (Levit. xi. 41) 'every creeping thing that creepeth on the earth shall be an abomination unto thee;' and what is all man's labour concerning the things of this life but a creeping thing on the earth? Wherefore Solomon might well say, ' *I hated all my labour.*'"

19. *And no one knoweth*, &c. And what is still more galling, is the fact that this stranger, to whom all the property, so wisely and prudently acquired, is to be left, may, for aught Coheleth knows, be a fool, and imprudently and wantonly squander all. This declaration about his ignorance of the character of the individual who is to be his heir, yields

20 wisely gained under the sun; this, too, is vanity. Thus I
turned to cause my heart to despair of all the gain which I

an additional proof to the one already
given in the preceding verse, that
Coheleth cannot refer to his son, and
thus exonerates him from the selfishness and meanness imputed to
him. It moreover shews that these
words could not proceed from Solomon, who knew his successor, and
well knew whether he was a wise
man or a fool. The ו before the interrogative מִי, is the regular conjunction, introducing an additional
reason to the one already given in
the preceding verse, why Coheleth
loathed his possessions, i. e., he must
not only leave his property to a
stranger, but does not even know
what he will be, whether wise or
foolish. Herzfeld's remark, that—
biefer Vers ift als integrirender Theil
bes mit שֶׁאַנִּיחֶנּוּ anfangenben Sahes
abverbialifch aufzufaßen als ftünbe:
„weil ich ihn hinterlaßen follte bem
Menfchen, ber nach mir fein wirb,
unb ich nicht weiß" ober: ohne zu
wiffen, „ob u. s. w." וּמִי, fteht nämlich eigentlich für מִי וַאֲשֶׁר, "this verse
must be taken adverbially, as an integral part of the sentence beginning
with שֶׁאַנִּיחֶנּוּ, i. e., 'because I must
leave it to the man who shall come
after me, and I know not,' or 'without knowing whether,' &c., &c. וּמִי
standing for וַאֲשֶׁר מִי," is both an unnecessary deviation from the regular
meaning of the ו, and weakens the
sense of the passage. The formula,
מִי יֹדֵעַ, who knows, is used for no one
knows, in the sense of the Latin
nescio an (comp infra, iii. 21; vi. 12;
Ps. xc. 11; Prov. xxiv. 22; and the
force of the interrogative in i. 16).
The Vulg.'s rendering of this clause,
QUEM IGNORO UTRUM, whom I know
not whether, &c., is an unwarranted
departure from the text. The disjunctive question, utrum-an? is here
expressed by the rare form הֲ—אוֹ,
instead of its usual אִם before the
second clause; a similar instance
occurs in Job xvi. 3. הֲקֵץ לְדִבְרֵי־רוּחַ אוֹ

מַה־יַּמְרִיצֲךָ, are the airy words at an
end? or what provoketh thee? (comp
Gesen. § 153, 2). The ו before יִמְלֹט,
is as frequently used adversatively,
i. e., and yet he shall rule (vide supra,
i. 4). The rendering of the Sept.,
καὶ εἰ ἐξουσιάζεται, and if he will rule,
taking the ו for וְאִם, as continuing
the interrogative from the preceding
clause, is both unjustifiable and inconsistent with the preceding verse,
where Coheleth said that a stranger
will have all his possessions; he
could therefore not be made to question again whether he will have the
power over it. That שֶׁעָמַלְתִּי וְשֶׁחָכַמְתִּי is
not to be translated wherein I have
laboured, and wherein I have shewn
myself wise (Sept., Geneva Version,
Auth. Version, and most modern
commentators), nor wherein I have
sweated and been solicitous (QUIBUS
DESUDAVI ET SOLLICITUS FUI, Vulg.),
but which I have wisely laboured or
gained, the second verb being subordinate to the first (vide supra, i. 16),
is evident from verse 20, where
Coheleth, referring to it, explains it
by עֲמָלִי בְּחָכְמָה. The Chaldee has
therefore rightly rendered it דְאַתְקֵנִית
בָּחוּכְמְתִי; so also Ibn Ezra, עמלתי ושחכמתי
תחת השמש ורע שמלח חכמתי מדהשעלים השועמדים
בחכמה שעמלתי ופירוש; Luther, bie ich
weislich gethan habe; Coverdale and
the Bishops' Bible, which I with such
wisdom have taken.

20. Thus I turned, &c. This and
the following verse are a rhetorical
epanalepsis, resuming and repeating,
in a somewhat different form, the
statement made in verses 18 and 19.
Not perceiving this, commentators
have experienced great difficulty in
their attempts to connect these verses
with what precedes. The ו before
סַבֹּותִי introduces the epanalepsis, and
must therefore be rendered thus,
סָבַב, to turn, to leave one thing and
turn to another, to turn in order TO
DO something (infra, vii. 25; 1 Sam.
xxii. 17, 18), and thus differs from

21 gained under the sun ; for here is a man which hath laboured wisely, and prudently, and dexterously, and to a man who hath not worked at it at all he must leave it as

שׁוּב and פָּנָה, *to turn in order* TO SEE (*vide*, ver 12 ; iv. 1. 7 ; ix. 11 ; Fürst, Lex. *s. v.* סָבַב). יְאֵשׁ is not the *Pahel* (Preston), but the infinitive *Piel* — the vowel of the first radical being prolonged to compensate for the Dagesh forte, which is lost from the middle letter (comp. Gesen. § 64, 3) — of יָאֵשׁ, *to relinquish, to abandon as hopeless, to despair ;* the Piel as frequently has a *causative* significa- tion (Gesen. § 52, 2, b ; Ewald, § 120, c). This word only occurs five times more in the Old Testament (1 Sam. xxvii. 1 ; Isa. lvii. 10 ; Jer. ii. 25, xviii. 12 ; Job vi. 26), but is frequently used in this sense in Rabbinic writings. עַל, *upon*, like ἐπί in Greek, also marks the object of a discourse or action, hence signifies *in reference to, concerning, of* (comp. שָׁמַעְתִּי עָלֶיךָ, *I have heard concerning thee*, Gen. xli. 15 ; ὅτι ταῦτα ἦν ἐπ᾽ αὐτῷ γεγραμμένα, *these things were written respecting him*, John xii. 16). The Sept., καὶ ἐπέστρεψα ἐγὼ τοῦ ἀποτάξασθαι τῇ καρδίᾳ μου ἐπὶ παντὶ τῷ μόχθῳ, *and I turned to bid farewell to my heart respecting all my labour*, though languid, yet gives the sense of the original ; whilst the Vulg., UNDE CESSAVI, RENUNCIAVITQUE COR MEUM ULTRA LABORARE, *wherefore I ceased, and my heart renounced to labour any more*, is an unjustifiable violation of the text. The Syriac ܟ̇ܣ ܩܡ̈ܦ̇ܟ݂ ܐܢܐ ܟ̇ܦܣܘ, *and I turned to relax my heart*, does not give the true meaning of יָאֵשׁ ; Luther's rendering, barum wandte ich mich, daß mein Herz abließe von aller Arbeit, which is followed by Cover- dale and the Bishops' Bible ("so I turned me to refrain my mind from all such travail"), adhering to the primary sense of יָאֵשׁ ; and the Geneva version ("therefore I went about to make my heart abhor all the labour"), ignore the preposition עַל. Hodgson's

translation, "I turned my heart to pensive musing on all the works," is preposterous.

21. *For here is a man, &c.* In resuming here the statement made in ver. 18, Coheleth leaves it beyond the shadow of a doubt that he did not intend to express, by the words אֲנִיחֶנּוּ לָאָדָם שֶׁיִּהְיֶה אַחֲרָי, *I must leave it to the man who shall be after me*, a misanthropic feeling, begrudging his very children the enjoyment of his amassed wealth ; but, on the con- trary, deplored the fact that the acquired property cannot sometimes even be bequeathed to one's own children, but must be left to strangers. This is evident from the synonymous phrase, לְאָדָם שֶׁלֹּא עָמַל־בּוֹ יִתְּנֶנּוּ, *he leaves it to a man who has not worked for it at all*, which undoubtedly means a stranger, in contradistinction to children, who, in the East especially, always *co-operate* with their parents in the acquisition of wealth. The Chaldee has therefore rightly para- phrased it וִימוּת בְּלָא וְלַד וְלִוְבַר דְּלָא טְרַח בֵּיהּ יִתְנְיֵיהּ, *and he dies without children, and leaves it to a man who has not worked at it*. כִּי, *for*, is causal, assigning a reason for the despair expressed in the preceding verse. The verb עָמַל is to be supplied from the second clause before שֶׁעָמְלוֹ, *i. q.*, שֶׁעָמַל עֲמָלוֹ, *who has laboured his labour*, here used metonymically for *who has gained his gain.* The preposition בְּ before דַעַת הַכְמָה, and כִּשְׁרוֹן, nouns of quality, forms a periphrasis for the *adjective* or *adverb* (comp. קוֹל־יְהוָֹה, בַּכֹּחַ, *the voice of the Eternal is with power*, i. e., *is powerful*, Ps. xxix. 4; Exod. xii. 11 ; 1 Chron. xxvi. 14; Gesen. § 106, 1, Rem. 1; Ewald, § 217, f.) The rendering of Ewald, dessen Mühe sich um Weisheit und Wissen, und Tüchtigkeit dreht, taking the בְּ as marking *the object for which* he expended his labour, is contrary to the scope of the passage, which

22 his portion; this, too, is vanity, and a great evil. For man
hath nothing from all his labour and the striving of his heart

speaks of the bequeathing of *riches*,
and not of *mental capacities;* of these
Coheleth himself complains that they
cannot be transmitted. Besides, if
this were the meaning, the following
clause would undoubtedly have been
וּלְאָדָם שֶׁלֹּא עָמַל בָּהֶם, in the *plural*. As
בְּשָׁרוֹן (from בָּשָׁר, kindred with יָשָׁר,
אָשָׁר, *to be straight, to be right,*
physically or morally, Esth. viii. 5,
infra, x. 17, with the termination וֹן,
according to the analogy of יִתְרוֹן,
vide supra, i. 2), means both that
which is done in a right manner,
*dexterity, adroitness, industry (vide
infra, iv. 4)*, and by metonymy, that
which is gained by acting aright,
success, prosperity; hence the Syriac

(ﺍﻟﺰﺪﻳﻘﺎ), the Chaldee (וּבְצִדְקֹן),

the Geneva Bible, the Authorised
Version, Geier, Rambach, Van der
Palm, Hodgson, Noyes, &c., retain
the primary sense of *straight, right,
equity;* the Sept. (ἐν ἀνδρείᾳ), Symm.
(ἐν γοργότητι), Vulg. (*sollicitudo*), Luther
(Geschicklichkeit), Coverdale and the
Bishops' Bible (*opportunity*), Hodgson, Herzfeld, Ewald, Hitzig, Stuart,
Philippson, Fürst, Elster, &c., adhere
to the idea of that which is done
aright, *i. e., dexterity, industry;*
whilst Gesenius, Holden, Rosenmüller, Knobel, Preston, &c., render
it *success, prosperity*. But as the
scope of the passage is to set forth
the deplorable fact that wealth
acquired by *toil* must be left to one
who *has not toiled* for it at all, the
meaning *industry* or *dexterity* is
preferable to *success* or *equity*, and
also agrees better with חָכְמָה, *wisdom*,
and דַּעַת, *intelligence*. עָמָל־בּוֹ, *i. e.,*
בֶּעֲמָלוֹ, *he has not laboured in the
labour* (comp. Ps. cxxvii. 1; Jonah
iv. 10). The suffix in יִתְּנֶנּוּ also
refers to עָמָל, and the suffix in חֶלְקוֹ to
the second אָדָם, *i e., to the man who
has not worked therein* (בַּעֲמָלוֹ); *he
must leave it* (עֲמָלוֹ) *as his portion;*

the verb נָתַן, *to bestow*, being one of
the verbs which are construed with
two accusatives (compare אֶתְּנָה גוֹיִם
נַחֲלָתֶךָ, *I shall give the heathen for
thine inheritance*, Ps. ii. 8, xviii. 41;
Gesen. § 139, 2; Ewald, § 283, b;
so the Chaldee יִתְּנִינֵיהּ לְמַלְכֵיהּ חוּלְקֵיהּ,
Luther, Auth. Ver., Knobel, Herzfeld,
Noyes, Hitzig, Heiligstedt, Elster,
&c.) Others, however, take the
suffix יִתְּנֶנּוּ to be the same as in חֶלְקוֹ,
*i. e., he gives it, namely his portion, to
another* (the Sept., Vulgate, Geneva
Version, Ewald, &c.), or refer it to
the first אָדָם, *i. e.,* יִתֵּן לוֹ, to the man
who has not worked therein, to him
he must give his portion (Ibn Ezra,
Bauer, Stuart, &c.) But as the first
of these constructions creates a pleo-
nasm, which is only used to give
special emphasis, as is not the case
here, and the second involves the
clogging repetition of the dative, as
well as the taking of the suffix for
the dative, after the verb נָתַן, which
is of very rare occurrence, the one
we have adopted is preferable.

22. *For man hath nothing*, &c.
But as for the man who thus exerts
his powers of body and mind to
obtain solid happiness here, he reaps
in this respect no advantage of all
his efforts. Thus Coheleth, in concluding the first section of his
disquisition, repeats the very words
with which he began (*vide supra*,
i. 3). מֶה־הֹוֶה לָאָדָם, *what is there to
man?* is the same as מַה־יִּתְרוֹן לָאָדָם,
what advantage is there to man? in
i. 3,—where the use of the interrogative for an emphatic denial is
explained,—and is well rendered by
the Vulg. *quid enim proderit homini*,
and still better by the Chaldee אֲרוּם
מָה הַנָּאָה אִית לֵיהּ לִגְבַר, *for what advantage hath man?* The Sept. ὅτι γίνεται
τῷ ἀνθρώπῳ ἐν παντὶ μόχθῳ αὐτοῦ, *for it
happens to a man in all his labour*, is
an unwarranted departure from the
text, without yielding any sense.
הֹוֶה is not a later Hebrew or Aramean

23 that he laboureth under the sun, since his business grieveth
   and irritateth him all his days, and his mind doth not rest
24 even at night; this also is vanity. There is nothing better for

form, instead of הָיָה (Knobel, Hitzig,
Heiligstedt, Stuart, Elster, &c), but
is the part. of הָיָה=הָוָה, *to blow, to
breathe;* hence *to have life, to exist,
to be,* a primitive form, as is evident
from its onomatopoetic nature, and
its use in the earliest Hebrew (comp.
Gen. xxvii. 29 ; Isa. xvi. 4, &c.)
The words עָמֵל שֶׁהוּא לְבּוֹ וּבְרַעְיוֹן עֲמָלוֹ are
generally rendered *his labour and
the vexation or striving of his heart,
wherein he hath laboured;* but this
is incongruous, inasmuch as עָמֵל can
only be predicated of עָמֵל, and not
of רַעְיוֹן ; nor can this rendering be
defended by resorting to the figure
Zeugma, where two subjects have a
verb in common, which can with
propriety predicate the action of
only *one;* for, in such a case, the
verb *immediately* follows the subject
of the action which it properly or
legitimately expresses (comp. Gen.
xlvii. 19 ; Isa. lv. 3 ; Job iv. 10).
Accordingly, the construction would
have been רַעְיוֹן לְבּוֹ וּבְכָל-עֲמָלוֹ שֶׁהוּא עָמֵל.
It is therefore more consistent, with
Herzfeld and Philippson, to take the
שֶׁ = אֲשֶׁר in שֶׁהוּא, not as ᾽a relative
pronoun, but as a *conjunction, that,*
in which sense it is frequently used
(*vide infra,* v. 4 ; vii. 29, &c.) For the
signification of רַעְיוֹן, *striving,* as well as
for its form, see i. 14 ; and for the use
of עָמֵל in the present tense, see ii. 18.

23. *Since his business,* &c. To
strengthen the conclusion submitted
in the preceding verse, Coheleth
adduces an additional fact, that not
only has man no future and abiding
advantage from all his toil, but that
it does not even yield *present* enjoyment whilst engaged therein, for
man's labour is accompanied with
grief and irritation in the daytime,
and deprivation of rest in the night.
כִּי is not to be taken as *truly* introducing emphatically the direct diction
(Ewald, Hitzig, Elster, &c.), but has
its usual sense *for,* only in a more

intense degree, by virtue of the
implied negation in the preceding
verse (comp. Micah vi. 4 ; Job xxxi.
18 ; Gesen. § 155, 1 e d). כָּל-יָמָיו, *all
his days,* is *the accusative of time,* in
an adverbial limitation. This is
evident — 1. From chap. v. 16, where
the same phrase occurs, and is
acknowledged to be so ; 2. From
the *Quametz* under the וְ in וְכַעַם,
which, being used to join words in
pairs, connects it inseparably with
מַכְאֹבִים (comp. תֹהוּ וָבֹהוּ, Gen. i. 2 ;
יוֹם וָלַיְלָה, *ibid.* viii. 22 ; see also *infra,*
iv. 8 ; Gesen. § 104, 2, d ; Ewald,
§ 243, a) ; and 3. From the antithesis
בַּלַּיְלָה, which is the accusative of
time. The whole clause is therefore
rightly explained by Ibn Ezra כל היום
שהוא בהקיץ כל ענינו בכאב נפש וכעם, *the
whole day whilst awake, all his labour
is grief of mind and irritation;* so
also the Vulg., which, omitting מְעִנְיַי,
has, CUNCTI DIES EJUS DOLORIBUS ET
ÆRUMNIS PLENI SUNT, *all his days
are full of sorrow and grief;* substantially the same is the loose
paraphrase of Luther, benn alle feine
Lebtage Schmerzen mit Grämen unb
Leib, followed by Coverdale and the
Bishops' Bible (*but heaviness, sorrow,
and disquietness all the days of his
life*), which mistake the word עִנְיַנוֹ,
and Herzfeld. מַכְאֹבִים, *grief,* the abstract, which, as in Greek and Latin,
is frequently expressed in Hebrew
by the *plural* (comp. חַיִּים, *life,* Gen.
ii. 9 ; סַנְוֵרִים, *blindness, ibid.* xix. 2 ;
Gesen. § 108, 2, a ; Ewald, § 179, a),
and כַּעַם, *irritation,* are used as *intensive adjectives* (*vide infra,* x. 6 ; Ps.
v. 9 ; Song of Songs v. 16 ; 1 Cor.
ii. 14 ; Phil. iii. 2 ; Gesen. § 106, 1,
Rem. 1 ; Ewald, § 296, b).

24. *There is nothing better,* &c.
Seeing that neither the exertions of
wisdom (i. 12 - ii. 11) nor the pursuits after pleasure (ii. 12 – 23) can
satisfy the cravings of the soul,
Coheleth concludes that there is

man than to eat and drink, and let his soul enjoy pleasure in

nothing left for man but calmly and cheerfully to enjoy the present; yet this, too, he finds is not always in the power of man. Much difficulty has been experienced in the rendering of the first part of this verse. The Sept. translates it, οὐκ ἔστιν ἀγαθὸν ἀνθρώπῳ, ὃ φάγεται καὶ πίεται καὶ ὃ δείξει τῇ ψυχῇ αὐτοῦ ἀγαθὸν ἐν μόχθῳ αὐτου, *man has not the good which he shall eat and drink. and which he shall shew his soul as good in his labour;* substantially the same, Geier, Dathe, and Knobel, fein Glück (wird) durch den Menschen, daß er esse und trinke und seine Seele Glück schauen lasse bei seiner Mühe ; Mendelssohn, Friedlander, and Preston, *it is no great good for a man to eat and drink and enjoy himself in his employment ;* Desvoeux, *no good in man that he eateth and drinketh, and maketh his soul see good in his labour;* Rosenmüller, Herzfeld, and Philippson ; nicht in des Menschen Befähigung liegt es, daß er esse und trinke und seine Seele Gutes genießen lasse für alle seine Mühe. But against these renderings is to be urged, that they are contrary to the scope of the whole argument. Coheleth having shewn the utter vanity of all exertions to secure abiding good, evidently intends to prove that enjoyment of the present *is* the only good thing left for man ; the contrast between this clause and the preceding verse puts this beyond the shadow of a doubt. Moreover, these renderings are against iii. 12. 22 ; v. 17 ; viii. 15 ; ix. 7 – 9, where the same or similar language is employed to recommend present enjoyment as the best thing for man. The Vulg., feeling this difficulty, has rendered it interrogatively, NONNE MELIUS EST COMEDERE ET BIBERE ET OSTENDERE ANIMÆ SUÆ BONA DE LABORIBUS SUIS ? *is it not better to eat and drink, and to shew his soul the good things of his labours ?* so also Luther, Coverdale, the Bishops' Bible, Hodgson, Boothroyd, Hengstenberg, &c.

But though this rendering gives the sense of the passage, yet the difficulty of assigning to אִין here an interrogative meaning in the face of the similar phrase אֵין טוֹב, in iii. 12. 22 ; viii. 15, &c., as well as the awkwardness of an interrogative sentence in this connection, will always be against it. The rendering of the Syr.

ܟܝܬ ܕܛܒ ܠܓܒܪܐ ܐܠܐ ܕܢܐܟܘܠ

there is nothing good for man except to eat, &c., the Chaldee וְאָכְלָה לֵית דִּשַׁפִּיר אֱלָהֵן דִּי יֵיכוּל, St. Jerome, *non est bonum homini, nisi quod comedit,* &c., Rashbam and Ibn Ezra, which is followed by the Geneva and Auth. Versions, De Wette, Ewald, Hitzig, Heiligstedt, Stuart, Elster, Vaihinger, &c , is the most preferable. A comparison of this clause with iii. 12 will shew that the מ, which this rendering supplies before שֶׁיֹּאכַל, has been dropped in transcribing, because the word which immediately precedes it ends with מ. For a similar instance, where the meeting of the same letter has been the cause of the dropping of one, see Job xxxiii. 17. The בְּ before אָדָם, as well as in iii. 12, has the same signification as the לְ in vi. 12; viii. 15 ; allied to this is the use of the בְּ, to denote *the object* in doing a thing =*for,* in x. 17. בַּמֶּה רָאִיתִי אֲנִי כִּי stands for רָאִיתִי אֲנִי כִּי בַּמֶּה, by an attraction which takes the subject of the dependent clauses into the governing one as the object; this takes place especially after verbs of *observing, knowing, shewing,* or *declaring* (compare וַיַּרְא אֱלֹהִים אֶת־הָאוֹר כִּי־טוֹב, *and God saw the light that it was good,* instead of וַיַּרְא אֱלֹהִים כִּי־טוֹב הָאוֹר, *and God saw that the light was good,* Gen. i. 4, vi. 2, xlix. 15 ; Exod. xxxii. 22 ; 1 Kings v. 17 ; comp. also Mark xi. 32, xii. 34; Acts iii. 10 ; Ewald, § 336, b; Winer, § 66, 5). Not perceiving this construction, which is of very frequent occurrence in this book (iii. 21 ; v. 19 ; viii. 17;

25 his labour; even this I saw cometh from God: for who should

xi. 8), expositors have found great difficulty in explaining these passages, and have often obscured the sense, which is obvious enough when the attraction is solved.

25. *For who should eat, &c.* The two assertions made in the preceding verse, viz., that the best thing for man is to enjoy the fruit of his labour, and that this enjoyment is a gift of God, are now accounted for in this and the following verses. "Nothing is better for man than to enjoy his labours, for who except the labourer (חוּץ מִמֶּנִּי) has the first claim to do so? To render this statement more striking and vivid, Coheleth places himself in the position of the labourer, and says, "If I toil, who should enjoy the fruit of my toil more than I?" A similar instance occurs in iv. 8. So Rashi מי ראוי לאכול את יגיעי ומי ימהר לבולעה מבלעדי, *who is entitled to eat my labours, and who should hasten to partake of them, except I?* Rashbam שהרי מי הוא שראוי לאכול ולמהר לשמוח בעמלי מבלעדי ועל כן יש לאכול ולשתות ולשמוח בטוב בעמלו, *for who is entitled to eat and hasten to rejoice in my toil, except I? therefore man (the labourer) should eat and drink and rejoice in his labour,* and Ibn Ezra היש מי שהוא ראוי לאכול אותו כמוני, *is there any one so entitled to eat it as I am?* This appears to be the most natural explanation, and most consonant with the scope of the passage. Others, however, maintain that this verse contains a proof, from Solomon's personal experience, of the assertion made in *the latter* part of the preceding verse, viz., *that the enjoyment of things is a gift of God,* and explain it, "Who shall eat, or who shall drink, more than I? no one! and if I, abounding in all good things more than any one (ii. 1 – 10) found that it was not in my power to enjoy them (ii. 2 – 11) surely the ability to enjoy the fruits of our labour must be from God" (Luther, Mendelssohn, Herzfeld), or "I who have so richly enjoyed life can testify

from my own experience, that it is a gift of God" (Patrick, Knobel, Hengstenberg, &c.) But the very fact that, according to these explanations, this verse simply raises a question without furnishing us with the clue for its solution, and that these diametrically opposite interpretations are therefore to be urged with equal right, shews the preferableness of the view we advocate. St. Jerome, again, who is followed by Coverdale, Desvoeux, Spohn, Ewald, Hitzig, Heiligstedt, Stuart, Philippson, Elster, Vaihinger, &c., renders this verse, QUIS ENIM COMEDIT, ET QUIS PARCIT SINE ILLO, QUI HOMINI BONO CORAM SE DEDIT? *for who eats, and who forbears it without him, who gives to the man that is good in his sight?* But this alteration of מִפֶּנִּי, *the first person,* into מִמֶּנּוּ, *the third person,* is both unnecessary and unwarranted. The appeal to the Sept. and Syriac is nugatory, for these ancient versions may simply have resolved the figure by which Coheleth places himself in the position of the labourer, and refer direct to the labourer, which is also done by Ibn Ezra, when explaining it (כי מי יאכל ממוני לבד ממנו). This is corroborated by the fact that the ancient Latin version, which is retained in the Vulgate, has *ut ego,* the first person. כִּי, *causal,* assigns a reason for the first statement made in the foregoing verse. The interrogative מִי is used as an emphatic denial, *vide supra,* i. 3. חוּשׁ, *to hasten,* is of frequent occurrence in the Old Test., and is used with other verbs or nouns, to intensify their meaning (comp. Ps. xxii. 20; cxix. 60); the full construction would be מִי יֹאכַל וּמִי יָחוּשׁ לֶאֱכֹל; hence Symmachus' rendering of יָחוּשׁ by ἀναλώσει, *shall consume;* the text, however, by leaving the verb to be mentally supplied from the first clause, renders the construction more forcible. A similar instance of חוּשׁ being construed with אָכַל, is to be found in

26 eat, and who should hasten thereunto, except I? For
to the man who is good before him, he giveth wisdom,
and knowledge, and joy; but to the sinner he giveth the
business to gather and to amass, to give it to him who

Hab. i. 8, כְּנֶשֶׁר חָשׁ לֶאֱכוֹל, *like an eagle
hasting to eat.* So Rashi, Rashbam,
Ibn Ezra, Geneva, and Auth.Version.
The Septuagint πίεται, and the Syriac
ܢܫܬܐ, *shall drink*, has evidently
arisen from a desire to make it
conform with the preceding verse.
Aquila φείεται, and Jerome PARCIT,
confounding יָחוּשׁ with the assonant
יָחוּס, is undoubtedly owing to a conceit of making this clause an antithesis to the former, *i. e., who shall
eat, and who shall refrain from eating,*
or *not eat it?* The Vulgate DELICIIS
AFFLUET, *shall abound with delights,*
which is followed by Luther (ſich
ergöᵗt), Knobel, Gesenius, Herzfeld,
Hitzig, Heiligstedt, Stuart, Philippson, Fürst, Elster, &c., who try to
justify it by appealing to the Aramean
or Mishnaic usage of this word, is
contrary to its uniform signification
in the Old Testament, and is rendered
nugatory by the passage in Hab.
quoted above. חוּץ מִן, *except*, which
occurs nowhere else in the Old
Testament, is a well-known Talmudic
phrase (comp. הכל בידי שמים חוץ מיראת
שמים, *everything is from God, except
the fear of God, i. e.,* man is a free
agent; God, who gives him every
blessing, does not *make* him religious;
Berach. 32, 2. 71; Nidah, 16, 72;
comp. also כל מצוה שהיא תלויה בארץ אינה
נוהגת אלא בארץ · · · חוץ מן הערלה וכלאים,
all the commandments which are local
(for Palestine) *are not to be practised
but in the land,* EXCEPT *circumcision
and the sowing of diverse seed* (Kid.
1. 9, see also Middoth, 2, 3).

26. *For to the man,* &c. The
second assertion, made in the latter
part of verse 24, is now substantiated. Having had more wisdom,
knowledge, and enjoyment than any
one else (1. 16, &c.), and having received these as a gift from the Lord,

who was pleased with him (1 Kings
iv. 12, 13), Coheleth can therefore
testify, from his own experience, that
these blessings are bestowed by God
on the righteous, and are withheld
from the wicked. Whilst the spiritual capacities are described as being
communicated directly from the Lord,
the earthly materials are given to us
through the medium of men, whom
God uses as instruments to effect his
great purposes. The wicked are also
represented as amassing wealth for
the righteous, in Job. xxvii. 13–17;
Prov. xiii. 22; xxviii. 8. כִּי, *causal, for,*
introduces the reason for the second
assertion, viz., that the capacity to
enjoy earthly possessions (מִיַּד הָאֱלֹהִים
הִיא) *is from God;* the intimate connection of this statement, with the
reason given for it in the verse before
us, is evident from the pronoun לְפָנָיו,
which refers to הָאֱלֹהִים, *God,* in
ver. 24, b. Herzfeld will not admit
that טוֹב לִפְנֵי אֱלֹהִים and חוֹטֵא have any
reference to *the moral* character of
the individuals thus described; חוֹטֵא,
he says, bezeichnet Einen, der die Gnade
Gottes verfehlt, ihrer nicht theilhaftig
wird; Herzfeld, therefore, makes this
verse to set forth God's arbitrary
granting or withholding the power of
enjoying earthly good, as he likes or
dislikes any one, irrespective of his
moral worth. But vii. 26, and especially viii. 12, 13, where the same
two characters are contrasted, and
where חוֹטֵא is defined by עֹשֶׂה רַע, *an
evil-doer,* and אֵינֶנּוּ יָרֵא מִלִּפְנֵי אֱלֹהִים, *one
who does not fear God,* are subversive
of this interpretation. The Vulgate's
paraphrase of וְלַחוֹטֵא נָתַן עִנְיָן, PECCA-
TORI AUTEM DEDIT AFFLICTIONEM ET
CURAM SUPERFLUAM, *but to the sinner
he has given vexation and superfluous
care,* is both an unwarranted departure from the text, and does not at all
improve the sense.

is good before God.   This, too, is vanity, and striving after
the wind.

This, too, is vanity, &c., *i. e.,* this
wisdom, knowledge, and joy, are
utterly unable to satisfy the mind,
which is disturbed by the contemplation of the fact, that whilst all the
objects of nature are abiding, man
vanishes and is buried in oblivion.
That נַּם־זֶה הֶבֶל refers to חָכְמָה וְדַעַת וְשִׂמְחָה
is evident, from the fact that these
are the very things, and the very

Words, which Coheleth has already
characterised as vain, and unable to
secure for him lasting good, in i. 16;
ii. 1.   Thus Coheleth concludes the
first portion of his enquiry, by shewing that wisdom, knowledge, and enjoyment of earthly blessings, which
are the best things for short-lived
man, cannot satisfy the cravings of
the human soul.

SECTION II.

CHAPTER III. 1—V. 19.

All the events of life are immutably fixed (1-8), hence the fruitlessness of
human labour (9). God has indeed prescribed bounds to man's employment, in harmony with this fixed order of things, but man through his
ignorance often mistakes it (10, 11); thus again shewing that there is
nothing left for man but the enjoyment of the things of this world in
his possession, and that even this is a gift of God (12, 13).   The
cause of this immutable arrangement in the events of life is, that man
may fear God, and feel that it is he who orders all things (14, 15). The
apparent success of wickedness (16) does not militate against this conclusion (17); but even if, as is affirmed, all terminates *here*, and man
and beast have the same destiny (18—21), this shews all the more
clearly that there is nothing left for man but to enjoy life, since this is
his only portion (22).   The state of suffering (iv. 1), however, according
to this view, becomes desperate, and death, and not to have been born
at all, are preferable to life (2, 3).   The exertions made, in spite of the
prescribed order of things, often arise from jealousy (4), and fail in their
end (5, 6), or are prompted by avarice (7, 8), and defeat themselves
(9—16).   Since all things are thus under the control of an omnipotent
God, we ought to serve him acceptably (17—v. 6), trust to his protection
under oppression (7, 8), remember that the rich oppressor, after all, has
not even the comfort of the poor labourer (9—11), and that he often
brings misery upon his children and himself (12—16).   These considerations, therefore, again shew that there is nothing left for man but to
enjoy life the few years of his existence, being the gift of God (17—19).

iii. 1 There is a fixed time for all things, and an appointed
2 season for all undertakings under heaven; a time to be
born, and a time to die; a time to plant, and a time to pluck

1. *There is a fixed time*, &c. Having
shewn, in the preceding section, that
neither wisdom nor pleasure can
avert the gloomy fate of man, and
that enjoyment, the only thing left
for man under these circumstances,
is utterly insufficient to cheer his dejected mind, Coheleth now shews that
industry, another favourite experiment which is frequently made, is
equally fruitless in its efforts to alter
this state of things. All the events
of life are permanently fixed (1 – 8),
and hence the abortiveness of human
labour (9). That לַכֹּל, *to all*, does not
refer to the *rerum creatarum universi-
tas* (Geier, Rosenmüller, &c.), but to
the affairs of *human life* (comp. i. 2
with 14), is evident from the second
clause, where חֵפֶץ is added to determine its meaning, as well as from
the sequel, which enumerates some
of the things denoted thereby. זְמָן
(from מָנָה, *to number, to measure, to
determine, to fix*), *a fixed time* (זמן קביע
מתי יהיה, Rashi, Ibn Ezra), is a word belonging to later Hebrew, and is used
for the earlier expression מוֹעֵד; it only
occurs in Nehem. ii. 6; Esth. ix. 27,
31; and in Chaldee, Dan. ii. 16, 21; iii.
7' 8; iv. 33; vi. 11; vii. 12. 22. 25;
Ezra v. 3. Gesenius' explanation
of לַכֹּל זְמָן by *cuique rei tempus certum
quoddam*, i. e., *nihil est quod perpetui-
tate gaudeat, omnia fluxa sunt et
caduca* (Thesa. and Lex., *s. v.*, זְמָן), is
against the scope of the passage,
which is not to describe *the frailty
and fleetness of all things*, but, on
the contrary, the immutable fixed-
ness of the things to be mentioned.
The meaning of עֵת must of course
be determined by זְמָן. חֵפֶץ (from חָפֵץ,
to incline, to bend, to desire), prop.
desire, metonymically the object one
desires, anything for which we strive,

business, undertaking. So ܩܒܥ,
business, undertaking, thing, in Syriac,

from ܩܒܥ, *to desire*, and שְׁאֵלָה or
שְׁאֵלָא, *a thing, a matter*, in Chaldee
(comp. Dan. iv. 14, &c.), from שְׁאַל,
to ask, to desire. The word is therefore well rendered by the Septuagint
πρᾶγμα, and Symmachus χεῖρα. The
Vulgate's rendering of this clause
by ET SUIS SPATIIS TRANSEUNT UNI-
VERSA SUB CŒLO, *and in their periods
all things pass under heaven*, is a
lame paraphrase. Still more objectionable is Desvoeux's version, " all
the determinations of man's will
under heaven have their proper time."
2. *A time to be born*, &c. Coheleth
begins his series of proofs in illustration of the general proposition made
in the foregoing verse, by referring
to the commencement and end · of
life. Both the hour of our birth
and of our death are preordained by
a power over which we have no
control, and no exertion on our part
can hasten on the fixed time to be
born, or delay the appointed day of
death. The preposition לְ prefixed
to the *infinitives* in this enumeration, gives them the force of the
Latin *Gerund* (comp. Gesen. § 45, 3 ;
Ewald, § 292, b). The Septuagint,
the Chaldee, Gesenius (Lex, *s. v*),
Knobel, Herzfeld, Hitzig, Philippson,
Stuart, &c., take לֶדֶת in its usual
active meaning, *giving birth;* but the
antithetical expression מוּת, *to die*,
requires it to be taken in the sense
of הִוָּלֵד, *to be born*, which the *infin.
active* sometimes has (compare מָלְאוּ
יְמֵיכֶם לִטְבּוֹחַ, *the days for you to
slaughter are accomplished*, Jerem.
xxv. 34; Ewald, § 304, c). עֵת לָלֶדֶת is
therefore well rendered by the Vulg.
tempus nascendi; so also Rashbam,
Luther, Coverdale, the Geneva
Bible, Auth. Version (text), Ewald,
Noyes, Heiligstedt, Elster, &c.
A time to plant, &c. The illustration from human existence is followed
by another taken from vegetable life,

3 up that which is planted ; a time to kill, and a time to save ;
4 a time to break down, and a time to build up houses ; a time
   to weep, and a time to laugh ; a time to mourn, and a time

in order to evince more strikingly the utter inability of man's efforts to affect the immutably fixed condition of things. Not only our life, but even that of vegetables, has its beginning and end predetermined. Rashi, who is followed by some Christian commentators, regards this clause as metaphorically describing the planting and uprooting of nations and kingdoms (comp. Jerem. xviii. 6, &c.) ; but this is too far-fetched. Although מֶטַע is more in accordance with the rule of forming infinitives from verbs (פ״נ), yet this is the only place where this form occurs : elsewhere the infin. is נְטֹעַ (comp. Gesen. § 166, 2, Rem. 1 ; Ewald, 238, c). עָקַר has here its primary signification, *to pluck out, to uproot ;* in the other passages where it occurs (Gen. xlix. 6 ; Josh. xi. 6. 9 ; 2 Sam. viii. 4 ; 1 Chron. xviii. 4 ; Zeph. ii. 4), it is generally used in a metaphorical sense. That it here refers to the uprooting at the appointed time of harvest, when the vegetables are gathered in, and not in order to transplant or to destroy an enemy's plants (entweder um es zu verſetzen, oder : Pflanzung eines Feindes, Hitzig) is evident from the parallel hemistich, which speaks of the natural termination of human life, and therefore demands that the termination of the vegetable life should be understood in a natural manner, *i. e.,* the ordinary ingathering of it when matured.

3. *A time to kill,* &c. Having averred, in the foregoing verse, that the natural termination of life is immutably fixed, Coheleth now submits that the bringing about of violent death and destruction, which seem fortuitous and to be in the power of man, is also predetermined. The common rendering of עֵת לַהֲרוֹג וְעֵת לִרְפּוֹא by *a time to kill and a time to heal,* is rightly rejected by Ibn Ezra,

inasmuch as it does not comport with the antithesis, which is so strictly adhered to in this description of events, since the opposite of *killing* is not *healing ;* he therefore explains לַהֲרוֹג by לִמְחוֹץ, *to strike, to wound,* which would well agree with *to heal.* But as this explanation does away with *the different kinds of death* which Coheleth manifestly intends to describe, as is evident from the words לָמוּת and לַהֲרוֹג, the Syriac version ܐܢܐ ܘܟܐ ܟܠ݂ܫܐ݂ܠ ܐ ܘܟ݂ܐ ܟ݂ܫܐ݂ܠ, which takes רְפָא, *to heal,* in the sense of *preserving* or *saving life,*is preferable. The Chaldee, which is followed by some Christian commentators, refers this verse to the time of war, when destroying and saving life, demolishing and erecting buildings, take place ; but this is too restricted an application of this passage. It is therefore better to take it in a more general sense, as descriptive of *all accidents,* affirming that every apparently fortuitous loss or preservation of life, or of the abode which shelters the living, is predetermined. Rashbam's explanation, which refers the whole description contained in 2 - 8 to *peace* and *war,* is still more objectionable.

4. *A time to weep,* &c. The sorrow and joy here mentioned are intimately connected with, and are the natural consequence of, the events described in the preceding verse. The expression לִבְכּוֹת, *to weep,* in the beginning of this verse, is designedly chosen for its proximity in sound to the word לִבְנוֹת, *to build,* at the end of the last verse ; so also רְקוֹד, *to leap, to dance,* is used in the sense and instead of שְׂמוֹחַ, *to rejoice,* because of its assonance with סְפוֹד, *to mourn.* The omission of the לְ before the two last infinitives is probably intended to give variety to the

5 to rejoice ; a time to cast away stones, and a time to gather
up stones ; a time to embrace, and a time to refrain from
6 embracing ; a time to seek, and a time to lose ; a time to
7 keep, and a time to cast away ; a time to rend garments, and
a time to sew them together ; a time to be silent, and a time

construction. Such omissions are not unfrequent (*vide infra*, xii. 12).

5. *A time to cast away stones*, &c. The Chaldee, Ibn Ezra, &c., take the casting away and the gathering of stones to refer to the time when these building materials are useless and dispersed, and to the time when they become useful again, and are carefully collected for the erection of dwellings. This well comports with the argument, inasmuch as it shews that the apparently opposite treatment of one and the same material, which seems to be at the arbitrary disposal of man, has nevertheless its cause, and is ordained by the same uncontrollable power. This explanation does not at all encroach upon the statement made in the latter part of the third verse, for there the fate of *houses* is described, whilst here that of *building materials* is mentioned. Others, however, understand it as describing the time of war and peace, when the invading enemy *casts stones* over arable land to render it unfit for cultivation (comp. 2 Kings iii. 19. 25), and when the stones are gathered up in order to restore the land to its useful state (Isa. v. 2), so Knobel, Hitzig, Heiligstedt, Stuart, Elster, &c. ; or, as referring to the demolishing and erecting of buildings or fortresses (De Lyra, Reynolds, Rosenmüller, Noyes, &c.) ; or to the work in plantations and vineyards, when there is a time for clearing these cultivated spots of stones, and when we must gather them to make fences (Patrick, Vaihinger, &c.) ; or to the casting away and gathering stones *for any purpose whatsoever* (Holden, Kitto, &c.) לַהֲבוֹק and מִכְנּוֹס, the *Kal* and the *Piel*, are, as frequently, used indis-

criminately, without any distinctive shade of meaning, *vide infra*, ver. 6 ; viii. 10 ; Ewald, § 120, b.

6. *A time to seek*, &c. Even the ever-changing desire in man to seek after new objects, and carelessly losing them as soon as they are obtained, the whimsical grasping of a thing, and then to reject it, all these are not done from choice, but are predetermined. Though the Piel of אָבַד, *to be lost*, *to lose*, signifies *to destroy*, in all other places where it occurs in the Old Testament, its Kal signification is here rightly retained by the Sept., Vulg., Luther, Coverdale, Geneva Version, Bishops' Bible, Auth. Version, and the majority of modern commentators, as is evident from the antithetical בַּקֵּשׁ, *to seek*. We had a similar instance in the foregoing verse, where the Piel retains the Kal signification. The

Syriac ܐܒܠܐ ܒܿܩܿܬܐ܂ ܘܡܐܒܕ

ܠܡܐܒܕ, transposing the words *seeking* and *losing*, has evidently arisen from the carelessness of the transcriber.

7. *A time to rend*, &c. The sustaining of losses, and the parting with that which is dear to us, mentioned in the preceding verse, suggested the allusion here made to the time of mourning, as indicated by the rending of garments, and the silence consequent upon deep grief. It was a custom which obtained at a very early period, to rend one's garments, or to tear them in the front of the breast, as an expression of grief, and, when the time of mourning was over, the rent (see *infra*, vii. 2) was repaired (comp. Gen. xxxvii. 29, xliv. 13 ;

8 to speak ; a time to love, and a time to hate ; a time of war,
9 and a time of peace. He who laboureth hath therefore no
10 advantage from that wherein he laboureth. I have considered
the business which God hath given to the sons of men to

Judg. xi. 35 ; 2 Sam. i. 2. 11, iii.
31, xiii. 31 ; 1 Maccab. ii. 14, iii. 47;
Judith, xiv. 16. 19 ; Joseph. Wars,
2. 15, 2 ; Mishna, Moed Katon, iii.
17 ; Shabbath, xiii. 3 ; Winer, Real=
wörterbuch, and Saalschütz, Archäo=
logie der Hebräer, s. v. Trauer). The
Jews to the present day still rend
the front of their garments at the
death of a parent, child, brother, or
sister, as an expression of deep grief,
and this act of rending is called
קְרִיעָה. The Chaldee has therefore
rightly rendered the words קְרֹעַ? and
לִתְפֹּר by לְמִקְרַע לְבוּשָׁא, to tear the garment, and לְאֶחָא בִּזְיָעָה, to repair the
rent. When Herzfeld maintains
that there can be no allusion here
to the rending of garments at the
time of mourning, because this custom
did not exist in Coheleth's time, we
oppose to this the foregoing quotations. For an instance of silence
under deep grief, see Job ii. 12, 13.

8. A time to love, &c. Our loving
a person and then hating him again,
or being at war with a nation to-day
and at peace to-morrow, are also
predetermined by the same Omnipotent Disposer of all things. In
all the instances adduced from the
events of life, Coheleth used the
infinitive mood, with the exception
of the last clause, where nouns are
employed, probably to mark the end
of the list. The sacred writer began
with birth and death, and finished
with war and peace, as if to indicate
that we enter upon the battle of life
at our very birth, and that death
alone terminates the conflict and
secures peace.

9. He who laboureth, &c. Having
confirmed the general proposition by
twenty-eight illustrations from the
common events of life, that nothing
is within the power of man, but that
all things are immutably fixed by

Omnipotence, Coheleth now submits
that all the exertions of the industrious to alter his circumstances and
to secure to himself abiding good
(יִתְרוֹן), must of necessity be ineffectual.
The interrogative, as is frequently
the case (vide supra, i. 3), is used for
an emphatic denial; Luther has therefore rightly rendered it so (Man
arbeite, wie man will, so kann man
nicht mehr ausrichten), though led
astray by the wrong version of the
Vulgate, (QUID HABET AMPLIUS HOMO
DE LABORE SUO? what more has man
from his labour?) he mistook its
connection with what precedes.

10. I have considered the business,
&c. In this and in the following verse,
Coheleth assigns a reason why the
efforts of man to secure lasting good
are ineffectual. He prefaces this
reason, which is contained in the
following verse, by telling us here
that what he is going to say is the
result of a minute inspection of the
different employments which God
has assigned to the children of men.
The difficulty experienced in the
interpretation of the following verse
has been greatly increased by the
Vulgate's mistranslation of this verse,
Vidi afflictionem, quam dedit Deus
filiis hominum, ut distendantur in ea,
which is followed by Luther, Daher
sahe ich die Mühe, die Gott den
Menschen gegeben hat, daß sie darinnen
geplagt werden ; Coverdale and the
Bishops' Bible, for as touching the
travail and carefulness which God
hath given unto men, I see that he
hath given it them, to be exercised in
it ; the Geneva Version, I have seen
the travail that God hath given to the
sons of men to humble them thereby ;
Authorised Version, I have seen the
travail which God hath given to the
sons of men to be exercised in it, and
which Bishop Reynolds, Knobel,

11 busy themselves therewith; he hath made it all beautiful in

Vaihinger, &c., explain that man's propensity to exertion, in spite of the immutably fixed order of things, has been implanted by God in order to exercise, humble, or plague him therewith. Against this we urge — 1. That this verse makes a simple assertion, without drawing or remotely implying any inference to complete it; and 2. That עֲנוֹת does neither mean *to afflict*, nor *humble*, nor *exercise*, but simply *to work*, *to toil*, as is evident from the noun עִנְיָן, *work*, with which it is connected, and which determines its meaning, *vide supra*, i. 13. The phrase is therefore well explained by Rashi and Rashbam המנהג להתנהג, and Ibn Ezra ענייני האדם שיתעסקו בו, who has rightly pointed out the intimate connection between this verse and the following one. רָאָה, *to see*, is used here as in ii. 12, in the sense of *examining*, *investigating*.

11. *He hath made it all*, &c. On examining the employments which God has assigned to man, Coheleth found that the benign Creator has made them beautiful in their respective seasons; that in addition to this excellent order of things, he has also implanted in the hearts of men a desire for that which is beyond time, and that the failure of man's efforts to secure lasting good, is owing to his ignorance of the works of God. As the verb עָשָׂה, *he has made*, refers to אֱלֹהִים, *God*, in the preceding verse, thus shewing the intimate connection between these two verses, it will at once be perceived that אֶת־הַכֹּל, *all*, at the beginning of this verse, refers to אֶת־הָעִנְיָן, *the employment*, *business*. Ibn Ezra has therefore well explained the connection, כאשר ראיתי כל עניני האדם שיתעסקו בו הכרתי שהכל עשה האלהים יפה בעתו *when I examined all the works of men wherewith they are occupied, I found that God has made it all beautiful in its season*. יָפֶה, *beautiful*, *appropriate*, *proper*, *well* (*vide infra*, v. 17). The suffix in בְּעִתּוֹ, *in its season*, refers to הַכֹּל, *all*. גַּם, *also*, has here its natu-

ral *accessory* signification, *i. e.*, " he not only made those employments beautiful, but he *also*, or *in addition* to this," &c. הָעֹלָם, *remote time*, *the unmeasured past*, or *future*, hence *eternity*, in which sense it is always used in the Old Testament, and is here contrasted with עֵת, *time*. The suffix in בְּלִבָּם, *in their heart*, refers to לִבְנֵי הָאָדָם, *the children of men*, in the preceding verse, just as אֶת־הַכֹּל, *all*, refers to עִנְיָן, *work*, and עָשָׂה, *he has made*, to אֱלֹהִים. *God*, in the same verse. מִבְּלִי (a compound of בְּלִי with the preposition, which this word attaches to itself without affecting its meaning, comp. בִּבְלִי, Deut. iv. 42; Job xxxv. 16; xxxvi. 12; לִבְלִי *ibid*. xxxviii. 41; xli. 25; Isa. v. 14), *without* (Deut. ix. 28; Isa. v. 13; Lam. i. 4), like חוּץ, *without*, denotes anything standing outside the circle of its fellows, forming an exception, being the only one in that position, hence is used metaphorically as an adverb of restriction, *except*, *only*. אֲשֶׁר, like ὅτι in Greek, and *quod* in Latin, is a *conjunction* attached to this adverb, just as the conjunction כִּי is to אֶפֶס (Deut. xv. 4), so that מִבְּלִי אֲשֶׁר signifies *only that* (comp. Ewald, § 354, b). Coheleth has evidently chosen this more difficult adverb of restriction because of its assonance with בְּלִבָּם, the word which immediately precedes it. מָצָא, *to find*, *to find out*, *to discover*, *to comprehend* (*vide infra*, vii. 24. 27; viii. 17, &c.). מַעֲשֵׂי הָאֱלֹהִים, *the works of God*, i. e., *his providential dealings*, *moral government* (compare *infra*, viii. 17), where the same thing is affirmed. The *beginning* and *end* of a thing are idiomatically used to express *the whole*, *entirely*, *all in all*, *eternity*, like ἀπὸ τῆς ἀρχῆς μέχρι τέλους in Greek. Thus the phrase, beginning and end of a speech, is used in x. 13 for *the whole of it*, the two ends of the day for *the entire day*, *always* (*infra*, xi. 6; Gen. xlix. 27; Ps. xcii. 3); hence God is called *the beginning and the end*, *the first and the last*, i. e., *all in all*, *eternal* (Isa. xli. 4;

its season; he hath also put eternity into their heart, only that

xliv. 6; xlviii. 12), which is also expressed by *Alpha* and *Omega* (Rev. i. 8), being *the first* and *the last* letters of the Greek alphabet, thus corresponding to the Rabbinic usage of א and ת, *the first* and *the last* letters of the Hebrew alphabet, to designate *the whole* (comp. "Adam transgressed the whole law from א to ת" in Yalkut Rubeni, p. 174). The words "man cannot comprehend the work which God worketh from beginning to end," therefore mean ' the work of God is entirely or altogether incomprehensible to man.' Having analysed the text and context, we proceed to examine some of the innumerable explanations which have been given of the clause גַּם אֶת־הָעֹלָם נָתַן בְּלִבָּם מִבְּלִי אֲשֶׁר לֹא־יִמְצָא הָאָדָם אֶת־הַמַּעֲשֶׂה אֲשֶׁר־עָשָׂה הָאֱלֹהִים, which constitutes the great difficulty of this ve‌rse. The Sept. renders it καίγε σὺν τὸν αἰῶνα ἔδωκεν ἐν καρδίᾳ αὐτῶν, ὅπως μὴ εὕρῃ ὁ ἄνθρωπος τὸ ποίημα ὃ ἐποίησεν ὁ Θεός, *and also the world* (σὺν = אֶת) *he has put into their heart, in order that man might not find out the work which God has worked;* so also the Syriac, ܐܰܘ

ܟܽܠܦܳܐ ܗܟ ܚܰܟܡܬܗ̄ ܐܰܘ ܗܠܳ; ܬܰܥܒܶܕ ܐܢܳܐ ܚܟ̄ ܘܰܟܳ ܦܳܙܳܠ

the Vulg., St. Jerome, Rashi, Luther, the Bishop's Bible, the Geneva Version, the Authorised Version, and many modern commentators; all these agree in rendering עֹלָם *world*, but generally differ about the particular meaning of *world* in this connection. Thus the Vulgate explains it as denoting *the problems* or *affairs* of the world: ET MUNDUM TRADIDIT DISPUTATIONI EORUM, UT NON INVENIAT HOMO OPUS, QUOD OPERATUS EST DEUS, *and he has delivered the world to their disputation, so that man cannot find out the work which he has worked,* &c.; hence Luther, unb läßt ihr Herz sich ängsten, wie es gehen soll in ber Welt; benn ber Mensch kann boch nicht treffen bas Werk, bas Gott

that; St. Jerome takes it to mean *the pleasures* or *enjoyments* of this world, and explains it: *Dedit Deus mundum ad inhabitandum hominibus, ut fruantur varietatibus temporum, et non quærant de causis rerum naturalium, quomodo creata sunt omnia, quare hoc vel illud ab initio mundi usque ad consummationem fecerit crescere, manere, mutari;* Luther, in his Comment., Gott hat bem Menschen nicht allein bie Welt gegeben, baß sie mögen ber gegenwärtigen Gaben brauchen, sonbern auch so geben, baß sie bes mit Freube unb Lust mochten brauchen, baß sie Freube unb Lust bavon hätten, unb kann boch ber Mensch bie Creaturen nicht nach seinem Willen regieren, in Zeit ober Maß fassen, wie er sagt, boch kann er nicht treffen bas Werk bas Gott thut, weber Anfang noch Enbe; and the Geneva Bible, *also he hath set the world in their heart, yet cannot man find out the work,* &c., *i e.,* though God has done so much for man, making the world without beautiful, and implanting capacities of enjoying it in his heart, yet (מִבְּלִי אֲשֶׁר) man, &c. Whilst some interpreters, mentioned by Ibn Ezra, (כי זה) ויש מפרשים העולם כמו שהוא בלשון קדמונינו ז"ל זה ענין (האות העולם) Knobel, De Wette, Gesen., Noyes, &c., take the expression *world* in a grosser sense, as denoting Weltsinn, *worldly-mindedness,* like αἰών in Eph. ii. 2, and explain the passage " God has made everything beautiful in its season, but he has put the love of this world into their heart, in order that they might not be able to discover the work which God works," &c., submitting that, according to the same idiom by which God is said to harden the heart of Pharaoh, he may also be said to put worldly-mindedness into the hearts of men, to prevent them seeing the beautiful harmony of his dispensations. Rashi, again, takes *world* to denote *the wisdom of the world,* and explains the passage גם את חכמת העולם אשר נתן בלב הבריות לא נתי הכל בלב כל אחד ואחד אלא זה קצת וזה קצת כדי שלא ימצא האדם את כל מעשה

man understandeth not the work which God hath made from

הק׳׳בה לדעת אותו ולא ידע את עת סקודתו ובמה
יכשל כדי שיתן לב לשוב שידאג ויאמר היום או מחר
אמות ולכך כתוב כאן העלם חסר לשון העלמה
שאם ידע האדם יום מיתתו קרובה לא יבנה בית
ולא ישע כרם לכך הוא אומר שהכל יפה עשה
בעתו זה שיש עת למיתה דבר יפה הוא שסומך
האדם לומר שמא עדיין עת מיתתי רחוק ובונה בית
ונוטה כרם וזו יפה שנעלם מן הבריות, *also the
wisdom of the world which he put into
the heart of his creatures, he has not
put it all into the heart of each one
separately, but gave every one a little,
so that man might not find out and
know all the work of God, that he
might not know the day of his visita-
tion, and what may cause him to
stumble in order that he may give his
heart to repentance, for he might grieve
and say, I shall die to-day or to-
morrow. Therefore is* העלם *written
here defectively, signifying* HIDDEN,
*for if man knew that the day of his
death is near, he would not build
houses, nor plant vineyards, hence it is
said that' he made everything beautiful
in its season,'* i.e., *it is a good thing that
there is a fixed time to die, that man
may be inclined to say, 'my appointed
time may still be far off,' and go on
building houses and planting vineyards, and thus it is beautiful that it
is hid from the creature,* evidently to
escape the difficulty of the preceding
explanation. Whilst Lord Bacon,
Ewald, Elster, &c., take the expression *world* more literally, and explain
it that man is *a microcosm* reflecting
the macrocosm; " God," says our immortal philosopher, "has framed the
mind like a glass, capable of the
image of the universe, and desirous
to receive it as the eye to receive the
light" (Advancement of Learning,
p. 30, Bohn's ed.). But against
these explanations we urge—1. That
the expression עלם occurs upwards of
three hundred times in the Old Testament, and never denotes *world,* or
worldly affairs, or *worldly pleasures,*
or *worldly wisdom,* but invariably
signifies *time past* or *present, unmeasured time, eternity,* and is so used in
all the other passages of this very

book (i. 4 ; ii. 16 ; iii. 14; ix. 6 ; xii. 5).
2. These explanations are precluded
by the evident antitheses between עלם
and עת. 3. The accessory particle גם,
also, which introduces this clause,
shews beyond doubt that there is *a
gradation* in the description of the
doings of God, *i. e.,* ' he has not only
made everything beautiful, in its season, but has done something greater
or grander still;" and to say that
this consists *in infatuating man* by
implanting in his heart the world, or
worldly wisdom, or cares, or pleasures,
is most incongruous. Rashbam tries
to adhere to the literal meaning of
עלם, inasmuch as he explained it by
time as composed of different seasons,
of prosperity and adversity, described
in verses 1 – 8, viz., גם את הזמן נתן להם
הק׳ בלבם של בני אדם שידעו ויבינו שעתים שהם
לטובה ויש עתים לרעה לפי שלא ימצא ולא ידע
האדם את המעשה אשר יעשה הק׳ מראש ועד
סוף שאם יהיו כל העתים לטובה או כולם לרעה
לא ישוב אדם בתשובה לפני הק׳ לפי שיאמר בלבו
אחרי שמקרה אחד בעולם או הכל לטובה או
הכל לרעה על זה אניח רוע מעשי ואיזה הנאה
תגיע לי בתשובתי, *he has also put time
into the hearts of the children of men,
that they may know and understand
that there are different seasons, seasons
of prosperity and seasons of adversity,
so that man might not find out the
work which God works from beginning
to end. For, if all the seasons were
alike, either wholly good or wholly evil,
man would not repent before God ; as
he might say in his heart, since there is
one fate in the world, all are either
unalterably good or evil, I shall relinquish my work, and what good shall I
have by repenting ?* Ibn Ezra adheres
still more closely to the literal meaning
of עלם, and says that ועניו גם את העלם
נתן בלבם שבני אדם מתעסקים כאילו יחיו לעולם
ובעבור התעסקם לא יבינו מעשה האלהים מראש
ועד סוף, *the meaning of' he has also put
eternity into their heart,' is, the children of men are so engrossed in business
as if they were to live eternally, and
because of their engrossing business they
do not understand the work of God
from beginning to end. But these ex-*

12 beginning to end. I knew, then, that there was no good for them but to rejoice and do themselves good all their life; 13 and also that if a man eat and drink, and see pleasure in all

planations, besides being extremely forced and artificial, incur the third objection which we urged against the other interpretations. The rendering of Coverdale ("He hath planted ignorance also in the hearts of men, that they should not find out the ground of his works"), which is followed by Parkhurst, Hodgson ("also I viewed the darkness which he spreadeth over men's hearts"), and Holden ("yet he hath also put obscurity into the midst of them"), has evidently originated from the second sense which Rashi has assigned to עֹלָם, and deserves no refutation. Whilst the alteration of עֹלָם into עֶלֶם, to which is assigned the meaning of *wisdom, understanding*, by appealing to the Arabic signification of this root (Gaab, Spohn, Hitzig, Stuart, &c.) must be repudiated as arbitrary and unwarranted.

12. *I knew that there was nothing better*, &c. Two things became evident to Coheleth from these facts; first, since man cannot secure to himself any abiding good, there is nothing left for him but to enjoy the present. Each of these two things is introduced with יָדַעְתִּי, *I knew*, i. e., *I came to know, I discovered*. אֵין טוֹב בָּם is explained by Rashbam בכל העתים ובכלה מעשים הללו כזה, and is rendered by Luther baß nichts Bessers darinnen ist; Coverdale and the Bishops' Bible, "in these things there is nothing better for a man," &c., referring the pronoun בָּם, to *the works of God;* so also Desvoeux, Holden, &c.; but it is evident from אֵין טוֹב בָּאָדָם in ii. 24, and from אֵין טוֹב לָאָדָם in viii. 15, where ל is used instead of the ב, that it refers to הָאָדָם,* *mankind*, in the preceding verse, which, being a noun of multitude, is followed by a relative pronoun in the plural. The Chaldee has therefore well rendered it לֵית טָב בְּהוֹן בִּבְנֵי אֵינָשָׁא, *there is nothing better for the*

children of men, &c., so also Rashi אֵין טוֹב בבריות, Ibn Ezra, Mendelssohn, Knobel, Herzfeld, De Wette, Hitzig, Stuart, Philippson, Elster, Hengstenberg, &c. The Vulg., ignoring the pronoun בָּם, as it ignores בָּאָדָם in ii. 24, leaves the sense ambiguous. That לַעֲשׂוֹת טוֹב, *to do good*, is not here used in a moral sense, i. e., *to do right* (the Sept., Vulg., Chaldee, Rashi, Reynolds, Patrick, Rosenmüller, Elster, Vaihinger, Hengstenberg, &c.), but means *to do oneself good, to procure pleasures*, like רָאָה טוֹב in ii. 24; v. 17 (Rashbam לעשות טובה לעצמו, Ibn Ezra שיחיה חיים טובים, Luther sich gütlich thun, Hodgson, Spohn, Knobel, Herzfeld, De Wette, Gesenius, Hitzig, Heilegstedt, Stuart, Fürst, &c.), is evident from ii. 24; iii. 22; v. 17; viii. 15; ix. 7, where the same physical enjoyment is spoken of without mixing it up with moral dealings, and especially from the following verse, where Coheleth, in resuming what he has said in this verse, explains לִשְׂמוֹחַ, *to rejoice*, by שֶׁיֹּאכַל וְשָׁתָה, *to eat and drink*, and לַעֲשׂוֹת טוֹב, *to do good*, by רָאָה טוֹב, וְכָל עֲמָלוֹ, *to see happiness* or *be happy in his work*. The suffix in בְּחַיָּיו, *his life*, refers to הָאָדָם, *man*, in the preceding verse. The sudden transition from the singular to the plural, and the plural to the singular (יִמְצָא, ver. 11, בָּם and בְּחַיָּיו, ver. 12), arises from the fact that the singular has here a plural meaning, inasmuch as the individual man is spoken of as the representative of the whole human race (comp. Gen. vi. 1; Exod. i. 20, xxxiii. 4; Gesen. § 146, 1; Ewald, § 317, c).

13. *And also that if a man*, &c. This verse forms an integral part of the preceding one, intensifying its statement. Not only is there nothing left for man but present enjoyment, but even for this man is dependent upon God. וְגַם, *and also*, is still

14 his labour, it is a gift of God. I knew that whatever God
hath made, the same continueth for ever; to it nothing can
can be added, and from it nothing can be taken, and God

dependent upon יָדַעְתִּי, *I knew.* The
conditional particle כִּי, *if,* is to be
supplied after וְאִם, and "מַתַּח וְגוֹ", is its
appadosis (comp. *infra,* v. 18; Ewald,
§ 357, c.) The construction is peculiar; it begins with the imperfect
יֹאכַל, and continues with the præterite שָׁתָה and רָאָה, with ו conversive;
the Syriac and Chaldee have the imperfect throughout. For the phrase
רָאָה טוֹב, see ii. 1. Coverdale and
the Bishops' Bible (*for all that a
man eateth and drinketh, yea whatsoever a man enjoyeth of all his labour,
that same is a gift of God*) mistook
the text for "וְגַם כָּל שֶׁיֹּאכַל הָאָדָם וְגוֹ.

14. *I knew that whatever,* &c. The
second lesson which Coheleth learned
from the facts described in 1–9 is,
that all the affairs of human life
alluded to, which God has preordained, are *immutably* fixed, that no
ingenuity or industry, however great,
can affect it in the slightest degree,
and that God has so ordained it, in
order to make man feel how entirely
dependent he is upon the Disposer
of all things, and to arouse in him
a reverential awe. יָדַעְתִּי, *I know,* as
in ver. 12, marks the introduction of
the second thing which became apparent to Coheleth. כָּל־אֲשֶׁר יַעֲשֶׂה
אֱלֹהִים, *whatever God hath made,* does
not denote *the works of creation*
(Rashi, Grotius, Le Clerc, &c.), which
is contrary to the scope of Coheleth
— who evidently points out man's
inability to affect any change in the
circumstances of his life contrary to
the preordained plan of God — but
refers to לַכֹּל זְמָן, *God has fixed a time
for all things,* and to the ensuing
description. עָשָׂה, *to do, to make,*
has here the sense of *to appoint, to
ordain, to fix.* The pronoun הוּא has
here the force of αὐτός in Greek,
and *idem* in Latin, and is used for
the sake of emphasis (comp. Gesen.
§ 124, 2, Rem. 3; Ewald, § 314).
Herzfeld's remark, that the use of it

here makes כָּל־אֲשֶׁר יַעֲשֶׂה הָאֱלֹהִים, a
nominative absolute, is contrary to
the particle כִּי by which this clause
is preceded. For the use of עַל, in
the sense of accession, see Gen.
xxviii. 9; Levit. v. 16; Gesenius,
§ 154, 3, Rem. 2. The suffix in עָלָיו
refers to כָּל־אֲשֶׁר יַעֲשֶׂה הָאֱלֹהִים. The
negative particle אֵין, when placed
before an infinit. with לְ, expresses
inability or *impossibility* (comp. אֵין
כֹּחַ לְהִתְיַצֵּב, *nothing is able to stand
before thee,* 2 Chron. xx. 6; Gesen.
§ 132, 3, Rem. 1; Ewald, § 321, c).
The construction of יָרֵא with מִלִּפְנֵי,
used here and in viii. 12, 13, instead
of the more regular one יָרֵא מִפְּנֵי
(2 Kings i. 15, xix. 6; Jerem. i. 8),
or יָרֵא with the *accusative* of person
or thing feared (Numb. xiv. 9; Job
ix. 35), need not be regarded as
belonging to later Hebrew (Herzfeld
and others), since it also occurs in
1 Sam. xviii. 12. שֶׁיִּירְאוּ, *that they
may fear,* refers to אָדָם, *men,* in the
preceding verse, which must be
supplied in the translation, being
too far removed from the verb. The
reading שיראו with one *Yod,* which
is found in many MSS., and noted
by the Masorites instead of שייראו,
does not alter the sense of the word.
According to the Hagadic interpretation, this verse is to be rendered *I
know that whatsoever God hath made
shall be for ever, man cannot add to it
or take from it* (*i. e.,* cannot alter it),
but God doth it (*i. e.,* does alter it),
that man might fear before him (see
the Midrash *in loco*). So also the
Chaldee, and Rashi, who refers to
the Deluge and to the days of Ahaz
and Hezekiah, when God altered the
course of the sea and of the sun,
"which he hath established for ever,"
in order that man might fear before
him. But this rendering is both
contrary to the scope of the passage
and to the meaning of עָשָׂה, in the
first clause of this very verse. The

15 hath so done it that men may fear before him. What hath been was long ago, and what is to be was long ago, for God

Vulg., NON POSSUMUS EIS QUISQUAM ADDERE NEC AUFERRE, QUÆ FECIT DEUS UT TIMEATUR, *we cannot add anything, nor take away from the things which God has made that he may be feared*, violently construes the text כַּאֲשֶׁר עָשָׂה אֱלֹהִים וְגו׳.

15. *What hath been*, &c. That God's ordinances are immutably fixed, is evident from the undeviating occurrence of the same events. For מַה־שֶּׁהָיָה, *what hath been*, see *supra*, i. 9. The Sept. and Vulg. have rightly rendered it here τὸ γενόμενον, *quod factum est*, though they mistranslated it in i. 9; whilst Desvoeux and Hodgson, to be consistent in their error, render it here also interrogatively. The pronoun הוּא, as in the preceding verse, is used for the sake of emphasis, and the auxiliary הָיָה, as usual, is to be supplied, so that מַה־שֶּׁהָיָה refers to that which *recently* took place, whilst הוּא כְּבָר הָיָה or כְּבָר הָיָה הוּא describes the same thing as already having occurred long before. So the Syriac version,

ܡܳܐ ܕܰܗܘܳܐ ܡܶܢ ܟܰܕܽܘ ܗܽܘ,

what was, has been long ago; Rashi, מה שהיה מלפנינו כבר הוא עשוי וראינוהו או שמענוהו מאחרים שראוהו, *that which happened before our eyes had happened long before, and we have seen it, or heard of it from others who saw it.* The Vulg. (QUOD FACTUM EST, IPSUM PERMANET, *that which has been made, the same remains*), Luther (Was Gott thut, das stehet da, *that which God does, remains*), the Geneva Bible (*what is that that hath been? that is now*), Coverdale, the Bishops' Bible, and the Auth. Version (*the thing that hath been is now*), which are followed by Knobel, Ewald, Heiligstedt, Elster, Vaihinger, &c., violate the meaning of כְּבָר, which invariably denotes time *long past* (*vide supra*, i. 10). Whilst De Wette, Noyes, Hitzig, Stuart, &c. (*that which is, was long ago*), most inconsistently

ascribe a sense to הָיָה here which they rightly deny in i. 12. אֲשֶׁר לִהְיוֹת exactly corresponds to our phrase *that which is to be*, and to the French *ce qui est à être* (comp. Gen. xv. 12 ; Prov. xix. 8 ; Gesen. § 132, 3, Rem. 1; Ewald, § 237). Luther's rendering of this clause und was er thun will, das muß werden, *and that which he will do must come to pass*, is an unwarranted paraphrase.

For God recalleth, &c. The reason why the events of every period are alike is because God, having fixed a time for everything (לְכֹל זְמָן, *vide*, ver. 1), that which has transpired at a certain season, must return with the return of that season. The ו before הָאֱלֹהִים is *causal*, assigning a reason for the assertion made in the preceding clause. בִּקֵּשׁ, *to seek out, to recall.* נִרְדָּף, part. Niphal of רָדַף, *to run after, to pursue*, is *that which is chased away, put to flight, that which is gone and past.* This term is here designedly chosen because of its connection with time, whose rapid march overtakes and speedily leaves behind every event which God has predetermined for every season. Having referred to the miraculous passage of the *I*sraelites through the Red Sea, to illustrate its interpretation of the preceding verse that God suspends the laws of nature, the Hagada, in harmony with that interpretation, explains וְהָאֱלֹהִים יְבַקֵּשׁ אֶת־נִרְדָּף, *and God avenged the persecuted Israelites*, i. e., he inflicted punishment upon the Egyptians who pursued the Jews into the sea (comp. the Midrash, the Chaldee Paraphr., and Rashi). That the Sept. (καὶ ὁ Θεὸς ζητήσει τὸν διωκόμενον), Symmachus (ὁ δὲ Θεὸς ἐπιζητήσει ὑπὲρ τῶν ἐκδιωκομένων), and the Syriac version (ܘܰܐܠܳܗܳܐ ܢܶܒܥܶܐ ܠܪܰܕܺܝܦܳܐ), should follow this sense of נִרְדָּף, is what might have been

16 recalleth what is past. And, moreover, I saw under the sun,
   in the place of justice there was iniquity, and in the place of
17 equity there was iniquity. I said to my heart, God will

expected, but that Seb. Schmidt, Rambach, Döderlein, Holden, Heinemann, Hengstenberg, &c , should have adopted this Hagadic interpretation is surpassing strange, for it is contrary to the former part of the verse, with which it is evidently connected; it anticipates what follows, and has, as we have seen, arisen from the Midrashic explanation of the preceding part of this verse. Luther's version denn er trachtet und jaget ihm nach, is both contrary to the text and unintelligible.

16. *And moreover I saw*, &c. The conclusion — that enjoyment of the present is the only thing left for man—at which Coheleth arrived from the contemplation of the inability of industry to counteract the immutably fixed events of human life, is now corroborated by another insurmountable difficulty, which our exertions to secure lasting good have to encounter. Man's exertions are not only baffled by the inscrutable laws of God, but are defeated by the lawlessness and wickedness of those who are appointed under God to uphold and protect the rights of the community. וְעוֹד, *and again, moreover*, indicates the commencement of another difficulty. The omission of it by the Vulgate weakens the sense. מְקוֹם, *place*, is not the object of רָאִיתִי, *I saw* (the Sept., Luther, Geneva Bible, Authorised Version, Desvoeux, Hodgson, De Wette, Knobel, Ewald, Vaihinger, &c.), which is contrary to the accents, and imparts a tameness to the diction, but is simply *an adverb of place* for בִּמְקוֹם, *in the place* (*vide infra*, xi. 3; Job i. 4; Ezek. vi. 13; Gesen. § 118; Ewald. § 204, a), thus leaving the whole circumstance as the accusative of the verb: so the Vulg., Coverdale, the Bishops' Bible, Herzfeld, Hitzig, Noyes, Stuart, Elster, &c. שָׁמָּה, *i. q.*, שָׁם, with the

demonstrative הָ, (*vide* Jerem. xviii. 2; Ps. cxxii. 5; Gesen. § 150, 1; Ewald, § 216, d) is used after מְקוֹם הַמִּשְׁפָּט and מְקוֹם הַצֶּדֶק for the sake of emphasis, just as הוּא in ver. 14, and is therefore wrongly omitted by the Vulg. The remark of Mendelssohn, Herzfeld, and Philippson, that מִשְׁפָּט—die Strafe des Ungerechten, צֶדֶק der Lohn des Gerechten sei, und daß also רֶשַׁע, auf מִשְׁפָּט bezogen, das Ungestraftbleiben des Ungerechten, dagegen auf צֶדֶק bezogen, das Unbelohntbleiben des Gerechten bedeute — denotes *the punishment of the wicked*, and צֶדֶק *the reward of the righteous*, and that רֶשַׁע when referred to מִשְׁפָּט, signifies *the withholding of punishment* from the wicked, whilst, with reference to צֶדֶק, it means *the withholding of reward* from the righteous, is very artificial. The simplest way is to take the clause מְקוֹם הַצֶּדֶק שָׁמָּה הָרֶשַׁע as a mere repetition after מְקוֹם הַמִּשְׁפָּט שָׁמָּה הָרֶשַׁע, to give intensity to the statement; this is frequently done in Hebrew to describe a continued state of things (*vide infra*, iv. 1; Isa. liii. 7; Ewald, § 313, a). The Sept. καὶ ἔτι ἴδον ὑπο τὸν ἥλιον τόπον τῆς κρίσεως, ἐκεῖ ὁ ἀσεβής· καὶ τοπόν τῶν δικαίων, ἐκεῖ ὁ εὐσεβής, *and moreover, I saw under the sun the place of judgment, there was the impious; and the place of the righteous, there was the pious;* both confounds *the abstracts* רֶשַׁע and צֶדֶק with *the concretes* רָשָׁע and צַדִיק in the following verse, in which Luther (da war ein gottloses Wesen; und Stätten der Gerechtigkeit, da waren Gottlose) partly shares, and has הַצַדִיק for הָרֶשַׁע, which the Arabic follows, but which has evidently arisen from the transcriber mistaking ἀσεβής for εὐσεβής.

17. *I said to my heart*, &c. Under these distressing circumstances, finding that there is no protection of right or administration of justice here, Coheleth at first tried to com-

judge the righteous and the wicked, for there is a time for
18 every thing and deed there.   Yet I said to my heart respecting

fort himself with the thought that there may be an infallible tribunal hereafter, when the righteous Judge will redress every grievance, and reward the just and the unjust, according to their merits. Whether we take שָׁם as an adverb of *place, there, i. e.,* with God (comp. Gen. xlix. 24), who is mentioned in the preceding clause (the Sept., Syriac, Ibn Ezra, the Geneva Bible, the Auth. Version, Reynolds, Heiligstedt, Elster, Hengstenberg, &c.), or regard it as an adverb of *time, then* (the Vulg., St. Jerome, the Chaldee, Knobel, De Wette, &c.), the context shews beyond all doubt that the retribution in question refers to *a future* bar of judgment. This is evident from the antithesis (verse 18 – 21), where Coheleth expresses a doubt about what he has here advanced, and where it is admitted, on all hands, that he discusses *a future state of existence :* rightly, therefore, the Chaldee יְדִין יְיָ בְּיוֹם דִּינָא רַבָּא, *God will judge in the great day of judgment ;* St. Jerome, IN TEMPORE JUDICII, IN FUTURUM JUDICIUM, *future judgment ;* Ibn Ezra, שם רמז לעולם הבא. The alteration of שָׁם into שָׂם, præt. of שׂוּם, *to appoint* (Archbishop Secker, Houbigant, Döderlein, Van der Palm, Dathe, Hodgson, Boothroyd, Holden, Ewald, Hitzig, Stuart, &c.), must be rejected as arbitrary. Equally arbitrary is the assertion of Herzfeld, which is followed by Fürst (Concordance, *s. v.*) and Vaihinger, that שָׁם is the part. of the Talmudic verb שׂוּם, *to estimate, to judge.* The Vulgate's omission of וְעַל כָּל־הַמַּעֲשֶׂה, and Luther's omission of שָׁם, will no more surprise us after what we have seen of their proceedings with the text. Coverdale and the Bishops' Bible, " Then thought I in my mind, God shall separate the righteous from the ungodly, and then shall be the time and judgment of all counsels and works," can neither

be reconciled with the original, nor with any of the ancient versions.

18. *Yet I said to my heart,* &c. The momentary consolation found in the thought of a future judgment, as expressed in the preceding verse, being based upon assigning *a priori* a superiority to man over other creatures, now disappears, when Coheleth comes to think that the only dignity with which God has endowed the human race above the brute creation is, that he has enabled man to understand that he is like the beast. The formula, אָמַרְתִּי אֲנִי בְּלִבִּי, which is repeated at the beginning of this verse, shews that the continuation of this thought takes a different turn, which is best indicated in the translation by supplying *again, yet.* As the preposition עַל is used to denote, 1. *The object* of a discourse, *concerning* (*vide supra,* ii. 10), 2. *The standard* by which a thing is measured, *according to* (Gen. xlviii. 6 ; Exod. xii. 5), 3. *The cause* for which a thing is done, *because* (Ps. xliv. 23 ; Job xxxiv. 36), and as דָּבָר, or the fem. דִּבְרָה, signifies both *a word, speech,* or *language,* and *a thing, a matter, affair* (*vide supra,* i. 8) ; hence the Sept. and the Syriac render עַל־דִּבְרַת, περὶ λαλιᾶς,

ܥܠ ܡܡܠܠܐ, *concerning the speech ;* or Herzfeld, *according to the language* of the children of men ; the Vulg., Coverdale, the Bishop's Bible, Auth. Ver., Knobel, Noyes, &c., *concerning,* or *with respect to, the affairs* of man : Ibn Ezra, Ewald, De Wette, Hitzig, Stuart, Elster, &c., *on account of* the children of men. Whichever of these meanings be adopted, the sense of the passage, according to our view, remains substantially the same, and the choice must be determined by the remainder of the verse, and the use of this phrase in the other passages of this book (*infra,* vii. 14 ; viii. 2). לְבָרָם is the *infinit.* Kal בָּר from בָּרַר = בּוּר, *to separate, to select, to choose* (according to the analogy of רָד. infinit. of

the children of men, God hath chosen them to shew that

רָדָה, Isa. xlv. 1; שַׁדְ of שָׁכַן, Jer. v. 26; comp. Gesen. § 67, Rem. 3; Ewald, § 238, b; § 255, d), with the suffix ם in the accusative; the לְ before it introduces *the indirect* speech, which is frequently the case after the verb אָמַר (comp. אָמַר יְהוָה לְהַשְׁמִיד אֶתְכֶם, *the Eternal said he would destroy you* (Deut. ix. 25; Esth. i. 17; iv. 13; *infra*, viii. 17; Ewald, § 338, a). The Sept., ὅτι διακρινεῖ αὐτούς, *that he may judge them*, has evidently arisen from exchanging it for יִשְׁפֹּט in the preceding verse, which, *like* לְבָרָם, is *the eighth* word of the parallel line, both of which begin with exactly the same words; whilst the Syriac ܠܡܶܒܪܳܐ mistook לברם for לברא. הָאֱלֹהִים, the subject of the infinit. בַּ, follows the verb between which the accusative ם is inserted. The proper order would be לְבָר הָאֱלֹהִים אֹתָם, but instances where the object precedes the subject are not unfrequent (comp. כֶּאֱכֹל קַשׁ לְשׁוֹן אֵשׁ, *as fire consumes straw*, Isa. v. 24; בִּשְׁלֹחַ אֹתוֹ סַרְגּוֹן, *when Sargon sent him*, *ibid.* xx. 1; Gesenius, § 133, 3; Ewald, § 309, a). As the ו before לִרְאוֹת, the second infinitive, shews that it is intimately connected with the first infinitive, and that it must refer to the same subject; the word, as it now stands in the text, yields a most awkward sense, *i. e.*, God has chosen the children of men that he might see they are beasts. There can, therefore, be little doubt that the Sept.

(τοῦ δεῖξαι), the Syriac (ܠܡܶܚܘܳܝܽܘܬܗܘܢ), the Vulg., and St. Jerome (*ut ostendere*), are right in reading it לְהַרְאוֹת, *the Hiphil*, instead of לִרְאוֹת, the Kal; nothing is more easily mistaken by a transcriber than the insignificant ־ and ־. Hence Rashi rightly explains it by להראותם. The *Sh'va* under שׁ, instead of שֶׁ=אֲשֶׁר, is most probably owing to one of the Segol points having been dropped, as the sacred writer always uses שׁ before the ה (*vide* ii. 22; vi. 10; xii. 9). בְּהֵמָה, *beast*, as frequently is used for

beasts. שְׁהֶם־בְּהֵמָה, *that they are beasts*, *i.e.*, LIKE *beasts.* To express strongly the resemblance of one thing to another, the Hebrews omit the כְּ *comparison*, and make the thing wherewith the subject is compared the predicate of the subject (comp. רֹאשׁוֹ כֶּתֶם פָּז, *his head is the finest gold*, *i.e.*, AS the finest gold, Song of Songs, v. 11; אִם־חוֹמָה הִיא, *if she be a wall*, *i. e.*, LIKE *a wall*, *ibid.* viii. 9). The accumulation of the relative pronouns הַמָּה לָהֶם · · · הֵם, yields that ironical climax which is expressed in Latin by *ipsissimi*, and in German by ſöchſtſelbſt (comp. Ewald, § 315, a). The rendering of the Sept., Vulg., and Syriac, with the exception of the mistake adverted to, is substantially the same which we advocate. Rashi's explanation, which is evidently the basis of the Turkey merchant's rendering, " Oh ! that God would enlighten them, and make them see that even they themselves are like beasts," and is followed by Adam Clark, &c., &c., referring it to the corrupt judges mentioned in ver. 16, is contrary to the form and signification of לְבָרָם, as well as to the scope of the passage. The explanation of Ibn Ezra, " I said in my heart, because of the children of men, God has chosen them (from among all creatures), and yet I saw that they are like beasts to themselves," *i. e.*, in their own estimation (אמרתי בלבי בעבור בני האדם שבחרם האלהים מכל תולדות הארץ וראיתי שהם כמו בהמות הם לנפשם במחשבותם); the Geneva version, " I considered in mine heart the estate of the children of men, that God had purged them ; yet to see to, they are in themselves as beasts;" Broughton, " I said in my heart, after the manner of the sons of men, when God made them known, that I saw how they are beasts; they to themselves ;" and the Authorised Version (text), " I said in my heart concerning the estate of the sons of men, that God might manifest them, and that they might see that they

19 they, even they, are like beasts. For man is mere chance, and the beast is mere chance, and they are both subject to

themselves are beasts;" besides the objections which they individually incur, are alike guilty of assigning two different subjects to the two inseparable infinitives. Luther's version (Jd) fprad) in meinem Herzen von dem Wesen der Menschen, darinnen Gott anzeiget und läßt es ansehen, als wären sie unter sich selbst wie das Vieh), Coverdale and the Bishops' Bible (" 1 communed with my own heart also concerning the children of men, how God hath chosen them, and yet letteth them appear as though they were beasts"), escape this objection, but they can neither be harmonised with the text nor context. De Wette, Knobel, Ewald, Heiligstedt, Vaihinger, Hengstenberg, &c. (I spake in my heart, it is because of the children of men — i. e, that the perversion of justice described in ver. 16, happens — that God may prove them, and that they may see that they are beasts) violently connect this verse with verse 16, assign two different subjects to the two infinitives, and create a harsh ellipsis, which is inadmissible. Still more objectionable is Philippson's violent rendering, Jd) fprad) in meinem Herzen über das Gerede der Menschensöhne, wohl um Gott zu erforschen ist's und zu sehen, daß sie Vieh find, making הָאֱלֹהִים the accusative of לְבָרָם. i. q., לְבָרֵר לָהֶם אֶת־הָאֱלֹהִים, which has been anticipated in the marginal reading of the Auth. Ver.

19. *For man is a mere chance, &c.* Coheleth assigns a reason why he put man and beast upon the same level in the foregoing verse: for both, he says, are the offspring of, and the victims to, the same blind chance; *their bodies* are alike subject to death, and *their souls* are the same; man has no advantage whatever over the beast, for both are alike vain; hence the correctness of the remark, that "men are like beasts." The fact that מִקְרֶה is written all the three times

with a *Segol*, shews beyond doubt that it is in the *absolute*, and must be taken as the *predicate, i. e.*, 'a mere chance are the children of men,' they are .the offspring of blind accident. For the meaning of מִקְרֶה, see ii. 14. וּמִקְרֶה אֶחָד לָהֶם, *and the same chance is to them both*, i. e., both are subject to the same chance, is not explanatory of מִקְרֶה בְּנֵי־הָאָדָם וּמִקְרֶה הַבְּהֵמָה, *man is a mere chance, and the beast is a mere chance* (Hengstenberg), but expresses an additional idea, *i. e.*, man and beast are not only the offspring of the same blind chance, but are alike subject to it during their life. For אֶחָד, *one, the same,* see ii. 14. To make this statement orthodox, the Hagada restricts it to the wicked, who, according to its exegesis, are described at the end of the preceding verse to be like beasts (*vide* Midrash, *in loco*). Hence the Chaldee paraphrase, אַרְעִין אֵינָשָׁא חַיָּבָא וְאַרְעִין בְּעִירָא, מְסָאֲבָא אַרְעִין חַד לְכוּלְּהוֹן, *as for the fate of the wicked and the fate of the unclean beast, both have the same fate;* hence also the Sept., καίγε αὐτοῖς συνάντημα υἱῶν τοῦ ἀνθρώπου καὶ συνάντημα τοῦ κτήνους συνάντημα ἓν αὐτοῖς· and the Syriac,

ܠܗܘܢ ܡܛܐ ܚܕ ܐܢܦܐ ܕܥܝܕ ܠܗܘܢ ܢܦܐ, *these*

(*i. e.*, the wicked mentioned in the preceding verse) *meet with the fate of the children of men and the fate of the beast; one fate have they.* The Vulgate: IDCIRCO UNUS INTERITUS EST HOMINIS ET JUMENTORUM, ET ÆQUA UTRIUSQUE CONDITIO, *therefore the death of man and of beasts is one, and the condition of both is the same;* Luther, benn es geht bem Menschen wie bem Vieh, omitting a clause; who is literally translated by Coverdale, " for it happeneth unto men as it doth unto beasts, even one condition unto them both," supplying the omission of Luther and Coverdale; the Geneva Version, " for the condi-

─the same chance; as is the death of one, so is the death of
the other, and both have the same spirit; and the advantage
20 of man over the beast is nothing, for both are vanity : both
go to the same place, both were made of dust, and both turn
21 into dust again : no one knoweth whether the spirit of man

tion of the children of men, and the condition of beasts are even as one condition unto them;" and the Auth. Version, "for that which befalleth the sons of men befalleth beasts ; even one thing befalleth them ;" are tame paraphrases, and do not express the sense of the original.

As is the death of one, &c. Not only are man and the beast alike the objects of chance in their *birth* and *life,* but, having the same perishable body and spirit, they are also alike as far as *death* and the *soul* are concerned, so that man has no advantage whatever over the beast. Similarly the Psalmist —

Man in, or despite of, his glory, abideth not;
He is like the beasts which perish.
xl. 13. 21.

מוֹת is a *noun* in the construct state before זֶה, and describes the state of the *body.* The double כְּ — כְּ, denoting similarity, is used for *as — so* (comp. Gen. xviii. 25, xliv. 18 ; Jud. viii. 18; Gesen. § 154, 3, f. ; Ewald, § 360, a). So also the repeated זֶה — זֶה is used for *this — that; one — the other* (comp. Job i. 16 ; Ps. lxxv. 8). As the two nouns בְּנֵי־הָאָדָם and הַבְּהֵמָה, to which these pronouns refer, are of different genders, we ought, correctly speaking, to have זֶה — זֹאת ; but, as we have already seen (*vide supra,* i. 11), strict attention to these matters is not always to be expected. וְרוּחַ אֶחָד לַכֹּל, *and both have the same spirit,* like וּמִקְרֶה אֶחָד לָהֶם, *and they are both subject to the same chance,* in the preceding clause, expresses an additional idea, *i. e.,* not only are their bodies alike a prey to death, but their spirits are the same. That רוּחַ denotes *the living principle, the spirit, the soul,* is evident both from the context and from verse 21, where

this expression is unquestionably used in this sense. For הַכֹּל, *all, both,* see ii. 14. The Sept. renders "וּמוֹתַר וגו׳, καὶ τί ἐπερίσσευσεν ὁ ἄνθρωπος παρὰ τὸ κτῆνος; Οὐδέν, *and what advantage has man over the beast? nothing;* so also Symmachus, καὶ τί πλέον ἄνθρωπος κτήνους; and Theodotion, καὶ τίς περίσσεια τῷ ἀνθρώπῳ; making וּמוֹתַר a compound of וּמֶה יתר.

20. *Both go to the same place,* &c. The declaration made in the preceding verse, that both man and the beast have the same *body* and *spirit,* is substantiated in this and the following verses. As the perishing body was mentioned first (כְּמוֹת זֶה כֵּן מוֹת זֶה), Coheleth explains it first. The bodies of both man and beast are made of earth, and, when they cease to live, turn into earth again (Gen. i. 24, ii. 7. 19, iii. 19 ; Ps. xxii. 16, civ. 29, cxlvi. 4 ; Job x. 9, xxxiv. 15, Sirach, xl. 11, xli. 10). הַכֹּל, *both,* and אֶחָד, *the same,* as in the preceding verse. What this " same place " is to which both go, we are told in the next clause. הָיָה מִן, *to be from, to come from, to proceed out of, to originate from* (comp. מַלְכֵי עַמִּים מִמֶּנָּה יִהְיוּ, *kings of nations shall come out of her,* Gen. xvii. 16), *to be made of,* is well rendered by the Sept. ἐγένετο ἀπὸ τοῦ χοός, *were made of dust,* and still better by the Vulgate, *de terra facta sunt ;* and by Luther, *von Staub gemacht.* שׁוּב אֶל־עָפָר, *to return to dust, to be converted or changed into dust again* (comp. Gen. iii. 19).

21. *No one knoweth,* &c. Having substantiated the first assertion, that both man and the beast have the same perishable body, Coheleth now proceeds to account for his second remark (וְרוּחַ אֶחָד לַכֹּל), that they have

goeth upward, and whether the spirit of the beast goeth down-

both also the same spirit, or that their respective spirits have the same destiny. The penetrating Rashbam has here again beautifully pointed out the connection of this verse with ver. 19, which many modern critics of greater pretensions have failed to see. *This verse*, says this Rabbi of the middle ages.—מוסב על ורוח אחד לכל על כן אני אומר רוח אחד לשניהם כי מי הוא שיודע שרוח שרוח האדם עולה למעלה ורוח בהמה יורדת למטה ועל כן אני אומר רוח אחד להם והכל הבל,—*is explanatory of the words,* " and both have the same spirit." *Why I say they have both the same spirit is because who knows whether the spirit of man goes upward, and whether the spirit of the beast goes downward? Therefore I maintain that they have both the same spirit, and that all is vanity.* For the question about the destiny of the body which is capable of ocular demonstration, Coheleth could refer to that which every one might see for himself. But the question about the destiny of the soul is of a different nature, and is beyond our ken; Coheleth therefore throws the burden of the argument upon his opponents, by maintaining that no one can shew that the spirit of man and the beast are not the same; that the one is destined to soar up to and be with the Father of our spirits, and that the other is doomed to descend into the earth, and be mingled with the dust, like the body. מִי יוֹדֵעַ רוּחַ בְּנֵי הָאָדָם הָעֹלָה הִיא לְמַעְלָה וְרוּחַ הַבְּהֵמָה הַיֹּרֶדֶת הִיא לְמַטָּה לָאָרֶץ, *who knoweth the spirit of man, whether it goeth upward, and the spirit of the beast, whether it goeth downward to the earth?* is again a contraction of מִי יוֹדֵעַ הָעֹלָה הִיא רוּחַ בְּנֵי הָאָדָם לְמַעְלָה וְהָרֹוּחַ הִיא הַיֹּרֶדֶת הַבְּהֵמָה לְמַטָּה לָאָרֶץ, *who knoweth whether the spirit of man goeth upward, and whether the spirit of the beast goeth downward to the earth?* (comp. ii. 24), which is beautifully solved by the Syriac, as may be seen below. The interrogative מִי יֹדֵעַ, *who knoweth*, as frequently, is used for an emphatic

denial (*vide* ii. 19, vi. 12, and the remark on i. 3). רוּחַ, *the vital spirit, the soul*, as is evident from verse 19, which is here taken up again. That לַשָּׁמַיִם, *to heaven*, is to be supplied after עֹלָה הִיא לְמַעְלָה, *goeth upward*, which the Chaldee very properly expresses (לִרְקִיעָא), and that it denotes *immortality*, is placed beyond a doubt by the antithetical phrase יֹרֶדֶת הִיא לְמַטָּה, *goes downward*, which is defined by the additional לָאָרֶץ, *to the earth*, and which unquestionably denotes *mortality*, the abode of the destroyed body. עֹלָה and יֹרֶדֶת, as well as the copula הִיא (*vide infra*, v. 18 ; Gesen. § 121, 2 ; Ewald, § 297, b), are feminine, because רוּחַ, to which they refer, is usually feminine. Though the present pointing of the ה in הָעֹלָה and הַיֹּרֶדֶת does not militate against our rendering, inasmuch as the *He*-interrogative has not unfrequently a *Pattach* followed by a *Dagesh*, like the article (compare הַיֵּיטַב בְּעֵינֵי יְהֹוָה, *should it have been accepted in the sight of the Eternal?* Levit. x. 19 ; Job xxiii. 6 ; Isa. xxvii. 7 ; Gesen. § 100, 4 ; Ewald, § 104, b), yet it can hardly be. doubted that the Masorites have designed it as the article-pronoun, in order to remove the denial of the immortality of the soul. All the ancient versions, however, take the *He* interrogatively; thus the Sept., καὶ τίς οἶδεν τὸ πνεῦμα υἱῶν τοῦ ἀνθρώπου εἰ ἀναβαίνει αὐτὸ εἰς ἄνω; καὶ πνεῦμα τοῦ κτήνους εἰ κΡΤΑβαίνει αὐτὸ κάτω εἰς τὴν γῆν; *who has seen the spirit of the sons of men whether, it goes upwards, and the spirit of the beast, whether it goes downwards to the earth?* the Vulg., QUIS NOVIT, SI SPIRITUS FILIORUM ADAM ASCENDAT SURSUM, ET SI SPIRITUS JUMENTORUM DESCENDAT DEORSUM? *who knows whether the spirit of the sons of Adam ascends upward, and whether the spirit of beasts descends downward?* the Syr.,

ܣܟܠܐ ܡܢ ܐܢ ܢܦܫ ܚܢܝܢܬܐ
ܗܠܟܐ ܠܥܠ ܘܢܦܫ ܚܝܘܬܐ

22 ward to the earth. Wherefore I saw that there is nothing
better for man than to rejoice in his labours, for this is his
portion, since no one can bring him to see what will be here-
iv. 1 after. Then I saw again all the oppressed who are suffering
under the sun, and beheld the tears of the oppressed, and

ﬦﬣ ﬨﬧﬤ ﬤﬣ ﬥ﬩ﬡ ﬡﬧﬦ, *and
who knows whether the spirit of man
goes upward, and whether the spirit
of the beast goes downward to the
earth?* the Chaldee, בָּן הוּא הַבִּינָה דַיָּדָע
אִין רוּחַ נִשְׁמְתָא בְּנֵי אֲנָשָׁא הַסַּלְקָא לְעֵילָא לִרְקִיעָא
וְרוּחַ נִשְׁמְתָא דִּבְעִירָא הַנַּחְתָא הִיא לְרַע לְאַרְעָא,
*who is wise enough to know whether
the soul of man goes upward to
heaven, and whether the soul of the
beast goes downward to the earth?*
So also Luther, the Geneva Version,
Knobel, Herzfeld, De Wette, Ewald,
Hitzig, Heiligstedt, Stuart, Elster,
Vaihinger, and almost all modern
commentators. The unnatural construction of Rashi, " He who has
understanding understands that the
spirit of man goes upward, and the
spirit of the beast goes downward,"
referring to מִי יוֹדֵעַ יָשׁוּב in Joel, ii. 14,
for this sense of מִי יוֹדֵעַ, which is followed by Mendelssohn and Preston;
and the far-fetched explanation of
Ibn Ezra, "Who knows, who among
men can understand, the immense
difference between the spirit of man
that goes upward, and the spirit of
the beast that goes downward, not
one in a thousand" — מִי שֶׁיָּדַע בְּנֵי הָאָדָם
הַדְּפֵרַשׁ שֶׁיֵּשׁ בֵּין רוּחַ הָאָדָם וְרוּחַ הַבְּהֵמָה וְהָעִנְיָן
כִּי לֹא אֶחָד מִנִּי אֶלֶף וְדַעַת הָרוּחַ עֲמוּקָה וּצְרִיכָה
לִרְאִיּוֹת וְלֹא יוּכְלוּ לְהָבִין אֲפִילוּ קְצָתָהּ כִּי אִם
הַמַּשְׂכִּילִים—which is followed by Cover-
dale, the Bishops' Bible, Reynolds,
Patrick, Hodgson, Holden, Hengstenberg, &c., are contrary to the
scope of the passage, and violate the
intimate connection which subsists
between this verse and verse 19.
Even Mr. Ayre, in *the orthodox* edition of the second volume of Horne's
Introduction (p. 745), disapproves of
Hengstenberg for not admitting that
the *He* is interrogative, and rightly

remarks, " that a distinct assertion
here of a future life would have been
premature; *that* the author reserved
for his conclusion." The denial of
the immortality of the soul contained
in this verse forms the very basis of
Coheleth's disquisition, as we have
seen in i. 2 – 11.

22. *Wherefore I saw,* &c. Since this
is the condition of man, Coheleth again
shews that there is nothing left for
him but to enjoy the present, as this
is his only portion, and as no one
can shew what will take place after
our death. The וְ in וְרָאִיתִי, as frequently, is inferential. חֵלֶק, *portion,
lot,* as in ii. 10. Though this verse
is an inference from the preceding
verses, and therefore has its cause
there, yet, to make it more impres-
sive, Coheleth repeats the reason in
a different form. The interrogative,
מִי יְבִיאֶנּוּ לִרְאוֹת, *who shall bring him to
see?* is the same as מִי יוֹדֵעַ, *who knows?*
in the preceding verse, and is used
for an emphatic denial. For the
construction בְּ רָאָה, see ii. 1. כָּה שֶׁיִּהְיֶה
אַחֲרָיו, *what will be after him? i.e.,*
after his death, hereafter (*vide infra,*
x. 14), whether there be a future
state of existence and enjoyment or
not.

1. *Then I saw again,* &c. From
this point of view, viz., that there
is no future state, Coheleth again
returns to contemplate the bitter
state of sufferings, the violation of
social laws, and the perversion of
justice which he alluded to in iii. 16.
שַׁבְתִּי וָאֶרְאֶה, literally *I turned and saw,*
i.e., *I again saw,* indicates the return
to the subject from another point of
view; for the adverbial use of שׁוּב,
see i. 7. The Vulg., VERTI ME AD
ALIA, ET VIDI, *I turned myself to other
things and saw,* is a loose paraphrase,

they had no comforter, and from their oppressors there was

and mistakes the connection. עֲשֻׁקִים, in the first clause, is taken by the Sept. (συκοφαντίας), Vulg. (calumnias), Chaldee (אֲנִיסִין), and after them Coverdale, Geneva Version, Luther, Auth. Version, Knobel, Hodgson, Hitzig, De Wette, Heiligstedt, Stuart, Elster, &c., as the abstract, oppression; whilst, in the second clause, these same authorities render it as concrete, oppressed. But the inconsistency of taking the same expression in the same verse in two different senses is most glaring; and as there can be no doubt that עֲשֻׁקִים, in the second clause, means oppressed, which is evident from the expression דִּמְעָה, tears, which can only be predicated of persons; its meaning in the first clause must therefore be determined thereby. · Hence Sym. (τοὺς συκοφαντουμένους), Rashi, Rashbam, Jermin, Herzfeld, Philippson, &c., are consistent in taking it as concrete in both clauses. The objection of Knobel, Hitzig, Holden, Elster, &c., that נַעֲשִׂים does not well agree with this rendering, has no force, for it is just as appropriate to say עָשָׂה עֲשֻׁקִים, to make oppressed ones, as to say עָשָׂה עֲבָדִים, to make slaves, or עָשָׂה נְפָשִׁים, to make souls. דִּמְעָה, tear, is used collectively.

And they had no comforter. The manifestation of sympathy with sufferers in the East was and still is more formal than in the West (compare iii. 7, vii. 2, and xii. 5). Friends even travelled great distances, and stayed with the sufferer for days, in order to comfort him. The Jews in the present day still regard it as an imperative duty to visit the afflicted, which is called מְנַחֵם אָבֵל, comforting the mourners, the very word used in our text, and the sufferers look forward to these condoling visits as a great relief. This will shew the force of the passage before us. The individuals in question are not only suffering from cruel injustice, but are left to bewail their gloomy fate without the customary and the highly-prized condolence,

which renders their sufferings still more poignant. The clause מִיד עשֻׁקֵיהֶם כֹּחַ continues to depend upon הִנֵּה, i. e., and behold, from the hand of their oppressors there is violence. כֹּחַ, power, is here used in a bad sense, for force, violence. The repetition of the words, " and they had no comforter," describes pathetically the continued state of things (vide supra, iii. 16). The Hagadic explanation of this clause, as given in the Chaldee paraphrase, לֵית לְמִפְרְקְהוֹן מִן יַד דְּאוֹנְסֵיהוֹן בִּתְקוֹף יָדָא וּבְחֵילָא וְלֵית דִּי יַנְחֵים לְהוֹן, and there is none with a strong hand and power to deliver them from the hand of their oppressors, and none to comfort them, which is followed by the Vulgate, NEC POSSE RESISTERE EORUM VIOLENTIÆ CUNCTORUM AUXILIO DESTITUTOS, nor were they able to resist their violence, being destitute of help from any; Coverdale, and there was no man to comfort them, or that would deliver and defend them from the violence of their oppressors, and others, not only require us to supply the negative particle אֵין, but also the principal verb מֵצִיל, to take כֹּחַ in a double sense, viz., power to resist, and violence, according to the Hagadic laws of exegesis (vide supra, p. 30), and to reconstrue the whole sentence, which none but the rabid opponents of the received text would do. Neither does Luther's version (und bie ihnen Unrecht thaten, waren zu mächtig, baß sie keinen Tröster haben konnten, and those that did them injustice were too powerful, so that they (the sufferers) could not be comforted) express the sense of the text. The usual interpretation is supported by the Sept., ἀπὸ χειρὸς συκοφαντούντων αὐτοὺς ἰσχύς, from the hand of their oppressors was violence; Rashi, עושקיהם מכריחים ותוקפים אותם בכח, their oppressors subdued and overpowered them violently, Rashbam, Ibn Ezra, and most modern commentators. The Syriac, which rightly translated the first מְנַחֵם ܡܒܝܐܢܐ, comforter, in-

2 violence, and they had no comforter; and I esteemed happy
the dead who have died long ago, more than the living who
3 are still alive; and happier than both, him who hath not
been born, who hath not seen these evil doings which are

consistently renders the second מְנַחֵם,

مَسَاعِد, *helper*.

2. *And I esteemed happy the dead*,
&c. These heart-rending and har-
rowing miseries, brought upon the
helpless and innocent by the very
men who were appointed to ameliorate the condition of the community,
were so intolerable, that Coheleth
regarded those whom death had
relieved from these bitter sufferings
as happier than those who endured
them. This lamentable description
of the misery to which Coheleth was
an eyewitness (וָאֶרְאֶה), and which so
frequently calls forth his indignation
against the authors of it (*vide infra*,
v. 8, viii. 4. 10, x. 5 – 7), shews that
Solomon could not have written this
book, for in his days no such misery
was prevalent, as is evident from
1 Kings iv. 20 – 25; x. 6 – 9. Besides, even if the books of Kings and
Chronicles had not given us the
history of this monarch's enlightened
and peaceful reign, it could not be
imagined that such a mighty and
wise potentate, who had given such
a signal evidence of the administration of justice in the case of the two
mothers, would so bitterly complain
of the judges of his land who were of
his own creation, when it was in his
power to crush the miscreants and
avenge the cause of the injured, who
are represented as "having no comforter." שַׁבֵּחַ, according to Ibn Ezra,
Herzfeld, &c., is a *verbal adjective*,
like מָאֵן, and, as is frequently the
case, is used with a personal pronoun for a finite verb (comp. Exod.
vii. 27, ix. 2, *al.*); according to
Gesen., Knobel, Heiligstedt, Elster,
&c., it is the *participle Piel* for מְשַׁבֵּחַ,
the מ having dropped, as in Zeph.
i. 14; and, according to Rashbam,
Mendelssohn, Ewald, Hitzig, &c., it

is the *infinitive absolute*, continuing
the construction which began with the
finite verb (compare Ewald, § 351, c).
The first of these views is the least
objectionable, since the examples
adduced to shew that the Piel part.
drops the מ are questionable, and
since the pronoun אֲנִי, with which
שַׁבֵּחַ is connected, is against its being
an infinitive. The additions שֶׁכְּבָר מֵתוּ,
who have died long ago, to הַמֵּתִים, *the
dead*, and אֲשֶׁר הֵמָּה חַיִּים עֲדֶנָה, *who are
still living*, to הַחַיִּים, *the living*, which
appear tautological in a modern
translation, give peculiar emphasis
to the original, *i. e.*, Coheleth not
only regarded those who have *recently*
been deprived of life as happier than
the living, but he praised those who
had long been forgotten (a fate which
was so much dreaded by the Easterns), as happier than those who were
not only living, but were in vigour,
and had the prospect of a long life.
The Septuagint's rendering of אֲשֶׁר
הֵמָּה חַיִּים עֲדֶנָה by ὅσοι αὐτοὶ ζῶσιν ἕως τοῦ
νῦν, *as many of them as are living
until now*, cannot be reconciled with
the text; the Vulg., Coverdale, and
the Bishops' Bible most arbitrarily
omit both additions. עֲדֶנָה is a contraction of עַד הֵנָּה (Gen. xv. 16; 1 Sam.
vii. 12; Gesenius, § 150, 2; Ewald,
§ 217, e).

3. *And happier than both*, &c.
The comparison of the death-relieved
sufferers with the living martyrs is
here extended to the yet unborn,
who are pronounced as happier still,
because they have not suffered at
all, whilst those relieved by death had
suffered for some time. A parallel
passage with the one before us, where
the dead and the unborn are preferred to the living sufferers, is to be
found in Job

Why died I not from the womb,
Come forth from the belly, and depart?

4 done under the sun. Then I saw that all the toil, and all the dexterity in work, are from jealousy of one toward the other, this also is vanity and striving after the wind;

Wherefore did knees meet me,
And why breasts, that I should suck?
For now I should have sank down and rested,
I should have slept, and then have reposed
With kings and counsellors of the earth,
Who built themselves pyramids ;
Or with princes rich in gold,
Who filled their houses with silver ;
Or like a hidden abortion I should not have been,
Like infants who have never seen the light.
iii. 11-16.

So also Theognis—

Πάντων μὲν μὴ φῦναι ἐπιχθονίοισιν ἄριστον,
Μηδ᾽ ἐςιδεῖν αὐγὰς ὀξέος ἠελίου·
Φύντα δ᾽, ὅπως ὤκιστα πύλας ᾽Αἰδαο περῆσαι,
Καὶ κεῖσθαι πολλὴν γῆν ἐπαμησάμενον.

"Not to be born, never to see the sun,
No worldly blessing is a greater one !
And the next best is speedily to die,
And, lapt beneath a load of earth, to lie !"
425-428.

שָׁבֵחַ must be mentally supplied before וְטוֹב, as it still governs the accusative אֵת אֲשֶׁר. The Sept., Syriac, Luther, the Authorised Version, &c., make אֵת to be the *nominative*, which both weakens the force of the passage and involves an anomaly ; whilst the Vulg., ET FELICIOREM UTROQUE JUDI-CAVI, QUI NECDUM NATUS EST, *and I judged him happier than both of them who has not yet been born*, which is followed by the Geneva Version, &c., unnecessarily introduces another verb to govern the accusative. רָאָה רָע, *to see evil*, i. e., *to experience it, to suffer under it* (comp. the opposite phrase רָאָה טוֹב, *to see good*, ii. 1).

4. *Then I saw that all the toil*, &c. The industry and dexterity mani-fested in the pursuits and avocations of life, in spite of the unalterably fixed destinies of man, and to the neglect of the enjoyment of the pre-sent, which is the only portion of man, arise from a mean desire to outdo one's neighbour, whose pro-sperity is looked upon with a jealous eye ; yet this base competition fre-quently terminates in the loss of the object eagerly pursued, and in

striving after the wind. וְרָאִיתִי אֲנִי אֶת־כָּל־עָמָל וְאֵת כָּל־כִּשְׁרוֹן הַמַּעֲשֶׂה כִּי הִיא קִנְאַת וְגוֹ״, *and I saw all the toil and all the dexterity in work, that they are from jealousy*, &c., is again an attraction instead of וְרָאִיתִי אֲנִי כִּי־כָל־עָמָל וְכָל־כִּשְׁרוֹן הַמַּעֲשֶׂה הִיא קִנְאַת וְגוֹ״, *and I saw that all the toil and the dexterity in work are from jealousy*, &c. (*vide supra*, ii. 24). The solution of this attraction shews that כִּי is a *conjunc-tion*, depending upon the verb רָאִיתִי, *I saw* (comp. Gen. i. 4 ; Job xxii. 12 ; Gesen, § 142, 4, Rem. 2 ; § 155, 4, c ; Ewald, § 336), and that the copula הִיא refers to עָמָל וְכִשְׁרוֹן. This is, more-over, evident from the preposition מִן in מֵרֵעֵהוּ, which indicates *the cause* of this industry and dexterity, and must be construed with אֶת־כָּל־עָמָל וְאֵת כָּל־כִּשְׁרוֹן הַמַּעֲשֶׂה, for it never goes with קִנְאָה ; this noun is invariably con-strued with לְ (1 Kings xix. 10), or with בְּ (Prov. iii. 31 ; xxiii. 17 ; xxiv. 1), and from the fact that קִנְאָה is not *passive, being envied*, das Beneiden-werden, but *active, the envying*, das Beneiden. Hence the the Vulg., RUR-SUM CONTEMPLATUS SUM OMNES LABO-RES HOMINUM, ET INDUSTRIAS ANI-MADVERTI PATERE INVIDIÆ PROXIMI, *again I considered all the labours of men, and I noticed that their industries are exposed to the envy of their neigh-bour ;* Luther, ich sahe an Arbeit und Geschicklichkeit in allen Sachen : da neidet einer den andern ; Coverdale, " again I saw that all the travail and diligence of labour was hated of every one ;" the Authorised Version, in the text, " again I considered all travail and every right work, that for this a man is envied of his neighbour ;" in the margin, " this is the envy of a man from his neighbour ;" and Hodg-son, " Then I viewed every ingeni-ous and excellent work ; but such caused a man to be envied by his neighbour," do not give the sense of the original.

324   COHELETH.   [CHAP. IV

5 the sluggard foldeth his hands and yet eateth his meat;

5. *The sluggard foldeth his hands,*
&c. To show the vain efforts of the
mean characters mentioned in the
preceding verse, Coheleth points to
the fact that, while industrious and
dexterous jealousy, attempting greedily to grasp the object of her eager
pursuit, finds frequently that she has
striven after the wind, the slothful
man quietly enjoys his repast. Much
difficulty has been experienced by
commentators in explaining this
verse, and multifarious are the opinions respecting its meaning. This
perplexity, I believe, is not owing to
any real difficulty in the text or context, but is to be ascribed to the fact
that interpreters have too implicitly
followed the traditional explanation.
Thus the Chaldee paraphrases this
verse, שַׁטְיָא אָזִיל וּמְנַפִּיךְ יַת יְדוֹי בְּקַיְטָא וְלָא
צָבֵי לְמִפְלַח וּבְסִתְוָא יֵיכוּל יַת כָּל מַה דְּאִית לֵיהּ
וַאֲפִילוּ כְּסוּ מֵעַל מְשַׁךְ בִּסְרֵיהּ, *the fool goes
and folds his hands in summer and
will not labour, and in winter eats
all he has, even the garment from the
skin of his flesh;* taking it to mean
that the fool, unwilling to work at
opportune seasons, when labour is to
be got, is obliged, at the time when
employment is not to be found, and
when hunger-bitten, as a penalty,
to sell his very garments in order to
satisfy the cravings of nature. It is
this explanation which has influenced all the commentators. The
Vulg. (STULTUS COMPLICAT MANUS SUAS
ET COMEDIT CARNES SUAS, DICENS: *the
fool foldeth his hands together, and
eateth his own flesh, saying.* &c.) takes
it in the same sense, and puts the
words of the following verse into the
mouth of the fool; thus also Ibn
Ezra, גם יש באדם כסילים עצלים אין להם קנאה
ולא יתעסקו במלאכה שיחיו ממנה רק חובקים את
ידיהם ואוכלים מה שיש להם וישארו בלא מחיה
ואחר שהוא אוכל כל מה שיש לו ולא יעמול להוסיף
כאילו אוכל את בשרו בעבור שימות ברעב: טוב
דברי הכסיל הוא האומר די לי, *there are also
sluggard fools among men, who are
not jealous, and do not engage in
work to live thereby, but fold their
hands, and eat up all they have, and*

are left without support; and having
eaten up all he had, and not laboured
to replenish, he is like one consuming
his own flesh, for he dies of hunger
(ver. 9); these are the words of the
fool, who says, I have plenty, &c.
Hence Coverdale: *the fool foldeth
his hands together, and eateth up his
own flesh; one handful (saith he) is
better with rest, &c.;* and Mendelssohn; and hence the various attempts to connect it with the preceding verse. Bishop Reynolds says
that this envy has for its consequence, that foolish and slothful
men refuse to take pains, and prefer
poverty rather than to be envied.
Mendelssohn takes this verse to be
an address of the diligent to the
indolent, to blame him. Knobel,
Preston, Philippson, Elster, &c.,
maintain that this verse describes
the opposite extreme; the preceding
verse depicted a man driven by
jealousy to laborious industry, whilst
this verse speaks of one who, through
indolence, lives on his patrimony,
and consumes it without taking any
steps to repair the inroads he makes
upon it. Gesenius and others take
it as still descriptive of jealousy, and
explain the words אֹכֵל בְּשָׂרוֹ, *the fool
devoured by envy,* comparing with it
ὃν θυμὸν κατέδων (Hom. Il. vi. 202).
Against all these interpretations we
urge that they are forced and unnatural, that some are against the
genius of language, and some against
the context. This will be seen from
an analysis of the words of the verse,
and their relation to each other, כְּסִיל
(from כָּסַל, *to be thick, fat, fleshy, to
be inactive, lazy,* or *languid, either in
body* or *mind,* as the latter is generally the result of the former) denotes
a sluggard, a fool, a sinner, whose
heart is overlaid with fat, and is
obdurate, so that he is rendered dull
and callous to the commandments
of God (Deut. xxxii. 15; Ps. xvii.
10; lxxiii. 7; cxix. 70; Isa. vi. 10;
comp. Prov. xv. 20; xix. 1; *infra,*
ver. 17. *al.*). That the idea of *inac-*

6 better a handful of enjoyment than two handsful of labour

tivity in labour, viz., עָצֵל, is here intended, is evident from the immediately following words, חֹבֵק אֶת־יָדָיו, *folds his hands*, which are used as descriptive of *a lazy man, i.e.*, עָצֵל (comp. Prov. vi. 10; xxiv. 33), and not *a fool*, in the ordinary meaning of this word; and from the preceding verse, where the opposite character is described, viz., *one active and industrious.* This last remark also shows that כְּסִיל, *the slothful*, is not to be taken *absolutely*, but *relatively;* when compared with this wide-awake activity, impelled by envy, which is always on the alert, he, who is contented with enjoying what he has, without attempting to replenish what he consumes, is inactive, slothful. אָכַל בָּשָׂר, *to eat meat*, is frequently used in Scripture as indicative of an ample and delicate repast (Exod. xvi. 8; xxi. 28; Isa. xxii. 13; Ezek. xxxix. 17), just as the abstinence from it is mentioned in cases of humiliation and fasting (Dan. x. 3), and we have no right to depart from its natural signification here, and force upon it the sense of *consuming one's own flesh*, especially as the words, הֶבֶל וּרְעוּת רוּחַ, *vanity and striving after the wind*, predicated in the preceding verse of the enviously industrious, show that the words אֹכֵל אֶת בְּשָׂרוֹ, *eating his meat*, the predicate of the easy sluggard, are intended as an antithesis, the one *repining*, the other *enjoying;* just as the *enviously industrious* is contrasted with *the reposingly slothful.*

6. *Better a handful of enjoyment*, &c. Coheleth, therefore, submits that he who quietly enjoys his scanty patrimony, without harassing cares and useless pursuits after gain, is to be preferred to him who succeeds in amassing wealth, but cannot enjoy it for want of tranquillity of mind. This verse has shared in its interpretation the fate of the preceding one. The Vulg., Ibn Ezra, Coverdale, the Bishops' Bible, Reynolds, Mendelssohn, &c., as we have seen, put it

into the mouth of the sluggard, as an apology for his laziness; whilst Preston, Philippson, Elster, and others, maintain that it contains a recommendation of Coheleth to avoid both extremes, viz., envious and toilsome industry, and careless slothfulness, and to choose the middle course. But how such a middle course is to be got out of the words in this verse, I am at a loss to divine. כַּף נָחַת, *a handful of quiet*, manifestly describes the כְּסִיל, *sluggard*, who quietly enjoys his repast, as is evident from עָמָל וּרְעוּת רוּחַ, *labour and striving after the wind*, which depicts the עָמָל וּכִשְׁרוֹן הַמַּעֲשֶׂה, *man of labour and dexterity*, in verse 4. Hence this verse must be taken as giving the estimate of the respective merits of the two classes described in verses 4 and 5. מְלֹא in both clauses is followed by כַּף, *a handful*, and חָפְנַיִם, *two handsful*, genitives of measure, and נָחַת, *enjoyment*, and עָמָל, *toil*, accusatives of the things measured (comp. אִם־יִתֶּן־לִי בָלָק מְלֹא בֵיתוֹ כֶּסֶף וְזָהָב, *if Balak would give me his house full of silver and gold*, Numb. xxii. 18; מְלֹא כַף־קֶמַח, *a handful of meal*, 1 Kings xvii. 12; Judges vi. 38; Gesen. Lex., *s. v.*, מְלֹא; Gram. § 118; Ewald, § 287, h; so the Sept., Syriac, Knobel, Herzfeld, Ewald, Gesenius, De Wette, Heiligstedt, Hitzig, Stuart, Philippson, Elster, Hengstenberg, and most modern critics). The rendering of Symmachus, μετὰ ἀναπαύσεως, the Chaldee, Rashi, Rashbam, Ibn Ezra, בְּנַחַת, בְּעָמָל; Vulg., *cum requie, cum labore;* Luther, mit Ruhe, mit Mühe; Coverdale, the Bishops' Bible, the Geneva Version, the Authorised Version, *with quietness, with travail*, supplying a בְּ before נָחַת and עָמָל, the accusative depending upon מְלֹא, are contrary to grammar. Auerbach ingeniously remarks that the difference between כַּף and חָפְנַיִם is כַּף הוא החלל, האמצעי שביד וחותך הוא כל היד עם העצבעות, *the former denotes the hollow of the hand, whilst the latter signifies the whole hand, including the fingers.* נָחַת (from נוּחַ, *to settle down, to rest*)

7 and striving after the wind   And again I saw a vanity under
8 the sun; here is one who hath no one with him, hath not
   even a son or brother, and yet there is no end to all his

denotes *quiet, rest,* and hence also *happiness, enjoyment, pleasure, delight,* from the great luxury which rest is to Orientals (comp. נַחַת שֻׁלְחָנֶךָ, *the enjoyment* or *delight of thy table,* Job xxxvi. 16, and *infra,* vi. 5 with 3, where it is used as a synonym with טוֹב in the sense of *good,* which meaning it frequently has in post-Biblical Hebrew. We need only refer to the well-known phrase, נוּחַ לוֹ לָאָדָם, *it is good with that man;* and see also *infra,* ix. 17).

7. *And again I saw,* &c. From jealousy Coheleth proceeds to *avarice,* as the two features are intimately connected with each other; both are described as the cause of hard labour, undertaken in spite of the immutably fixed order of things, and as neglecting the enjoyment of the present, which is the only portion of man; the former is instigated to work by envying the possessions of others, whilst the latter is impelled to toil by an insatiable desire of filthy lucre. For the adverbial use of שׁוּב see i. 7. The Vulg., CONSIDERANS REPERI ET ALIAM VANITATEM SUB. SOLE, *considering I also found another vanity under the sun,* is a loose paraphrase, and an inconsistent departure from its tame rendering of the same phrase in verse 1.

8. *Here is one,* &c. The miser is now introduced. Here is a solitary being, without connection, either by blood or ties of friendship, to inherit his amassed wealth, yet is he actuated by the greedy love of money to toil incessantly, and does not endure two mouths in his house, or even suffer his own mouth to enjoy the fruit of his labours. The pronoun לוֹ, *to him,* from the second clause, must be supplied after שֵׁנִי, *second,* i. q., וְאֵין שֵׁנִי לוֹ, *and has not a second.* But who is meant by this *second?* According to St. Jerome, St. Ambrose, &c., it is *Christ;* according to Rashi,

Rashbam, &c., it is (אדם שני לסייעו), *a companion* or *a partner in business;* according to Ibn Ezra, it is (אשה שהיא עזר כנגדו), *a wife;* according to Holden, &c., it is *a son to inherit the fruit of his labours;* according to Bishop Reynolds, Knobel, &c., it is *a second generally, associate, wife, friend,* or *partner;* and, according to Heiligstedt, Stuart, Elster, &c., it is simply exegetical of the emphatic meaning of אֶחָד, viz., *one only.* The following verse, however, which unquestionably restricts it to the union of social polity, corroborates the opinion of Rashi and Rashbam, that *a partner* is thereby intended. גַּם, with the negative particle אֵין, gives intensity to the statement, *i. e., not even* a son or a brother (comp. *infra,* viii. 16; 2 Sam. xvii. 12, 16; Ps. xiv. 3; liii. 4; Ewald, § 352, b); as much as to say, not to find a companion or friend is strange enough, but *not even* to have a brother or son, which everybody has, this is indeed astonishing; and yet this solitary individual labours without end to amass wealth. For the *Quametz* under the וְ in וָאֶרְאֶה, being used to join words in pairs, see ii. 23. Herzfeld regards the second גַּם, before עֵינָיו, as synonymous with וְ. *and;* but this is an unnecessary deviation from its meaning, and weakens the force of the passage; it is used as in the former clause for emphasis, shewing that this lonely being does not only labour incessantly, but that his greedy eye is *not even* satisfied with his great wealth. Owing to the apparent inconsistency of construing תִּשְׂבַּע, *sing.* with עֵינָיו, *the dual,* 54 of Kennicott's MSS., the Sept., Chaldee, St. Jerome, the Syriac, and the Keri have עֵינוֹ in the *singular.* There is, however, no need of resorting to a different reading for rectifying this anomaly, since עֵינַיִם not unfrequently takes a *sing.* fem. verb after

labour, even his eyes are not satisfied with riches; and for whom do I labour and deny my soul any of my riches? this,
9 too, is vanity, and an evil business. Happier two than one,
10 because they have a good reward for their labour; for if one

it (comp. וְעֵינָיו קָמָה, 1 Sam. iv. 15; 1 Kings xiv. 6. 12; Micah iv. 11; Gesen. § 146, 5; Ewald, § 317, a). For the phrase שָׂבַע עַיִן, to satiate the eye, see i. 8.

And for whom do I labour, &c. To render the statement more striking and vivid, Coheleth places himself in the condition of such a friendless and childless miser, and exclaims, "If I were such a solitary being, for whom would I toil?" &c. For a similar instance of personification, see ver. 15; ii. 15. The Chaldee, however, supplies וְלָא יֵמַר בְּלִבֵּהּ, *and does not say in his heart*, putting it into the mouth of the miser; so also the Vulgate, NEC RECOGITAT, DICENS: CUI LABORO? which is followed by Coverdale, the Bishops' Bible, the Geneva Version, the Authorised Version, &c.; but this unnecessary insertion of words does not at all improve the sense. חָסֵר, *to be wanting*, intransitive, is, like all other verbs denoting *want* or *fulness*, construed with the accusative in Kal, and in Piel, the causative of Kal, with two accusatives, one of the *person* (אֶת־נַפְשִׁי), and the other of the thing or *object*, which is to be supplied from the noun מְטוֹבָה, as indicated by the *partitive* מִן (comp. יִשָּׁקֵנִי מִנְּשִׁיקוֹת, *let him kiss me* — i. e., מִנְּשִׁיקָה, *a kiss — of the kisses*, Song of Songs, i. 2; Ps. cxxxii. 11; Gesen. § 154, 3, c; Ewald, § 217, b, 1, b). The full construction would therefore be חָסֵר. וּמְחַסֵּר אֶת־נַפְשִׁי כָּל־טוּב מְטוֹבָה, followed by מִן, with the double accusative fully expressed, also occurs in Ps. viii. 6; וַתְּחַסְּרֵהוּ מְעַט מֵאֱלֹהִים, *and thou makest him want* (הוּ ָ, accusat. of person) *but little* (מְעַט, accusat. of thing or object) *of God* (see Hupfeld, *in loco*). The opinion of Gesenius (Lex, *s. v.*), Herzfeld, Hengstenberg, Fürst (Lex, *s. v.*), &c., that חָסֵר is construed with מִן instead of the

accusative, is contrary to the *usus loquendi*. Equally objectionable is the artificial explanation of Knobel and Elster, that חָסֵר מְטוֹבָה, Mangel von etwas weg leiben laffen ift prägnant gefagt für: Mangel leiben und entfernt fein laffen, u. s. v. For עָנָה רָע, see i. 13.

9. *Happier two than one*, &c. This solitary and selfish miser, who thinks to increase his happiness by increasing his wealth, defeats by his own conduct the very object which he has in view. Since the alliance which he so much shuns, for fear of having his riches diminished and his happiness lessened, is the very thing which promotes happiness, inasmuch as two labouring together effect, by mutual counsel and assistance, much more than a solitary being could do, and have therefore "good reward for their conjoint labour." The abhorrence with which a lonely life was regarded among the Hebrews, and the high estimation in which friendship was held, gave rise to the following proverbs :— אוֹ חַבְרוּתָא אוֹ מִיתוּתָא, *either friendship or death*, Talmud, Tanith, 23; אָדָם בְּלָא חֲבֵרִים כִּשְׂמֹאל בְּלָא יָמִין, *a man without friends is like a left hand without the right*, Mibchar Peninim (comp. Dukes, Rabbinifche Blumenlefe, p. 89). אֲשֶׁר, like the Latin *quippe, qui*, has frequently a *causal* meaning (comp. Gen. xxx. 18, xxxiv. 27; Josh. iv. 7; Gesenius, Lex. *s. v.*)

10. *For if one fall*, &c. To illustrate the benefit accruing from social life, Coheleth adduces an example of two travelling together, one of whom happens to fall; and, because he has an associate, he has some one to help him up, of which the solitary being is deprived. So it is in the journey of life; union is strength; the misfortune of one is relieved by

fall, the other will lift up his fellow; but woe to the solitary
11 one who falleth and hath no fellow to help him up. Moreover,
if two sleep together they are warm; but a solitary one, how

the opportune assistance of the other.
The Chaldee, Ibn Ezra, Mendelssohn,
&c., restrict the term *falling* to drop-
ping down ill; whilst Reynolds,
Holden, Preston, Stuart, &c., extend
it *to all sorts of misfortunes* arising
from temporal, physical, or spiritual
distress. But it is far more natural
to take it in its literal sense, as
referring to travelling. In the East,
where travelling on foot is general,
the bad state of the roads, and the
long and slovenly dresses of the
Orientals, often occasion falling;
hence the benefit of journeying in
company. A similar passage, where
the advantage of two going together
is set forth, occurs in the Iliad,
x. 224 – 226.

Σύν τε δύ' ἐρχομένω, καί τε πρὸ ὅ τοῦ ἐνόησεν,
Ὅππως κέρδος ἔη· μοῦνος δ' εἴπερ τε νοήση,
Ἀλλά τε οἱ βράσσων τε νόος λεπτὴ δέ μῆτις.

*if two walk together one will always
see better than the other what is advantageous; but one alone, though he sees
it ever so well, is more tardy in his
resolution, and limited in his view.*
יִפֹּל is used *distributively*, referring
to *either* of the two (comp. Prov.
xxviii. 1), and is well rendered by
the Chaldee אִין יִפֹּל חַד מִנְהוֹן, *if one of
them fall;* the Vulg., *si unus ceciderit;*
Luther, *fällt ihrer einer;* Coverdale,
and the Bishops' Bible. The Geneva
Version, "if they fall," which is
adopted by the Authorised Version,
does away with the help which this
passage is designed to express, for if
both the travellers fall, no helper is
left. אִילוֹ, *woe to him,* stands for
אִי לֹו (comp. Ewald, § 241), which indeed is the reading of many MSS.
The interjection אִי, *woe,* only occurs
once more (*vide infra,* x. 16), but
is frequently used in post-Biblical
Hebrew. The Chaldee reads it וְאִילוֹ
or וְאִילוֹ, *if, i. e.,* "if a solitary one
fall, then there is not a second to
raise him up;" but this reading,

though it yields good sense, is not
supported by MSS. וְאִי הָאֶחָד stands
for וְאִי לָאֶחָד, the pronoun לוֹ, for the
sake of emphasis, precedes the noun
which stands in apposition to it
(comp. וְכֹל אֲשֶׁר יִקְרָא־לוֹ הָאָדָם נֶפֶשׁ חַיָּה הוּא
שְׁמוֹ, *and whatsoever man called every
living creature, that was its name*
(Gen. ii. 19; Exod. ii. 6; Deut.
xxxiv. 10; Gesen. § 121, b, Rem. 3;
Ewald, § 309, c).

11. *Moreover, if two sleep together,*
&c. The instance here adduced has
been suggested by the one in the
foregoing verse, and sets forth another
benefit which these fellow-travellers
mutually derive from union. They
not only support each other in their
onward march in the heat of the
day, but cheer and warm one another
in their repose in the cold of the
night. The heat of the day in
Palestine renders individuals very
susceptible to the cold in the night,
which, in times bygone, was not so
effectually excluded as with us.
Oriental houses had no glass windows, and the lattices, made to admit
the light in the day, let in the cold
in the night, which was felt all the
more severely by reason of the
Easterns sleeping on a floor-mat,
and their outer-garments being all the
covering they usually had (comp.
Exod. xxii. 26). Hence sleeping
together was and still is very common, and was regarded as such a
comfortable thing that it is especially
mentioned in the Mishna among the
things not to be indulged in, if one
has vowed to derive no benefit from
his neighbour (Nedarim, iv. 4). This
striking injunction illustrates the passage before us, without resorting to
the explanation of the Chaldee,
Rashi, Mendelssohn, &c., that it
refers to husband and wife, which is
against the tenor of the passage; or
to the fanciful opinion of Harmer
(Observations, i. p. 269), that it

12 can he be warm? And if an enemy overpower the solitary one, two surely will withstand him, and a threefold cord is

refers to sleeping together *for medical purposes*. שָׁכַב, *to lie down*, in order to sleep; hence *to sleep* (comp. וַיִּשְׁכַּב אוּרִיָּה פֶּתַח בֵּית הַמֶּלֶךְ, where the Authorised Version has rightly rendered it, *but Uriah slept at the* door *of the king's house*, 2 Sam. xi. 9; 1 Kings xxi. 27; Prov. xxiii. 34), whilst it has weakened the force of the passage here, by translating it *to lie*, thus deviating from Coverdale, the Bishops' Bible, and the Geneva Version, which translate it here, *when two sleep together*. The וְ in וְחַם, which introduces the apodosis after אִם, is better left untranslated, in accordance with the genius of the English language. חַם, the third person, with לוֹ, the pronoun, is used impersonally, which is often the case with neuter verbs (comp. צַר לִי, *I am distressed*, Ps. xxxi. 10; יָטַב לִי, *I am happy*, Job xxxii. 20; Gesen. § 137, 2; Ewald, § 295, a). יֵחַם is the future A of חָמַם, *to be warm*, with *Tsere* under the preformative, like יֵמַר, from מָרַר, *to be bitter* (Isa. xxiv. 9; Gesen. § 67, Rem. 3; Ewald, § 138, b). The interrogative, as frequently, is used for an emphatic denial (*vide supra*, i. 3).

12. *And if an enemy*, &c. A third instance, to illustrate the advantage of union, still suggested by these fellow-travellers. The nightly repose alluded to in the preceding verse is frequently disturbed in the East by marauders (Job i. 15, with Gen. xvi. 12; Song of Songs iii. 8), who subsist on plunder and rapine, and are always on the alert for travellers. Now, if this lonely miser were assaulted by such a robber, he would succumb, whereas two would successfully resist the assailant. The same idea is strikingly set forth by Lokmân, in the beautiful fable about the lion and the two bulls—

Un lion attaqua un jour deux taureaux; mais ceux-ci se réunirent, et le frappant de

leurs cornes, ils l'empêchèrent de pénétrer entre eux deux; alors il aborda l'un d'eux et le trompa en lui promettant de ne plus rien entreprendre contre lui, quand bien même il se séparerait de son compagnon. Sur cette promesse les deux taureaux s'étant séparés, le lion les mit en pièces l'un après l'autre.

Cette Fable signifie,

que lorsque les habitans de deux villes se réunissent à un même avis, leurs ennemis font contre elles de vains efforts; mais que, si la discorde les divise, elles périssent toutes deux. — FABLES DE LOKMAN, par Charles Schier. Fable I.

The subject of action to יְקֹף must be supplied from the act, as is frequently the case (compare אִם־יַחֲרוֹשׁ בַּבְּקָרִים, *will* (the husbandman) *plow with oxen?* Amos vi. 12; Ewald, § 294, b). The suffix וֹ in יִתְקְפוֹ is a contraction of הוּ; by the dropping of the feeble ה arose â — u, and thence ô (comp. יָרְדֻפוֹ, Hos. viii. 3; Ps. xxxv. 8, *infra*, vi. 10; Gesen. § 58, 2; Ewald, § 249, b). That הָאֶחָד, *the one*, is not *the subject*, referring to *the assailant*, "and if one prevail" (the Syriac, Chaldee, Rashbam, Ibn Ezra, the Geneva Version, the Authorised Version, Hodgson, &c.), but is *the object*, still describing the solitary miser, "if an enemy overpower the solitary one" (the Septuagint, Symmachus, the Vulgate, Rashi, Luther, Coverdale, the Bishops' Bible, De Wette, Knobel, Ewald, Herzfeld, Hitzig, Noyes, Heiligstedt, Stuart, &c.), is evident from verses 8-11; from the term גְּנֵדוֹ, which can only refer to the subject in יִתְקְפוֹ; and from the successful *two*, which are manifestly contrasted with the unsuccessful *one*. For the anticipation of the noun (הָאֶחָד) by the pronoun (וֹ in יִתְקְפוֹ), see verse 10. עָמַד, *to stand*, is used with נֶגֶד or לִפְנֵי, *before*, to express *resistance*, *to withstand* (comp. Josh. x. 8; Ps. cxxx. 3; cxlvii. 17).

And a threefold cord, &c. This clause is added, to set forth still more strikingly the strength and the advantage of combined effort. The lonely

13 not easily broken.   Happier a poor and wise youth than an

miser, who shrinks from having a *single* individual with him, for fear of having his advantages lessened, is shewn that the larger the number of associates the greater the benefit. The alliance of *three* is mentioned, because this number was regarded as representing unity and completeness. Hence the complete adoration of God, both by his angels in heaven and man on earth, consisted in the invocation of a *threefold* " holy " on the part of the celestial beings (Is. vi. 3), and *three* annual visits to Jerusalem, and *three* daily prayers at home on the part of the terrestrial worshippers (Exod. xxiii. 14 ; Ps. lv. 18; Dan. vi. 11).   מְהֵרָה is a later Hebrew form for מְהֵרָה, without the preposition (comp. Ewald, § 315, c).

13. *Happier a poor and wise youth,* &c.   A fourth illustration, to shew the benefits accruing from sociableness, and the disadvantages arising from a solitary and selfish life. The full force of this comparison will be seen more easily if we bear in mind the esteem in which old age and youth were respectively held in the East. Owing to a natural feeling, as well as to the advantages connected with it, old age has always been held in reverence.   In ancient days, when books were exceedingly scarce, and instruction and knowledge were obtained by oral communication, the aged, being the depositaries of the traditions of their fathers, having had intercourse with the wise men of preceding generations, and possessing large experience of their own, were naturally looked upon as the guides and teachers of the people. " With the aged," we are told, " is wisdom, and in length of days understanding" (Job xii. 12; xv. 10).   Hence God himself, when appearing to Moses in the bush, and commissioning him to deliver Israel from bondage, enjoined the deliverer to " go and gather the aged of Israel," and communicate with them first (Exod. iii. 16 ; comp. also *ibid.* xxiv. 1 ; Numb. xi. 16).

The young, on the contrary, were taught to regard grey hairs as " a crown of glory," to rise from their seats when an old man entered the room (Lev. xix. 32 ; Prov. xxiii. 22 ; Siruch iii. 13, vi. 35, viii. 6), and to let him occupy the head of the table at meals (Baba-Bathra, 119 ; Winer, Realwörterbuch; Saalschütz, Archäologie der Hebräer, *s. v.*, Alter; Smith, Dictionary of the Bible, *s. v.*, *age*). Yet, notwithstanding all the privileges belonging to old age, *a young man though poor,* if wise and social, is to be esteemed more than the *hoary aged though rich,* if he be a lonely, foolish, and incorrigible miser. This idea is beautifully illustrated in a Midrashic legend.   The coin which Abraham bequeathed to his posterity as a memorial, we are told, has engraven on one side a hoary aged male and female, and on the other a young man and woman, to teach us that, on the one side, man may be old in mind and young in body, and, on the other, that he may be young in mind and old in body (*vide* Tanshuma on Chayeh Sarah, p 27 ; Hamburger, Geist der Hagada, *s. v.*, Alter) ; or, as the Book of Wisdom has it, " Honourable age is not that which standeth in length of time, nor that which is measured by number of years, but wisdom is the grey hair unto men, and an unspotted life is old age" (iv. 8, 9).   Much ingenious speculation has been expended in the attempts to divine whom Coheleth meant by the old and young kings. From the Chaldee, which merely refers to Abraham and Nimrod, Jeroboam and Rehoboam, and from the Midrash and Rashi, who simply adduce Joseph, David, and Zedekiah to illustrate the declaration before us, modern commentators have affirmed that Coheleth *alludes* to these parties. Others, again, have maintained, with equal assurance, that Amaziah and Joash (so Kaiser), or the high priest Onias and his nephew Joseph, who flou-

old and foolish king who does not as yet know to be
14 admonished. For a prisoner may go from prison to a
throne, whilst a king may become a beggar in his own

rished 246 – 221, B C. are meant (Hitzig). But these expositors might, with equal propriety, endeavour to fix the name of the solitary miser depicted in verse 8, or try to identify the two social individuals mentioned in verse 9. If it be admitted that the sacred writer exposes there an evil feature prevalent in his days, why not concede the same thing here? יֶלֶד, prop. NATUS, one born, a child, a boy, and also a young man (comp. Gen. iv. 23, where it is in parallelism with אִישׁ, man; Gen. xxxvii. 30, xlii. 22, where Joseph, seventeen years old, is called יֶלֶד; and 1 Kings xii. 8, where even the friends of Rehoboam's youth, who, according to xiv. 21, was forty-one years old, are called יְלָדִים. Though the form מִסְכֵּן (from סָכַן, to be bent down, to be low, poor) only occurs here and in ix. 15, 16, yet its signification, poor, wretched, is firmly established by the use of other forms of this root in the Old Testament (comp. מִסְכֵּנוּת, poverty, Deut. viii. 9; מִסְכֵּן, Isa. xl. 20); by the meaning of ܡܣܟܢ, to make poor, in Syriac, and other cognate languages, and by the renderings of the ancient versions and modern lexicographers. Desvoeux's rendering of it by experienced, and Hodgson's by feeble, are therefore to be rejected. מֶלֶךְ, king, is used tropically for one possessing grandeur or riches, as is evident from its antithesis מִסְכֵּן, poor, and from the contrast so minutely observed in the other terms, viz., זָקֵן, old man, and יֶלֶד, young man, חָכָם, wise man, and כְּסִיל, fool.

Who does not as yet know, &c. i.e., who, though having attained to so advanced an age, has led such a selfish and solitary life that he did not gain a kind friend or companion to counsel or admonish him. יָדַע, *to know*, i.e., *to come to know, to learn*, as in iii. 12. זָהַר, *to shine, to have light;* Niphal, *to be enlightened,*

to be instructed, or *warned, to beware* (comp. infra, xii. 12; Ezek xxxiii. 4, 5). The Vulg., QUI NESCIT PRÆVIDÉRE IN POSTERUM, is a loose paraphrase.

14. *For a prisoner may go,* &c. The assertion made in the preceding verse is now corroborated, by adverting to the fact that poverty and riches may change their owners. The history of all nations shews that some, who have been born in meanness and poverty, have, by wisdom and magnanimity, raised themselves to honour and riches; whilst others, who have inherited kingdoms and renown, have, by their foolish and selfish conduct, been reduced to dishonour and poverty. כִּי, *for,* assigns a reason for the preference given to the poor but wise youth. The subject of יָצָא, the third person singular, must be supplied from the action or condition described, *i.q.,* מִבֵּית הָאֲסוּרִים אָסוּר יָצָא לִמְלֹךְ, *a prisoner may go from prison to reign* (vide ver. 12). הָסוּרִים stands for הָאֲסוּרִים, *dungeon* (from אָסַר, *to bind, to put in prison*), as is indicated by the Quametz under the ס, the radical א in the feeble verbs פ״א is not unfrequently dropped (compare הָרַמִּים for הָאֲרַמִּים, 2 Chron. xxii. 5 with 2 Kings viii. 28; מָקֹרת for מְאֹרת, Ezek. xx. 37; Gesenius and Fürst, Lexicons, *s. v.* א; Ewald, § 53, c, § 86, b); so the Sept., Sym., Syriac, Vulg., Rashi, Rashbam, Ibn Ezra, Luther, Coverdale, the Bishops' Bible, the Geneva Version, the Auth. Version, De Wette, Knobel, Herzfeld, Gesenius, and most modern commentators. The derivation of it from סוּר, *to turn aside,* hence *revolters, political rebels* (Parkhurst, Holden), *outcasts, menials* (Ewald), *fugitives* (Hitzig, Stuart, &c.), are contrary to the punctuation. The expression *out of the dungeon,* is used figuratively for *low condition, abject circumstances.*

Whilst a king may become, &c.

15 kingdom. I see all the living who walk under the sun,

As the *first* clause of this verse began with the *causative* כִּי, to assign a reason for the superiority ascribed to the poor but wise youth in the *first* part of the foregoing verse, so this *second* clause also begins with the *causative* כִּי, to assign a reason for the inferiority ascribed to the rich but foolish king in the *second* part of the preceding verse. נוֹלָד, *to be born*, like γίνομαι in Greek, also denotes *to be made, to become*, and is well explained by the Chaldee אִתְעֲבִיד, Rashi נוֹלד, נעשה ולשון הוה הוא, Herzfeld and Philippson. Here, again, the subject of the verb is to be supplied from the tenor of the passage, *i. q.*, גַּם בְּמַלְכוּתוֹ מֶלֶךְ נוֹלַד רָשׁ, *in his very kingdom a king may become a beggar.* Simple and obvious as the sense of this clause appears, yet interpreters greatly differ in their explanation of it. Thus the Chaldee (אֲרוּם אַף בְּיוֹמֵי מַלְכוּתֵיהּ דְּאַבְרָהָם אִתְעֲבִיד נִמְרוֹד מִסְכֵּינָא בְּעָלְמָא, *for even in the days of Abraham's reign Nimrod became poor in the world*) still refers בְּמַלְכוּתוֹ to the young man, and takes נוֹלַד רָשׁ as the only part in this verse belonging to the foolish king, *i. e.*, " for during his reign (*i. e.*, the young man's) he (*i. e.*, the old king) became poor." Rashi refers it entirely to *the youth* (כי גם במלכותו הוא נהפך ממנהג השררה ומקטין עצמו אצל החכמים כמדת הרשים), *i. e.*, " for he was worthy to go from the prison to reign, since even in his own kingdom he made himself poor." Ibn Ezra, again, who is followed by Mendelssohn and Preston, maintains that it is explanatory of the preceding part of this verse, אִיךְ אל תחמה יצא החכם מדבר להפך כי גם הזקן שהוא מלך נולד רש כענין ערום יצאתי מבטן אמי, *wonder not* at the origin of this wise youth, since this old man, who is king, was also born poor, according to the passage, " naked came I out from my mother's womb " (Job i. 21) ; whilst Rashbam refers the first part of this verse to the old and foolish king, who, like the poor and wise young man, came out poor from his mother's womb (בֵּית אַסוּרים), and the clause before us

to his son born during his reign, who is as poor and as foolish as himself. Desvoeux renders it, " and because he was born poor in the kingdom that became his ;" Hodgson, Knobel, De Wette, Heiligstedt, &c., " yet in his own kingdom was he born poor ;" Vaihinger, " yea even in his own kingdom he was born poor." But all these renderings violate the relationship of the two causal particles at the beginning of the two clauses of this verse, and destroy their connection with the two characters referred to in the foregoing verse. The exposition we defend is substantially the same as that of Symmachus, the Vulgate, Luther, Coverdale, the Bishops' Bible, the Geneva Version, the Auth. Version, Reynolds, Hengstenberg, &c.

15. *I see all the living*, &c. Here, again, Coheleth transports himself into the midst of the scene which he depicts, in order to render the illustration more vivid and striking. So great is the popularity of this social and wise young man, that, notwithstanding his humble origin, Coheleth can see all the people desert the standard of the old and foolish king, in spite of his high birth, and flock to this upstart. Luther, Coverdale, the Bishops' Bible, Desvoeux, &c., connect הַמְהַלְּכִים with עִם הַיֶּלֶד, *i. e.*, *walking with the young man* ; but this is against the accents, and against the article before מְהַלְּכִים, which clearly shews that it is in apposition to הַחַיִּים, and that תַּחַת הַשֶּׁמֶשׁ is the same as תַּחַת הַשֶּׁמֶשׁ is the same as רְאִי הַשֶּׁמֶשׁ in vii. 11 ; grammatically, therefore, the predicate can only begin with עִם, before which the *substantive verb*, as usual, is omitted (so the Sept., Vulg., the Syriac, the Chaldee, the Geneva Version, the Authorised Version, and most modern commentators). Why Holden says that " the authorised translation is inadmissible," I cannot divine ; since, in English as in Hebrew, the verb substantive is frequently omitted. עִם, with the substantive verb implied or ex-

16 with the sociable youth who standeth up in his place; there is no end to all the people, to all over whom he ruleth.

pressed, is used for *being on the side of one*, or *belonging to his party, to succour, to help him* (comp. אֱלֹהִים עִמָּךְ, *God is with thee*, i.e., *to help thee*, Gen. xxi. 22; אֶהְיֶה עִמָּךְ, *I shall be with thee*, ibid. xxvi. 3; and εἶναι μετά τινος, Matt. xii. 30). Ewald and Heiligstedt take עִם as denoting *comparison*, and translate the verse, Doch, ich sah all die Lebenden, so unter der Sonne wandeln, in Vergleich mit dem Jüngling, dem Zweiten, der statt seiner herrschen sollte, which they explain, auch dieß Glück ist näher betrachtet nicht eben zu beneiden, sobald man ihn nur mitten im Strom der Weltgeschichte denkt (עם wie ii. 16; vii. 11) wo sein Andenken bald erlöschen wird, *yet even this fortune* (of this young man who has thus raised himself to the throne) *will not be envied if we examine it more closely, and bear in mind that he is in the stream of the world's history* (עַם), *where his memory will soon be extinguished.* But this explanation involves a most unnatural ellipsis; besides, as Elster rightly remarks, had this been the meaning of the sacred writer, he would not have said, "I saw all the living in comparison with this youth," but ".I considered this youth in comparison with all the living." Still more strange is Hodgson's rendering, "I contemplate all the armies which, with the heir, are in motion under the sun." The article in הַיֶּלֶד shews that it refers to the young man spoken of in ver. 13. That הַשֵּׁנִי denotes here one who *forms a second, i.e.*, one endowed with the feelings and happy knack of associating himself with people, *the sociable*, is evident from verses 8 and 10, where it is used in contrast with אֶחָד, *the solitary being.* The common rendering of שֵׁנִי by *second, i.e.*, the man who follows the old one, regarding it as an "explicative," so far from explaining, only obscures, the text, which would be

far more intelligible if this so-called explicative were omitted. עָמַד, *to stand up*, in the sense of ascending the throne, only occurs in later Hebrew (comp. Dan. viii. 23, xi. 2, 3. 20). The pronoun in תַּחְתָּיו refers to the old and foolish king, whom this upstart succeeds.

16. *There is no end, &c.* A further description of the great popularity of this wise youth: the people that gather around him, and whose sovereign he becomes, are innumerable. The phrase, לְ קֵץ אֵין, *there is no end to anything*, is of such frequent occurrence, and the לְ before the object so clearly points out the thing described, that we are utterly astonished how Tremellius, De Dieu, Patrick, Reynolds, Henry, &c., could insert the word "fickleness" before people, as the object designed by the sacred writer, especially as אֵין־קֵץ לְכָל־הָעָם, *there is no end to all the people*, is so manifestly intended to correspond to כָּל־הַחַיִּים, *all the living*, in the preceding verse. It is equally surprising that Mendelssohn should explain it, "there is no end, in the opinion of all the people, to all that they have in their own time," which is followed by Preston, taking the לְ in לְכָל־הָעָם as denoting *according to, in the opinion of*, and לִפְנֵיהֶם to mean *in their own time*, and regarding the whole clause as describing the dissatisfaction and impatience of the people with what they have in their own time, and constantly wishing for new changes, as this would require לְ בְּעֵינֵי כָל־הָעָם. Besides, the second לְכָל before אֲשֶׁר־הָיָה, as the לְ shews, is still depending upon אֵין־קֵץ, and must therefore be taken in the same sense as the first, which is also against the artificial renderings of Herzfeld, kein Ende nahm allem Volke ein Zeder, der ihnen gegenwärtig war, and Philippson, kein Ende war des Volkes, das früher war, auf Jedes Seite. The pronoun אֲשֶׁר, as often, merely

Yet those who will live afterwards shall not rejoice in him, for
17 even this is vanity and striving after the wind.   Keep thy

serves as *a sign of relation*, giving to
the suffix הֶם in לִפְנֵיהֶם a relative signification, *i. e., before whom, whose;* and,
in such a case, is separated from the
word which it thus affects, by one or
more words (comp. אֲשֶׁר הָיָה שָׁם, Gen.
xiii. 3; Gesen. § 123, 1; Ewald,
§ 331, c). הָיָה, *he was,* therefore
refers to the youth.   The phrase
הָיָה לִפְנֵי, *to be before any one,* means
to be his leader, just as הָיָה אַחֲרֵי, *to be
behind any one,* means *to follow one
as being led* (1 Kings xvi. 21), and as
יָצָא וּבָא לִפְנֵי, *to go out and in before
one* means *to command, to lead,*
Numb. xxvii. 17; 1 Sam. xviii. 16;
2 Chron. i. 10; Mic. ii. 13; Gesen.
Lex., *s. v.,* פָּנֶה.   The Chaldee has
therefore rightly rendered it וַהֲוָה
מְדַבַּר קֳדָמֵיהוֹן, *whose leader he was,* so
also Dathe, Holden, Knobel, De
Wette, Gesenius, Hitzig, Stuart,
Elster, Vaihinger, Hengstenberg, &c.
The Vulgate, *infinitus numerus est
populi omnium, qui fuerunt ante eum;*
Luther, unb beš Volks, baš vor ihm
ging, war fein Enbe, unb beß, baš ihm
nach ging; Coverdale and the Bishops'
Bible, " as for the people that have
been before him, and that come after
him, they are innumerable ;" are
contrary to the text.
Yet those who will live hereafter.
Having been led to shew the advantage of sociableness and magnanimity
over selfishness, that the former may
raise the meanest subject to royal
dignity, whilst the latter may reduce
to beggary even a potentate, Coheleth
recurs to his grand theme that, however great the position and the renown which this obscure individual
may acquire, this will not exempt
him from the common fate of all
men.   He, too, will soon be gone,
will quit the theatre upon whose
stage his prudence enabled him to
play so grand a part, never to be
remembered by posterity.   Thus
Coheleth returns to the deplorable
fact, which is the burden of the

prologue (i. 11) and of the whole
book.   For the *adversative* meaning
of גַּם, *yet, nevertheless,* see ii. 14; for
הָאַחֲרֹנִים, *those that will live afterwards,
posterity, future generations,* see i. 11,
and for רוּחַ, see i. 17.
  17. *Keep thy feet,* &c.   Since all
things are thus under the control of
an Omnipotent Power, so that no
exertion of ours can secure for us
lasting good, or avert the evils common to all men, Coheleth submits
that the best thing we can do is to
submit to the laws of God, and serve
him acceptably upon whom we inevitably depend.   In speaking of the
worship of God, the sacred writer
refers to three things — 1. *The going
to the Temple,* taken up in this verse;
2. *Prayer,* discussed in v. 1, 2; and
3. *Vows,* in 3 – 6.   Like all other
terms employed in ordinary life to
describe the physical world, the
expressions *way* or *path, foot,* and
walking, have been transferred to
our moral life.   Hence *the way of
the Lord, i. e.,* the path of obedience
ordained by and leading to the
Lord, wherein the righteous walk,
thus also becoming their way (Ps. i.
6, v. 9, xviii. 21, xxv. 4, xxvii. 11,
cxix. 1. 33, cxxviii. 1), which is
through Christ, who is " the way "
(John xiv. 6), and leads to happiness
(Matt. vii. 14).   Sinners have their
way, which runs counter to the commandments of God (Judg. ii. 19;
Job xxii. 15; Ps. i. 1. 6, cxlvi. 9;
Prov. ii. 12, iv. 19, xii. 26), and leads
to misery (Prov. vii. 27; Matt. vii.
13).   Obedience is therefore described
as " *running in the way* of God's
commandments" (Ps. cxix. 32); and,
as the *foot* is the chief instrument in
this race, its attitude and movements
are used to indicate the moral acts
of man.   Speaking of his obeying
God's Word, the Psalmist says that
he was enabled to do so because " I
have refrained *my feet* from every evil
way" (Ps. cxix. 101); and the Apostle

feet when thou goest to the house of God, for it is nearer to obey than to offer the sacrifice of the disobedient, as they

Paul, in exposing the conduct of those who dissembled, says, "When I saw that they walked not uprightly (with *a straight foot*, as the original has it), according to the truth of the Gospel" (Gal. ii. 14). It is therefore evident that, by the admonition *keep thy feet* is meant that they should be *straight*, and *running in the way of God's commandments ;* or, in other words, that the individual should be obedient; and that it has no reference whatever to the ancient custom of discalceation when entering upon the performance of religious ordinances (Exod. iii. 5 ; Josh. v. 15), as is affirmed by the Midrash Mede, Patrick, Holden, &c. The vowels in רַגְלֶיךָ are intended to shew that the word is *singular*, hence the Masoretic note tells us that the *Yod* is superfluous, which the Sept., Vulg., Syriac, Chaldee, many of Kennicott's MSS., and some modern critics follow ; but, like most of the *Keris*, this emendation is unnecessary, and has probably arisen from a desire to make it conform to Prov. i. 15, iv. 26.

For it is nearer to obey, &c. As regards going to the Temple, Coheleth remarks that to keep one's feet in the way of obedience, which prevents doing evil, is a much nearer way to appear before God than the roundabout path of sinning, and bringing sin-offerings. The adjective קָרוֹב, like its opposite רָחוֹק (comp. Prov. xxxi. 10), is used for *comparison* (comp. קָרוֹב מִמֶּנִּי, *nearer than I*, Ruth. iii. 12). The rendering of Aquila ʹκαὶ ἔγγιζε ὅστε ἀκούειν), the Vulg., St. Jerome (*et appropinqua ut audias*), the Syriac (ܘܩܪܘܒ ܠܡܫܡܥ), the Chaldee (וּתְהֵי מְקָרֵב אוּדְנָךְ לְקַבָּלָא), Luther, Coverdale, the Bishops' Bible, the Geneva Version, the Authorised Version, Hodgson, Rosenmüller, De Wette, &c., and *be nearer*, or *draw nigh to hear*, &c., taking קָרוֹב as an

infinitive absol., *with an imperative signification*, and of Knobel, Hitzig, Stuart, Elster, Vaihinger, &c., *to draw near to hear is better than*, &c., who not only take קָרוֹב as *an infinitive absolute*, but also retain its literal meaning, are contrary to the uniform usage of קָרוֹב, which never occurs as *an infinitive absol.*, but is always *an adjective*, or is used for *comparison*. Still more objectionable is the explanation of Rashbam (והק' יהי לך קרוב לשמיע תפלתך יותר מנתינת וזבחי הכסילים), *and God will be nearer to thee to hear thy prayer than to the bringing of a sacrifice by a fool*) and Ibn Ezra (יותר קרוב לקבל דבריך) אם תקריאנו באמת מזבח שיתנוהו הכסילים, *God is nearer to accept thy prayer, if offered sincerely, than the sacrifice which fools bring*), which, though admitting קָרוֹב to be used for *comparison*, impose too harsh an ellipsis upon the text. Had this been the meaning of the sacred writer, he would undoubtedly have written וְקָרוֹב לְשְׁמֹעַ כְּסִיל. כְּסִיל, *fool*, as frequently is used in a moral sense (*vide* ver. 5) for *sinner, transgressor, disobedient*, thus forming a contrast with שְׁמֹעַ, *to obey*.

As they who obey know not, &c. This clause is explanatory of the remark made in the preceding one, shewing how it is that obedience is the nearer way to God. Those that obey can appear at once before God, as they have not to go and bring a sin-offering first, for they know not how to commit sin. Referring אֵינָם יֹדְעִים, *they know not*, to כְּסִילִים the disobedient, commentators have experienced the greatest difficulty in explaining this clause. According to the Hagadic explanation (הכסיל אינו יודע להפריש בין נדר לנדר, *vide* Midrash *in loco*), it is to be rendered, *for fools know not to distinguish evil*, i. e., from good ; hence the Chaldee, ארום ליחיׁדון דָּיְעִין לְמֶעְבַּד בְּהוֹן בֵּין טָב לְבִיׁשׁ; the two readings of the Sept., ὅτι οὐκ εἰσὶν εἰδότες τοῦ ποιῆσαι κακόν, and κακόν· and hence also the rendering of the Syriac,

v. 1 who obey know not to do evil.   Do not hasten on thy
mouth, and do not urge thy heart to utter words before God,
for God is in heaven and thou art upon earth, therefore let

כֹּהֵ֤נוּ דָ֣עַ֨ מְי֣דֵ֨ לֵמֹכֵ֨דֵ֨ דָּ֣ה,

for they know not to do or *distinguish
good;* but as עָשָׂה רָע is a well-known
phrase, which uniformly denotes *doing*
or *practising evil,* this Hagadic interpretation must be rejected. To escape
this, the Vulg. and St. Jerome, who
are followed by Luther, Coverdale,
the Geneva Bible, the Authorised
Version, Hodgson, Desvoeux, De
Wette, &c., render it *for they know not
that they do evil,* or *when they do this
evil,* or *what evil they do,* which is
interpreted, " for they make no conscience of or do not concern themselves about doing evil, or they understand not when they do it;" but this
interpretation is quite as unwarranted
as the former, inasmuch as יָדַע by
itself never signifies *to concern oneself, to enquire;* and as the *infinit.*
לַעֲשׂוֹת cannot grammatically be translated *that,* or *what they do.*   Still
more untenable are the explanations
of Rashi אין הכסיל מבין שהוא עושה רע לעצמו,
*the fool knows not that he does himself
injury,* Rashbam, שהרי אינם יודעים כסילים
הללו לעשות מעשים טובים, ועל כן הם מזומנים
לעשות רע, *for these fools know not how
to do good works, therefore they do
evil,* and of those mentioned by Ibn
Ezra (יש אומרים כי פירוש רע כמו רצון), *they
know not to do His will,* or *pleasure,*
who are followed by Pagninus, Mercer, &c., taking רַע as synonymous
with רֵעַ (Ps. cxxxix. 2. 17).   Ibn
Ezra, indeed, eludes all these difficulties, by supplying רק, *i. e.,* כִּי אֵינָם
יוֹדְעִים רַק לַעֲשׂוֹת רָע, which is followed by
the Bishops' Bible, *for they know
nought but to do evil;* but an omission
or ellipsis of the most important word
in the clause, which transforms *good*
into *evil,* cannot be imagined. Neither
can the forced renderings, zu nichte
werden bie, bie nur Frevel zu üben
wiffen, *destroyed shall they be who know
nought but to do evil* (Kaiser, Schmidt,

Nachtigal); benn fie verftehen nicht
traurig zu fein, *for they know not how
to be sad* (Hitzig and Stuart), be reconciled with the *usus loquendi* or the
context.   The easiest solution, therefore, is the one suggested by Herzfeld
and Philippson, who refer אֵינָם יוֹדְעִים
they know not, to the subject implied
in לִשְׁמֹעַ, *to obey,* i. e., *those that obey
commit no sin,* as the subject of the
action is frequently supplied from
the act (see verses 12 and 14).

1. *Do not hasten,* &c.   From the
caution given how to appear before
God, Coheleth passes to the mode in
which our requests should be made
known to him.   Two things are to
be observed in offering up our
prayers.   We are, in the first place,
not to hurry on *our mouth* to speak
as much and as fast as it can; and
secondly, we are not to allow *our
heart* to produce its thoughts precipitately; we are to exercise reverence
and godly fear in the manner, and
forethought and discretion in the
matter of our supplications; both
our *words* and our *thoughts* are to be
simple and *few* at a time.   If those
who appear before earthly potentates
arrange their thoughts and words in
an intelligent manner and in small
compass, how much more ought we to
do it, as we ought to remember the
infinite distance between the Majesty
who is enthroned in heaven, and his
subjects upon earth.   *Fewness of
words,* in the presence of our superiors, indicates a due reverence for
their elevated position, and a modest
acknowledgment of our inferiority.
Hence the advice of Sirach, " If thou
be among great men, make not thyself equal with them, and when aged
men are in a place, *use not many
words* " (xxxii. 9), " use not much
speech in the assembly of elders, and
multiply not words in thy prayer"
(vii. 14), and the injunction in the
Talmud, לעולם יהיו דבריו של אדם מועטין

2 thy words be few; moreover, dreaming cometh through the
multitude of things, and foolish talk through the multitude

לִפְנֵי הקׂ״בה, *the words of a man should always be few in the presence of God* (Berachoth, 61, a), based upon this verse, which our Saviour also urged his disciples to observe (Matt. vi. 7). אַל, like the Greek μή, is *hortatory*, and is best translated *do not*, whilst לֹא, like the Greek οὐ, οὐκ, expresses a direct and absolute negative (Gesen. § 127, 3, c; Ewald, § 320, a). בָּהֵל, intransitive in Kal, *to be afraid, to flee in trepidation, to be in haste*, is causative in Piel (comp. Ps. ii. 5, lxxxiii. 6; Job xxii. 10); the prepositions עַל here, and בְּ in vii. 2, with which it is construed, express the *weight* and *constraint* included in the idea of *driving* or *hasting* one onwards (compare Ewald, § 217, i); אַל־תְּבַהֵל עַל־פִּיךָ therefore means, *do not cause thy mouth to hurry or run*, referring to the rapid utterance of a multitude of words, whilst וְלִבְּךָ אַל־יְמַהֵר, *and do not urge on thy heart*, refers *to speaking quickly and precipitately*. The Vulgate, *ne temere quid loquaris*, Luther, ſei niĉht ſĉnell mit deinem Munde, which is followed by Coverdale (*be not hasty with thy mouth*), the Bishops' Bible, the Geneva Bible, the Authorised Version, and many modern commentators, is contrary to the *causative* signification of בָּהֵל. לִפְנֵי הָאֱלׂהִים, *before God*, is a well-known formula, describing *the place where God is present, his sanctuary* (Exod. xvi. 9, xviii. 12; Deut. xiv. 26, xv. 20), hence the phrase נִרְאָה אֶת־פְּנֵי יְהׂוָה, *to appear before the Eternal*, which describes those who go up to the sanctuary (Exod. xxiii. 15; Ps. xlii. 3; Isa. i. 12; Ewald, § 217, l). The plural מְעַטִּים only occurs once more in Ps. cix. 8, יִהְיוּ־יָמָיו מְעַטִּים, *let his days be few;* generally the singular is used (comp. מְעַט וְרָעִים, *few and evil*, Gen. xlviii. 9; Jorem. xlii. 2; Neh. ii. 12; Ewald, § 296, d).

2. *Moreover, dreaming*, &c. Another reason to enforce the caution given in the preceding verse. Not only does the reverence due to an ordinary sovereign require of us to be simple and brief in our thoughts and words, when we address the King of Kings, but the evil resulting from engaging in too many things, or speaking too much on any occasion, forbids us to pursue such a line of conduct in the presence of the Majesty of heaven. For surely, if engaging the mind in a variety of things brings it into a dreamy and confused state, and if indulging the tongue in voluble talk engenders folly, frothy and wordy addresses to God must be an evil. As כִּי gives an additional reason, it must be rendered *moreover*. חֲלוׂם denotes the series of thoughts occupying the mind of *a sleeping person*, as well as *the idle thoughts* entertained in *a wakeful state*, hence *extravagances, incoherent conceits, follies*, which arise from allowing the faculties to dwell upon a multitude of things at a time (*vide* ver. 6); and the בְּ in בְּרוׂב, following a verb of *coming*, may either denote coming *with* something or *through* it. Accordingly, בָּא חֲלוׂם בְּרׂב הָעִנְיָן may either be translated, *moreover, a dream cometh with a multitude of things, i. e.*, it brings with it, is attended with, or makes its appearance under a confused multitude of objects; and קוׂל כְּסִיל בְּרׂב דְּבָרִים, *the voice of the fool cometh with a multitude of words, i. e.*, comes out in an incoherent quantity of words (the Chaldee, Ibn Ezra, Mendelssohn, Gesenius, Noyes, Preston, &c.); or, *dreaming cometh through a multitude of things, the voice of a fool through a multitude of words*, so the Vulg., Rashbam, Luther, Coverdale, the Bishops' Bible, the Geneva Bible, the Authorised Version, and many modern commentators, which we prefer, as it is more in accordance with the scope of the passage. These two parts of the verse are taken by

3 of words.   When thou vowest a vow to God, hesitate not to
pay it, for fools have no fixed will; pay that which thou hast

the Chaldee, Rashbam, Ibn Ezra,
Reynolds, Mendelssohn, Hodgson,
Holden, Knobel, De Wette, Noyes,
Hitzig, Stuart, Elster, Vaihinger,
Hengstenberg, &c., as including a
comparison, i. e., "just as is the case
with the one, so it is (וְ) with the
other." But this has arisen from
ignoring the fact that *two* distinct
objects are mentioned in the preceding verse, *i. e.*, the multiplication *of
words* as well as *of things*, the one
connected with (פֶּה) *the mouth*, and
the other with (לֵב) *the heart*, and that
the two clauses in this verse refer to
those two objects respectively. Besides, our explanation not only leaves
to the וְ its natural meaning, but
solves the otherwise inexplicable
sixth verse.   For עִנְיָן, see i. 13 ;
Symmachus (ἀποβήσεται ὄνειρος διὰ πλῆθος
ἀνομίας) mistook it for עָוֺן. קוֹל, *voice*,
by metonymy here and ver. 5, *speech,
prattling*. כְּסִיל, prop. a noun, is also
used as an adjective (comp. אִישׁ כְּסִיל,
a foolish man, Prov. xiv. 7).

3. *When thou vowest,* &c. Having
spoken of the requisite state of mind
when *going to* the Temple, and of the
reverence and godly fear to be exercised *in it,* Coheleth now speaks of the
conduct of worshippers when *out of
it.* In the Temple, standing before
the Lord, and stimulated by the
conviction that a self-imposed sacrifice has a special merit in the sight
of God, vows were frequently made *to
do* or *not to do* certain things, which
the worshipper sometimes refused
to perform, after leaving the scene
of religious excitement, as the sacrifice appeared too great upon calm
reflection. Such voluntary promises
to God obtained at a very early
period of religious life. Jacob, we
are told, made a solemn *vow* to
devote himself to God, if the Lord
would bring him home safely (Gen.
xxviii. 20). These self-imposed
vows consist of two kinds — I. Positive (נִדְרֵי הֶקְדֵּשׁ), wherein things are

consecrated for religious purposes.
1. *Men,* who are to be redeemed
according to certain prices fixed for
different ages and sexes; a boy from
a month to five years, at five shekels,
a girl at three shekels; a boy, from
five to twenty years, at twenty shekels,
and a girl at ten; a man, from twenty
to sixty, at fifty shekels, and a woman at thirty shekels; a man above
sixty, fifteen shekels, and a woman
ten : if the person is poor, the value
is proportionately lessened (Levit.
xxvii. 3–8). 2. *Animals,* which
could only be redeemed when the
animal vowed was unclean, and hence
was unfit for sacrifice (*ibid.* 9–13) ;
and 3. *Houses* or *fields,* which had
also to be valued by the priest, and
could be redeemed.   II. NEGATIVE
(נִדְרֵי אִסָּר), wherein one promised to
abstain from enjoying or doing a
certain thing, which was solemnly
binding upon all, except a daughter,
when still under the roof of her
father, and a wife, whose vow the
father or husband could disannul
the day it was made, but not later.
Though the Bible nowhere regards
vows as duties, but, on the contrary,
distinctly declares that he who makes
no vows has not neglected any duty
(Deut. xxiii. 23), yet it demands
that what has thus been voluntarily
promised should be strictly performed (Deut. xxiii. 22–24). כַּאֲשֶׁר
תִּדֹּר, at the beginning of this verse,
corresponding to כַּאֲשֶׁר תֵּלֵךְ in iv. 17,
shews that another part of Divine
worship, different to that described
in verses 1 and 2, is here intended.
For the construction תִּדֹּר נֶדֶר, see i. 3.

For fools have no fixed will, i. e.,
it is only fools who waver in their
determination, and do not know
their own will.   The Chaldee (לֵיה
רַעֲוָא דַי בְּמִפְשָׁיָא), the Vulg. (*displicet
enim ei infidelis et stulta promissio*),
Rashi (אין חפץ הק״בה ברשעים הנודרים ואין
משלמים), and Rashbam, who are
followed by Luther, Coverdale, the

4 vowed. Better that thou shouldest not vow, than that thou
5 shouldest vow and not pay. Do not suffer thy mouth to

Bishops' Bible, the Geneva Bible, the Authorised Version, and most modern commentators, take חֵפֶץ as the predicate of God. But had this been the sense of the passage, the words supplied by Rashi would undoubtedly have been in the text, or we should at least have had חֶפְצוֹ instead of חֵפֶץ. In addition to this grammatical difficulty, it is to be urged that the statement, *God has no pleasure in fools*, is too trivial, and tamely anticipates the forcible declaration upon this subject in verse 5, its appropriate place. The Sept. (ὅτι οὐκ ἔστιν θέλημα ἐν ἄφροσιν), St. Jerome (*quia non est voluntas in insipientibus*), Ibn Ezra (ולא תהיה מן הכסילים כי אין חפץ בם), Desvoeux, Mendelssohn, Herzfeld, Preston, Philippson, &c., have therefore rightly taken כְּסִילִים as the subject to חֵפֶץ.

4. *Better that thou*, &c. Since vows are not enjoined in the Word of God, and he who makes none is guilty of no dereliction of duty; and since, once made, vows are as binding as oaths, it is the height of delusion to suppose that God would be pleased with a mere promise for which he did not ask, when the non fulfilment of it involves a violation of his law. Better, far better, not to vow at all, than to vow and not to pay. For the injunction here, see Deut. xxiii. 21–23. The Talmud also cautions against rash vows, and tries to prevent their frequent occurrence, by minutely interpreting the law respecting them (Numb. vi.), and by rigidly enforcing their payment (comp. Tr. Nazir). Hence it is related of Simon the Just (*ibid.* iv. 6), that because vows are often made rashly and afterwards regretted, and the sacrifice is not given with a willing and pure heart, he said, " I have never in my life eaten of the sin-offering brought by a Nazir who became defiled, except of one brought by a very handsome youth, with

richly-curled hair, who came from the South. ' My son,' said I to him, ' what led thee to determine to destroy such beautiful hair?' ' I tended my father's flock,' quoth he, ' and as I went to draw water I saw my reflection in it, and forthwith the evil spirit (vanity) laid hold of me and wanted to ruin me; I exclaimed, Miserable being! why be proud of a property which does not belong to thee? thou wilt soon become the portion of maggots and worms! By the Temple, I will cut it off as a sacrifice to God!' I stood up and kissed the youth's head, and said, ' May many in Israel be like thee; thou hast indeed done according to the words of the law, and made the vow for God.' " Would that there were many among those that profess to follow a higher standard of morality, who, if their right eye offended them, or their right arm, would be as ready to pluck it out or cut it off, and cast it from them! For the use of אֲשֶׁר instead of כִּי, compare 2 Sam. xii. 6, with ver. 10, where עֵקֶב אֲשֶׁר and עֵקֶב כִּי are interchanged (Fürst, Lex, *s. v.*, אֲשֶׁר, 5; Ewald, § 336, a).

5. *Do not suffer thy mouth*, &c. From *the positive*, Coheleth proceeds to the *negative vows*. If an individual has once made a vow to abstain from eating certain food, or from indulging in certain pleasures, he is not to allow his mouth, by partaking of these abjured things, to cause his flesh to sin in gratifying its desires. נָתַן, *to give*, like ܢܬܠ in Syriac, δίδωμι in Greek, and *dare* in Latin, also denotes *to permit, to allow, to suffer*, and is construed with the accus. of the object and the infin. c. ל (comp. לֹא נָתַתִּי לַחֲטֹא חִכִּי, *I suffered not my mouth to sin*, Job xxxi. 30; Gen. xx. 6; Judges i. 34). לְחֲטִיא, the Hiphil of חָטָא, *to sin*, is *to cause to sin*, and is rightly rendered so by the

cause thy flesh to sin, and do not say before the angel that it

Sept., Vulg., and most modern commentators; it stands for לְהַחֲטִיא; the characteristic ה of the Hiphil, though generally retained before prepositions in the infinit., is sometimes dropped by contraction (compare לַחְתֹּם for לְהַחְתֹּם, Exod. xiii. 21; לַאֲדִיב for לְהַאֲדִיב, 1 Sam. ii. 33; לַרְאוֹת for לְהַרְאוֹת, supra, iii. 18; Gesen. § 53, 3. 7; Ewald, 244, b). בָּשָׂר, flesh, like σάρξ in the New Testament, denotes the seat of carnal appetites and lusts (comp. Gen. vi. 3; Ps. lxxviii. 39, and the approximation to this sense, supra, ii. 3). The rendering of לַחֲטִיא אֶת־בְּשָׂרֶךָ by to bring punishment upon thy body (לְמִגְרַם דִּין גְּהִנָּם עֲלֵי בִּסְרָךְ, Chaldee, Ibn Ezra, Mendelssohn, Hitzig, Stuart), or thy progeny (שִׁיפְקוּד הֶעָוֹן עַל בניך, Rashi), or to cause thy flesh to be accused of sin (Gesenius and Fürst, Lexicons, s. v., הָטָא) are unwarranted departures from the signification of this Hiphil.

And do not say, &c. If the mouth has been indulged, and the vow violated, the sin of prevarication is not to be added to it, by declaring, in the presence of the angel presiding over the altar, that it was (מֵרִי שְׁגָגָה) *a mistaken vow;* erroneous vows (נִדְרֵי שְׁגָגוֹת) being one of the four kinds of vows which were not obligatory (compare Nedarim iii.). The God of all the inhabitants of the earth, is also the Lord of the angelic hosts who people the heavens (צְבָא הַשָּׁמַיִם, 1 Kings xxii. 19; 2 Chron. xviii. 18; Ps. ciii. 21, cxlviii. 2), and who, like the abodes which they occupy, have been created by the Divine fiat (Ps. xxxiii. 6; Chagiga, 14). Like their Creator, who is a spirit (πνεῦμα, John iv. 24), the angels are spiritual beings (πνεύματα, Acts viii. 26, with 29. 39; 1 Cor. xiv. 12. 32; Heb. i. 14; Rev. v. 6), and hence are immortal (Luke xx. 36); their number is exceedingly great, " thousands of thousands," " ten thousand times ten thousand," and " myriads," occupy the plains of heaven (Deut. xxxiii. 2; 2 Kings vi. 16, 17; Ps. lxviii. 17; Dan. vii. 10;

Matt. xxvi. 53; Luke ii. 13; Heb. xii. 22; Jude 14; Rev. v. 11, ix. 16), they are always ready to do the will of their Lord (מֲלְאֲכֵי הַשָּׂרֵת, Ps. ciii. 20, 21; Job ii. 1; Heb. i. 14), who manifests his power, his acts of mercy, and his judgments upon this earth, through their agency, thus forming a connecting link between heaven and earth, by their perpetual ascending and descending the ladder which Jacob saw.

The angels occupy different ranks and offices in the various departments of God's government. Seven of them, as the highest functionaries (שָׂרִים, *princes* or archangels) of the innumerable company, surround the throne of God, and form the cabinet (Ezek. ix. 2; Tobit xii. 15; Rev. i. 4, iv. 5, v. 6, viii. 2); viz., 1. MICHAEL, the prime minister (הַשָּׂר הַגָּדוֹל, Dan. xii. 1; Rev. xii. 7. 9), the high priest of heaven, the guardian and protector of the Jewish nation (Dan. x. 13), called by the Jews רבהון דישראל (Targum, Song of Songs viii. 9), and is regarded by Targum Jonathan as the angel who wrestled with Jacob (Gen. xxxii. 25); he attends to the welfare of the Jews (Zech. i. 8 ‒ 14), rebukes Satan for his malignant intentions towards Joshua, the high priest (*ibid.* iii. 1, 2). As the protector of the Jews, Michael contested with the Prince of Persia for their liberty (Dan. x. 13. 20); secured the body of Moses, the chief of the nation, from the grasp of Satan (Jude 9) (a passage which has been greatly misunderstood by Christian commentators, not knowing that this is recorded in Jewish writings; compare Midrash Petirath Moshe, p. 115, ed. Jellinek); and at the head of his angels also contends with the dragon and his angels, who are in pursuit after the child Jesus, "who is caught up to heaven" (Rev. xii. 7). 2. RAPHAEL, who presides over the sanitary affairs (Tobit iii. 17, xii. 15; Enoch xl. 8). " When God would cure any sick

was error: why should God be angry on account of thy idle

person," says St. Jerome, " he sends the archangel Raphael, one of the seven spirits before his throne, to accomplish the cure" (Dan. viii. comp. Arnald's Com. on Tobit, iii. 17), and there can be but little doubt that this is the angel who went down at certain seasons to move the waters of the pool (John v. 4), to cure the impotent people. 3. GABRIEL, the messenger, to announce or effect deliverance. He therefore appears to Daniel, to explain to him the vision of deliverance (Dan. viii. 16), and to reveal to him the remarkable prediction about the coming Deliverer (*ibid.* ix. 21); it is Gabriel who also appears to the praying Zacharias, announcing himself as a *presence-angel*, and predicting the birth of the Deliverer's forerunner (Luke i. 11 – 20), and it is he who six months later comes to the Virgin Mary, to tell her of the birth of the Deliverer himself (*ibid.* i. 26 – 35). 4. URIEL, mentioned in 2 Esd. iv. 1, v. 20; Enoch xix. 1, xx. 2; Targum Jonathan, Deut. xxiv. 6; Bemidbar Rabba, c. 2; Pirke R. Eliezer, c. 4. In the two places last mentioned, these four archangels are described as surrounding the throne of the Divine Majesty — Michael at the right, Uriel at the left, Gabriel before, and Raphael behind; Pirke R. Eliezer places Gabriel at the left and Uriel in the front; whilst the Book of Enoch (xl. 8, 9) gives 5. PHANIEL, instead of Uriel, as one of the four archangels who, with 6. RAGUEL, and 7. SARAKIEL, mentioned in xx. 4. 6, constitute the seven archangels.

Next to the cabinet comes the privy-council (סוֹד הַקְּדוֹשִׁים, Ps. lxxxix. 6 – 8; 1 Kings xxii. 19; Dan. iv. 14, vii. 10), composed of four-and-twenty crowned elders (Rev. iv. 4, &c., vii. 13, &c., viii. 3, &c., and comp. v. 8), who surround the throne of God (Rev. xi. 16; Isa. xxiv. 23), before whom Christ will confess those who confessed him, and deny those who denied him (Luke xii. 8, 9).

Then comes the council, consisting of the seventy angel-princes, the provincial governors presiding over the affairs of the seventy nations into which the human family is divided. Hence Targum Jerashalmi, and Targum Jonathan ben Uziel's paraphrase on Gen. xi. 7, 8, אָמַר יְיָ לְשַׁבְעִין מַלְאֲכַיָּא דְקַיְמִין קוֹמוֹי אֵיתוּן כְּדוּן וְנָחִית וּנְעַרְבְּבָן תַּמָּן לִישָׁנְהוֹן דְּלָא יִשְׁמְעוּן אֵינַשׁ לִישַׁן חַבְרֵיהּ: וְאִינְגְלִיאַת כֵּימְרָא דַיְיָ עֲלוֹי קַרְתָּא וְעָמֵּיהּ שׁוּבְעִין מַלְאֲכַיָּא כָּל קְבֵל שׁוּבְעִין עַמְמַיָּא, *the Lord said to the seventy presence-angels, Come, now, and let us go down, and there let us confound their language, so that one may not understand the language of the other. And the Lord manifested himself against that city, and with him were the seventy angels, according to the seventy nations* (see also Rashi and Ibn Ezra on this passage). Hence the Septuagint's translation of Deut. xxxii. 8, ὅτε διεμέριζεν ὁ ὕψιστος τὰ ἔθνη . . . . ἔστησεν ὅρια ἐθνῶν κατ' ἀριθμὸν ἀγγέλων θεοῦ, *when the Most High divided the nations . . . he set the boundaries of the nations according to the number of the angels,* explaining this passage by Gen. xi. So also Targum Jonathan, בְּאַחֲסָנוּת עִלָּאָה עַלְמָא לְעַמְמַיָּא דִי נְסָקוּ מִבְּנוֹי דְנוֹחַ בְּאַסְפָּרְשׁוּתְהּ מַכְתָּבִין וְלִישָׁנִין לִבְנֵי נָשָׁא בְּעִדָּנָא דְפַלִּוּתָא בֵּי הִיא זִמְנָא רָמָא פִּיצָתָא עִם שׁוּבְעִין מַלְאֲכַיָּא רַבְרְבֵי עַמְמִין דְּאִתְגְּלִי עִמְּהוֹן לְמֶחֱמֵי קַרְתָּא וּבֵי הִיא זִמְנָא אָקִים תְּחוּמֵי אוּמַיָּא בְּסְכוּם מִנְיַן שׁוּבְעִין נַפְשָׁתָא דְיִשְׂרָאֵל דִּנְחָתוּ לְמִצְרָיִם, *when the Most High caused the world to be inherited by the nations who proceeded from the sons of Noah, when he distributed writing and language to the children of men at the dispersion, at that time the Most High descended with the seventy angel-princes of the nations, who appeared with him to see the city; and at that time he fixed the boundaries of the nations, according to the seventy souls of Israel that went down into Egypt* (see also Rashi and Ibn Ezra *in loco*); and hence Sirach, alluding to this passage, says, " For in the division of the nations of the whole earth, he set a presiding angel over every people, but Israel is the

Lord's portion," xvii. 17 (comp. also Tobit v. 6; Targum on the Song of Songs, i. 2; Ibn Ezra and Gesen. on Isa. xxiv. 2). We therefore find that when Joshua advanced on Jericho, and saw the defending angel, he immediately exclaimed, "Art thou ours, or our adversary's?" (v. 13), and the angel replied that he came as the Prince of the Eternal's host; it was Michael, the defender of the Jews, and not the guardian angel of the adversary (comp. Rashi and Kimchi, *in loco*). Hence we also find Michael, the prince and guardian angel of the Jews, come to support Daniel against the guardian angel of Persia, who is to be overthrown by the guardian angel of Greece (comp. Dan. x. 13. 21; and St. Jerome and Ibn Ezra, *in loco*); and hence the four guardian angels of the four monarchies which Zecharias saw (comp. Zech. vi. 1 – 8, the Targum, Rashi, and Ibn Ezra, *in loco*).

Then comes the innumerable company of presence-angels, since every individual has a guardian angel as well as every nation. Thus Targum Jonathan on Gen. xxxiii. 10, says, בְּגִין כֵּן חָמִית סְבַר אַפָּךְ וּדְמֵי לִי הֵי כְמֶיחֱמָא אַפֵּי כַּלְאָכָא דִידָךְ, *for this reason I saw the benignity of thy face, and it is to me like the sight of the face of thy angel* (see also Rashi on this passage). Christ, in speaking of the care and tenderness we ought to manifest for children, says that their angels do always behold the face of my Father which is in heaven (Matt. xviii. 10), upon which St. Jerome remarks: MAGNA DIGNITAS ANIMARUM, UT UNA · QUÆQUE HABEAT AB ORTU NATIVITATIS IN CUSTODIAM SUI ANGELUM DELEGA- TUM, *great is the dignity of these little ones, for every one of them has from his very birth an angel delegated to guard him* (Patav. de Angelis, ii. c. 6). When St. Peter was chained in prison, his angel released him (Acts xii. 7 – 11); and when he knocked at the door, the damsel, who had recognised his voice, and wished to let him in, was told that it was his angel (*ibid.* xii. 14, 15).

Then there are angels who preside over all the phenomena of nature; an angel presides over the sun (Rev. xix. 17); angels guard the storm and lightning (Ps. civ. 4; Heb. i. 7); four angels have charge over the four winds (Rev. vii. 1, 2); an angel presides over the waters (Rev. xvi. 5); an angel also presides over the altar in the Temple (*ibid.* xiv. 18).

Wherever the presence of God is manifested in an especial manner, the angelic hosts attend the Divine Majesty. Ten thousands were present at the giving of the law (Deut. xxxiii. 2; Ps. lxviii. 17; Acts vii. 53; Gal. iii. 19), upon them God comes down as on chariots (Ps. xviii. 10, lxviii. 17), by them his throne is borne (1 Sam. iv. 4; 2 Sam. vi. 2; Ps. xcix. 1; Isa. xxxvii. 16), in their presence God meets his people, and from among them he declares his will (Exod. xxv. 22). Hence the manifestation of God in any place premises the presence of angels, and the appearance of angels betokens the presence of God in an especial manner. Thus, when Jacob in a vision saw angels at Luz, he at once exclaimed, "It is none other but the house of God" (Gen. xxviii. 12 – 17). It is therefore evident that, in places where God is worshipped, and where he manifests himself as he does not unto the world, there angels are present. Hence the Sept. translates נֶגֶד אֱלֹהִים אֲזַמְּרֶךָ, καὶ ἐναντίον ἀγγέλων ψαλῶ σοι, *in the presence of the angels will I sing praise unto Thee* (Ps. cxxxviii. 1), referring to the service of the Temple, where God's presence is manifested; so also the Vulg., *in conspectu angelorum psallam tibi.* Not only were God and the ministering angels present at the worship in the Temple, but, wherever two or three met together to study the Word of God, the Shechinah and the angels were in the midst of them; hence the reverential behaviour, "because of the angels." It is related in the Talmud that R. Jochanan ben Zakkai, being on a journey with R. Eliezer ben Erech, asked for an exposition of the vision of Ezekiel. מיד ירד רבן יוחנן בן זכאי מעל החמור ונתעטף וישב על האבן תחת הזית אמר לו רבי מפני מה ירדת מעל החמור אמר איפשר אתה דורש במעשה מרכבה ושכינה עמנו ומלאכי השרת מלוין אותנו ואני ארכב על חמור, *whereupon R. Jochanan ben Zakkai got down from the ass, and wrapped himself in the fringed garment, and sat down on a stone under an olive tree. And R. Eliezer said to him, Rabbi, wherefore didst thou go down from the ass? And he replied, whilst thou explainest the vision of the chariot, the Shechinah is in the midst of us, and the angels accompany us, and shall I ride upon an ass?* (Chagiga, 14, b.) Hence, also, the much disputed injunction in 1 Cor. xi. 10. The Apostle having shewn in 7–9 the relation of the woman to the man, she — being subordinate to the man, having been created for him, and her δόξα being derived from the man — is to have the mark of being under power, *i. e.*, a covering upon her face, "because of the angels," who, as we have seen, are present at Divine worship, and who would be offended at the woman that haughtily discards the badge of being under the power of man. See also on the presence-angel, 1 Tim. v. 21.

It is therefore obvious that when Coheleth enjoins reverential and ingenuous conduct in the Temple, in the presence of (מַלְאָךְ) *the angel*, he means *a celestial being*, which is rightly maintained by the ancients. Their difference of opinion as to the particular angel here intended, arose from the fact that the angels present in the Temple occupy different offices, and as our text assigns no special office to the angel in question, every interpreter felt at liberty to choose from the different angelic officials any one he liked. Thus, because an angel, being the ambassador of God, is often put for God, the Sept., the Syriac, and Rashbam translate לִפְנֵי הַמַּלְאָךְ, *in the presence of God;* St. Jerome's teacher took it to be the guardian angel of the worshipper, noting down and carrying the uttered

words unto God (comp. St. Jerome, *in loco;* Tobit xii. 12); so also Ibn Ezra, Grotius, Le Clerc, &c. The Chaldee understands by it *the evil angel*, who is in the heart of every one, and who shall arraign us before the bar at the great day of judgment; Bishop Reynolds, again, thinks that it has "some allusion to the history of Balaam, who, when the angel stood in the way against him, made such an excuse as this: It was an error, I knew not that thou stood against me, if it displeases thee I will go back" (Numb. xxii. 34); whilst others think it means Christ, the Angel of the Covenant, who is in the midst of the people. It seems, however, more probable that מַלְאָךְ, like many other nouns, is used collectively for the *angels* who attend the Divine Majesty (so Mede and Patrick); or, which is still more literal and in accordance with the scope of the passage, that *the angel presiding over the altar* is here intended. The opinion of Rashi, that מַלְאָךְ is *the priest* or *messenger who comes for the thing vowed* (שליח הבא להובעך צדקה), which is also followed by Desvoeux, Mendelssohn, Gesen., Knobel, Holden, Hitzig, Noyes, Heiligstedt, Stuart, Elster, Vaihinger, Hengstenberg, &c., is contrary to the general usage of the word. The appeal to the solitary passage in Malachi ii. 7 is nugatory, for there it is the predicate of כֹּהֵן, *priest*. Besides, if a *human* messenger or priest were meant, we should undoubtedly have had אַל־תֹּאמַר אֶל־הַמַּלְאָךְ, *do not say* to *the messenger*, and not לִפְנֵי, *before, in the presence of* (comp. Deut. xxvi. 3, 5, where God and the priest are severally addressed, the former by אָמַרְתָּ לִפְנֵי, and the latter by אָמַרְתָּ אֶל). As to the etymology and form of מַלְאָךְ, it is from לָאַךְ, *to send, to depute, to do anything*, kindred with הָלַךְ, יָלַךְ and שָׁלַךְ, having its primitive root in the biliteral לְךְ, *to move, to be in motion*, and is an abstract noun, signifying *function, mission, deputation*, then *deputy, messenger, angel.* לָמָּה, *why*, is the intensitive interroga-

6 talk, and destroy the work of thine hands? For it is through
the multitude of idle thoughts, and vanities, and much
7 talking; but fear thou the Lord. If thou seest oppression
of the poor, and perverting of justice and equity in the land,

tive used for dissuading or rebuking.
For קוֹל, *prattling*, see verse 2. The
destruction of property (מַעֲשֵׂה יָדֶךָ) is
mentioned, not because it is in keeping with the threats of the Old
Testament, which primarily refer to
chastisements in the present world
(Stuart), but, because the transgressor thinks that, by indulging in the
abjured pleasures, he will be cheered
and strengthened to prosecute his
work successfully, whereas God, by
destroying the transgressors' handi-
work, defeats the very object in view.
6. *For it is through the multitude*, &c. In concluding this paragraph about Divine worship, Coheleth
gives, in a general summary, the
source of all the mischief connected
therewith, against which he has cautioned. The indulgence in the things
abjured, the plea that the vow has
been made inadvertently, as well as
the wrath of God, and the punishment consequent thereupon; all this
arises from being thoughtless and in-
cautious in the presence of God. כִּי,
for, assigns a reason for what is
mentioned in the foregoing admonition, the substantive verb הִיא, as is
frequently the case, is omitted after
it. רֹב חֲלֹמוֹת וַהֲבָלִים refers to the confused and vain *thoughts*, while דְּבָרִים
הַרְבֵּה to the many and unmeaning
words of the worshipper. The particle
כִּי, in the second clause, obtains an
adversative force by virtue of the
negative אַל־תִּתֵּן אֶת־פִּיךָ וְגוֹ in the preceding verse, with which it is connected, *i.e.*, " do not suffer thy mouth
to cause thy flesh to sin . . . . but
fear God, for he punishes sin" (comp.
Gen. xlv. 8; 1 Kings xxi. 15; Gesen.
§ 155, 1, e; Ewald, § 354, a). This
simple construction of the text is
supported by the Sept., the Syriac,
Rashbam, and Herzfeld. The artificial rendering of the Vulg., UBI

MULTA SUNT SOMNIA, PLURIMÆ SUNT
VANITATES, ET SERMONES INNUMERI,
*where there are many dreams, there
are many vanities and innumerable
words*, which is followed by Luther
(wo viele Träume sind, da ist Eitelkeit
und viele Worte), Ewald, Heiligstedt,
Hengstenberg, &c., taking וַחֲבָלִים וְגוֹ
as the predicate of בְּרֹב חֲלֹמוֹת; of Coverdale and the Bishops' Bible, who try
to connect it with the preceding verse
by adding words ("and why? whereas
there are many dreams and many
words, there are also divers vanities"),
the Geneva Bible, and the Authorised Version, making וּדְבָרִים הַרְבֵּה the
predicate of בְּרֹב חֲלֹמוֹת וַהֲבָלִים; of
Reynolds, Holden, Knobel, De Wette,
Noyes, Stuart, Elster, Vaihinger, &c.,
" for in a multitude of dreams there
are vanities, and so in many words;"
of Desvoeux, " for it is in the multitude of dreams that both vanities
and words are multiplied;" Mendelssohn and Friedlander, Bey allen
deinen Träumereyen, Eitelkeiten und
Worten verletze die Ehrfurcht gegen
Gott nicht; Hodgson, "since as in the
multitude of dreams, so in the multitude of words, there are vanities;"
and of Preston, " for in the multitude
of dreamy and vain matters words
also may be multiplied," deviate from
the natural signification of the copula
and the simple order of the words.
7. *If thou seest oppression*, &c.
Closely connected with the service
due to the Supreme Being, is *the
confidence* we ought to repose in his
protection and moral government.
When we see those who are deputed
to maintain and defend justice wrest-
ing from the people that which belongs to them, we are not to despair,
for the power of injustice is limited;
the lawless tyrant is not absolute,
there is another magistrate above
him, who will check his violence and

be not alarmed at the matter; for there is a superior

unjust conduct, and there are still higher magistrates to watch even over this superior one, to call him to account for duties neglected. For מְדִינָה, *kingdom*, see ii. 8. תָּמַהּ, *to be astonished, to be struck with fear* (comp. Ps. xlviii. 6; Jer. iv. 9); the common rendering of it by "*do not marvel*," is incongruous, inasmuch as the assurance here given, that the power of oppressors is limited, and their unjust acts will not escape unpunished, can only be a reason for sufferers not to be frightened or to despair, but does by no means suffice to remove the cause for marveling at seeing justice perverted by the very men who are appointed to uphold it. For חֵפֶץ, which is rightly rendered by the Septuagint, πρᾶγμα, Vulg., *negotium*, Luther, the Bishops' Bible, the Geneva Bible, the Authorised Version in the text, and modern commentators, *matter* or *thing*, see iii. 1. The explanation of the Chaldee (אֵיכְדִין) רְעוּתָא דַיָי עַל כָּל אֵלֵין, *do not wonder how the will of God can tolerate it;* Rashi, אל תתמה על הפצו של מקום כשיביא עליהם רעה, *do not wonder at the determination of God when he punishes them;* and Ibn Ezra, שתאמר מה הפץ יש למקום שלא יושיע, *do not wonder at the purpose of God in not avenging it*, which is followed by the Authorised Version in the margin, Reynolds, Desvoeux, and Mendelssohn, taking חֵפֶץ for *will, purpose, dispensation*, and referring it to God, requires a harsher and more intolerable ellipsis than the one repudiated in verse 3.

For there is a superior, &c. This clause has been variously interpreted. The Chaldee renders it אֲרוּם אֵל אַדִּיר עַל שְׁמֵי מְרוֹמָא נְטִיר עוֹבָדֵי בְּנֵי אֲנָשָׁא בֵּין טָב לְבִישָׁתָא וּמִן קֳדָמוֹ מִשְׁתַּלְחִין גֻּבְרִין נַוְתָנִין וְתַקִּפִין לְמֶרְדֵּי בְּרַשִׁיעַיָא וּלְמֶהֱוֵיהוֹן מְתַמַּן רַבָּנִין עֲלֵיהוֹן, *for the Mighty God* (גָּבֹהַּ) *from on high* (מֵעַל גָּבֹהַּ) *watches* the deeds of the sons of men, whether good or evil, and from his presence are sent forth proud and strong men to rule over the wicked, and are appointed masters over them (וּגְבֹהִים עֲלֵיהֶם), taking the

first גָּבֹהַּ for *the High One*, the second גָּבֹהַּ for his *high habitation*, and the plural גְּבֹהִים for *high rulers*, whom God appoints upon earth to restrain the deeds of the wicked; so also Rashi. The assertion of Knobel, that the Chaldee refers גְּבֹהִים *to God*, is therefore incorrect. Ibn Ezra explains it to mean angels, who, rising one above the other in rank, are all watching the evil conduct of the wicked. For his words, and Dr. Gill's misrepresentation of them, see Introduction, p. 175. Bishop Reynolds takes גָּבֹהַּ מֵעַל גָּבֹהַּ שֹׁמֵר after the Chaldee, *the High One from above is looking down;* and the plural, גְּבֹהִים, he refers to *the angels*, after Ibn Ezra; Bishop Patrick explains it "the king from on high (*i. e.*, his throne, or seat of judgment) observes and will punish it; and if he does not do it, God and his angels will punish both the oppressors and the king;" taking the first גָּבֹהַּ to denote *the king*, the second גָּבֹהַּ his *high throne*, and the plural גְּבֹהִים to signify *God and his angels*, Dr. Gill interprets גָּבֹהַּ מֵעַל גָּבֹהַּ שֹׁמֵר according to the Chaldee, and גְּבֹהִים he takes to denote *the three Divine persons;* Holden, again, paraphrases the Auth. Ver., "for [he that is] higher than the highest *angel in heaven and most powerful potentate in the world* regardeth; *so that nothing happens without his permission;* and [there be] higher than they, *i. e., there are the High Ones of the Holy Trinity, above the princes of the earth and the hierarchy of heaven;*" whilst Knobel, Elster, and Vaihinger maintain that the first גָּבֹהַּ denotes *the king*, the second גָּבֹהַּ *the unjust magistrate*, and the plural גְּבֹהִים means *God*. But, apart from the objections which might be urged against each of these interpretations separately, we submit — 1. That they are all alike guilty of assigning to the same expression, and in the same verse, *three different* meanings, which is a most unjustifiable mode of proceeding; and, 2. The following verse manifestly refers

8 watching the superior, and superiors again over them; and
the advantage for the people is, that it extendeth to all; even

to the king as the climax of the different dignitaries mentioned in this
verse, and it would be preposterous
to suppose that Coheleth puts an
earthly monarch above God. The
Sept. has therefore rightly rendered
it ὑψηλὸς ἐπάνω ὑψηλοῦ φυλάσσει, καὶ ὑψηλοὶ
ἐπ' αὐτοῖς, superior watches over superior, and superiors again over them;
so also the Vulg. (excelso excelsior est
alius, et super hos quoque eminen-
tiores sunt alii), the Syriac, Rashbam,
Luther, Herzfeld, Hitzig, &c. The
substantive verb, as in the preceding
verse, and frequently in other places,
is omitted after כִּי. The preposition
מִן, from, in מֵעַל, expresses the height
from which the other superior looks
down (comp. Esth. iii. 1; Nehem.
iii 28; Ewald, § 219, a). The plural
גְּבֹהִים is used to indicate that there
are a number of other officials, so
that there is always one to correct
the other. עֲלֵיהֶם, over them, refers to
the immediate antecedent, the superiors just mentioned.

8. And the advantage, &c. Having
shewn in the preceding verse that
the power of the unjust magistrates
is checked by those superior officials
who are in authority over them,
Coheleth now shews that even the
monarch himself, who is above all,
and seems to be absolute in his
power, is subject to laws; that he is
dependent upon the industry of his
people, so that even he cannot commit violence with impunity; and
herein consists "the advantage of
the people." For יִתְרוֹן, advantage,
see i. 3. אֶרֶץ, earth or land, is used
synecdochically for its inhabitants
(comp. Gen. ix. 19, xi. 1; Isa. xxvi.
18). The great advantage of the
people is, that this restriction of
power and subordination are not
simply confined to the various officials of state, but are to be seen in
all (בַּכֹּל הִיא) without exception. נֶעֱבָד
is a denominative from עֶבֶד, a servant,
and hence signifies to become a ser-

vant, to be subject (לְשָׂדֶה) to the field.
Rashi has therefore well paraphrased
this clause שאפילו הוא מלך צריך הוא להיות
נעבד לשדה אם עשתה הארץ פירות יש לו מה יאכל
ואם לאו מת ברעב, for though he is a king,
yet is he subject to the field; if it produces fruit, he has to eat, and if not,
he must die of hunger; so also Ibn
Ezra. אפילו המלך שאין למעלה ממנו נעבד
לשדה בעבור צרכו כי ממנו מחיתו, even the
king, who has no superior, is subject
to the field for his maintenance, for
he subsists thereby. The different
explanations given of this verse
are almost innumerable. Without
pausing to refute the Vulgate (ET
INSUPER UNIVERSÆ TERRÆ REX IM-
PERAT SERVIENTI, and, moreover,
there is the king who reigns over all
the land subject to him), Luther
(Ueber das ist der König im ganzen
Lande, das Feld zu bauen, for this
is the king over the whole land, to
cultivate the field), Coverdale (" the
whole land also, with the fields and
all that is therein, is in subjection
and bondage unto the king"), the
Bishops' Bible (" the increase of the
earth upholdeth all things, yea, the
king himself is maintained by husbandry"), and Hodgson (" lo! the
earth is most bountiful of all things;
kings from the earth are supplied"),
which are loose paraphrases, and
cannot be reconciled with the text;
we have to remark that the Syriac
(ܣܘܼܠܛܵܢ ܘܐܝܼܟ ܚܲܩܠܵܐ ܗܘ ܦܵܠܚܵܐ
ܕܢܸܬܒܲܩܪ ܡܲܠܟܵܐ) affords no
help, inasmuch as it is exactly the
same as the Hebrew, and pass on to
examine some of the different versions which have been deduced from
the text. The Sept. translates it
καὶ περίσσεια γῆς ἐπὶ παντί ἐστιν, βασιλεὺς
τοῦ ἀργοῦ εἰργασμένου, the advantage of
the earth is for all, the king of the
tilled field (has it); similarly Sym., καὶ
περίσσεια γῆς ἐπὶ παντὶ αὐτός ἐστι βασιλεὺς
τοῦ ὀργοῦ εἰργασμένου, which the Geneva

9 the king is subject to the field.   Whoso loveth money is

Bible, the Auth. Version, Reynolds, Holden, &c. follow, without, however, taking the לְ in לְשָׂדֶה as the genitive to מֶלֶךְ, and נֶעֱבָד as an adjective or part. passive belonging to שָׂדֶה   The Chald. paraphrases it וּמוֹתַר שְׁבַח פּוּלְחָנוּת אַרְעָא עַל כּוֹלָּא הִיא דְּבִעִידָן דְּכִירוֹדִין בְּנֵי מַלְכוּתָא וּמַלְכָּא מִתְיְהֵב בְּפַצָּחֵיהוֹן כֵּן,קָרָמֵיהוֹן אִין לֵית לֵיהּ עִיבּוּר לְמֵיכַל הַהוּא מַלְכָּא לְגְבַר פָּלַח בְּחַקְלָא מִיתְעֲבֵיד עֶבֶד מְשַׁתַּעֲבֵיד, and the great advantage of cultivating the land is above all, for when the subjects of a country revolt, and the king flees from them into the country, if he has nothing to eat, this very king becomes subject to a labourer in the field.   According to Rashi, שְׂכַר עֲבוֹדַת אֲדָמָה חֲשׁוּב הוּא עַל הַכֹּל שֶׁאֲפִילוּ הוּא מֶלֶךְ צָרִיךְ הוּא לִהְיוֹת נֶעֱבַד לְשָׂדֶה, the profit of cultivating the ground is above all, for even the king is subject to the field; according to Rashbam the meaning is וְיִתְרוֹן אֶרֶץ בַּכֹּל בְּנֵי אָדָם הוּא שָׁוֶה שֶׁיֵּשׁ לְכוּלָּם לַעֲבוֹד אֲדָמָה לְמַעַן יִחְיוּ וְיִתְפַּרְנְסוּ מֵעָמָל יְדֵיהֶם וְאַף הַמֶּלֶךְ יֵשׁ לוֹ לִהְיוֹת עוֹבֵד אֲדָמָה לְשָׂדֶה נֶעֱבָד, as for the produce of the earth, it is for all men alike, i. e., for all men have to till the ground to support themselves by labour, and even the king cultivates the ground, i. e., inasmuch as he deputes his people to do it for his sustenance, therefore he is called a husbandman ; whilst, according to Ibn Ezra, it means כִּי יִתְרוֹן עֲבוֹדַת הָאָרֶץ בַּכֹּל דָּבָר הוּא אֲפִי' הַמֶּלֶךְ שֶׁאֵין לְמַעְלָה מִמֶּנּוּ נֶעֱבַד לְשָׂדֶה בַּעֲבוּר צָרְכוּ כִּי מִמֶּנּוּ מְחִיָתוֹ, for the advantage of cultivating the ground is in every respect, since even the king, who is the greatest in rank, is dependent upon the field for his subsistence. The point in which all these expositors agree is, that this verse is a commendation of husbandry. But, against all these interpretations is to be urged — 1. That they most unnaturally take אֶרֶץ for עֲבוֹדַת הָאָרֶץ, for which not a single instance is adduced from the hundreds of passages where this term occurs ; and, had this been the meaning of the sacred writer, he would undoubtedly have used the regular phrase עָבַד אֲדָמָה, to till the ground (comp. Gen. iv. 2 ; Prov. xii.

11), or at least אֲדָמָה instead of אֶרֶץ (comp. Gen. xlvii. 19. 22, 23 ; Ps. cv. 35) ; 2. That it is contrary to the usus loquendi to connect יִתְרוֹן with בְּ, and render it advantage in, or above, or for, in such cases it is invariably construed with עַל or מִן ; and 3. That it severs this verse from the preceding one, with which it is manifestly connected. The rendering of Knobel, Gesenius (Thesaur. s. v, עָבַד), De Wette, Noyes, Vaihinger, &c., an advantage to a land, in all respects, is a king who is honoured by the land, takes the two manifestly distinct expressions אֶרֶץ and שָׂדֶה as synonymous, makes, contrary to usage, the לְ in לְשָׂדֶה dependent upon the passive נֶעֱבָד, and violates the connection of this verse with the preceding one, so much so, that even Knobel is constrained to say, Der Satz gehör genau genommen nicht hierher, sondern ist als beiläufig eingeschoben zu betrachten, this sentence, strictly speaking, does not belong to this place, but must be regarded as incidentally introduced here. Ewald and Elster's translation, und ein Vortheil des Landes bei alle dem ist ein König der Landschaft gesetzt, and an advantage of the land, in every respect, is a king appointed over the land, i. e., the worst monarchy is better, in every respect, than anarchy, as well as that of Hitzig and Stuart, "an advantage of a land in all this, is a king to a cultivated field," also incur the above-named objections.

9. Whoso loveth money, &c. Not only are the oppressed to be consoled by the fact that the power of the oppressor is restricted, but be assured that these greedy tyrants do not even enjoy the comforts of the humble labourer. For the sinful love of money, which causes them to adopt such criminal means to obtain it, only engenders desires in them which can never be satisfied. That this is the doom of money-lovers experience fully verifies, so much so, that it has become an axiom, expressed in the proverbs of every nation: SEMPER

never satisfied with money, nor he who loveth riches with

AVARUS EGET, *the covetous is always in want.* For parallel passages, see Juvenal —

Interea pleno quum turget sacculus ore
Crescit amor nummi quantum ipsa pecunia
   crevit;
Et minus hanc optat qui non habet.

"Besides, while thus the streams of affluence roll,
They nurse the eternal dropsy of the soul,
For thirst of wealth still grows with wealth increased,
And they desire it less, who have it least."
SAT. xiv. 138–140.

and also Od. iii., xvi. 28; and Ovid Fast., i. 211. כֶּסֶף prop. *silver*, like ἀργύριον in Greek (Matt. xxv. 18. 27; Mark xiv. 11), and *argent* in French, is used metonymically for *money* in general (Gen. xxiii. 13, xliii. 15. 21; Exod. xxii. 6; Deut. xxiii. 20), which in ancient times was not coined, but consisted in bars or ingots of silver, the value of which was ascertained by weight (compare Gen. xxiii. 16; Exod. xxii. 17; 2 Sam. xviii. 12; Strabo, iii. 155), and which does still take place in many parts of China and Abyssinia (comp. 𝔚iner, 𝔑eal 𝔚örterbuch, *s. v.* 𝔊elð; Kitto Cyclop. Bib. Lit. under *Money*). Rashi's explanation of לֹא־יִשְׂבַּע כֶּסֶף by *cannot eat money, cannot feed upon it* (לא יאכל כסף), which is followed by Broughton, Mendelssohn, &c., is incompatible with the reason assigned in the following verse for the remark here made, inasmuch as it is there stated that the increase of wealth brings with it an increase of expenditure, and that this constant coming and going *cannot satisfy* him who loves to hoard up his money. מִי־אֹהֵב is the same as the simple אֹהֵב in the previous clause, מִי, as frequently, being used for the *indefinite pronoun*, *whoso* (vide supra, i. 9), and is rightly rendered so by the Vulgate (*qui*), the Chaldee (מַן דִּי), the Syriac, Rashi, Ibn Ezra, Luther, Coverdale, the Bishops' Bible, the Geneva Bible, the Authorised Version, and most modern commentators. The Sept.'s translation of it by τίς, *interroga-*

tively, which is followed by Rambach, Desvoeux, Schmidt, Spohn, &c., is against its use in such connections. הָמוֹן, from הָמָה, *to hum, to sound, to make a noise,* is properly *a noise,* especially of a multitude (1 Sam. iv. 14, xiv. 19; Job xxxix. 7), hence *a noisy multitude, a great multitude,* either of *people* or *things, a mass, riches* (Ps. xxxvii. 16; Isa. lx. 5; Jerem. iii. 23; 1 Chron. xxix. 16). The distinction which Ibn Ezra makes between הָמוֹן and כֶּסֶף, that the former denotes riches, consisting in a *multitude of garments and merchandise* (ממון בבגדים ומיני סחורות), or, according to others whom he quotes, in *the multitude of slaves and servants* (המון קנות עבדים ושפחות ושמשים רבים), whilst the latter denotes wealth as consisting in *metal,* is too artificial. Hengstenberg's assertion, that הָמוֹן never signifies directly riches, but always noise, or *that which is scraped together with noise, tumult, cunning, and force,* is contradicted by passages cited above. The construction of אָהַב with the preposition בְּ, has no parallel in the Old Testament. תְּבוּאָה denotes the *produce* of the earth (Josh. v. 12; Isa. xxx. 23), or of an investment, hence *profit, gain, revenue* (Prov. x. 16, xv. 6; Isa. xxiii. 3), and is the *accusative* after יִשְׂבַּע, which is to be supplied mentally from the preceding clause, *i. e.,* לֹא־יִשְׂבַּע תְּבוּאָה. This interpretation seems to be the most simple and consonant with the scope of the passage, and is adopted by the Auth. Version, Hodgson, Herzfeld, Ewald, Heiligstedt, Philippson, Stuart, Elster, Vaihinger, &c. The clause, however, is variously rendered; the Sept. has, καὶ τίς ἠγάπησεν ἐν πλήθει αὐτοῦ γέννημα; *who has loved, in its fulness, gain?* i. e., *who has fully loved gain?* taking הָמוֹן as a noun of quality, the בְּ before it as forming a periphrasis for an adjective or adverb (*vide supra,* ii. 21), and exchanging the negative לֹא for the pron. לוֹ. The Chaldee (מַן דִּי רָחִים לְמִכְנוֹשׁ מָמוֹן יַתִּיר לֵיהּ וְגוֹ'), the Vulg. (*qui amat divitias, fructum*

10 what they yield; this, too, is vanity.   For when riches
increase, those that consume them increase; what advantage,
therefore, hath the owner thereof, except the looking thereon
11 with his eyes?   Sweet is the sleep of the husbandman,

non capiet ex eis), and Rashbam, who
are followed by Luther, Coverdale, the
Bishops' Bible, the Geneva Bible,
Knobel, De Wette, Noyes, Heugsten-
berg, &c., supply לוֹ after תְּבוּאָה, *i. e.*,
*whoso loves riches, there is no profit
to him, or has no profit from them ;*
Rashi and Ibn Ezra render it, *and
whoso loves riches, not fruit, shall not
be satisfied* (אהב לקבץ ממון בבנדים ומיני
סחורות ולא יאהב תבואה), supplying אֹהֵב
after the negative particle לֹא, and
making the whole clause dependent
upon יִשְׂבַּע in the preceding clause.
Desvoeux has, *who loveth numerous
company? no income shall be sufficient
for him*, Hitzig, unb wer liebt eine
Fülle bie nichts einbringt, supplying
אֲשֶׁר before לֹא.

10. *For when riches increase*, &c.
One source of dissatisfaction to the
money-lover arises from the fact that
when his wealth increases his outlay
also increases — children, relations,
friends, servants, all flock around
him to take part in its consumption;
where the carcass is, there the eagles
gather together. Pheraulas, who was
born poor, and afterwards acquired
great wealth, though the very reverse
of the mean character here described,
replied to the young Sacian, who
admired his riches and splendour,
and thought that this noble-minded
Persian must now be as happy as he
was wealthy, " Do you think, Sacian,
that I live with the more pleasure the
more I possess? Do you not know,
that I neither eat, nor drink, nor
sleep, with a particle more pleasure
now than when I was poor? But,
by having this abundance, I gain
merely this, that I have to guard
more, to distribute more to others,
and to have the trouble of taking
care of more; for a great many
domestics now demand of me their
food, their drink, and their clothes;

some are in want of physicians; one
comes and brings me sheep that
have been torn by wolves, or oxen
that have been killed by falling over
a precipice, or tells me of a distemper
that has fallen on the cattle; so that
I seem to myself, in possessing abundance, to have more afflictions than
I had before in possessing but little.
. . . If to possess riches were as
pleasant as to obtain them, the rich
would very much exceed the poor in
happiness. But it is obligatory on
him that possesses abundance to
expend abundance, both on the gods,
on his friends, and on strangers.
Whoever, therefore, is greatly pleased
with the possession of riches, will, be
assured, feel much annoyed at the
expenditure of them." Xenophon,
Cyropæd. viii. 3. 35 – 44. Bohn's
Classical Lib. To give in the translation the connection of the original,
we must supply the causative particle
for before בִּרְכוֹת, as this verse assigns
a reason for the assertion made in
the preceding one. טוֹב, *good*, i. e.,
goods, wealth (comp. מִלֵּא בָתֵּיהֶם טוֹב,
he filled their houses with wealth,
Job xxii. 18; 1 Kings x. 7). For
בַּשִּׁרוֹן, see ii. 21. בְּעָלֶיהָ, *the owner
thereof*, is *plural of power* (compare
verse 12, vii. 12, viii. 8; Exod. xxi.
29; Isa. i. 3; Gesen. § 108, 2, b;
Ewald, § 178), with the meaning of
the singular, hence the ו *sing.* in
עֵינָיו, which refers to it. The Masoretic reading, רְאוּת instead of רְאִית, is
immaterial, as this may simply be
another form of the same noun, like
שְׁבִית and שְׁבוּת. The words רְאוּת עֵינָיו,
seeing it with his eyes, refer to his
seeing the increased number of de-
vourers; the Vulg., CERNIT DIVITIAS
OCULIS SUIS, *he sees the riches with
his eyes*, is less appropriate.

11. *Sweet is the sleep*, &c. The
troubles which the light of the day

whether he eat little or much; whilst abundance doth not

discloses to the sight of the money-lover (רְאוֹת עֵינָיו) do not close with the day, since night affords him no relief. Sleep, which gives the weary plough-man repose, whether he lives lavishly or frugally, is scared from the chamber of abundance by cares and fears. The refreshing sleep enjoyed by those who lead a rural life has often been celebrated by poets, both of ancient and modern times. Thus Horace

> Somnus agrestium
> Lenis virorum non humiles domos
> Fastidit umbrosamque ripam,
> Non Zephyris agitata Tempe.

> " Sleep, gentle Sleep, with no disdain,
> Is looking on the roof
> Low nestling of the rural swain,
> Or bank embower'd in shades,
> Not Tempe's breeze-fann'd glades."
> Od. iii. 1. 21 – 24.

עֹבֵד is well explained by Rashi, Rashbam, Ibn Ezra, and most modern commentators, by עֹבֵד אֲדָמָה, *one who tills the ground, husbandman* (comp. Gen. iv. 2; Prov. xii. 11), rural life with the ancients being the type of natural happiness and tranquillity. The Septuagint's rendering of it by δοῦλος, *slave*, as if the original were עֶבֶד, which some moderns have followed, is both incorrect and inapposite. The phrase אִם־מְעַט וְאִם־הַרְבֵּה יֹאכֵל, *whether he eat little or much*, as Rashi rightly remarks (כי כבר הורגל בכך), shews *his contented habits*, his indifference to the fact that he lives lavishly or frugally. אִם — וְאִם, like אִם — אִם, *if — if*, without the וְ, is used disjunctively for *whether — or*, like εἴτε — εἴτε, ἐάντε — ἐάντε in Greek (comp. 1 Cor. xii. 26; 2 Cor. i. 6; *infra*, xi. 3, xii. 14; Gen. xxxi. 52; Josh. xxiv. 15; Ewald, § 361). For the adverbial use of הַרְבֵּה, see i. 16.

Whilst abundance, &c. The disturbed rest of the avaricious and careworn money-lover has also been set forth by the classical writers as a melancholy contrast to the sweet repose of the humble labourer —

An vigilare metu exanimen, noctesque diesque
Formidare malos fures, incendia, servos,

Ne te compilent fugientes; hoc juvat? horum
Semper ego optarim pauperrimus esse
bonorum.

" But, with continual watching almost dead,
House-breaking thieves, and midnight-fires to dread,
Or the suspected slave's untimely flight
With the dear pelf; if this be thy delight,
Be it my fate, so Heaven in bounty please,
Still to be poor of blessings such as these."
HORACE. SAT. i. 1. 76 – 79.

שָׂבָע, *satiety*, like שָׂבָע (Deut. xxxiii. 23), denotes *abundance of things, riches* (comp. Gen. xli. 29; Prov. iii. 10); so Rashi (שובע נכסים), Rashbam (הון רב), Ibn Ezra (רוב ממון), Knobel, Heiligstedt, &c. St. Jerome, however, takes it to mean *abundance of food* (*incocto cibo in stomachi angustiis æstuante*), the repletion of the stomach with various delicacies, which, being more than he can digest, keeps the rich man awake; this explanation is also suggested by Ibn Ezra (או יהיה שב אל המאכל), and is adopted by Reynolds, Mendelssohn, Desvoeux, Hodgson, Herzfeld, Hitzig, Elster, Vaihinger, Hengstenberg, &c., but is incompatible with the scope of the passage. The character here depicted is a greedy money-lover, who is tormented by every item of increased expenditure, and it is therefore not very likely that *such an one* will live *so abundantly* as to be kept from sleeping by " overloading his stomach." Besides, this interpretation mars the contrast here drawn, which is not between faring sumptuously and living meanly, but between *the quiet* repose of the labourer and *the disturbed, the anxious* nights of the money hunter. The simple order of the words in this clause would have been וְהַשֹּׂבָע אֵינֶנּוּ מַנִּיחַ לָעָשִׁיר לִישׁוֹן, but to give prominence to the antithesis, וְהַשֹּׂבָע לָעָשִׁיר is placed at the beginning of the sentence (comp. Gesen. § 145, 1; Ewald, § 309, a). The לְ in לָעָשִׁיר is not the *dative* of *appurtenance*, standing for שֹׂבַע הֶעָשִׁיר, *the abundance of the rich* (the Sept., Vulg., Rashi, Rashbam, Luther, Coverdale, De Wette, Gesenius (Lex. *s. v.*, לְ, 4, c), Ewald (§ 292, a), Hitzig, Heiligstedt,

12 suffer the rich to sleep. There is a sore evil which I have seen under the sun — riches hath been hoarded up by the
13 rich for the owner thereof to his hurt. For the riches perish in some unfortunate business, and he begetteth a

Stuart, Elster, Vaihinger, Hengstenberg, &c.), but is the dative of person, belonging to the verb חִיחַ, with which it is often construed (comp. Exod. xxxii. 10; 2 Sam. xvi. 11; 1 Chron. xvi. 21) The repetition of the dative (לֹו) has been occasioned by the interposition of אֵינֶנּוּ, which, as Herzfeld rightly remarks, makes וְהַשָּׂבָע לֶעָשִׁיר a *nominative absolute*. The genius of the English language does not admit of imitating the order in the Hebrew; in German the construction can be retained: aber der Ueberfluß den Reichen — er läßt ihn nicht schlafen.

12. *There is a sore evil*, &c. The corroding desire for more wealth (ver. 9), the mortification by day in seeing the increased drains upon it (10), and the anxious and sleepless nights (11) which this wicked money-lover has to endure, are aggravated by the fact that his iniquity is visited upon "his children and children's children" (Exod. xxxiv. 7), inasmuch as he hoards up riches for his son, for the next owner of it (לִבְעָלָיו), to his son's harm (לְרָעָתוֹ). The fem. part. חוֹלָה, here and in verse 15, is used adjectively, the relative pronoun אֲשֶׁר as frequently being implied after רָאִיתִי (comp. *infra*, vi. 1), where the full construction is to be found. עֹשֶׁר שָׁמוּר לְ, *riches kept for*, the subject of the verb עָשִׁיר as frequently must be supplied from circumstance (*vide supra*, iv. 12. 14), i. e., *riches kept by the rich man for*, &c. (comp. כִּי לַמּוֹעֵד שָׁמוּר־לְךָ, *for until this time hath it been kept for thee*, 1 Sam. ix. 24, the only other passage where שָׁמוּר לְ occurs, and where, as here, the subject (טֶבַח) is to be supplied from the connection. בְּעָלָיו, *its owner*, i. e., *the o e who now owns it, the heir*, to whom the suffix in לְרָעָתוֹ refers. The rendering of עֹשֶׁר שָׁמוּר לִבְעָלָיו, *riches kept by its owner* (Knobel), Ewald, De

Wette, Herzfeld, Noyes, Hitzig, Heiligstedt, Elster, Vaihinger, Hengstenberg, &c.) is ungrammatical, and is contradicted by the passage already cited, where this phrase occurs. The rare instances of a *passive* participle being followed by לְ which are adduced in justification of this rendering, prove nothing, for even if their correctness be admitted, it is most unjustifiable to create more irregularities because similar ones are to be found, and especially as the regular construction yields good sense. Besides, this rendering, as well as the interpretation which commentators generally give of this passage, are contrary to the scope of the passage, inasmuch as they refer לְרָעָתוֹ to עָשִׁיר, *the rich man* who hoards up riches *to his own injury*, whereas the passage speaks of *two* distinct persons, one hoarding up the riches, and the other possessing them, and the context describes the misery of his *progeny*. The *plur.* בְּעָלִים, as in verse 10, is used for the *singular*, hence לְרָעָתוֹ, *to his harm*, with *sing.* suffix; the Sept., Vulg., Rashi, Rashbam, Ibn Ezra, Luther, Coverdale, the Bishops' Bible, and almost all modern versions, render it in the singular, whilst the Authorised Version, following the Geneva Bible, wrongly translates it "for the *owners* thereof *to their* hurt."

13. *For the riches perish*, &c. Coheleth now shews how those riches have been hoarded up by the money-lover, to the hurt of the owner thereof, or heir. Having come into the possession of wealth, as well as of an unquenchable thirst for more, which is its concomitant, he is led to speculate, and by some important undertaking loses all. This punishment is felt all the more bitterly, because he begets a son in these impoverished

14 son when he hath nothing in his possession.   As he cometh
forth from the womb of his mother, even as he cometh
naked, he returneth again, and taketh nothing from his work

circumstances, whom he must leave in utter destitution. בְּעִנְיַן רָע, literally *in an employment of evil,* i. e., *in an evil* or *unlucky business,* for עִנְיָן, being in the construct before רָע, see i. 13, and iv. 8.   The incorrect and unhappy rendering of the Vulg., *afflictione pessi.na,* has unfortunately been followed by the Geneva Bible in the meaningless phrase, " evil travail," which the Authorised Version has adopted.   Still worse is Luther's paraphrase, denn der Reiche kommt um mit großem Jammer, which Coverdale and the Bishops' Bible ("for ofttimes they perish with his great misery and trouble ") follow.   The pronoun in בְּיָדוֹ does not refer to בֵּן, *the son* (the Chaldee, the Vulg., Luther, Coverdale, the Bishops' Bible, Mendelssohn, Herzfeld, Gesenius (Lex. *s. v.* יָד, i. aa), Preston, &c., but to *the father;* as is evident both from the following verse, which continues to describe the condition of the father, and from the scope of the passage, which is manifestly to set forth the additional grief of the father, who not only loses all, but begets a son when unable to leave him anything. Rashbam has therefore rightly explained והוליד בן אחרי כן שאין בידו מאומה, שאין לו מה יתן לבנו להורישו ולהנחילו, *and he begets a son when he has nothing in his possession, when he has nothing to leave him ;* so also Döderlein, Kaiser, Heinemann, Knobel, Noyes, &c.   בְּיָדוֹ, *in his hand,* i. e., *that which one takes with him, which belongs to him,* hence, like *penes* in Latin, denotes *possession, property.*
14. *As he cometh,* &c.   The riches which this greedy money-lover lost he never recovered throughout the whole of his life, so that he died and returned to the womb of the common mother earth as stripped of all he had as when he came from his mother's womb.   The innermost recess of the earth is represented as the bosom

where the embryo of all things living is generated.   The earth receives us at our birth, nourishes us when born, and ever afterwards supports us, and finally receives us into her embrace when we are rejected by the rest of nature, and covers us with special tenderness (Plin. ii. 63).   Hence the Psalmist speaks both of the womb of his mother (בְּטֶן אֵם) and of the earth (תַּחְתִּיּוֹת אָרֶץ) as the place where he was formed.

For thou hast created my reins,
Thou hast woven me in the womb of my
     mother;
I praise thee because I was wonderfully
     distinguished.
Wonderful are thy works,
And my soul knoweth it full well ;
My substance was not hid from thee
When I was formed in the secret place,
When I was wrought in the womb of the earth
                              cxxxix. 13-15.

And Job, when deprived of all things, spake of his departure as returning *to the bosom of the earth,* in as destitute a condition as when he came from the *bosom of his mother,* using the very words of the passage before us —

Naked came I forth from the bosom of my
     mother,
And naked I return thither.   i. 21.

So also Sirach, " Great travail is created for every man, and a heavy yoke is upon the sons of Adam, from the day that they go forth of their mother's womb, till the day that they return to the mother of all things" (xl. 1).   For שׁוּב לָלֶכֶת, *to return again;* and for בּוֹא, *to come,* and הָלַךְ, *to go,* in the sense of *to be born,* and *to die,* see i. 4 ; כְּשֶׁבָּא is added to כַּאֲשֶׁר יָצָא, for the sake of emphasis, *vide supra,* iv. 2.   נָשָׂא בַּעֲמָלוֹ is not *receive,* or *take away* FOR, BY, or THROUGH *his work* (the Chaldee, Knobel, De Wette, Ewald, Stuart, Philippson, Elster, &c.), but *take* OF or FROM *his work* (the Vulgate, Ibn Ezra, Luther, Coverdale, the Bishops' Bible, the Geneva Bible, the Auth.

15 which he may carry away as his possession. And even this
is a sore evil, just as he cometh so must he go, and what
16 advantage hath he who laboureth for the wind? Yet he

Version, Noyes, &c.), the בְּ in בַּעֲמָלוֹ,
as Ibn Ezra rightly remarks (ראב"ע
בעמלו מקום מ"ם כמו והנותר בבשר ובלחם),
stands for מ, i. e., is partitive, comp.
Levit. viii. 32, " that which remains
of the flesh and of the bread ;" and
especially וְנָשְׂאוּ אִתְּךָ בְּמַשָּׂא הָעָם, and
they shall carry with thee A PORTION
OF the burden of the people (Numb.
xi. 17), and יִשָּׂא בְשִׂיחִי מִשְׁכָּבִי, my couch
shall bear A PART OF my complaints
(Job vii. 13), where the same construction of בְּ נָשָׂא occurs. For the
form יֵלֵךְ instead of יוֹלִיךְ, see Ewald,
§ 131, b. בְּיָדוֹ, in his possession, as in
the preceding verse.

15. And even this is a sore evil, &c.
Having described, in the foregoing
verse, the miserable end of this covetous money-lover, Coheleth submits
that, had it been nothing else, had he
lived a happy life, in the enjoyment of
all his acquired wealth, and only been
reduced to such a condition at the
close of it, even this alone (וְגַם־זֹה)
would be a sore evil, to be obliged
to depart this life in as destitute a
condition as he came, after having
toiled for years, and used all manner
of unjust means to obtain riches.
גַּם, at the beginning of this verse, is
intimately connected with גַּם at the
beginning of the following verse as
protasis and apodosis, as is evident
from the whole scope of the passage;
גַּם — גַּם are therefore to be rendered
even — yet. The Vulgate, Luther,
Coverdale, and the Bishops' Bible
have therefore wrongly ignored this
particle. For זֹה, this, see ii. 2, and
רָעָה חוֹלָה, see verse 10 of this chapter.
עֻמָּה (from עָמַם, to bring together, to
unite, to connect), like עָם (vide ii. 16),
is properly a noun, signifying a gathering, a union, a connection, and, like מִעַן,
is never found without the prefix לְ
(comp. לְעֻמָּתָם, in connection with them,
i. e., corresponding to them, according
to their manner, like them, Ezek. i. 20;
זֶה לְעֻמַּת־זֶה, this one in connection with,

corresponding to, like, the other, infra,
vii. 14). That עֻמָּה should be here
without the לְ, thus forming a solitary
exception to the thirty-one places
with the prefix (comp. Exod. xxv.
27, xxviii. 27, xxxvii. 14, xxxviii. 18,
xxxix. 20; Levit. iii. 9; 2 Sam. xvi.
13 (twice); 1 Kings vii. 20; 1 Chron.
xxiv. 31 (twice), xxv. 8, xxvi. 12. 16;
Nehem. xii. 24; Coheleth vii. 14;
Ezek i. 20. 21, iii. 8 (twice), 13; x.
19, xi. 22, xl. 18, xlii. 7, xlv. 6. 7,
xlviii. 13. 18 (twice), 21), will hardly
be admitted, especially when we bear
in mind the inseparableness of the prefixes from certain nouns when used
as prepositions. To לְמַעַן we add בַּעֲבוּר.
Hence Ibn Giat rightly remarks, לעמת
לא יבא מבלי הלמד כמו למען שלא תחסר ממנו
הלמד ובית בעבור וכלעמת שבא הכף כף הדמיון
והלמד מן לעמת והיה ראוי להיות מלה אחת
כלעמת ונפרד כמו הרבה מן הדבקים שנפרדו כמו
ולאסורים פקח קוח שהם שתי מלות ועניגם מלה
אחת, that כָּל־עֻמַּת is a separation of
כְּלְעֻמַּת, according to the analogy of
מִלְעֻמַּת, the בְּ being changed into בְּ before another letter with Sheva. This
is, moreover, corroborated by the
Septuagint (ὥσπερ γὰρ), the Syriac
(ܐܟܡܐ), which, however, take
the בְּ in כְּלְעֻמַּת as the causative particle,
the Vulgate, Kimchi, Solomon ben
Melech, &c. בֵּן — בְּ, as — so (comp.
Ps. cxxvii. 4; Joel ii. 4; Gesen. § 154,
3, f; Ewald, § 360, a). בּוֹא and הָלַךְ,
as in the former verse, signify to be
born, and to die. For יִתְרוֹן, advantage,
see i. 3. לָרוּחַ, for the wind, i. e., to no
purpose. The untangible and fleeting
wind is frequently used in Scripture
to represent that which has no substance, is empty, hollow, and eludes
the grasp; hence such phrases as " to
inherit the wind" (Prov. xi. 29), " to
bring forth wind" (Isa. xxvi. 18),
" words of wind" (Job xvi. 3), &c.

16. Yet he eateth all his days, &c.
The case, however, is different; so
far from simply dying divested of all

eateth all his days in darkness, and is much disturbed, and

his property, the greedy money-getter has nothing but anxiety, trouble, and vexation *all his lifetime*, both in obtaining and keeping his wealth. For גַּם, *yet*, see the preceding verse. כָּל־יָמָיו, *all his days*, is as usual the accusative of time, with an adverbial signification (*vide supra*, ii. 23). בַּחֹשֶׁךְ, *in darkness, in obscurity*, either because he avoids company for fear of the expenses connected therewith, or he is avoided by every one in consequence of his mean and niggardly disposition, thus forming a contrast to לָהֲלֹךְ נֶגֶד הַחַיִּים, *to walk before the living*, in vi. 8. The Chaldee has therefore aptly paraphrased it, כָּל יוֹמוֹהִי בַּחֲשׁוֹכָא שָׁרֵא בְּדִיל דְּלָחְמוֹהִי בִלְחוֹדוֹהִי יֵיכוֹל, *he dwells in obscurity all his days, so that he may eat his bread alone.* Ibn Ezra's explanation (ביום שהוא אור לא יאכל כי אם בחשך והענין מרוב עסקיו ועמלו לקבץ ממון לא יאכל עד בוא הלילה), *he does not eat in the daytime when it is light, but in the night*, i. e., *owing to his multitudinous undertakings and work to obtain money, he cannot eat till the evening comes*, is too far-fetched, and does not comport with the following clause. Still more objectionable is Mendelssohn's interpretation, viz., the miser eats in the dark to save the light; or, " he consumes all his day in gloom" (Durell, Hitzig, Stuart, Elster, &c.), taking כָּל־יָמָיו, contrary to the *usus loquendi*, as the *object*. As to the Septuagint's changing יֹאכַל into וְאָכַל, καὶ ἐν πένθει, which is followed by Spohn, Ewald, Heiligstedt, &c., it is rightly rejected by the Syriac, the Chaldee, and most modern commentators; and though it is in perfect harmony with the exegetical rules according to which that version was made, we wonder that critics who reject these rules should have adopted this alteration of the text.

And is much disturbed, &c. These are the natural consequences. One who robs the poor and perverts justice, to fill his bag, will be haunted by the sighs and cries of the sufferers, and, however steeled the heart of the

delinquent may be, he will nevertheless experience many a grievous and agonising hour. כָּעַס is an intransitive verb, third person sing., signifying *to be disturbed, irritated, vexed* (comp. vii. 9 ; Nehem. iii. 33), hence the noun כַּעַס, i. 18, vii. 9. For הַרְבֵּה, infinit. absol. used *adverbially*, see i. 16. חָלְיוֹ stands for לוֹ חֳלִי, literally *grief is to him*, i. e., *he has grief;* the suffix, which is generally the accusative, is not unfrequently also used for the *dative* (comp. אֹהֲבוֹ שִׁחֲרוֹ מוּסָר, *whoso loves him (i. e.,* his son), *seeks him (i. e., for him) correction*, Prov. xiii. 24; Job xxxi. 18, xl. 22; Isa. xliv. 21, lxv. 5; Gesen. § 121, 4 ; Ewald, § 315, b). The Sept. (καὶ θυμῷ πολλῷ καὶ ἀῤῥωστίᾳ καὶ χόλῳ, *and in much vexation, and infirmity, and wrath*), the Vulgate (ET IN CURIS MULTIS, ET IN ÆRUMNA ATQUE TRISTITIA, *and in many cares, and in misery and sorrow*), and the Syriac

ܣܿܓܝܐ ܒܪܘܓܙܐ ܘܒܚܡܬܐ ܘܒܐܒܠܐ ܘܒܟܘܪܗܢܐ, *and in much anger, and wrath, and in mourning, and sickness*), which are followed by Luther (unb in großem Grämen unb Krankheit unb Traurigkeit), Coverdale, and the Bishops' Bible (*with great carefulness, sickness, and sorrow*, i. e., *he eats in much vexation*, &c.), making this clause dependent upon יֹאכַל in the preceding clause, are loose paraphrases, and have given rise to the unwarranted alterations of the *verb* כָּעַס into כַּעַס, the *noun*, and וְחָלְיוֹ into וְחָלִי. (Desvoeux, Spohn, Ewald, Heiligstedt, &c.) The Geneva Version, " he eateth in darkness with much grief, and in his sorrow and anger," is only guilty of altering כָּעַס, the *verb*, into כַּעַס, the *noun*, whilst the Authorised Version, "and he hath much sorrow and wrath with his sickness," not only makes the same unwarranted alteration, but also changes וְחָלְיוֹ into בְּחָלְיוֹ, and most unjustifiably construes the text וְכָעַס הַרְבֵּה וְחָלְיוֹ וְקָצֶף. Equally arbitrary and violent are the

17 hath grief and vexation. Behold, that which I have seen is
good, that it is well for man to eat and to drink, and to
enjoy the good in all his labours which he laboureth under
the sun, the numbered days of his life which God hath

renderings, "and anger, sickness, and
wrath multiply," taking הִרְבָּה as " *the
præterite Hiphil,* which agrees with
each of the singular nouns separately,
and the ו final in וחליו is plainly a
mistake" (Durell) ; " and what the
better for having toiled for the wind,
and for having lived all his days in
gloom and great care, in disquiet and
vexation?" (Hodgson) ; " in darkness
he consumes all his days, and much
anger in his sickness and irritation,"
altering פָּעַם, the *verb,* into פַּעַם, the
noun, making it the *accusative* after
יֹאכֵל, and changing וְחָלְיוֹ into לְחָלְיוֹ
(Hitzig) ; or " and is much irritated,
and his infirmity is matter of indigna
tion," taking the ו in וְקָצַף as *explica
tive* or *intransitive* (Herzfeld, Stuart,
and Philippson).

17. *Behold that which I have seen,*
&c. Having shewn that all things
are immutably fixed (iii. 1 – 22), and
that the mistaken exertions made
by men to alter their destinies arise
from impure motives, and defeat
themselves (iv. 1 – v. 16), Coheleth
concludes this section by again sub
mitting that there is nothing left for
man but to enjoy life the few years
of his existence. הִנֵּה, *lo, behold,*
calls attention to what the writer
has previously asserted upon the
same subject. אֲשֶׁר־רָאִיתִי אָנִי, *what I
have seen, i. e.,* what I have found
and propounded before (ii. 24 – 26).
טוֹב, *is good, holds good,* namely, that
it is well to eat, &c. For יָפֶה, *beauti
ful, good,* and then *well* (see iii. 11).
The Septuagint's rendering of this
clause, ἰδοὺ εἶδον ἐγὼ ἀγαθὸν, ὅ ἐστι καλὸν
κ.τ.λ., *behold I have seen good which is
beautiful,* &c., connecting טוֹב with
רָאִיתִי אָנִי, and making אֲשֶׁר־יָפֶה expli
cative of אֲשֶׁר טוֹב, which is followed
by the Authorised Version in the
margin, Geier, Rambach, Rosenmül
ler, &c., who appeal to עָוֹן אֲשֶׁר חֵטְא,

an evil, which is sin (Hos. xii. 9), is
inadmissible, because of the *Quametz*
under אָנִי, which shews that it must
be connected with הִנֵּה. The same
objection is to be urged against Des
voeux, Hitzig, and Stuart, who regard
אֲשֶׁר יָפֶה simply as a resumption of
אֲשֶׁר טוֹב, referring to Zech. ix. 17.

The Syriac, ܗܐ ܡܕܡ ܕܚܙܝܬ ܐܢܐ
ܩܘܗܠܬ ܛܒ ܗܘ ܘܫܦܝܪ,
*behold this which I, Coheleth, have
seen, it is good and beautiful,* and the
Chaldee paraphrase, וְהָא דִּי חֲזֵית אֲנָא
טָבָא הוּא לִבְנֵי אֲנָשָׁא וּדְשַׁפִּיר לְהוֹן, *and be
hold that which I have seen is good, and
that which is comely for them,* which
take אֲשֶׁר as a *copula,* and are followed
by the loose versions of Coverdale
and the Bishops' Bible (" therefore
we think it a better and a fairer thing
for a man to eat," &c.), the Autho
rised Version in the text, Hodgson,
&c., and which have caused Houbigant
and Spohn to alter the text into
טוֹב וְיָפֶה, are most arbitrary and un
justifiable. The loose renderings of
the Vulgate (HOC ITAQUE VISUM EST
MIHI BONUM, UT, *this, therefore as
seemed good to me, that,* &c.), Luther
(So sehe ich nun das für gut an daß es
fein sei, wenn man isset und trinket),
and the Geneva Bible, " behold, then,
what I have seen good, that it is
comely to eat," &c., cannot be recon
ciled with the text. For the phrase
רָאָה טוֹב, *to see good,* see ii. 1. The
suffix in עֲמָלוֹ refers to the implied
אָדָם ; relative pronouns are frequently
used instead of nouns, when the sub
ject is obvious from the context
(comp. *infra,* vii. 1 ; Prov. xxvii. 9 ;
Ps. xviii. 15, xliv. 3; Ewald, § 294, b).
מִסְפַּר יְמֵי־חַיָּיו, as in ii. 3, and כָּל־יָמָיו in
the preceding verse, is the accusative
of time.

18 given him; for this is his portion; and I have also seen,
that a man to whom God hath given riches and wealth, and
if he hath enabled him to eat thereof, and to take his portion,
19 and to rejoice in his labour, this is a gift of God. He should
remember that the days of his life are not many, that God
causeth him to work for the enjoyment of his heart.

18. *And I have also seen, &c.* This
verse forms an integral part of the
preceding one, intensifying its statement. Not only is there nothing
left for man but present enjoyment,
but even for this he is dependent
upon God. גַּם, *also,* is dependent
upon רָאִיתִי אָנִי in the preceding verse,
and the particle כִּי is to be supplied
after it. זֶה מַתָּת וְגו׳ is the apodosis
to the protasis, which begins with
וְהִשְׁלִיטוֹ. The two synonymous terms
עֹשֶׁר וּנְכָסִים, *riches and wealth,* are used
to describe great abundance, and,
being inanimate things, are followed
by מִמֶּנּוּ, the *neuter* in the *singular.*

19. *He should remember, &c.* To
urge us on to the enjoyment of the
present, the only thing left for
man, as stated in verse 17, Coheleth
submits that we ought always to
remember two things; first, the
shortness of our life, and hence the
necessity of enjoying it whilst it
lasts. The prominence which the
sacred writer has given to the first
part of this hemistich (לֹא הַרְבֵּה) gave
rise to the frequently occurring at-
traction; so that כִּי לֹא הַרְבֵּה יִזְכֹּר אֶת־יְמֵי
הַיָּיו stands for יִזְכֹּר כִּי לֹא הַרְבֵּה יְמֵי חַיָּיו
(comp. ii. 24, iii. 21, and especially
xi. 8, where this attraction takes
place in a similar phrase). So also
Rashi, Ibn Ezra (for Gill's misrepresentation of these Rabbins, see
p. 175), Mendelssohn, Herzfeld, and
Philippson. The Septuagint, not
perceiving this attraction, renders
this clause, ὅτι οὐ πολλὰ μνησθήσεται
τὰς ἡμέρας τῆς ζωῆς αὐτοῦ, *for he shall
not much remember the days of his
life,* which is followed by the Vulgate (*non enim satis recordabitur
dierum vitæ suæ*), Luther (denn er
denkt nicht viel an das elende Leben),

who, by way of explanation, has
miserable life instead of *the days of
his life,* Coverdale, and the Bishops'
Bible ("for he thinketh not much
how long he shall live"), the Geneva
Bible ("surely he will not much
remember the days of his life"), the
Auth. Version in the text, Desvoeux,
Hodgson, Knobel, Gesenius, (Lex.
under עָנָה), Ewald, De Wette, Stuart,
Elster, &c., and which is explained
" in the enjoyment of the special
gifts of God, his reflections on the
sombre part, or on the shortness of
his days, will cease to be painful and
distressing to him!" The marginal
reading of the Authorised Version,
"though he give not much, yet he
remembereth the days of his life," is
a literary curiosity.

That God causeth, &c. The second
thing we are to remember is, that
the design of God, in assigning to
us the various pursuits of life, is
present enjoyment. כִּי, *that,* is the
conjunction following the verb of
remembering, as in the preceding
clause. The rendering of it by
because, for, forasmuch (the Septuagint, Vulgate, Luther, Coverdale, the
Bishops' Bible, the Geneva Bible,
the Authorised Version, &c.), or *when*
(Stuart, &c.), is owing to their misunderstanding of the preceding part
of the verse. מַעֲנֶה is the Hiphil
participle of עָנָה, which is so frequently used in this book for *to
occupy, to work;* the literal meaning
of the Hiphil, therefore, is *to cause
to work;* the pronoun אֹתוֹ, *him,* as
frequently, is omitted. בְּשִׂמְחַת לִבּוֹ, *in*
or *for the enjoyment of his heart, i.e.,*
he assigns to him work wherein is
enjoyment of heart, or makes him
work for, or that he might have,

enjoyment. So some interpreters mentioned in the Michlal Jophi יש מפרשים אותו לשון עסק מענין לענות בו והוא פועל יוצא ופירושו כי האלקים נותן לו עסקו (וענין במה שישמח לבו), the Septuagint (ὁ Θεὸς περισπᾷ αὐτὸν ἐν εὐφροσύνῃ καρδίας αὐτῷ, *God occupies him in the joy of his heart*), and the more paraphrastic Vulgate (DEUS OCCUPET DELICIIS COR EJUS, *God occupies his heart with delights*), which gave rise to Luther's version (Gott erfreuet sein Herz), and to the rendering of Coverdale and the Bishops' Bible (" God filleth his heart with gladness," taking *occupet* in the sense of *filling*), De Wette, Gesenius, Vaihinger, &c.; others, however, translate it, *God leaves him to sing in the joy of heart* (הק' נתן לו כמין זה למען יהי' משורר ושמח)

בלבו ולהיות שמח בחלקו בחיו ,מענה לשון מפעיל ,הוא לשון שמחה וזמרה כמו ותען להם מרים Rashbam, Köster, &c.), or *God answers him with the joy of his heart*, *i. e.*, bestows upon him joy, as it were, in answer to his desire (יש אומרים הוא מלשון ענה ועניינו יענה השואל והמבקש כפי שאלתו, some interpreters mentioned by Ibn Ezra, the Geneva Bible, the Auth. Ver., Geier, Döderlein, Rosenmüller, Noyes, Elster, Hengstenberg, &c.), or, *God helps thee in the enjoyment of heart* (מענה עניניו ממציא כמו אענה את השמים והם יענו את הארץ ,והענין שהמקום מסייע לו בשמחתו כי הוא נתן לו והשליטו לאכול ממנו, Ibn Ezra, Mendelssohn, Preston, Hitzig, &c.) But these renderings do not comport with the *Hiphil*, nor do they affect the argument.

SECTION III.

CHAPTER VI. 1—VIII. 15.

Coheleth now shews that wealth is utterly unable to secure real happiness (vi. 1-9), since the rich man can neither overrule the order of Providence (10), nor know what will conduce to his well-being (11, 12). And lastly, *prudence*, or what is generally called *common sense*, is examined, and shewn to be as unsatisfactory as all the preceding experiments. Coheleth thought that to live so as to leave a good name (vi. 1-4); to listen to merited rebuke (5-9); not to indulge in a repining spirit, but to submit to God's Providence (10-14); to be temperate in religious matters (15-20); not to pry into everybody's opinions (21, 22), lessons of prudence, or common sense, higher wisdom, being unattainable (23, 24); to submit to the powers that be, even under oppression, believing that the mightiest tyrant will ultimately be punished (viii. 1-9), and that, though retribution is sometimes withheld (10), which indeed is the cause of increased wickedness (11), yet that God will eventually administer rewards and punishments (12, 13); that this would satisfy him during the few years of his life. But as this did not account for the melancholy fact that the fortunes of the righteous and the wicked *are often reversed all their lifetime*, this common-sense view of life too often proved vain (14), and Coheleth therefore recurs to his repeated conclusion, that there is nothing left for man but to enjoy the things of this life (15).

vi. 1 There is an evil which I have seen under the sun, and it
2 weigheth heavily upon man. Here is a man to whom God
hath given riches, and wealth, and abundance, so that his
soul lacketh nothing of all that it desireth, and God hath
not given him the power to eat thereof, but a stranger eateth

1. *There is an evil*, &c. Coheleth now shews that wealth, too, is utterly unable to secure real happiness. As רַב, like πολύς in Greek, is used both for the amount of numbers, *many*, *much*, and tropically for degree, *much*, *great*, hence interpreters are divided as to the rendering of רַבָּה הִיא עַל־הָאָדָם. Thus the Vulgate (*frequens apud homines*), Rashi (בהרבה כי אדם היא נדהגת), Luther (es ist gemein bei den Menſchen), Coverdale, the Bishops' Bible, the Geneva Bible, the Authorised Version, Hodgson, De Wette, Noyes, Preston, &c., translate it, *it is common, general*, or *much among people*, whilst Rashbam, Ibn Ezra, Knobel, Herzfeld, Ewald, Hitzig, Heiligstedt, Philippson, Stuart, Elster, Hengstenberg, &c., render it, *it weighs heavily upon man*. But as the preposition עַל, *upon*, which expresses the *pressure* or *weight* of a grievance (*vide supra*, ii. 17), and especially as the phrase רָעַת הָאָדָם רַבָּה עָלָיו in viii. 6, denoting undoubtedly *the evil of man is great*, or *weighs heavily upon him* (compare also Isa. xxiv. 20), are against the first rendering, we must decide for the second.

2. *Here is a man*, &c. To illustrate the inability of riches to yield satisfaction, Coheleth refers to a type of man — instances of which we may daily see in abundance among the money-men of our day — whose schemes of emolument have largely prospered, and who has succeeded in procuring all the luxuries that the heart can desire and that wealth can command, yet God has not given him the capacity of enjoying these overflowing resources of earthly good. כָּבוֹד is not *glory*, *honour* (Sept. δόξα, Vulgate, Syriac,

Luther, Coverdale, the Bishops' Bible, the Geneva Bible, the Authorised Version, Desvoeux, Knobel, Gesenius (Lex. *s. v.*), Ewald, De Wette, Heiligstedt, Noyes, Elster, Vaihinger, Hengstenberg, &c.), which is incompatible with the verb לֶאֱכֹל, inasmuch as it would be preposterous to say, *he cannot eat his honour*, but *abundance* (Rashbam, Hodgson, Herzfeld, Philippson, Stuart, Fürst, &c.), in which sense it is frequently coupled with עֹשֶׁר (compare כִּי־יַעֲשִׁיר אִישׁ כִּי־יִרְבֶּה כְּבוֹד בֵּיתוֹ, *when a man becomes rich*, *when the abundance of his house increases*, Ps. xlix. 17; Prov. iii. 16, viii. 18; Isa. x. 3, lxvi. 12). Whether we take אֵינֶנּוּ to stand for אֵין (compare Gen. xxx. 33, xxxix. 9), construe חָסֵר with the dative, as in Deut. xv. 8, and translate אֵינֶנּוּ חָסֵר לְנַפְשׁוֹ מִכֹּל אֲשֶׁר־יִתְאַוֶּה, *nichts fehlt seiner Seele von allem was ihn gelüstet*, *nothing lacketh to his soul of all that he desires* (the Vulg., Hodgson, Noyes, &c.), or retain the usual rendering, *he denies nothing to his soul of all* (the Sept., the Geneva Bible, the Authorised Version, &c.), the preposition מִן does not stand for the object of חָסֵר, but is *partitive* (*vide supra*, iv. 8). As נֶפֶשׁ is of a *common* gender, the verb יִתְאַוֶּה is better referred to it. For מִמֶּנּוּ, the *neuter pronoun singular*, referring to several nouns, see v. 18.

But a stranger, &c. The poignancy of the grief is enhanced by the fact that he who inherits his property, and possesses the power of enjoying it, is not even a son, but a total stranger. To depart this life without issue, and to leave one's possessions to strangers, was one of the greatest calamities that could befall an Eastern. When God appeared to

3 it; this is vanity, and a sore evil. Though one beget a hundred children, and live many years, yea, numerous as may be the days of his years, yet, if his soul is not satisfied

Abraham (Gen. xv. 1–5), and told him that he was his shield, and promised to reward him greatly, the aged patriarch at once exclaimed, מַה־תִּתֶּן לִי, "what canst thou give when I am going off childless, and when the owner of my house is to be Dammesek Eliezer?" No blessing could compensate the absence of children, and no sorrow was greater to him than to leave his acquired property to a stranger, though this stranger was his faithful servant. אִישׁ נָכְרִי, a stranger, one of another family, in contradistinction to one's own son. The explanation of it by foreigner, enemy, plunderer (Reynolds, Ewald, Heiligstedt, &c.), is contrary to the scope of the passage which speaks of a man who did not lose his wealth, but retained it through life, and could not enjoy it. Moreover, the contrast in the next verse plainly shews that a childless parent is here intended. When describing the inability of the owner of the property to enjoy, the sacred writer used the partitive יֹאכַל מִמֶּנּוּ, eat of it, enjoy any part of it; but, when speaking of the stranger who comes into possession of the property, he is described as יֹאכְלֶנּוּ, without the partitive, enjoying it all.

3. Though one beget, &c. So great, however, is the misery of not being able to enjoy one's property, that, even if the case were the very reverse of what it was stated to be in the preceding verse; if, instead of being childless and leaving one's possessions to a stranger, one had been blessed with an unusually large number of children; and if, instead of departing this life, and bequeathing one's property at the ordinary time allotted to man, one lived an extraordinary number of years in the possession of his wealth, yet, if he had not the power of enjoying it, an abortion is far better

than he. אִם, as often, is used concessively, and, as is generally the case, is followed by the imperfect (comp. אִם־יַעֲלֶה לַשָּׁמַיִם שִׂיאוֹ, though his height were to mount up to heaven, Job xx. 6; Isa. i. 18; Ps. cxxxix. 8; Gesen. § 155, 2, g; Ewald, § 362, b). אִישׁ, a man, any one, one (comp. Gen. xiii. 16; Exod. xvi. 29; Song of Songs viii. 7). מֵאָה is neither here nor elsewhere used adverbially for a hundred times (Knobel, &c.), but invariably signifies a hundred; the object, as is frequently the case with numerals, is implied, and must be taken from the context. Here, of course, with the Chaldee, Rashi, Ibn Ezra, &c., we must supply בָּנִים (compare עֲקָרָה יָלְדָה שִׁבְעָה, the barren woman hath born seven, i. e., children, 1 Sam. ii. 5, and vide infra, viii. 12). Durell's construction of אִישׁ with מֵאָה, i. e., though he beget a hundred males, is ungrammatical, as מֵאָה cannot stand after a noun singular. Besides, בָּנִים is used in such a case, and not אִישׁ. Though some have had nearly as many children (comp. 2 Chron. xi. 21; 2 Kings x. 1), yet it will hardly be questioned that מֵאָה is used as a round number for a great many (comp. Gen. xxvi. 12; 2 Sam. xxiv. 3; Prov. xvii. 10; 1 Cor. xiv. 19; and see infra, viii. 12). רַב, much, many, is used adverbially, and like כְּמַט (vide supra, v. 1) is joined to substantives plural (comp. בְּרָקִים רַב, lightnings much, i. e., a great many, in great number, Deut. xxxiii. 7; Ps. xviii. 15. The וְ in וְרַב is cumulative, augmenting and intensifying the concession made in the first clause, i. e., numerous as may be, &c. Overlooking this, many interpreters have found it difficult to explain this hemistich, without producing a truism or tautology. The unhappy rendering of the Vulg., ET VIXERIT MULTOS ANNOS ET PLURES DIES ÆTATIS HABUERIT, and live many

with good, and even if the grave did not wait for him, I say,

years, and have many days of years,
which is followed by Luther (unb
hätte so langes Leben, baß er viele
Jahre überlebte), Coverdale, the
Bishops' Bible, the Auth. Version
(" and live many years, so that the
days of his years be many "), Reynolds, Preston, &c., or, " and live
many years, and the days of his
years be multiplied" (the Geneva
Bible, De Wette, &c.), must strike
every reader, as if one could live
many years *without living many
days.* To avoid this awkwardness,
the Chaldee explains this clause,
וּבִשְׁלָטָנוּתָא וְרַבָּנוּתָא הוּא דִי יְהוֹן יוֹמֵי שְׁנוֹהִי,
*and if he had been in power and domi-
nion all the days of his life,* taking רַב
to denote a *chief, leader, a great man,*
which is followed by Desvoeux,
Knobel, Vaihinger, &c. But against
this is to be urged, that רַב as a
substantive, in the sense of *chief,* is
invariably followed by the *genitive of
that over which he is the chief.* Rashi
and Ibn Ezra, again, explain רַב by
plenty, abundance (רב הון וכל טוב ימי שלו),
i. e., if he had plenty of riches, and
all manner of good the days of his
life. But this requires too great and
too harsh an ellipsis; and, if the
sacred writer had intended to convey
this sense, he would undoubtedly
have written וְרַב טוב לו. Gill's assertion, that Rashi interprets it " *sufficient,* he lives as long as is desirable,"
when Rashi's words are רב ורב לשון די
די לכל טובה, meaning *plenty of all sorts
of good,* is another lamentable proof
of his misrepresenting the Rabbins.
Whilst Durell, dissatisfied with all
these explanations, alters שֶׁיִּהְיוּ into
שְׂיָחוּ (compare 1 Sam. xiv. 34), and
translates it, " and his sheep (here
taken for substance in general) be
great all the days of his life." This
requires no refutation.

And even if the grave, &c. The
augmentation, rising in scale, has
here reached its climax. Not only
would numerous years not compensate for the inability of enjoying one's
property, but even (וְגַם, see ver. 5) if

the grave were not to exist for such
a man, if he were never to die, an
untimely birth, which has had no life
at all, would be preferable to him,
though in the possession of perpetual
life, so extraordinary and great a
boon. Great difficulty has been experienced in the exposition of this
clause. Already St. Jerome mentions
different explanations of it — 1. It
means that, having been occupied
for so many years in amassing wealth,
and having laid up so much for many
years to come, the rich man did not
think of death or burial, and hence
" has no burial" in his mind, does
not remember that he must die, and
is not prepared for it. 2. It means
that his covetous heart does not
allow him to provide a respectable
sepulchre for his remains (so also the
Chaldee, Patrick, Clark, Knobel,
Stuart, &c.) 3. It means that he
is assaulted and murdered for his
wealth, and his body is cast away
without interment (so also Rashi).
4. It means that he has no burial,
because he has not lived; having
done no good or worthy thing whereby
to perpetuate his memory among his
posterity, but having allowed his life
to pass away in silence like a beast.
This opinion St. Jerome himself
adopts. 5. According to Rashbam,
again, it means that he has lost his
money, and therefore was not buried
(so also Desvoeux, Ewald, &c.) 6.
It means that his heirs deny him an
honourable interment for want of respect (Reynols, Mendelssohn, Holden, Elster, Philippson, &c.) 7. It
is a marginal gloss, put inadvertently
into the text (Hitzig). Passing over
the emendations of the text as unwarranted and arbitrary, we submit
that these explanations, making Coheleth speak of interment, or of funeral honours, or of a monument to
perpetuate his memory, are totally at
variance with the argument before
us. 1. The object of the sacred writer
is not to contrast the ignominy of a
graveless corpse with the blessedness

4 Better than he is an untimely birth ; for this cometh in
　nothingness and goeth in darkness, and with darkness is its
5 memory covered ; it doth not even see, and doth not know

of a long and fruitful life, but to shew
that nothing, *not even a long and
fruitful life*, can compensate for the
inability of enjoying one's possessions. He therefore puts a prosperous, fruitful, and *long life* in the
balance with the want of power to
enjoy overflowing riches, and finds
the latter so miserably wanting, that
he prefers nauseous *lifelessness* to such
a *long life*, as the fifth verse unmistakeably shews. 2. קְבוּרָה invariably
means a *burial-place*, a *grave*, a
sepulchre. Jer. xxii. 19, the only instance which Gesenius adduces in his
lexicon to shew that it signifies *burial*,
the action of burying, *sepulture*, forms
no exception, inasmuch as קְבוּרַת חֲמוֹר
יִקָּבֵר is better rendered *in the sepulchre
of an ass he shall be buried*. Besides,
the Jews had too great a respect for
their dead to deny a grave to one
who happened to be a miser, or to lose
his money. 3. The concessive particle גַּם shews, beyond doubt, that the
climax is here reached by the concessions. These facts are also against
those who interpret this clause as. referring to *accidental absence of funeral
honours*, or *of a grave*. Now, in
Scripture language, *very long life* is
hyperbolically described by *not seeing
death*, or *the grave* (comp. the phrases
לֹא יִרְאֶה מָוֶת, μὴ ἰδεῖν θάνατον, *not to see
death*, Ps. lxxxix. 49; Heb. xi. 5),
and לֹא רָאָה שָׁחַת, *not to see the grave*
(Ps. xvi. 10, xlix. 10), whilst a *speedy
death* is described by *the grave waiting for one* (comp. לִי קְבָרִים, *graves wait
for me*, Job xvii. 1). In the face of
the last-cited passage, the sense of
קְבוּרָה לֹא הָיְתָה לוֹ, *the grave is not waiting
for him*, will at once be obvious.
אָמַרְתִּי, the *perfect*, like *novi, memini,
odi*, in Latin, and οἶδα, μέμνημαι in
Greek, is used for the *present* (comp.
infra, viii. 14, ix. 16; Gesen. § 126,
3; Ewald, § 135, b). The comparison
of one in great misery with an untimely birth also occurs in Job iii. 16.

4. *For this cometh*, &c. The fate
of the untimely birth is preferable,
because it is a mere nothing when
born; it is immediately and quietly
put out of sight, and nothing is
known about it. בָּא, *to come*, *i. e.*,
into existence. הֶבֶל, *nothingness*, *i. e.*,
a mere nothing in size and form.
יֵלֵךְ, *it goes*, *i.e.*, to be buried. בַּחֹשֶׁךְ,
in darkness, in obscurity, as untimely
births are removed and interred
without its being known, whilst the
funerals of grown-up and aged people
are attended with much noise and
great ceremonies. שֵׁם, when used
in connection with the departed,
denotes *memory* = זֵכֶר (comp. Deut.
ix. 14; 1 Sam. xxiv. 22; 2 Sam.
xiv. 7; Ps. lxxii. 17). That it is
here *memory*, and not " name," is
evident from the fact that, being an
untimely birth, it had no name
given to it. Some indeed (the Vulg.,
the Chaldee, Luther, Coverdale, the
Bishops' Bible, the Geneva Version,
the Authorised Version, Jermin, &c.)
refer this verse to the man who has
no ability to enjoy his property, and
others (Rashbam, Reynolds, Patrick,
Gill, Desvoeux, &c.) to both *the
joyless man* and *the untimely birth ;*
but the following verse, which continues this subject, as is evident from
the expression גַּם, leaves it beyond
the shadow of a doubt that it refers
to the abortion, the immediate antecedent. (So Rashi, Ibn Ezra, Mendelssohn, Scott, Clarke, Holden,
Knobel, De Wette, Herzfeld, Ewald,
Gesenius, Preston, Noyes, Stuart,
Elster,Vaihinger, Hengstenberg,&c.)
For Jermin's remarkable explanation of this verse, see p. 140.
　5. *It doth not even see*, &c. And
not having lived at all, the untimely
birth is free from all the ills and
sufferings of life with which the joyless rich man is loaded, and hence it
has more rest than he. Bearing in
mind what a luxury rest is with

6 the sun; it hath more rest than he. And if he live twice a thousand years and see no good, do not both go to the same

Orientals, how eagerly they desire it, and how highly they prize it; that from this circumstance the rest promised in the land of Canaan, as well as in the heavenly Canaan, has borrowed its imagery; we shall be able to enter more fully into the preference here given to the reposing abortive. Of course the contrast is between the ever-busy, careworn, and annoyed speculator, who is *living*, and active, and the untimely birth, which is *dead*, and resting; for in death both rest alike. We should have deemed this remark superfluous had not some interpreters mistaken the comparison. גַּם denotes *accession*, augmenting and intensifying what has already been said, setting forth more definitely and largely the idea commenced with the words בְּהֶבֶל בָּא, *i. e.*, it is not only a mere nothing in its size and form, but has no life as well, being dead prior to its birth. רָאָה שֶׁמֶשׁ, *to see the sun* (i. q., רָאָה אוֹר חָזָה שֶׁמֶשׁ), is an established phrase denoting *to live* (comp. *infra*, vii. 11, xi. 7; Job iii. 16; Ps. xlix. 20, lviii. 9), and has its analogy in the Greek ὁρᾷ φάος ἠελίοιο (Hom. II. Σ 61), ὃ λαμπρὸς αἰθήρ, ἡμέρας ἀγνὸν φάος ὡς λεύσσειν (Eurip. Hippol.), and in the Latin, *luminibus uti, diem videre* (Ovid. Frist. v. 4, 44), as well as in our phrase *to see the light of the day*, and is evidently chosen because of חֹשֶׁךְ in the preceding verse. יָדַע, as frequently, is added to רָאָה, to augment and inten- sify the idea (comp. 1 Sam. xii. 17, xxiii. 23, xxv. 17; 2 Sam. xxiv. 13; 1 Kings xx. 7. 22; 2 Kings v. 7). The explanation, *not felt any worldly happiness*, which Reynolds, Mendels- sohn, Herzfeld, &c., give to this pas- sage, is therefore contrary to the usage of this phrase. The compli- cated rendering of the Sept., καὶ οὐκ ἔγνω ἀνάπαυσις τούτῳ ὑπὲρ τοῦτον, *and has not known rest to this above that*, detaches יָדַע from רָאָה, and connects it with the following part of the

hemistich, against the accents and the usual connection of these two verbs. So does also the traditional paraphrase of the Chaldee, וְלָא יְדַע בֵּין טָב לְבִישׁ לְמִבְחָן בֵּין עָלְמָא הָדֵין לְעָלְמָא דְאָתֵי, *and he does not know between good and evil, to choose between this world and the world to come*, which is fol- lowed by the Vulg. (NEQUE COGNOVIT DISTANTIAM BONI ET MALI, *nor does he know the difference between good and evil*), Luther (und weiß keine Ruhe weder hie noch da), Coverdale ("and knoweth of no rest, neither here nor there"). Ibn Ezra, too, separates it from the preceding verb, and is consequently obliged to supply the word מְאוּמָה, which is followed by the Bishops' Bible, the Geneva Ver., the Authorised Version, &c. נַחַת, *rest*, and then *good* as resulting therefrom, as is evident from טוֹב מִמֶּנוּ הַנָּפֶל in verse 3, for which the synonymous נַחַת לָזֶה מִזֶּה is here used (comp. also iv. 6). For מִזֶּה, standing for מִזֶּה, see ii. 7.

6. *And if he live*, &c. But after all the concessions made in verse 3, however extraordinarily long the life of this rich man may be, it must eventually terminate, and he go to the same place as the abortion; so that his long life, joylessly spent, not only placed him below the un- timely birth as long as it lasted, but is of no advantage to him in death, since he must share the same doom as the abortion. אִלּוּ, *if* (a contrac- tion of אִם, *if*, and לוּ, *if*), which only occurs once more in the Old Testa- ment (Esth. vii. 4) is a particle of later Hebrew, and is frequently used in the Targums, the Mishna, and the Syriac. The subject of חָיָה, *he lived*, is still אִישׁ, *a man, one*, men- tioned in verse 3, to whom the rela- tive pronoun מִזֶּה refers, with which the preceding verse concludes. אֶלֶף פְּעָמַיִם is not *many thousand* (אלף אלפים, Ibn Ezra), but *two thousand*, the dual פְּעָמַיִם, *two times*, is·used adver-

7 place? All the labour of this man is for his mouth, and yet
8 the soul cannot be satisfied; for what advantage hath the

bially, like our *twice*. The phrase is
a paraphrase of וֹל הָיָה־אֹל הָרוּבְק,
hyperbolically expressing unusually
long life. The interrogative אֹלַה is
used for an emphatic assertion (comp.
i. 3). For םוֹקָמ, *place*, i. e., *the grave,
sheol*, as well as דָחֶא, *the same*, and
לֹבַּה, *both*, see iii. 20.

7. *All the labour*, &c. This verse
shews how the untimely birth has
more rest than this man, inasmuch
as it states that his life is a protracted
scene of toil, turmoil, and dissatisfaction, ever labouring to satisfy his
soul, which cannot be satisfied,
whilst the abortion escapes all this.
םָדָאָה does not refer to *man generally*,
as most commentators take it, but
to the particular individual described
in the preceding verses, as is evident
from the context, and especially from
the phrase אָלָמִת אֹל שֶׁפֶנ, *i. q.*,
עָבְּשִׂת in verse 3, which is applied to
the case in question. וּהיִפְל, *for his
mouth*, i. e., *for his enjoyment*. הֶפ,
mouth, is used metonymically for the
food and dainties put into it. Luther
strangely renders this clause einem
jeglichen Menschen ift Arbeit aufgelegt
nach feiner Maße, *to every man work
is allotted, according to his measure*,
taking וּהיִפְל as a *particle* with suffix;
so also Holden, who however translates it, *all the labour of this man is
with respect to* or *for himself*, or *his
own account;* but this, to say the
least, is an unnecessary departure
from the meaning הֶפ, and does not
improve the sense. For םַג, *yet*, see
ii. 14. To be consistent with his
mistranslation of the former clause,
Luther renders this part of the verse,
aber das Herz kann nicht daran bleiben,
but his heart cannot abide by it, i. e.,
the heart cannot keep to the work
allotted to man, but runs away from
it after greater things.

8. *For what advantage*, &c. To
shew more strikingly that all the exertions of this rich man fail to satisfy
the cravings of his soul, Coheleth ap-

peals to the fact that no efforts of any
man can do this; for the wise man in
this respect has no advantage over the
fool, nor the poor man over the chief.
יִּכ assigns a *reason* for the assertion
made in the last clause of the preceding verse. For the interrogative
רֵתוֹי־הַמ, *what advantage?* for an emphatic denial, see i. 3. ןִמ, from the
first clause, must be supplied before
עֵדוֹי, *i. e.*, "וֹגְו עַדֹי ןִמ יִנָעֶל־הַמ *what advantage has the poor man over him
who knows*, &c. םיִיַחַה־דֶגֶנ ךֵלֹה, *to walk
before the living*, denotes *one who leads
a public life*, in contradistinction to
the ךֶשֹׁחַב לַכָא, *him who spends his life
in obscurity* (v. 16); *one who is a
leader, a chief, a magnate* (compare
iv. 16). For םיִיַח, *the living*, denoting
men, see iv. 15. The difficulty experienced in the interpretation of this
verse has been increased by the discordant and loose paraphrases of the
ancient versions. Thus the Sept.
renders it ὅτι τίς περίσσεια τῷ σοφῷ ὑπὲρ
τὸν ἄφρονα; διότι ὁ πένης οἶδεν πορευθῆναι
κατέναντι τῆς ζωῆς, *for what advantage
is there to the wise man above the fool?
since the poor man knows to walk before life.* The Vulg. has, QUID HABET
AMPLIUS SAPIENS A STULTO? ET QUID
PAUPER, NISI UT PERGAT ILLUC, UBI
EST VITA? *what has the wise man more
than the fool? and what the poor man
but that he go thither where life is?*
which has evidently arisen from the
Hagadic explanation given by the
Chaldee, אָמְלָעְב אָמיִפֲחַל תיִא אָרֲחוֹמ הַמ םוּרֲא
לֵבַּקְתִמ אָלְד אָרַד אָשיִבּ ןיִגְבּ אָיָתַּשׁ ןִמ רֵתַּי ריִגַּה
ןֵהֵלֲא דָבְעֶמְל אָיָנֲע אוּהַהְל תיִא הַמוּ ןוֹהְיֵלֲע
ריִתָע ןיִרְכִיַּה עַדְיַ יִד ןיִגְבּ יָד אָתיִרְיוֹאָבּ ךְסָפְמְל
ןֶרֵע ןיִגְבּ אָיָקַּיַּדִצ לֵבֵּל ,ךְדִמְל *for what advantage has the wise man in this world
over the fool, because of the wicked
generation by which he is not accepted?
and what is this poor man to do but
to study the law of the Lord, that he
may know how he will have to walk
before the righteous in paradise?*

The Syriac translates it ܡܬܠ ܕܐ

wise man over the fool? what the poor man over him who

ܣܵܐܲܠܕܢܵ ܠܡܣܓܝܐ ܡܢ ܕܚܟܡܬܐ

ܠܡܚܢܵܐ ܘܡܚܒܢܵܐ ܒܝ ܠܡܚܝܼܠ

ܕܝܢܐ, *for there is an advantage to the wise man over the fool, why? for the poor man knows to go to life.* So also the Vatican copy of the Sept., ὅτι περίσσεια τῷ σοφῷ ὑπὲρ τον ἄφρονα. The Rabbins, though adhering more to the text, also differ greatly in their interpretation of this verse. According to Rashi, it means " for what has this wise man more than the fool, and what has the poor man less than the rich man, since he, too, knows how to walk before the living?" ואהרי שכן הוא מה יתר לו בחכמתו משאם היה כסיל ומה לעני חסרון מן העשיר שאין לו קורת רוח גם הוא יודע להלוך בארץ אצל החיים, *and since it is so (i.e., the appetite is insatiable), what more has he through his wisdom than if he were a fool? and what has the poor man less than the rich man who has no rest of mind, since he, too, knows how to proceed in the land by the living?* which is followed by Broughton, who renders the verse, " then what hath the wise man more than the fool? and what less hath the poor man of knowledge, to walk before the living?" But as this interpretation restricts חָכָם to *the money-getter* in the preceding verse, and necessitates the extraordinary ellipsis of חסרון מן העשיר, it cannot be entertained. Similarly Rashbam, " what has the wise man more than the fool? what has this poor man less than the wise man? since he, too, knows how to walk before the living." שהרי מה יתרון לחכם יותר מן הכסיל בעולם ששניהם חיין ועומדין בעולם באחד ועל כן אמרתי הכל הבל : מה לעני יודע·באיזה דבר התחיל עני זה גרוע מן החכם שהרי הוא יודע לילך בעולם עם שאר החיים כאחד סן החכמים *for what advantage has the wise man above the fool in the world, wherein they both live and maintain themselves alike? and therefore I said that all is vanity.* " *What to the poor man,*" &c., i. e., *wherein does this poor man*

begin to be less than the wise man? since he, too, knows how to proceed in the world, with the rest of the living, like one of the wise; but as this explanation also imposes similar harsh ellipses upon the text, it must likewise be rejected. According to Ibn Ezra, it means, " what advantage is there to the wise man above the fool? why should the intelligent poor man walk like the rest of the living?" which he explains, אם יבקש החכם ממון אין קץ ונפשו לא תמלא כנפש הכסיל מה יתרון יש לו • וענין מה לעני יודע העני שהוא יודע ומבין מה לו להלוך בדרך· הכסילים כנגד החיים, *if the wise will always be looking after money, and his desire is as insatiable as the desire of the fool, what advantage has he? And the meaning of* מה לעני יודע *is, the poor man who knows and is intelligent, why should he walk in the way of fools like the living?* taking יוֹדֵעַ as an adjective joined to עָנִי, and as synonymous with חָכָם in the preceding clause, which few interpreters will follow. Equally discordant are the versions of the Reformers. Thus Luther has, denn was richtet ein Weiser mehr aus weder ein Narr? Was untersteht sich der Arme, daß er unter den Lebendigen will sein? *for what does the wise man accomplish more than the fool? what does the poor man dare, that he will be among the living?* Coverdale, " for what hath the wise more than the fool? what helpeth it the poor that he knoweth to walk before the living?" substantially the same the Bishops' Bible, " for what hath the wise more than the fool? what helpeth it the poor that he knoweth to walk with fools before the living?" and the Geneva Version, which is followed by the Authorised Version, " for what hath the wise man more than the fool? what hath the poor that knoweth how to walk before the living?" Neither has modern criticism succeeded in lessening this divergency of opinions. According to Bishop Patrick, it is the

9 knoweth to walk before the living?　Better, indeed, is that
which is seen by the eyes, than that which is pursued by the

language of the wretch mentioned
before, who asks, " What excellence
is there in the wise man more than
in a fool, especially if he become poor,
though he knows," &c.　According
to Dr. Durell, " the latter part of
this verse is an answer to the question
in the former part, and ought to be
rendered, ' for what hath the wise
more than the fool? that which the
poor hath who knoweth to walk
before the living;' i.e., in point of
morals, the wise has no advantage
over the poor who knows and practises his duty."　Herzfeld, though
he also takes the answer to be contained in this verse, reduces it to a
still shorter compass, inasmuch as
he translates it, denn was hat der
Kluge voraus vor dem Thoren? was
sogar der Arme? Er versteheet, vor
den Lebenden zu wandeln, what advantage has the wise above the fool?
what even the poor? He knows to
walk before the living.　Desvoeux,
Spohn, Knobel, Ewald, De Wette,
Hitzig, Noyes, Heiligstedt, Stuart,
Elster, Vaihinger, Hengstenberg,
&c., like the Geneva Version and
the Authorised Version, take יֹדֵעַ לַהֲלֹךְ
נֶגֶד הַחַיִּים as descriptive of עָנִי, i.e.,
the poor who knows to walk before
the living.　But against this is to be
urged — 1. That it destroys the symmetry of the verse, inasmuch as the
first clause is made to describe two
individuals, whilst the whole of the
second clause, only one; 2. That the
object of comparison is wanted in
the second clause; and 3. That as
חָכָם, the wise man, is compared with
כְּסִיל, the fool, in the first clause, it is
evident that עָנִי, the poor, in the
second clause, must also have an
opposite wherewith to be compared,
which our rendering supplies.

9. Better, indeed, is that which, &c.
It is indeed better to make the best
of what we see and is present, than
to let our soul wander after gratifications which might be secured, but

are looming in the future.　Luther
aptly paraphrases this clause, es ist
besser, das gegenwärtige Gut ge-
brauchen, denn nach anderm gedenken,
it is better to enjoy the present good than
to think about other good, and rightly
remarks, in his commentary, Salomo
will, daß wir sollen brauchen des
Gegenwärtigen, und Gott dafür danken
und nicht auf anders denken; wie der
Hund in Aesopo nach dem Schatten
schnappet, und ließ das Fleisch fallen,
Solomon submits that we should enjoy
the present, thank God for it, and
not speculate about getting other
things; like the dog in Æsop, which
snapped at the shadow and dropped
the meat.　Substantially the same
sentiment is expressed in iv. 6.
מַרְאֵה עֵינַיִם, the sight of the eye, i.e.,
that which is the object of sight,
that which we can see (infra, xi. 9;
Levit. xiii. 12; Deut. xxviii. 34) is
before us, is present, which we possess,
and can enjoy, is well paraphrased
by the Chaldee, טָב לִגְבְרָא לְמֶחֱדֵי עַל מַה
דְּאִית לֵיה, it is better for a man to rejoice
over what he has, and is contrasted
with הֲלָךְ־נָפֶשׁ, the wandering of the
desire, after things at a distance;
ever dissatisfied with what it has,
and always running after that which
it has not.　הֲלָךְ, to go, to go to and
fro, to wander (comp. Exod. ix. 23;
Ps. lxxiii. 9, xci. 6), is evidently
chosen because of לַהֲלֹךְ in the preceding verse, by way of paranomasia.
The loose paraphrase of the Vulg.,
MELIUS EST VIDERE QUOD CUPIAS,
QUAM DESIDERARE QUOD NESCIAS, it
is better to see what thou desirest than
to desire what thou knowest not, and
the explanation of Rashi, טוב היה
חוכנשר לה לראות עושרו למראה עיניו ממאכל
ומישתה ההולך בנפש, it would have been
better for him to look at his riches
with the sight of his eyes, than to eat
and drink, which goes into the body,
are irreconcileable with the text, and
weaken the sense.　Coverdale's version, " the sight of the eyes is better

soul; yet this, too, is vanity and striving after the wind.
10 What hath been was long ago called by name; moreover, it
is known that he is a man, and cannot contend with Him
who is mightier than he; what advantage then hath man?

than that the soul should so depart away," is unintelligible, and is rightly rejected by the Bishops' version.

Yet this, too, is vanity, &c. Yet even this enjoyment of the present, however pleasant for the moment, is unable to allay the cravings of the mind, and to impart lasting happiness. That נַם־זֶה refers to מַרְאֵה עֵינַיִם, *that which the eyes see, i. e.,* the enjoyment of the present, is evident from ii. 1, and the following verses. Ibn Ezra's rendering of this verse, " better that which the eyes can see than the wandering of the soul, though it is vanity and striving after the wind," as if Coheleth had said, מה לחכם שתהלוך נפשו בדרך הכסלים שנפשם לא תמלא די לו הנמצא הנראה לעין אף על פי שהנראה ואשר יעלה במחשבת הנפש הבל, *why should a wise man's desire walk in the way of fools, whose desire is never satisfied? enough for him that which is tangible and seen with the eye, though that which is seen and enters into his mind is vanity,* is therefore inadmissible.

10. *What hath been,* &c. Coheleth now gives the cause why all the efforts of riches fail to secure solid happiness. It is because that everything which has happened has been immutably fixed beforehand, and because the opulent is, after all, only a frail creature, unable to contest with the Almighty. The Vulg.'s rendering of מַה־שֶּׁהָיָה by QUI FUTURUS EST, *he who shall be,* is contrary to the signification of מָה, which is used for *things* and not for *persons,* unwarrantably converts הָיָה, the *præterite,* into the future, and is against the usual meaning of this phrase (comp. i. 9, iii. 16, &c). כְּבָר נִקְרָא שְׁמוֹ, *it was long ago called by name, i. e.,* its very nature and fate have been predetermined. The Masorites mark in the margin the ה in שֶׁהַתַּקִּיף as

superfluous, not because " the Punctuators failed to discover the idea which the writer meant to convey," as Stuart asserts, but because they, for some unknown reason, deemed the article unnecessary after אֲשֶׁר, as is evident from x. 3. For מִמֶּנּוּ, being a contraction of מִמֶּנְהוּ, see iv. 12. Somewhat remarkable are the interpretations which the Rabbins give of this verse. According to Rashi, the meaning is, " what he was, his fame has long since been proclaimed, and it is now known that he was but a man, and could not contend with him who is stronger than he," and he explains it, מה־שהיה חשיבותו וגדולה שהיתה לו בחייו · כבר נקרא שמו ,כלומד כבר היה ועבר כבר יצא לו שם בשורה ועתה חלף ונודע שהוא אדם ולא אל וסופו שמת ולא יוכל לדין עם מלאך המות שהוא תקיף ממנו, "what has been," i. e., to him, the distinction and eminence he had in his lifetime. " Long since has his name been called," i. e., has been long since, and is now past, long since has his name been famous for it, but it is now vanished. " And it is known that he is a man," i, e., and not a god, and that his end was to die, and could not contend with the angel of death, who was stronger than he. According to Rashbam, it means, " he who was mighty, whose name is proclaimed, and it is known that he was a mighty man, yet he could not contend with him who is stronger than he," which he explains, אתו שהי' גביר ונקרא שמו ונודע שהוא אדם חשוב וגבור בשעת המיתה לא יכול לדין ולהלחם עם מלאך המות שהוא תקיף ממנו, *he who was strong, and his name proclaimed, and it is known that he was a distinguished and powerful man, could not, in the hour of death, contend with the angel of death, who is stronger than he.* Ibn Ezra, again, who takes verses 8 and 9 as a caution given to the poor but pru-

11 Moreover, there are many things which increase vanity;
12 and who knoweth what is good for man in life, the numbered
days of his vain life, which he spendeth as a shadow? and

dent man, regards this verse as a
continuation of this advice, and
explains it, כבר נקרא שמו ונודע מה שהיה,
שהוא אדם כך וכך ולמה יבקש הליכת הנפש עד
שהיה כפלוני ויתכן שלא ישיגנו ואין ראוי לאיש
שכל שידין עם שתקיף ממנו על כן אין ראוי לו
לבקש מה שהחיים מבקשים ויעשה זאת כנגדם
שיהיה כמו הם, *what he was, his name
has long since been called, and it is
known that he is such and such a
man; and why should he* (*i.e.*, the
poor and wise man) *seek the desire
of his heart till he be like that man,
and probably without attaining to it?
Now it does not become a wise man to
compete with one who is richer than
he, hence he ought not to seek that
which the living* (*i.e.*, the rich fools) *seek,
and act so before them to be like them.*
There can be little doubt that the
traditional explanation contained in
Rashi and Rashbam, has given rise
to Luther's version, was ift es, wenn
einer gleich hoch berühmt ift, fo weiß
man doch, daß er ein Menfch ift, und
fann nicht hadern mit dem, das ihm
zu mächtig ift, which, as usual, is
followed by Coverdale, " what is
more excellent than man? yet can
he not, in the law, get the victory
over him that is mightier than he."
Hodgson's translation, "what is that
in the creation most mighty? Let
its name be mentioned. Confessedly
it is man. Yet how unable is he to
contend with the power that is above
him," competes with any of the
Rabbinic expositions.

11. *Moreover, there are many things,*
&c. Another reason why all the labour
and accumulated riches of man fail
to satisfy his soul (as stated in ver. 7)
is, that there are so many things
which are got to yield comfort, but
which from their nature only increase
the void in his heart, and his disappointment. כי as frequently introduces an additional reason for the
assertion made in verse 7, and must
therefore be translated *moreover* (*vide*

supra, v. 2). For דְּבָרִים, *things*, see i.
8. 10. מַה־יּוֹתֵר לָאָדָם, *what advantage
hath man?* as will be shewn in the
following verse, belongs to the end of
the preceding verse. For the interrogative used as an emphatic denial,
vide supra, i. 3. The Vulgate renders
this verse, VERBA SUNT PLURIMA MUL-
TAMQUE IN DISPUTANDO HABENTIA VA-
NITATEM, *there are many words, and
they have much vanity in disputing*,
taking דְּבָרִים to denote *arguments*, or
murmurings against God. Hence the
rendering of Coverdale, "a vain thing
is it to cast out many words, but
what hath a man else?" the explanation of Jermin, Spohn, and others,
" for many words increase vanity, *i.e.*,
if man were to murmur or complain
before God about his lot, he would
only contract greater misery;" and the
interpretation of Desvoeux,"for there
are many arguments to shew the
multitude of vanities, *i. e.*, that prevail on this earth;" Ewald and
Elster, again, will have it that "the
many words" refer to the scholastic
philosophy which was then current
among the Jews to propound the
summum bonum; whilst Hitzig and
Stuart maintain that it means "truly
there are many words increasing
vanity, *i.e.*, however, I will say no
more, since much speaking has already been condemned, see v. 6."
But, apart from the violation which
these interpretations do to the text,
the rendering of דְּבָרִים הַרְבֵּה, *by many
words*, is contrary to the scope of the
passage, which manifestly speaks of
the insufficiency of *the many things*
tending to increase or diminish happiness, but of which man is ignorant, as is evident from the next
verse.

12. *And who knoweth*, &c. The
shortsightedness and ignorance of
man render him utterly incapable of
knowing what things will yield him
comfort during the few years of his

who can tell man what shall be after him under the sun?
vii. 1 A good name is better than sweet perfume, and the day of

earthly existence; so that the very objects which he toils to acquire in order to make him happy, may turn out to belong to the "many things which increase vanity." *The shadow*, playing so important a part in the comforts of Oriental life, owing to the refreshing coolness aɴd shelter which it affords in scorching climates, became, in consequence of its transient and fugitive nature, an appropriate metaphor of the fleeting life of man. Hence we frequently find the days of man's existence upon earth so rapidly over and gone, compared with the shadow which hurries over the fields, flies away, and disappears. Thus David, speaking of human life, says, " our days upon earth are like a *shadow*" (1 Chron. xxix. 15), " his days are like the *passing shadow*" (Ps. cxliv. 4); and Job, " our days upon earth are a *shadow*" (viii. 9), "he flies like a *shadow*, and doth not abide (xiv. 2). See also *infra*, viii. 13. כִּי here, being continuative of כִּי in the former verse, must be rendered *and*. This is frequently the meaning of this causal particle when it is repeated (comp. כִּי אֱלֹהִים הוּא כִּי שִׂיחַ, *for he is a god, and is meditating*, 1 Kings xviii. 27; כִּי־צָרָה קְרוֹבָה כִּי־אֵין עֹזֵר, *for trouble is nigh, and there is no help*, Ps. xxii. 12, so also γὰρ . . . γὰρ, Matt. vi. 32, xviii. 10, 11, xxiv. 27. 28; Gesenius and Fürst, Lex. *s.v.*, כִּי). For the phrase מִי יוֹדֵעַ, *who knows?* i.e., *nobody knows*, see iii. 2. The close connection of this clause with the former part of the preceding verse, leaves no doubt upon my mind that the words מַה־יּוֹתֵר לָאָדָם belong to the end of verse 10. Coheleth assigned a reason, in verse 11, why it is that the acquisition of many things does not yield happiness, " because there are many things which yield the reverse," which by itself is no reason at all, unless we connect this verse with it, " and because no one knows what is good for man," hence, in

their ignorance, they alight upon that which brings the opposite to what they desire. Nothing can therefore be more plain; thus construed, כִּי יֵשׁ־דְּבָרִים הַרְבֵּה מַרְבִּים הָבֶל כִּי מִי־יוֹדֵעַ מַה־טּוֹב לָאָדָם וְגוֹ׳ *for there are many things which increase vanity, and who knows what is good for man, i.e.*, so that, in the selection of things, he may avoid those " which increase vanity," everything is plain. If we want any more proofs of the correctness of this construction, we need only refer to the violent and arbitrary means which commenᵣtators have adopted to trace the connection of these verses, and to explain the meaning of מַה־יּוֹתֵר לָאָדָם in its present position. מִסְפַּר, being *accusative of measure*, requires no preposition (*vide supra*, ii.). Hengstenberg's remark, that the בְּ from בַּחַיִּים is to be supplied before it, is therefore gratuitous. Durell's alteration of it into מִסְפֹּר, " *who knoweth what is better in life for a man than to number the days of his life?* &c , that is, to take account of them so as to turn them to profit," is preposterous. עָשָׂה יָמָיו, *to spend his days*, has its analogy in the Greek ποιεῖν χρόνον (Acts xv. 33), ποιεῖν ἐνιαυτόν (James iv. 13), and δίκαιοι ποιήσουσιν ἔτη πολλά (Prov. xiii. 23, Sept.). The וְ in וְיַעֲשֵׂם as frequently stands for the relative pronoun (comp. Gen. xlix. 25; Job xxix. 12; Ps. lv. 20; Isa. xiii. 14; Gesenius, Lex. *s. v.*, וְ e c). As אֲשֶׁר is used instead of כִּי (*vide infra*, viii. 13; Ewald, § 353, a, § 362, b), which is still connected with the two preceding causative particles, viz , כִּי=אֲשֶׁר . . . כִּי . . . כִּי, it must also be rendered by *and*.

1. *A good name*, &c. Seeing, then, that wealth was also unable to avert the doom of man, and to secure lasting good, Coheleth resorted to the last experiment, viz., *prudence*, or what is generally called the *common sense* view of life, thinking that he might thereby secure the desired end. The particular features of this

2 death than the day of his birth. It is better to go to the
house of mourning than to go to the house of feasting,
because this is the end of all men, and the living will lay it

view are given in this chapter and in
the following one. Like the enumeration of the general events of life in
iii. 2 – 8, the description of this view
begins with the commencement and
end of life. Paramount to all other
considerations, is to lead such a life
as to secure a good name. In tropical
climates perfumes are in great requisition, and are used especially on
occasions of social gatherings, or on
visits to persons of rank (2 Sam. xii.
20; Ruth iii. 3; Ps. xlv. 8; Prov.
vii. 17; Dan. x. 3; Amos vi. 6;
Matt. vi. 17) to prevent the offensiveness of the profuse perspiration
to which the melting heat subjects
those who are under its influence, as
well as to regale and refresh the
company. The sweet odour, therefore, diffused by perfumes, became a
very beautiful and expressive metaphor for the excellencies of character
(comp. Song of Songs i. 3), and an
offensive smell is used to express the
contrary idea (Gen. xxxiv. 30; Exod.
v. 21). שֵׁם, *name*, without any adjunct, also means *a good name* (comp.
נִבְחָר שֵׁם מֵעֹשֶׁר, *a good name is preferable to riches*, Prov. xxii. 1; Zeph.
iii. 19), and, as in the Song of Songs
i. 3, forms a paranomasia with שֶׁמֶן,
which is beautifully imitated by
Knobel and De Wette, beſſer gut
Gerücht, als gute Gerüche, and less
successfully by Ewald, beſſer deß
guten Namens Luft als guter Salben
Duft. Our language, however, does
not admit of an imitation. טוֹב,
good, when connected with שֶׁמֶן, *perfume*, denotes *sweet, delicious*, in which
the goodness of the aromatic consists (comp. Ps. cxxxiii. 2; Song of
Songs, i. 2).

And the day of death, &c. To
such a man who has striven to live a
praiseworthy life and has succeeded,
the day of his death, which is the
day wherein the battle is decided,
and he goes off the conqueror, is

better than the day of his birth,
when he enters upon the field, ignorant of the strength and snares of
the enemy, and doubtful of victory.
A story told in the Midrash beautifully illustrates this passage. "Two
vessels met at sea, one was going
into the harbour and the other was
just starting for a long voyage; in
the former silence prevailed, whilst
in the latter the voice of jubilee
was heard. A wise man who witnessed this scene exclaimed, in great
astonishment, What a perverted
world! the vessel which has safely
returned ought to rejoice, inasmuch
as it has overcome the perils of the
sea, but not the one which is starting
and has to weather all the dangers!
So we are also not to rejoice when a
man is born, when he starts upon
the journey of life, and goes to meet
the dangers of temptation, but when
he is freed from these dangers, finishes
his earthly course, and enters peaceably and with a good report into the
haven of rest" (compare Leopold
Löw, המפתח, i. p. 106). And since it
is death alone which decides the
victory, hence Sirach says, "Judge
none blessed before his death," and
the Jewish sages caution, in the
Mishna, אל תאמין בעצמך עד יום מותך, *do
not trust thyself till the day of thy
death* (Aboth, ii. 4). Failing to see
this, Knobel refers this clause to
the *fool*, for whom the day of death
is better than the day of his birth,
because it frees him from the contempt which he experiences in life;
whilst Hitzig, Stuart, &c., regard the
first clause as comprising a common
apothegm, introduced here to illustrate the assertion in the second
clause, viz., "a good name is better
than sweet perfume, so is the day of
death better than one's birth."

2. *It is better*, &c. To obtain and
maintain such a name in life and
victory in death, means must be

3 to heart.   Better is thoughtful sadness than wanton mirth,

chosen and used adequate to this purpose. Visits to houses of mourning and to the graves were and still are regarded by the Jews as productive of a serious and beneficial state of mind, influencing the moral conduct of the visitor, by reminding him of his own frailty and mortality, and the necessity of preparation for it. Hence the Talmudic proverb, אגרא דבי טעמא שתיקותא, *the profit from the house of mourning is silent reflection* (Berachoth, vi. 72). Thus also the beautiful mediæval poet, Moses Ibn Ezra —

הֱקִיצוּנִי סְעִיפֵי לַעֲבוֹר עַל
מְלוֹן הוֹרַי וְכָל אַנְשֵׁי שְׁלוֹמִי
שְׁאֵלְתִּימוֹ (וְאֵין מַקְשִׁיב וּמֵשִׁיב)
הֲבָנְרוּ בִּי עֲדֵי אָבִי וְאִמִּי
בְּלִי לָשׁוֹן קְרָאוּנִי אֲלֵיהֶם
וְהֶרְאוּנִי לְצִדֵּיהֶם מְקוֹמִי

I sought the abode where all my kindred sleep,
Parents and friends, in their sepulchral home,
I spoke, but none replied. In silence deep,
I seem'd to hear a voice that bade me come,
And lay me on that couch, where none embrace,
And make, with them, my own last resting place.

MOSES BEN EZRA, *Darstellung von Leopold Dukes, Altona*, 1839, p. 101.

In addition to what has already been said upon mourning (*vide supra*, iii. 7), we must remark here that the time of mourning begins as soon as the mourners have returned from the grave, and lasts *seven days* (Gen. l. 10), hence is called שִׁבְעָה among the Jews, during which time the mourners sit barefooted on the ground or footstools, and are visited by their relations, friends, and acquaintances (comp. Sirach, xxii. 12). For מְלֵכָח instead of מְלֶלֶכָח, see ii. 7. בֵּת מִשְׁתֶּה, *house of drinking*, is a general term for a *jovial place*, hence it is called בֵּית שִׂמְחָה, in verse 4. הוּא, *this is*, refers to מָוֶת, *death*, which is involved in אֵבֶל, *mourning*. Less appropriate is the paraphrase of the Vulgate, IN ILLA ENIM FINIS CUNCTORUM ADMONETUR HOMINUM, *for in that we are admonished of the end of*

all men ; or the explanation of Rashi (בשביל שהאבל הוא סוף כל האדם), who refers it to the mourning itself. The phrase נָתַן אֶל־לֵב, *to take it to heart*, which also occurs in ix. 1, like שִׂים עַל־לֵב, *to lay it to heart* (Isa. xlii. 25, lvii. 11), is used for *serious consideration, reflection*, and is strangely rendered by the Sept. ὁ ζῶν δώσει ἀγαθὸν ἐν καρδία αὐτοῦ, *the living will put good into his heart;* so also the Syriac,

ܘܚܝܐ ܢܬܠ ܛܒܬܐ ܒܠܒܗ,

which has evidently arisen from taking over יִתֵּן from the following verse, as this verb stands in the Hebrew copy in the following line under יִתֵּן. The Vulgate, ET VIVENS COGITAT, QUID FUTURUM SIT, *and the living thinks what is to come*, is a good paraphrase.

3. *Better is thoughtful sadness, &c.* The pensive reflections arising from visits to the house of mourning are far preferable to the levity produced by resorts to the haunts of pleasure, inasmuch as seriousness is beneficial to the heart. That כַּעַס here is *sad thoughtfulness, sober reflection*, is evident from the fact that this verse describes the state of mind produced by visits to the house of mourning, spoken of in the preceding verse, which is not an *angry*, nor even a *simply sorrowful* one, but is a *reflecting*, a *thoughtful* state of mind. This is, moreover, corroborated — 1. By the words וְהֵחַי יִתֵּן אֶל־לִבּוֹ, *and the living will lay it to heart = reflect upon it*, which most unquestionably describes this state of mind; 2nd, By the term שְׂחוֹק, *wanton mirth, levity* (*vide supra*, ii. 2), which gives the *opposite result*, produced by frequenting the haunts of pleasure; and 3. By its explicative רֹעַ פָּנִים, which means *sad thoughtfulness*, arising from dwelling or reflecting upon thoughts suggested by painful scenes or sufferings, as is evident from the question מַדּוּעַ פְּנֵיכֶם רָעִים, *why are your countenances sad or thoughtful ?* (Gen. xl. 7) put to

4 for by a serious countenance the heart is improved. The
heart of the wise, therefore, is in the house of mourning, and
5 the heart of fools in the house of mirth. It is better for a
man to listen to the reproof of a wise man, than to hear the
6 song of fools; for as the crackling of thorns is under the pot,

Pharaoh's butler and baker, who dwelt upon the dream they had in the night, which Hengstenberg seems to have overlooked in his assertion that Nehem. ii. 2, is the only place where רַע פָּנִים occurs in the sense of *sadness, pensiveness.* יִיטַב לֵב is well rendered by the Sept. (ἀγαθυνθήσεται καρδία), the Syriac, Rashi (יהפוך לב האדם להטיב דרכיו), Rashbam, Luther, the Bishops' Bible, the Geneva Version, the Auth. Ver., Hodgson, Knobel, Herzfeld, Philippson, Vaihinger, &c., *the heart is made better,* inasmuch as his thoughts are directed to himself; he thinks of the fleetness of life, and the necessity of preparing himself for a speedy departure, and hence is led to regulate his conduct accordingly. The rendering, *the heart is joyful* or *made glad* (Coverdale, Desvoeux, Umbreit, Rosenmüller, Stuart, Elster, &c.) is at variance with the scope of the passage, which speaks of the *moral effect* produced by the visits to the house of mourning. The Vulgate's strange rendering of this verse, MELIOR EST IRA RISU; QUIA PER TRISTITIAM VULTUS CORRIGITUR ANIMUS DELINQUENTIS, *anger is better than laughter, because through the sadness of the countenance the mind of the offender is corrected,* taking כַּעַס as the indignation either of God or of pious men, manifested against sin, originated from the Hagadic interpretation given in the Midrash, the Chaldee, and Rashi. It is surprising that Mercer, Grotius, and several other commentators should have followed this interpretation.

4. *The heart of the wise,* &c. This being the case, because such great and solid benefits are to be derived from visits to, and reflections upon

the house of mourning, therefore the wise man will dwell upon it, whilst the fool, who craves after sensuous pleasures, will think of the abodes of mirth. The construction לֵב בְּ, *to have the heart in it,* expresses *both* facts mentioned in the preceding verses, viz., *the going to* the respective places, and the consequent *thinking thereupon.*

5. *It is better for a man,* &c. From the lessons of the *dead,* Coheleth passes on to those of the *living.* The wise man not only learns salutary lessons from the silent yet eloquent rebukes of the dead, but will profit by the wholesome corrections of the living, which are sometimes as distasteful as visits to the dead. He will prefer the reproving voice of the prudent, however disagreeable for the moment, to the mirthful notes of the fool. The proper construction of this verse is טוֹב לָאִישׁ לִשְׁמֹעַ גַּעֲרַת חָכָם מִשְׁמֹעַ וְגוֹ׳, *it is better for a man to hear the reproof of a wise man, than to hear,* &c.; אִישׁ, of the first clause, is by carelessness of style put into the second clause. In earlier and more energetic Hebrew, אִישׁ would have been omitted altogether, and we should have had טוֹב לִשְׁמֹעַ . . . מִשְׁמֹעַ וְגוֹ׳. The Vulgate's paraphrase of מֵאִישׁ שֹׁמֵעַ שִׁיר כְּסִילִים, QUAM STULTORUM ADULATIONE DECIPI, *than to be deceived by the adulation of fools,* taking שִׁיר to denote a *plaudit song,* which is followed by Reynolds, Patrick, Desvoeux, Stuart, &c., is contrary to the following verse, where שִׁיר כְּסִילִים is explained by שְׂחֹק הַכְּסִיל, *the mirth of the fool.*

6. *For as the crackling of thorns,* &c. We have here a reason for the assertion made in the *second* clause of the preceding verse. The wise

7 so is the laughter of a fool; this, also, is vanity; for extortion maketh the wise man foolish, and bribery corrupteth the

man shuns the merry songs at the compotations of fools, because he knows that they are as transient and unprofitable as the flashy and useless noise of kindled thorns, which for a moment seems very fierce, but suddenly disappears. The charcoal, generally used as fuel in the East (Ps. xviii. 8; Isa. xlvii. 14; Jerem. xxxvi. 22, 23; John xviii. 18), is comparatively slow in burning up, and hence those who were impatient of obtaining their meals in the ordinary way were tempted to employ dried thorns. But it was soon found that the ardent blaze snapt fiercely, made much noise, and went out immediately, without producing the desired end (Ps. cxviii. 12; Joel ii. 5). Hence this striking comparison between the crackling of ignited thorns under a kettle, and the merry noise of an excited fool over his pot. פִּי, *for*, gives the reason why the wise man acts as described in the foregoing verse. סִירִים, *thorns*, and סִיר, *kettle*, form a paronomasia, and are evidently selected because of their assonance with שִׁיר in the preceding verse. Knobel (wie das Geräusch der Nessel unter dem Kessel), and Ewald (wie unter dem Topf der Dornen Knistern, so des Thoren Kichern), have again imitated the paronomasia, which might also be done in English, viz., *as the noise of nettles under the kettle*.

7. *For extortion*, &c. Having given, in the preceding verse, the reason for the assertion made in the *second* clause of verse 5, Coheleth gives here the reason for the allegation in the *first* clause of that verse. The prudent man, when he is guilty of misdemeanour, will prefer the reproofs of the wise, however unpalatable, because he knows, in his better moments, that the sin of taking bribes, into which he has fallen, is so pernicious that it infatuates even the wise, and that bribery besots

the heart. The same evil consequences, attending the acceptance of gifts by judges, are mentioned in Exod. xxiii. 8 and Deut. xvi. 19. פִּי, *for*, introduces the reason for the assertion made in the *first* clause of verse 5. Instances where two subjects are proposed, and the latter is treated first and the former second, are of frequent occurrence. Thus—

1 The wicked draw the sword
2 And stretch their bow
2 To shoot down the poor and the needy,
1 To cut in pieces the upright in conduct.
Ps. xxxvii. 14.

Here לְהַפִּיל, *to shoot*, in the *third* hemistich, takes up קֶשֶׁת, *the bow*, in the *second*, and לִטְבּוֹחַ, *to cut down*, in the *fourth* hemistich, takes up חֶרֶב, the *sword* of the *first*.

Behold how good and how pleasant
When brethren dwell together,
[*Pleasant.*] Like sweet perfume upon the head
Flowing down upon the beard,
The beard of Aaron,
[*Good.*] As the dew of Hermon
Flowing upon the mountains of
    Zion.   Ps. cxxiii. 1-3.

Here, again, "*pleasant*," the second remark, is taken up first, and "*good*," the first, is taken up second (comp. also Isa. lvi. 3, 4, 5; and *infra*, x. 11, xi. 4). עשֶׁק, from עָשַׁק, *to oppress, to defraud*, literally *oppression, extortion*, and metonymically *the thing* obtained by oppression, fraud, or extortion (comp. הָעשֶׁק אֲשֶׁר עָשָׁק, Lev. v. 23; Ps. lxii. 11; Isa. xxx. 12). Here, however, it corresponds more to שׁחַד, *bribery*, as is evident from מַתָּנָה, *gift*, with which it stands in parallelism. מַתָּנָה, *a gift*, generally, is often used in a specific sense, a present given in order to bribe, hence *bribery* (comp. Prov. xv. 27). The nonconformity of וִיאַבֵּד, third person *masc.*, and מַתָּנָה, a noun *fem.*, is owing to the predicate preceding the subject, in which case there is a frequent departure from the general rule (comp. בָּא עָלַיִךְ רָעָה Isa. xlvii. 11; 1 Kings xxii. 36; *infra*, x. 1, xii. 4; Gesen. § 147, a; Ewald, § 316, a). The traditional

8 heart. The end of a reproof is better than its beginning,

explanation, as preserved in the Chaldee, which paraphrases this verse, אֲרוּם אֱנִישָׁא יְחַתְּ בְּחַפִּימָא בְּנִין דְּלָא אָזִיל בְּאוּרְחָתֵיהּ וּמְהוֹבֵד בְּמִלוֹי בִּישַׁיָּא יָת חוּכְמַת לֵב חַכִּמַיָּא דְּאִתְיְהִיבַת לֵיהּ בְּמַתְּנָא מִן שְׁמַיָּא for the robber mocks at the wise man, because he goes not in his way, and destroys with his evil speech the prudent heart of the wise, which was given to him as a gift from heaven, has been followed by the ancient versions and subsequent expositors. Thus the Septuagint translates it, ὅτι ἡ συκοφαντία περιφέρει σοφὸν καὶ ἀπολλύει τὴν καρδίαν εὐτονίας αὐτοῦ, for calumny carries about the wise man and destroys his heart, and, like the Chaldee, takes עשֶׁק for בְּמִלוֹי בִּישַׁיָּא, regarding it as the subject of both verbs, viz., יְהוֹלֵל and יְאַבֵּד, and מַתָּנָה as the genitive of לֵב; so also the Vulgate (CALUMNIA CONTURBAT SAPIENTEM, ET PERDET ROBUR CORDIS ILLIUS, calumny confounds the wise and destroys the strength of his heart), Rashi, and Rashbam, who, like the Chaldee, say that by לֵב מַתָּנָה is meant a wise heart, because it is a gift to man (comp. Prov. ii. 5). Similarly Luther (ein Widerspenstiger macht einen Weisen unwillig, und verderbet ein mildes Herz), who, as usual, is followed by Coverdale (" whoso doeth wrong maketh a wise man to go out of his wit, and destroyeth a gentle heart"). Against this, however, is to be urged, that it severs this verse from its connection, that it is against the parallelism, and that the predicates יְהוֹלֵל חָכָם, makes foolish the wise, and יְאַבֵּד אֶת־לֵב, corrupts the heart, undoubtedly refer to bribery, as will be seen from a comparison of this passage with Exod. xxii. 8 and Deut. xvi. 19. The Bishops' Bible (" the wise man hateth wrong dealing, and abhorreth the heart that coveteth rewards"), Desvoeux (" surely oppression shall give lustre to a wise man, but the gift corrupteth the heart"), and Hodgson (" though influence may sway a wise man to do imprudently, yet it is the bribe which corrupteth the heart"), are as curious

as they are irreconcileable with the text. Ewald's alteration of עשֶׁק, extortion, into עשֶׁר, riches (Jahrb. viii. p. 175), is purely conjectural, and does not improve the sense or the connection.

8. The end of a reproof, &c. The wise man submits to it because he knows that the end of merited reproof is better than we are at first inclined to think. At the outset of a rebuke flesh and blood will sometimes rise, excited feelings will rebel, but when the reproof is over we calmly reflect upon it, and find that, however disagreeable at the beginning, the end of it is profitable. Hence the advantage of a patient and forbearing spirit over a haughty and rebellious temper. Expositors, having overlooked the connection of the preceding verse with verse 5, and translated דָּבָר here, thing, have found great difficulty in the interpretation of this verse, for it is not true that the end of things generally is better than the beginning, and other passages of Scripture affirm the very reverse. We are told of the beginning of things which seems good, but the end is bad (Prov. v. 3, 4, xvi. 25). The attempts to particularise and defend it here are either at the expense of the context or against the genius of the language. The Septuagint and Vulgate therefore rightly render דָּבָר by λόγος, oratio, speech, though St. Jerome, in loco, through his misinterpretation of the preceding verse, was at a loss what to make of it, and hence submitted that " the end of a speech is better than the beginning," 1. Because with the end the speaker's anxiety is over, and with the beginning it begins. 2. Because when the speech is ended the hearer can reflect upon what has been said, but at the beginning he has not as yet got any benefit. 3. Because it is better to be quiet than to speak. 4. It may mean as long as we are in this world our knowledge is all a beginning, but when that which is perfect is

9 forbearance is better than haughtiness. Do not, therefore,
hasten on thy spirit to be angry, for anger is cherished in
10 the bosom of fools. Do not say what was it that former
days were better than these? for thou wouldst not ask from

come, we shall in the end be made
perfect. This patristic exposition
may fairly compete with any Rabbinic
interpretation of this verse. Adhering, then, to דָּבָר, signifying *speech*,
the connection, as we have traced it,
at once shews that the speech here
intended is of *an admonitory kind*,
rebuke, reproof. דָּבָר, *a word*, is also
used for *words collectively*, *a speech*,
in Gen. xliv. 18; Job iv. 2, xv. 3,
an advice, an admonition, in Prov.
iv. 4. 20; 2 Sam. xvii. 6; 1 Kings
i. 7. אֶרֶךְ רוּחַ, *long of spirit*, like
μακρόθυμος in Greek, and *longanimus*
in Latin, is a spirit that can bear
long, hence *patience, forbearance ;*
its proper antithesis is קְצַר רוּחַ, *short
of spirit* (Prov. xiv. 29), a spirit that
bears a short time, *impatience, un-
forbearance;* here, however, גְּבַהּ רוּחַ,
haughty of spirit, is contrasted therewith, because it is *pride*, which makes
reproof intolerable, and resists it in
every form. According to the analogy of the double forms, גָּדוֹל, and
גָּדֵל, קָטֹן, and קָטָן, there is a form גָּבֵהַּ, as
well as גָּבוֹהַ, and גְּבַהּ, is the *construct*
of the former.

9. *Do not, therefore, hasten*, &c.
This, then, being the case, since the
issue of a reproof is so profitable,
our pride ought never to excite our
tempers to rise and be irritated under
such circumstances, especially as it
is the fool who, not being able to
perceive the end of such rebukes,
will harbour anger against those
that administer reproof unto him.
For the causative use of תְּבַהֵל, and
the בְּ, expressing the force involved
in the idea of hurrying, see v. 1.
חֵיק, *bosom*, is regarded as the seat of
the *affections, feelings*, &c. (compare
Ps. xxxv. 13; Job xix. 27), *i. e., the
breast, the heart*, so that the phrase
יָנוּחַ בְּחֵיק, is the same as יָנוּחַ בְּלֵב, *to
rest* or *be cherished in the heart*

(comp. בְּלֵב נָבוֹן תָּנוּחַ חָכְמָה, *wisdom rests
in the heart of the intelligent*, Prov.
xiv. 33).

10. *Do not say*, &c. This common-
sense view of life not only shews
how benefits are to be derived from
apparently unpleasant subjects, such
as visiting houses of mourning, in
preference to places of mirth (1 – 4),
and submitting patiently to reproof
(5 – 9), but teaches us quietly to bear
all things, and to make the best of
the circumstances in which we are
placed (10 – 14). We are not to
indulge a repining disposition, employing ourselves in searching after
causes why bygone days were better,
to the neglect of present enjoyments,
since such a line of conduct is contrary to wisdom. The tendency to
praise the past above the present,
which Coheleth here denounces, is
common to the aged of every clime
and age. When man grows old, the
recollection of past sufferings grows
faint, whilst any present affliction is
keenly felt and greatly magnified.
The striking example of this in the
case of the Israelites, who, when in
the wilderness, having the presence
of God and heavenly food, soon
forgot their past bondage and extraordinary sufferings in Egypt, and felt
so acutely the comparatively little
inconveniences in the Desert, that
they wished to have back the former
days (Exod. xvi. 3; Numb. xi. 5, 6,
xiv. 1 – 4), is only a type of man generally. Thus Aristotle, in his description of those advanced in life (Rhet.
ii. 13), says that "they never cease
talking of that which has taken place,
since they are delighted in awaken-
ing the recollections of things."
And Horace, speaking of the many
inconveniences which encompass a
man of years, says, evidently having
the passage of Aristotle in his mind—

11 wisdom after them.   Wisdom is as good as riches, and
moreover hath an advantage over it for those who see the

Difficilis, querulus, laudator temporis acti
Se puero, castigator censorque minorum.

" Morose, complaining, and with tedious
praise
Talking the manners of their youthful days."
                          DE ARTE POET. 173–4.

הַיָּמִים הָרִאשֹׁנִים, *former days, the bygone
days of one's life.* אֵלֶּה, *these, the
present days.* The מִ in מֶהָכְמָה denotes
the *source* whence the question does
not proceed. שָׁאַלְתָּ has here a *sub-
junctive* signification, *thou wouldst
not ask,* as is evident from the context, which alone must decide it, since
the indicative form of the verb is
used to express the different moods.
The construction of שָׁאַל with עַל־ only
occurs once more in later Hebrew
(Nehem. i. 2), in the earlier stages of
the language it is construed with
לְ (Gen. xliii. 7). זֶה, *these,* refers to
הַיָּמִים הָרִאשֹׁנִים, as is evident from the
preposition עַל, *concerning, after.* The
paraphrastic rendering of the Vulgate, (STULTA ENIM EST HUJUSCEMODI
INTERROGATIO), which is followed by
Luther (benn bu fragſt ſolches nicht
weislich), Coverdale and the Bishops'
Bible (" for that were no wise question "), the Geneva Version and the
Authorised Version (" for thou doest
not enquire wisely of this thing or
concerning this "), and most commentators, refers שָׁאַלְתָּ עַל־זֶה to the
question מֶה הָיָה, and thereby confounds it with שְׁאֵלָת־זֶה.
11. *Wisdom is as good, &c.* Wisdom is not to be violated by dwelling upon the imaginary good of
former days, since having her is in
some respects as good as possessing
wealth, and, in other respects, she
has a decided advantage over wealth,
for those who lead an active life.
The Septuagint renders the first
clause, ἀγαθὴ σοφία μετὰ κληρονομίας,
wisdom is good with an inheritance,
so also the Vulgate, the Chaldee,
Rashbam, Ibn Ezra, Luther, the
Bishops' Bible, the Geneva Bible,
the Authorised Version in the text,

which Ibn Ezra explains, ואם יתכן
שתהיה להכם נחלה טוב הוא לו וייחר טוב
לרואי השמש כי יכבדו אותו בעבור עשרו, *and
if it be desirable that a wise man
should have property, it will be good
for him, and especially good with
regard to those who see the sun, since
they will respect him for his riches,*
and which Rashbam explains, חשובה
וטובה חכמתו של אדם עם נהלה עם שנשתיירו
לו מאביו שלא יתקיימו בידו אם אין לו חכמה
כדי לשמור נכסיו וטובה החכמה יותר מן הממון
לרואי השמש ההולכים ומתנהגים בעולם שחכמתן
מסייעתן ותומדת להן *a man's wisdom is
more respected, and is more advantageous, when it goes together with the
patrimony and property bequeathed to
him by his father, which will not
abide unless he has wisdom to manage
his riches ; but still better than riches
is wisdom for those who lead a public
life, for their wisdom assists and maintains them.* But whichever interpretation we adopt, this rendering is
contrary to the scope of the passage,
as this verse evidently gives the
reason why we are not to complain
of the disappearance of better and
wealthier days, by shewing that there
is an equivalent for riches, and more
than an equivalent to those who are
active upon the stage of life. To
translate, therefore, טוֹבָה חָכְמָה עִם־נַהֲלָה,
wisdom is good WITH *riches,* is to imply
that it is not good without riches,
thus praising up wealth above wisdom, the very thing which Coheleth
denied in the preceding verse, and
combats in the following verse. The
forced explanations of Rashi (עם נחלת
וכות אבותם), *wisdom is good with the
inherited merits of the parents,* taking
נַחֲלָה in a spiritual sense for *merits;*
Mendelssohn, *if wisdom is good with
the possession of an inheritance, it is
found better when that is gone;* and
Spohn, Weisheit iſt heilſam bey Jam-
mertagen und Vorzug benen, welche
heitere Tage haben, *wisdom is salutary
in days of mourning, and an advantage to those who have cheerful days,*

12 sun. For to be in the shelter of wisdom is to be under the
shelter of riches, and the advantage of wisdom is, that

only shew the difficulty arising from
the rendering of עִם, *with.* We avoid
all this if, with the Syriac, Coverdale, Authorised Version in the margin, Desvoeux, Hodgson, Knobel,
De Wette, Herzfeld, Hitzig. Noyes,
Stuart, Elster, Vaihinger, Hengstenberg, &c., we take עִם as a *comparison,*
a sense which it frequently has, and
and in which it occurs in this very
book (see *supra,* ii. 16). נַחֲלָה, *possession, wealth* (comp. Prov. xx. 21).
The Syriac ܠܐ ܘ ܡܬܚܟܡܐ

ܡܢ ܙܝܢܐ ܛܒ ܚܟܡܬܐ *wisdom is better
than weapons,* has evidently arisen
from mistaking נַחֲלָה for נְחִילָה, an *instrument.* The translator has no
doubt fallen into this error through
the passage טוֹבָה חָכְמָה מִכְּלֵי קְרָב, *wisdom
is better than instruments of war* (ix.
17). The וְ in וְיוֹתֵר as often is *aug-
mentive* (comp. Job v. 15; Ps lxxiv.
11; and *supra,* vi. 3). יוֹתֵר is not an
adverb, more (Gesenius, Lex. *s. v.,*
Hitzig, Stuart, &c.), which is against
the parallelism and the structure of
the following verse, but is a participial *noun* (comp. *supra,* vi. 8. 11).
For the phrase רֹאֵי הַשֶּׁמֶשׁ, see vi. 5.

12. *For to be in the shelter,* &c.
Here we have the reasons for the
two assertions made in the preceding
verse respecting wisdom, viz., its
being sometimes as useful as money,
and sometimes having the advantage
over it. That wisdom is in some
cases as good as riches, is evident
from the fact that it is as much a
defence as money. If "riches are
sometimes the ransom of a man's
life" (Prov. xiii. 8) wisdom will deliver a whole city from destruction
(*infra,* ix. 15). And that, in other
cases, wisdom has a pre-eminence
over riches, is also evident, inasmuch
as it has the power of affecting the
inner man, it makes him serene and
cheerful, which the former cannot
do. כִּי, *for,* introducing the reason

for the assertion made in the foregoing verse. The verb *to be,* as
frequently, is to be supplied after it.
From the refreshing coolness which
the *shadow* of overhanging cliffs or
spreading branches of trees afford to
the Eastern in his scorching climate,
צֵל is used metaphorically for *shelter,
protection, defence* (compare Gen. xix.
8; Numb. xiv. 9; Ps. xvii. 9). The
figure has evidently been suggested
by the phrase רֹאֵי הַשֶּׁמֶשׁ, *those who
see* THE SUN, which immediately precedes it. Symmachus (σκέπει σοφία
ὡς σκέπει τὸ ἀργύριον, *wisdom protects
just as money protects*), and the Vulgate (SICUT ENIM PROTEGIT SAPIENTIA,
SIC PROTEGIT PECUNIA), who are followed by Luther (denn die Weisheit
beschirmet, so beschirmet Geld auch),
Coverdale and the Bishops' Bible
("for wisdom defendeth as well as
money"), and the Authorised Version
("for wisdom is a defence and money
is a defence"), ignoring the בְּ, have
made some modern commentators to
to regard it here as the so-called בְּ
essentiæ. But this, to say the least,
is an unnecessary deviation from the
natural signification of this preposition, and necessitates us to supply
the בְּ *comparison.* The explanation
of Rashi (כל מי שישנו בצל החכמה ישנו בצל
הכסף שהחכמה גורמת לעשר שיבא, *whoso is
under the protection of wisdom is under
the protection of money, because it is
wisdom that brings riches*), and Ibn
Ezra (או יהיה החכם חוסה בצל החכמה ובצל
הכסף, *then—i. e.,* when he has riches
with wisdom, according to Ibn Ezra's
view of the preceding verse—*will
the wise man be protected both by the
shelter of wisdom and the shelter of
money*), are as far-fetched as they are
at variance with the scope of the
passage. וְיִתְרוֹן דַּעַת, *and, moreover, an
advantage of wisdom is,* takes up וְיוֹתֵר
of the preceding verse, and hence
shews that the latter is a *noun,* and
that דַּעַת is the same as חָכְמָה, *wisdom,*
of which וְיוֹתֵר, *and there is an advan-*

13 wisdom enliveneth the possessor thereof. Consider, moreover, the work of God, since no man can straighten that
14 which he hath made crooked. In the day of prosperity be
therefore in prosperity, and in the day of adversity consider
that God hath also made this as well as that, to the end that

tage, is the predicate. The Septuagint's rendering of וְיִתְרוֹן דַּעַת הַחָכְמָה "
by καὶ περίσσεια γνώσεως τῆς σοφίας, *and
the advantage of the knowledge of
wisdom, &c,* which is that of the
Chaldee וּמוֹתַר מַנְדְּעָא חוּכְמְתָא דְאוֹרַיְיתָא,
taking דַּעַת as the *construct* with
הָחָכְמָה, is contrary to the accents, and,
if admitted, would yield the same
sense which we have given to the
passage. The Vulgate's paraphrase
(HOC AUTEM PLUS HABET ERUDITIO
ET SAPIENTIA, QUOD VITAM TRIBUUNT
POSSESSORI SUO, *but learning and
wisdom have this more, that they give
life to the possessor thereof*), is a muti-
lation of the text, whilst Luther
(aber die Weisheit gibt das Leben dem,
der sie hat, *but wisdom gives life to
the possessor thereof*) entirely omits
the words וְיִתְרוֹן דַּעַת.

13. *Consider, moreover, &c.* Another reason for obeying the injunction given in verse 10. Complaining
is vain; God has ordained it so, and,
however crooked it may appear to
us, no man can rectify it. רְאֵה, *see,
consider, bear in mind, remember.*
The expression *moreover,* which is
often omitted in Hebrew, must be
supplied in the translation. מַעֲשֵׂה,
work, i. e., *of providence, appointment,
ordaining;* so also לְתַקֵּן, *to rectify,*
and עִוַּת, *to make crooked,* are used in
a spiritual sense. The interrogative,
in which the last clause is expressed,
is tantamount to an emphatic denial,
i. e., *no one can, &c. (vide supra,* i. 3).
For the pleonastic suffix in עִוְּתוֹ, see
ii. 12. The Septuagint's rendering
of כִּי מִי יוּכַל לְתַקֵּן אֵת אֲשֶׁר עִוְּתוֹ by ὅτι τίς
δυνήσεται τοῦ κοσμῆσαι ὃν ἂν ὁ Θεὸς διαστρέψῃ
αὐτόν; *for who is able to make him
straight, if God has distorted him?*
which is followed by the Vulgate,
QUOD NEMO POSSIT CORRIGERE, QUEM

ILLE DESPEXERIT, *that no man can
correct him whom He has despised,*
has evidently originated from the
traditional explanation, as contained
in the Chaldee, which paraphrases
this verse הוי מסתכל ית עובדא דיי וגבורתיה
די עבר ית סמיא ית גביגא וית חגירא למהוייהון
פרישן בעלמא ארום מן הוא הכימא די יכיל לתקנא
ית חד מנהון אלהן מרי עלמא די עתיה *consider the work of God and his power,
who made the blind, the hunch-backed,
and the lame, to be a wonder in the
world; for who is so wise that he can
make straight one of these, except the
Lord of the world who made them
crooked?* and is precluded by the
scope of the passage. For the complaints against which Coheleth speaks
are not about *corporeal defects,* but
those of a repining spirit which is
dissatisfied with the present order
of Providence. Luther's rendering
(denn wer kann das schlecht machen, das
Er krümmet? *for who can make that
bad which He makes crooked?*) is
irreconcileable with לְתַקֵּן.

14. *In the day of,* &c. Having
shewn that dissatisfaction with the
present is contrary to the common-
sense view of life, inasmuch as it
only mars the enjoyment of what
one possesses, without being able to
effect any change in the order of
God's providence, Coheleth deduces
therefrom the necessity of being contented and submissive, in whatever
circumstances of life we are placed,
since God designedly so interweaves
his providences that no man may
be able to foresee the future, in order
that all should live in constant dependence upon him. The sentiment
here propounded, not to mar present
blessings by undue anxiety for the
impenetrable future which a benign
Providence has concealed from the

man should not discover anything which will be after him

human eye, was also the maxim of
the ancient philosophers, and is
beautifully expressed by Horace

Prudens futuri temporis exitum
Caliginosa nocte premit deus
Ridetque, si mortalis ultra
Fas trepidat. Quod adest, memento
Componere æquus; cetera fluminis
Ritu feruntur, nunc medio alveo
Cum pace delabentis Etruscum
In mare, nunc lapides adesos.

" But God, in goodness ever wise,
  Hath hid, in clouds of depthless night,
All that in future prospect lies
  Beyond the ken of mortal sight,
And laughs to see vain man opprest
With idle fears, and more than man distrest.

" Then wisely form the present hour,
  Enjoy the bliss that it bestows;
The rest is all beyond our power,
  And like the changeful Tiber flows,
Who, now, beneath his banks subsides,
And peaceful to its native ocean glides."
                            Od. iii. 29 ; 29–36.

The phrase הֱיֵה בְטוֹב, which the Sept.
rightly explains ζῆθι ἐν ἀγαθῷ, means
live, as it were, in the atmosphere of
contentment or in a state of contentment; be so — do not allow anything
to make you feel or think otherwise,
and is designedly chosen for the sake
of alliteration with טוֹב , so also רְאֵה,
see, consider, bear in mind—the thing
to be considered being given in the
following clause — is used to form a
paranomasia with רָעָה. For לְעֻמַּת, in
connection with, like, see v. 15, and
for עַל דִּבְרַת giving the motive or
occasion of the action, see iii. 18.
The various interpretations given of
almost every word of this verse by
modern commentators, have chiefly
been occasioned by the ancient versions which, as usual, are to be
traced to Hagadic influence. Thus
the Chaldee paraphrases it בְּיוֹם דְּיוֹטִיב
לָךְ יְיָ תְּהֵי אַף אַנְתְּ בְּטִיבוּתָא וְתִיטַב לְכָל עַלְמָא
בְּגִין דְּלָא יֵיתֵי עֲלָךְ יוֹמָא בִּישָׁא חֲזֵי וְאַסְתַּכַּל וְאַף
יָת דֵּין כָּל קֳבֵיל דֵּין עֲבַד יְיָ בְּגִין לְאוֹכָחָא אֱינָשֵׁי
עַלְמָא מִן בְּגִלַל דְּלָא יִשְׁכַּח אֱינַשׁ בַּתְרוֹהִי מִדַּעַם
בִּישׁ לְעַלְמָא הַהוּא, in the day when the
Lord does thee good, be thou also happy
and do good to all the world, that the
evil day may not come upon thee, see
and behold; and also this against
that, God has made to reprove the
men of the world, so that men should

not find after him any evil in the
world to come, construing רָאֵה before
בְּיוֹם רָעָה, i.e., " in the day of prosperity look to the day of adversity,"
referring the pronoun in אַחֲרָיו to both
God and man, and taking it as well
as מְאוּמָה in a double sense, viz., אַחֲרָיו
to denote after Him, against Him,
i.e., God, and after him, after he
(i.e., man) has departed, hereafter,
and מְאוּמָה to signify nothing and
blemish, i.q., מוּם (comp. Dan. i. 4).
Hence the Vulgate, IN DIE BONA
ERUERE BONIS, ET MALAM DIEM PRÆ-
CAVE ; SICUT ENIM HANC, SIC ET
ILLAM FECIT DEUS, UT NON INVENIAT
HOMO CONTRA EUM JUSTAS QUERI-
MONIAS, in the good day enjoy good
things, and beware of the evil day,
for God has made both this and that,
so that man may not find against
Him a just complaint, also makes
the בְ in בְּיוֹם dependent upon רָאֵה (so
also Ibn Ezra, Coverdale, the Bishops'
Bible, Hodgson, Noyes, &c.), refers
the pronoun in אַחֲרָיו to God (so also
Sym., Rashi, Ibn Ezra, Luther,
Mendelssohn, Durell, Herzfeld, &c.),
and takes מְאוּמָה to denote fault (so
also Symmachus, Rashi, Ibn Ezra,
Döderlein, Spohn, Nachtigal, &c.)
Against this is to be urged — 1. That
the advice הֱיֵה בְטוֹב, be happy, which
refers to the conduct of man in the
day of his prosperity (בְּיוֹם טוֹבָה), absolutely requires that the antithetic
רָאֵה should be taken as an admonition
how one is to demean himself in the
day of adversity (בְּיוֹם רָעָה) ; 2. אַחֲרָיו
or אַחֲרֵי is invariably used in this
book as a preposition of time, the
suffix referring to the future of the
individual (ii. 18, iii. 22, vii. 12, ix.
3, x. 14), which is also against
Philippson, who refers it to the
manner of God's dealings, and translates the clause ſo baß ber Menſch
nichts barüber hinauß finbe; and 3.
מְאוּמָה always, without exception, signifies something (see v. 13, ix. 5),
which sense the Septuagint (μηδέν),
the Syriac (ܡܕܡ), and most modern

15 I have seen in my fleeting days, both the righteous die in his righteousness, and the wicked live long in his wickedness.

16 Be not therefore very righteous, and make not thyself too

commentators rightly assign to it here.

15. *I have seen both*, &c. The *passive* submission to the decrees of God's providence, which Coheleth has propounded according to the common-sense view of life (10–14) is now followed by wholesome directions with regard to *active* life (15–20). The golden lesson is not to run into intemperance in religion or irreligion, but to keep to the happy medium. To inculcate this, the sacred writer relates his experience, and then draws the conclusion from it to shew the soundness of this rule. In his fleeting days Coheleth has seen both the righteous, who has the promise of long life, die prematurely, though he consistently maintained his integrity; and the wicked, who is to be cut off suddenly, prolong his days in spite of his persisting in wickedness. הַכֹּל, as frequently, signifies *both* (comp. ii. 14), and is rightly referred by the Vulg., Mendelssohn, Herzfeld, Preston, &c., to the following cases:—בִּימֵי חֶבְלִי, *in the days of my vanity*, i. e., *in my vain* or *fleeting days*; the noun in the genitive expressing the quality of the nominative, has the suffix which refers to the whole idea (comp. הַר קָדְשִׁי, *the mountain of my holiness*, i. e., *my holy mountain*, Ps. ii. 6; Song of Songs viii. 2; Gesenius, § 121, 6; Ewald, § 291, b). Though the בְּ sometimes signifies *for, though* (see the following verse), and is so translated here by Symmachus (τῇ δικαιοσύνῃ αὐτοῦ), Ibn Ezra, Coverdale, the Bishops' Bible, Reynolds, Patrick, Hodgson, Hitzig, Stuart, &c., yet it is more consonant with the scope of the passage to render it with the Septuagint, Vulgate, Syriac, Chaldee, Luther, the Geneva Version, the Authorised Version, &c., by *in*, which, as Desvoeux and Knobel rightly remark, has here the sense of *although*,

notwithstanding (comp. Ewald, § 217, f. 3). הֶאֱרִיךְ, *to make long, to prolong*, is generally followed by the *accusative* יָמִים, *days* (*vide infra*, viii. 13; Deut. v. 30), but sometimes is without it (compare Prov. xxviii. 2; Gesen. § 153, 2; Ewald, § 122, d). The same ellipsis exists in German, *es lange machen, lange treiben*, instead of *lange leben*.

16. *Be not therefore very righteous*, &c. This, then, being the case, since the fortunes of life are not distributed according to the merits or demerits of man, Coheleth submits that we are not to be too rigid and scrupulous in our religious and moral conduct, which, whilst it secures no special blessing, will only alienate our friends from us, and thus mar our enjoyment of the present, the only thing left for man. Much ingenuity has been expended by commentators of all ages, in their attempts to make this verse orthodox. Thus the traditional view, as given in the Midrash and the Chaldee, and followed by Rashi, refers it to *judges*. לָא תְהֵא וַאי יַתִּיר בְּעִדָּן דְּאִתְחַיֵּיב חַיָּיבָא קְטוֹל בְּבֵית דִּינָךְ בְּדִיל לְחַיָּסָא עֲלוֹהִי דְּלָא לְמִקְטְלֵיהּ, *be not too righteous when the criminal is found guilty of death in thy court of justice, so as to have compassion on him and not execute him*, taking צַדִּיק in the sense of *clemency*. Mercer, Geier, Mendelssohn, Hodgson, Rosenmüller, &c., who also restrict this injunction to magistrates, take צַדִּיק in the opposite sense, to denote *rigid*. Ibn Ezra, who is followed by Grotius, Lord Bacon (Adv. of Learning, viii. c. 2, Apho. 31), Paley in one of his sermons, Le Clerc, Reynolds, Desvoeux, Patrick, Noyes, understands by צַדִּיק, *hermitical piety*, one who, by seclusion, entirely neglects the maintenance of his body, הענין חסור מדרך הישוב כמו שיעשו הר'ומיסי בארץ אדום וישמעאל. But 1. These explanations are contrary to the usual meaning of צַדִּיק,

17 wise, for thou wilt only make thyself to be forsaken.   Be not
very wicked, and be not foolish, lest thou die before thy

which always signifies *a man acting
morally* IN ALL *things*, and is so
defined in verse 20, עֹשֶׂה־טּוֹב.   2. The
preceding verse, which contains the
premises to this, describes the fate of
men *really* pious and *really* wicked.
Now, to make Coheleth say that
because some who were *sincerely*
good died prematurely, in spite of
their goodness, therefore be not thou
affectedly good, is most preposterous. The only legitimate conclusion
is, that he cautions us against being
very righteous, pursuing piety much,
in a *good* sense.   Dr. Hammond
(Answ. to Cawdry, chap. ii. § 2).
Holden, Adam Clarke, Stuart, and
others, who saw that " these interpretations are strained and far-fetched,"
resorted to their favourite but equally
arbitrary expedient of putting these
words into the mouth of an objector.
We need not, however, adopt any
violent means to make this verse
harmonise with orthodoxy, inasmuch
as the " politic precept unto neutral-
ity and indifference in good courses"
here propounded, is in accordance
with the so-called *common-sense view
of life* discussed in this section, and
is *not the final* opinion of Coheleth.
That comes at the end of the book,
and must not be anticipated here.
For הַרְבֵּה, *much*, see i. 16, and the
adverbial signification of יוֹתֵר, see ii.
15.   תִּתְחַכָּם is rendered by Gesenius,
Fürst (Lex. *s. v.*), and most modern
commentators, *to be wise in one's
own eyes;* but this is contrary to הֵנֵּה
נִתְחַכְּמָה לּוֹ, Exod. i. 10, the only other
passage where the Hithpael occurs,
and where it incontestably signifies
*to make one's-self wise, to shew one's-
self wise, to act with wisdom*, in
reality, which signification this conjugation frequently has (comp. הִתְחַוִּי,
to shew one's-self strong, 2 Sam. x. 12;
2 Chron. xiii. 7, 8; הִתְאַנֵּף, *to shew
one's-self angry*, Deut. i. 37, iv. 21,
ix. 8. 20; Gesen. § 54, 3; Ewald, §
124). Besides the antithesis אַל־תְּהִי סָכָל,

which speaks of *real*, and not *affected*
foolishness, shews beyond doubt that
the *wisdom* under consideration must
also be *real*. We thus obtain another
proof that the *piety* against which
Coheleth cautions is *sincere*, and not
affected, piety.   For the Pattach
under the final syllable of תִּתְחַכָּם
instead of תִּתְחַכֵּם with a Tzere, see
Gesen. § 54, 3, note. תִּשּׁוֹמֵם is the
Hithpael fut. for תִּתְשׁוֹמֵם— the ת of
the syllable הִת being assimilated
before ז, ט, כ, ג, ד, and ת (compare
Gesen. § 54, 2, 6; Ewald, § 124, c)—
and means *make thyself desolate,
deserted*, or *lonely* (comp. Job xvi. 7,
where all his friends desert him for
his piety), so the Geneva Bible, the
Authorised Version in the margin,
Desvoeux, Durell, Hodgson, Hitzig,
Stuart, &c. The Septuagint's rendering of it by μήποτε ἐκπλαγῇς, *lest
thou be confounded*, which is followed
by the Vulgate NE OBSTUPESCAS, *lest
thou be stupified*, does not at all
militate against our explanation of
the argument.   Luther, Coverdale,
the Authorised Version in the text,
and others, who translate it, *destroy
thyself*, sever the connection of this
verse with the preceding one, since
the death of the righteous mentioned
there is not caused by themselves,
through imprudence, but is permitted by an inscrutable Providence.
The interrogative, as often, is used
for an emphatic affirmation (*vide
supra*, i. 3), and the sense of the
passage is better expressed by rendering it, with the Septuagint and
Vulgate, in the affirmative.

17. *Be not very wicked*, &c. But,
on the other hand, we are to be as
moderate in the indulgence of sin as
we are to be temperate in the practice
of virtue. For, whilst it is true that
a man may live a long life in spite
of his wickedness, yet it is also true
that there are certain laws of nature
which cannot be transgressed with
impunity, violation of these will most

18 time. It is better that thou shouldest lay hold of this, and also not let go thy hand from that, for whoso feareth God

assuredly be visited with premature death. It is almost needless to say that this verse shared the fate of the preceding one. Ibn Ezra's forced attempt to get over the difficulty will shew to what tortures the text of Scripture is put, to wring from it sentiments which should be compatible with the interpreter's pre-conceived notions. "Know," he says, (ודע כי הרשעות היא להתעסק בדברי העולם) "that wicked here means to be engaged in worldly matters." Strange that Herzfeld should follow this interpretation. עֵת, time, also the right time, proper time (comp. infra, x. 17; Prov. xv. 23), which is rendered still more emphatic by the pronoun (comp. Ps. i. 3, civ. 27). The interrogation, as in the former verse, is used for an emphatic assertion.

18. It is better that, &c. Since great piety causes isolation, and great wickedness brings about premature death, we must not give ourselves up entirely to either, but strive to take the middle course. A God-fearing man will know how to avail himself of both. The repeated זֶה . . . זֶה, this . . . that, is rightly referred by the Chaldee, Rashi, Rashbam, Ibn Ezra, Knobel, Herzfeld, Vaihinger, &c., to צֶדֶק, piety, and רֶשַׁע, sin, their immediate antecedents, although, as we have seen, these commentators differ in their interpretation of these terms. Most modern commentators, however, (e.g., Reynolds, Patrick, Hodgson, Holden, Noyes, Stuart, &c.), refer this to the counsel given in verse 18 to avoid wickedness, and that to the advice in verse 16 to abstain from over-righteousness. But, 1. According to this interpretation, this verse contains no farther development of the precepts already given in verses 16 and 17, and is mere tautology. 2. Coheleth nowhere refers to several precepts by distinct pronouns; and 3.

This explanation proceeds from a misunderstanding of the view here propounded. יָרֵא אֱלֹהִים, one who fears God, according to this theory. יָצָא, to go, to go along, to proceed with. אֶת־כֻּלָּם, both, i.e., צֶדֶק, righteousness, and רֶשַׁע, sin, to which the two pronouns זֶה . . . זֶה, referred in the preceding clause. Rashbam beautifully explains the whole verse טוב לך שתאחז בזה בצדק להיות צדיק וגם מזה מן הרשע אל תנח ולא תסיר ידך ממנו כי אותו אדם שהוא ירא שמים יוצא ידי חובתו בכולם שהוא שומר את עצמו שאינו צדיק הרבה ואינו רשע יותר מדי וגו' it is good that thou shouldest take hold of this, i.e., on righteousness, to be righteous, and also from that, i.e., from sin, do not withdraw thine hand from it; for whoso fears God will proceed properly in both, as he takes care not to be very righteous, nor to sin above measure. &c. The Vulgate, which renders יֵצֵא אֶת־כֻּלָּם by NIHIL NEGLIGIT, gives the same meaning to this phrase in the negative. So also the Syriac, Rashi, Ibn Ezra, Durell, Hitzig, Stuart, &c. The rendering of יָצָא by escape (Luther, Coverdale, &c.), come forth of (the Bishop's Bible, the Geneva Version, and the Auth. Version, &c.), avoid (Desvoeux), will be guided by (Hodgson), &c., are contrary to the usus loquendi, inasmuch as it is an intransitive verb, and cannot govern the accusative. The appeal to the phrase יָצָא אֶת־הָעִיר (Exod. ix. 29. 33), is inapposite, as this case is not exactly analogous. The rendering of the Septuagint, ἀγαθὸν τὸ ἀντέχεσθαί σε ἐν τούτῳ, καίγε ἀπὸ τούτου μὴ μιάνῃς τὴν χεῖρά σου, it is good that thou hold fast to this, and also by this defile not thine hand, changing מֵידֶךָ into תְּמֵמְאָא; and the Vulgate, BONUM EST TE SUSTENTARE JUSTUM, SED ET AB ILLO NE SUBTRAHAS MANUM TUAM; QUIA QUI TIMET DEUM, NIHIL NEGLIGIT, it is good for thee to sustain the just, nay, from him withdraw not thine hand; for whoso fears God neglects nothing, taking טוב in a double sense, viz, it

19 will make his way with both.   Wisdom alone is greater
  strength to the wise, than many mighty men who have been
20 in the city; for there is not a righteous man upon earth who

is good, and, a *good* or *upright man*,
according to the Hagadic rule of
interpretation, evidently proceed
from a desire to make this verse orthodox.

19. *Wisdom alone*, &c.   In concluding this lesson of moderation,
Coheleth submits that it is wisdom
alone, or this common sense view of
life, which will shew itself more
powerful in him who acts according
to it, to resist the extremes of life,
than the combined strength of a numerous army in a beleagured city.
חָכְמָה, *wisdom*, is the view of life under
consideration.   תָּעֹז is rendered *actively* by the Sept. (βοηθήσει, *will help*),
Aquila (ἐνισχύσει, *will strengthen*), Vulgate (*confortavit*), which is followed
by Luther, Coverdale, the Bishops'
Bible, the Geneva Version, the Auth.
Version, and most modern commentators, but without any example to
substantiate it, as עָזַז is invariably
used *intransitively*, *to become strong,
to be strong, to shew itself strong, to
have protection*.   This may be seen
by referring to Gesenius (Lex. *s. v.*),
who strangely enough makes this
passage a solitary exception, though
the uniform signification of the Kal
yields excellent sense, and is rightly
given by Ibn Ezra יותר עוז וכֹח יש לחכמה
מעוז שליטים רבים, *wisdom has more
strength and power than many mighty
men*, Knobel, Lee (Lex. *s. v.*), &c.
עֶשֶׂר, *ten*, is frequently used for a
round number (Gen. xxxi. 7; Numb.
xiv. 22; Job xix. 3), and exactly corresponds to our expression *many*,
which ought to be given in a version
to convey the proper sense of the
original, as Rashbam and Ibn Ezra
rightly maintain and substitute רבים,
many.   Desvoeux's objection, that
" ten mighty men would be a poor
garrison for a besieged city," which
led him to interpret שַׁלִּיטִים, *princes,
chiefs*, including the forces they command (Comment. p. 570), is owing

to an oversight of this idiom, and of
the similar comparison cited above.
The phrase עִיר גִּבֹּרִים, *a city of mighty
men*, i. e., *defended by mighty men*
(Prov. xxi. 22), puts it beyond a doubt
as to what שַׁלִּיטִים בָּעִיר in this verse
means.   With this well-known comparison before us, and the simple
meaning of the text, we may well be
astonished at the extraordinary and
most unnatural interpretation which
Mendelssohn gives to this verse, viz.,
" this maxim will be confirmed to a
wise man from any ten rulers that
have been in a city, that there is no
just man," &c., taking חָכְמָה to denote
a *piece of wisdom*, a *wise maxim*, and
the מ in מְעַשָׂרָה as descriptive of *place*.
Strange that Preston should follow
this interpretation.   The præterite
הָיוּ, and the article in בָּעִיר, make the
illustration מְעַשָׂרָה שַׁלִּיטִים appear as if
it had actually taken place.   But
such personifications are frequently
resorted to by Coheleth in order to
render the statement more vivid and
striking (comp. ii. 15, iv. 8. 15, &c.)

20. *For there is not*, &c.   The
reason why wisdom was stated in the
foregoing verse to be effectual in aiding the wise to avoid extremes is, that
righteousness, the only other thing
which might have been thought able
to assist in this respect, is impracticable, inasmuch as there is not a
single righteous man who can in-
violably follow its precepts.   כִּי is not
surely, truly (the Geneva Version,
Hodgson, Noyes, &c.), nor *although*
(Holden, &c.), but *for*, assigning a
reason for the eulogy passed upon
wisdom in the preceding verse.   For
the position of the *negative* particle
אֵין, see Ewald, § 321, b.   Rashbam's
explanation, ועכשיו אמרתי לך שאין דבר
חשוב בעולם כהחכמה ,ועל כן זאת לבך להבין
שהרי אין אדם חכם בארץ אשר יעשה טוב בכל
ימיו שלא יחטא .ועל כן יש לך לשמור עצמך
שמירה גדולה שלא תבוא לידי חטא בקל וחומר
מן החכם *having said that there is no-*

21 doeth good and sinneth not. Moreover, give not thy heart
to all the words which are uttered, lest thou hear thy servant

*thing in the world so excellent as
wisdom, Coheleth now wants it to be
understood that there is, nevertheless,
not a single wise man upon the earth
who does good and errs not. Hence
the necess·ty of being exceedingly careful not to fall into error, especially
when one is a wise man,* assigns to כִּי
the abnormal sense of *nevertheless*,
takes צַדִּיק in this verse to be synonymous with חָכָם in the preceding one,
and does not improve the sense.
Equally objectionable is Ibn Ezra's
interpretation, חזר לבאר ענין אל חזי צדיק
הרבה וענינו דע כי לא תוכל שלא תחטא כי אין
אדם אשר לא יחטא בפועל או בדבור או במחשבה,
*Coheleth now returns to explain verse
16, " Be not very righteous," and his
meaning is, know that it is impossible
for you not to sin, for there is not a
man existing who does not sin either
in deed, words, or thought,* regarding
verse 19 as parenthetical, which is
followed by Mercer and others. Still
more artificial is the explanation of
Reynolds, Spohn, Holden, Knobel,
Heiligstedt, &c., connecting it with
the following verse, viz., " Because
there is not a just man upon earth
that doeth good and sinneth not,
therefore it is also *the part of wisdom*
to take no heed unto all words," &c.,
as כִּי never begins a new subject, and
is never construed with גַּם as *cause*
and *effect*.

21. *Moreover, give not thy heart,*
&c. · Another lesson which wisdom
teaches, is to abstain from prying
into everybody's sentiments, as this
frequently results in hearing things
which mar the peace and happiness
of the curious. The transition from
the former lesson to this is apparent.
In the preceding admonition, reference had to be made to the imperfections of the best of men, it is
therefore natural that Coheleth should
pass on to a propensity in man, which,
if indulged, would bring to his ears
the very failings of which he is guilty.
Lord Bacon beautifully remarks upon

this passage, " It is scarce credible
what uneasiness is created in life by
an useless curiosity about the things
that concern us; as when we pry into
such secrets, as, being discovered,
give us distaste, but afford no assistance or relief. For— 1. There follows
vexation and disquiet of mind, as all
human things are full of perfidious-
ness and ingratitude. So that, though
we could procure some magic glass,
wherein to view the animosities, and
all that malice which is any way at
work against us, it were better for
us to break it directly than to use it.
For these things are but as the
rustling of leaves, soon over. 2. This
curiosity always loads the mind with
suspicion, which is a violent enemy
to counsels, and renders them unsteady and perplexed. 3. It also
frequently fixes the evils themselves,
which would otherwise have blown
over: for it is a dangerous thing to
provoke the consciences of men,
who, so long as they think themselves
concealed, are easily changed for the
better ; but, if they once find themselves discovered, drive out one evil
with another. It was therefore
justly esteemed the utmost prudence
in Pompey that he directly burnt
all the papers of Sertorius, unperused
by himself or others " (Advancement
of Learning, viii. 2, Aphorism 4,
pp. 301,302,Bohn's ed.) *Servants* are
adduced as an illustration, because
they are generally acquainted with
the faults of their masters, and are
often prone to speak about them to
others; and because from them an
insult is felt more keenly, and the
master has the best opportunity of
resenting it. נָתַן לֵב לְ, *to give one's
heart to anything,* i. e., *to search it
out.* For יְדַבֵּרוּ. *they spake,* third person
plural, used *impersonally* or *passively,*
see i. 10. אֲשֶׁר לֹא, *that not, lest* (comp.
Esth. i. 19, ii. 10). מְקַלְלֶךָ is well
rendered by Symmachus λοιδοροῦντός σε,
the Vulg. MALEDICENTEM TIBI, Cover-

22 speak evil against thee; for thy heart knoweth that oftentimes
23 thou also hast spoken evil of others. All this have I tried
by wisdom; I wished to be wiser, but it was far from me.

dale, the Bishops' Bible, &c., *reviling,
abusing,* or *speaking evil of thee*; the
Piel of קָלַל is often used in this sense
(comp. *infra*, x. 20; Levit. xix. 14;
2 Sam. xvi. 5). For the construction
of מְקַלֶּלְךָ, see Ewald, § 284, 6. The
Hagadic explanation of this verse,
אוּף כָּל מִילַיָּא דִימַלְּלִין לָךְ רַשִּׁיעָא לָא תִּמְסוֹר לִבָּךְ
לְקַבָּלוּתְהוֹן דְּלָא יֵיתוּן יוֹמִין דִּי תִשְׁמַע יָת עַבְדָּךְ
מְלַיֵּט לָךְ, *also all the words which
the wicked speak to thee, give not
thy heart to accept them, lest the
days come when thou shalt hear thy
servant curse thee*, gave rise to the
rendering of the Septuagint, καίγε
εἰς πάντας λόγους οὓς λαλήσουσιν ἀσεβεῖς
μὴ θῇς καρδίαν σου, and also the Syriac

Version, ܣܘܦ ܟܠܗܘܢ ܡ̈ܠܐ
ܘܡܚܕܐ ܢܦܫܟ ܠܐ ܬܬܠ ܠܟ

*and also do not give thy heart to all
the words which the wicked speak.*

22. *For thy heart knoweth, &c.*
To prove what has been said, Coheleth appeals to our own experience.
We know that we frequently dwell
upon the faults of our neighbours,
and it is but natural that they should
do the same. If we therefore like to
be inquisitive, we must expect to hear
the same free expression of unpleasant things about ourselves which
we exercise with regard to others,
and which they would hear if they
instituted the same inquiries. גַּם,
also, before פְּעָמִים, *times*, belongs to
אַתָּה, *thou*, where, however, it is
repeated, because the intervening
words are too many. The subordi-
nate פְּעָמִים רַבּוֹת, *many times*, depending
upon קִלַּלְתָּ, *thou hast spoken evil of*, is
placed first, for the sake of emphasis.
The regular construction would be
כִּי יָדַע לִבְּךָ גַּם־אַתָּה אֲשֶׁר קִלַּלְתָּ אֲחֵרִים פְּעָמִים
רַבּוֹת, which is rightly given by the
Vulgate SCIT ENIM CONSCIENTIA TUA,
QUIA ET TU CREBRO MALEDIXISTI
ALIIS, Rashbam שהרי גם אתה יודע בעצמך

אֲשֶׁר רַבּוֹת פְעָמִים קִלְּלָה אֲחֵרִים, Luther denn
dein Herz weiß, daß du andern auch
oftmals geflucht haft, Coverdale and
the Bishops' Bible "for thine own
heart knoweth, that thou thyself also
hast oft-times spoken evil by other
men," Hodgson, Herzfeld, &c. The
Geneva Version ("for oftentimes also
thine heart knoweth that thou likewise hast cursed others"), which is
followed by the Authorised Version,
is a departure from Coverdale and
the Bishops' Bible for the worse.
The rendering of Knobel, De Wette,
Hitzig, Stuart, Vaihinger, &c., *for
thou knowest many times* or *many
instances when*, &c., taking פְּעָמִים רַבּוֹת
as the accusat. of the *object* governed
by יָדַע, is owing to a misunderstanding
of this emphatic construction. To
connect this verse with its rendering
of the former one, the Septuagint
translates it ὅτι πλειστάκις πονηρεύσεταί
σε καὶ καθόδους πολλὰς κακώσει καρδίαν σου,
*for many times he will do thee evil,
and will repeatedly afflict thy heart,*
&c.; it substitutes, according to the
Hagadic mode of interpretation, יָרַע,
he shall do thee evil, shall afflict thee,
for יָדַע, which is similar in appearance, making ἀσεβής (רָשָׁע), *the sinner,*
which was supplied in the preceding
verse, the subject, and doubly ex-
plains the clause, first פְּעָמִים רַבּוֹת יָרַע לָךְ,
and then פְּעָמִים רַבּוֹת יָרַע לִבֶּךְ, because
the Hiphil יָרַע signifies both *to do
evil, morally,* and *to afflict.* We have
had such modes of explanation before,
see verse 18.

23. *All this have I tried, &c.* This
line of conduct thus set forth, Coheleth tells us he had tried himself
by means of *practical* wisdom, which
he had so largely acquired, and therefore could speak experimentally upon
the subject (comp i. 12). He, moreover, tells us that, stimulated by her
salutary assistance in *practical* life,
he wished for her help in another
direction; he wanted to obtain still

24 Far remaineth what was far, and deep, deep! who can find
25 it out? I and my heart turned to know and diligently to

greater wisdom, so as to be able to fathom and comprehend the myste-ries of Providence, but that in this he utterly failed. For הִי, *that*, see ii. 2, and נִפָּה, *to try*, see ii. 1. אָמַרְתִּי, *I said*, also *I thought, I wished*, is closely connected with the *future* (אֶחְכָּמָה) which is subordinate to it, and must be rendered, *I thought to be wise*, or *wiser* (comp. לֹא יָדַעְתִּי אֲכַנֶּה, *I know not I shall flatter*, i.e., *I know not to flatter*, Job xxxii. 22; Isa. xlii. 21; Gesen. § 142, 3, c.; Ewald, § 285). The phrase is well explained by Ibn Ezra, בקשתי שאחכם יותר ומצאתי שהוא דבר רחוק, *I wished to be wiser, but I found that this is too remote an object*.

24. *Far remaineth what was far*, &c. To shew the failure of his attempt to fathom by wisdom the counsels of the Almighty, Coheleth says, that that which had appeared to him inexplicable in the moral government of God prior to his obtaining wisdom still continued to be so afterwards. The same sentiment is expressed in viii. 17. The repetition עָמֹק, in the second clause, shews that רָחוֹק must also be repeated in the first clause, and that it has been omitted for the sake of brachylogy. Fully expressed, the verse would be רָחוֹק הוּא מַה־שֶּׁהָיָה רָחוֹק וְעָמֹק מַה־שֶּׁהָיָה עָמֹק וְגוֹ׳, *far remains what was far, and deep remains what was deep*. The Septuagint, connecting it with the preceding verse, renders it εἶπα Σοφισθήσομαι καὶ αὕτη ἐμακρύνθη ἀπ᾽ ἐμοῦ μακρὰν ὑπὲρ ὅ ἦν καὶ Βαθὺ βάθος, *I said I will be wise, but it was far from me, beyond what it was, and great measure;* thus also the Vulgate, *dixi: Sapiens efficiar; et ipsa longius recessit a me, multo magis quam erat, et alta profunditas*, and the Syriac

ܐܶܡܪܶܬ݂ ܐ݈ܙܳ̈ܠ ܘܰܢܒܶܟ݂ܰܡ ܣܳܘ ܗ݈ܝ ܪܰܚܺܝܩܳܐ

ܘܥܰܡܺܝܩܳܐ ܗ݈ܝ ܘܡܰܢ ܡܶܫܟܰܚ ܠܳܗ̇

referring the whole verse to wisdom, which is fol-lowed by Coverdale and the Bishops' Bible, "I thought to be wise, but she went further from me than she was before, yea and so deep that I might not reach unto her." But this is inadmissible, because it cannot be taken as a *comparative*, and because the *feminine* רְחוֹקָה and the *masculine* רָחוֹק cannot both be the predicate of the same subject. Luther's Version, es ist ferne, was wird es sein? und ist sehr tief, wer will es finden? which is literally adopted in the Geneva Bible, "it is far off, what may it be? and it is a profound deepness, who can find it?" and explained in the margin "meaning wisdom," the Authorised Version, Knobel, De Wette, Noyes, Hitzig, Stuart, Vai-hinger, &c., "that which is far off, and exceeding deep, who can find it out?" besides referring the *fem.* רְחוֹקָה and the *masc.* רָחוֹק to the same subject, violate the uniform meaning of the phrase מַה־שֶּׁהָיָה, and render the præterite הָיָה in the present. The loose renderings of Desvoeux, "what-ever is so far off, nay removed to the greatest depth, who shall find it?" and Hodgson, "how distant is it, and deep! Deep! who can reach it?" incur the same objections.

25. *I and my heart turned*, &c. From this vain attempt to speculate about remote and profound things (23–24) Coheleth returned with greater eagerness than ever (לָדַעַת וְלָתוּר וּבַקֵּשׁ) to the teachings of *practical* wis-dom, setting forth her salutary coun-sels. The caution now given is to be guarded against *women* (25–29), for they engender and perpetuate evil and misery. For סָבַב, *to turn from one thing*, construed with לְ *to*, indi-cating *the other thing*, to which the transition is made, see ii. 20. וְלִבִּי is not *sensu meo* (Symmachus), nor *animo meo* (the Vulgate), לְחֶשְׁבָּנָא בְּלִבִּי

3 D

examine practical wisdom, in order to know the cause of

(the Syriac, the Chaldee, Knobel, Heiligstedt, Hitzig, Elster, Vaihinger, &c.) making it the instrumental accusative, as if it were בְּלִבִּי, *with my heart*, which twenty-eight of Kennicott's, and fourty-four of De Rossi's MSS. actually have, as this is contrary to the וְ ; nor ich kehrte mein Herz, *I applied my mind* (Luther, Coverdale, the Bishops' Bible, the Authorised Version in the text, Spohn, Noyes, &c.), as if it were אֶת־לִבִּי ; nor is it *my desire*, the copula הָיָה being implied after it, and the infinitives (*nominascent*) that follow are the complement or predicate, *i. e., and my purpose or desire was to know*, &c. (ומה שבותי לדעת וגו' Ibn Ezra), und meine Begehr war zu erkennen (Herzfeld, Stuart, &c.), but *and my heart* (καὶ ἡ καρδία μου, Sept.) *as a companion*, in accordance with the uniform apostrophising of the heart or the soul, which is always appealed to and summoned when a new thing is to be undertaken (*vide*, i. 13, ii, 1. 20). The predicate סַבּוֹתִי is *singular*, though referring to both אֲנִי and לִבִּי, because it is placed at the beginning of the sentence (comp. Gen. xxiv. 55 ; 1 Sam. xxvii. 8 ; Jer. xxx. 19 ; Gesenius, § 147 ; Ewald, § 339, c). For the use of הוּר and בִּקֵּשׁ, verbs of similar import to express *intensity*, see i. 13. The omission of the לְ before בַּקֵּשׁ is harsh and uncommon, and is therefore rightly supplied in the Syriac and the Chaldee paraphrase. The לְ is however also omitted in וְהָיוּ לְאֹתֹת וּלְמוֹצֲדִים וּלְיָמִים וְשָׁנִים (Gen. i. 14). חֶשְׁבּוֹן, from חָשַׁב, *to bind, to knit together, to interlace* (Exod. xxvi. 1. 31, xxviii. 6, xxxv. 35), *to combine skilfully*, like all other verbs of binding, knitting, &c. (see Fürst, Lex. under אָרַג, חָשַׁב, זָמַם, כָּנַב), is transferred to the combining of thought, either in a good or bad sense; hence *to think, to think out, to devise, to plot*, means *combination, device, the summing up of combinations, explanation, the sum, result, estimate, decision* (*vide infra*, ver. 27,

ix. 10). חֶשְׁבּוֹן defines חָכְמָה, wherewith it is connected by the copula, thus constituting the figure hendiadys = ἕν διὰ δυοῖν, in which case the defining noun may either stand before or after the one it defines (comp. לְאֹתֹת וּלְמוֹעֲדִים, *for signs and for seasons, i. e.,* for signs of seasons Gen. i. 14 ; בְּשָׂמִים וּמִינִים, *odours and kinds, i. e.,* divers kinds of odours 2 Chron. xvi. 14, *infra*, viii. 5, 6; ix. 11; Gesen § 155, 1, a. The וְ in וְלָדַעַת, as frequently, marks the *end* or *aim* of this enquiry (comp. Gesen. § 155, 1, e; Ewald, § 347). That רֶשַׁע, כֶּסֶל, and הַסִּכְלוּת, *wickedness, vice,* and *folly*, are here used metonymically for the *origin, source,* or *cause* of these evils is evident from the following verse. The article in הַסִּכְלוּת shews that it is a special kind of folly, and that הוֹלֵלוֹת *defines it*, i. q., וְהַסִּכְלוּת אֲשֶׁר הוֹלֵלוֹת, *and that folly which is madness*, i. e., that mad or infatuated folly. What this is, Coheleth tells us in the following verses. The Vulgate renders לָדַעַת רֶשַׁע כֶּסֶל וְהַסִּכְלוּת הוֹלֵלוֹת by UT COGNOSCEREM IMPIETATEM STULTI ET ERROREM IMPRUDENTIUM, which is followed by Luther (zu erfahren der Gottlosen Thorheit, und Irrthum der Tollen), Coverdale and the Bishops' Bible (" to know the foolishness of the ungodly, and the error of doting fools "); but against this is to be urged — 1. That it is contrary to the signification of כֶּסֶל and הוֹלֵלוֹת, which are *abstracts ;* and 2. That it is against the construction of the words רֶשַׁע and הַסִּכְלוּת, which are in the *absolute*, as is evident from the absence of the article in the nouns supposed to be in the genitive. The

Syriac ܠܡܕܥ ܪܘܫܥܐ ܕܣܟܠܐ ܘܣܟܠܘܬܐ ܘܓܘܪܐ *to know the wickedness of the fool, and folly and adultery*, incurs these objections with regard to the words רֶשַׁע כֶּסֶל ; whilst Rashbam (רשע של סכלות וכסולות של הוללות), and the Geneva Bible (" to know the wickedness of folly

26 wickedness, vice, and mad folly, and I found the woman
more bitter than death ; she is nets, her heart snares, and
her hands are chains ; whoso is good before God shall escape
27 from her ; but the sinner shall be caught by her. Behold
what I have found, saith Coheleth — taking one thing by one

and the foolishness of madness"),
the Authorised Version (" to know
the wickedness of folly, even of
foolishness and madness"), Desvoeux
(" to know the wickedness of ignorance and the foolishness of that
which is in the greatest esteem "),
and Hodgson (" to make likewise
the evil of folly and the madness of
vice "), only incur the second objection. The rendering of Knobel,
Herzfeld, Ewald, Hitzig, Heiligstedt,
Philippson, Stuart, Elster, Vaihinger,
Hengstenberg, &c., "to know wisdom
as folly, and folly as madness," taking
כֶּסֶל and הוֹלֵלוֹת as second accusatives
depending upon the verb לָדַעַת, is very
artificial, and has not been substantiated by any really parallel instances
in Ewald's Grammar, § 284, b.

26. And I found, &c. Coheleth
soon found that it is woman who
is the cause of all the mischief,
employing her arts and snares to
inveigle man ; that only the God-
fearing can be delivered from her,
whilst the sinner is irretrievably
caught. That woman is the cause
of man's sin is quite in harmony
with the earliest notions of the female
sex, and with the opinions of Orientals to the present day. The conduct
of the first man, who tried to exculpate his crime by ascribing the
culpability to the woman (Gen. iii.
6. 12), has been faithfully copied by
his sons in all ages, to the detriment
of themselves, the female sex, and
society at large ; so that the woman
became the embodiment of wickedness (Zech. v. 8 ; Sirach xxv. 24,
xlii. 13, 14 ; 1 Tim. ii. 14 ; Testament of the Twelve Patriarchs,
Ruben, § 5). מוֹצֵא is one of the verbs
ל״א which adopt the vowel points of
ל״ה by virtue of their intimate con-

nection, in consequence of which
these two classes of verbs not unfrequently flow into one another (comp.
infra, viii. 2. 12, ix. 18, x. 5 ; Gesen.
§ 75, vi. ; Ewald, § 116, b ; § 142, c).
מַר does not agree with אִשָּׁה, because
it precedes it for the sake of emphasis,
as in the foregoing verse. לִבָּהּ and
יָדֶיהָ may either be the accusative of
the manner or the respect in which
she is snares, &c., i. e., who is nets
and snares as to her heart, and bands
as to her hand (comp. Gen. xxxvii.
21 ; Deut. xxii. 26, xxxiii. 11 ; Ps.
lxxxiii. 6 ; Gesen. § 139, 2 ; Ewald, §
281, c) ; or, which is still better, they
are to be taken as the subject or
nominative, הִיא, as frequently, being
used for the sake of emphasis (vide
supra, iii. 14) to describe the whole
sex ; so the Septuagint, Vulgate, the
Syriac, Desvoeux, Holden, &c. The
omission of the ו before אֲסוּרִים is
owing to the fact that when three or
more nouns or clauses are connected,
the copula is sometimes only inserted
between the first and second, and not
before the subsequent ones (comp.
מֹר וַאֲהָלוֹת קְצִיעוֹת, myrrh, and aloes,
and cassia, Ps. xlv. 9 ; Deut. xxix.
22 ; Job xlii. 9 ; Isa. i. 13).

27. Behold what, &c. The allegation made in the foregoing verse
respecting the great wickedness of
woman, Coheleth here assures us is
not owing to his ignoring the faults
of his own sex, but is the result of
unbiassed and minute observations
of both sexes. Having examined
both man and woman, and taken
everything (אַחַת לְאַחַת) belonging to
their respective conditions into consideration, he now tells us both what
he has found and what he has not
found among them to substantiate
the foregoing assertion. In giving

28 to find the result — and what my soul is still seeking, and I
have not found; one man among a thousand I have found,

his reasons, Coheleth begins with
רְאֵה, *see, behold*, to secure special
attention. That by זֶה, *this*, the
sacred writer points to what *follows*
(Desvoeux, Knobel, Heiligstedt, Hitzig, Stuart, Elster, &c.), and not to
what precedes (Mendelssohn, Rosenmüller, Vaihinger, Hengstenberg,
&c.), is evident from verse 29, where
the same words (רְאֵה זֶה) are used to
call attention to what he is *going to
say*. Grotius, Durell, Houbigant,
Michaelis, Van der Palm, Spohn,
Knobel, Heiligstedt, Stuart, Elster,
&c., alter אָמְרָה קֹהֶלֶת into אָמַר הַקֹּהֶלֶת,
maintaining that the words are
wrongly divided, and that the article
ה has, by a mistake, been detached
from הַקֹּהֶלֶת and attached to אָמַר. In
support of this they submit — 1. That
קֹהֶלֶת is construed with the masculine
verb אָמַר in all the other passages
where it occurs (compare i. 1, 2. 12,
and xii. 8, 9, 10) ; 2. That the phrase
אָמַר הַקֹּהֶלֶת actually occurs in xii. 8,
where קֹהֶלֶת has the article ; and 3.
That this is supported by the Sept.
and the Syriac. But this emendation
is arbitrary, as well as unnecessary,
and proceeds from a misunderstanding of the word קֹהֶלֶת, which describes
Solomon as *personified wisdom*, and
hence may be construed both with
masculine and feminine verbs, according to the nature of the case
(*vide supra*, p. 7). The article in
xii. 8 has a special significance there,
and would be useless here. As to
the appeal to the ancient versions,
it is preposterous to seek support for
this emendation from the rendering
εἶπεν ὁ ἐκκλησιαστής of the Septuagint,
since the Greek verb has no distinction between masculine and feminine, and the masculine article ὁ
before ἐκκλησιαστής only shews that
ἐκκλησιαστής is a masculine noun in
Greek, just as the article ἡ before
καρδία shews that καρδία is feminine ;
and no one would ever try to establish
therefrom, by the same parity of

reasoning, that לֵב is feminine in
Hebrew. The Syr. ܐܡܪ ܩܘܗܠܬ
proves nothing, inasmuch as it only
shews that in the copy from which
this version was made, the ה was
altogether wanting. The feminine
אַחַת is used in a *neuter sense* for *one
thing* (*vide supra*, i. 11), and the
verb substantive הָיְתָה, which, as frequently, is omitted, must be supplied
after it, *i. e.*, אַחַת לְאַחַת הָיְתָה, *one thing
to one thing was to find*, &c., that is
to say, *every individual thing peculiar
to either sex was, or came in, to make
up the result*, thus shewing that all
partiality has been carefully excluded.
In the translation this clause is better
put in parenthesis, to mark the intimate connection of this verse with
the following one, which the improper division of verses has entirely
destroyed.

28. *And what*, &c. Coheleth now
tells us what he has found and what
he has not found in the course of
his examination. A man virtuous
and upright, and deserving this appellation, he has found among a
thousand, but a woman possessing
these characteristics which make her
worthy of this name he has not found
among a similar number ; or, in
other words, though upright men
are not very numerous, yet they are
to be found, but upright women are
scarcely to be met with. This, then,
being the case, the allegation in
verse 26 is fully established. For
the Eastern notions of women we
must refer to verse 26, and my commentary on the Song of Songs, pp.
14–19, and add here the remarks of
St. Chrysostom, that the devil, when
depriving Job of his substance,
children, and health, left his wife,
" because he thought that she would
be a great furtherance unto him to
conquer that saint of God " (Homel.
38 in Epistol. ad Corinth.) ; " what
is woman, but a punishment that

29 but a woman among all that number I have not found : only
behold this have I found, that God made man upright, but

cannot be driven away, a necessary evil, a natural temptation, a desirable calamity, a domestic danger, one beloved for the colour of good ?" (Homel. 6 in Matt., quoted by Jermin, p. 243) ; and the saying of Mohammed, that among men there were many perfect, but among women only four — Asiah, the wife of Pharaoh ; Mary, the mother of Christ ; Cadijah, his wife ; and Fatima, his daughter" (Pocock, Specimen Hist. Arab. p. 188, ed. White, Oxon. 1806; Prideaux, Life of Mahomet, p. 61, quoted by Holden, p. 124). אֲשֶׁר, that, at the beginning of this verse, depends upon רְאֵה זֶה, behold this, in the foregoing verse ; so that וְזֶה, and this, or the simple copula וְ, is to be supplied before it, and is properly given by the Syriac, Luther, and the Geneva Bible ; hence the Sept., the Vulgate, the Authorised Version, also rightly connect this verse with the preceding one. Holden's assertion, that by doing this these versions " produce the contradiction of saying that the Preacher had not found what before he asserted that he had found," proceeds from his having mistaken the sense of the sacred writer ; since the *finding* and *not finding* refer to *two separate subjects*, the former to men, the latter to women. To us it is a matter of great surprise that commentators should not have alighted upon this simple and natural explanation of the text, but have resorted to a multitude of forced and conflicting interpretations too numerous to be repeated. The words עֹד־בִּקְשָׁה נַפְשִׁי, *my soul is still seeking*, are added, to shew the difficulty of the task. Coheleth had not only devoted the same space of time in his search after a good woman which he gave to his search after a good man, but he tells us that *he is still in quest of her*. The absence of the *Dagesh* in בִּקְשָׁה here, and in בִּקְשׁוּ in the following

verse, is owing to the peculiarity that the radical letters in the forms of Piel and Pael, which have *Sheva* under them, may drop the characteristic *Dagesh* (comp. Ps. lxxiv. 7 ; Ezek. xvii. 7 ; Gesenius, § 20, 3 ; Ewald, § 64). That אָדָם and אִשָּׁה stand for אִישׁ יָשָׁר, *an upright man*, and אִשָּׁה יְשָׁרָה, *an upright woman*, is evident from verse 26, and especially from the following verse. אָדָם is not unfrequently used for אִישׁ, like ἄνθρωπος for ἀνηρ in Greek, and *homo* for *vir* in Latin (comp. Ps. cv. 14, with 1 Chron. xvi. 21, and Matt. xix. 10). אֶלֶף, *a thousand*, is put for a *large round number* (comp. Ps. l. 10, lxxxiv. 11, xc. 4, cv. 8), and hence the phrase one in a thousand became an idiomatic expression for *something rare* (compare Job ix. 3, xxxiii. 23). אֲנָשִׁים, *men*, is to be supplied after מֵאֶלֶף, *in a thousand.* בְּכָל־אֵלֶּה, *among this*, i. e., *large number.* Though the number *thousand* has evidently been suggested by the number of Solomon's wives and concubines (1 Kings xi. 1 – 9), yet it would be contrary to the scope of the passage to refer this description to *them*. For if the *thousand men* refer to the *male sex generally*, the common laws of language and exegesis demand that the *thousand women* should be interpreted of the *female sex generally.* Bishop Patrick's attempt to elude this dilemma by trying to restrict the thousand men to the multitude who attended upon Solomon in the court, is simply gratuitous, inasmuch as there is not the slightest intimation that Solomon's *courtiers* or *servants* are here intended ; but, on the contrary, the following verse clearly shews that mankind generally are meant.

29. *Only, behold,* &c. To avoid, however, all misunderstanding as regards the origin of this state of things, and to shew that the degeneracy of both men and women, great

viii. 1 they seek out many devices.   Who is like the wise
man ? and who like him that understandeth the meaning of

in the one case and great in the
other, has no other source than the
human heart, Coheleth finds it necessary to add that when man left
the hands of the Creator he was not
so; God created men upright, but
they corrupted themselves. לְבַד, *only*,
is used for singling out the subject
to which particular attention is drawn
(comp. Isa. xxvi. 13).   That הָאָדָם is
here used in a generic sense for *mankind*, is evident from the *plural* pronoun הֵמָּה, *they*, thus affording another irrefragable proof that the
characteristics mentioned in the preceding verses do not belong to *particular classes*, but to *mankind*.   For
the Piel יְבַקְשׁוּ without the *Dagesh* in
the ק, see the foregoing verse. חִשְּׁבֹנוֹת,
devices (*vide* verse 25), has what is
called the *Dagesh dirimens* or *euphonic*
(comp. Gesen. § 20, 2; Ewald, §
188, f).   The Vulgate's rendering of
וְהֵמָּה בִּקְשׁוּ חִשְּׁבֹנוֹת רַבִּים, ET IPSE SE IN-
FINITIS MISCUERIT QUÆSTIONIBUS, *and
he has entangled himself with an in-
finity of questions*, connecting it with
the following verse; which is followed
by Coverdale, " God made man just
and right, but they seek diverse
subtilties, whereas no man hath
wisdom and understanding to give
answer thereunto;" and Ewald, who
explains it doch wenn das wahrhaft
tugendhafte Weib sehr selten sein mag
(B. 28) so ist doch nicht weniger gewiß,
daß der Mensch, von Geburt (Natur)
unschuldig und einfach, gerade und
redlich erschaffen, im Gewirre des Lebens
sich selbst viele unnöthige Fragen und
Grübeleien schafft, welchem Hange zum
Klügeln man nicht einseitig nachgeben
soll (B. 29) aufgebend vielmehr unnütze
Spitzfindigkeiten (z. B. die über
schlechtere Natur des Weibes, welches
doch vielleicht näher betrachtet ein
Irrthum ist vergl. ix. 9), soll man die
reine Wahrheit und Weisheit suchen,
*though a really virtuous woman may
be very rare* (verse 28), *yet it is not
less certain that man in his birth*

*(nature) is made innocent and simple,
upright and honest; that he creates
for himself, in the turmoil of life,
many unnecessary questions and en-
quiries, and that we are not to yield
one-sidedly to this propensity of prying
into things* (verse 29), *but, relinquish-
ing useless speculations — such as about
the more degenerate nature of woman*,
which, perhaps, *if more closely examined would not be true* (comp. ix. 9)
—*we are to pursue real truth and
wisdom* (chap. ix.) — destroys the
manifest antithesis between יָשָׁר and
חִשְּׁבֹנוֹת, and is against the scope of
the passage, which has nothing to
do with *speculation*, but with *moral
degeneracy*.

1. *Who is like the wise man?* &c.
The next lesson which this common
sense view of life teaches is gentle
submission.   He who is truly wise,
who understands the import of this
matter, or of this view of life, has no
compeer.   The abnormal כְּהֶחָכָם, instead of the normal כֶּחָכָם, with the ה
dropped, and its vowel under the כ
comparison, is not of unfrequent occurrence, especially in later books
(comp. Ezek. xl. 25, xlviii. 22; 2
Chron. x. 7, xxv. 10, xxix. 27; Nehem.
ix. 19, xii. 38; Gesen. § 52, 2; Ewald,
§ 244, a). יוֹדֵעַ stands for כְּיוֹדֵעַ, the כְּ
comparison, as usually, is to be supplied before it from the preceding
noun כְּהֶחָכָם.   The expression פֵּשֶׁר is
purely Chaldaic, and only occurs in
Daniel, and denotes *interpretation,
signification, import, meaning*.   דָּבָר,
thing, matter (see *supra*, i. 10), refers
to the view of life under consideration.   The phrase פֵּשֶׁר דָּבָר exactly
corresponds to the Hebrew נְבוֹן דָּבָר in
1 Sam. xvi. 18.   The interrogative,
as frequently, is used for an *emphatic
negative, i.e*, 'no one can be compared with the wise man, and with
him who knows the import of this
view of life.'   The rendering of the
Septuagint, τίς οἶδεν σοφούς or σοφίαν;
καὶ τίς οἶδεν λύσιν ῥήματος; *who knows the*

the thing ? The wisdom of this man enlighteneth his
2 countenance, and his stern visage is changed. I say, then,
Obey the king's command, and especially because of the oath

wise or *his wisdom ? and who knows the interpretation of the word ?* dropping the כְּ comparison from כְּהֶחָכָם, making it the accusative to יוֹדֵעַ, which is taken over from the following clause, as well as referring it to the wisdom of God, and understanding by דָבָר the Scripture, is as usual to be traced to Hagadic influence, as may be seen from the Chaldee, which paraphrases it כְּמַאן הוּא חַכִּימָא דְיָכִיל לְמֵיקַם, קֳבֵיל חוּכְמְתָא דַיָ וּלְמֵידַע פִּשָׁר מִילַיָא כִּנְבִיאֲיָא, *who is the wise man, that can stand before the wisdom of God, and fathom the import of his word, like the prophets ?* and especially from the Midrash Rabba, and Yalkut.

The wisdom of this man, &c. This clause gives the reason for the sentiment expressed in the former one. He has no equal, because his wisdom, or the prudent view of life according to which he regulates his conduct, makes him cheerful, and teaches him submission, to endure that which he cannot cure. As the face is the mirror of the soul, it is especially mentioned in describing the state of our innermost feelings. הָאִיר פָּנִים, *to light up the countenance,* i. e., *to brighten, to cheer, to make happy* (comp. Numb. vi. 25; Ps. xix. 9; Prov. xvi. 15, and the synonymous expression, נָהַר, *to brighten up, to be cheerful,* Ps. xxxiv. 6; Isa. lx. 5). That עֹז פָּנִים, *strength of face,* means *resolutensss, sternness,* or *rigour of his face,* as Holden, Herzfeld, Philippson, Elster, &c., rightly maintain, is evident from Deut. xxvii. 50, where גֹּז עַז פָּנִים is explained by אֲשֶׁר לֹא־יִשָׂא פָנִים לַזָקֵן, *which does not regard the pe. son of the old,* inasmuch as it could not properly be said that an enemy is *impudent to the young,* and therefore must mean a foe treating with rigour both old and young. יֵשָׁנֵא stands for יְשֻׁנֶה (comp. 2 Kings xxv. 25, and Jer. lii. 33, with Lam. iv. 1); for the cause of it, see *supra,* vii. 26. The Septuagint's rendering

וְעֹז פָּנָיו יְשֻׁנֵּא by καὶ ἀναιδὴς προσώπῳ αὐτοῦ μισηθήσεται, *and his shameless face will be hated,* altering יְשֻׁנֵּא into יִשָּׂנֵא, the Niphal future of שָׂנֵא, *to hate,* which is followed by Luther (wer aber frech ift, der ift feindfelig), Coverdale (" but malice putteth it out of favour"), Desvoeux (" whereas a sullen look would make him an object of hatred "), Durell (" but he that bath an impudent countenance shall be hated "), Hodgson (" but austerity in the looks is hateful "), &c., is both unjustifiable, and mars the connection of this verse with the sequel. The Vulg., ET POTENTISSIMUS FACIEM ILLIUS COMMUTABIT, *and the omnipotent will change his face,* taking עֹז as *nominative,* and *subject,* and פָּנָיו as the *accusative,* governed by the verb which follows it, and altering יְשֻׁנֵּא, the future *Pual,* into יְשַׁנֶּא, *Piel,* is to be repudiated, because — 1. It assigns to עֹז a sense which it never has, since the term is invariably used as an *abstract* and not a *concrete ;* 2. It disjoins the idiomatic and well-known phrase עֹז פָּנִים ; and 3. It arbitrarily alters the text. The same objections are to be urged against Hitzig's rendering, unb Trotz fein Antlitz entftellt, espoused by Stuart (" but haughtiness disfigureth his face "), which follows the construction and emendation of the Vulgate, though assigning a different but equally unjustifiable sense to עֹז, and adopts the antithetic form of the Septuagint.

2. *I say, then, Obey,* &c. Having submitted that this prudent view of life will make us adapt ourselves and cheerfully yield to the pressure of circumstances, Coheleth deduces therefrom the lesson of submission and obedience to the authority reigning over us for the time being, and especially as submission and obedience have been solemnly promised with an oath invoking the name of God. The oath referred to alludes

3 of God. Do not go away hastily from his presence, do not
even stand up because of an evil word, for he doth whatsoever

to the covenant at the coronation of
the king, when the sovereign solemnly
promises to govern the people according to the law of God, and the
people in return swear fealty and
allegiance to their monarch (comp.
2 Kings xi. 17; 1 Chron. xi. 3, xxix.
24). Hence we are told by Josephus,
that when Ptolmey Lagi settled the
captive Jews in Egypt, he made them
take an oath of allegiance (Antiq.
xii. 1.) The pronoun אֲנִי has caused
much difficulty to interpreters, as it
has no predicate connected therewith.
The Septuagint, the Syriac, and the
Chaldee ignore it altogether, which
made Dathe strike it from the text,
Durell alter it into אנא or אנה, I pray
thee, and Spohn change it into אַף.
The Vulgate (ego os regis observo)
leaving אֲנִי, alters שְׁמֹר, the imperative,
into שֹׁמֵר, the participle, which is followed by Luther, the Bishops' Bible,
Hitzig, Stuart, &c.; whilst Ibn Ezra,
Coverdale, the Geneva Version, the
Authorised Version, Desvoeux, Hodgson, Knobel, De Wette, Noyes, Heiligstedt, Elster, Hengstenberg, &c.,
regard it as an ellipsis, and supply
the verb אַזְהִירְךָ, אֲצַוְּךָ or אֹמֵר. But
as the first and second interpretations
alter the text, which is always to be
avoided, and the second has an additional difficulty, viz., making Coheleth represent himself as acting,
whereas, in all the other instances,
he advises others how to act,, we
prefer the third explanation, especially as ellipses are not uncommon
(comp. בְּאָזְנָי יְהוָֹה צְבָאוֹת, in mine ear
(said) Jehovah of hosts (Isa. v. 9;
Jerem. xx. 10; 2 Cor. ix. 6). כֶּה,
mouth, is used metonymically for
that which proceeds from it, word,
command (comp. Gen. xlv. 21; Exod.
xvii. 1; Job xxxix. 27, and the
phrases מָרָה אֶת פֶּה, to disobey the
command, Numb. xvii. 14, xxx. 24;
1 Sam. xii. 15, and עָבַר פֶּה, to transgress the command, Numb. xiv. 21,
xxii. 18; 1 Sam. xxv. 24; Prov.

viii. 29). The ו in וְעַל introduces an
additional and special motive for obedience, i. e., not only are we obliged
to submit, because of this common-
sense view of life, but also because
of the oath. For עַל דִּבְרַת, because,
see iii. 18. Rashi's explanation of
it by with, making it restrictive of
the command given in the preceding
clause ועצל דברת שבועת אלהים אשמור פי
המלכים, and BY or WITH the oath of
God will I keep the command of
kings, ובלבד שלא יעבירונו את השבועה
שנשבענו למקום, obeying earthly monarchs
only as far as their commands do not
make us transgress the oath of obedience to God, instancing the three
Hebrew youths (Dan. iii.), which is
followed by Bishops Reynolds and
Patrick, is contrary to the usage of
this phrase. Still more arbitrary is
Mendelssohn's translation, " I counsel thee to observe the king's word;
thy prince fulfilleth the duty promised to God," which is followed by
Friedländer, Jch warne dich, vollstrecke
des Königs Willen; dein Fürst erfüllt
die Gott geschworene Pflicht, and by
Preston, who, misunderstanding his
Hebrew guide (אני מזהיר ומצוה את כל)
א' מהעם לשמור את פי המלך כי הוא שליט
בעמו לעשות כרצונו ואולם העל הוא חמושל
(אשר הוקם על ישמור דברת שבועת האלהים),
makes him say, " I advise thee to
observe the king's word, and an elevated person, the subject-matter of
the oath of God"—as nothing can be
more preposterous than to take עַל to
denote prince, sovereign. שְׁבוּעַת אֱלֹהִים,
oath of God, i. e., an oath made by
the name of God, in which his sacred
name is solemnly invoked as witness
to the transaction (Exod. xxii. 10;
2 Sam. xxi. 7; 1 Kings ii. 43).

3. Do not go away hastily, &c.
This obedience must not be restricted
to ordinary occasions, when everything demanded on the part of the
sovereign is in accordance with the
feelings of the subject; but we are to
be submissive even when the king

4 pleaseth him; inasmuch as the word of a king is powerful

treats us harshly. If he chooses to rebuke us, we are not, in consequence of this insult, hastily to quit his service and throw off our allegiance to him; nor are we to manifest our disapprobation of it, since he can do with the resenter whatever he likes. הָלַךְ מִפְּנֵי, *i. q.*, יָצָא מִלְּפְנֵי, *to go away from one's presence* (Gen. iv. 16), i. e., *to withdraw from him, to quit his service, to throw off allegiance to him* comp. הָלְכוּ מִפְּנֵיהֶם, *they withdrew from their presence* (Hos. xi. 2; and see *infra*, x. 4). אַל־תִּבָּהֵל מִפָּנָיו תֵּלֵךְ, *do not be hasty, withdraw from his presence*, stands for אַל־תִּבָּהֵל לָלֶכֶת מִפָּנָיו *do not hastily withdraw from his presence;* תִּבָּהֵל, the first verb, as frequently, is used *adverbially*, to qualify תֵּלֵךְ, the second verb (comp. נֵדְעָה נִרְדְּפָה, *we shall know, we shall pursue,* i. e., *we shall know to pursue.* Hos. vi. 3; אַל־תַּרְבּוּ תְדַבְּרוּ, *do not multiply speak*, i. e., *do not multiply to speak*, 1 Sam. ii. 3; see also *supra*, i. 16; and *infra*, x. 1, xii. 9). Rashi and Ibn Ezra's explanation of this lingual peculiarity, יותר נכון הוא שיחסר שי׳׳ן שהוא במקום אשר ויהיה כן ונדיצה שנרדפה אל הרבו שדברו. אל תבהל מפניו שתלך. אל ימהר לבך שתחשוב שתוכל ללכת מפניו that שֶׁ=אֲשֶׁר is to be supplied in these cases before the second verb, comes to the same thing. Whilst the Septuagint, καὶ περὶ λόγου ὅρκου θεοῦ μὴ σπουδάσῃς, ἀπὸ προσώπου αὐτοῦ πορεύσῃ, and the Syriac,

ܣܓܠܐ ܡܛܠ ܡܘܡܬܐ ܕܐܠܗܐ ܠܐ

ܬܣܬܪܗܒ ܡܢ ܩܕܡܘܗܝ ܬܐܙܠ

and because of the word of the oath of God thou shalt not be hasty; go away from his presence; the Chaldee, וּבְעִידָן רוּגְזָא דַיָי לָא תְּנוּחַ לְצַלָּאָה קֳדָמוֹהִי אִתְבְּהֵיל קֳדָמוֹהִי אֱזִיל וְצַלֵּי וְהִבְעֵי רַחֲמִין מִנֵּהּ, *and in the time of the anger of the Lord, do not cease to pray before him, tremble before him, go and pray and ask for mercy from him;* and Rashbam, לא תהי׳ בהול מפניו של הק׳ להתרחק מעליו אבל לפניו תלך לשמור מצותיו *do not with-*

draw from his presence, but walk before him, which detach תִּבָּהֵל from תֵּלֵךְ, and which have given rise to the rendering of Desvoeux, "Be not hasty. Go out of his presence. Stay not whilst he gives wrong orders;" Durell, "Rush not hastily from his presence: go thy way, stand not in an evil thing;" Hodgson, "Thou shalt not escape from his view; go, persist not in perverseness," and others; impose too artificial a sense upon the passage, and are rightly rejected by the Vulgate, Luther, Coverdale, the Bishops' Bible, the Geneva Bible, and almost all modern critics. עָמַד, *to stand up,* as frequently, means *to protest, to oppose, to resent* (Ps. lxxvi. 8, cxxx. 3; cxlvii 17), the בְּ in בְּדָבָר denotes *the cause* for this standing up, as well as for the action described in the first clause (comp. Gen. xviii. 28; Exod. x. 12). The rendering of the Vulg. (NEQUE PERMANEAS IN OPERE MALO, *and do not persist in an evil work*), which is followed by Luther, Coverdale, the Bishops' Bible, &c., and of the Geneva Bible (" stand not in an evil thing "), which is followed by the Authorised Version, are contrary to the scope of the passage, inasmuch as *the hasty going away* (תִּבָּהֵל תֵּלֵךְ) evidently shews that עָמַד is a limitation of it, restricting the dissuasion to *the standing up* in a passion, the step preceding the hasty departure. Besides, verse 5 proves incontestably that דְּבַר רָע does not mean *an evil work*, but signifies a *sore rebuke.* Hitzig's version (bleibe nicht stehen bei schlimmen Befehl), which is followed by Stuart (" do not make delay in regard to a command which is grievous," *i. e.*, never hesitate to execute his orders, whatever they are), is contrary to the phrase בְּ עָמַד, which never means *to hesitate, to delay.*

4. *Inasmuch as the word*, &c. This verse assigns a reason for the assertion made in the second half of the foregoing verse, " the king can do

5 and who shall say unto him, What doest thou? Whoso
keepeth the commandment knoweth not an evil word. More-

whatever he pleases," because, or inasmuch as (בַּאֲשֶׁר), his royal mandate (דְּבַר מֶלֶךְ) is power itself, and no one can call into question his doings, or bring him to account for them. How useless and hazardous, therefore, for a subject to disrespect or bid defiance to the person or power of a sovereign. בַּאֲשֶׁר, not *wherever* (the Chaldee בְּאַתַר דְּ), *in every place, where* (בכל מקום שׁ. באיתו מקום אשר, Rashbam, Ibn Ezra, the Geneva Bible, the Authorised Version, &c.), which makes this clause a needless repetition of the sentiment expressed in the second clause of the preceding verse, but *because, since, inasmuch as* (comp. ii. 16, vii. 2), as Rashi (בשביל אשר) and almost all modern commentators rightly render it. The Sept. (καθὼς βασιλεὺς ἐξουσιάζων λαλεῖ), and the Svr.

ܐܝܟ ܡܢ ܕܡܡܠܠ ܐܝܟ ܡܠܟ

he speaks like a powerful king, which have evidently given rise to Coverdale's rendering, "like as when a king giveth a charge, his commandment is mighty; even so, who may say unto him," &c., adopted in the Bishops' Bible, are irreconcileable both with the text and context. The Vulg. (ET SERMO ILLIUS POTESTATE PLENUS EST, *and his word is full of power*). Luther (in des Königs Wort ist Gewalt), and Hodgson entirely ignore בַּאֲשֶׁר. Rashi's explanation (דבר הק׳בה מושל הוא), which is adopted by Desvoeux, who renders it, "*the word of a king is a despotic commander*," submitting that "*the word of a king* seems to be personified by a very intelligible prosopopœia," is not only, as he himself concedes, too bold in our Western languages, but also too bold and incongruous for Eastern languages, and, at all events, ought not to be ascribed to them without incontestable proof, which, however, Desvoeux has failed to adduce. His argument, that שִׁלְטוֹן

has *a personal signification in Chaldee, which is a sufficient inducement to retain it in Hebrew*, is untenable, inasmuch as in Chaldee too שִׁלְטוֹן is originally an *abstract* noun, and, like many other abstracts, both in that language and in Hebrew, obtained a *concrete* signification. This is especially the case with those nouns which denote *authority*, and the very word *authority* is so used in our language.

5. *Whoso keepeth the commandment*, &c. But though the part of wisdom is not to defy the power of a potentate, even if that power is abused, and is made to weigh heavily upon us, yet such abuses are not the rule, but the exception. Generally speaking, a peaceful and obedient subject, who submits to the institutions of the sovereign, will not experience evil words. מִצְוָה, *i. e.*, מִצְוַת הַמֶּלֶךְ, *the commandment of the king*, so that שׁוֹמֵר מִצְוָה is the same as פִּי מֶלֶךְ שְׁמֹר in verse 2. יָדַע, *to see, to observe, to perceive, experience*, either with the *eye, ear*, or *feelings*; hence, also, *to hear* (comp. Gen. ix. 24; Levit. v. 1). That דָּבָר רָע cannot mean here *an evil thing, an evil work, a wrong action*, is evident from the words שׁוֹמֵר מִצְוָה; for to say, "whoso keepeth the commandment shall know no evil thing," is simply to say, *whoso keeps the commandments does not transgress them*, or, *the obedient are not disobedient*. To avoid this truism, the Vulgate was constrained to resort to an inconsistency, and translate it here *non experietur quidquam mali*, which is followed by Luther (wird nichts Böses erfahren), Coverdale and the Bishops' Bible ("shall feel no harm"), the Geneva Bible and the Authorised Version ("shall feel or know no evil thing"), thus making the same words דָּבָר רָע to signify two different things, *a wrong action*, and *infliction, punishment*, which is against all rules of

over the heart of the wise man knoweth a time of judgment;
6 for there is a time of judgment for everything, when the

language; a careful comparison of verses 3 and 5 will shew that the same thing is intended.

Moreover the heart, &c. Another reason why a wise man will yield the obedience enjoined in verse 2 is because he knows that there is an appointed time of judgment, when the tyrant shall be brought to retribution by a power infinitely above the strength of any potentate; knowing this, he submissively and patiently bides his time, and does not attempt to raise his feeble arm. The וְ in וְעֵת being connected with a clause which gives an additional reason, has, as frequently, the meaning of *moreover.* עֵת וּמִשְׁפָּט is a *hendiadys*, and is well translated by the Sept., καιρὸν κρίσεως, *time of judgment.* For this figure, see vii 25. The rendering of the Vulgate (TEMPUS ET RESPONSIONEM, *time and answers*), and of Hodgson ("the right time and use of judgment"), are both contrary to the text and context. Ibn Ezra rightly remarks (ועניין עת ומשפט דבק עם הפסוק שלאחריו) that this clause must be connected with the following verse.

6. *For there is a time, &c.* The time of judgment is sure to come as soon as the subjects find their sufferings intolerable; revolt, and heavy retribution for every evil which the tyrant has perpetrated, will then be the result of his lawless and outrageous conduct. For חֵפֶץ, see iii. 1. Of course עֵת וּמִשְׁפָּט is a *hendiadys*, as in the preceding verse. We should have deemed it superfluous to make this remark had not the Septuagint, which has rightly rendered it so there, most inconsistently translated it here καιρὸς καὶ κρίσις, *time and judgment;* the Vulgate, too, has rendered it differently *(tempus et opportunitas).* כִּי, in the second clause, is rightly rendered by the Chaldee (כַּד) and Rashi (כאשר) as a particle of *time,* in which sense it is frequently used

(comp. פִּי־יִהְיֶה לָהֶם דָּבָר בָּא אֵלַי, *when they have a case they come to me,* Exod. xviii. 16; Ps. xxxii. 3; Gesenius, § 155, 1, c, b; Ewald, § 337, c). רָעַת הָאָדָם רַבָּה עָלָיו is taken as—1. *The wickedness of a man is great upon him, i.e.,* when the measure of his iniquity is full, regarding רָעַת הָאָדָם as the evil which a man commits, רַבָּה as *great, sufficient, full,* and עלי as referring to הָאָדָם, *the sinner* (so the Chaldee, Rashi, Rashbam); 2. *The evil of man is heavy upon him, i.e.,* the evil which is inflicted upon man by the tyrant becomes intolerable; or, 3. *The evil of man (i. e.,* of the tyrant) *is heavy upon him (i.e.,* upon the oppressed). As the first view is precluded by the phrase רַבָּה עָלָיו, which describes the weight of oppression upon the sufferers, and the second leaves no natural subject to the predicate in the following verse, we must adopt the third interpretation. הָאָדָם is not the king *exclusively,* but refers to oppressors generally, including the tyrannical monarch This generic term is evidently chosen because a despotic sovereign necessarily has a host of lawless and debased officials. The rendering of the Septuagint ,and Theodotion (ὅτι γνῶσις τοῦ ἀνθρώπου πολλὴ ἐπ' αὐτόν, *for the knowledge of man is great upon him,* taking רָעַת for דַּעַת), and the Vulgate *(et multa hominis afflictio),* which has evidently given rise to the rendering of Coverdale and the Bishops' Bible ("for everything will have opportunity and judgment, and this is the thing that maketh man full of carefulness and sorrow"), and the Auth. Version ("because to every purpose there is a time and judgment, therefore the misery of man is great upon him"), and is explained by Bishops Reynolds and Patrick "because to every purpose or enterprise there is a proper season, and peculiar manner of acting; upon which narrow points

7 tyranny of a man is heavy upon him.   Because he knoweth
  not what will be, and because no one can tell him when it
8 will be.   No man is ruler over his spirit to retain the spirit,
  and there is no power over the day of death ; and there is no

the happy success of such undertakings do depend ; and this cannot
without much wisdom be duly observed ; hence it cometh to pass that
the misery of man is great upon
him," are contrary to the text and
context, for פִּי — פִּי is never used as
cause and *effect*. Ibn Ezra's explanation, אע"פ שידע כי עת לכל חפץ ולא ידע
מתי חגיע העת וזו רעה רבה, *although he
knows that there is an appointed time
for everything, yet he knows not when
that time will come, and this is a great
evil*, taking פִּי to signify *although*, is
too far-fetched. Still more objectionable are the renderings of Desvoeux
(" because man's evils are multiplied
upon him by his not knowing futu-
rity ; for who will shew him what
turn things shall take ? ") and Hodgson (" for in every transaction there
is a crisis, and a need of dexterity ;
yet great is man's misfortune therein,
that he knoweth not how a matter
shall turn out, and who shall tell
him what will come to pass ? ")

7. *Because he knoweth not*, &c.
This righteous retribution is sure to
overtake the guilty (פִּי), because his
infatuation, connected with the determination to carry out his evil designs
(אֵינֶנּוּ יֹדֵעַ), disables him from seeing
(מַה־שֶּׁיִּהְיֶה) *what* disastrous consequences his criminal conduct will
bring forth ; (פִּי) and because no one
else can tell him (כַּאֲשֶׁר יִהְיֶה) *when* all
this will come to pass. פִּי . . . פִּי,
before the first and second clauses,
are *causal* and *co-ordinate*, assigning
reasons for the inevitable day of
retribution spoken of in the foregoing
verse, and, as usually, are to be rendered *because . . . and because* (*vide
supra*, vi. 11, 12). The pronoun in
אֵינֶנּוּ refers to הָאָדָם, the immediate
antecedent. The contrast between
the wise and submissive man in
verse 5, and the infatuated oppressor

in this verse, is exceedingly beautiful
and striking ; of the former it is
said that (יֵדַע לֵב חָכָם) *he knows* a time
of retribution, and of the latter, that
(אֵינֶנּוּ יֹדֵעַ) *he knows not* what will
happen to him. כַּאֲשֶׁר, like כִּי in the
preceding verse, is used as a particle
of *time*. The interrogative, as usual,
is for an emphatic denial, which
is best expressed in the translation.
Rashi well explains this verse, כי איננו
ידע מה שיהיה ׃ כשהרשע עובר עבירה איננו נותן
לבו למה שעתיד הק"בה להביאו במשפט ואוי לו
בכך ׃ כי כאשר יהיה ׃ הפורענות מי יגיד לו
להמלך בו ולימול בו עצה ולישול רשות כי פתע
פתאום, " *because he knoweth not*," &c.,
*when the wicked sins he does not think
that God will bring him* to judgment,
and woe to him for it ; " *because when
it shall be*," &c., i. e., *the retribution*,
" *who can tell him ?*" *to advise or
consult with him, and take respite, for
it shall come upon him very suddenly.*
The Vulgate's paraphrase (QUIA IGNO-
RAT PRÆTERITA, ET FUTURA NULLO
SCIRE POTEST NUNCIO, *because he is
ignorant of things past, and things
to come, he is unable to know through
any messenger*), is most arbitrary,
and confounds שֶׁיִּהְיֶה, the *future*, with
שֶׁהָיָה, the *præterite* (which is also
done by St. Jerome, the Syriac, and
several MSS.), and כַּאֲשֶׁר, *when*, with
כַּמֶה־שֶׁ ; so also Luther (benn er
weiß nicht, was gewesen ift, unb wer
will ihm fagen, was werben foll ?)
Equally arbitrary are the renderings
of Coverdale, " and why ? a man
knoweth not what is for to come,
for who will tell him ? " and the
Bishops' Bible, " and why ? a man
knoweth not what is for to come,
for who can tell when it shall be ? "

8. *No man is ruler*, &c. And when
the day of retribution does come, as
it assuredly will come, no man, however great his power, will be able to
retain his spirit ; no dominion, how-

furlough in this battle, and no cunning will save the wicked;
* 9 all this I have seen, having given my heart to all the doing

ever wide, will control the day of
death; there will be no leave of
absence from this death-battle, and
no wicked subterfuge will secure the
escape of the crafty; neither tyranny
nor cunning will save the tyrant or
the wicked from this appointed doom.
אֵין אָדָם, no man, i. e., not even the
powerful despot. רוּחַ is rightly translated by the Vulgate, the Chaldee
(רוּחַ נִשְׁמְתָא), Rashi (הרוח שבגופו),
Rashbam (ונשמתו), Luther, Coverdale,
the Bishops' Bible, the Geneva Bible,
the Authorised Version, Hodgson,
Knobel, De Wette, Herzfeld, Heiligstedt, Elster, Hengstenberg, &c., *the
spirit, the breath of life* (comp. Gen.
vi. 17; Job xii. 10); the rendering
of it by *wind* (Schmidt, Desvoeux,
Mendelssohn, Friedlander, Spohn,
Boothroyd, Preston, Hitzig, Stuart,
Vaihinger, &c.), taking this clause to
form a comparison with the following
one, viz., "just as man has no power
over the wind, so he has none in the
day of death "), is—1. Contrary to the
parallelism שִׁלְטוֹן בְּיוֹם הַמָּוֶת; 2. Obliges
us to take the copula וְ in the abnormal
sense of comparison; and 3. Leaves
the latter clause of the verse, which
shews that all the clauses are *co-ordinate*, unaccounted for. The Vulg. (NON
EST IN HOMINIS POTESTATE PROHIBERE
SPIRITUM, it *is not in man's power to
retain the spir*it), is a languid paraphrase, neither giving the force of
אֵין אָדָם, in which it is followed by
Luther, &c., nor substituting an
equivalent for the words לִכְלוֹא אֶת־הָרוּחַ.
The word מִשְׁלַחַת has called forth a
greater variety of opinions; the
Chaldee has (מָנֵי וְיָנָא) *weapons;* so also
Ibn Ezra, who explains it by נשק,
weapon, and regards it as synonymous with שֶׁלַח (Job xxxiii. 18, xxxvi.
12); the only other instance, however,
where מִשְׁלַחַת occurs (Ps. lxxviii. 49),
and undoubtedly signifies *a sending,*
as well as its parallelism מַלְאָ, are
decidedly against this rendering.
Less objectionable, but still requiring

too great an ellipsis, are the explanations *substitute* (זו לאמר אשלח בני און
עבדי במקומי, i. e., *I will send my son or
servant in my stead,* Rashi) *martial
host* (אין כוח בידו לשלוח משלחת חייליו,
להלחם עם מלאך המות שלא יקח נשמתו ממנו,
*he cannot send the host of his soldiers
to wage war with the angel of death
to prevent him taking away the soul,*
Rashbam), and *embassy* (" there is
no embassy admitted during the
war," Desvoeux). Whereas the rendering, *sending away, discharge, let
go on furlough,* is naturally deduced
from the root, requires no ellipsis,
and suits the context and the parallelism. There is no necessity for
resorting to the far-fetched interpretation of רָשַׁע by *agitation, anxiety,*
according to the example of Ibn
Ezra (פירוש רשע רוב התנועה והנצוה), in
order to deduce therefrom the meaning of a *wily disposition,* which is
ever fertile in schemes and resources
(Preston), for this word not unfrequently means *wicked deeds, fraud,
cunning* (comp. Job xxxiv. 26; Prov.
viii. 7, xvi. 12). By גְּעָלָיו is meant
רָשָׁע הָרָשֵׁע. For the plural רְשָׁעִים, see
v. 10.

9. *All this have I seen,* &c. This
retributive justice overtaking the
tyrant, spoken of in verses 6 - 8, Coheleth assures us is what he has himself seen, having carefully examined
the transactions of men. אֶת־כָּל־זֶה, *all
this,* i. e., all which is stated in verses
6 - 8, about righteous retribution.
The construction רָאִיתִי וְנָתוֹן, the *finite*
verb, with the *infinitive,* instead of
רָאִיתִי וְנָתַתִּי, is of frequent occurrence.
When several successive acts or states
of the same subject are enumerated,
it often happens that the first of the
verbs takes the required form in respect to *tense* and *person,* whilst the
others are in the *infinitive absolute* or
construct, with the same distinctions
implied (comp. וַיַּרְכֵּב אֹתוֹ . . . וְנָתוֹן,
*and he made him ride . . . and gave
him,* &c., Gen. xli. 43; Exod. xxxii.

that is done under the sun. There is a time when a man
10 ruleth over men to their injury; and thus I have seen wicked •

29; Levit. x. 9 - 11; 1 Sam. ii. 28;
Esth. ix. 6. 12; *infra*, ix. 1. 11; Gesen.
§ 131, 4; Ewald, § 351, c).

There is a time when, &c. Coheleth,
however, has also seen instances
where retributive justice is wanting;
man is sometimes permitted all his
life long to tyrannise over and crush
his fellow-men with impunity. עֵת, *a
time = sometimes* (*vide infra*, ix. 8), is
well rendered by the Vulg. *interdum;*
Luther, זu Ʒeíten; עֵת, as usually,
is implied; the Septuagint (τὰ ὅσα,
all things) exchanges it for אֶת,
the sign of the *accusative*, and supplies לֵב after it from the first part of
this verse. The pronoun לוֹ is referred
by Symmachus (εἰς κακὸν αὐτοῦ), the
Vulgate (*in malum suum*), Rashi,
Rashbam, Luther, Coverdale, the
Bishops' Bible, the Geneva Bible,
the Authorised Version, Le Clerc,
Grotius, Hodgson, Herzfeld, Philippson, Stuart, &c., to the *first* אָדָם, *the
ruler's own heart;* i. e., the despot by
his tyrannic sway ultimately brings
misery upon himself; whilst the Septuagint (τοῦ κακῶσαι αὐτὸν), the Syriac,
the Chaldee, Ibn Ezra, Knobel,
Ewald, De Wette, Hitzig, Heiligstedt, Elster, Vaihinger, &c., refer it
to the *second* אָדָם, i. e., *man rules over
his fellow-men* to their *misfortune and
ruin*. Against the first explanation,
however, is to be urged that — 1. It
does not harmonise with the following verse, where the wicked is said
sometimes to escape with impunity;
2. שָׁלַט by itself does not mean *to
tyrannise*, but simply to rule in a lawful sense; 3. Chap. v. 12, to which
Philippson appeals for support, is
against this interpretation; and, 4.
It takes away the pronoun from its
immediate antecedents, and is obliged
to refer it to the more remote subject.

10. *And thus I have seen*, &c. He
not only saw tyrants succeed in practising their tyranny the *whole of their
life* without being visited by retributive justice, but that these wicked

ones are perpetuated by their children
when they die; whilst the righteous
depart this life, and, leaving no issue,
are totally forgotten in the city. The
difficulty which commentators have
experienced in the interpretation of
this verse, has been greatly increased
by the arbitrary and senseless renderings of the Ancient Version. Thus
the Septuagint has καὶ τότε ἴδον ἀσεβεῖς
εἰς τάφους εἰςαχθέντας, καὶ ἐκ τοῦ ἁγίου, καὶ
ἐπορεύθησαν καὶ ἐπῃνέθησαν ἐν τῇ πόλει, ὅτι
οὕτως ἐποίησαν, *and I saw the wicked
brought to the graves and from the
holy place, and they departed and they
were praised in the city, because they
had acted in this manner*, altering
יַהֲלֵכוּ, הַבִיאוּ לִקְבָרִים וָבָאוּ into קְבָרִים וָבָאוּ into
וְהָלְכוּ, and וְיִשְׁתַּכְּחוּ into וְיִשְׁתַּבְּחוּ. The
last alteration, as will be seen below
from Rashi's remark, is based upon
the Hagadic explanation of this verse.
The Vulgate has VIDI IMPIOS SEPUL-
TOS, QUI ETIAM, CUM ADHUC VIVE-
RENT, IN LOCO SANCTO ERANT, ET
LAUDABANTUR IN CIVITATE QUASI JUS-
TORUM OPERUM, *I saw the wicked
buried, who, while they lived, were in
holy places, and were praised in the
city as if men of just works*, dropping
the word וָבָאוּ, inserting אֲשֶׁר עֵינָו חַיִּים,
changing וּמִמְּקוֹם into וּבִמְקוֹם, and, like
the Septuagint, וְיִשְׁתַּכְּחוּ into וְיִשְׁתַּבְּחוּ.
Passing over these arbitrary altera-
tions of the text, we come to St.
Jerome, who renders it ET TUNC VIDI
IMPIOS SEPULTOS, ET VENERUNT, ET
DE LOCO SANCTO EGRESSI SUNT, ET
LAUDATI SUNT IN CIVITATE QUIA SIC
FECERUNT, *and then I saw the wicked
buried, and they came and went forth
from the holy place; and they were
praised in the city because they had
done so*, which he explains, " I have
seen the wicked buried in such a
manner, and such an opinion was
entertained about them, that they
were esteemed holy on the earth,"
thus taking בָּאוּ and יַהֲלֵכוּ in an *impersonal sense*. Hence the explanation of Rambach and Gill, " Multi-

men buried and come again, and· those who did right depart

tudes came to attend the funeral of
such rich and mighty men, and
walked after or followed the corpse
(וּבָאוּ); and even the priests and
Levites from the Temple made a part
of the funeral procession (וּמִמְּקוֹם קָדוֹשׁ
יְהַלֵּכוּ), and walked in great solemnity
from thence to the place of interment,
which was usually without the city;
all their evil deeds were forgotten
(וְיִשְׁתַּכְּחוּ בָעִיר), their acts of oppression
and injustice, as if this had never
been done by them." But, 1. It is
most arbitrary to detach the verbs
from their immediate antecedents,
and make them refer to *subjects not
at all mentioned in the* context; and,
2. The simple expressions וּבָאוּ and
יְהַלֵּכוּ can never be forced to mean to
*come to a funeral procession, to walk
after the corpse.* The importance of St.
Jerome's version consists in proving
that the present Hebrew text is the
same which he used; a fact which
is also corroborated by the Syriac

Version, ܣܘܬܡܢܝ ܣܪܕܐ ܐܡܝܟܐ

ܝܨܠ ܣܡܝ ܥܙܠܝ ܥܠܨܝܕܒܝ

ܚܝܕܠܟܐ ܐܢܟ ܝܣܥܕܘ

and thus ܕܒܨ ܝܗܡܟܐ ܚܡܝܢܟܠܐ

*I saw the wicked who were buried, and
they went out of the holy place and
were forgotten in the city who acted so;*
and the quaint Chaldee paraphrase,
וּבְקוּשְׁטָא חֲזֵית חַיָּבַיָּא דְּאִתְקְבָרוּ וְאִשְׁתְּצִיאוּ
מֵעַלְמָא מֵאֲתַר קַדִּישׁ דְּצַדִּיקַיָּא שָׁרָן תַּמָּן וַאֲזָלוּ
לְאִיתוֹקָדָא בְּגֵיהִנָּם וְאִתְנַשְׁיָן מִבֵּין יָתְבֵי קַרְתָּא
וְהֵיכְמָא דַעֲבָדוּ אִתְעֲבֵיד לְהוֹן *and indeed I
have seen sinners who were buried and
blotted out of the world, from the holy
place where the righteous dwell, and
went to be burned in Gehenna, and are
forgotten from among the inhabitants
of the city; and as they have done, so
it is done to them,* which requires no
refutation. According to Rashi, this
verse is to be translated, "And I saw
the wicked, deserving to be buried,
rule in the place of the Holy One,

and when they went away from it
they were praised in their city because they had done so; or, but they
were forgotten in the city where they
had acted so;" which he explains ראיתי
רשעים קברים שהיו ראויין להטמן בעפר שהיו
נבוים בין שאר אומות שנאמר עליהם זה העם לא
היה ושלטו בביתו של הק"בה שהוא מקום קדוש
ובלכתם משם אל ארצם היו משתבחים בעירם
אשר כך וכך עשו בביתו של מקום אל חקרי
וישתכחו אלא וישתבחו · כך דרשוהו רז"ל ולעניין
השכחה כך נדרש באגדה וסופו שישתכח שמם
וזכרם מן העיר עצמה אשר כן עשו בה שנאמר
וקבצתי את כל הגוים אל עמק יהושפט במקום
שניאצו לפני יפרע מהם· וכן הוא אומר ה' בעיר
צלמם תבזה " *I saw the wicked buried,"*
i.e., *who deserved to be hidden in the
ground, for they were despised among
other nations, just as it is said of
them,* " *this people does not deserve to
be a people*" (Isa. xxiii. 13); *and yet
they ruled in the house of the Lord
(for this is the meaning of* מקום קדוש),
*and when they went from it into their
own country they were praised in their
city, because they have done this and
that in the house of the Lord; do not
read* וישתכחו *but* וְיִשְׁתַּבְּחוּ. *So our
Rabbins of blessed memory have interpreted it. According to the reading
FORGETTING, however, it is thus explained in the Hagada: yet their end
is that their name and memory are
blotted out from* THE VERY TOWN
wherein they had thus acted; comp.
" *and I will gather all nations into
the valley of Jehoshaphat*" (Josh.
iv 2), i. e., *they shall be punished in*
THE VERY PLACE *where they despised
me; and,* " *Lord, thou shalt despise
their image in the city*" (Ps. lxxiii. 20).
Similarly Rashbam, ראיתי בעולם רשעים
שראויים למיתה וחורבות וקבורה שהיו באים והולכים
ממקום קדוש וחורבות ורעות רבות היו עושים בו
וסופן נשכח שמם וזכרם באותו עיר אשר כן עשו
*I have seen wicked men in the world,
who deserved to be buried, coming and
going from the place of the Holy One,
and committing therein destruction
and great evil; and their end was that
their name and memory were blotted
out in the very town where they had
acted so.* Against this interpretation

from the place of the holy, and be forgotten in the city.

is to be urged — 1. That קְבוּרִים does not mean *who deserve to be buried,* but always describes those *who are actually buried.* 2. It violently construes וְבָאוּ וַיְהַלֵּכוּ as an expression of the *exercise of office,* in which sense it is never used. Preston's appeal to 1 Sam. xxix. 6 is nugatory, for there and everywhere else the established phrase צֵאת וָבוֹא is used, which is quite different from the words in question. 3. Had the sacred writer intended to convey by these words the idea of *bearing office,* he would undoubtedly have written וָבָאוּ וַיְהַלֵּכוּ, and not have separated them by the insertion of מִמְּקוֹם קָדוֹשׁ, producing thereby so unnatural a construction. 4. The parallelism קְבָרִים וָבָאוּ and יְהַלֵּכוּ וִישְׁתַּכְּחוּ בָעִיר shews that they are two distinct and antithetical clauses. The proper explanation, as frequently, is given by Ibn Ezra, who says, ראיתי רשעים שׁשׁלטו באדם והרעו להם מתו בלא יסורין קבורים בקברם כענין כי אין חרצובות למותם ובאו לעולם שׁנית והענין שׁיבואו בניהם ויעמדו במקומם ויעמוד זכרם ואשׁר ממקום קדוש יהלכו והענין כי הקדושׁים שׁימותו בלא בן וישׁתכחו בעיר שׁהיו שׁמה והם אשׁר עשׂו כן האמת כני כן בנות צלפחד דוגברות, *I saw the wicked who rule over their fellow-men, and tyrannise over them, die without anguish;* "they are buried in their graves" is like "there are no pains in their death" (Ps. lxxiii. 4), *and they came into the world a second time,* i. e., *their children succeed to their places and perpetuate them; whilst those who departed from the holy place, that is, the holy ones, die without issue, and are forgotten in the city where they were, and these are they who executed justice* (כֵּן=אֵמֶת), *taking.* בָּאוּ *and* יְהַלֵּכוּ *in the legitimate sense of coming into the world and departing from it* (vide supra, i. 4), *and* כֵּן with Symmachus (ὡς δίκαια πράξαντες), and the Vulgate for *right, well;* so also Coverdale, the Bishops' Bible, the Geneva Bible, &c. (comp. Exod. x. 29; Numb. xxviii. 7; 2 Kings vii. 9). For the indiscriminate use of the Piel הִלֵּךְ, and the Kal הָלַךְ, see iii. 5; and for

the passive signification of the Hithpael וַיִּשְׁתַּכְּחוּ, comp. Judg. xx. 15. 17; Gesen. § 54, d; Ewald, § 124, c. Luther's version — und da sahe ich Gottlose, die begraben waren, die gegangen waren, und gewandelt hatten in heiliger Stätte, und waren vergessen in der Stadt, daß sie so gethan hatten, *and then I saw the godless that were buried, who had gone and had walked in holy places, and were forgotten in the city,* which he explains, sie waren in der heiligen Städte, das ist, sie regierten in Gottes Volk, Da sahe ich Gottlose die begraben waren, das ist, ich sahe daß die Tyrannen verstorben waren, und daß ein frommer Fürst an die Stadt kam, als nach Saul, David, also vergessen die Leute bald frommer treuer Regenten, "they were in the places of the holy," i. e., *they ruled the people of God.* "Then I saw the godless who were buried," i. e., *I saw that the tyrants were dead, and that a pious prince came to the city; and as, after Saul, David was forgotten, so the people soon forgat pious and faithful rulers,* which has given rise to Coverdale's translation, and to the marginal notes in the Bishops' Bible, "for I have often seen the ungodly brought to their graves, and yet they have returned into the city again" (that is, the ungodly hath been praised after their burial), "from the place of holy men, which in the city were grown out of memory" (that is, the holy men, after their burial, grew out of memory), "as were those also that lived well," — is most arbitrary, and irreconcileable with the text. That which is of importance in these versions is the fact that they distinguish *two* classes of men in this verse, the righteous and the wicked. The Geneva Bible alone has faithfully followed Ibn Ezra's explanation, "And likewise I saw the wicked buried, and they returned" (Marg. Gloss, that is, others as wicked as they); and they that came from the holy place" (Marg. Gloss, they that

11 also this is vanity. Because sentence is not forthwith
executed for evil work, the heart of the sons of men is full

feared God, and worshipped him according as he had appointed) " were
yet forgotten in the city where they
had done right;" whilst the Authorised Version (" and so I saw the
wicked buried, who had come and
gone from the place of the holy, and
they were forgotten in the city where
they had done so"), following Rashi,
is guilty of the violent proceedings
with the text mentioned above in
the analysis of this Rabbi's interpretation. The renderings of Desvoeux
(" nay, then I saw wicked men buried.
Though they came even from the
place of prostitution, they shall go
and be praised in the city where
they have done so "), and Hodgson
(" for hereby have I seen wicked
men brought to their graves ; yea,
forth have they been led, from the
seat of royalty conducted, and consigned to death in that city where so
they had acted "), are an additional
evidence that learned men may be
ignorant of the laws of exegesis.
Knobel, Ewald, Herzfeld, De Wette,
Hitzig, Heiligstedt, Elster, Philippson, Vaihinger, &c., who adopt Ibn
Ezra's interpretation without mentioning it, have successively marred
it by their attempts to improve upon
it. Thus Knobel and De Wette
(und alsdann sah ich Frevler bestattet
werden ; und es kamen an und vom
heiligen Orte gingen hinweg und
wurden vergessen in der Stadt, welche
redlich gehandelt halten),though rightly
taking בוא and הָלַך to denote *being
born* and *dying*, totally destroy the
antithesis, by referring both to אֲשֶׁר
כֵּן־עָשׂוּ, *those who acted uprightly ;*
Ewald, Hitzig, Heiligstedt, Elster,
Philippson, and Vaihinger do the
same thing by a more violent process,
inasmuch as they take וְבָאוּ as an
ellipsis for וְבָאוּ שָׁלוֹם, *they entered into
peace*, as in Isa. lvii. 2, or for וְבָאוּ
לִקְבָרִים, *they entered their graves*, and
יְהַלְכוּ, the *Piel*, to be here used for the
Hiphil יוֹלִכוּ, *they drove away;* Herzfeld,

who does not join in this arbitrary
rendering of יְהַלֵּכוּ, explains it by *emi-
grating ;* whilst Hitzig alters it into
יַחֲלֵפוּ, *the perished.* According to
Fürst (Concordance, *s. v.*, שָׁכַח, ii.),
this verse ought to be rendered, "and
whilst I saw the wicked peacefully
buried, and go [to their fathers] and
depart from the place of the holy, yet
were those found (*i. e.*, remembered)
in the city who acted uprightly,"
taking שָׁכַח to denote *to find, to exist,*
to *be found*, which, as will be seen
from Ibn Ezra's remark (וישתכחו ויפרשו
מתרגום וימצאו), has been proposed and
rejected long ago. The many ellipses,
however, which this explanation presupposes, and the forced meaning it
assigns to the several expressions,
will, we believe, prevent its having
many followers. Stuart's version,
" and I saw the wicked buried, for
they had departed, even from a holy
place did they go away ; and then
they were forgotten in the city where
they had so done," taking וְבָאוּ as
pluperfect, and the ו before it as
standing in a kind of apodosis, is
simply preposterous ; for to say *the
wicked were buried, for they had
departed*, is nonsense ; since they
could not be buried without dying
first. Besides, Stuart makes the
verbs בוא and הָלַך, which denote *two
opposite* things, express the *same
idea*, and destroys the antithesis of
the hemistiches.

11. *Because sentence*, &c. This
melancholy absence of retributive
justice induces many fearlessly to
commit sin, inasmuch as they have
no apprehension of punishment
(comp. Ps. cxxv. 3). The heart,
being the seat of reason and feelings
(*vide supra*, i. 13), is represented as
becoming *replete* with thoughts which
tend to and alternately ripen in the
perpetuation of evil (comp. *infra*,
ix. 3 ; Esth. vii. 5, and see the
similar expression in Acts v. 3).
אֲשֶׁר, *because*, is used instead of כִּי

12 in them to do evil, because a sinner doeth evil a hundred

(comp. vi. 12). אֵין by no means necessitates the alteration of נַעֲשָׂה the
præterite Niph., third per. masc., into
נַעֲשָׂה, the *participle fem. ;* for, though
it is true that this negative particle
is *generally* construed with the participle, yet we also assuredly find it
joined with a *finite verb* (comp. הַסְּנֶה
אֵינֶנּוּ אֻכָּל, *the bush was not consumed,*
Exod. iii. 2 ; אֵין הַמֶּלֶךְ יוּכַל אֶתְכֶם דָּבָר,
*the king cannot do anything against
you,* Jer. xxxviii. 5 ; Job xxxv. 15 ;
Gesen. Lex., *s. v.*) This construction
is moreover corroborated by the fact
that פִּתְגָם is *masculine,* as is evident
from וְנִשְׁמַע פִּתְגָם, Esth. i. 20, and
can therefore only agree with נַעֲשָׂה,
third per. *masc.,* but not with the
alteration of it into נַעֲשָׂה, the *fem.
part.* פִּתְגָם, *sentence,* is a later Hebrew
word ; it only occurs once more in
Hebrew (Esth. i. 20), and may either
be derived from פְּתַג in Aramæan,
פְּתַק = פְּתַג = פְּסַק, to *make known, to
announce, to pronounce, to pronounce
sentence,* or it may be kindred with
the Aramæan פְּסַק, *to adjudicate, to
decide,* with the termination ם‿ like
סֻלָּם, *ladder,* סָלְעָם, *locust.* Both the
pause-accent upon it, and the *Quametz*
under the ‏ ‎, shew that it is the *absolute
form ;* מַעֲשֵׂי הָרָעָה must therefore be
taken as *accusative absol.* (compare
Job i. 5 ; Ps. cxxii. 4, cxliv. 12 ;
Gesen. § 118, 3 ; Ewald, § 300, c).
The Septuagint (ὅτι οὐκ ἔστιν γινομένη
ἀντίῤῥησις ἀπὸ τῶν ποιούντων τὸ πονηρὸν ταχύ,
*because there is no contradiction made
from them who do evil quickly*), is
exceedingly obscure, the translator
evidently could not catch the meaning of the original, and, as is usual
in such cases, determined to follow
the very order of the words in the
Hebrew, altering, however, מַעֲשֵׂה,
work, into מֵעֹשֵׂי, *from the doers of,*
which the Vulgate, St. Jerome, the
Syriac, &c., follow, and which is
adopted by Spohn. The noun מְהֵרָה,
prop. *haste, speed,* is used adverbially
for בִּמְהֵרָה, *in speed, forthwith, quickly*
(comp. Numb. xvii. 11 ; Judg. ix. 54 ;
Ps. xxxi. 3). Schmidt, Ewald, and

Hengstenberg, however, take it in
the adject. sense, and, as both *substantives* and *adverbs* may be employed
for adjectives (see Gesen. § 106, 1 ;
Ewald, § 296, d), translate it, aber
wo fein ftrafenbes Urtheil ergeht, ba
nimmt bie Bosheit fchnell überhanb,
unb bas menschliche Herz füllt fich
mit Planen, Böfes zu ftiften, *but
where no sentence is executed, there
wickedness soon has the upper hand,
and the human heart is filled with
schemes to do evil* (Schmidt) ; weil
nicht gefchieht ber höchfte Wille, kommt
leicht ber Bosheit That ; barum ift bas
Herz ber Menfchenkinber in ihnen voll,
Böfes zu thun, *because the supreme
will is not executed, deeds of wickedness are soon done, therefore is the
heart of men full to do evil* (Ewald) ;
weil nicht ergehet ein Ausfpruch, eilet
bas Werk ber Bosheit ; barum wirb
bas Herz, u. f. w., *because a sentence
is not executed, the work of wickedness
hastens, therefore the heart,* &c. (Hengstenberg). But this division of the first
clause into two sentences renders the
words, " therefore the heart of men,"
&c., superfluous, since the second
sentence is already the apodosis, and
gives the result of the first, so that
the third sentence is thereby made
mere tautology. Besides, had this
been the meaning of the sacred
writer, he would undoubtedly have
placed עַל־כֵּן before מַעֲשֵׂה הָרָעָה. The
Septuagint's rendering of מָלֵא לֵב וְגוֹ׳
by ἐπληροφορήθη καρδία, *the heart is fully
persuaded,* does not exactly express
its meaning ; the Vulgate, ABSQUE
TIMORE ULLO FILII HOMINUM PER-
PETRANT MALA, *the children of men
commit evils without any fear,* is still
more languid and paraphrastic.

12. *Because a sinner,* &c. This
clause resumes the statement made
in the first clause of the preceding
verse to render it more intense and
emphatic. What is there summarily and simply characterised as a
delay in the execution of the sentence
upon the wicked, is here more particularly set forth in the striking

instances of a sinner who is both spared for many years to perpetrate crime, and is perpetuated in his wicked progeny. אֲשֶׁר is therefore *causal*, and co-ordinate with אֲשֶׁר in the foregoing verse, both having the same sense. That "אֲשֶׁר אֵין־נַעֲשָׂה וְגוֹ and "אֲשֶׁר חֹטֶא עֹשֶׂה וְגוֹ express the *same thing* is moreover evident from the two phrases אֲשֶׁר יִהְיֶה־טּוֹב and אֲשֶׁר יְרֵאוּ מִלְּפָנָיו, which are used to express the *same thing*, when the *opposite character* is described. Hence the Vulgate, Rashi, and Ibn Ezra's rendering of אֲשֶׁר by *although*, which is followed by Luther, Coverdale, the Geneva Bible, the Auth. Version, Hodgson, Knobel, Herzfeld, Stuart, Elster, Vaihinger, Hengstenberg, &c., is contrary to the evenness of the construction. When we moreover add that אֲשֶׁר never means *although*, that Gesenius (Lex. *s. v.* אֲשֶׁר B. 4), and Ewald (Gram. § 362, b), who assign to it this concessive signification, have not adduced a single instance to justify this unnatural sense, the correctness and necessity of our rendering will be obvious. For חֹטֶא with a *Segol* instead of חֹטֵא with *Tzere*, see vii. 26. מֵאַת is not used *adverbially* for *a hundred times* (Gesen. Lex. *s. v.*; Ewald, § 269, d; Knobel, Herzfeld, Heiligstedt, Stuart, &c.), as there is no analogy for this usage (*vide supra*, vi. 3), but, as Rashi and Rashbam rightly remark (מקרא קצר הוא ורבוק הוא על חתיבה החסירה), is used *brachylogically*, and is the construct to an omitted word (comp. שָׁבְרֵת וְלֹא מִיָּן, *drunken with—i.e.* חֲמַת יְהֹוָה, *the wrath of the Eternal*, as is evident from ver. 17—*and not with wine*, Isa. li. 21). The expression to be supplied in the passage before us may either be שָׁנִים יָמִים, *years* (the Chaldee, Rashi, Rashbam, &c.), or פְּעָמִים, *times* (the Vulg., St. Jerome, Ibn Ezra, Luther, Coverdale, the Bishops' Bible, the Geneva Bible, the Auth. Ver., &c.); the former, however, is preferable, for it agrees better with the *delay* of the execution of retributive justice mentioned in the preceding verse,

which undoubtedly implies *waiting many years*, and which is not necessarily implied in the latter, inasmuch as one may commit *a hundred sins*, or a large number of them, in *a very short time*. That מַאֲרִיךְ, part. Hiphil, is here used as a noun, and signifies *one who makes long*, or *perpetuates*, *a prolonger*, *a perpetuator*, the wicked progeny which perpetuates his family, referring רְשָׁעִים קְבֻרִים וָבָאוּ, *the wicked being buried, and appear again in their wicked descendants, who perpetuate them, are their perpetuators* (verse 10), is evident from the לוֹ by which it is followed, thus making an essential difference between its signification here and in vii. 5, where it is used absolutely. All that is to be supplied here is the *substantive verb*, which, as is well known, is generally omitted. The literal translation of וּמַאֲרִיךְ לוֹ, [therefore, is, *and there is a perpetuator to him;* the passive rendering, however, and *he is perpetuated*, suits our idiom better. The Septuagint's rendering of this clause, ὃς ἥμαρτεν ἐποίησεν τὸ πονηρὸν ἀπὸ τότε καὶ ἀπὸ μακρότητος αὐτῶν, *whoso has sinned has done evil from that time and from the length of them*, meaning, most probably, *from the whole length of their existence*, takes אֲשֶׁר as a pronoun, changes מֵאַת into מֵאָז, and מַאֲרִיךְ לוֹ into מֵאָרְכָם, and yields no sense. Equally senseless is the translation of Symmachus, ἁμαρτών γὰρ] ὁ κακοῦργος ἀπέθανεν μακροθυμίας γενόμε-ης αὐτῷ, *for a sinner doing evil is dead, long-suffering being granted unto him*, which St. Jerome (Com. *in loco*) tells us was explained, " he who does evil and sins is dead in sin, although his days be prolonged to an old age," exchanging מֵאַת for its assonant מֵת, which is also done by Aquila and Theodotion, κακοῦργος ἀπέθανεν. More literal is the rendering of St. Jerome, QUIA PECCATOR FACIT MALUM CENTIES, ET ELONGAT EI DEUS, EX HOC COGNOSCO EGO, QUOD ERIT BONUM TIMENTIBUS DEUM, QUI TIMENT A FACIE EJUS, *because a sinner does evil a hundred times, and yet God lengthens his days, hence I know that*

years and is perpetuated.   But I also knew that it shall be well with those who fear God, who truly fear before him ; 13 and it shall not be well to the wicked, and, like a shadow, he shall not prolong his existence, because he doth not fear

it shall be well with those who fear God, who fear before his face, which he explains, "from the fact that God grants time for repentance to him who sins very much, this being meant by a hundred times, and does not immediately punish him for his wickedness, but waits that he may return ; I understand how merciful and gracious God will be to them who fear him and tremble at his word." Hence the Bishops' Bible, "because an evil person offendeth an hundred times, and God deferreth, giving him long life, therefore am I sure that it shall go well with them that fear God," &c., and Desvoeux, "because the sinner dieth, committing evil, even from the delays granted to him, thus I know that it shall be well," &c., who, however, alters מְאַת into מֵת, and מַאֲרִיךְ into מֵאָרֶךְ, supplying נָתַן after it.   But this interpretation is both contrary to מִשָּׁם, which never means *from hence,* and to the evenness of the structure, as shewn above.

But I also knew, &c.   But though Coheleth *has seen* (רָאִיתִי) the wicked triumph in their wickedness, which encourages men to practise evil (9 – 12, a), yet he was also *persuaded* (יֹדֵעַ אָנִי) that what he has asserted (5 – 8) is also true. viz., that there is an appointed time for righteous retribution, when it shall be well with those who truly fear God.   For the adversative meaning of כִּי, *but,* see v. 6.   The participle יֹדֵעַ is placed before אָנִי for the sake of emphasis. The repetition אֲשֶׁר יִהְיֶה־טּוֹב לְיִרְאֵי הָאֱלֹהִים אֲשֶׁר יִרְאוּ מִלְּפָנָיו, characterising the God-fearing, corresponds to the repetition in the description of the godless.   It is one of Coheleth's favourite modes of imparting emphasis to an allegation, and has its parallel in the New Testament (comp. χήρας τίμα, τὰς ὄντως

χήρας, *honour widows, who are truly widows,* I Tim. v. 3).   For the construction of יָרֵא with מִלְּפָנֵי, see iii. 14.

13. *And it shall not,* &c.   The discrepancy between the allegation in the preceding verse, that *wicked men do live long in spite of committing sin,* and the assertion here that *they shall not live long,* is a natural consequence of limiting the bar of judgment to this side of the grave ; and this limitation, be it remembered, formed the starting-point, and is all along the basis of Coheleth's reasoning.   With the promise of temporal rewards and punishments, a believing Old Testament philosopher could say (יֹדֵעַ אָנִי) "*I know,* I have been assured, that the righteous shall have a prosperous and long life, and the wicked a miserable and short existence;" but when he looked at the mysterious administration in the moral government of God, he also was constrained to exclaim (רָאִיתִי), "*I see* the very reverse often take place." Hence the discrepancy which weighed so deeply upon the minds of the chosen people, which led to such disastrous consequences, with which Coheleth deeply sympathises (*vide* p. 21, &c.), and which he ultimately reconciles. There is therefore no need to resort to the arbitrary rendering of the Vulgate, ET BONUM NON SIT IMPIO, &c., *and let it not be well with the wicked,* &c., and the explanation of St Jerome, which make this verse an imprecation, in order to obviate the discrepancy. לֹא־יַאֲרִיךְ יָמִים כַּצֵּל, *man shall not prolong his days like a shadow,* is merely a negative mode of expressing the well known phrase, יִבְרַח כַּצֵּל . . . אָדָם, *man, or his days, shall flee away like a shadow,* and is well rendered by Luther (unb wie ein Schatten nicht lange leben), Spohn unb feine Lebenszeit wird wie ein

14 before God. Still there is this vanity happening upon the earth, that there are righteous men who have wages like that of the wicked, and there are wicked who have wages like that of the righteous; I said that this, too, is vanity. 15 And I praised mirth, because there is nothing better for

Schatten), and others. The Sept., οὐ μακρυνεῖ ἡμέρας ἐν σκιᾷ, *he shall not prolong his days in, or under, a shadow,* which is followed by Desvoeux; and the Chaldee paraphrase, וְלָא יְהֵי לַהּ אַרְכָּא לְעָלְמָא דְאָתֵי וּבְעָלְמָא הָדֵין יִתְקַטְעִין יוֹמֵי חַיּוֹהִי וְיִעְרְקוּן וְיֵחַלְפוּן כְּטוּלָּא, *and there shall be no space for him in the world to come, and in this world the days of his life shall be cut off, they shall flee and pass away like a shadow*; the Vulgate, NEC PROLONGENTUR DIES EJUS, SED QUASI UMBRA TRANSEANT, *neither let his days be prolonged, but like a shadow let them pass away*; the Auth. Version, " neither shall he prolong his days, which are as a shadow;" and Noyes, " he shall be like a shadow, and shall not prolong his days," dividing it into two distinct clauses; as well as Coverdale and the Bishops' Bible, " neither shall he prolong his days, but even as a shadow so shall he be," &c.; and the Geneva Bible, " neither shall he prolong his days; he shall be like a shadow, because," &c., connecting כַּצֵּל, contrary to the accents, with the closing part of the verse, which is followed by Hitzig, Stuart, Elster, &c., are inadmissible. For the comparison of the fleeting life of man with the transient shadow, see vi. 12. יָמִים, *years,* is, as frequently, used for *years of life, lifetime, life, existence.* Here, too, יְרֵא is construed with מִלִּפְנֵי, for which see iii. 14.

14. *Still there is this vanity,* &c. The conflict which has been carried on in verses 5 – 13, between Coheleth's *knowledge* or *assurance* (יָדַע אָנִי) of righteous retribution and his *experience* (רָאִיתִי) of its absence in this world, is now decided in favour of the latter, by an appeal to the melancholy fact that the very reverse of retributive justice is to be seen, since

the righteous endure the sufferings wherewith the wicked are threatened, whilst the wicked enjoy the earthly blessings promised to the righteous. יֵשׁ, belonging to all numbers and genders, is construed with the *sing.* הֶבֶל, *vanity,* and the *plur.* צַדִּיקִים, *the righteous.* עַל־הָאָרֶץ, *upon the earth,* used here, in verse 16, and in xi. 2, is the same as תַּחַת הַשֶּׁמֶשׁ, *under the sun,* or תַּחַת הַשָּׁמַיִם, *under heaven* (comp. i. 3). מַעֲשֶׂה, *work,* is also used metonymically for the *effect, fruits,* or *wages* of work generally, and the special name for these fruits must be determined by the nature of the employment in question (comp. Exod. xxiii. 16; 1 Sam. xxv. 2; Isa. xxvi. 12; Jer. xlviii. 7). As the work here spoken of is the moral and immoral conduct of the righteous and the wicked (מַעֲשֶׂה), the wages of course must be *reward,* or *happiness,* and *punishment,* or *misery,* the *destiny* or *fate* consequent upon such modes of living. The כְּ comparison in כְּמַעֲשֵׂה, shews that מַעֲשֵׂה is implied before it, *i. e.,* מַעֲשֵׂה כְּמַעֲשֵׂה הָרְשָׁעִים and כְּמַעֲשֵׂה הַצַּדִּיקִים (comp. *supra,* ii. 15). הִגִּיעַ with אֶל or עַל, as in Esth. ix. 26, is *to reach to any one, to come to, to have.*

15. *And I praised,* &c. Having shewn the utter inability of wealth to secure lasting happiness (vi. 1 – 12), and the impossibility of *prudence,* or a life regulated according to the teachings of *common sense,* to overrule the mysterious dealings of Providence, or to account for the melancholy fact that the fortunes of the righteous and the wicked are often reversed all the days of their lives (vii. 1. – viii. 14), Coheleth recurs to his repeated conclusion, that there is nothing left for man but to enjoy

man under the sun than to eat, and drink, and rejoice, and
this will follow him in his work during the days of his life
which God giveth him under the sun.

the things of this life. אֲשֶׁר is not a
conjunction introducing the clause
"אֲשֶׁר אֵין־טוֹב וגו, as an explanatory
periphrase of וְשִׁבַּחְתִּי אֲנִי אֶת־הַשִּׂמְחָה,
unb id) preiſe bie Freube, baß nämlid)
nid)tß gut ſei für ben Menſd)en, *i. e.*,
*I praise enjoyment that, namely, no-
thing is good for man but*, &c. (Herzfeld, Philippson, Hengstenberg, &c.),
but is *causal*, as is evident from the
connection of this verse with the preceding one, and from the fact that
we have here the conclusion from
the foregoing experiments. The
singular וְהוּא may either refer to the
eating, drinking, and rejoicing comprised in *one*, or, which is still better,
to טוֹב. לָוָה, *to incline, to join one's-self
to any one, to attend, to follow*, is here
construed with the *accusative*, like
דָּבַק in Gen. xix. 19. בַּעֲמָלוֹ is the same
as בְּכָל־עֲמָלוֹ in iii. 13; the בְ expresses
proximity, nearness ; when man is engaged *in* or is *at* his work, this good

or enjoying spirit which he cultivates
will accompany him to his sphere of
labour. The phrase is well rendered
by the Septuagint, καὶ αὐτὸ συμπροσέσται
αὐτῷ ἐν μόχθῳ αὐτοῦ, Herzfeld and
Philippson, unb bieß begleitet ifm bei
ſeiner Müfe. The paraphrase of the
Vulgate, *et hoc solum secum auferret
de labore suo*, followed by Luther,
unb ſold)eß werbe ifm von ber Arbeit;
Coverdale, and the Bishops' Bible,
" for that shall he have of his labour ; " the Geneva Bible, " for this
is adjoined to his labour ; " Desvoeux,
" for this shall borrow him from his
labour," which he explains, " man is
the property of labour ; if ever that
tyrannical owner parts with him, it
is only by way of *loan ;* pleasurable
enjoyments may sometimes *borrow*
him for a while, but he must be returned ; " and Hodgson, " and these
are to comfort him in his labour,"
are contrary to the meaning of לָוָה.

SECTION IV.

CHAPTER VIII. 16 — XII. 7.

Coheleth now recapitulates the investigations contained in the preceding
section, and gives us his final conclusion. Having found that it is
impossible to fathom the work of God by wisdom (viii. 16, 17) ; that
even the righteous and the wise are subject to this inscrutable Providence, just as the wicked (ix. 1, 2) ; that all must alike die and be
forgotten (3 – 5), and that they have no more participation in what
takes place here (6) ; that we are therefore to indulge in pleasures
here while we can, since there is no hereafter (7 – 10) ; that success
does not always attend the strong and the skilful (11, 12) ; and that
wisdom, though decidedly advantageous in many respects, is often
despised and counteracted by folly (13 – x. 3) ; that we are to be patient
under sufferings from rulers (4), who by virtue of their power frequently

pervert the order of things (5 – 7), since violent opposition may only tend to increase our sufferings (8 – 11) ; that the exercise of prudence in the affairs of life will be more advantageous than folly (12 – 20) ; that we are to be charitable, though the recipients of our benevolence appear ungrateful, since they may, after all, requite us (xi. 1, 2) ; that we are always to be at our work, and not be deterred by imaginary failures, since we know not which of our efforts may prove successful (3 – 6), and thus make life as agreeable as we can (7), for we must always bear in mind that this is the only scene of enjoyment; that the future is all vanity (8) ; but as this, too, did not satisfy the craving of the soul, Coheleth at last came to the conclusion, that *enjoyment of this life, together with belief in a future judgment, will secure real happiness for man* (9, 10), and that we are *therefore to live from our early youth in the fear of God and of a final judgment,* when all that is perplexing now shall be rectified (xii. 1 – 7).

16 As I gave my heart to know wisdom, and to see the work which is done under the sun, how that one doth not see

16. *As I gave my heart, &c.* To shew more strikingly the force of the final conclusion, submitted at the end of this section, Coheleth gives first a *résumé* of the investigations contained in the foregoing three sections. He tells us, that in the course of his enquiry he found it utterly impossible to fathom the work of God by wisdom. The expression כַּאֲשֶׁר marks the beginning of a new subject (comp. v. 3). For נָתַן לֵב and עִנְיָן, see i. 13; and for יָדַע חָכְמָה, *to know,* i. e., *to acquire wisdom,* see i. 16. כִּי, the *relative conjunction,* introduces the explanatory clause גַם בַּיּוֹם וּבַלַּיְלָה וְגוֹ׳, explicative of הָעִנְיָן, and is still depending upon וְלִרְאוֹת (comp. תַּעֲלֻמוֹת חָכְמָה כִּי־כִפְלַיִם לְתוּשִׁיָה, *and that he may reveal* or *disclose to thee the depths that they are double for thy wisdom,* i. e., they doubly surpass thy wisdom, Job xi. 6, where כִּי introduces כִפְלַיִם לְתוּשִׁיָה, explanatory of תַּעֲלֻמוֹת חָכְמָה, and is dependent upon וְיַגֶּד, see also *ibid.* xii. 12). This explanation, besides relieving this clause from the complicated position in which it is placed, by those who assign to כִּי a *causal* signification, makes it evident that the much disputed suffix in בְּרִיָו, which the Chal-

dee, Reynolds, &c., refer to *Solomon,* and Rashbam, Ibn Ezra, Rosenmüller, De Wette, &c., to his *heart,* refers to man engrossed in this (עִנְיָן) "work which is done upon the earth" (comp. ii. 23, v. 16, ix. 12). גַם. with the *negative,* gives intensity to the statement, *i. e., not even* (comp. iv. 8). After what has been said in i. 8, upon the ascription of *hope* to the eye, the phrase *the eyes see sleep* will at once be intelligible (comp. also Gen. xxxi. 40 ; Ps. cxxxii. 4 ; Prov. vi. 4). The same phrase is also used in Latin, comp.

Somnum hercle ego hac nocte oculis non vidi meis.

"I' faith, I have not seen sleep this night with my eyes."

TERENT. HEAUTONTIM., III. i. 82.

By the figure *Zeugma,* the words שֵׁנָה בְּעֵינָיו אֵינֶנּוּ רֹאֶה, *he sees no sleep with his eyes,* which can with propriety be predicated only of בְּלַיְלָה, the nearer noun, refers also to בַּיּוֹם, the more remote one. This figure of speech is of frequent occurrence in the Old and New Testament, as well as in profane writings (comp. קוֹל שָׁחַל וְשִׁנֵּי כְפִירִים נִתָּעוּ, *the roaring of the lion, and the teeth of the young lion are*

17 sleep with his eyes by day and by night, I then saw that
man cannot find out all the doing of God which is done
under the sun; wherefore man laboureth to search it, and
cannot find it out; and even if the wise man saith he under-

broken, Job iv. 10; where the *breaking* can be said only of the teeth; see also Isa. lv. 3; Jer. xv. 8; Hos. i. 2, and γάλα ὑμᾶς ἐπότισα, οὐ βρῶμα, *I have fed you with milk, not with meat*, 1 Cor. iii. 2, where ἐπότισα, which properly is the predicate of γάλα, is also applied to βρῶμα; so also Luke i. 63; Hom. Il. viii. 546).

17. *I then saw, &c.* Having acquired this eagerly sought for wisdom, and ascertained the value of the utmost human exertions to scrutinise God's dispensations, Coheleth was fully convinced that it is utterly impossible for any man to fathom the mysterious dealings of Providence, and that the greatest efforts, be they physical or intellectual, are totally useless and vain. The וְ in וְרָאִיתִי, as frequently, introduces the *apodosis*, the foregoing verse being the *protasis*, and is to be rendered *then* (comp. ix. 3. 16, x. 10, 11; Gesenius, § 129, 1 Rem.; Ewald, § 230). We have here, again, an attraction, the ordinary construction of which would be וְרָאִיתִי כִּי לֹא יוּכַל הָאָדָם לִמְצוֹא אֶת־כָּל־מַעֲשֵׂה הָאֱלֹהִים אֲשֶׁר נַעֲשָׂה וְגוֹ, *I then saw that man cannot find out all the doing of God which is done, &c.* (compare iii. 21). For מַעֲשֵׂה הָאֱלֹהִים, denoting *God's providential dealings*, and מָצָא, *to find out, to fathom*, see iii. 11. Luther, misunderstanding this attraction, erroneously translates it, und ich fahe alle Werke Gottes. Denn ein Mensch kann das Werk nicht finden, u. s. w. Equally erroneous are the Bishops' Bible ("I understood of all the works of God, but it is not possible for a man to attain unto the works that are done," &c.), the Geneva Bible, which is followed by the Auth. Ver., Desvoeux ("then I understood that this is all God's own work, that man

is not able to find out the end of this work that is done under the sun"), Hodgson ("I perceived also, in every work of God, that man can account for nothing which is done under the sun"), &c. That שֶׁל, *i. q.*, אֲשֶׁר ל, corresponding to the Aramæan דְּדִיל, compounded of דִּי בְּ, means *on account of, because of*, is sufficiently established from בִּשְׁלְמִי, *on whose account*, in Jonah i. 7, for which verse 8 has בַּאֲשֶׁר לְמִי, as well as from בְּשֶׁלִּי, *on my account* (*ibid.*, verse 12; Ewald, § 222, e). Accordingly, בְּשֶׁל אֲשֶׁר signifies *on account of that, on this account, wherefore, therefore, hence*, and has its exact analogy in the frequently-occurring phrase of accumulated relatives in Aramæan, בְּ דִּי ל דִּי = בְּדִיל דִּי, *on this account, hence*. The rendering of it by *whatsoever*, or *however, in that, wherein that* (Septuagint ὅσα ἐάν, the Syriac كُوْ ?, Rashbam באותו דבר ש, Gesen. Lex., Philippson, Vaihinger, &c.), making it equivalent to בְּכָל אֲשֶׁר, which some maintain was the original reading of the text (Ewald, § 362, b; Heiligstedt, &c.), is both contrary to the undoubted existence of the analogous phrase, and to its signification. For the same reasons, we must reject the paraphrastic rendering of the Vulgate, *et quanto plus laboraverit ad quærendum, tanto minus inveniat*, which is adopted by Luther, und je mehr der Mensch arbeitet zu suchen, je weniger er findet, the explanation of Rashi, the Geneva Bible, Hodgson, &c., בשביל אשר, *for the which;* the translation of Coverdale and the Bishops' Bible. "and though he bestow his labour . . . yet," &c., the Authorised Version, "though seek though . . . yet," &c. For the ל in לָדַעַת, introducing the *indirect* speech, see iii. 18.

ix. 1 standeth it, he cannot find it out. For all this have I taken
to heart, and proved all this, that the righteous and the wise,
and their labours, are in the hand of God ; these men know

1. *For all this,* &c. The validity
of his assertion, that all human
efforts to fathom the moral government of God are vain and useless,
is evident from the fact, that if any
man or thing could render the mysterious dealings of Providence more
apparent, it would be the conduct of
the righteous and the wise, yet they
themselves and their works are subject to this arbitrary and inscrutable
Providence, and are totally ignorant
of the issue of their good and prudent works; they cannot tell whether
their labours will secure for them
love or hatred, happiness or misery,
since both prosperity and adversity
come upon them irrespective of their
conduct. כִּי, *for,* assigns a reason
for the allegation in the foregoing
verse about the inscrutable nature
of God's dealings, and is wrongly
omitted by the Vulgate.   For the
phrase *to take it to heart,* see vii. 2 ;
and for לָבוּר, the *infinitive construct,*
continuing the discourse after a finite
verb, with the signification of בֵּרְתִּי,
the finite verb, see viii. 9.   The
Septuagint's rendering of וְלָבוּר אֶת־כָּל־זֶה
by καὶ καρδία μου σύμπαν ἴδεν τοῦτο,
and my heart has seen all this, which

is followed by the Syriac, ܘܿܚ̣ܙ
ܠܒܼܝ ܗܿܢܐ ܟܿܠ ܗܿ ܣܼܘ, evidently proceeds from having inadvertently separated ולבוראת into ולבי ראה, mistaking
ח for ה, and the ו for י.   The צַדִּיקִים
וְהַחֲכָמִים, *righteous and the wise,* are
mentioned, because they might have
been supposed to overrule or explain
this mysterious incongruity in the
administration of retributive justice.
עֲבָד, with *Quametz* impure, *labour,
work,* is wrongly taken by the
Chaldee, Rashi, Luther, the Bishops'
Bible, &c., for עֶבֶד *servant.* בְּיַר הָאֱלֹהִים,
to be in the hand of God, is not *to be
under a special Providence* (Rashi,
Bishop Patrick, Gill, &c.), which is

contrary to the scope of the passage,
but means absolutely depending
upon his arbitrary power, entirely
subject to his inscrutable dealings
(comp. Ps. xcv. 4 ; Prov. xxi. 1 ;
Job xii. 10), *i. e.,* the works of the
good and the wise will not produce
that which they desire, but that
which the unfathomable will of God
decrees ; so much so, that retributive justice is reversed, as is manifest
from the following verse, where the
same idea is more largely dwelt upon.
This determines the sense of the
much disputed גַּם־אַהֲבָה גַם־שִׂנְאָה אֵין יוֹדֵעַ
הָאָדָם to be, that as the dealings of
Providence are so irrespective of
merit, the righteous and the wise
cannot know from their own conduct
whether they will meet with the
expressions of love or hatred, *i. e.,*
prosperity or adversity, both await
them indiscriminately, since they
are distributed without any regard
to holy and prudent life.   Thus אַהֲבָה
and שִׂנְאָה may either be taken metonymically for the expression of God's
love and hatred, *i. e., prosperity* and
adversity, happiness and *misery ;* or,
with Ibn Ezra, may be regarded as
the *object* of love and hatred, כל מה
שהם אוהבים או שונאים אינם יודעים מתי יבואם
הכל לפניהם, *i. e., they know not when
the things which they love or hate
may come upon them, both are before
them.*   The repeated גַּם . . . גַּם is
equivalent to the Latin *tum . . tum,
both . . . and* (comp. *infra,* verse 6,
Gen. xxiv. 25 ; Exod. xii. 31;
Gesen. Lex. *s v. ;* Ewald, § 359) ;
but as the literal rendering, " both
prosperity and adversity man knoweth not,''. would be awkward in
English, we must substitute the
disjunctive particles *neither . . . nor.*
הַכֹּל, *all,* as frequently, also *both,* i. e.,
happiness and *misery,* as the two
conditions, comprise the *totality* of
man's feelings (comp. ii. 14).   A
tyro in Hebrew knows that לִפְנֵיהֶם

3 G

2 neither love nor hatred, both are before them, both just as
  before all others ; the same fate happeneth to the righteous
  and the wicked ; to the good and pure, and to the impure ;
  to him who sacrificeth and to him who doth not sacrifice ; as
  is the good so is the sinner, he that sweareth as he who

refers to הָאָדָם, which is used *collectively* for הַצַּדִּיקִים וְהַחֲכָמִים, *the righteous and the wise* ; yet Dr. Gill explains it, "*yet all things are before him ;* Elohim, the three divine Persons."

2. *Both just as before all others,* &c. This verse is intimately connected with the preceding one, being a continuation of the same sentiment, and ought not to have been separated from it. Both happiness and misery, which, as said at the end of the foregoing verse, indiscriminately await the righteous and the wicked, come to them just in the same arbitrary manner as to all other men ; there is no difference in this respect between the good and the bad, the pious and the impious meet with the same fate. That הַכֹּל, which is simply a further explanation of הַכֹּל in the preceding verse, should have called forth such a diversity of opinions, must be ascribed to the confusion which reigns in the ancient versions on this clause. The Septuagint renders הַכֹּל כַּאֲשֶׁר לַכֹּל by ματαιότης ἐν τοῖς πᾶσιν, *vanity in all,* omitting כַּאֲשֶׁר, and alters הַכֹּל לַכֹּל into הֶבֶל בַּכֹּל. Symmachus, who also takes הַכֹּל for הֶבֶל, connects it with הַכֹּל לִפְנֵיהֶם at the end of the foregoing verse, viz., τὰ πάντα ἔμπροσθεν αὐτοῦ ἄδηλα, *all before him is uncertain ;* so also the Vulgate, SED OMNIA IN FUTURUM SERVANTUR INCERTA, *but all things are kept uncertain for the future.* The Syriac

ܟܠ ܩܕܡܝܗܘܢ ܗܒܠܐ ܟܠ ܐܝܟ, *all before him is vanity, all as to all,* has both the correct reading of the text and this emendation, the latter has evidently been inserted into the text from a marginal gloss. Hitzig's explanation of this clause is

truly marvellous ; he takes מִקְרֶה אֶחָד both as the *predicate* of הַכֹּל and the *subject* of כַּאֲשֶׁר לַכֹּל ; the full construction, according to him. is הַכֹּל מִקְרֶה אֶחָד כַּאֲשֶׁר לַכֹּל מִקְרֶה אֶחָד, Alle finb gleich= wie Alle trifft Ein Zufall. These arbitrary emendations and far-fetched expositions appear all · the more monstrous when compared with Ibn Ezra's simple and natural explanation of this clause, הכל יבא לחם כמו שיבא לכל, *all* or *both things happen to them* (*i. e.,* to the righteous and wise) *just as to every one else ;* similarly Rashbaum הכל כאשר לכל פי' הוא של הכל לפניהם כל הרעות והפורעניות באות כמות שהן לכל בני האדם לפניהם, which follows הַכֹּל at the end of the preceding verse, belongs also to הַכֹּל at the beginning of this verse, and the verb substantive, as is usually the case, is omitted after כַּאֲשֶׁר ; the full construction is הַכֹּל לִפְנֵיהֶם כַּאֲשֶׁר יִהְיֶה לַכֹּל, *both await them just as they await all others.* מִקְרֶה אֶחָד, *the same fate,* refers to the same indiscriminate fortunes spoken of in the preceding verse, which meet alike the righteous and the wicked, without any regard to merit or demerit. For מִקְרֶה, *fate,* and אֶחָד, *the same,* see ii. 14. טוֹב, *good,* is placed before לַטָּהוֹר וְלַטָּמֵא, to shew that the purity and impurity are not *Levitical* but *moral.* The Septuagint's insertion of רַע, *evil,* after it, thus making it a separate couplet, viz , לַטּוֹב וְלָרַע, which is also done by the Vulgate and Syriac, and adopted by Desvoeux, Spohn, &c., has no MS. authority, and would, if admitted, be a needless tautology, inasmuch as טוֹב כַּחֹטֵא are mentioned in the next couplet but one. כְּ — כְּ is used when two things are compared, *as — so* (comp. כַּחַטָּאת כָּאָשָׁם, *as is the sin-offering, so is the trespass-offering,* Levit. vii. 7; Ewald,

3 feareth an oath.　This is the greatest evil of all that is done under the sun, that there is the same fate for all, and that, although the heart of the sons of men is full of evil, and madness is in their hearts during their life, yet, after it, they
4 go to the dead; for who is excepted?　To all the living there

§ 360). The בְּ comparison is omitted before הַנִּשְׁבָּע, and כַּאֲשֶׁר is used before שְׁבוּעָה instead of בְּ, to give variety to the construction. The antithetic שְׁבוּעָה יָרֵא, *he who fears an oath*, shews beyond doubt that *careless swearing*, the habit of using an oath at every declaration made, is intended by שְׁבוּעָה, and not *perjury* (Vulgate, Rashi, Rashbam), compare Matt. v. 34, and Talmud, Gittin, 34, b, 35. a, where swearing generally is discouraged.

3. *This is the greatest*, &c. What is worst of all is, that this absence of all distinction between the righteous and the wicked, during the whole of man's life-time, is also visible in death; that those who had their hearts full of wickedness and folly all the days of their life, at the end of their journey enter into the realm of the dead, like the rest of mankind. The preposition בְּ in בְּכֹל gives to רַע the force of the superlative, making it stand forth prominently as evil in the midst (בְּ) of all other evils; none of all those by which it is surrounded can eclipse it, hence its superlative idea (comp. אַלְפִּי הַדַּל בִּמְנַשֶּׁה, *my family is the weakest in Manasseh*, Judg. vi. 15 ; Song of Songs i. 8 ; Lam. i. 1 ; Amos iii. 16 ; Ewald, § 313, c. The Vulgate has therefore rightly rendered it, PESSIMUM INTER OMNIA, *the worst of all things*, and Ibn Ezra אין בכל מהשנעשה תחת השמש דבר יותר קשה מזה, *among all things done under the sun nothing is more difficult than this*, &c.; so also Knobel, Herzfeld, Vaihinger, &c. That מִקְרֶה אֶחָד refers to *death*, to which all men, good and bad, are alike subject, as in ii. 14, iii. 19, is evident from its explicative וְאַחֲרָיו אֶל־הַמֵּתִים at the end of the verse. וְגַם

is still dependent upon כִּי, which must be mentally supplied before it, *i. e*, וְכִי גַם. *and that even if, although*, they have led such a wicked life, there is no distinction made between them and the righteous (מִקְרֶה אֶחָד לַכֹּל), the same fate is for all alike. The ו before וְאַחֲרָיו must therefore be regarded as introducing the *apodosis*, וְגַם being the *protasis* (*vide supra*, viii. 17). The suffix in וְאַחֲרָיו refers to הַחַיִּים, *life*, which, like many other abstract nouns, is expressed by the *plural* (comp. Gesen. § 108, 2, a ; Ewald, § 179, a). For מָלֵא לֵב, see viii. 11. The omission of הֹלְכִים, *they go*, before אֶל־הַמֵּתִים, *to the dead*, which imparts great energy to the diction in the original, must be supplied in the translation, as our idiom does not admit of such an ellipsis. The traditional explanation of this clause, taking אֶל־הַמֵּתִים, *to the dead*, for *hell*, which is given in the Midrash, the Chaldee, Rashi, &c., and which, as usual, is followed by the Vulgate (ET POST HÆC AD INFEROS DEDUCENTUR, *and afterwards they shall be brought down to hell*), Gill, &c., requires no refutation.

4. *For who is excepted?* In corroboration of the mournful fact with which the preceding verse concluded, viz., that all men, good and bad, die alike, Coheleth appeals to our own experience, asking us whether any, no matter what their conduct, can be adduced as being exempted from this fate common to all men. Some difference shewn in this awful event between the righteous and the wicked would indeed be a slight satisfaction, since the living, however low and contemptible their condition, possessing some rays of hope, are preferable to the dead, however great

and honoured. To enter into the full force of the adage with which Coheleth illustrates the advantage of life over death, we must advert to the respective positions which the dog and the lion occupied in the estimation of the Hebrews. Now that we hear it affirmed "that, with the exception of woman, there is nothing on earth so agreeable, or so necessary to the comfort of man, as the dog" (Jesse's Anecdotes of Dogs, Introd., Bohn's ed.); when we see this animal, a most faithful and cheering companion to the beggar in his solitude, and the monarch in his exile; the first to defend us in danger, the last to desert us in distress; tenderly guarding the infant, and gently guiding the blind; when we read some of the sweetest lines composed to celebrate his noble deeds and generous feelings, we could hardly understand the contemptible allusion to the dog, both here and elsewhere in the Scriptures, did we not bear in mind the Jewish treatment of the dog. The Jews excluded dogs from all familiarity, and entirely banished them from their premises. These animals without owners had therefore to take up their abode in some desolate part of the town, had to subsist on offal, carrion, and human corpses (Exod. xxii. 31; 1 Kings xiv. 11, xvi, 4, xxi. 19. 23; 2 Kings ix. 36; Ps. lix. 6). From this disgusting way of subsistence, and their repulsive habit alluded to in Prov. xxvi. 11, and 2 Pet. ii. 22, dogs were looked upon as the most *unclean, debased,* and *despicable* creatures; and the very term dog became a metaphor for uncleanness, debasement, and despicableness (1 Sam. xvii. 43, xxiv. 14; 2 Sam. ix, 8, xvi. 9; 2 Kings viii. 13; Sirach xiii. 22; Matt vii 6, xv. 26; Rev. xxii. 15). Hence the Jews called the Gentiles *dogs,* because of their abasement and abominations, and hence our Lord, when speaking of Jews and Gentiles, calls the former children and the latter *dogs* (Matt. xv. 26), and Mohammedans to this day call

Christians dogs by way of contempt. The lion, on the contrary, was regarded as the *king* of animals, in consequence of his strength and invincible courage, and became the symbol of *might* and *majesty.* The royal tribe of Israel is compared to a lion (Gen. xlix. 9); God, in his power and majesty, is frequently spoken of as a lion (Job x. 16; Isa. xxxviii. 13; Lam. iii. 10; Hos. xiii. 7); and the Messiah is distinguished as "the lion of the tribe of Judah" (Rev. v. 5). Mohammed called his uncle Homza, *the lion of God* (Gesen. Comment. on Isaiah xxix. 1). Hence the force of the passage. Notwithstanding the debased condition of the one, and the majestic position of the other, a despicable living dog is preferable to an exalted but dead lion. The same proverb exists in Arabic (comp. Golii Adag. Cent. ii. 3). כִּי is *causal,* assigning a reason for the previous allegation, and is therefore wrongly translated *surely, truly,* in the Geneva Bible, by Stuart, &c. מִי, as usually, is the interrogative *who,* with the substantive verb implied, hence מִי אֲשֶׁר means *who is it that.* יְבָחַר (the Pual of בָּחַר, *to prove, to approve, to select, to choose*) is *selected, excepted, exempted;* the interrogation is used for an emphatic denial, and is therefore well rendered by Symmachus τίς γὰρ εἰς ἀεὶ διατελέσει ζῶν; *who shall always continue to live?* and better still by the Vulgate, NEMO EST QUI SEMPER VIVAT, ET QUI HUJUS REI HABEAT FIDUCIAM, *there is no one who lives for ever, or hopes for it* — making, however, of אֶל כָּל־הַחַיִּים יֵשׁ בִּטָּחוֹן in the Hebrew אוֹ יֵשׁ לְכָל־הַחַיִּים בִּטָּחוֹן —Rambach, Michaelis, Rosenmüller, Knobel, De Wette, Gesenius, Noyes, Philippson, Vaihinger, Fürst, &c. Others, however, who adhere to this construction, and deduce the same sense from this clause, unnecessarily change the vowel-points of the Pual יְבָחַר either for יִבְחַר the Kal (Elster, &c.), or יֵחָבַר the Niphal (Hengstenberg, &c.) The *Keri* יְחֻבַּר, which is adopted by the Septuagint, Symmachus, the Syriac,

5 is hope, for a living dog is better than a dead lion. For the living know that they shall die; but the dead know not anything; and there is no more any advantage to them, for

the Chaldee, Rashi, Rashbam, Ibn Ezra, the Geneva Bible, the Authorised Version, Desvoeux, Hodgson, Ewald, Hitzig, Stuart, &c., and which is to be found in ten of Kennicott's MSS., and thirteen of De Rossi's, connects it with the following part of the verse, *i. e., for to him who is joined to all the living there is hope.* But — 1. This construction severs the manifest connection of this verse with the preceding one; 2. It renders בָּל before הַחַיִּים superfluous and intolerable, so much so, that it even called forth the remark from Stuart, that "the phrase has no parallel in the Hebrew," and yet, strange to say, he adopts it; and 3. The *Keri* evidently proceeds from an intentional transposition of the letters ב and ח, which was one of the Hagadic rules of exegesis, thereby to obtain the supposed seventy different meanings of the text (*vide supra*, p. 31). Luther (denn bei allen Lebendigen ist, das man wünſcht, nehmlich Hoffnung, *for to all the living there is that which is desired, namely, hope*), defies the Hebrew text. Equally arbitrary is the strange version of Coverdale, "and why? as long as a man liveth he is careless; for a quick dog (say they) is better than a dead lion," which is adopted in the Bishops' Bible, and has given rise to Broughton's translation, "for all that be yet accompanied unto all the living (say the men of an evil heart) they have assurance. For it is better with the dog alive than with the lion that is dead." According to the explanation we defend, the expression בָּל before הַחַיִּים is not only tolerable but necessary, inasmuch as by הַחַיִּים, *all the living*, the sacred writer means *irrational* as well as *rational* life, as is evident from the illustration which he introduces of the *dog* and the *lion.* There is no necessity for appealing to the doubtful usage of the לְ to intro-

duce the *subject*, and to regard לְפְּלֶב as the *nominative* (Hitzig), nor for taking it in the sense of QUOD ATTINET AD, · *in respect to, as to* (Knobel, Preston, Heiligstedt, Stuart, Hengstenberg, &c.), which it undoubtedly has elsewhere (comp. Ewald, § 310, a), but which would produce a harsh construction here, nor for assigning to it the signification ſogar, *even* (Ewald, Gramm. § 310, b), which has not a single parallel, but is to be taken in its usual sense as standing before the *dative* (so Symmachus, κυνὶ ζῶντι βέλτιόν ἐστιν ἢ λέοντι τεθνηκότι, the Geneva Bible, Rashi, Desvoeux, Rosenmüller, Herzfeld, &c.), and is omitted before הָאַרְיֵה, not from an inadvertency of the transcriber (Desvoeux, p. 332), but because of מִן, which precedes it, so that הָאַרְיֵה stands for לָאַרְיֵה (comp. ii. 7, vi. 5. 8, vii. 2, xii. 12). However, it is better with the Septuagint, the Vulgate, the Syriac, the Chaldee, Desvoeux, &c., to translate *as if it were* in the nominative, since it conveys more forcibly the sense of the original.

5. *For the living know*, &c. The ray of hope dimly shining in the breast of the living, mentioned in the foregoing verse to shew the advantage of life over death, is here concentrated in the consciousness of death which the living possess, and which, as the antithesis shews, has its concomitant faculties, enabling the living to enjoy some earthly pleasures when they do come, though they be rare and arbitrary. The dead, however, are entirely unconscious, and can therefore share no more in the pleasures of this earth, since the faculties capable of enjoyment are destroyed in them. כִּי, *for, because*, assigns a reason for the assertion in the foregoing verse, that *there is hope to all the living*, which we are here told consists in their consciousness, together with the *feelings and passions* belong-

6 their memory ceaseth to be ; also their love as well as their
hatred and their zeal have long perished, and there is no
more any portion for them for ever in all that is done under

ing thereto. Hodgson's rendering,
" it is true the living know that they
shall die, but the dead know nothing,"
is both contrary to the signification
of כִּי, and is against the scope of the
passage. That the bare fact of consciousness and unconsciousness is
not all which forms the contrast and
constitutes the advantage of the
living over the dead, is evident from
the other feelings denied to the latter,
and of course must be affirmed of the
former. The expression שָׂכָר, *reward*,
here *advantage*, is used instead of
יִתְרוֹן or חֵלֶק of the following verse, because of its forming a paranomasia
with זֵכֶר, just as קִנְאָתָם and שִׂנְאָתָם are
employed in the sequel. נִשְׁכַּח זִכְרָם is
generally rendered *their memory is
forgotten*, i. e., *the remembrance of
them is gone*. Now, we can understand Luther and Coverdale doing
so, because they are consistent, and
translate the following verse daß man
sie nicht mehr liebet, noch haſſet, noch
neidet, " for their memorial is forgotten, so that they be neither loved,
hated, nor envied ;" but we can
neither understand nor exculpate the
inconsistency of almost all modern
commentators, who, whilst taking
the suffix in זִכְרָם to express the *object*,
regard the suffixes in שִׂנְאָתָם, אַהֲבָתָם
and קִנְאָתָם, so closely connected with
the former both by form and the accessory particle גַּם, as the *subject*.
For these obvious reasons we must
take the suffixes of *all the four* nouns
in the same sense; and as the suffixes
of the following three nouns supply
the place of *possessive pronouns*, which
is generally conceded, as will be seen
in the following verse, the suffix of
the first noun must also express the
possessive. זֵכֶר, therefore, like שִׂנְאָה,
אַהֲבָה, and קִנְאָה, refers to *the faculty
itself*. שָׁכַח, *to forget*, also *to discontinue, to cease to exist* (comp. Ps.
lxxvii. 10 with verse 9, where it is
used in parallelism with אָפֵס לָנֶצַח, *to*

terminate *for ever*, and גָּמַר, *to end ;*
and see also the following verse,
where אָבַד, *to perish*, stands in parallelism with שָׁכַח here).

6. *Also their love*, &c.   The destruction of the retentive faculty is
not the only result of this unconscious
state of the dead ; all the affections
and feelings perish likewise. Love,
hatred, and zeal, the triad in which
all human passions are comprised,
also become extinct. Hence the dead
can no more have any participation
in sublunary affairs ; the faculties requisite for this are gone. The accessory גַּם, *also*, intimately connects
this verse with the preceding one,
from which it ought not to have been
separated, shewing that the subjects
which it introduces *share the same
fate* as the one mentioned before.
The repetition of it three times
(גַּם־גַּם־גַּם) corresponds to our *also —
as well as — and* (comp. Isa. xlviii. 8,
and *supra*, verse 1).   That שִׂנְאָתָם,
אַהֲבָתָם, and קִנְאָתָם are the *affections*,
and not, by metonymy, the objects
upon which these passions are exercised (woran sie mit Liebe hingen, was
sie mit Abscheu verfolgten, was sie mit
Eifer betrieben, u. s. w., Knobel), is
evident from the fact that the *things*
we love, hate, or are zealous for are
not annihilated when we die.   זֵכֶר
has here again been rendered incorrectly and inconsistently in the Auth.
Version by *now*.   אָבַד determines the
meaning of שָׁכַח, with which it stands
in parallelism.   For the *singular*,
אָבְדָה, referring to *several nouns*, see
i. 10.   The Vulgate's rendering of
וְחֵלֶק אֵין־לָהֶם עוֹד לְעוֹלָם by *nec habent
partem in hoc sæculo*, followed by
Luther (und haben kein Theil mehr
auf der Welt), Coverdale, the Bishops'
Bible, &c., taking לְעוֹלָם for בְּעוֹלָם
הַזֶּה, which is explained by St. Jerome,
that " the hypocritical love of the
wicked towards God, their professed
hatred of sin, making them exclaim

7 the sun. Go, then, eat with gladness thy bread, and drink
thy wine with cheerful heart, as God hath long since been
8 pleased with thy works; let thy garments be white at all

with the Psalmist, ' do not I hate
them, O Lord, who hate thee,' &c.,
and their feigned zeal for goodness,
representing it to be as great as that
of Phineas; all this perishes," is as
usual to be traced to the Hagadic interpretation of this verse, which, to
obviate the absolute denial of the
survival of any feelings after the de-
mise of the body, restricts it ·to the
wicked. Hence the Chaldee, בָּתַר
בוֹחֲיהוֹן דְּרַשִׁיעַיָא לֵית בְּהוֹן צְרוּךְ אַף רְחִימְתְהוֹן
אַף שְׂנָאֲתְהוֹן אַף קִנְאֲתְהוֹן הִיא כְּבַר הוֹבְדוּן מִין
עַלְמָא וְחוּלָק טָב לֵת לְהוֹן עוֹד עִם צַדִּיקַיָא לְעַלְמָא
דְאָתֵי וְלֵית לְהוֹן הַנָיָא מִן כָּל מַה דְאִתְעֲבֵיד
בְּעַלְמָא הָדֵין תְּחוֹת שִׁמְשָׁא, *the wicked after
their death are useless; their love, as
well as their hatred and jealousy, behold they have perished long ago from
the world! and they have no more a
good part with the righteous in the
world to come, and they have no enjoyment from all that is done* (לְעוֹלָם)
in this world under the sun. (Compare
also the Midrash and Rashi *in loco.*)
  7. *Go, then,* &c. Since death destroys all the capacities of enjoying
the fruition of our earthly toil, and
since God does not regulate our enjoyments here according to merit or
demerit, as is evident from the arbitrary distribution of fortunes, we
must enjoy life whilst we can, and
not let our pleasures be interrupted
or marred by allowing doubts to enter
our minds as to whether we please or
displease God. God, who indulges
the *wicked,* must surely have *long
since* (כְּבַר) been pleased with *our*
works; we must therefore not be
troubled with it *now. Bread* and *wine,*
being the staff and comfort of life, are
frequently used together as including
all things necessary to support and
cheer us (comp. *infra,* x. 19; Gen. xiv.
18; 1 Sam. xvi. 20, xxv. 18; Nehem.
v. 15; Lam. ii. 12; Tobit iv. 15–17).
The imperative לֵךְ is used emphatically, and has an inferential force,
i. e., this being the case, go then, &c.

The expressions טוֹב, *good,* and רַע, *evil,*
are frequently used to describe *cheerfulness* and *sadness;* hence the phrase
לֵב טוֹב, *a cheerful heart* (Esth. v. 9,
Judg. xvi. 25), יֵטַב לֵב, *to cheer the heart*
(1 Kings xxi. 7; Ruth iii. 7), לֵב רַע,
a sad heart (Nehem. ii. 2; Prov. xxv.
20). כִּי כְּבָר רָצָה הָאֱלֹהִים אֶת־מַעֲשֶׂיךָ, *for
God has long since been pleased with
the works,* is not the principal reason
why Coheleth appeals to us in the
former part of the verse to enjoy life,
i. e., because he has loved us and
blessed us with these good things (the
Chaldee, Rashi, Rashbam, Grotius,
Rosenmüller, &c.), nor because we
can judge, from our being able to do
so, that our words are pleasing to God
(Le Clerc, Van der Palm, Noyes,
Philippson, &c.), which severs this
verse from the preceding one, and
contradicts the whole scope of the passage, wherein it is denied that God rewards those with whom he is pleased;
nor is it, as Ibn Ezra affirms, כי אלה
המעשים רצה האלהים שתעשה, *for God desires you to do so, i. e.,* indulge in
these enjoyments, who is followed by
Reynolds, Geier, Schmidt, Hodgson,
Nachtigal, Umbreit, Hitzig, Stuart,
Vaihinger, &c., as this is incompatible
with the words of the text, inasmuch
as the general term מַעֲשֶׂיךָ cannot be
specifically and exclusively referred
to *enjoyment;* to convey this idea, the
words of the text would undoubtedly
have been כִּי כְּבָר רָצָה הָאֱלֹהִים שֶׁתִּתְעַצֶּה
אֶת־כָּל־זֶה—but a subordinate one.
  8. *Let thy garments be,* &c. From
the recommendation of *dainty food,*
Coheleth passes on to *festive raiment.*
The wearing of white garments in
hot climates has its origin in the
fact that they are cool and pleasant.
From the great expense, however,
connected with the perpetual cleaning
of them, they could only be worn
daily by persons of wealth, rank, or
office, who are distinguished by them
(2 Chron. v. 12; Matt. vi. 29; Joseph.

9 times, and let no perfume be lacking upon thy head ; enjoy
life with the woman whom thou lovest, all the days of thy
vain life which He giveth thee under the sun, all thy vain
days, for this is thy portion in life, and in the labour where-

Antiq. viii. 7, 3), whilst ordinary
people reserved them for visits to the
great (Esth. viii. 15) and festive occasions. Hence white garments became
the emblem of *purity* and *festivity.*
The pure and happy angels are
clothed in white garments (Mark xvi.
5 ; John xx. 12) ; and the glorified
saints at their feast in heaven are clad
in white robes (2 Esdras ii. 39. 44,
45 ; Enoch lxi. 18; Rev. iii. 4, 5. 18,
vi. 11, vii. 9, xix. 8; Bähr, Symbolik
i. 338). Perfuming, too, was an indulgence reserved for occasions of
rejoicing (*vide supra,* vii. 1). Hence
both white garments and perfuming
were studiously avoided in times of
sorrow (2 Sam. xii. 20, xiv. 2, xix.
24; Dan. x. 3). Similar customs
prevailed among the Greeks and
Romans. Thus Horace tells us

Licebit
Ille repotia, natales aliosve dierum
Festos albatus celebret.

" When rob'd in white he mark'd with festal
mirth
His day of marriage, or his hour of birth."
Sat. ii. 2, 59 – 61.

See also Hom. Odyss. iv. 49, x. 360 ;
Horat. Od. ii. 7. 7, 8, iii. 29, 4, 5 ;
Ovid. Heriod. xv. 76 ; and especially
Cicero, in Orat. in Vatin. c. 13. To
wear always white garments, and to
have always one's head perfumed,
therefore means to be constantly
cheerful and *happy,* to regard life as
if it were a holiday. The *moral* interpretation of this verse, applying it
to a *pure* and *sinless* life, which is
given in the Midrash, the Chaldee,
the Talmud, Rashi, &c., and which
is followed by St. Jerome in his
spiritual application of these words,
and more recently by Hengstenberg,
who says that " *white garments are
to be put on as an expression of lively
faith in the future glory of God's
people,*" is rightly rejected by Ibn

Ezra, and almost all modern commentators, as contrary to the scope
of the passage. As the *singular* עֵת,
time, is used in Hebrew in the same
sense in which we employ the *plural*
(*vide supra,* viii. 9), the latter must
be given in our idiom to convey the
force of the original.

9. *Enjoy life with the woman,* &c.
To festive enjoyments are to be added
the gratifications with those who
are " the delight of man," which
formed an essential part in Eastern
pleasures (*vide supra,* ii. 8). The
discrepancy which some have found
between the recommendation here to
enjoy life with women, and the assertion made in vii. 26 – 28 about their
wickedness and the mischief arising
from intercourse with them, proceeds
from overlooking the different stages
of the argument. Here, in the
résumé, Coheleth has reached that
point from which he could see no
moral government at all, no retributive justice, and nothing left for man
but momentary enjoyment and the
gratification of every desire which
is calculated to impart pleasure.
Whereas, there, in the *disquisition,*
Coheleth has passed this stage, and
gone on to the *prudent* or *common-
sense view of life,* which enjoined
moderation, and therefore precluded
every indulgence which was incompatible with that view. For the
phrase רְאֵה חַיִּים, *to see,* i. e., *to enjoy
life,* see ii. 1. אֵם־אֲשֶׁר is rightly
explained by St. Jerome, QUÆCUM-
QUE TIBI PLACUERIT FÆMINARUM EJUS
GADUE COMPLEXU, *whosoever among
women shall please thee, rejoice in her
embrace;* so also Ibn Ezra (עם שמח
אשה שהשיקת בה), Mendelssohn, Holden,
Herzfeld, &c. The opinion of Bishops
Reynolds and Patrick that this refers
to the enjoyment of the marriage
state is against the context; for, as

10 with thou labourest under the sun. Whatever thine hand
findeth to do, whilst thou art able, do it; for there is no
work, nor device, nor knowledge, nor wisdom in Hades,
11 whereunto thou art going.　Then again I saw under the

Holden rightly remarks, that " an
exhortation to pass a life of pleasure
and voluptuous ease is in perfect
harmony with the counsel given
immediately before, ' eat thy bread
with joy,'" &c. This is moreover
corroborated by the absence of the
article in אִשָּׁה, which does not mean
wife, but *any woman*. אֲשֶׁר־אָהַבְתָּ refers
to *amor vulgivagus*; and, from the
nature of the case recommending,
as it does, a *favourite* woman, is
another evidence that sensual gratification, and not " the enjoyments of
the matrimonial state," is here urged.
אֲשֶׁר before נָתַן does not refer to the
woman (Geier, Rambach, Michaelis,
Rosenmüller, Heinemann, Vaihinger,
&c.), but to כָּל־יְמֵי חַיֵּי הֶבְלֶךָ (the Septuagint, the Vulgate, Le Clerc, Hodgson,
Nachtigal, Umbreit, Knobel, Herzfeld, Hitzig, Elster, Hengstenberg,
&c.); the adverbial clause belongs
to חַיִּים, as is evident from viii. 15,
where we also see that the *subject* of
הָאֱלֹהִים is נָתַן. The words כָּל יְמֵי הֶבְלֶךָ,
all thy vain days, are repeated for
the sake of *emphasis*, to indicate that
not *a single day* ought to be permitted to pass unenjoyed, and are
therefore wrongly omitted by the
Septuagint, Syriac, Chaldee, several
of Kennicott's and De Rossi's MSS.,
who have overlooked that this is one
of Coheleth's favourite modes of imparting force to an assertion (comp.
viii. 11, 12). הוּא, *this*, is for the
neuter, as in iii. 22, v. 17, and refers
to the enjoyment of life.

10. *Whatever thine hand*, &c. The
principal and specific cases of indulgence adduced in the recommendation of pleasure are wound up with the
general remark that we are to have recourse to (כֹּל) *any* and *every* source of
voluptuous gratification (בְּכֹחֶךָ) *whilst
we have the power* to do it; since, in
the realm of death to which we are

all hastening, all labour and device,
all knowledge and wisdom cease ;
we have no more power to enjoy.
מָצָא, *to find, to gain, to possess, to
have;* hence יָד מָצָא, *the hand gains* —
either by *picking up, labour*, or *victory*, wherein the hand is the agent —
denotes *possession, power, ability,* i. e.,
QUODCUMQUE FACERE POTEST MANUS,
whatever the hand is able to do, as
the Vulgate rightly has it (comp.
Levit. xii. 8, xxv. 28). The בְּכֹחֶךָ is
not to be construed, against the
accents, with עֲשֵׂה, i. e., *do it as in
thy power, as well as thou canst* (ὡς ἡ
δύναμίς σου ποίησαν, the Sept., Grotius,
Le Clerc, Desvoeux), or, *do it with
all thy power*, or *with thy might*
(עֲבִיד בְּכָל חֵילָךְ, the Chaldee, Coverdale,
the Bishops' Bible, the Geneva Bible,
the Auth. Version, Geier, Michaelis,
Schmidt, Nachtigal, Van der Palm,
Rosenmüller, Heinemann, Noyes,
Vaihinger, &c.), or *do it instantly*
(INSTANTER OPERARE, the Vulgate,
Luther, Reynolds, &c.); nor is it to
be rendered *through thy power*,
i. e., whatever thy hand finds to do
through thy power (De Wette, Knobel,
Herzfeld, Hitzig, Stuart, Hengstenberg, &c), but *whilst thou art in thy
strength, whilst thou art living*, as is
rightly explained by Rashi (בעוד
שאתה בכחך), and Rashbam (בעודך בחיים),
which, as the latter well remarks, is
evident (מוסב על בשאול אשר למטה), from
the powerless state of the dead in
the following hemistich, with which
it is contrasted. For חֶשְׁבּוֹן, see
vii 25.

11. *Then again I saw*, &c. Having
affirmed in verse 1 that *both* the
righteous and the wise are subject
to the same inscrutable and arbitrary Providence as the wicked, and
having established his position with
regard to the *pious* in 2 – 10, Coheleth
now proceeds to establish his allega-

sun, that the race is not to the swift, nor the battle to the
strong, nor yet bread to the wise, nor riches to the intelligent,
nor favour to the learned; that the time of misfortune meeteth
12 all, and that man doth not even know his time; like fish
which are taken in a destructive net, and like sparrows which
are caught in a snare, like these are the sons of men ensnared
in the time of misfortune, when it suddenly cometh upon them.

tion with regard to the *wise and
intelligent.* Like piety, wisdom cannot counteract that arbitrary state
of things according to which the
very reverse of what we expect from
the means employed takes place.
For the formula שַׁבְתִּי וְרָאֹה, *I turned
and I saw,* i. e., *I saw again,* marking
the transition to the other part of
the subject, see iv. 1, where also
שׁוּב, as here, is used *adverbially;*
and for וְרָאֹה. the *infinitive absolute,*
instead of וָאֶרְאֶה, the *finite verb.* see
viii. 9. That מֵרוֹץ, *race,* and מִלְחָמָה,
battle, mean a *successful issue* in these
engagements is evident from the
context. The climactic גַם marks gradation in the scale of importance, and
shews that the *principal* design of the
verse is to set forth the *powerlessness
of wisdom,* swiftness and strength
being introduced as mere stepping
stones whereby to ascend to the
highest capacities of man. כִּי before
the last clause, like the one preceding
it, is dependent upon רָאֹה, and must
therefore be translated *that,* and not
for. עֵת רָעָה, which is substituted in
the following verse for עֵת וָפֶגַע עֵת here,
shews that פֶגַע, *chance, fortune,* denotes *misfortune,* and that the ו before
it indicates that it serves to define
עֵת, constituting the figure hendiadys,
vide supra, vii. 25. This simple
explanation relieves the sentence
from the awkward and meaningless
rendering that "time meets all," and
also accounts for the verb יִקְרֶה, *it
happens,* being in the *singular.*
    12 *And that man,* &c. Of how
little value wisdom is in this matter
is evident from the humiliating fact,
that it is not only utterly unable to

exempt the wise from the day of
calamity, but that it does not even
enable him to *foresee it;* and thus,
with the rest of mankind, the wise
are as suddenly, as ignorantly, and
as inextricably ensnared by misfortunes as the simple fish or bird. כִּי
is still a *conjunction,* depending upon
רָאֹה, so that כִּי — כִּי — כִּי is to be translated *that — that — and that* (vide
supra, vi. 11, 12). גַם, with the
negative particle, is used with peculiar emphasis for *not even* (comp. iv.
8, viii. 16), i. e., the wise man is not
only subject to the same fate as the
fool, but *cannot even* foresee it. הָאָדָם,
when used after the description of a
particular class of men, refers *to them
especially,* see verse 1, and *infra,* x.
14). עִתּוֹ, *his time,* is not *time of
death* (NESCIT HOMO FINEM SUUM,
the Vulgate, Grotius, Nachtigal,
Hitzig, Heiligstedt, Hengstenberg,
&c.), nor *seasons of prosperous and
adverse fortunes* (Holden, &c), nor
proper time for working (Knobel, &c.),
but *the time of misfortune,* which is
determined by the last clause of this
verse. כְּהֵם,, the *masculine,* refers
both to the *masculine* דָּגִים and the
feminine צִפֳּרִים, giving preference to
the masculine gender, as is generally the case in such instances.
יוּקָשׁ may either be regarded as a
verbal adjective, formed from the
future Hophal of קוּשׁ, or may be
taken as standing for מְיֻקָּשׁ, the
participle Pual of יָקַשׁ, the preformative מ being omitted, and the absence
of the *Dagesh forte* in the ק being
compensated for by the lengthening
of the preceding vowel (comp. Exod.
iii. 2; Judg. xii. 8; 2 Kings ii. 10;

13 Even this wisdom have I seen, and it seemed great to me:
14 There was a little city, and few men in it; and a powerful
king came against it, and besieged it, and built great towers

Gesen. § 52, 2, Rem. 6; Ewald, § 169, d). כַּאֲשֶׁר תִּפּוֹל = כְּשִׁתְּפוֹל is *feminine*, referring to עָר, and still keeps up the figure of the snare which is made to fall over its victims.

13. *Even this wisdom have I seen*, &c. The assertion made in verse 11 about the inability of wisdom, and subordinately also of physical prowess, is now illustrated by an example. Coheleth relates an anecdote to shew a display of wisdom which even to him, *the wisest of men*, appeared very great, yet it could not secure favour to the wise man. The best rendering of the involved גַּם־זֹה רָאִיתִי חָכְמָה, and the one most consonant with the context, is that of the Vulgate (*hanc quoque sub sole vidi sapientiam*), Rashbam (אף חכמה זאת ראיתי בעולם), Luther (id) habe auch biefe Weischeit gefecten), Coverdale and the Bishops' Bible ("this wisdom have I seen also"), the Geneva Bible, the Authorised Version, &c. The Septuagint (καίγε τοῦτο ἴδον σοφίαν, *also in this I saw wisdom*), making זֹה and חָכְמָה a double accusative to רָאָה, which is followed by Spohn, Köster, Hengstenberg, &c., as well as the rendering of Herzfeld, &c. ("I have also seen this; there is wisdom," &c.), supplying the substantive verb before חָכְמָה; of Knobel, De Wette, &c. (aud) biced natjm id) watjr: Weisheit unter ber Sonne, u. δ. w., *also this I saw, namely wisdom under the sun*, &c.), and of Stuart, Elster, &c. ("I have also seen this, I have seen wisdom," &c.), repeating mentally the verb רָאִיתִי before חָכְמָה, require harsh ellipses, and interrupt the manifest connection of this passage with verse 11. אֵלַי, *to me*, i. e., *appeared to me*, the substantive verb, as usual, is to be supplied, which must be rendered *is*, *appears*, or otherwise, according to the requirement of the connection (comp. Ewald, § 217, c).

14. *There was a little city*, &c.

The occasion upon which this extraordinary wisdom was displayed was when a small and defenceless city was attacked by a large and powerful army, which, in addition to its immense superiority in numbers, had the advantage of occupying the rising ground round the city, thus affording it capital ground for building bulwarks overlooking the walls into the very heart of the place. Desperate and hopeless indeed appears the state of the devoted inhabitants. The substantive verb הָיְתָה, *there was*, must be supplied after עִיר קְטַנָּה, *a small city*. וַאֲנָשִׁים בָּהּ מְעָט, *and few men within it*, is added to shew *the very small number* of defenders, which is not necessarily implied in the simple mentioning of a little city, for the inhabitants might have hired soldiers to assist them. מֶלֶךְ גָּדוֹל, *a great king, a powerful king*, leading a large army (comp. Jer. xxvii. 7). The rendering of עָלֶיהָ by *against it* does not convey the exact idea of the original, which means *over* or *above it*. Hence Ibn Ezra rightly remarks, that היא במקום נמך שיוכל לבנות עליה מצודים ונבוהים ממנה, *the city was built on an incline, so that the enemy could build the bulwarks overlooking it, and higher than it*. מְצוֹד, i. q., מְצָד, not from מָצַד (Ibn Ezra), which does not occur, but from צוד, *to lie in wait*, is *siege work, intrenchments, a bulwark* (1 Chron. xi. 7, xii. 8. 16), here the idea of *tower* is more prominent, just as בָּחוּן (Isa. xxiii. 13), and דָּיֵק (2 Kings xxv. 1; Jer. lii. 4; Ezek. iv. 2), which also signify *tower*, are derived from בָּחַן and דּוּק, *to look out*. The reading מְצוֹרִים, which is to be found in two of De Rossi's MSS., and which is adopted by Döderlein, and Gesenius in his Thesaurus and Lexicon, has too little authority to support it, is unnecessary, and has manifestly arisen from mistaking the ר for ר. The addition of the Vulgate,

15 over it. And there was found in it a poor-wise man, and he
saved the city by his wisdom ; and yet no one remembered
16 that poor man. Therefore I say, wisdom is indeed better
than force, yet the wisdom of the poor is despised, and his

at the end of this verse, ET PERFECTA
EST QBSIDIO, *and the siege was perfect,*
owes its origin most probably to a
marginal gloss, giving another version of וְסָבַב אֹתָהּ.

15. *And there was found,* &c. In
this critical state, when defence by
force of arms was utterly impossible,
a poverty-stricken wise man came
forward, and by his prudence saved
the people and the place from destruction And yet, notwithstanding his
great wisdom and the services he had
rendered, the poor man was left in
his impoverished circumstances without ever being noticed. We thus
see that the battle is not to the
strong, nor riches or favour to the
wise, and the allegation in verse 11 is
fully substantiated. The Midrashic
interpretation of the preceding verse,
and the one before us, again shews
how completely the Hagadic mode
of allegorising the Scriptures has
been Christianised. According to
the Midrash, the Chaldee, &c., which
is also mentioned by St Jerome,
Rashi, Ibn Ezra, and De Lyra, "the
little city" means *the human body;*
"the few men within it," *the component parts of man;* "the great
king," *the evil propensity;* "the great
bulwarks," *the snares of hell;* "the
poor wise man," *the good spirit in
man.* St. Jerome and De Lyra adopt
this explanation, and Dr. Gill, in
accordance " with some Christian
interpreters," explains it "*to better
purpose* concerning the Church attacked by Satan and delivered by
Christ, who, notwithstanding, is un-
kindly and ungratefully used." מָצָא
is rightly rendered by the Vulgate,
the Syriac, the Chaldee, Rashbam,
Luther, Coverdale, the Bishops'
Bible, the Geneva Bible, the Authorised Version, and most modern
commentators, *inventus est;* the third

person being used for the *impersonal*
or *passive* (*vide supra,* i. 10). Less
appropriate is the translation of
Desvoeux, Herzfeld, Hengstenberg,
&c., " he found," regarding מֶלֶךְ, *king,*
as the subject of מָצָא, *he found,* since
the king, being repelled and defeated,
and hence having had no opportunity of seeing the interior of the
place, could not be said to have
found this man in it. The omission
of the וְ before חָכָם is not owing to
an oversight of the transcriber, but
shews the close union of the two
nouns, *i. e., poor — wise.* There is
therefore no necessity, with Spohn,
&c., to adopt the וְ from some MSS.,
which will always be found to supply
or to take away letters, especially וְ
and וֹ. For אָדָם, *man,* used collectively, *men at large,* and *no man, vide*
vii. 29, x. 4. Ibn Ezra's explanation
of שלא היה לאותו החכם by וְאָדָם לֹא זָכַר
המסכן זכר בפי אנשי העיר לפנים קודם שימלט
אותם, *there was no mention made of
this poor wise man in the mouth of
the men of the city prior to his saving
them,* which is followed by Mendelssohn, Schmidt, Friedländer, Rosenmüller, &c., as well as the one adopted
by Döderlein, Spohn, &c., *no one
thought of this poor-wise man in this
critical moment,* are contrary to the
meaning of זָכַר, which denotes remembering *something past,* and to the
scope of the passage. The Vulgate
has therefore rightly rendered it, ET
NULLUS DEINCEPS RECORDATUS EST
HOMINIS ILLIUS PAUPERIS, *and none
afterwards remembered that poor
man;* so also the Chaldee, Rashbam,
Knobel, Herzfeld, Hitzig, Elster, &c.

16. *Therefore I say,* &c, This
therefore shews that though indeed
wisdom is superior to strength, yet
it is despised, and the wise men are
neglected, thus establishing the allegation made in the first verse that

the *wise*, like the *righteous*, are subject to an arbitrary Providence, and cannot overrule the destiny common to all, which has no respect for merit or demerit. The וְ in וְאָכְרְתִּי, is *inferential*, indicating that this verse contains the inference drawn from the anecdote related in verses 14 and 15 ; whilst the וְ in וְחָכְמַת, as frequently, introduces the *apodosis* (compare viii. 17, ix. 3. 16, x. 10). The participles בְּזוּיָה, *despised*, and נִשְׁמָעִים, *listened to*, describe what is *generally* and *permanently* done (compare Ewald, § 168). Desvoeux's rendering, " the wisdom of this experienced man is despised, and his deeds are not mentioned," is contrary to the signification of מִסְכֵּן (see iv. 3), and נִשְׁמָעִים.

17. *Though the words of the wise,* &c. Having remarked, in the preceding verse, that wisdom is *generally* despised, Coheleth concedes that there are *particular* cases which form an *exception*. There are times when the words of the wise are listened to with greater satisfaction than is the behest of a foolish ruler ; as he himself has shewn (verses 14 and 15) in the instance adduced to set forth the power of wisdom. This verse, therefore, and the first part of the following verse, take up the momentary respect paid to wisdom, indirectly noticed in the anecdote which Coheleth related, shewing, as we shall see in the sequel, that it does not at all militate against his position, but, on the contrary, confirms it. Failing to see this, commentators have been greatly perplexed to account for the apparent contradiction between this and the preceding verse. Of course the Hagadic mode of interpretation, as seen in the Midrash and the Chaldee paraphrase, finds no discrepancy whatever, inasmuch as this verse simply means כְּלֵי דִצְלוֹתָא דְחַכִּימַיָא בְּנַחַשָׁא מִתְקַבְּלִין קֳדָם מָרֵי עָלְמָא יַתִּיר מִקַבְּלַת קָל גַּבְרָא רַשִׁיעָא דְהוּא שַׁלִיט עַל שַׁטְיָין דְּפָנִין וְלֵית

מְקַבֵּל, *the words of prayer of the wise, offered in silence, are accepted before the Lord of the world, above the vociferations of the wicked rulers over fools, who speak much and are not accepted.* Similarly Rashi, and St. Jerome, who as usual Christianises it by applying it to *wise and foolish preachers in the Church.* . " Whatever declaimer," says the Father, " thou seest in the Church exciting applause, moving laughter, or stirring up the feelings of mirth among the people by inciting and elegant words, know that it is a sign of folly both in the speaker and in the hearer, for the words of a wise man are heard in quiet and moderate silence." Those, however, who adhere more closely to the text have tried to reconcile the discrepancy by torturing every word, making a distinction between אֵינָם נִשְׁמָעִים in the preceding verse, which they say means *are not heard* AT ONCE, and נִשְׁמָעִים in the verse before us, which, according to them, signifies *they are heard* ULTIMATELY, or hinging it upon the difference between the *singular* (חָכְמַת הַמִּסְכֵּן) in the preceding verse, and the *plural* (חֲכָמִים) in this verse, viz., the words of *one* wise man are not listened to, but when uttered by *many* are listened to; or, by laying stress upon the word מִסְכֵּן, referring the preceding verse to *poor* wise men, who are not obeyed *because of their poverty.* These opinions are mentioned and rightly rejected by Ibn Ezra, which has nevertheless not prevented some modern commentators espousing them. Ibn Ezra himself tries to remove the difficulty by supplying אִם before חָכְמַת in the foregoing verse, making it the *protasis*, and this verse the *apodosis*, which is followed by Coverdale, the Bishops' Bible, " a wise man's counsel that is followed in silence, is far above the crying of a captain among fools," Philippson (16) unb wirb auch bie Weisheit bes

18 foolish ruler, and wisdom is better than instruments of war,
x.1 yet one fool destroyeth much good ; a dead fly maketh sweet

Armen veractet, und werben feine
Worte nicht gehört, (17) die Worte
der Weifen, in Ruhe angehört, find
beffer als, u. f. w. But this explanation — 1. Harshly and unwarrantably supplies טוֹבִים before מַזְעֵקַת ; 2. It
violates the idiomatic construction
מ נַחַת, as is evident from vi. 5 ; and,
3. Is at variance with the scope of
the passage, which is not to shew the
value of wisdom, but, on the contrary,
to set forth *its utter inability* to cope
with an arbitrary Providence, and
how entirely it is even under the
subjection of folly, as will be seen in
the next verse. Le Clerc, Desvoeux,
&c., who render it "the words of the
wise are more minded among men of
quiet dispositions," &c., incur the
additional censure of taking most
arbitrarily and unnaturally the word
נַחַת, the *abstract* for the *concrete*
plural, in the sense of *men of quiet
dispositions;* so also Bishop Reynolds,
Durell, Hodgson, Spohn, Knobel,
Herzfeld, &c., who render נִשְׁמָעִים by
ought to be heard, or *merit attention,*
besides the above-named objections,
are guilty of taking the same word
in *two different* senses. All these
difficulties are avoided by identifying
the obedience spoken of in this verse
with the instance of obedience narrated in verse 15. דִּבְרֵי; *the words of,*
is opposed to וַעֲקַת, *the vociferous command,* and חֲכָמִים, *the wise,* to מוֹשֵׁל
בַּכְּסִילִים, *a foolish ruler.* The בְּ prefixed to nouns gives them sometimes
the force of *adjectives* (comp. אֲדֹנָי
בְּסֹמְכֵי נַפְשִׁי, *the Lord is among my supporters,* i. e., *is my supporter,* Ps. liv. 5;
יְהֹוָה בְּעֹזְרִי, *the Eternal is among my
helpers,* i. e , *is my helper,* ibid. cxviii.
7; Job xxiv. 13). Hence the Sep-
tuagint rightly translates מוֹשֵׁל בַּכְּסִילִים
by ἐξουσιαζόντων ἐν ἀφροσύναις, *those who
rule in folly;* so Geier, Patrick,
Knobel, Noyes, Heiligstedt, &c. בְּנַחַת
qualifies נִשְׁמָעִים, and is the point of
comparison.

18. *And wisdom is better than,* &c.

Coheleth, moreover, refers to the
other point in which wisdom shewed
itself very powerful in the anecdote
which he related. Not only did this
poor man's wise counsel inspire more
confidence than the command of a
martial chief, but his wisdom shewed
itself superior to all the weapons of
war and the bulwarks raised against
the defenceless city. Yet all this
does not enable the wise man to
overrule the destiny common to all
men, and render him more distinguished than the fool; on the contrary, his very wisdom is subject to
folly, and a single fool may entirely
destroy all the good which wisdom
has effected. As the first part of this
verse continues the concession, the
concessive particle, or the simple *conjunction,* must be expressed in the
translation to give the force of the
original. חוֹטֵא (from חָטָא, *to miss, to
err,* in point of *knowledge* or *virtue*),
one who is in error, intellectually or
morally, a *fool,* a *sinner.* That the erring is here *intellectual* and not moral,
is clearly indicated by the context.
The Vulgate, ET QUI IN UNO PECCA-
VERIT MULTA BONA PERDET, *and he
who shall offend in one, shall lose
many good things,* alters וְחוֹטֵא אֶחָד
into וְחוֹטֵא בְּאֶחָד, and is at variance
with the context. The reading חֲטָא,
which the Syriac and nine of Kennicott's MSS. have, and is adopted by
Döderlein, Spohn, Schmidt, Mendelssohn, Friedländer, &c., is rightly
rejected by Knobel, De Wette, Herzfeld, Hitzig, Elster, Vaihinger, &c.,
as incompatible with the context.
How Preston could say that "the
Rabbinical commentators are inclined to take it to be a noun abstract., signifying *defect,*" when the
Sept., the Chaldee, Rashi, Rashbam,
Ibn Ezra, &c., explain it by *sinner,* or
fool, is most unaccountable.

1. *A dead fly,* &c. This verse
illustrates and confirms the allegation in the immediately preceding

ointment stinkingly to ferment; a little folly is more mighty

clause, and ought not to have been interrupted by the separation of chapters. To shew more strikingly the subjection of wisdom to folly, Coheleth alludes to an every-day occurrence which has passed into a proverb. Just as the insignificant fetid fly has the power of corrupting a quantity of precious perfume by imparting unto it its offensive smell, so a little folly has often shewn itself more weighty and powerful than glorious wisdom. From the disagreeable effect which the presence of dead flies in precious mixtures produces in the sultry climate of the East, arose the Arabic proverb, "A fly is nothing, yet it produces loathsomeness." This will shew the force which the illustration here used has to an Oriental. The genitive being used to describe the *operation* as well as the *quality* of a noun, זְבוּבֵי מָוֶת, *flies of death* may either mean *death-working* or *deadly flies*, according to the analogy of כְּלֵי מָוֶת, *instruments of death*, i. e., *deadly instruments* (Ps. vii. 14, xviii. 5, cxvi. 3), and ἡ πληγὴ τοῦ θανάτου, *deadly-wounds* (Rev. xiii. 3. 12), so the Septuagint, the Chaldee, Luther, Geier, Schmidt, Nachtigal, Dathe, Knobel, Herzfeld, Fürst (Lex. *s. v.* זבוב), Vaihinger, &c.; or it may denote *dead flies*, according to the analogy of אֶבֶן חֵן, *a precious stone* (Prov. xvii. 8), יַעֲלַת חֵן, *a graceful ibex* (ibid. v. 19), so Symmachus, the Vulg., the Syriac, St. Jerome, Rashi, Rashbam, Ibn Ezra, Coverdale, the Bishops' Bible, the Geneva Bible, the Auth. Ver., Desvoeux, Hodgson, Durell, Mendelssohn, Friedländer, De Wette, Ewald, Gesenius, Hitzig, Preston, Heiligstedt, Noyes, Stuart, Philippson, Elster, Hengstenberg, &c.; the latter is more compatible with the context, inasmuch as the simple settling down of *poisonous* flies upon perfume would not corrupt its odour, whereas *dead* flies corrupt it. As to the *singular* verb יַבְאִישׁ following the *plural* noun זְבוּבֵי Ibn Ezra rightly remarks that עניני

כל זבוב יבאיש במקומו כמו בנות צעדה עלי שור כל בת צעדה כל אחת ואחת במקומה ותקח האשה את שני האנשים ותצפנו צפנה כל אחד .... ואחד במקומו ויקח הזקיהו את הספרים ויפרשהו קרא כל אחד ואחד לבדו, it is used *distributively*, referring to *each fly separately*, as is often the case (comp. בָּנוֹת צָעֲדָה עֲלֵי שׁוּר, *each branch separately spreads over the wall*, Gen. xlix. 22; וַתִּקַּח הָאִשָּׁה אֶת־שְׁנֵי הָאֲנָשִׁים וַתִּצְפְּנוֹ, *and the woman took the two men and hid each of them*, Josh. ii. 4; וַיִּקַּח חִזְקִיָּהוּ אֶת־הַסְּפָרִים ... וַיִּפְרְשֵׂהוּ, *and Hezekiah took the letters and read them ... and spread each of them*, 2 Kings xix. 14; see also *supra*, iv. 10; *infra*, verses 13. 15; Gesen. § 146, 4; Ewald, § 319). יַבְאִישׁ is used *adverbially*, to qualify יַבִּיעַ, i. e., *makes it stinkingly to ferment;* for examples of this construction, see viii. 3. The absence of יַבִּיעַ in the Septuagint, the Vulg., Symmachus, and the Syriac, does not prove that it was originally a marginal gloss, and was afterwards inserted in the text, but only shews that those translators thought that the omission of it in the translation would give more faithfully the *force* of the original. שֶׁמֶן רוֹקֵחַ, *ointment of the perfumer*, i. e., *ointment prepared or spiced by the perfumer*, which is expressed more clearly in Exod. xxx. 35, xxxvii. 29, by רֹקַח מַעֲשֵׂה רוֹקֵחַ, i. e., *perfumed ointment ;* hence the Septuagint appropriately renders it σκευασίαν ἐλαίου ἡδύσματος, *a preparation of sweet ointment, sweetly prepared ointment*, and the Vulg., SUAVITATEM UNGUENTI, *the sweetness of oil*, or *sweet oil.* The assertion, therefore, of Desvoeux (p. 185) and others, that the Septuagint read רֶקַח instead of רוֹקֵחַ, and the Vulgate מַבִּיעַ, *exhalation*, instead of יַבִּיעַ, is gratuitous. *A little folly*, &c. The great power which the insignificant fly has over the precious ointment, a little folly has over honourable wisdom. The great difficulty which commentators have experienced in interpreting this verse is chiefly confined to this clause, and to its connection with the preceding hemistich. The Septuagint has, τίμιον ὀλίγον σοφίας ὑπὲρ δόξαν ἀφροσύνης μεγάλην, *a little wisdom is more honour than the great glory of folly*, dropping the מ from מֵחָכְמָה, connecting the latter with מְעָט, and construing the clause יָקָר חָכְמָה מְעָט מִכְּבוֹד סְכְלוּת. The Vulgate — PRETIOSIOR EST SAPIENTIA ET GLORIA PARVA ET AD TEMPUS STULTITIA, *wisdom and glory are more precious than small and short-lived folly*, taking the מ from מֵחָכְמָה and מִכָּבוֹד, and prefixing it to סְכְלוּת, assigning to מְעָט a double sense, viz., *little, insignificant*, and *short, short-lived*, and construing the text as if it were יָקָר חָכְמָה וְכָבוֹד מִסְכְלוּת מְעָט; and St. Jerome's version, PRETIOSA EST SUPER SAPIENTIAM ET GLORIAM STULTITIA PARVA, *precious above wisdom and glory is a little folly*, taking the מְעָט סְכְלוּת, *a little folly*, as something recommendable either as possessing *few faults*, or having *simplicity*, which, this Father says, is to be preferred to wisdom, because the latter is frequently connected with craftiness, and is to be chosen rather than glory, which is accompanied by pride — proceed as usual from the Hagadic interpretation, as may be seen from the Chaldee, וְכַמָּא יָאֵי וְיָקָר יַתִּיר מָן הוּכְמְתָא חַכִּימִין וְעוֹתָר עַתִּירִין גְבַר דְּסַכְלְוּתֵיהּ זְעֵיר וְקַלִּיל, *and how much more beautiful and precious than the wisdom of the wise, and the riches of the rich, is the man whose folly is slight and insignificant!* and from the Midrash: hence also Luther's translation, darum ift zuweilen beſſer Thorheit denn Weisheit und Ehre, *therefore folly is sometimes better than wisdom and honour*, which the Reformer says is intended as a consolation for those who are sometimes obliged to choose the position of fools, and keep back their good counsel in the presence of cunning statesmen, who have been raised to posts of honour. Coverdale's strange version, " dead flies that corrupt sweet ointment and make it to stink, are something more worth than the wisdom and honour of a fool," is a literal translation of the Zurich

Bible. Passing over these emendations, which are both arbitrary and contrary to the scope of the passage, we come to Ibn Ezra, who explains it והענין כמו הזבובים המתים יבאישו מדן השמן הרוקח כן יש לאדם שהוא יקר מחכמה ומכבוד שיש בו סכלות מעט כי סכלות מעט לחכם ישחית זכרו ויבאישנו, *as dead flies make the sweet ointment to stink, so is it with the man who is in estimation for wisdom and for glory that has a little folly, since the little folly of the wise man destroys his reputation, and makes it to stink*, taking the verb יַבְאִישׁ, *causes to stink*, from the first clause to govern the second member, regarding יָקָר as its subject, in the sense of *estimation, renown*, and the מ in מֵחָכְמָה and מִכָּבוֹד as *causative;* and is followed by the Bishops' Bible, " a dead fly doeth corrupt sweet ointment, and maketh it to stink: even so ofttimes he that hath been had in estimation for wisdom and honour, is abhorred because of a little foolishness;" the Geneva Bible, " dead flies cause to stink and putrefy the ointment of the apothecary; so doth a little folly him that is in estimation for wisdom and for glory," the Authorised Version, Grotius, Le Clerc, Mendelssohn, Friedländer, Michaelis, Holden, Rosenmüller, Preston, Philippson, Hengstenberg, &c. But we submit — 1. That this interpretation is at variance with the argument, which is to shew how completely the wise man is subject to the folly of *others*, how " one fool" may subvert all his wise plans, and not to demonstrate how a little folly, or a slight oversight *on the part of the wise man*, will destroy his reputation ; 2. That it unwarrantably separates the assyndic יַבְאִישׁ יַבִּיעַ, and makes יָקָר depend upon יַבְאִישׁ only ; 3. That it is thereby necessitated to resort to a very harsh ellipsis ; and 4. That it departs from the natural sense of the construction יָקָר מִ, which all the ancient versions, however strange their explanations, rightly take to express the *comparative*. The easiest rendering, and the most compatible with the context, is that of the Syriac

2 than honourable wisdom. Still the mind of the wise man
3 is at his right hand, but the mind of the fool at his left; and
even when the fool walketh on the road he lacketh his mind,

ܡܰܝ ܡܝܬܐ *ܕܝܡܘܬܐ* ... (Syriac text) ... *as the dead flies make to stink
the vessel of sweet ointment, so a little
folly is more weighty than wisdom and
great glory ;* so also Rashi, Rashbam,
Knobel, De Wette, Ewald, Noyes,
Heiligstedt, Hitzig, Stuart, Elster,
Vaihinger, &c. יָקָר, as is rightly explained by Rashi and Rashbam,
לשון כבד הוא כבד ושקול יותר מן ההכמה
retains here its original signification,
weighty, heavy, and is construed with
מִן, comparison, *i. e., it is heavier and
weighs more than wisdom ;* it is *masculine,* though referring to סִכְלוּת, *fem.,*
because it is placed at the beginning
of the sentence (*vide supra,* vii. 7).
מִכָּבוֹד is in apposition to מֵחָכְמָה, which
it qualifies, so that מֵחָכְמָה מִכָּבוֹד, literally *from wisdom, from honour,* means
from honourable wisdom (comp. וְבָחִים
שְׁלָמִים, *sacrifices, eucharists,* i. e.,
eucharistic sacrifices, Exod. xxiv. 5 ;
1 Sam. xi. 15 ; אֲמָרִים אֱמֶת, *words,
truth,* i. e., *truthful words,* Prov. xxii.
21 ; Gesen. § 113 ; Ewald, § 287, c).
This is more in accordance with the
scope of the passage than the common rendering, "wisdom and glory,"
supplying the copula, as Coheleth
does not treat upon *glory* or *renown,*
but *wisdom exclusively.*

2. *Still the mind of the wise man,*
&c. The utter inutility and inability of wisdom to *exempt* the wise
from the destiny common to all men,
hitherto demonstrated, does by no
means imply that it is *absolutely*
powerless and useless. If wisdom
can do as little as folly to affect an
arbitrary Providence which has no

regard for merit or demerit, yet it
has a great advantage over folly in
many other respects. The mind of
the wise man is at his right hand,
ready to guard and defend him from
a thousand dangers, whilst that of
the fool is out of its proper place,
and is useless in cases of emergency.
Here again, as in ii. 13, Coheleth,
after having shewn the powerlessness
of wisdom *relatively,* guards us against
taking his assertion *absolutely.* To
indicate this in the translation, we
must supply the expression *nevertheless, still,* or *yet.* לֵב, *heart,* also
mind, see i. 13. The use of the
phrase *to be at one's right,* for *to stand
by one, to be ready to assist, to defend*
(comp. כִּי מִימִינִי, *for He is at my right
hand,* i. e., *to defend me,* Ps. xvi. 8 ;
אֲדֹנָי עַל־יְמִינֶךָ, *the Lord is at thy right
hand,* i. e.. *to protect thee,* Ps. cx. 5),
shews that *to be at the left hand*
means the reverse, *to be out of its
place, missing.* That this is the
sense is moreover evident from חָסֵר
לִבּוֹ, *he misses his mind, it is absent,*
which is used in the following verse to
describe the condition of a fool ; thus
shewing beyond doubt that we are to
understand by לִשְׂמֹאלוֹ, *at his left hand,*
to be absent from its proper place.

3. *And even when,* &c. Nor can
this want of wisdom be concealed ;
it is so glaring that everybody sees
it as soon as the fool leaves his house
and sets his foot on the street to go
somewhere, inasmuch as he is bewil-
dered and ignorant of the commonest
roads, in the very place where he has
spent all his life. בַּדֶּרֶךְ, *on the way,*
is not used figuratively for his *undertakings* and *intercourse with men*
(עסקיו ודבריו, Ibn Ezra ; fein Thun,
Luther; Coverdale, Reynolds, Patrick,
Knobel, Heiligstedt, Stuart, Elster,
Vaihinger, Hengstenberg, &c.), but
is used in its literal sense, *on the
road, when he has to walk to any
place* (Rashi, Rashbam, Grotius, Le

4 and yet he saith of every one, He is a fool! If the anger of
the ruler is kindled against thee, quit not thy place, for

Clerc, Herzfeld, Hitzig, &c.), as is
evident from verse 15, where the
same phraseology is used to illustrate
great stupidity; it depends upon הָלַךְ,
and is placed first for the sake of
emphasis; the regular construction
would be וְגַם־כַּאֲשֶׁר הַסָּכָל הֹלֵךְ בַּדֶּרֶךְ.
For כְּשֶׁ = כַּאֲשֶׁר, used as a particle of
time, i. e., when, see viii. 7; and for
the Massoretic remark, that the
article in כְּשֶׁהַסָּכָל is redundant (יתיר ה")
because of כַּאֲשֶׁר, which precedes it,
see vi. 10. לִבּוֹ is generally taken as
the subject of חָסֵר, and is rendered
his heart or understanding fails, or is
lacking. Against this, however, Herzfeld and Philippson rightly urge that
חֲסַר לֵב is a phrase of frequent occurrence, and that חָסֵר is, in this phrase,
the epithet of the man, and not of
the heart. Accordingly לִבּוֹ must be
taken as the object, חָסֵר as the predicate, and סָכָל as the subject. אָמַר, to
speak, to speak inwardly, to wish, to
think (comp. Exod. ii. 14; supra,
vii. 23). לַכֹּל, as frequently, to every
one. סָכָל הוּא, he is a fool, is the
purport of his thoughts about, or
his address to, every one. So Symmachus, as mentioned by St. Jerome
(in loco), SUSPICATUR DE OMNIBUS
QUOD STULTI SUNT, he suspects all
men that they are fools; the Vulgate,
OMNES STULTOS ÆSTIMAT, he thinks
all men fools; Luther, Coverdale, the
Bishops' Bible, Desvoeux, Knobel,
Hitzig, Heiligstedt, Stuart, Elster,
Vaihinger, Hengstenberg, &c., and
this seems also to be the sense of the
Septuagint's strange version, καὶ ἅ
λογιεῖται πάντα ἀφροσύνη ἐστίν, and all
that he will think is folly, which is
followed by the Syriac version ܣܘܟ
ܕܗ ܃ܘܢܐܣܒܢ̈ܣ ܗܡܒܠܬܐ, and
which has given rise to the rendering of סָכָל by thöricht, foolish, i. e.,
er spricht zu Allem; es ist thöricht
(Knobel, Ewald, Vaihinger, Hengstenberg, &c.), contrary to the uni-

form signification of סָכָל, which is
always used of persons (comp. ii. 19.
vii. 17, x. 14; Jer. iv. 22, v. 21).
The Chaldee paraphrase וְכֹלָּא אָמְרִין
דְּשַׁטְיָא הוּא, and all say that he is a
fool, cannot be reconciled with the
words of the text. The explanation
of Rashi, Rashbam, and Ibn Ezra,
כְּאִלּוּ הוּא קוֹרֵא עַל נַפְשׁוֹ וּמַרְאֶה קְלוֹנוֹ וּמוֹדִיעַ
חֶסְרוֹנוֹ לַכֹּל, he, as it were, proclaims
against himself, displays his folly,
and makes known his shortcomings to
all, taking it as oratio obliqua, which
is followed by the Geneva Bible, the
Authorised Version, Reynolds, Hodgson, Herzfeld, De Wette, Noyes,
Philippson, &c., is inadmissible, inasmuch as it would require either
סָכָל אֲנִי or כִּי סָכָל הוּא.

4. If the anger of the ruler, &c.
Another lesson which Coheleth deduced from the awful absence of
retributive justice — wherewith this
résumé begins, viii. 16. 17 — was
patiently and submissively to bear
the anger of a tyrannical ruler, since
gentleness will effect that which the
existence of retribution would have
done, viz., prevent the despot from
committing still greater outrages.
רוּחַ, like its equivalent spirit in English, also signifies excitement of mind,
temper, anger (comp. Isa. xxv. 4,
xxxiii. 11; Zech. vi. 8, and especially Judg. viii. 3, where the opposite phrase רָפָה רוּחַ is used for anger
subsiding), עָלָה, with עַל or בְּ, expresses
the rising of the passion against any
one (comp. אַף אֱלֹהִים עָלָה בָהֶם, the anger
of the Lord rose against them. Ps.
lxxviii. 21. 31). That מְקוֹמְךָ אַל־תַּנַּח,
do not leave thy place, is not to be
taken figuratively for laß dich nicht
entrüsten, lose not thy self-possession
(Luther, Knobel, Hitzig, Stuart,
Elster, Vaihinger, &c.), but means a
sudden surrendering of one's post or
office, thus inculcating the idea of
self-possession, but not making it
the exclusive one, is evident from
the phrase אַל־תַּבָהֵל מִפָּנָיו תֵּלֵךְ, do not

5 gentleness preventeth greater outrages. There is an evil
which I have seen under the sun ; an outrage as that which

hastily leave his presence, in viii. 3.
There is no necessity for taking
מַרְפֵּא as standing for מַרְפֵּה (Ibn Ezra,
Grotius, Le Clerc, Knobel, Herzfeld,
Fürst, &c.), as the regular root yields
the required sense. רָפָא, *to mend, to
cure, to assuage pain of body*, like
SOLOR, CONSOLOR, *healing, solacing;*
in Latin, for *solus,* ὅλος, and אָסָא in
Chaldee, signifies also *to allay pain
of mind, to quiet, to soothe ;* hence
מַרְפֵּא, *what is allaying, quieting*, or
soothing, i. e., *quietness, gentleness.*
יַנִּיחַ, *will leave at rest, will not stir up,
will not provoke, will prevent.* It is
therefore evident that חֲטָאִים גְדוֹלִים,
greater errors or *outrages*, does not
refer to *offences of the subject*, but is
the same as דָּבָר רָע in viii. 3, and
characterises the *ill-treatment from
the ruler.* The several Hagadic in
terpretations of this verse contained
in the Midrash, one of which is
adopted in the Chaldee paraphrase,
and espoused by St. Jerome and
other fathers, viz., " ' the spirit of the
ruler,' *i. e.*, the prince of this world,
the spirit that now worketh in the
children of disobedience, ' riseth up
against thee,' *i e.*, enters into our
heart and inflicts the wound of evil
thought ; ' do not leave thy place,'
i. e., we must not easily give place,
but must fight against this evil
thought, strive to be freed from this
sin, so that the thought does not become an action;" and the other which
was entertained by St. Jerome's
teacher, and is followed by Ibn Ezra,
viz.: אם עלית בחכמתך עד מעלת הממשלה
מקומך אל תנח והענין שפלת רוח או ענינו
שיתעסק גם בהכנעה תמיד כמו שהיה בתחילה
כאילו לא זז ממקומו ולא עלה למדרגה עליונה
כנגד בני האדם ' מרפא פועל מהבנין הכבד
שממנו הרפה לה והא'לף במקום ה'א כא'לף על
כן הוא מרפא שהוא מהבנין הכבד והענין כי
העוב הממשלה יזוב חטאים גדולים, "if the
spirit," *i. e.*, *if thou hast risen, through
thy wisdom, to the dignity of a ruler,*
" leave not thy place," *i. e , thy humility, or cease not to be always occupied*

*with wisdom, just as thou didst prior
to the removal from thy place, and
elevation to that high position.* מרפא
is *part. Hiphil,* from רָפָה, *to leave*
(comp. הַרְפֵּה-לָהּ, *leave her,* 2 Kings
iv. 27), *and the* א *stands for* ה, *as in
the Piel,* מַרְפֵּא (Jer. xxxviii. 4), *and
the meaning is, for whoso leaves ruling
leaves great sins —* as well as the
strange rendering of the Zurich Bible,
literally adopted by Coverdale, " if
a principal spirit be given thee to
bear rule, be not negligent then in
thine office ; for so shall great wickedness be put down, as it were, with
medicine," and the alteration of the
last clause in the Bishops' Bible,
" for he that can take care of himself
avoideth great offence," are as curious
as they are irreconcileable with the
text and context. Equally curious
is Desvoeux's translation of the last
clause, " for power kept in thy hands
will make an atonement for great
offences."

5. *There is an evil*, &c. The displeasure of the monarch, summarily
mentioned in the foregoing verse, is
now illustrated by the manifestation
of it in such an outrage of justice as
can only proceed from a despot. אֲשֶׁר
is omitted before רָאִיתִי, as in vi. 1.
The כְּ in כִּשְׁגָגָה is not ὡς ἀκούσιον,
QUASI NON SPONTANEUM, *as if done
unwillingly ;* QUASI PER ERROREM, *as
if through an error ;* QUASI IGNO-
RANTIA, *as if it were ignorance* (the
Septuagint, Aquila, Theodotion, the
Vulgate, St. Jerome, &c.) *i. e.*, it
appears to people as if it were an
error, but it is not so; trying *to ex-
tenuate it* (Ibn Ezra, Mendelssohn,
Preston, Hengstenberg, &c.); or being
so flagrant and outrageous that it
appears more as if it were an error
than intentional; trying to *enhance
it* (Herzfeld, &c.); nor *as if it were
owing to an error*, &c. (Rashbam); nor
is it *namely* (Luther, Coverdale; the
Bishops' Bible, Spohn, Ewald, &c.);
nor is it *caph veritatis* (Bishop Rey-

6 proceedeth from a ruler ; a great fool is placed in many high‑

nolds, Noyes, Hitzig, Elster, &c.) ;
nor can it signify *according to ;* nach
Maaßgabe, in Folge eines Versehns,
was vom Fürsten ausgeht, gibt es
einen Uebelstand im Leben (Döderlein,
Holden, Knobel, De Wette, Heiligstedt, Vaihinger, &c.); but means *an
error* or *outrage like that which,* &c. ;
*such an outrage as despots only can
commit,* שׁגָגָה being implied before
כְּשׁגָגָה, as is evident from the signification of the כְּ when preceding substantives (compare ii. 15). יֹצֵא is
doubly anomalous, it stands for יוֹצְאָה,
which again is pointed as the part.
fem. of verbs ל"ה (compare Ewald,
§ 189, f). The allegorisers see no
inconsistency in making the ruler
here spoken of to be both *God* and
the *devil.* Thus St. Jerome was
told by his Rabbi, HEBRÆUS POTEN-
TEM ET PRINCIPEM A CUJUS FACIE,
IGNORATIO VIDEATUR EGREDI, DEUM
EXPOSUIT, QUOD FUTENT HOMINES IN
HAC INÆQUALITATE RERUM ILLUM NON
JUSTE ET UT ÆQUUM EST JUDICARE,
*that the Jews explain this ruler to be
God, from whose presence error seems
to go forth, since men think that there
is no justice in these inequalities ;* this
Hagadic interpretation is also given
by the Chaldee paraphrast and Rashi,
and is pronounced by Hengstenberg
to be the *true one.* Others, however,
according to the same Father, take
the *ruler* to be the *devil,* who rules
under the sun, and hence derive
from it this comfort, NE SIMUS ITAQUE
TRISTES SI IN HOC SÆCULO HUMILES
VIDEAMUR, SCIENTES A FACIE DIA-
BOLI STULTOS SUBLEVARI, ET DIVITES
DEJICI, SERVOS INSIGNIA HABERE
DOMINORUM ET PRINCIPES SERVORUM
INGREDI VILITATE, *let us therefore
not be sad, if we have to appear low
in this world, knowing that it is from
the devil that fools are exalted and
the rich degraded, that servants have
the distinctions of master, and princes
walk in the degradation of servants.*
6. *A great fool is placed,* &c. The
outrage committed by the despot
consists in his elevating consummate

fools to high positions, and degrading
the wise and the noble. נָתַן, *to give,*
also *to place* (comp. Deut. xvii. 15 ;
Esth. vi. 8). סָכָל is not a *concrete*
according to the analogy of יֶלֶד, as
Ibn Ezra explains it, ויתכן היות סכל
שם התאר כמו ילד, but is the *abstract,*
as Rashi rightly has it (השטות), used
instead of the concrete סָכָל, to intensify the idea, and is tantamount to
extremely or *intensely foolish* (*vide
supra,* ii. 23): the Septuagint, Aquila,
Symmachus, the Vulgate, the Syriac,
St. Jerome, the Chaldee, &c., rightly
give the concrete in their versions.
מָרוֹם, *altitude, height,* metaphorically,
high station, high condition (comp.
Job v. 11) ; the article in בַּמְּרוֹמִים
indicates the *well-known* high offices
of state, just as it points in בַּשֵּׁפֶל to
the acknowledged opposite extreme
established by society. The absence
of the article in רַבִּים shews that it is
an adverbial addition to בַּמְּרוֹמִים (*vide
supra,* vi. 3), intimating that *many*
offices of responsibility are conferred
upon the fool ; whereas בַּמְּרוֹמִים הָרַבִּים,
as Herzfeld rightly remarks, would
denote *in the many high places,* thus
introducing a complaint about the
large number and *great revenue* of
these offices, which is foreign to the
design of the passage. Less appropriate and forcible is the rendering
of the Septuagint (ἐν ὕψεσιν μεγάλοις),
the Vulgate (*in dignitate sublimi*),
Rashi (במרומי גובה), and Ibn Ezra,
which is followed by Luther, Coverdale, the Bishops' Bible, the Geneva
Bible, the Authorised Version, &c.,
assigning to רַבִּים the secondary sense
of *great.* מְשִׁירִים. as opposed to הַסָּכָל,
folly = the foolish, are the spiritually
rich, QUI DIVITES SUNT SERMONE ET
SAPIENTIA, *the rich in eloquence and
wisdom,* as St. Jerome remarks,
hence the *wise,* the *noble ;* just as
שׁוֹעַ denotes both *rich* and *noble* (Job
xxxvi. 19 ; Isa. xxxii. 5), and הֹר,
noble, also signifies *elevated in mind,
wise* (*vide infra,* verse 16). There is
therefore no necessity for resorting
to any violent means, in order to

7 positions, and the noble sit in degradation. I have seen
servants upon horses, and masters walking on the ground
8 as servants. Yet he who diggeth a pit shall fall into it,

produce the antithesis between the two clauses; such, for example, as adopted by those mentioned by Ibn Ezra, מפרשים אמרו שהיה ראוי להיות בש״ץ והענין שבעלי השכל ראויים לשבת במרומים רבים והעשירים בהפך, who maintain that the ס stands for ש, and submit that the contrast is between the שכל, the *wise* and the *rich* (so also Kimchi, *s. v.*), or taking רַבִּים over to the second hemistich, and translating it, "while the noble and the rich sit in low places" (Döderlein, Bauer, Van der Palm, Boothroyd, &c.)

7. *I have seen servants*, &c. A further description of the tyrannical and outrageous proceedings of the despot. Riding on horses has been, and still is, a mark of distinction and honour among the Eastern as well as other nations (comp. Esth. vi. 8, 9; 2 Chron. xxv. 28; Jer. xv. 25). Justin tells us that among the Parthians, HOC DENIQUE DISCRIMEN INTER SERVOS LIBEROSQUE EST, QUOD SERVI PEDIBUS, LIBERI NON NISI EQUIS INCEDUNT, *the difference between slaves and freemen is, that the former go on foot, and the latter ride on horseback* (xli. 3). Maillet and Pocock record in their travels, that Europeans generally are obliged to ride on asses or mules, and that the consuls alone are permitted to ride on horseback. And Maundrell, speaking of his trip to see the beautiful gardens at Damascus, says, " on visiting these gardens Franks are obliged either to walk on foot, or else to ride upon asses, the insolence of the Turks not allowing them to mount on horseback " (Journey from Aleppo to Jerusalem, Bohn's ed. of Early Travels in Palestine, p. 492; Harmer, Observations, &c., ii., p. 410; Rosenmüller, Orient. iv., p. 172). This being the custom, we can see how great is the outrage, and subversion of all decency and law, committed by the tyrant in the cases before us. As

these extraordinary changes and violations proceed from (שַׁלִּים) *a ruler*, שָׂרִים cannot mean *princes* in the strict sense of the word, but as frequently simply denotes *prefects, leaders, masters* (comp. Exod. i. 11; 1 Sam. xxii. 2; 2 Sam. xxiii. 19).

8. *Yet he who diggeth*, &c. The twelfth verse, which concludes with the counsel given in verse 4, viz., the advantage of submitting patiently to and of conciliating the anger of the ruler, shews, beyond doubt, that the intervening adages in vv. 8 – 11, are designed to set forth the dangers to which the opposite conduct might expose the suffering *subjects*. The metaphor from the *digging of a pit* must have been very striking to those who were familiar with the fact that huntsmen, to secure their prey, dug deep ditches, covered them over with foliage, and put some alluring meats on the covering, and when the animals stepped on them to get the food the cover gave way and they fell in, and that it frequently happened that those who were engaged in this dangerous digging were themselves buried by the falling in of the earth. Hence the admonition, that by trying to undermine the despot for the sufferings he inflicts upon us, we may be utterly ruined in this hazardous process, by bringing upon ourselves the whole weight of the tyrant's anger; whereas " gentle submission will prevent greater outrages" (comp. Prov. xxvi. 27; Ps. vii. 16, lvii. 7). The second adage originated from the well-known habit of serpents to make their abodes in walls. Hence it not unfrequently happened that when a man " went into a house, and *leaned his hand on the wall*, a serpent bit him " (Amos v. 19). The danger was infinitely greater when a man inadvertently tried to *pull down the wall* and disturbed the nest of these venomous reptiles. Thus, by attempt-

9 and whoso breaketh down a wall a serpent shall bite him;
he who breaketh up stones shall be hurt therewith; whoso

ing to destroy the fabric of despotism, we may provoke the deadly poison of the tyrant, whereas " gentle submission will prevent greater outrages." גּוּמָץ, *a pit*, is ἅπαξ λεγόμενον, from גָּמַץ, *to dig*, a root of frequent occurrence in Syriac and Chaldee; .it is a participial noun of Pual, standing for מְגֻמָּץ; the prefix מ is not unfrequently dropped in the participle of this conjugation, as well as of the Piel, in which case it is distinguished by the *Quametz* in the final syllable (comp. יֻלָּד for מְיֻלָּד, Judg. xiii. 8; רֻחָמָה for מְרֻחָמָה, Hos. i. 6. 8; Gesen. § 52. 2, 6; Ewald, § 169, d). The warning which the Massoretic note gives us, that (דגש אחר שורק) *there is a Dagesh after a Shurek*, is unnecessary, since the ו is not a proper *Shurek*, but merely orthographic, and is short, as in יֻלָּד, Judg. xiii. 8; and יֶאֶשׁ, *supra*, ix. 12. That גָּדֵר here is not a *hedge* (the Sept. and the Vulg., followed by Luther, Coverdale, the Bishops' Bible, the Geneva Bible, Desvoeux, Hodgson, Noyes, &c.) but a *stone wall*, is evident from וְגֶדֶר אֲבָנָיו נֶהֱרָסָה, *and the stone wall thereof was broken down*, Prov. xxiv. 31; גֹּדֵר פֶּרֶץ, *repairer of the breach*, Isa. lviii. 12; גָּדַר דְּרָכַי בְּגָזִית, *he hath enclosed my ways with hewn stones*, Lam. iii. 9; and especially from the following verse, where the illustration of plucking up stones has undoubtedly been suggested by, and is connected with, the breaking down of stone walls.

9. *And whoso breaketh down*, &c. The illustrations adduced in this verse are taken from the same employment, mentioned in the second part of the foregoing verse. With the breaking down of walls are connected the *pulling out of stones* and the *cutting down of timber*, both of which are dangerous occupations, and sometimes cripple for life those who are thus engaged. When it is borne in mind that the appliances with which art and science have so

profusely enriched us for pulling down huge stone buildings did not exist in the times here spoken of, and that the dangers of this employment were consequently far greater, and the accidents far more numerous, than we can now imagine, the beauty and force of the metaphor, borrowed therefrom to set forth the peril of attempting to subvert the structure of a despotic government, will be obvious. As נָסַע, which primarily means *to pull up, to pluck up*, anything fast, has, from its being frequently used in connection with the pulling up of tent-pins or stakes to take down and remove the tents, also come to signify *to remove*, expositors are divided about the meaning of מַסִּיעַ here; the Sept. (ἐξαίρων λίθους), Symmachus (μετεωρίζων λίθους), Hodgson, Gesenius, Ewald, Hitzig, Heiligstedt, Stuart, Elster, Fürst, Vaihinger, Hengstenberg, &c., adhere to the primary meaning of *breaking up, pulling out*, whilst Aquila (μετατιθῶν λίθους), the Vulgate (*qui transfert lapides*), the Syriac (ܡܫܰܢܶܐ), Rashi, Rashbam, Ibn Ezra, Luther, Coverdale, the Bishops' Bible, the Geneva Bible, the Auth. Version, Desvoeux, De Wette, Noyes, &c., take it in the secondary sense of *removing*. The former sense, however, is warranted by the phrase הִסִּיעַ אֲבָנִים, *to pull up stones*, in 1 Kings v. 31, and is more consonant with the scope of the passage, inasmuch as *breaking up* agrees better with the parallelism *cleaving*. For בָּהֶם, *masc.*, referring to the *fem.* אֶבֶן, see ii. 6. There is no necessity, with Gesenius, Hitzig, Elster, &c., for taking יִסָּכֶן as a denominative from שַׂכִּין, *coulter* (Prov. xxiii. 2), in order to obtain the meaning *shall be cut*, or *wounded*, which the Vulgate (*vulnerabitur*), Luther (wird verletzt werden), Coverdale, the Bishops' Bible (*shall be hurt*), Desvoeux, Spohn, &c., rightly give, since סָכַן

10 cleaveth wood shall be cut thereby.   If the axe be blunt,

itself denotes *cutting* in Aramæan
(comp. Fürst, Lex. *s. v.*) Less appropriate is the rendering *shall be endan-
gered* (the Septuagint, Ibn Ezra, the
Geneva Bible, the Authorised Version,
Knobel, Herzfeld, Ewald, De Wette,
Noyes, Stuart, Vaihinger, &c), which,
as Hitzig rightly remarks, is too
general and indefinite, when compared with the other predicates. Still
more objectionable is the rendering
shall be burned (the Chaldee עֲתִיד
(לְאִתְחוֹקְדָא בְּנוּרָא), *heated* or *warmed*,
Rashi (יחממם), and Rashbam, which
is followed by Broughton, deducing
it from סֹכְנָת in 1 Kings i. 2, to which
the meaning of *warming, heating*, is
wrongly assigned, as will be seen
from a comparison of it with Isa.
xxii. 15.

10. *If the axe be blunt*, &c. To
shew more forcibly the folly of
attempting to raise a feeble arm
against the mighty trunk of despotism, Coheleth takes up, from another point of view, the illustration
used in the second hemistich of the
foregoing verse. If one will go to
work with a blunt axe, and does not
take due precaution to sharpen the
instrument before using it, he will
only make the tyrant increase his
army, and thereby augment his sufferings. But it is the prerogative of
wisdom to repair the mischief which
such precipitate folly occasions. The
different renderings of this verse are
very numerous and most conflicting.
The Septuagint has ἐὰν ἐκπέσῃ τὸ
σιδήριον, καὶ αὐτὸς πρόσωπον ἐτάρξεν, καὶ
δυνάμεις δυναμώσει, καὶ περίσσεια τοῦ ἀνδρείου
σοφία, *if the axe should fall, and it
troubled his face, and he shall
strengthen the forces; and the advantage of man is wisdom*, altering קְהָה
into נָפַל, omitting לא before פָּנִים, assigning to קַלְקַל the Chaldee sense of
hurting, and changing הַכְשִׁיר for אִישׁ.
The Vulgate, SI RETUSUM FUERIT
FERRUM, ET HOC NON UT PRIUS, SED
HEBETATUM FUERIT, MULTO LABORE
EXACUETUR; ET POST INDUSTRIAM
SEQUETUR SAPIENTIA, *if the iron be*

*blunt, and it be not as before, but if
it be dull, it may be sharpened with
much labour, and after industry shall
follow wisdom*, doubly translating
קְהָל, viz., *light, smooth, edgeless*, and
to make smooth, sharpen, assigning
to יַבֵּר the sense of *imparting strength,
sharpening*, altering וַחֲיָלִים into בַּחֲיָלִים,
taking יְתְרוֹן to denote *after*, and
הַכְשִׁיר, *industry*. St. Jerome translates
it, SI RETUSUM FUERIT FERRUM ET
HOC NON UT PRIUS, SED CONTUR-
BATUM FUERIT, VIRTUTIBUS CORRO-
BORABITUR, ET RELIQUUM FORTITU-
DINIS SAPIENTIA EST, *if the iron be
blunt, and it be not as before, but is
troubled, it shall be strengthened by
virtues, and the remainder of strength
is wisdom;* which he explains, "if
any one finds that, through negligence, he has lost the knowledge of
the Scriptures, has become dull, and
does not continue as he began, — for
it frequently happens that when one
gets a smack of knowledge he becomes elated with pride, leaves off
to learn, — his knowledge gradually
decreases, and the mind gradually
becomes empty, *the iron is dulled*,
sloth and idleness being as it were
a rust of wisdom; if this be the
case with any one, let him not be
troubled, but go to his teacher and
be instructed again, and after labour,
and industry, and much sweat —
for this is meant by the Hebrew
(בחילים יגבר), 'he shall be strengthened
by forces,' *i. e.*, by toil, industry, and
sweat, and daily readings — he shall
obtain wisdom, and his strength shall
have this end, that he shall get wisdom." The source of this interpretation may be seen in the Midrash
and the Chaldee. The Syriac Version

ܐ ܦ݂ܽܘܠ ܦ݂ܶܙܠܶܐ ܘܣܘ ܐ ܘܟ݂ܶܣܣ
ܘܣܩܠܐ ܡܣ̈ܩܐ ܘܣܦ݂ܩܠ݂ܐ
ܟܶܣܒ݂ܶܝ̈ܢ ܢܬ݂ܣܩܡܐ, *if the axe be
blunt, and it troubles the face and
increases the slain, and the advantage*

and he do not sharpen it beforehand, he shall only increase

of the upright or *diligent is wisdom*,
omits, like the Septuagint, לֹא before
פָּנִים, and takes קִלְקַל to denote *trouble;*
but, unlike any other version, mistakes וַחֲיָלִים for וַחֲיָלִים.   Passing on
from these arbitrary alterations of
the text and meaningless versions,
we come to the Rabbinic expositors
of the middle ages, who, though more
literal, are not less divergent in their
opinions as to the meaning of the
verse.   According to Rashi and
Rashbam, אם קהה חברול · חרובת צורים
שקהו פיהם וחדודם : והוא לא פנים קלקל · ואינם
למושים ימרוטים למען היות להם ברק אע׳׳פכ
וחיילים יגבר כגביר הוא במלחמה את גבורי
החיילים לנצח : ויחרון הכשיר חכמה ומעלה כשרון
יש עוד לחכמה יותר מן הברול ; the meaning
is, "though the sword, even if it be
blunt, and have not its edge sharpened, is vanquishing armies, yet
has wisdom a greater advantage,"
making it substantially the same as
the assertion, "wisdom is better
than weapons of war," in ix. 18.
According to Ibn Ezra again, אף כי
קהה הברול ולא קלקל פניו והענין שלא יחיד
ממורט וקלקל הוא מפעלי הכפל והוא כפול והוא
מענין נחשת קלל אז יתיש כח הבוקע ומלח יגבר
כמו ינצח כמו וגברתי את בית יהודה וחיילים
יגבר כמו כח כענין אלהים ה' חילי אנשי חיל ·
ויחרון הכשיר חכמה והענין שיש לחכמה יחרון
על כל עצב כי תכשיר האדם ותיישרנו בלא עצבון
והתשות כח וכשר הדבר פועל עומד מן הבנין הקל
והכשר פועל יוצא מן הבנין הכבד הנוסף, it
ought to be rendered, "if the axe
be blunt, and he do whet the edge,
then it will overcome his strength
(*i. e.*, the cleavers), but wisdom has
an advantage (*i. e.*, over all labour)
for securing success."   Neither are
the Reformers less discordant in
their renderings.   Luther has, wenn
ein Eisen stumpf wird und an der
Schneide ungeschliffen bleibt, muß man
es mit Macht wieder schärfen; also
folgt auch Weisheit dem Fleiß, which
is literally adopted by Coverdale,
"when an iron is blunt, and the
point not sharpened, it must be whet
again, and that with might; even so
doth wisdom follow diligence," and
followed by the Bishops' Bible;

whereas the Geneva Bible translates
it, "if the iron be blunt, and one
hath not whet the edge, he must
then put to more strength; but the
excellency to direct a thing is wisdom," which, with very little varia-
tion, is adopted in the Authorised
Version.   Nor has this difference
of opinion been diminished by the
progress of modern criticism, as may
be seen from the following specimens: Desvoeux renders it, "if an
iron instrument be blunt, though
the edge is not quite off, and he who
wanteth to make use of it increaseth
his strength, skill is more profitable
to succeed;" Spohn, wenn eine Art
stumpf ist, und man schleift sie, so
kann man desto mehr damit ausrichten.
Aber noch besser glückts der Weisheit,
if an axe be blunt, and is sharpened,
much more can be done therewith;
yet wisdom has still greater success;
Hodgson again has, "if iron be
rusty and its edge blunt, no strength
will avail to make it cut; yet still
wisdom will find out how to make it
execute its office;" .whilst Hitzig,
who is followed by Stuart and Elster,
renders it, wenn er das Eisen abge-
stumpft hat, und es ohne Schneide ist,
so schwingt er und strengt die Kräfte an.
Besser ists, triftig Weisheit handhaben,
if he has blunted the iron, and it is
without edge, he swings it and exerts
his strength; it is better dexterously
to use wisdom.   Against all these
interpretations we urge — 1. That if
the connection of these adages with
the general argument is as we have
stated at the beginning of this verse,
they are totally at variance with the
scope of the passage; and 2. That
they all more or less force meanings
upon the words which are contrary
to the *usus loquendi*, as will be seen
from the following analysis of the
text.   That קֵהָה, the Piel, like the
Kal, is used *intransitively* is established beyond doubt, from the kindred
כֵּהָה, which has an intransitive sense
(comp. וְכָהֲתָה כָל־רוּחַ, *and every spirit*
became faint, Ezek. xxi. 12), and is

the army; but the advantage of repairing hath wisdom.

rightly rendered so by the Vulgate, St. Jerome, Rashi, Rashbam, Ibn Ezra, Luther, Coverdale, the Bishops' Bible, the Geneva Bible, the Auth. Version, and most modern commentators. The Piel, קֵהָה, which only occurs here, has evidently been chosen in preference to the Kal, קָהָה, because of its forming a paranomasia with בַּרְזֶל, which Hitzig, Stuart, Elster, &c., who take it *actively*, have failed to see, and hence have also been driven to give a forced explanation to the following words, as will be seen in the sequel. The Septuagint's rendering of it by ἐκπέσῃ, *shall fall*, is simply arbitrary, as is evident from the fact that all the other ancient versions have the word as it is in the Hebrew. The quadriliteral בַּרְזֶל, *iron, an iron, an iron tool, an axe* (2 Kings vi. 5; Isa. x. 34), is not derived from בָּרַז, *to pierce*, with the ל annexed at the end (Gesenius, &c.), as *transfixing* does not describe the property of the *metal*, but is from בָּלַל, *i. q.*, פָּלַל in Aramæan, *to be hard, solid* (with ל inserted after the first radical, according to the analogy of זַלְעָף from זָעַף), whence the Greek βασάλτης, *iron-marble*, of which Pliny says, *quem vocant baselten, ferrei coloris atque duritiei, unde et nomen ei dedit* (*vide* Fürst, Lex. *s. v.* בַּלַל). The pronoun וְהוּא, *and he*, refers to בּוֹקֵעַ עֵצִים, *the cleaver of wood*, mentioned in the preceding verse, and would have been useless if קֵהָה had been *transitive*, inasmuch as the latter would express the *subject*, viz., "*if he* blunted the axe." The omission of the negative לֹא by the Sept. and the Syriac is owing to their peculiar interpretation of this clause. פָּנִים here is an *adverb* of time, being an abbreviation for לְפָנִים (compare Ewald, § 220, a), and is well rendered *before, beforehand*, by the Vulgate, St. Jerome, Ewald, Philippson, &c.; the ל is omitted because of its close connection with לֹא. The meaning, *edge*, which is assigned to it by Rashi, Rashbam, and Ibn Ezra,

and which is followed by Luther, Coverdale, the Bishops' Bible, the Geneva Bible, the Auth. Version, and most modern commentators, is contrary to the sense in which this word is uniformly employed in Scripture. פֶּה, *mouth*, which *lacerates and destroys*. is figuratively used for a *destructive edge*, and not פָּנִים, *the face*, this being no symbol of *destruction*. To appeal to the prosopopœia in Ezek. xxi. 21, as those do who maintain that פָּנִים here denotes *edge*, is most unjustifiable. We quote the passage —

Collect thyself! turn to the right!
Attend! turn to the left!
Whither is thy face directed?
And I also will clasp my hands together,
And cause my fury to rest upon thee;
I, the Eternal, have spoken it.

The fearful sword, described in verses 19 and 20, which is to make the devastations, seems, as it were, still to slumber, and is therefore summoned, in verse 21, by a bold apostrophe, to rouse itself, to collect, to unite all its powers, to dash to its right hand and to its left, and is rebuked for its *drowsy face* or appearance. We ask whether we can legitimately appeal to this highly figurative passage, where hands, and feet, and face, and powers of action are ascribed to the sword, for proof that פָּנִים signifies *edge* in the prosaic and calm language of our text? קָלַל (the Pilpel of קָלַל, *to be light*) is to *set in motion* (κέλλω, CALLO), *to turn* (Ezek. xxi. 26), *to turn quickly so as to produce brilliancy* (comp. מִתְהַפֶּכֶת, Gen. iii. 24), *to polish* (comp. קָלָל, *to polish*, Ezek. i. 7; Dan. x. 6), hence *to sharpen*. The Chaldee signification of *troubling, hurting*, which is assigned to it by the Septuagint and Syriac, as well as the meaning *smooth, blunt*, which the Vulgate and St. Jerome give it, are contrary to the *usus loquendi* and the scope of the passage; whilst the meaning *to swing* in the air so as to increase the force of the blow, which is given to it by Hitzig and Elster, proceeds from a misunderstanding of

11 if the serpent bite without enchantment, there is no advan-

the design of this verse, and involves an unnecessary violation of the pause-accent over the next clause. The rendering of חֲיָלִים by *physical power, strength, force,* is contrary to its uniform signification. When Hengstenberg declares that " חֲיִל occurs also elsewhere in the sense of *strength, force* kommt auch sonst in der Bedeu-tung Kräfte vor," we submit that neither he, nor Gesenius in his Thesaurus and Lexicon, nor any one else has been able to adduce a single instance to substantiate the assertion. Besides here the plural חֲיָלִים occurs twenty times more (1 Kings xv. 20; 2 Kings xxv. 23. 26; 1 Chron. vii. 5. 7. 11, xi. 26; 2 Chron. xvi. 4; Isa. xxx. 6; Jerem. xl. 7. 13, xli. 11. 13. 16, xlii. 1. 8, xliii. 4. 5; Dan. xi. 10), and, with the exception of the disputed passage in Isa. xxx. 6, invariably denotes *military hosts, armies,* and is so rendered in all versions of the Bible and by all lexicographers. We have therefore no right to depart from this meaning here, especially when its regular signification yields excellent sense. Coheleth tries to expose the folly of raising a blunt and ineffective weapon against a monstrous despotism, and, to render this exposure more striking and effectual, he reminds the feeble sufferer that, by attempting to subvert this tyrannical power with inefficient means, he would only cause the tyrant to increase and strengthen his armies, and thereby also augment his own sufferings. For the וְ before חֲיָלִים, introducing the apodosis, see viii. 17. יְגַבֵּר, the Piel of גָּבַר, *to be strong,* is *to make strong, to strengthen, to increase the strength,* &c. (comp. Zech. x. 6. 12). The signification *to strengthen, to sharpen,* which is assigned to it by the Vulgate and St. Jerome, followed by Luther, Coverdale, the Bishops' Bible, &c., regarding בַּרְזֶל as its *object,* and וַחֲיָלִים as used *adverbially,* does violation both to the text and context. As כָּשֵׁר, *to be right,* is also

used to denote the *result* of being right, *i. e., success* (*vide supra*, ii. 21). Rashi, Rashbam, and Ibn Ezra, who are followed by Gesenius, De Wette, Knobel, Noyes, Preston, Vaihinger, &c., take it in its secondary sense, *i. e., success;* whilst Herzfeld, Philippson, Hengstenberg, &c., retain the primary meaning *right,* which yields excellent sense, and is therefore preferable, not however in the shade of meaning which they give it. הַכְשִׁיר, *Hiphil infinit. absolute,* accordingly signifies *making right, repairing, mending;* it is in the genitive, depending upon יִתְרוֹן, *i. e., the advantage of repairing;* it is the prerogative of wisdom to repair the mischief which the folly of raising a feeble arm against deeply-rooted tyranny brings about. The Septuagint's rendering of it by *man,* the Vulgate's and St. Jerome's rendering *diligence,* which is followed by Luther, Coverdale, the Bishops' Bible, &c., as well as Hitzig's alteration of it into הַכְשִׁיר, *the infinitive construct,* are inadmissible and arbitrary.

11. *If the serpent bite,* &c. As the preceding verse concluded with the remark that it is the prerogative of wisdom to repair the mischief caused by the precipitate conduct of the foolish, Coheleth now urges upon the wise that unless their wisdom is exerted for the good of the sufferers, unless the serpent provoked to come from its habitation to sting the assailants, is prevented by the superior skill of the wise from infusing its deadly poison, their wisdom will be useless. Just as the illustration used in the preceding verse was suggested by the second clause of verse 9, so the one in this verse has been suggested by the second clause of verse 8, the second suggestion being taken up first, and the first second. For similar inversions, see vii. 7. From the remotest antiquity to the present day we find throughout the East a large number of itinerant serpent charmers. These charmers

travel about towns and villages to
tame serpents, which they effect
either by cantillating certain forms
of exorcism, or by some other mysterious adjuration, alluring them to
come forth from the fissures in the
walls of houses, and rendering them
incapable of darting at any one.
" As the serpent seeks the darkest
place in which to hide itself," says a
modern traveller, " the charmer has
in most cases to exercise his skill in
an obscure chamber, where he might
easily take a serpent from his bosom,
bring it to the people without the
door, and affirm that he had found
it in the apartment, for no one would
venture to enter with him after
having been assured of the presence
of one of these reptiles within ; but
he is often required to perform, in
the full light of day, surrounded by
spectators, and incredulous persons
have searched him beforehand, and
even stripped him naked, yet his
success has been complete. He
assumes an air of mystery, strikes
the wall with a short palm-stick,
whistles, makes a clucking noise
with his tongue, and spits upon the
ground, and generally says, ' I adjure you by God, if ye be above, or
if ye be below, that ye come forth ;
I adjure you by the most great
name, if ye be obedient, come forth ;
and if ye be disobedient, die, die,
die !' The serpent is generally dis-
lodged by his stick from a fissure in
the wall, or drops from the ceiling
of the room. I have often heard it
asserted that the serpent-charmer,
before he enters a house in which he
is to try his skill, always employs a
servant of that house to introduce
one or more serpents; but I have
known instances in which this could
not be the case, and am inclined to
believe that the durweeshes above
mentioned are generally acquainted
with some real physical means of
discovering the presence of serpents
without seeing them, and of attracting
them from their lurking places"
(Lane, Modern Egyptians, ii. p. 106).
" I have seen many serpent-charmers,"

says Dr. Thomson, "who do really exercise some extraordinary power over
these reptiles. They carry enormous
snakes, generally black, about them,
allow them to crawl all over their persons and into their bosoms, always,
however, with certain precautions,
either necessary or pretended to be
so. They repeatedly breathe strongly
into the face of the serpent, and
occasionally blow spittle, or some
medicated composition upon them"
(The Land and the Book, London,
1859, p. 154). The Psalmist, speaking of the malignity of the incorri-
gibly wicked, compares it to the
venomous serpent which is proof to
all the efforts of the charmer (Ps.
lviii. 5) ; and God declares that he
will send serpents against his people " which are not to be charmed"
(Jer. viii. 17; compare also Sirach
xii. 13; Bochart. Hieroz., part ii. lib.
3, c. 6, where this subject is most
elaborately treated ; Hengstenberg,
Egypt, and the Books of Moses,
p. 100, English ed.; Winer, Realwörterbuch, s. v. Zauberei). The wisdom and skill of such a charmer
will be useless, if they are not exerted
to prevent the reptile from darting
upon the people. The article in
הַנָּחָשׁ, the serpent, refers to the serpent
mentioned in verse 8. בְּלֹא, literally
in not, not in, i. e., without (comp.
הַאֲזִינָה תְפִלָּתִי בְּלֹא שִׂפְתֵי מִרְמָה, give ear to
my prayer, with no feigned lips, Ps.
xvii. 1 ; 1 Chron. xii. 33 ; 2 Chron.
xxx 18). לַחַשׁ, from לָחַשׁ, to whisper,
to mutter magic formulas, to charm, is
incantation, charm, as is evident from
Jer. viii. 17, where, as here, it is used
with regard to the charming of serpents; so Aquila, ἀπούσης ἐπῳδῖς, and
Symmachus, ἐν οὐκ ἐπαοιδῷ, without
contentment. The ו in וְאֵין, as in the
foregoing verse, introduces the apodosis. בַּעַל הַלָּשׁוֹן, master of the tongue,
i. e., one who has such a mastery of
his tongue as to deprive by its mysterious murmurings the venom of
serpents, hence an enchanter, a
charmer. Durell's suggestion, that
הלשון may be a mistake for לחשון,
caused by a transposition of letters,

12 tage to the charmer.   The words from the mouth of the
wise man gain him favour, but those from the lips of the

is as unnecessary as it is gratuitous,
The verse is well rendered by the
Septuagint ἐὰν δόκη ὄφις ἐν οὐ ψιθυρισμῷ,
καὶ οὐκ ἔστιν περίσσεια τῷ ἐπᾴδοντι, and the

Syr. ‍‏ܐܢ ܢܟܬ ܚܘܝܐ ܕܠܐ ܚܘܫܒܐ
ܠܝܬ ܝܘܬܪܢܐ ܠܚܪܫܐ‍‏, if the
serpent bites, being unenchanted, there
is no advantage to the enchanter; and
beautifully explained by Rashbam,
אם הנחש נושך את האדם בשביל שהלוחש
לא ליחש עליו לחש הוא נושך ואין לו יתרון לבעל
הלשון, if the ser-
pent bites one because the charmer
has not charmed it, there is no advantage to the charmer who knows how
to charm, and does not do it, who
rightly remarks that (לחש נופל על הנחש)
נָחָשׁ and לָחַשׁ form a paranomasia.
The rendering of the Vulgate, SI
MORDEAT SERPENS IN SILENTIO, NIHIL
EO MINUS HABET QUI OCCULTE DE-
TRAHIT, if a serpent bite secretly, he
is nothing better who backbites slily,
which St. Jerome explains, SERPENS
ET DETRACTOR SUNT ÆQUALES; QUO-
MODO ENIM ILLE SECRETO MORDENS
VENENUM INSERIT, SIC ILLE CLAM
DETRAHENS, VIRUS PECTORIS SUI IN-
FUNDIT IN FRATREM, a serpent and
a slanderer are alike, for just as the
serpent stealthily infuses its poison, so
he who is secretly slandering instils the
venom of his breast into his brother;
and the explanation of Ibn Ezra,
אין יתרון לבעל הלשון מי הנחש הצפעוני שלא
ישמע לחש שיזיק ולא יהנה, if the unenchanted serpent bites and has no
advantage, no more has the backbiter;
which are followed by Luther (ein
Wäscher ist nichts besser denn eine
Schlange, die unbeschworen sticht, a
babbler is nothing better than a serpent which bites without enchantment),
misrepresented by Holden (p. 149),
who affirms that Luther renders it
"without provocation;" Coverdale
and the Bishops' Bible ("a babbler
of his tongue, or a backbiter, is no
better than a serpent that stingeth

without hissing"); the Geneva Bible
("if the serpent bite when he is not
charmed, no better is a babbler");
the Authorised Version ("surely the
serpent will bite without enchantment, and a babbler, or the master
of the tongue, is no better"), Hodgson
("though the serpent sting without
hissing, yet doth not he who hath a
double tongue bite still more cun-
ningly?") &c., owe their origin, as
usual, to the Hagadic interpretation
of this verse (comp. the Talmud,
Erchin, 15, b; Tanith, 8, a; the
Chaldee paraphrase, and the Midrash,
in loco), and are both against the
genius of the language and contrary
to the scope of the passage.

12. The words from the mouth, &c.
Having exposed the folly of attempting to raise a feeble opposition
against a powerful despot, Coheleth
recurs to the remark he has made in
verse 4, that it is the part of the wise
man patiently to bear that which
cannot be removed, and to use conciliatory language, which will, after
all, secure favour, whilst the words
which the fool employs will bring
him into ruin.   חֵן is not grace in the
sense of graceful, the abstract for the
adjective (Luther, Coverdale, the
Bishop's Bible, the Geneva Bible,
the Authorised Version in the text,
Holden, Knobel, Ewald, De Wette,
Heiligstedt, &c.), but favour, i.e.,
favour procuring; his words are such
as conciliate or procure favour or acceptance (Rashbam, Hodgson, Herzfeld, Noyes, Hitzig, Stuart, Vaihinger,
Hengstenberg, &c.), as is evident
from the antithesis.   The construct
דִּבְרֵי, from the first clause, is to be
supplied before שִׂפְתוֹת in the second
hemistich, i.e., וְדִבְרֵי שִׂפְתוֹת, and the
words of the lips of, &c.; cases in
which words are taken over from one
hemistich into the other are of frequent occurrence (comp. the following verse; xi. 5, xii. 11, 13; Ps. xx. 7;
Prov. iii. 12), and inattention to this

13 fool destroy him ; the beginning of the words of his mouth
is folly, and the end of the words of his mouth is mischievous

fact, on the part of translators, has
produced inextricable confusion in
the translations of different passages
of Scripture ; as, for instance, Isa.
xxxi. 5, כְּצִפֳּרִים עָפוֹת כֵּן יָגֵן יְהֹוָה צְבָאוֹת
עַל־יְרוּשָׁלַ͏ם, *us birds protect their chickens,
so Jehovah of Hosts protects Jerusa-
lem*, to which the tender expressions
of our Saviour in Matt. xxiii. 37 seem
to allude, but which yields no sense
in the common renderings. Failing
to see this in the passage before us,
commentators are not only compelled
to take שִׂפְתוֹת metonymically for
speech, but to make the *masculine verb*
תְּבַלְּעֶנּוּ the predicate of the *feminine
noun* שִׂפְתוֹת. The *plural* const. שִׂפְתוֹת,
instead of the *dual* שִׂפְתֵי, which also
occurs in Ps. xlv. 3, lix. 8 ; Song of
Songs iv. 3. 11, v. 13 ; Isa. lix. 3, is
owing to the fact that the dual form
is gradually dropped in the later
phases of development in the language (comp. Gesen. § 88, 2 ; Ewald,
§ 180). The pronoun in תְּבַלְּעֶנּוּ does
not refer to *the wise man*, or *any one
else*, as the Hagadic interpretation
will have it (comp. the Midrash, the
Chaldee, and Rashi), which is adopted
by St. Jerome, who remarks, ET RE-
VERA PRÆCIPITATUR SAPIENS QUANDO
IN AUREM LOQUITUR IMPRUDENTIS, ET
VERBA EJUS IN PROFUNDO UT ITA
DICAM GURGITE PEREUNT, *a wise man
is as if he were thrown down when he
speaks in the hearing of a fool, and
his words perish, if I may say so, in
a deep gulf*, and followed by Luther,
Bishop Patrick, Schmidt, Umbreit,
&c., but refers to the *fool himself*.
For the *verb singular* תְּבַלְּעֶנּוּ, referring
to the *plural noun* דְּבָרִים, see verse 1.
Mendelssohn's rendering of this verse,
" the words of a wise man's mouth
are, ' Shew mercy,' but of the lips of
the fool, ' Destroy him ! ' " taking
תְּבַלְּעֶנּוּ as the *second person*, and regarding it as the expression used by
the fool, which is followed by Friedländer and Preston, is simply preposterous, and is completely set aside

by the similar construction in the
following verse.
13. *The beginning of*, &c. The
reason why the words of the fool are
his ruin, is, that they are replete with
folly and mischief from beginning to
end. תְּחִלָּה and אַחֲרִית, like our phrase
" from beginning to end," denote the
whole, altogether (*vide supra*, iii. 11),
and are tersely explained by Ibn Ezra
אין טעם לדבריו התחלה וסוף, *there is no sense
in his words from beginning to end*.
Accordingly דִּבְרֵי, as in the foregoing
verse, is to be supplied before פִּיהוּ in
the second clause from the first hemistich, which is rightly done by the
Sept. (ἀρχὴ λόγων στόματος αὐτοῦ ἀφροσύνη,
καὶ ἐσχάτη στόματος αὐτοῦ περιφέρεια
πονηρά), the Chaldee (שֵׁירוּי מִלֵּי פוּמֵהּ,
שְׁטוּתָא וְסוֹף מֵימַר פּוּמֵהּ חוּלְחָלְתָּא בִּישָׁא),
Rashbam, Luther (der Anfang seiner
Worte ist Narrheit, und das Ende ist
schädliche Thorheit), who, like Ibn
Ezra, gives the same sense, by omitting the second פִּיהוּ, Coverdale, the
Bishops' Bible ("the beginning of his
talking is foolishness, and the last
word of his mouth is stark madness"), Ewald, &c. This shews beyond doubt that our construction of
the preceding verse is the legitimate
one. The inconsistency of taking
פִּיהוּ, in the second clause, metonymically for *his talk* (the Auth. Version,
Desvoeux, Knobel, De Wette, Noyes,
Heiligstedt, &c.), or of applying
אַחֲרִית to פִּיהוּ, i. e., *the end of his mouth*,
that is, *the end which his mouth makes
of its discourse* (the Vulg., the Geneva
Bible, Herzfeld, Hitzig, Stuart, Elster,
Vaihinger, Hengstenberg, &c.), is
evident from the parallel construction
in the first clause. Still more objectionable are the renderings, "the
consequence of his words is mischievous madness" (Mendelssohn,
Schmidt, Friedländer, Preston, &c.),
"the beginning of the words of his
mouth is folly, but the end of his
discourse is absurdity that bringeth
mischief" (Hodgson), &c.

14 madness. The fool also speaketh much, though no man

14. *The fool also*, &c. Another
characteristic of the fool is, that he
talks much upon everything, and
about the most profound and mysterious subjects, though no man knows,
nor can get to know, what events
will transpire here, and what will be
hereafter. The ו in וְהַסָּכָל introduces
an *additional* feature, and, as frequently elsewhere, signifies *moreover,
also*. יַרְבֶּה דְבָרִים, literally *he multiplies words*, i. e., *speaks much* ; the
subject upon which the fool here
exercises his loquaciousness cannot
be mistaken from the remainder of
the verse ; it is about מַה־שֶּׁיִהְיֶה וַאֲשֶׁר
יִהְיֶה מֵאַחֲרָיו, *what will take place here
and hereafter,* which no man, however
wise, can know, much less such a
fool. The particle *although*, or *yet*,
which is not unfrequently omitted,
must be supplied before לֹא. The
phrase לֹא־יֵדַע הָאָדָם means *no man
knows* or *can know* (comp. ix. 1. 12 ;
and לֹא־יִמְצָא הָאָדָם, *no man finds* or
can find, iii. 11, vii. 14, viii. 17).
מֵאַחֲרָיו, *from after him*, i. e., *from the
time when he will be no more, after
his death ;* the phrase יִהְיֶה אַחֲרֵי is of
frequent occurrence in this book, and
invariably signifies *what shall be after
life is finished, after death, hereafter ;*
whilst יִהְיֶה by itself denotes the *future ;*
so that מַה־שֶּׁיִהְיֶה means *what a day* or
the morrow may bring forth, and
אֲשֶׁר יִהְיֶה מֵאַחֲרָי, *what shall be hereafter,
after death.* The additional clause
מִי יַגִּיד לוֹ, which is used as an *emphatic
denial*, is to shew the total impossibility of knowing these things about
which the fool prattles ; men of far
greater capacities than he not only cannot get to know these things by their
own cogitations (יֵדַע), but are unable
to ascertain them from others (יַגִּיד).
The difficulty which commentators
have felt in developing the sense of
this verse, and in tracing its connection with the foregoing verse, it will, we
believe, appear groundless, from this
simple analysis of the text, and has
evidently arisen from the loose and
discordant paraphrases of the ancient

versions and mediæval expositors.
Thus the Septuagint has καὶ ὁ ἄφρων
πληθύνει λόγους· οὐκ ἔγνω ὁ ἄνθρωπος τί τὸ
γενόμενον καὶ τί τὸ ἐσόμενον· ὅ τι ὀπίσω αὐτοῦ
τίς ἀπαγγελεῖ αὐτῷ ; *and a fool multiplies words ; man knows not what has
been and what shall be ; what is after
him who can tell him ?* altering the
future שֶׁיִהְיֶה into שֶׁהָיָה, regarding the
מ in מֵאַחֲרָיו as a *pronoun*, and connecting it with the last clause. The
Vulg., STULTUS VERBA MULTIPLICAT ;
IGNORAT HOMO, QUID ANTE SE FUERIT ;
ET QUID POST SE FUTURUM SIT, QUIS EI
POTERIT INDICARE ? *a fool multiplies
words ; man does not know what was
before him, and what shall be after
him who can tell him ?* and St. Jerome,
ET STULTUS VERBA MULTIPLICAT ; IG-
NORAT HOMO QUID SIT, QUOD FACTUM
EST, ET QUOD FUTURUM EST POST EUM,
QUIS ANNUNCIABIT EI ? *and a fool
multiplies words ; man knows not what
has been, what is, and what shall be
after him ; who shall declare it unto
him ?* also alter מַה־שֶּׁיִהְיֶה into מַה־שֶּׁהָיָה ;
the latter, moreover, inserts מַה־שֶּׁהָיָה
and explains it QUUM STULTUS NEC
PRÆTERITORUM MEMINERIT, NEC FU-
TURA AGNOSCAT, ET IGNORANTIÆ
TENEBRIS VOLUTETUR, FALSAM SIBI
SCIENTIAM REPROMITTENS, IN EO DOC-
TUM SE PUTAT ET SAPIENTEM, SI
VERBA MULTIPLICAT, *when a fool
neither remembers the things which are
past, nor knows the things which are
to come, and stumbles in the darkness
of ignorance, he assures himself of a
false knowledge, and thinks himself
learned and wise if he only multiplies
words.* But, apart from the arbitrary
alteration of the text, this interpretation makes הָאָדָם, *man*, identical with הַסָּכָל, *the fool*, mentioned
in the first clause, which is both contrary to the uniform meaning of הָאָדָם
in such constructions, and clogs the
whole sentence. If the sacred writer
had intended to convey this idea, he
would undoubtedly have omitted
הָאָדָם altogether. The explanations
of Rashi, והסכל ירבה דברים גוזר ואומר מחר
אעשה כן לפלוני ואינו יודע מה יהיה מחר : ואשר

knoweth what shall be here nor what shall be hereafter;
15 who can tell him it? The work of a fool wearieth him,

יהיה מאחריו מי יגיד לו כלומר לא סוף דבר שאינו
יודע מה׳ יהיה לאחר זמן אלא אף ההווה עכשיו
מאחריו שלא כנגד עיניו אלא מאחורי טרפו מרחוק
צריך הוא שיהא מי יגיד לו, "and the fool
multiplies words," i. e., he fixes and
declares I shall do so and so to this
and that one tomorrow, and does not
know what may be tomorrow. "And
what shall be," &c., i. e., he not only
does not know what may happen after
the lapse of a little time, but does not
even know what is taking place behind
his back at this preseent moment; and
Rashbam, הכסיל מרבה דברים של כסילות
ואינו יודע ומבין הרעה אשר תבא ותגיע לו בסופו
וגם הרעה אשר עליו פתאום מאחריו כאשר
ילך בדרכו אינו יודע כי מי יגיד לו, the fool
talks much foolishness, and does not
know nor understand the evil which
will come upon him at his end; and
even the evil which may be close behind
his back, when walking on the road,
he does not know, for who can tell him
it? according to which the verse
ought to be translated "and the fool
talks much; the foolish man knows
not what the future will be, yea, not
even what is now going on behind
him," which are followed by Mendelssohn and Friedländer, incur the
additional censure of taking מֵאַחֲרָיו as
a preposition of place, i. e., behind
one's back, contrary to the sense
which it invariably has in this book,
as will be seen from the above-cited
passages. The Chaldee paraphrase,
וְשָׁטְיָא מַסְגֵּי פִתְגָּמִין סְרִיקִין דְּלֵית בְּהוֹן צְרוֹךְ עַד
דְּלָא יְנְדַע אֲנַשׁ מַה דַּעֲתִיד לְמֶהֱוֵי בְּיוֹמוֹהִי וּמָה
דְּעָתִיד לְמֶהֱוֵי בְּסֵיפֵיהּ מַאן יְחַוֵּי לֵיהּ, and the
fool multiplies empty and useless words,
so much so, that no man can know
what will be in his days, and what
will become of him at the end who can
tell him? which is followed by Preston, Hitzig, Stuart, &c., is contradicted by the indisputable signification of the same expressions in the
passages already quoted. Ibn Ezra's
explanation, והסכל יאמר אוכל ואשתה כי
לא אדע מה שיהיה בחיי ובמותי, and the fool
says, I will eat and drink, for I know

not what will happen here or hereafter,
taking מַה־שֶּׁיִּהְיֶה וְגוֹ׳ as a minesis or
representation of what the fool says,
which is followed by the Geneva
Bible ("for the fool multiplieth words,
saying, man knoweth not what shall
be," &c.), and others, is sufficiently
refuted by iii. 22, vi. 12, viii. 17,
where it is evident that it is the sentiment of Coheleth himself, and not
of the fool. Coverdale, "a fool is so
full of words, that a man cannot tell
what end he will make; who will then
warn him to make a conclusion?"
the Bishops' Bible, "a fool is full
of words, and a man cannot tell what
shall come to pass; who will then
warn him of it that shall follow after
him?" Geier and Hodgson, "though
the fool use many words, no man can
tell what they mean, and to what
purpose they tend no man can inform
him," are as curious as they are irreconcileable with the text.

15. The work of a fool, &c. As in
his sayings, so in his doings, the folly
of the fool manifests itself to his
detriment. The duties of a life
spent under a tyrannical government, which the wise man contrives
to discharge with comparative ease
by conciliatory words and deeds,
thoroughly weary the fool, because
of his utter ignorance of the things
easily come-at-able and familiar to
everybody. Cities being capitals of
all the adjacent country, are much
talked of and well known by the
surrounding inhabitants. As one
who does not know the high road
to the capital must be extremely
ignorant, the phrase not to be able
to discover the beaten and much-
frequented track to the town became
a proverbial expression to denote a
fool who is ignorant of the most
ordinary things appertaining to the
journey of life, just as we say, "He
has not wit enough to travel on a
broad open highway." We have had
similar language in verse 3. The

16 because he knoweth not how to go to the city. Woe to thee,
O land, when thy king is childish, and thy princes feast

Chaldee paraphrase עַל דְּלָא אַלִּיף לְמֵיזַל
לְהֵרְתָּא דְחַבִּימַיָא שָׁרֵי בְנַהּ לְמִחְבַּע מִנֵּיהּ אוּלְפָנָא,
*because he will not learn to go to the
city where the wise dwell to seek
instruction*, which takes "the city"
as *the seat of wisdom* where knowledge might be obtained; as well as
its offsprings, viz., "the work of the
fool wearies him who does not understand to go to the city, *i.e*, *who does
not know to bribe the great lords in
the city where justice is exposed for
sale* (Ewald), and "he does not know
to help himself in the right way,
since the city is the seat of the
government of the place, and it is
there that the countryman may hope
to find redress for his complaints"
(Elster), are too artificial. Still more
objectionable is the explanation of
Rashbam and Ibn Ezra. דמה הכסיל
שיעמוד לבקש גבוהות ונפלאות ממנו והוא לא
ידע הנראות והידיעות כאדם רוצה ללכת אל עיר
ולא ידע הדרך וייגע ולא יראה חפצו, *the fool
who attempts to search into things
which are too sublime and mysterious
for him, whilst he does know the things
which are obvious and well known, is
like a man wishing to go to the city
and does not know the way, and thus
wearies himself without seeing his
desire*, taking אֲשֶׁר in the sense of
כַּאֲשֶׁר, which is followed by Mendelssohn, Friedländer, Hodgson, Preston,
who translates it, "the work of the
fool wearies him; he is like one who
does not know the way to the city."
The construction of תְּיַגְּעֶנּוּ, the third
pers. *fem.* with עָמָל, a *masculine* noun,
shews the inattention to the agreement of *genders, numbers*, &c., mentioned in i. 10. The *sing.* suffix וּ
in תְּיַגְעֶנּוּ, as well as the *sing.* verb
יֵדַע, referring to the *plural* noun כְּסִילִים,
as frequently, are used *distributively*
(*vide* verse 1), and in such a case
the sentence may either be rendered
in the *singular*, as the Septuagint
and the Chaldee have it, or *plural*,
as the Vulgate, St. Jerome, and the
Syriac have it. It is therefore pre-

posterous to maintain, as Houbigant,
Spohn, and others do, that these
versions had different renderings,
and accordingly alter the text.

16. *Woe to thee, O land*, &c. Having
strongly urged the policy of not engaging in any feeble acts of rebellion,
but of patiently submitting to a
tyrannical and degraded government, Coheleth takes care that his
counsels should not be misunderstood, and perchance be taken as if he
approved of outrages from the powers
that be. In shewing, however, his
utter disapprobation of such abuses,
the sacred writer adroitly describes
the woeful plight of the *land* whose
princes and governors are despotic
and sensuous, instead of denouncing
the *prince and the rulers* themselves,
which might have been attended with
serious consequences to himself,
living as he did under such depraved
and grinding despotism. Dissipation and intemperance, the concomitants of infatuated despotism, are
described by *feasting in the morning*,
because indulging in sumptuous fare
at this early part of the day was
regarded as the height of sensuality
and depravity, and was therefore
abhorred by the Hebrews as well as
by other nations. Hence the prophet
Isaiah, in denouncing the woful
degradation of Israel, mentions their
feasting at an early hour (v. 11),
and St. Peter, standing up to repudiate the charge of drunkenness
against the disciples, pointed to the
fact that it was "the third hour of
the day" (Acts ii. 15), *i.e.*, about
nine o'clock in the morning, when
none but the most dissolute would
be found in such a state. Cicero,
describing the scenes of revelling
into which the place of Marcus Varro
was converted, says, AB HORA TERTIA
BIBETATUR, &c., *there was drinking
from the third hour*—nine o'clock in
the morning (Philipp. ii. 41; comp.
also Catull. Carm. xlvii. 5, 6; Juven.

17 in the morning! Happy thou, O land, when thy king is noble, and thy princes eat in proper time, for strength and

Sat. i. 49, 50). St. Jerome thinks that there is something very sacred concealed in the latter clause of this verse, and therefore takes "the king" to be the *devil*, who, in respect to God, "the ancient of days," as Daniel calls him (vii. 9), *is a child in understanding;* "the princes" are *the followers of the prince of this world,* who revel in earthly pleasures and say, Let us eat and drink, for to-morrow we shall die. VAE TERRÆ CUJUS EST DIABOLUS REX, QUI SEMPER NO-VARUM RERUM CUPIDUS, ETIAM IN ABSALON ADVERSUS PARENTEM RE-BELLAT, &c., *woe to the land where the king is the devil, who, always desiring something new, rebelled in Absalom against his father,* &c. This is one of the two solitary places where the interjection אִי is used in Biblical Hebrew (*vide supra,* iv. 10). נַעַר is not *slave* (Döderlein, Desvoeux, Dathe, Van der Palm, Spohn, Nachtigal, &c.), which despicable sense it never has; but, as is evident from the context, describes *one who is inexperienced, childish, foolish* (Rashbam, Mendelssohn, Knobel, Heiligstedt, &c.), just as נָשִׁים, *women,* is used for *effeminate* and *weak-minded men* (comp. Isa. iii. 4. 12, xix. 16; Jer. i. 6, 7). That אָכַל here means *feasting, immoderate indulgence,* is evident from the antithesis in the next verse, where the good princes are described as eating to live, and not living to eat.

17. *Happy thou, O land,* &c. To render the side-blow to despotism more heavy, Coheleth refers, on the other hand, to the happy state of a country whose prince and rulers are benign and moderate. Failing to see this, Spohn and others arbitrarily transpose whole sentences, whilst Vaihinger regards this verse as an interpolation, having made its way into the text from a marginal gloss. According to St. Jerome, "the king, the son of nobles," is *the Saviour,*

the son of the noble patriarchs, Abraham, Isaac, and Jacob, the descendant of the prophets and holy men; "the princes" are *the apostles and the saints, whose king is the son of the nobles;* these "do not eat in the morning," *i.e., do not run after the pleasures of this world,* "but eat in due season," *i. e., shall eat at the time of retribution,* "in strength and not in confusion," *i. e., every good thing of this world is confusion, but the good of the world to come is perpetual strength.* It need hardly be said that this is the Hagadic interpretation Christianised (compare Midrash Yalkut, *in loco,* and Talmud, Tanith, 6). אַשְׁרֵי, *the plural const.* of אֶשֶׁר, from אָשַׁר, kindred with כָּשַׁר, יָשַׁר, *to be right, physically* or *mentally* (*vide* ii. 21) is the abstract, according to the usage of plural nouns for abstracts (*vide* ix. 3), and signifies *blessedness, happiness;* it occurs only in this plural construct (אַשְׁרֵיהוּ in Prov. xxix. 18, stands for אַשְׁרֵיהוּ), and has its exact correspondence in the Aramæan טוּבֵי דְ, which has also the force of an *interjection.* Hupfeld's assertion, that אַשְׁרֵי never has an exclamatory sense (Comment. Ps. i. 1), is completely set aside by the fact that it stands here in parallelism with the interjection אִי. In אַשְׁרֵיךְ, which has a *masculine* pronoun, and refers to the *feminine noun* אֶרֶץ, we have another instance of colloquial inattention (*vide* i. 10). בֶּן־חוֹרִים is not *the son of,* or *come from, a noble* (St. Jerome, the Chaldee, Coverdale, the Bishops' Bible, the Geneva Bible, the Auth. Ver., Grotius, Le Clerc, Döderlein, Desvoeux, Hodgson, &c.), which in itself would by no means secure the happiness here spoken of, as those of noble blood may be of ignoble deeds, and a curse to the country, but *one who is of a noble character* (the Vulgate, *cujus rex nobilis est;* Rashbam, חשוב וחכם; Ibn Ezra, שיעשה כיתשה הראוים והפך כן

18 not for feasting! Through slothful hands the roof falleth

בְּלִיַּעַל ; Luther, Knobel, Noyes, Heiligstedt, Vaihinger, &c.) בֶּן, according
to a common idiom, when followed
by a genitive of a *quality* or *condition*,
denotes *one who possesses it* (comp.
בֶּן־חַיִל, *son of strength*, i e., *a hero*,
2 Sam. xiii. 28; בֶּן־עַוְלָה, *son of wickedness*, i.e., *a wicked man*, 2 Sam. vii. 10;
Ps. lxxxix. 23 ; Song of Songs vii. 2,
infra, xii. 4 ; John xii. 36 ; Eph.
ii. 2 ; Col. iii. 6 ; Gesen § 106, 2, a ;
Ewald, § 287. f). The *plural* חוֹרִים,
like אִשָּׁרֶיךָ in this verse, is used for
the *abstract* בְּעֵת, which corresponds
to the Latin *in tempore*, means *proper
time* or *season* (*vide* vii. 17), and
stands in apposition to בַּבֹּקֶר. The
בְּ in בִּגְבוּרָה and בַּשְׁתִּי denotes the
cause or *object* of the eating in question (comp. Ps. v. 11, vii. 7, xxxi. 10 ;
Jonah i. 14, *supra*, i. 24 ; Ewald,
§ 217, f, 3, a). שְׁתִי, from שָׁתָה, according to the analogy of דְּלִי from
דָּלָה, פְּרִי from פָּרָה, קְרִי from קָרָה, is not
drunkenness (the Geneva Bible, the
Auth. Version, Desvoeux, Noyes,
Vaihinger, &c.), since it is most
incongruous to say " princes *eat* for
drunkenness," but means a *feast*,
feasting inordinately, *revelry* (the
Vulgate, the Syriac, Rashbam, Ibn
Ezra, Luther, Coverdale, the Bishops'
Bible, Hodgson, Knobel, De Wette,
Herzfeld, Heiligstedt, Hitzig, Stuart,
Elster, &c.), like מִשְׁתֶּה from the same
root (Esth. i. 3 ; Isa v. 12), and the
Greek συμπόσιον. The Septuagint's
rendering of it by καὶ οὐκ αἰσχυνθήσονται,
and they shall not be ashamed, taking
it for בּוֹשׁ, from בּוּשׁ, which is followed
by St. Jerome (*et non in confusione*),
and the Chaldee בְּחַלָּשׁוּת *in weakness*,
deriving it from נָשָׁה, *failing in
strength*, are owing to their allegorical
explanation of this verse, and are
plainly against the form of the word
and the scope of the passage. בִּגְבוּרָה
וְלֹא בַשְּׁתִי are added to the verb יֹאכֵלוּ,
to qualify it, marking the difference
between its signification here and in
the foregoing verse.

18. *Through slothful hands*, &c.
The woe pronounced upon the land

whose king and princes are given to
folly and dissipation (verse 16) is
here continued. Through devoting
the time to inordinate pleasures and
profligacy, which ought to be given
to the maintenance of justice and
order of the body politic, the community becomes disorganised, and
the whole state is dilapidated and
ruined. Ibn Ezra, and after him
most modern commentators, rightly
take this verse to represent, under
the figure of a crumbling and leaky
building, the ruined and deplorable
condition of a community neglected
in the adjustment of its interests,
and drained of its resources by profligate rulers. Those who maintain
that it simply contains " a dissuasive
from idleness generally " (Le Clerc,
Sebastian Schmidt, Michaelis, Rosenmüller, Holden, &c.) are obliged to
sever this verse from the preceding
verses and verse 20, which is manifestly connected with it, without
being able properly to join it to anything else. עֲצַלְתַּיִם is not the dual of
עַצְלָה (Gesenius, Lex. *s. v.*, Preston,
&c.), which would be עַצְלָתַיִם, but of
עֲצֵלָה or עֲצַלְת (*vide* Fürst, Lex. *s. v.*),
and may either be regarded with Ibn
Ezra (חוזרות לידים כאלו אמר בידים עצלות),
as referring to יָדַיִם, as if the writer
had said *through slothful hands*, or
may be taken as an *epitheton perpe-
tuum* for hands (compare Ewald,
§ 180, a). The rendering of it by
double hands, i. e., *great* or *much slothfulness* (the Auth. Version, Knobel,
Gesenius, Noyes, Elster, Hengstenberg, &c.) is both incompatible with
the second hemistich, which would
decrease in force from *great* slothfulness to simple idleness, instead of
rising, and unnecessarily assigns an
abnormal sense to the dual. מְקָרֶה,
beam, like קוֹרָה, *beam*, also means
roof (comp. Gen. xix. 8 ; Song of
Songs i. 17) שִׁפְלוּת יָדַיִם, literally
the letting down of hands, i e., letting
them hang down instead of keeping
them at work, is the same as חִבֻּק יָדַיִם,
iv. 5, and is well rendered by the

19 in, and through lazy hands the house leaketh.   They turn

Septuagint ἐν ἀργίᾳ χειρῶν, *through the laziness of* = *lazy hands.*

19. *They turn bread,* &c.   These lazy rulers convert the blessings of God, bread which sustains and wine which cheers life, into means of revelry and profligacy, and the money which is extorted from the people is made to supply all this. For the use of *bread* and *wine* to represent the comforts of life, see ix. 7. שְׂחוֹק is *laughter, mirth, revelry* (*vide* ii. 2), the לְ before it, construed with עָשָׂה, a verb of *making,* denotes the *result* or *effect,* thus marking that which anything has been made or is *converted into ;* לֶחֶם וְיַיִן are the *accusative of the object,* both being governed by עָשָׂה, as the Septuagint, the Vulgate, the Syriac, St. Jerome, &c., rightly have it (compare שְׁאֵרִיתוֹ לְאֵל עָשָׂה, *the residue thereof he made into a god,* Isa. xliv. 17).   The pronoun אֲשֶׁר, which is frequently omitted, is to be supplied before יְשַׂמַּח, as is evident from the parallel passage, יַיִן יְשַׂמַּח לְבַב־אֱנוֹשׁ, *wine which maketh glad the heart of man,* Ps. civ. 15. חַיִּים may either be taken as a *noun,* i. e., *life,* or as an *adjective,* i. e., *the living ;* the former seems preferable, since it corresponds better to לֵבָב in the parallel passage.   וְהַכֶּסֶף, *and the money,* stands for וְכֶסֶף הָעָם, *and the people's money ;* הָעָם, *the people,* like the subject of יַעֲשׂוּ, *they make,* being designedly suppressed, because of the danger of speaking plainly to despots, and is in accordance with the caution given on this subject in the following verse.   עָנָה, *to answer,* also *to yield, to grant* (comp. Hos. ii. 23, 24), and the sense is the same whether we take יַעֲנֶה as Kal or Hiphil ; in the former case it is *yields,* in the latter, *is made to yield.* הַכֹּל, as frequently, when following two things spoken of, means *both* (*vide* ii. 14), and refers to לֶחֶם וְיַיִן, *the bread and wine.*   The conflicting opinions about the meaning of the verse are almost innumerable, and, as usual, have been largely promoted

by the different renderings of the ancient versions.   Thus the Septuagint has εἰς γέλωτα ποιοῦσιν ἄρτον καὶ οἶνος καὶ ἔλαιον τοῦ εὐφρανθῆναι ζῶντας, καὶ τοῦ ἀργυρίου ταπεινώσει, ἐπακούσεται σὺν τὰ πάντα, *for joy they make bread, and wine, and oil, that the living should rejoice, and to money all things will humble themselves, they will respond,* adding שֶׁמֶן, *oil,* after יַיִן, *wine,* taking יְשַׂמַּח, the well-known epithet of יַיִן, which cannot be predicated of לֶחֶם, for יְשַׂמֵּחוּ, referring it to both *bread* and *wine,* regarding הַחַיִּים as the subject of the three nouns לֶחֶם יַיִן וְשֶׁמֶן, doubly translating עָנָה, and making אֶת־הַכֹּל the *nominative ;* substantially the same is the Syriac Version

[Syriac text]

, *for joy they make bread, and wine, and oil, that they may rejoice the living, and money oppresses and leads them astray in all ;* and the Vulgate, IN RISUM FACIUNT PANEM ET VINUM, UT EPULENTUR VIVENTES ; ET PECUNIÆ OBEDIUNT OMNIA ; the clue to these versions will be found in the Chaldee, which paraphrases it לְהוֹנָא עָבְדִין צַדִּיקַיָּא לֶחֶם לְפַרְנָסָא עִנְיֵי כַּפְנִין וְחַמְרָא דִּמְזִיגִין לִדְצַחְיָין (ס״א לִצְחוּצִין) יְהֵי לְהוֹן לֶחֶדְוָה לְעָלְמָא דְאָתֵי וּכְסַף פּוּרְקָנְהוֹן יְסַחַר עֲלֵיהוֹן וְכוּתְהָא לְעָלְמָא דְאָתֵי בְּאַנְפֵּי כּוֹלָא, *in joy do the righteous make bread to feed the hungry poor ; and the wine which they mix for the thirsty (or the sufferers) will be a rejoicing to them in the world to come, and the redemption money will proclaim their merit in the world to come, in the face of all.*   Compare also the Midrash, *in loco,* where the Septuagint's double rendering of עָנָה will be found.   Passing over these Hagadic explanations, the object of which was not to give the literal meaning of the text, but to obtain some profound and mysterious doctrine from every

bread and wine, which cheereth life, into revelry, and the

detached sentence and word, we come to the Rabbins of the middle ages. According to Rashi, Rashbam, and Ibn Ezra, the meaning is, "a banquet is prepared for enjoyment, and wine that cheers the living; but money procures it all;" hence the necessity of labouring to acquire it, and not indulging in the laziness described in the foregoing verse. Against this explanation is to be urged — 1. That שְׂחוֹק, being simply another expression for שָׂמְחִי in verse 17, cannot be taken in a *good sense*. 2. That though עָשָׂה לֶחֶם, *by itself*, may mean *prepare a feast*, like לְחֶם אֲבַד in Chaldee (Dan. v. 1), to which Rashi appeals, yet its connection here with וְיַיִן precludes the idea of *giving an entertainment*. 3. To take this verse as holding forth the consequence of being able to give entertainments as a bait for industry, is utterly at variance with verse 18, and with the whole scope of the passage. The versions of the Reformers are more discordant and far-fetched than those of the Rabbins. Luther in his commentary translates it denn sie erlangen ihr Brot mit Lachen, und der Wein muß die Lebendigen erfreuen. und daß Geld muß ihr sein, u. s. w., *for they gain their bread by laughing; and wine must rejoice the living, and money must be theirs*, &c.; which he explains, *there are a large number of dangerous nobility in the courts of princes who have not the fear of God nor true wisdom, and gain their bread by flattering, by eating and drinking with the debased, &c., they think of nothing but eating and drinking, and are of no use to kings but to empty the purse and the cup; these look for money, and think of nothing but money*, &c. But this is at variance with the words of the text. In the last edition of his translation of the Bible, however, it is rendered das macht, sie machen Brot zum Lachen, und der Wein muß die Lebendigen erfreuen, und das Geld muß ihnen alles zuwege bringen, *hence they make bread for laughter, and*

wine must rejoice the living, and money must procure everything, which seems to favour the interpretation we defend. The rendering of the Zurich Bible, Speyß machet die menschen lachen; unnd weyn machet sy frölich: dem gelt aber sind alle ding ghorsam, which is literally adopted by Coverdale and the Bishops' Bible, " meat maketh men to laugh, and wine maketh them merry; but unto money are all things obedient;" the Geneva Bible (" they prepare bread for laughter, and wine comforteth the living, but silver answereth to all"), and the Authorised Version (" a feast is made for laughter, and wine maketh merry — marg., glad the life — but money answereth all things "), being substantially the same; and which is explained by Poole, Hodgson, Holden, Noyes, &c., *as commending that which is procured by diligence*, i. e., *money*, affirming that whilst other things, even the best of them, such as bread and wine, have a limited use, one making us laugh, the other *merry, money procures all*, is simply a modification of the Rabbinic view; and 1. Is guilty of taking שְׂחוֹק in a *good sense*, in common with the Rabbins; 2. Is contrary to the genius of the language, inasmuch as לִשְׂחוֹק עֹשִׂים can never have this sense in connection with לֶחֶם: had the sacred writer intended to convey this idea he would undoubtedly have written לְבַב־אֱנוֹשׁ יִסְעַד, which is the established description of לֶחֶם, just as יְשַׂמַּח לְבַב־אֱנוֹשׁ or יְשַׂמַּח חַיִּים is of יַיִן (comp. Ps civ. 15); and 3. The preceding verses, as well as the following verse, shew that it is not " a detached and isolated apophthegm, teaching the extensive sway and predominating power of wealth." Other explanations, which connect this verse with the preceding one by supplying *who, while, where,* or some other expression, as, for instance, " through idleness of the hands of those men the house droppeth through, who make feasts for laughter, and prepare wine to make

20 money of —— is made to supply both.   Still do not

their life merry, and whose money doth readily answer all these greedy lusts" (mentioned by Reynolds) ; "through idleness of hands the house will drop, while they make feasts to divert themselves, and spend their life in making themselves merry with wine and oil, money supplying with them the want of everything else " (Desvœux) ; " through negligence the house bursts, where feasting is made for revelry, where wine cheers the living, and all the money is spent for it" (Döderlein) ; " those who give entertainments from sheer sensuality, and cheer their carousing comrades with wine, with these money answers all things" (Mendelssohn and Friedländer) ; " through remissness of the hands a house drops through, to the derision of those who acquire by industry bread and wine that cheers the people, and money that furnishes everything" (Preston); &c., &c., are too far-fetched, and have deservedly been left to their respective authors. We have now to mention the interpretation generally adopted by the most respectable critics of the present day, viz., " for luxury they (i. e., the lazy rulers) make feasts; and wine cheers the living (i. e., these living ones), and their motto is, Money supplies all." To this effect, Nachtigal, Knobel, Herzfeld, De Wette, Hitzig, Heiligstedt, Stuart, Philippson, Elster, Vaihinger, &c. But against this is to be urged — 1. That the rendering of לִשְׂחוֹק עֹשִׂים by to make for luxury, is unnatural ; 2. That it violently separates יַיִן from לֶחֶם, its usual concomitant, as is evident from the adjunct יְשַׂמַּח חַיִּים (comp. the above-quoted passage from Ps. civ. 15); and 3. That to say "wine cheers the hearts of these living ones" amounts to nothing, inasmuch as it predicates nothing wrong, since this is the proper object of wine, whereas the sacred writer evidently intends thereby something bad.

20. Still do not revile the king, &c.

However, the very depravity and tyranny of the sovereign and rulers ought to make us very cautious in speaking against them, as no mercy can be expected from such an administration. This is the reason why Coheleth himself has spoken all along so covertly about the abuses in high places. To be plain is dangerous. No matter how hidden and safe we may think the place where we speak, the secret will escape ; there are spies in our families, in our innermost room, who will report; it will creep out in some unforeseen and surprising way, as if the bird which settles upon the window listened to what we said, and conveyed it to the despot. The phrase " the bird of air shall convey the report," is evidently proverbial, and corresponds to the many similar sayings of the same import, both in the Scriptures and classics. Thus, the stones of the wall, and the brick from the timber, are represented as declaring injustice perpetrated (Hag. ii. 11); and the stones, we are told, would forthwith proclaim the blessings of the King Messiah (Luke xi. 40). So also Juvenal : —

O Corydon, Corydon, secretum divitis ullum
Esse putas ? Servi ut taceant, jumenta lo-
    quentur
Et canis et postes et marmora ; " Claude
    fenestras
Vela tegant rimas, junge ostia, tollite lumen
E medio (clamant omnes) prope nemo recum-
    bat ;
Quod tamen ad cantum galli facit ille secundi
Proximus ante diem cauposi cet."

" And dost thou seriously believe, fond swain,
The actions of the great unknown remain ?
Poor Corydon! even beasts would silence
    break,
And stocks and stones, if servants did not,
    speak.
Bolt every door, stop every cranny tight,
Close every window, put out every light ;
Let not a whisper reach the listening ear,
No noise, no motion ; let no soul be near ;
Yet all that passed at the cock's second crow,
The neighbouring vintner shall, ere day-
    break, know."   Sat. ix. 102–108.

Comp. also Cicero pro Marcello 3 ; the Hebrew proverb, אָזְנַיִם בַּכֹּתֶל, the wall has ears, quoted in the Midrash on this passage; which also exists in German, die Wände haben Ohren;

revile the king even in thy thoughts, and do not revile the prince even in thy bed-chamber, for the bird of the air conveyeth the report, and the winged creature telleth the

and the similar sayings in our language, *hedges have ears, the walls will speak*, &c., &c. Others, however, think that allusion is here made to the *cranes* of Ibycus (the Midrash, Grotius, Le Clerc, Schmidt, &c.), or to the custom of employing carrier-pigeons to convey despatches (Paxton, Illustrations. ii.; Kitto, Daily Bible Illustrations, Poetical Books, p. 384, &c., &c.); but there is no necessity to depart from this common proverbial phrase. The accessory particle גַּם, as frequently, serves to mark the *gradation of the idea;* we are not only to abstain from reviling the great in veiled language before the public, as in the preceding verse, but *also*, or *even*, in private it is best to guard against it. מַדָּע is a word of later Hebrew, and only occurs in 2 Chron. i. 10, 11, 12; and Dan. i. 4. 17; in which passages it denotes *knowledge.* The signification *understanding, mind, thought*, however, assigned to it here by the Septuagint (συνείδησις), the Vulgate (*cogitatio*), the Chaldee (בְּמַדְּעָךְ בְּחַבְיוֹנֵי לָךְ), Rashi (במחשבותיך), Rashbam (בקיוב לבך), Ibn Ezra (בלבך ובמחשבותיך), Luther, the Zurich Bible, Coverdale, the Bishops' Bible, the Geneva Bible, the Authorised Version, and most modern commentators, is fully established by the usage of this word in the Chaldee and Syriac, to which alone we must appeal for the meaning of a doubtful word in the later books of the Hebrew Bible; the renderings, *thy kinsfolk, acquaintance, confidant* (Le Clerc, Nachtigal, &c.), *in confidential talk* (Döderlein), *although thou knowest it, on account of thy knowledge* (Bauer, Desvoeux, &c.), *in loco concubitus tui* (Van der Palm), *in thy study* (Hengstenberg), &c., &c., are contrary to the genius of the language. The assertion that קוֹל, which denotes *language audibly uttered*, precludes the rendering of מַדָּע by *thought*, is gra-

tuitous, since both קוֹל and דָּבָר are used *hyperbolically*, as is evident from the whole tenor of the verse, which is highly figurative. Equally untenable is the objection, that this rendering is contrary to the parallelism, for thoughts are represented by the Hebrews as occupying the *innermost recesses* of the heart, and forms a suitable parallelism with the *inner chamber* of the house used as the dormitory. For קָלַל, *to revile, to speak evil*, see vii. 21, and עָשִׁיר, *noble*, see verse 6 of this chapter. קוֹל, *voice*, also *report* (comp. Gen. xlv. 16; Jer. iii. 9); so also דָּבָר, *word*, means *rumour, report* (comp. Job xli. 4. [12]). The Massoretic remark, that the ה in הַכְּנָפַיִם is *redundant*, is as little to be regarded as in verse 6, or in vi. 10, since בַּעַל, like עוֹף, is a *generic* term, and, being in the *construct state*, has the article transferred to the noun in the genitive (comp. Gesen. § 111, 1; Ewald, § 277, d, 2). We expected that the Hagadic interpretation of this verse, which takes "the king" to be *the Lord of the heavens*, and "the winged tribe," *the angel Raziel* (comp. the Midrash and the Chaldee paraphrase), would be christianised by St. Jerome and applied to better purpose, making "the king" to be *Christ the King of the Church;* "the rich," *the saints enriched with wisdom and heavenly virtues;* and "the birds of the air," *the angels;* but we are surprised at the remark of Bishop Patrick, who says, "I am not satisfied whether Solomon had not respect to something else, and intimated that *some prophet* might make the discovery, as Elisha did of many things spoken of in the king's own chamber (2 Kings vi. 9). The Chaldee paraphrase, by 'that which hath wings,' understands the heavenly ministers; and so many of the Hebrews, about which though they talk many fabulous things, yet the meaning may be

xi. 1 story. Cast thy bread upon the surface of the water, for in

the angels shall one way or other bring it to light, and give occasion to the discovery," and quotes Bishop Taylor as being of the same opinion. We have here another proof of the fact that men may be very learned, and yet not know the principles of historico-grammatical exegesis.

1. *Cast thy bread,* &c. Having shewn the *evil* which we shall escape by the exercise of wisdom in our conduct towards those *who are above us,* towards perverse kings and governors, Coheleth now adverts, on the other hand, to the *good* which will accrue to us from our wise and kind dealings with those *who are below us,* with our apparently ungrateful fellow-creatures. Hospitality, so universally practised in the East, is here recommended under seemingly the most unpromising circumstances. Bread in the East is made in cake-like shape; it is very thin, and more like what we should call flaps. The passover-bread, to the present day, is not thicker than the blade of a knife, round or oval, and about nine or ten inches in diameter (Jahn, Biblical Antiq. § 140; Kitto, Cyclop. Bib. Lit., under *Bread*), so that, when put into a stream, it would float for a time and be carried away by the current. Hence the force of the allusion in this admonition. We are to be charitable to thankless people, when the bread we have bestowed seems as if cast upon the surface of the water, where it is irrecoverably borne away by the rapidly flowing stream, since we cannot tell whether in the process of time we may not reap the benefit of it. The Arabs have a similar proverb, *Do good, cast thy bread into the water, thou shalt be repaid some day* (comp. Diez, Denkwürdigkeiten von Asien, i. 106). The comparison of that which swiftly and irreclaimably disappears, with floating matter impetuously carried away upon the surface of water, is also to be found in other parts of the Scriptures. Thus the prophet Hosea com-

pares the perishing king of Samaria to a *chip irresistibly carried away upon the surface of the water* (x. 7); and Job speaks of the wicked as being suddenly carried off, *like floating upon the surface of the water* (xxiv. 18). The verse is therefore tersely explained by Rashi עשה טובה וחסד לאדם שיאמר לך לבך עליו אל תראנו צוד כאדם שמשליך מזונותיו על פני המים, *be benevolent and charitable, even to men respecting whom thy heart tells thee thou shalt never see again, just as if one had cast his benevolence upon the surface of the water;* so also Rashbam, Ibn Ezra, Grotius, Lê Clerc, Patrick, Durell, Umbreit, Rosenmüller, Knobel, Herzfeld, Heiligstedt, Noyes, Philippson, Elster, &c. The Chaldee paraphrase, אושיט לחם פרנסותך לעניי דאזלין בספינן על אפי מיא, *give thy nourishing bread to the poor, who go in ships upon the surface of the water,* apart from restricting the charity to *navigators,* assumes an ellipsis which is inadmissible. The offshoot of this interpretation, viz., the view that *merchants are here encouraged to send their goods by sea to distant lands* (Geier, Mendelssohn, Michaelis, Döderlein, Spohn, Preston, &c.), is still more untenable, since לחם can never mean *merchandise,* and since the following verse, with which it is intimately connected, undoubtedly shews that *charity* is here intended. For the same reasons we must also reject the opinion of those who, though regarding it as an admonition to be charitable, maintain that the language is borrowed from *maritime trade* (Hengstenberg, &c.) Neither can the explanation of those be admitted who take it as commending *agricultural pursuits,* with special reference to the practice in Egypt of sowing the seed previous to the complete recession of the waters of the Nile, &c., thus rendering it *sow thy seed by the water,* &c. (Van der Palm, Bauer, &c.); or *sow thy corn before the waters,* i. e., *before the rainy season* (Desvoeux, Nachtigal, Boothroyd, &c.); or, *sow*

2 the process of time thou mayest find the profit of it; give a
portion thereof to seven and even to eight, for thou knowest

thy seed when showers approach (Hodgson), because—1. To render שַׁלַּח לַחְמְךָ by *sow thy seed*, is contrary to the *usus loquendi*; this is expressed in Hebrew by the established phrase זְרַע אֶת־זַרְעֶךָ, which is used in verse 6. 2. עַל פְּנֵי can neither mean *by, before*, nor *when*. 3. The following verse shews that *charity* is here spoken of, and not the pursuit of agriculture. Those, therefore, who, whilst admitting that it refers to charity, take it as a proverbial form of speech drawn from the manner of husbandmen (Bishops Reynolds and Lowth, The Sacred Poetry of the Hebrews, Lect. x., p. 108, ed. 1835; Holden, &c.), incur the first and second objections. רֹב, *multitude, greatness, length, process*. יָמִים, *days*, also *time*, as consisting of a succession of days (comp. Gen. xlvii. 8; 1 Sam. xxvii. 11; 1 Kings ii. 11). The pronoun in תִּמְצָאֶנּוּ, referring to לֶחֶם, stands synecdochically for the *produce* or the *benefit* of the noun to which it refers (compare אֲרוּרָה הָאֲדָמָה בַּעֲבוּרֶךָ בְּעִצָּבוֹן תֹּאכֲלֶנָּה, *cursed be the ground for thy sake; in sorrow shalt thou eat it*, i. e., *the product of it*, Gen. iii. 17; Isa. i. 7, xxxvi. 16; Jer. v. 17.

2. *Give a portion*, &c. This charity is not to be restricted to these apparently unpromising circumstances; it should be of a general character. We are to help, by our diffusive liberality, as many as we possibly can, since we know not what a day may bring forth; reverses may come upon us, and we may then be relieved by the objects of our former benevolence. חֵלֶק, *portion*, refers to לַחְמְךָ, *thy bread*, in the foregoing verse, and must be supplied here (so Rashi, Rashbam, Heiligstedt, &c.) *To seven, and also to eight*, is an idiomatic phrase, denoting *many*. Two numerals are frequently coupled together, the latter rising in the scale above the former, to express an *indefinite number, some, several, many, e.g.,*

"once and twice," *i. e., several times* (Job xxxiii. 14; Ps. lxii. 12); "twice and thrice," *i. e., often* (Job xxxiii. 29; Isa. xvii. 6); "three and four," *i. e., frequently, many* (Exod. xx. 5, xxxiv. 7; Prov. xxx. 15. 18. 21; Amos i. 3. 6. 9. 11. 13, ii. 1. 4. 6); "four and five" (Isa. xvii. 6); "six and seven," *i e., many* (Job v. 19; "seven and eight" Micah v. 4). Similar idioms exist in Greek and Latin; comp. the τρὶς καὶ τετράκις of Homer; *bis et ter, bis terque* (Cicero. Quint. Fr. iii. 8; Cels. de re Med. iv. 12); *ter quaterque, ter et quater, ter aut quater* (Horat. Od. i. 31, 13; Sat. ii. 7. 76; Virg. Georg. i. 410; Ovid. Metam. i. 179). The persons, as often, are implied in the numerals (*vide supra*, vi. 3; 1 Sam. xviii. 7; Isa. xxxvii. 36; Ps. xci. 7); so Rashi (צריכי חסר) *needy persons*, Rashbam (לכמה בני האדם) *to many men*, and most modern commentators. The Chaldee paraphrase and Ibn Ezra, however, regard these numbers as referring to *time*, the former to the *seventh and eighth month*, when we are to sow our portion of seed, and the latter to the *sacred number seven*, and the *eight days of the week*; but this is contrary to the context and the genius of the language, as this would require בַּשְּׁבִעָה and בַּשְּׁמוֹנָה. Still more artificial and objectionable is the opinion that these numbers refer to *vessels*, thus cautioning those who trade by sea *not to stow all their property in one ship, but to divide it among seven or eight vessels* (Mendelssohn, Friedländer, Preston, &c.), or, which is substantially the same, *divide* or constitute thy portion into seven or eight portions (Nachtigal, Hitzig, Stuart, &c.); vereinige dich mit sieben oder achten, *unite thyself to seven or eight*, which Spohn explains, treibst bu dein Gewerbe allein, so bist bu in Gefahr, baß bey eintretendem Unglück bein ganzes Vermögen verlohren gehe. Trifft bu aber mit mehrern in Gesellschaft, so verliehrst bu bann nur ben

3 not what misfortune there may be upon the earth.   When

einen oder den andern Theil, *if thou carriest on business alone, thou art in danger of losing the whole of thy property when misfortune comes ; but if thou enterest into partnership with several others, thou wilt only lose a part,* thus cautioning us against risking all in one adventure. מה־יהיה רָעָה stands for מַה־רָעָה יִהְיֶה ; it not unfrequently happens that the accusative, which defines more closely the thing intended, is separated by intermediate words, especially from מָה, *what,* and אֲשֶׁר, *which* (compare 2 Kings viii. 12, xii. 6 ; Esth. vi. 3 ; Ewald, § 287, h). To take this clause as an admonition to be benevolent *because impending calamities may deprive us of the means of doing good* (Rashi, Reynolds, &c.), or *because thou little knowest what misery there exists upon earth, i. e.,* " being rich, thou art ignorant to what degree poverty and misery prevail upon the earth" (Holden), is against the scope of the passage, which propounds precepts of worldly wisdom, the observance of which will yield temporal advantages. St. Jerome's explanation of this verse is really marvellous. He finds in the two numbers the two Testaments composing the Holy Scriptures ; the number " seven" being the *Old Testament,* because of the Jewish Sabbath which is therein enjoined to be celebrated on the *seventh* day; the number "eight" the *New Testament,* because the Saviour rose on the *eighth* day; "the evil" *the tortures of the wicked after death,* and " upon earth" meaning *the heretics living upon the earth.* And after expatiating upon the fact that the Jews restrict their faith to the Old Testament, the *number seven,* and Marcion, the Manichees, and other heretics to the New, the *number eight,* the sainted Father deduces from it the solemn lesson, NOS UTRIQUE CREDAMUS INSTRUMENTO ; NON ENIM POSSUMUS DIGNOS CRUCIATUS, DIGNAMQUE PÆNAM JAM NUNC MENTE COMPREHENDERE, QUÆ REPOSITA EST HIS QUI VERSANTUR IN TERRA JUDÆIS ATQUE HÆRETICIS E DUOBUS ALTERUM DENEGANTIBUS, *let us therefore believe both instruments, for indeed we cannot now comprehend the merited tortures and punishment reserved for those who are upon earth, for the Jews and heretics who deny either of them.*

3. *When the clouds,* &c. From acts of benevolence Coheleth passes over to the common work of life ; and just as he recommends *general liberality* in the former case, because our shortsightedness might sometimes lead us to withhold our gifts, which, if bestowed, would perchance yield an ample return, so he tells, with regard to our every-day employment, that we are to be *generally active.* Our ignorance of the circumstances connected with our labours (verse 3) must not keep us from putting forth our exertions (4), inasmuch as they can never be known to us (5), but, on the contrary, ought to make us always active, since, for aught we know, one or the other effort may produce the desired effect (6). According to his usual manner, the sacred writer begins with stating facts, and then deduces from them the maxim he wishes to propound. Here then are the phenomena of nature ; the rain and the wind, both at times neutralising our efforts ; the former is detrimental to the harvest, the latter to the sowing; we see the one taking place *when the clouds are filled with rain,* and the other *when the trees are blown down ;* all that we know about it beforehand, Coheleth ironically remarks, is that the tree will lie on the spot where it falls ; we know as little about the phenomena of nature as we know about the objects of our charity. The perplexity which commentators have experienced in the interpretation of this verse is owing, we believe, to their attempts to connect it with the preceding verse. Thus Rashi regards it as still enforcing the lesson of charity by a reference to the objects

the clouds are full of rain they empty it upon the earth,
and when the tree falleth in the south or north, in the
4 place where the tree falleth there it lieth ; whoso therefore
watcheth the wind shall not sow, and he who looketh at the

of nature, which freely communicate their blessings to those who stand in need of them. אם ראית עבים מלאים גשם ידעת שסופם יריקו גשמיהם על הארץ במקום שהטובה צומחת וניכרת שם סופה לנוח, *when thou seest the clouds filled with rain thou knowest that they are destined to pour down their rain upon the earth ; in the place where the good flourishes and is cut down there it is destined to abide*, i.e., for the benefit of others; so should the rich man, whom God has filled with blessings, pour them forth to others : substantially the same are Ibn Ezra, Bishop Reynolds, Grotius, Knobel, Elster, Vaihinger, &c. Others, again, whilst adopting Rashi's explanation of the first clause, regard the second as referring to death, when we are unable to do good, just as the tree, when cut down, bears no more fruit (Bishop Patrick, Rosenmüller, &c.); or explain it as describing the uncertainty of riches, thus giving a reason for the admonition to be benevolent whilst we have the means (Schmidt, &c.). Rashbam, again, takes it to set forth *disinterested* benevolence, כשם שאם ימלאו העבים גשם שהם יריקו וישפחו על הארץ וכשם שאם יפול עץ בדרום או בצפון מקום שיפול שם יהי' הוא כך אי אפשר שלא תיהנה מאותן שתתן להם חלקים משלך, *just as the clouds that are filled with rain empty their contents upon the earth, and as the tree which falls in the south or north remains in the place, so it may be that thou wilt have no advantage from those to whom thou impartest a portion of what thou hast;* whilst Michaelis, Spohn, Umbreit, &c., maintain that the whole verse describes the impossibility of *preventing misfortunes.* Without entering into the particulars of each of these interpretations severally, we submit— 1. That all of them give a most unnatural sense to the second hemistich ; and 2. That the repetition of עָנִים in the following verse, and indeed the whole tenor of it, shew beyond doubt that verses 3 and 4 are intimately and inseparably connected. All the difficulties vanish if we regard עֵץ יִפּוֹל as descriptive of the *trees uprooted and prostrated by the wind*, the approach of which we cannot foretell, just as we cannot prognosticate when it will rain, thus forming the basis of the statement in the following verse. מָקוֹם, the *accusative* of *place*, has here the force of בִּמְקוֹם, as in iii. 16, and in Esth. iv. 3, viii. 17 ; Ezek. vi. 13, where it is also in the construct state before אֲשֶׁר, for which see i. 7, and Ewald, § 332, c. יְהוּא is the apocopated future of הָיָה, with otiant א (comp הָלְכוּא for הָלְכוּ, Josh. x. 24; אָבוּא for אָבֹא, Isa. xxviii. 12; Gesen. § 44, Rem. 4 ; Ewald, § 84, c).

4. *Whoso therefore watcheth*, &c. Inference from the fact stated in the foregoing verse. This then being the case, since we cannot foretell these phenomena ; since all we know of them is when we see them marshaling their strength and committing their ravages upon the objects around us, the husbandman who watches the wind and clouds before he ventures to sow and reap, will never engage in agricultural pursuits, and have no return at all ; just as in the case of charity mentioned in verses 1 and 2, he who is over-scrupulous in the distribution of alms may frequently lose a profitable return. As often, the second part of the preceding verse is taken up first, and the first part is here the second, for which see vii. 7. How this fact could have been so generally overlooked, when *the uprooting the tree* so manifestly answers to the *wind*, and when the very expression עָנִים of the preceding verse is here repeated, is

5 clouds shall not reap. As thou knowest as little the course
  of the wind as the formation in the womb of the pregnant,
  so thou knowest not the work of God who worketh all

really surprising, especially as interpreters have ever been puzzled to
explain this verse when detached
from the foregoing one, and are
obliged to regard it as an *imperfect
comparison*, as a *protasis without the
apodosis*, which we are told to supply.
5. *As thou knowest*, &c. Having
adverted in verse 3 to the impossibility of knowing beforehand the
state of the weather, and shewn in
verse 4 *what we ought not to do* under
these circumstances, Coheleth now
submits that, great as our ignorance
is of the course of the wind, and it
is as great as that of the foetus, this
ignorance extends to all the works
of God, and then shews us in the
following verse *what we ought to do*
in such a state of shortsightedness.
The reason why the sacred writer
mentions the course of the wind
alone, and does not also allude to
the *formation of the clouds*, which
we might be led to expect at first
sight, when comparing this verse
with the preceding one, will be found
upon a more close investigation of
the context. Now, though the clouds
as well as the wind were referred to
in the preceding verse (4), yet were
the *clouds alone expressly* mentioned
in verse 3, the wind being described
only *by its effects*. It is therefore to
be expected that Coheleth, in exposing our ignorance of that which
the husbandman allows to influence
his work, would also distinctly mention the wind, and thus, with the
clouds of verse 3, give *by name* the
two objects quoted in verse 4. The
comparison of our ignorance about
the course of the wind with that of
the foetus is most striking, and expresses the *intensity* of this ignorance.
A similar comparison is used in vi.
3 to convey a *thorough* absence of
happiness. עֲצָמִים, *bones*, constituting
the principal part of the body, is
used metonymically for *the body*

itself, the bodily form (comp. Lam.
iv. 7; Ezek. xxxii. 27), *the foetus*,
and is here evidently chosen for its
assonance with עֵץ in verse 3; it is the
subject, and the predicate אֵינְךָ יוֹדֵעַ
is to be mentally supplied from the
preceding clause, as is frequently the
case (*vide* x. 12). The Septuagint
connects the first clause with the
preceding verse, ἐν οἷς οὐκ ἔστιν γινάσκων
τίς ἡ ὁδὸς τοῦ πνεύματος, *among whom
(i. e.,* those who watch the wind, &c.)
*there is none knowing what is the way
of the wind*, arbitrarily altering the
text. The Vulg., QUOMODO IGNORAS,
QUÆ SIT VIA SPIRITUS ET QUA RA-
TIONE COMPINGANTUR OSSA IN VENTRE
PRÆGNANTIS: SIC, &c., *as thou knowest
not what is the way of the spirit, and
in what manner the bones are joined
together in the womb of the pregnant,
so,* &c., which St. Jerome explains
as describing *the mysterious entrance
of the soul into the body of the foetus,
as well as the formation of the latter,*
and which is followed by the Bishops'
Bible, the Geneva Bible, the Authorised Version, Holden, Gesenius,
Fürst, &c., proceeds as usual from
the Hagadic interpretation of this
verse, and may be seen in the
Chaldee, הֵיכְמָא דְלֵיתָךְ יָדַע אֵיכְדֵין יָהֲלֵךְ רוּחַ
נִשְׁמְתָא דְחַיֵי בְּגוּף עוּלֵימָא שְׁלִילָא דְשָׁרֵי בִּמְעֵינָא
דְאִמֵּיהּ מְעַבְּרָא וְהֵיכְמָה דְלָא הִינְדַע אוֹ דְכַר אוֹ
נוּקְבָא עַד זְמַן דְאִתְיְלִיד, *as thou knowest
not how the spirit of the breath of
life enters into the body of an infant
which rests in the womb of its pregnant mother, and as thou knowest
not whether it is a male or female
until it is born,* &c., &c., and the
Midrash. But this interpretation—
1. Severs the manifest connection
between this verse and the preceding
one, by assigning, contrary to the
laws of exegesis, different senses to
רוּחַ in these two verses; 2. Most
unjustifiably paraphrases כַּעֲצָמִים בְּבֶטֶן
הַמְּלֵאָה as if it were אַךְ הָעֲצָמִים יִהְיוּ בְּבֶטֶן
or אֵי זֶה דָרֶךְ הָעֲצָמִים מְלֵאָה, no instance

6 things. Sow, then, thy seed in the morning, and withhold
   not thine hand therefrom in the evening, since thou knowest
   not which shall prosper, this or that, or whether both shall
7 be alike good; and the light shall be sweet, and it shall be

having been adduced by Gesenius
and Fürst in their lexicons, where פ
is used in such a sense, and the פ by
which it is preceded plainly shewing
that it is the *Caph comparison*; and
3. It introduces a new subject, viz.,
our ignorance of the formation and
animation of the human body, which
is foreign to the scope of the passage.
The rendering, "as thou knowest
not what is the way of the wind, just
as [thou knowest not] the bones in
the womb of her who is with child,
so thou knowest," &c., now generally
given of this verse, puts an exceedingly forced construction upon the
words, which is by no means obviated
by Rashi, who takes פ . . . כַּאֲשֶׁר as
inverted (comp. Gen. xiii. 10; Isa.
xxiv. 2), *i.e.*, "just as thou knowest
not the formation in the womb
so thou knowest not what is the way
of the wind, and so also thou knowest
not the work of God," &c.

6. *Sow, then, thy seed*, &c. The
lesson deduced from our ignorance
of the operations of God is that we
are to be always diligent. Since we
know not the course of things, and
cannot foretell whether our labours
of the former or latter part, or both
parts of the day, will be opportune,
it is safest to be constantly at work,
in which case we shall be sure to
labour at the proper time. The *inferential particle*, as frequently, is
omitted at the beginning of the verse,
and must be supplied in the translation. For *morning* and *evening*, the
two ends of the day, denoting the
whole of it, constantly, vide iii. 11;
x. 13. The ל in לָעֶרֶב stands for עֵת,
and has therefore the same meaning
as the usual בָּעֶרֶב (comp. Gen. xlix.
27; Ps. xc. 6, with Gen. viii. 11).
מִזְּרֹעַ אֶת־זַרְעֶךָ, *from sowing thy seed*,
must be mentally supplied after
אַל־תַּנַּח יָדֶךָ *withhold not thine hand.*

אֵי זֶה, *which of the two*, refers to both
the morning and evening sowing here
recommended; to which also הֲזֶה אוֹ־זֶה,
this or that (comp. Job. i. 16; Ps.
lxxv. 8), and שְׁנֵיהֶם, *both*, refer. For
יִכְשָׁר, see ii. 21. כְּאֶחָד, properly *as one*,
is used for *alike*, because when two
or more things do or suffer the same
thing, they may be regarded as identical in this respect (comp. זְאֵב וְטָלֶה
יִרְעוּ כְאֶחָד, *the wolf and the lamb shall
feed like one*, i. e., *alike*, Isa. lxv. 25;
Ezra ii. 64). The Vulgate's rendering of the last clause by ET SI
UTRUMQUE SIMUL, MELIUS ERIT, *and
if both together, it shall be better*,
which is followed by Luther, Coverdale, the Bishops' Bible, &c., making
וְאִם־שְׁנֵיהֶם כְּאֶחָד depend upon יִכְשָׁר and
טוֹבִים, a separate clause, is contrary
to the word טוֹבִים, which is the *plural*.

7. *And the light*, &c. If we will
act in accordance with the foregoing
advice; if we will be benevolent to
all our fellow-creatures, and ever diligent in our business, we shall find life
sweet, and have pleasure in living.
The *light* and the *sun* are designedly
used for *life*, in harmony with the
clouds, wind, and especially the *day*
spoken of in the foregoing verses. In
addition to what has been said in
explanation of the phrase *to see light*,
for *to live*, in vi. 5, we quote a passage
from Euripides, which is a striking
parallel to the words in question —

Μή μ᾽ ἀπολέσῃς ἄωρον. ἡδὺ γὰρ τὸ φῶς
Λεύσσειν τὰ δ᾽ ὑπὸ γῆς μή μ᾽ ἰδεῖν ἀναγκάσῃς.

Destroy not my youth, to see the light
Is sweet, oh do not hurl me into the realm
       of darkness!
                    IPHIGIN. IN AULIS, 1219-19.

The ל in לָעֵינַיִם has retained the short
vowel *Pattach*, because the guttural ע,
which, like ה and ח, allows a sharpening of the syllable, though orthogra-
phically excluding the *Dagesh forte*
(comp. 1 Sam. xvi. 7; Ezek. xii. 12;

8 cheering to the eyes to see the sun. For even if a man should live many years, he ought to rejoice in them all, and to remember that there will be many dark days, that all

Ewald, § 50, b). To make this verse begin a new paragraph, *commending the enjoyment of life* (Mendelssohn, Knobel, Herzfeld, &c.), or to take it as giving a *reason* why the preceding verses urge that man should industriously provide for life, viz., since notwithstanding all the evils connected with it, life has many enjoyments (Hitzig, Stuart, Hengstenberg, &c.), or to regard it as furnishing "another argument in favour of charity, to this effect: However great may be the sweets and pleasures of life, and whatever delights a man may enjoy, yet seasons of pain, and sickness, and sorrow will occur; and the experience of human frailty should melt his heart to active benevolence towards every suffering child of the dust" (Holden), is doing violence to the text and context unnecessarily. The explanation we have given leaves to the words their natural meaning, and is in harmony with the scope of the passage. The Syriac version, "light is sweet, and is pleasant to the eyes, and especially to those who see the sun," is nonsense; for those who cannot see the sun have no pleasure in light.

8. *For even if a man*, &c. The reason why man should put forth all those exertions to make life comfortable is, that this is the only scene of enjoyment; we ought therefore to make of it an uninterrupted holiday, however long our earthly existence, since we must remember the many dark and joyless days that will succeed it, when we shall moulder in the dust. The Egyptians, too, urged death as a reason for enjoying life. Herodotus tells us that at their feasts "a servant carries round to the several guests a coffin, in which there is the image of a dead body carved in wood, and painted to resemble nature as nearly as possible, about a cubit or two cubits in length; and, shewing

this to each of the company, he says, 'Gaze here; then drink and be merry, for when you die, such will you be'" (ii. 78). This is the natural result, if a future state is denied. Compare Sirach ii. 24; Book of Wisdom ii. 1, &c.; 1 Cor. xv. 32; Hor. Od. lib. ii., od. iii. 13. כִּי, as usual, is *causal*, and assigns a reason *why every exertion should be made to procure enjoyment.* For רַבִּים, *masculine*, instead of רַבּוֹת, *feminine*, referring to שָׁנִים, a *feminine* noun, see ii. 6. יִשְׂמָח and יִזְכֹּר are not to be rendered *indicatively*, as Döderlein, Rosenmüller, De Wette, Noyes, &c., will have it, who regard this verse as giving a reason *why* life is called sweet in the preceding verse (viz., *because if a man live many years he rejoices in them all*, &c.), as this contradicts the frequent complaints made in this book about the unnecessary anxieties and trouble which men create for themselves, and the constant *admonition to enjoy life*, and is based upon a misunderstanding of the preceding verse, but are to be rendered *obligatory;* and the ו in וְיִזְכֹּר is also *causal*, and introduces the *principal reason*, i.e., life must be enjoyed, since we must bear in mind that this is the only scene of enjoyment, that a protracted, dreary, and joyless state is to follow it, וְיִזְכֹּר אֶת־יְמֵי הַחֹשֶׁךְ כִּי־הַרְבֵּה יִהְיוּ is, again, an attraction for וְיִזְכֹּר כִּי־הַרְבֵּה יִהְיוּ יְמֵי הַחֹשֶׁךְ, for which see ii. 24. כָּל־שֶׁבָּא is dependent upon כִּי וְיִזְכֹּר, *he must remember that all which is coming is vanity, i.e.,* that the hereafter is all nothing. The different interpretations of this verse are as conflicting as they are numerous. The Vulgate, SI ANNIS MULTIS VIXERIT HOMO, ET IN HIS OMNIBUS LÆTATUS FUERIT, MEMINISSE DEBET TENEBROSI TEMPORIS, ET DIERUM MULTORUM, QUI CUM VENERINT, VANITATIS ARGUENTUR, PRÆTERITA, *if a man live many years, and have rejoiced in them all, he ought to remember the dark*

9 which is coming is vanity! Rejoice, O young man, in thy
youth, and let thy heart cheer thee in thy youthful days,
and pursue the ways of thine heart, and the things which
are seen by the eyes, and know that, respecting all these,

*time, and the many days wherein, when
they shall come, the things passed shall
be accused of vanity,* is utterly at
variance with the text and context,
and evidently proceeds from the
Hagadic interpretation of this verse,
which converts it into an orthodox
remark cautioning us against sin
(comp. the Chaldee and the Midrash).
Hence also the explanation of Rashi,
" if a man live ;many years he will
rejoice in all good things, for he will
remember that the days of darkness
for the sinner shall be many ; all that
shall come upon him will be distress;"
and substantially the same Rashbam.
Ibn Ezra, again, submits that the
meaning of the verse is "even if a
man knew that he would live many
years, and rejoice in them all, yet
when he remembers the days of darkness in the grave that they will be
many, every one that comes into the
world is vanity. to him," which is
substantially followed by Desvoeux,
&c. These far-fetched explanations
are fully equalled by the rendering of
Luther, wenn ein Menſch lange Zeit
lebt, und iſt fröhlich in allen Dingen,
ſo gedenket er doch nur der böſen
Tage daß ihrer ſo viel iſt; denn alles
was ihm begegnet iſt, iſt eitel, *if a
man live a long time and rejoice in all
things, he still only remembers the evil
days that they are many, for all which
happened to him is vanity;* and Coverdale, " if a man live many years and
be glad in them all, let him remember the days of darkness, which shall
be many; and when they come, all
things shall be but vain." Equally
inadmissible is the interpretation of
those who regard this verse as admonishing those who enjoy life never
to forget that we must also *suffer*
(Holden, Stuart, &c.), since — 1. Coheleth could not so definitely affirm
that *every* man will suffer, and that,

too, *many years ;* 2. It is most incongruous to admonish a man to
rejoice every year of his life (בְּכֻלָּם),
and yet in the same breath tell him
that he will have many a 'long year
of afflictions, when he will be unable
to enjoy himself; and 3. The terms
light and *sun,* used in the preceding
verse for *life,* plainly shew that the
phrase *the days of darkness* is used
antithetically for death (comp. also
Ps. lxxxviii. 12, 13, cxliii. 3 ; Job
x. 21).

9. *Rejoice, O young man,* &c. The
appalling conclusion stated in the
foregoing verse, to which Coheleth
was driven again and again by reasoning upon the current view about
the destiny of man, and the fact that
there can be no true enjoyment here
with the prospect of annihilation
before us, which chills and mars our
earthly pleasures, leaves the cravings
of the soul unsatisfied, and wrings
from the agonising heart, panting
after something higher and imperishable, the desponding and repeated
cry, "Vanity of vanities ; all is
vanity!" leads him at last to the true
way of happiness. To be really happy,
we must not only lead a cheerful life,
and enjoy the earthly pleasures and
blessings wherewith a benign Creator
has so largely blessed us, but *look
forward to a future bar of judgment,*
which will regulate our conduct, restrain our enjoyments within lawful
bounds, and make them consistent
with our thoughts of a righteous
retribution from a holy God. This
enjoyment is to commence in that
period of life when pleasures are most
innocent, easily attainable, and un-
alloyed by cares and anxieties. It is
to begin at that age which influences
the whole of our after life; a cheerful
and happy disposition cultivated in
our youth will yield its rich harvest

10 God will bring thee into judgment.　Banish, therefore,
sorrow from thy mind, and put away sadness from thy body,

in old age. For similar reasons is piety urged upon the young especially, in xii. 1. The בְּ in בְּיַלְדוּתֶךָ does not mark the *object* at which one is to rejoice (Doderlein, Schmidt, &c.), but denotes the *time*, and stands for בִּימֵי (comp. Isa. ix. 2), as is evident from the parallelism. As the heart is regarded as the *source of happiness*, whence joy, as it were, gushes forth upon the whole body (Prov. xiv. 30, xv. 13), hence it is here represented as *making man cheerful*. For the *passive* signification of מַרְאֵה, see vi. 9. The Massoretic reading מַרְאֵה, *singular*, instead of מַרְאֵי, *plural*, which is also to be found in forty-one of Kennicott's MSS., has evidently arisen from a desire of making this passage uniform with vi. 9, as well as from taking it as an *abstract*, or for the *act of seeing*, which also accounts for the Septuagint, the Vulg., the Syriac, and the Chaldee renderings. Herzfeld justly remarks that the abnormal *Quametz* under the ר in וְרָע, instead of the normal *Pattach*, is owing to the accent *Sakefgadol*, which not unfrequently lengthens the *Segol* into *Pattach* (comp. וַיֹּאמַר, Gen. xliii. 29, xlvii. 30), and more especially to the sense, drawing our attention to the very momentous doctrine propounded in this clause, and constituting it, as it were, a separate clause calling for a pause and reflection (comp. Ewald, § 100, c). Thinking that the former part of this verse speaks too much about present enjoyment, the Hagada tried to modify the words of the text, explaining וְהַלֵּךְ בְּדַרְכֵי לִבְּךָ וּבְמַרְאֵי עֵינֶךָ by וֶאֱזִיל בְּעִנְוְתָנוּתָא עִם אָרְחֵי לִבָּךְ וּתְהֵי זָהִיר בְּחֶזְוָינִי עֵינָךְ וְלָא תַסְתַּכֵּל בְּבִישׁ, *and walk in meekness with the ways of thine heart, and be careful as to the seeing of thine eyes, and do not look upon evil* (comp. also the Midrash, *in loco*). Hence the rendering of the Septuagint, καὶ περιπάτει ἐν ὁδοῖς καρδίας σου ἄμωμος καὶ μὴ ἐν ὁράσει ὀφθαλμῶν σου, *and walk in*

the ways of thine heart blamelessly, and not after the sight of thine eyes,* which the Vulgate, the Syriac, and St. Jerome rightly reject. Rashi, Rashbam, and Ibn Ezra, who are also dissatisfied with such arbitrary treatment of the text, try to explain away this recommendation to enjoy life, by regarding it as *ironical*. But against this are — 1. All the parallel passages (ii 10. 24, iii. 12, 13. 22, v. 18, vi. 9, vii. 14, viii. 15, ix. 7 – 9), in which present enjoyment is *seriously* recommended; 2. The intimate connection of this verse with the immediately following one, where the same idea is expressed in a different form; and 3. The design of the whole book, which is to cure the *melancholy* state into which the people had at that time fallen, and to subvert the systems of *ascetic life* which many had reared in consequence of their temporal sufferings, and their limiting retributive justice to this side of the grave. The apparent contradiction between this recommendation and the prohibition in Numb. xv. 39, mentioned in the Midrash (see also *supra*, p. 56), which has given rise to this unnatural interpretation, is removed by the fact that *two different kinds of pleasure* are spoken of in these two places. Moses prohibits *illicit* gratifications, whilst Coheleth recommends *innocent* pleasures, which pleasures are to be in harmony with our preparation for a future account of all our doings at the bar of judgment.

10. *Banish, therefore, sorrow,* &c. Having shewn, in the foregoing verse, that true happiness consists in both *enjoying the present* and *looking forward to a future state*, Coheleth now submits that we ought to regulate our life accordingly. The first remark contained in the first clause, viz., about enjoying the present, is taken up first. Here it is expressed in a *negative* form, that we are to

xii.1 for youth and manhood are vanity; and remember thy

banish all sorrow and sadness from our minds and bodies; there it is stated in a *positive* form, that we are to enjoy all earthly happiness. The additional reason here given for enjoying this life is strikingly different from the one given in verse 8. In verse 8, starting from the view that there is no hereafter, the *vanity of the future* is urged as an argument for enjoying the present; here, after having asserted that there is a final day of judgment, the *vanity of the present life* is given as a reason for not leading a life of anxiety and care. That כַּעַס and רָעָה denote *care* and *trouble*, is evident from the context, and from i. 18, vii. 3. St. Jerome's explanation, IN IRA OMNES PERTUR- BATIONES ANIMI COMPREHENDIT; IN CARNIS MALITIA UNIVERSAS SIGNIFICAT CORPORIS VOLUPTATES, *in anger* (the Preacher) *comprehends all the passions of the mind, and by wickedness of the flesh he indicates all the pleasures of the body*, which is followed by the Geneva Bible, the Authorised Version, Reynolds, Patrick, Hodgson, Holden, &c , is preposterous, and is rightly rejected by Luther, the Zurich Bible, Desvoeux, Knobel, Herzfeld, and most modern commentators. שַׁחֲרוּת is not from שָׁחַר, *to dawn* (Gesenius, Knobel, &c.), as this would describe *early childhood*, which can- not be meant here, being incom- patible with cares and anxieties, but from שָׁחֹר, *to be black*, and accordingly denotes the *age when the hair of man is black = manhood*, as opposed to שֵׂיבָה, which describes the time of life when the hair is *white* or *grey = old age*. The Chaldee has therefore ap- propriately rendered it by יוֹמֵי אוּכָמוּת שְׂעַר, *the days of black hair*; so also St. Jerome, Rashi, Rashbam, Ibn Ezra, Herzfeld, and Philippson; the latter rightly appeal to the Talmudic phrase שחורי הראש, *black-haired heads* (Nedarim 30, b), to denote *manhood*. This derivation shews more definitely the distinction between יַלְדוּת and שַׁחֲרוּת; the former means *youth*, the

latter *manhood*. The Septuagint's rendering of it by ἄνοια, *folly;* the Vulgate *voluptas;* and the Syriac

ܠܐ ܝܺܕܰܥܬ݂ܳܐ, *and not knowledge*, are unwarrantable departures from the signification of the word. Hodgson's rendering, " for youth and its lusts are vanity," surpasses these versions.

1. *And remember*, &c. The second remark, contained in the second clause of xi. 9, is now taken up. Since God will one day hold us ac- countable for all the works done in the body, we are to set the Lord always before our eyes; we are to re- member that he made us, and not we ourselves, and hence the lives which he has given us are to be spent in accordance with the laws he has in- stituted. The youth especially is warned to remember his Creator, be- cause at this period of life the pas- sions are strong, and the powers of discretion and restraint are feeble; and nothing is so sure to save him from turning the innocent pleasures recommended to him into voluptuous- ness and sensuality, as constantly bearing in mind that there is a right- eous Judge, who holds us accountable for every action, from our very youth to the last moment of our existence. Moreover, the same reason which Coheleth used in urging cheerfulness upon the youth (xi. 9), also holds good with regard to religion. The youthful heart is more impressible, and the impressions received in tender age are hardly ever obliterated, and frequently influence the whole of one's after life. The ו in וּזְכֹר is not *inferential*, but is the regular *copula*, shewing the intimate connection of this verse with the preceding one; both resuming and elaborating upon the two remarks made in xi. 9. בּוֹרְאִים, like אֱלֹהִים, *God*, קְדֹשִׁים, *the Holy One* (Prov. ix. 10, xxx. 3; Hos. xii. 1), and several titles of *man* (Gen. xli., xlii. 30; Isa. xix. 4, xxxvii. 6) is plural; the ancients

Creator in the days of thy youth, before the days of evil
come, and the years arrive of which thou shalt say, I have
2 no pleasure in them : before the sun becometh dark, and

from time immemorial conceived
might, power, and *dominion* as something distributed and manifold, see
v. 10. The assertion of Holden and
others, that "the employment of a
plural appellation of God, in this
and other passages of Scripture, was
designed to indicate, though obscurely, a plurality of persons in the
Divine Essence," greatly injures the
true faith, and works into the hands
of the enemies of this doctrine. The
reading בְּרָאֶךָ, in the *singular*, which
is found in one hundred and forty-
two of Kennicott's MSS., and is
adopted by Houbigant, Spohn, &c.,
is contrary to the general usage of
the appellations, and has evidently
arisen either from a desire to do
away with an apparent anomaly, or
from an inadvertent dropping of the
insignificant י, than which nothing is
more easy and frequent. The appeal
to the ancient versions, which, we are
told (Houbigant, Spohn, Davidson,
the Hebrew Text Revised from Critical Sources, p. 195), have all the
singular, is preposterous. Who would
ever think of appealing to Luther,
Coverdale, the Geneva Bible, the
Authorised Version, all of which
have the singular, to prove that the
original from which they were made
had the singular? These languages
have not the same idiom, and to
express it literally would represent
the Hebrews as polytheists. Schmidt
and Nachtigal's rendering, freue dich
deines Daseins, *rejoice at thy existence*,
i.e., do not overlook that thou art created, comparing בּוֹרְאֶיךָ with γεννηθέντες,
which stands for βιωσάντες (Wisdom v.
13), or deriving it from the Arabic בּרא,
sanitas, and making it denote die
Jahre der Blüthe der Gesundheit, *the
years of blossoming health*, only shews
what learned blunders learned men
may commit.

Before the days of evil, &c. We
are to remember our Creator before

the vigour of life is wasted in carnal
pleasures and sensuous gratifications ; before we have contracted
the penalties of excess, and become
weary of our merited sufferings;
before we are constrained, in a
miserable old age, despondingly to
exclaim, "I have no pleasure in life!"
עַד is frequently used as a conjunction, *whilst*, joined to שֶׁ = אֲשֶׁר it
denotes *whilst that* (Song of Songs
i. 12), and to לֹא it means *while not*
(Prov. viii. 26), so that עַד אֲשֶׁר לֹא signifies *while that not*, i e., *before*, and
is well rendered by Symmachus πρίν,
the Vulgate *antequam*, the Syriac
ܠܐܡܬܝ , and the Chald. עַד דְּלָא, the latter
exactly corresponds to the Hebrew.
It is to be observed that this combination עַד אֲשֶׁר לֹא is repeated three
times in this description, viz., here,
in the following verse, and in verse 6,
to mark the transition from one subject to another   יְמֵי הָרָעָה, *the days
of evil* do not refer to *the ordinary
infirmities of old age*, the ills that
flesh is heir to, but characterise a
suffering old age brought about by
excess and lewdness, the result of
having spent the youth of one's life
in carnal gratifications, *in forgetfulness of the Creator*. For אֲשֶׁר הָאִמִיר,
see i. 10, and for בָּהֶם *masculine*,
instead of בָּהֵן, feminine, referring to
שָׁנִים, a *feminine* noun, see ii. 6.

2. *Before the sun*, &c. From this
miserable *old age* Coheleth passes
over to the *approach of death*, which
he describes, under the figure of a
gathering storm, when the splendour
of the heavenly lights (the whole
day, i. e., twenty-four hours) is obscured by the ever-returning clouds
charged with fresh rain. Nothing
could be more fitly compared with the
approach of death to seize its victim,
striking terror into all the inmates
of the house, and defying all efforts of
power and skill, than the threatening

the light, and the moon, and the stars, and the clouds
3 return after the rain; when the keepers of the house shall

tempest, which makes masters and servants, men and women, quake alike, and puts a stop to all business. Modern commentators, having implicitly followed the Hagadic opinion that this is an allegorical description of *old age*, have experienced the greatest difficulty, and advanced the most contradictory statements, in their expositions of this and the three following verses. The uniform calmness of diction which prevails throughout the book; the absence of even the slightest indication, on the part of the sacred writer, that he here intends to give us an allegory; the violation done to the text, to carry it through, which cannot be done after all, as will be seen in the sequel; the perfect confusion of opinions as to what the different parts of this supposed allegory mean; the tastelessness and obscenity palmed upon the beautiful and graphic description; and, above all, the fact that a *gathering tempest* is here depicted, shew the mistake which modern commentators have committed in not rejecting the Hagadic exposition here, which they have rightly rejected throughout the book. The best refutation, however, of this allegorical exposition is, we believe, to give in every place the tone and character of these conflicting views. עַד אֲשֶׁר לֹא, *before*, marks the transition from *old age* to the *day of death*, הָאוֹר is not *the dawn* (אור השחר שיעלה טרם וזרח השמש ויעמוד אחר בואו שעה וגו׳, Ibn Ezra), nor *the light shining between the setting of the sun and the rising of the moon, called the evening red*, Michaelis), nor is it inserted *simply for the sake of accumulation* (Knobel), but is *the light* which, according to the Bible and many nations of antiquity, and some modern philosophers, *exists independently of the sun* (comp. Kalisch on Genesis, p. 64). The Syriac wrongly takes it as the construct to the following

words, *i.e., the light of the moon and the stars*, whilst Spohn expunges it from the text altogether. The Talmud (Shabbath, 152, a) and Rashi take the darkening of the sun, the light, the moon and the stars, for the darkening of *the forehead, the nose, the soul, and the teeth;* the Chaldee for the obscuring of *the face, the eyes, the cheeks, and the apples of the eyes*, whilst Dr. Smith (The Portraiture of Old Age, pp. 27–47), for the decay of *all the mental faculties.*

And the clouds return, &c. Ordinarily the clouds depart, and the sky clears up after the rain, but in the threatening storm here described they return with fresh rain after having discharged their contents, thus obscuring the sun, light, moon, and stars. According to the Chaldee and Rashi, this refers to *the distilling of tears;* according to Rashbam, Bishop Reynolds, Grotius, Knobel, and others, it denotes a *perpetual succession of sufferings;* according to Ibn Ezra, it means *the constant dimness of the eyes;* according to Le Clerc and others, it means *a bad influenza, accompanied with never-ceasing snuffling.*

3. *When the keepers of the house,* &c. In that portentous day every one shall be seized with consternation, men and women, menials and superiors, shall quake alike. בַּיּוֹם, *in the day*, as frequently, is used as a conjunction of time, denoting *when* (comp. Gen. ii. 4, iii. 5, v. 1, 2; 2 Sam. xxii. 1), and refers to the four-and-twenty hours during which the darkness described in the preceding verse shall prevail. זוּעַ, *to tremble, to quake*, only occurs twice more in Biblical Hebrew (Esth. v. 9; Habak. ii. 7), but is frequently used in Aramæan. שֹׁמְרֵי הַבַּיִת, *the keepers of the house*, are *menial servants*, whose business it is to guard the premises against robbers or marauders, whilst אַנְשֵׁי הֶחָיִל, *the men of power*, are *supe-*

quake, and the men of power writhe, and the grinding-maids shall stop because they have greatly diminished, and the women who look out of the windows shall be shrouded
4 in darkness; and the door shall be closed in the street:

riors. עוה, *to bend* (*vide supra*, i. 15) in the Hithpael, *to bend one's-self, to twist, to writhe.* According to the Talmud (*l.c.*) and Rashi, "the keepers of the house" are *the ribs and the loins ;* according to the Chaldee, *the knees;* according to Ibn Ezra, Grotius, Knobel, &c., *the hands and arms;* according to Bishop Reynolds, *the head, the arms. and the ribs.* "The men of power," again, we are told by the Talmud (*l. c.*), Rashi, Rashbam, Ibn Ezra, mean *the thighs,* by the Chaldee paraphrast we are assured that they signify *the arms,* by Reynolds that they denote *the legs and thighs,* or *the back,* and by Holden and Knobel that they represent *the knees and legs,* or *the legs alone.*
And the grinding-maids, &c. The allusion here made to mills and grinding-maids will appear very striking, if we bear in mind the ancient customs connected therewith. A mill formed a most important and indispensable utensil in Eastern housekeeping, as there were no public mills or bakers except the king's (Gen. xl. 2; Hos. vii. 4–8), and as the warm climate, drying up the bread and rendering it insipid, made it necessary both to grind and bake daily. Hence the benevolent enactment of the Law to take no mill or millstone in pledge (Deut. xxiv. 6). The grinding was generally done in the evening, and the noise arising from the simultaneous performance in a large number of houses or tents was very great, so much so that allusion is made to it in the Scriptures (Jerem. xxv. 10; Rev. xviii. 22, 23), as indicative of an active and happy population. A stoppage of the mills, occasioned by a storm as described in the text, would be as terrible as a cessation of business in our towns under similar circumstances.

It was generally the custom to employ *women* at these mills; the labour was very hard, and menial female slaves, and sometimes captives taken in war, were made to perform it (comp. Exod. xi. 5; Job xxxi. 10, 11; Isa. xlvii. 2; Matt. xxiv. 41; Jahn, Bib. Antiq. § 139 ; Kitto, Cyclopædia of Bib. Lit. under *Mill*). "The women who look out of the windows" are women of a higher class, not engaged in rude labour, but who amuse themselves in this way, as is still done in the East. The *wives* and *daughters,* not having the liberty of going into the streets, find it a great source of amusement to look through the latticed windows in the houses of their confinement, to see what is going on outside. Hence we find that, under alarming circumstances, when fear would make Western women rush into the streets, "the mother of Sisera" is represented as "looking out at the window, and crying through the lattice" (Judg. v. 28). Thus the two classes of women mentioned in this clause, viz., *the grinding slaves* and *the ladies of the house,* exactly correspond to the two classes of men described in the former hemistich, viz., *the outdoor watches* and *the men of power.* בטל, *to pause, to rest, to stop,* only occurs here, but is frequently used in Aramæan. כי is *causal,* giving a reason why the women stopped grinding. מעטו, the Piel, is the *intensive* of Kal, and means *they have greatly diminished.* "The female-grinders," the allegorisers tell us, mean the *teeth,* and "the women looking out of the windows" are the *eyes;* but this is a very coarse and unpoetical name for teeth, and breaks down the allegory, inasmuch as the expression *grinders* vulgarly denotes teeth.
4 *And the door,* &c. Out of terror

when the noise of the mill shall grow faint, and the swallow
shall rise to shriek, and all the singing birds shall retire;

every door shall be barred, and the great noise of the mills, arising from simultaneous grinding in every house, shall grow very feeble, because the grinders shall hide themselves, frightened at this gathering storm. " The door shall be closed," we are assured with equal confidence, means the most opposite and contradictory things, *the pores of the body* (the Talmud, *l. c.*, Rashi, Rashbam, Dr. Smith, &c.), *the fettering of the feet* (the Chaldee), *the lips* (Ibn Ezra), *the eyes* (Hengstenberg) ; whereas " the sound of the mills shall be low" denotes *the mastication and the grinding of the food in the stomach* (Talmud, *l. c.*, Rashi, Rashbam, Ibn Ezra, Dr. Smith, Holden, &c.), *the appetite for food shall depart* (the Chaldee), *the human voice shall grow feeble*, or *the enunciation shall become difficult* (Geier, Grotius, Döderlein, &c.) The ב in בְּשִׁיק has here its natural *local* meaning, denoting the place where the closing of the doors takes place, *i. e.*, *in the street.* שְׁפַל is the *infinitive construct,* according to the analogy of שְׁכַב, with the preposition בְּ denoting *time* (compare Gesen. § 132, 2). טַחֲנָה is not *grinding-maid* or *miller* (the Septuagint, the Vulgate, Luther, the Zürich Bible, Coverdale, the Bishops' Bible, Desvœux, &c.), nor *grinding* (the Geneva Bible, the Auth. Version, Ewald, Noyes, &c.), but *mill* (Rashbam, Ibn Ezra, Hodgson, Spohn, Knobel, De Wette, Gesenius, Herzfeld, Heiligstedt, Hitzig, Stuart, Elster, Vaihinger, Philippson, Fürst, and almost all modern critics and lexicographers, Hengstenberg not excepted, for he, too, renders it bie Mühle, only that his English translator has mistaken it for bas Mahlen, and translates it " *grinding* "). Though the word occurs nowhere else in Biblical Hebrew its sense is indubitable, inasmuch as it is the common expression for *mill* amongst the Hebrews.

And the swallow, &c. Exceedingly beautiful and characteristic is the description of the change of birds in the gloomy atmosphere. The portentous swallows, in anticipation of the storm, quit their nests with shrieks to fly about; whilst the singing birds, which mount the air with their warbling songs, for the same reason descend and retire. That הַצִּפּוֹר is the subject of וְיָקֻם is evident from the following clause, where the parallel בְּנוֹת הַשִּׁיר is the subject of וְיִשַּׁחוּ, and from the whole tenor of the description. As the Hebrews use the generic term הַצִּפּוֹר, the *bird*, in descriptions, the *particular* bird intended must be gathered from the tone of the passage, and expressed in the translation. Here the *swallow* is most probably meant, which flies about shrieking before the approach of the storm. קוּם לְקוֹל, to *arise for a noise,* i. e., to *arise to make a noise,* just as קוּם לַמִּשְׁפָּט, *to rise for judgment,* means *to rise to execute judgment* (Ps. lxxvi. 10); קוּם לִמְנוּחָה, *to rise for rest,* is *to rise to take rest* (Ps. cxxxii. 8); קוּם לַמִּלְחָמָה, *to rise for war,* is *to rise to wage war* (Jer. xlix. 14). יִשַּׁחוּ, the Niphal of שָׁחַח, *to be brought low,* is *they lower themselves, they descend* (the reflexive being the primary signification of this conjugation, comp. Gesen. § 51, 2; Ewald, § 123, b), and forms a beautiful contrast to יָקֻם, one class of birds *rising,* the other *retiring.* For the *masculine* יִשַּׁחוּ, instead of the *feminine* תִּשַּׁחוּ, referring to the *feminine* noun בְּנוֹת, see vii. 7. בְּנוֹת הַשִּׁיר, literally *the daughters of song,* denotes, according to a common idiom, *song-stresses* (*vide supra,* x. 17), here *singing birds,* as is evident from the parallelism and the whole scope of the passage. In Syriac, too, בַּר זְמִירָא, is a *singing bird* (comp. Die Fabeln bes Sophos, herausgegeben von Julius Landsberger, S. 3). As this simple and natural construction, representing the commotion of the birds in

5 yea the people shall be frightened at that which is coming

anticipation of the storm, is fatal to the allegorical interpretation, which regards the whole description as " *a portraiture of old age*," the defenders of the allegory have been driven to force the most unnatural constructions upon this part of the verse. Thus the Hagadic explanation, as contained in the Talmud (*l. c.*), the Midrash, and the Chaldee, and followed by the Septuagint, the Vulgate, the Syriac, St. Jerome, Rashi, Rashbam, Ibn Ezra, Luther, the Zurich Bible, Coverdale, the Bishops' Bible, the Geneva Bible, the Auth. Version, and almost all modern critics, takes *the aged man* as the subject of יָקוּם, *and he shall rise*, which St. Jerome explains FRIGESCENTE JAM SANGUINE, ET HUMORE SICCATO QUIBUS MATERIIS SOPOR ALITUR, AD LEVEM SONITUM EVIGILAT, NOCTISQUE MEDIO QUUM GALLUS CECINERIT EXURGIT, NEQUAQUAM VALENS STRATO SÆPIUS MEMBRA CONVERTERE, *the blood now growing cold, and the moisture being dried up whereby sleep is nourished, he awakens at the slightest sound, and in the middle of the night when the cock crows he rises quickly, not being able frequently to turn his limbs in bed*, and which is espoused by almost all the allegorisers of the present day. But against this interpretation is to be urged — 1. That though aged people may easily be awakened by a slight noise, yet they do not *rise up* at the sound of a bird; if simple awaking were intended, Coheleth would undoubtedly have used יֵעוֹר and not יָקוּם. Ewald, Hitzig, Stuart, and Philippson saw this, but, adhering to the allegory, were constrained to resort to a still more unnatural explanation, and to refer יָקוּם to קוֹל הַצִּפּוֹר, *es sich zur Sperlingsstimme anläßt*, i. e., *the noise of the mill rises to the voice of a sparrow*, which is against the parallelism, and contrary to the expression יָקוּם, *rises*, inasmuch as it is preposterous to characterise the greater noise of the mill, *when reduced* to that of a sparrow, as *rising*, and

which would have been conveyed to us without יָקוּם, viz., בְּשָׁפַל הַטַּחֲנָה לְקוֹל הַצִּפּוֹר, *when the noise of the mill is lowered to the voice of a bird*. 2. The *plural* יִרָאוּ in the following verse shews that יָקוּם, the *singular*, and the *plural* יִרָאוּ, do not refer to the same subject, the *aged man;* and, 3. That it is contradicted by the following clause, where בְּנוֹת הַשִּׁיר, which answers to צִפּוֹר in the first clause, is the *subject*. But, apart from the violence done to the text, the deathblow to the allegory is the fact that it falls through in this clause, and that its defenders are obliged to give to the passage before us a *literal interpretation*, viz., that the voice of the bird is literally the voice of the bird, and that rising means rising up; whilst the immediately following clause is again explained *allegorically*, and the words וְיִשַּׁחוּ כָּל־בְּנוֹת הַשִּׁיר are made to signify *music and songs shall be a bore to him* (Talmud, *l. c.*) ; *the lips shall relax, so that he shall not be able to sing* (the Chaldee) ; *his ears shall be heavy* (St. Jerome, Grotius. Bishop Patrick); *he shall despise all singers and songstresses* (Rashi, Rashbam, &c.); *his throat shall be disabled* (Ibn Ezra) ; *all the organs employed in the production and enjoyment of music are rendered powerless to afford delight* (Dr. Smith, Holden, &c.) ; *all song-singing is low* (Hitzig, Stuart, &c.)

5. *Yea the people shall be frightened*, &c. All this consternation will arise from the dread which people shall have of the awful storm gathering over their heads, and of the terrors which are on their way. גַּם, as frequently, is used by way of *emphasis*, and can hardly be translated ; the nearest approach to it is our word *yea* (comp. Gesen. Lex. *s. v.*). גָּבֹהַּ. the *height*, because there storms gather. For יִרָאוּ, the third person plural used *impersonally*, see i. 10. הַתְחַת is not an *adjective* (Gesenius, Lex. *s. v.;* Herzfeld, &c.), as this is contrary to the analogous form גְּלִל, but is a noun (see Ewald, § 158. b), from חָתַת, *to*

from on high, and at the terrors which are on their way; and
the almond shall be despised, and the locust shall be loathed,

fear, denoting *fear, terror*, and is dependent upon the verb יִירָאוּ; the מִ from מִנְּבֹהַּ, is to be mentally supplied before it. Here, again, most commentators have been compelled to abandon the allegory, and take it as referring to the *incapacity of aged people to ascend high places, owing to weakness*, *shortness of sight and breath, and to the timidity of old people to walk in public ways*, arising either from apprehension lest anything should happen to them, or from the weakness of their limbs; so the Talmud (*l. c.*), St. Jerome, Bishop Reynolds, Holden, Knobel; or, as Ibn Ezra will have it, יראו מחשבותיו שהרוח חושבת שהיא נוסעת והולכת אל מקום גבה, *he shall be afraid of his thoughts, which dwell upon the fact that his spirit will soon depart and go to the high heaven.*

And the almond, &c. In the midst of such a confusing and terrifying scene the most delicate and inviting fruit will have no charm, but only create disgust and be left untouched. It is well known that the delicious almond is a highly prized fruit in the East, and great indeed must be the consternation of an Oriental which makes him disgusted with this delicacy. יָנֵאץ a contraction of the apocopated יָנֵץ, from יָאֵץ (compare Gesen. § 73, 2, Rem. 4) is, as Ibn Ezra has already remarked, from נָאַץ, *to deride, to despise, to disgust,* and in the Hiphil signifies *causes disgust;* so also the Zurich Bible, Coverdale, Michaelis, Desvoeux, Hodgson, Gesenius, Knobel, De Wette, Herzfeld, Noyes, Hitzig, Stuart, Elster, &c. The rendering, *and the almond tree shall blossom* (the Septuagint, the Vulgate, the Syriac, Rashi, Rashbam, Luther, the Geneva Bible, the Authorised Version, and many modern commentators), deriving it from נוץ or נָצַץ, *to flourish*, has entirely arisen from the allegorical interpretation, and is contrary to the form of the word, as יָנֵאץ for יָנֵץ has no

parallel in Hebrew. Besides, the predicates of the other two nouns, which express *the inability to enjoy that which has been highly esteemed*, as well as the scope of the passage, are utterly at variance with this derivation. The Syriac, ܣܘܒܠ

ܚܣܘܠܟ ܦܗܝ̈ܐ ܣܒ̈ܚܐ ܦܓܪܐ ܘܢܐܙܠ,

and the watch shall rush upon him, and the almond shall flourish, doubly translates וְיָנֵאץ הַשָּׁקֵד, taking יָנֵאץ from נוץ in the twofold sense of *to fly, rush, i.q.*, נוס, and *to flourish*, and assigning to שָׁקֵד, from שָׁקַד, *to watch* (comp. Ps. cxxvii. 1; Jer. v. 6; Ezra viii. 29), the meaning of *watch, keeper* (so also Symmachus, according to St. Jerome and Ibn Ezra), as well as of *almond*. As for the allegorical meaning of this clause, we are told that it denotes *the haunch bone shall come out from leanness* (the Talmud, (*l. c.*) the Chaldee, Rashi, Rashbam, &c.), *the hoary hair which comes quickly upon a man, just as the almond tree thrusts out her blossoms before any other trees* (Bishop Reynolds, Mendelssohn, &c.) Others, again, mentioned by Ibn Ezra and Salomon ben Melech, affirm that שָׁקֵד is האבר ששיבתו אחר הראש והזקן, *membrum gentilæ,* and translate it *reprobabitur coitus,* which is followed by Dr. Mead (*Medica Sacra,* p. 44), Desvoeux, Hitzig, and Fürst. We shall give the words of the latter in the original, as we forbear translating them. שָׁקֵד, ist bie Eichel, *glans virilis,* was bie fühlbare Lust in bem Zeugungsgeschäft barstellen soll, so baß auch וְיָנֵאץ הַשָּׁקֵד, unb bie (männliche) Eichel verschmähet (bie bargebotene Lust) überseßt werben kann; baß. bie eigenthüml. Schreibung, um Bild u. Abbild zugleich zu bezeichnen. But let those who are shocked with this explanation remember that, if it be once conceded that we have here an allegory, the defenders of this obscene

and the caper-berry shall be powerless; for man goeth to

exposition have as much right to maintain this to be its meaning, as those have who make the text declare a host of other most far-fetched and diametrically opposite things.

And the locust, &c. This locust (חָגָב) is one of the four kinds which the Jews were permitted by the Law to eat (comp. Levit. xi. 22). Locusts have been from all antiquity, and still are to the present day, very agreeable, wholesome, and nutritious food both in the East and in other countries. They are prepared in different ways; either boiled in salt water, head, feet, and wings taken off, and dried in the sun, or ground into flour and made into bread. We are told in the Talmud (Aboda Sara, 39, b) that after wine was poured upon them they were put into baskets and formed an extensive article of commerce. Diodorus Siculus says that a people of Ethiopia were called Æridophagi, *eaters of locusts*, because they were so fond of them (xxiv. 3), and Aristotle describes them as *delicacies* (Hist. Anim. v. 30). Modern travellers, too, testify to the agreeableness of this food. Dr. Shaw observes, that when the locusts are sprinkled with salt and fried, they are not unlike in taste to our fresh water cray-fish; and Russell says, "the Arabs salt them and eat them as a *delicacy*" (compare Harmer, Observations, ii. p. 58; Kitto, Cyclop. Bib. Lit.; Winer, Realwoerterbuch; Leyysohn, Die Zoologie des Talmud, *s. v*) This will suffice to shew that the locust is mentioned in conjunction with the almond as *a delicate viand*. יִסְתַּבֵּל, the Hithpael of סָבַל, to *bear a heavy burden*, signifies *to make itself a burden, to become burdensome, loathsome.* According to the Hagadic interpretation, יִסְתַּבֵּל, *to become a burden*, signifies *to become big either with fat or swelling*, and the meaning of the passage is וְיִתְנַפְּחוּן אִסְתַּוָרֵי רִגְלָךְ, *and the ankles of the feet shall be swelled* (the Chaldee); so also St. Jerome, *senum crura tumentia, et*

podagræ tumoribus pregravata, referring it to the swelled legs of old men, oppressed with the swellings of the gout. Hence the renderings of the Septuagint, καὶ παχυνθῇ ἡ ἀκρίς, *and the locust shall be made fat*, the Vulgate *impinguabitur locusta*, the Syriac ﺟﻤﻊ, and others. Then, again, we are assured that it signifies *the stomach*, swelled with undigested humours (De Lyra, Le Clerc, &c.); it denotes *the shoulders, hips, and back*, all bunching out (Bishop Patrick, &c.); it means *the dry, shrunk, shrivelled, crumpling, scraggy old man* (Dr. Smith, Holden, Vaihinger, &c.); it is *the powers hostile to life* which destroy it in old age (Hengstenberg). Then, again, Rashi, Rashbam, and the commentators mentioned by Ibn Ezra, who are followed by Dr. Mead, Desvoeux, Hitzig, and Fürst, maintain that it means חמבושים טימשכו למטה or כי החי"ת, במקום ע"י, und lästig ist der Schlauch, als Bezeichnung des männl. Gliedes.

And the caper-berry, &c. The caper-plant belongs to a tribe of plants, the species of which grow abundantly in Asia, Africa, and Southern Europe, out of the crevices of walls, in the rubbish of ruins, and in barren places, producing a striking effect, as it is a showy and ornamental plant. "It forms a much-branched, diffuse shrub, which annually loses its leaves. The branches are long and trailing; smooth, but armed with double curved stipulary spines. The leaves are alternate, roundish or oblong-oval, a little fleshy, smooth, of a green colour, but sometimes a little reddish. The flowers are large and showy, produced singly in the axils of the leaves, on stalks which are larger than the leaves. The calyx is fourleaved, coriaceous; the petals are also four in number, white, and of an oval roundish form. The stamens are very numerous and long, and their filaments being tinged with purple, and terminated by the yellow anthers;

his eternal home, and the mourners walk about the street:

give the flower a very agreeable appearance. The ovary is borne upon a straight stalk, which is a little longer than the stamens, and which, as it ripens, droops and forms an oval or pear-shaped berry, enclosing within its pulp numerous small seeds." Almost every part of this shrub has been used by the ancients as a condiment. The stalk and the seed were salted or preserved in vinegar or wine, and the buds or unexpanded flowers are esteemed at our tables as a pickle or sauce of a delicate flavour. The berries possess some irritant properties, and were taken as a provocative of appetite (comp. Kitto, Cyclop. Bib. Lit. under *Abiyonah*; Winer, Realwoerterbuch, *s. v.* Kapper). Hence the caper-berry was called אֲבִיּוֹנָה (from אָבָה, *to desire;* for the form, see Ewald, § 163, e), literally *desire, appetite,* and metonymically that which creates desire or appetite, *incentive, stimulant.* The mention of the caper-berry is exceedingly striking. Having stated that all desire for food, however tempting, shall vanish in this awful scene, Coheleth says that even the caper-berry, with all its provocative properties, will fail to excite appetite. That אֲבִיּוֹנָה, which in Biblical Hebrew only occurs here, means the *caper-berry,* and קפרים, the *covering* or *peel* of the fruit of צלף, the *caper-shrub,* is evident from the Septuagint, the Vulgate, the Syriac, St. Jerome, and the uniform signification of it in the Talmud (comp. Berachoth, 36, a; Buxtorf, Lex. Rabb. et Talm., pp. 12. 2098). Moreover, the parallels שָׁקֵד and חָנָב shew, beyond doubt, that it is a *fruit.* Hence Gesenius, Knobel, Ewald, De Wette, Noyes, Heiligstedt, Hitzig, Stuart, Fürst, Elster, Vaihinger, &c., rightly defend the signification of *caper-berry,* though their untenable explanation of the whole passage has led them wrongly to restrict it to a provocative *ad appetitum rei veneræ, ad irritandam venerem.* וְתָפֵר, Hiphil of

פָרַר. *to break, to abolish,* signifies *to cause its power to cease,* i. e., *to produce no effect, to be powerless.* The Syriac ܘܒܛܠ ܟܦܪܐ ܘܬܬܒܛܠ ܚܒܝܬܐ, *and the caper shall burst, and desire shall cease,* also translates וְתָפֵר אֲבִיּוֹנָה doubly, taking פָרַר both for *breaking, bursting,* and *destroying, ceasing,* and אֲבִיּוֹנָה for *caper,* and *want* = אֶבְיוֹן. Here again all the allegorisers have been obliged to drop the allegory, except Rosenmüller, who says, "the veteran who has reached the end of his days, and daily must expect to sink into his grave, is compared to such an over-ripe caper-berry, which is nearly falling off" (Biblical Mineralogy and Botany, Clark's edition, p. 107, &c.) Döderlein's rendering of this clause, da das Turteltäubchens Klagegetön verschmäht wird, *when the plaintive notes of the turtle-dove are despised,* which is followed by Schmidt, deriving אֲבִיּוֹנָה from יוֹנָה, *dove,* and אֲבִי *ah!* is as curious as it is preposterous.

For man goeth, &c. The cause of all this is, that death is on his way to seize his victim, and the professional mourners, who are hired to bemoan the departed, like sharks, are seen to follow closely at the heels of death, impatiently preparing themselves for the employment, before the sufferer has breathed his last. כִּי is *causal,* giving the cause of this consternation. The participle הֹלֵךְ expresses *the approaching future,* i. e., *he is about to go,* or *is in the act of going* (comp. Gen. xvii. 19, xviii. 18, xix. 13; Gesenius, § 134, 2; Ewald, § 335, b). בֵּית עוֹלָם, *the house of eternity,* i. e., *eternal* or *everlasting house* or *home,* is the common expression in later Hebrew for the *grave* or *graveyard,* and the Jews use it to the present day. The same phrase exists in the Chaldee, and the Targum which takes יָרֹנוּ יֹשְׁבֵי סֶלַע (Isa. xlii. 11) as referring to the inhabitants of the grave, renders it יְשַׁבְּחוּ מֵיתַיָּא כַּד יְפְקוּן

6 before the silver cord goeth asunder, and the golden bowl

מִבַּתֵּי עֲלָמֵיהוֹן, *the dead shall praise thee when they shall quit their eternal homes.* It also occurs in Tobit iii. 6, "command that I may be delivered from this distress (εἰς τὸν αἰώνιον τόπον) *into the everlasting place.* Knobel's assertion, ewige Wohnung nennt Koheleth das Grab, weil er keine Befreiung daraus annimmt, *that Coheleth calls the grave the everlasting abode, because he did not believe in a liberation therefrom,* is both contrary to the design of the book and to fact. Had this phrase been used in the early portions of the Old Testament such an assertion would have some force ; but, as it is, בֵּית עוֹלָם originated at a time when the belief in a resurrection was general, so much so that it became the great question of the day ; and the above-quoted passage from the Chaldee shews that the paraphrast used it not weil er keine Befreiung daraus annimmt, *because he did not believe in a liberation therefrom,* but IN CONNECTION with a liberation from the grave. The true explanation is given by Ibn Ezra, who remarks, אל בית עולמו הוא הקבר והוא הבית שידור שם לעולם ויש עולם קצין כמו וישב שם עד עולם ועבדו לעולם, *his everlasting home means the grave, for it is the abode where man dwells everlastingly. The word " everlasting," however, must here be taken in a restricted sense, just as in the phrases* "he shall abide everlastingly" (1 Sam. i. 22), and " he shall serve him everlastingly " (Exod. xxi. 6, &c.) The Syriac's rendering of בֵּית עוֹלְמוֹ by

ܟ݁ܰܡܶܐܠܳܐ ܕܒܶܝܬ, *his house of labour,* changes עלם into עמל, by transposing the ל and מ according to the Hagadic rules of interpretation (*vide supra,* p. 31); thus giving a reason why *all want shall cease,* as its rendering of וְתָפֵר אֲבִיּוֹנָה in the preceding clause ; it is because man goes to *his place of labour,* whence all his wants will be supplied. The phrase סָבְבוּ בַשּׁוּק, *walking up and down,* or *going about the street,* characteristically describes

these (סוֹפְדִים) *mercenary mourners* (comp. Jer. ix. 17; Mishna, Moed Katon, iii. 8 ; Joseph. De Bell. Jud. iii. 9, 5 ; Kitto, Cyclop. Bib. Lit., under *mourning* ; Winer, Realwoerterbuch, *s. v.* Leichen) who loiter about the house before the sufferer has expired, anxiously waiting to be employed. This accounts for the participle הֹלֵךְ being used with הָאָדָם, *man is about to die, is in the act of dying,* whilst the *præterite* סָבְבוּ is used with הַסּוֹפְדִים, *the mourners already go* or *loiter about* (בַשּׁוּק) *in the street,* not after the funeral.

6. *Before the silver cord,* &c. Having described the *approach* of death, Coheleth now passes on to its *arrival.* To impress upon our minds more deeply the awfulness of that encounter, and the necessity of remembering the Creator before death strikes the final blow, the sacred writer describes the dissolution of man under two different metaphors. In the first part of the verse the breaking up of the human machine and extinction of life are compared to the snapping asunder of the silver cord by which a burning lamp is suspended from the ceiling, dashing into pieces the golden reservoir of oil which imparts the vital fluid to the branches where the wicks are placed, and extinguishing the light. עַד אֲשֶׁר לֹא, *before,* is used for the third time in this description, and, as in the two former instances, marks a *new period ;* it indicates here the *transition* from the approach of death to its arrival, and is depending upon זְכֹר אֶת־בּוֹרְאֶיךָ וְגו׳, *remember thy Creator,* &c., in the first verse רָתַק, *to go asunder, to snap,* beautifully describes *the separating of the strands.* The reading יֵרָתֵק proposed by the Massorites, which is found in twenty-one of Kennicott's MSS., and perhaps five more, and is adopted by Rashi, Rashbam, Ibn Ezra, Spohn, &c., is both unnecessary and untenable, because — 1. A Niphal of רָתַק nowhere occurs; 2. Even if this conjugation be admitted,

the Niphal of רָתַק, *to bind, to chain*, can never mean *to be unbound, unchained ;* and 3. The verb רוּץ in the corresponding clause shews beyond a doubt that רָחַק is the proper reading. For the last mentioned reason, as well as for all want of authority, we must reject the reading יֵָחֵק, suggested by Pfaunkuche, Herzfeld, Gesenius, &c., or יֵחָרֵק, as Hitzig will have it, who is followed by Stuart, transposing the letters ר and ח. We must add that the vowel-points of יֵרָתֵק belong to יֵחַק in the *Keri*, and that the proper reading is יֵרָחֵק, as the vowels of the Ketib always belong in such cases to the marginal reading. חֶבֶל הַכֶּסֶף, *the cord of silver*, i. e., the cord composed of silvered strands for the sake of ornament; just as we have the chains silvered or gilt by which our chandeliers are suspended. As the derivation of חָרֵץ from רָצֵץ, *to break* (the Septuagint, Rashi, Rashbam, Ibn Ezra, the Zurich Bible, Coverdale, the Bishops' Bible, the Geneva Bible, the Authorised Version, Hodgson, Knobel, Gesenius, De Wette, Ewald, Noyes, Hitzig, Heiligstedt, Stuart, Elster, Vaihinger, &c.), creates two inadmissible anomalies, making, in the first place, תָּרִיץ, the regular future of רוּץ, the abnormal future of רָצֵץ, thus mixing up the verbs רָצֵץ and רוּץ, which are always distinct both in form and sense (Isa. xlii. 4 not excepted, see Hengstenberg, Christology, *in loco*) ; and secondly, assigning to רָצֵץ, which invariably signifies *to break*, an intransitive meaning, *to be broken ;* it is better to regard it as the regular future of רוּץ, *to run* (the Vulgate, Luther, Desvoeux, Hengstenberg, &c.), *to escape.* The idea of *escaping* forms an excellent parallelism with רָחַק, *to go asunder*, just as נִשְׁבַּר, *to be broken*, and נָרֵץ, *to be dashed*, correspond to each other in the second part of this verse, and preserves the evenness of the construction. גֻּלָּה (from גָּלַל, *to roll on, to swell*), properly *that which sends forth water, a spring, a fountain* (Josh. xv. 19; Judg. i. 15), *a reservoir* or *bowl of oil*, which sends

forth the oil into the branches containing the wicks. Hence the wick is called שׁוֹאֶבֶת, *the drawer* (Mishna, Sabbath, xxix. 9). Gesenius' remark, that *it is so called from its round form* (Lex. *s. v.*) is rightly rejected by Herzfeld, on the ground that an oil vessel is not necessarily round, and that it may assume any shape. The renderings of the Septuagint, ἀνθέμιον, *flower*, and the Vulgate, VITTA, *fillet*, are both contrary to the signification of גֻּלָּה, and at variance with the context. Hitzig, Stuart, and others take הַזָּהָב to mean *oil* which is of a *golden colour*, and appeal to Zech. iv. 12 in corroboration of this explanation. But though it is true that זָהָב is tropically used in the passage alluded to, yet, as the genitive הַכֶּסֶף, *silver*, connected with חֶבֶל, *cord*, is used in the former clause to describe the *material*, consistency demands that the genitive הַזָּהָב, *gold*, connected with גֻּלָּה, *bowl*, in the corresponding clause, should also be taken as descriptive of the *material*. Rashi, Rashbam, Ibn Ezra, Bishop Reynolds, Desvoeux (p. 193), Mendelssohn, Holden, Preston, and others, take the imagery here as part of that contained in the remainder of this verse, and maintain that the *whole* verse alludes to a *water apparatus*, viz., the *cord* or *line* (חֶבֶל), the *cistern* (גֻּלָּה) into which the water is emptied, the *bucket* or *pail* (כַּד) in which the water is brought up, and the *wheel* (גַּלְגַּל) by which it is got up. But against this is to be urged—
1. That גֻּלָּה never means *cistern ;*
2. That the adjectives *silver* and *gold* are most inappropriate to a *water apparatus ;* and 3. That the marked distinction drawn between this part of the verse and the following, by the use of adjectives here, and the entire absence of them in the next hemistich, indicates most clearly that two distinct metaphors are intended. As to the allegorical meaning of this clause, we are told that "the silver cord and golden bowl" mean *the tongue and the skull of the head* (the Chaldee), SPINA DORSI, *the backbone*

escapeth, or the bucket breaketh upon the fountain, and the
7 wheel is shattered at the well, and the body returneth to

or *the marrow of it*, and PIA MATER, *the brain* (Rashbam, Ibn Ezra, Dr. Smith, Bishop Patrick, Clarke, Holden, &c.), " *the urine*, whose stream resembles a silver thread, which is then broken, when it distils by drops, as it frequently doth in old men" (Gasper Sanctius, quoted by Bishop Patrick, *in loco*).

Or the bucket, &c. The second metaphor, under which the breaking up of the human machine is described, is taken from the working of a well. One of the methods most employed for drawing up water from wells or reservoirs is a wheel, which has a line and a bucket appended to it, and is turned by a man or an ox. Robinson, in his description of the water apparatus he saw, says that " a platform of very large stones was built up around the well, and there were many drinking troughs. On the platform was fixed a small reel for the rope, which a man, seated on a level with the axis, wound up by pulling the upper part of the reel towards him with his hands, while he at the same time pushed the lower part from him with the feet" (Palestine, ii. 22). And just as when the bucket or wheel is broken, the machine is incapable of service and useless, so man may be unable to draw comforts from the remembrance of the Creator, when the inroads of death have shattered his frame and impaired his faculties. Just as two verbs were used in the first part of this verse, רָחַק and רוּץ, which denote *separation, departure*, so there are two verbs employed in this clause, שָׁבַר and רָצַץ, which signify *to break, to dash in pieces*. The Septuagint's rendering of וְרוֹץ by καὶ συντροχάσῃ, *and shall run together*, arises from confounding it with וְיָרוּץ, which immediately precedes it. The two prepositions עַל and אֶל, are not promiscuously used for *at* (the Sept., the Vulgate, the Syriac, Luther, the Geneva Bible, the Auth. Version, Hodgson, Herzfeld, De Wette, Noyes, Hitzig, Stuart, Hengstenberg, &c.), but are designedly employed to describe the *different positions* occupied by the subjects with which they are respectively connected; the bucket (כַּד) generally stands *upon* the enclosure of the well, thus being, as it were, over or above it, hence it is עַל־הַמַּבּוּעַ, whilst the wheel (הַגַּלְגַּל) is *contiguous* or *joined to* it, hence אֶל־הַבּוֹר. Hence the Zurich Bible, Coverdale, the Bishops' Bible, Knobel, Heiligstedt, Elster, Vaihinger, &c., rightly translate the former *upon*, and the latter *at*. The reading אַל, which is to be found in twenty-one of Kennicott's MSS., is plainly a mistake. According to the allegorisers, " the bucket being broken over the fountain " means *the gall at the liver being broken* (the Chaldee, Ibn Ezra, &c.), *the veins at the right ventricle of the heart shall cease to act* (Dr. Smith, Bishop Patrick, Dr. Gill, &c.), *the individual and general life shall terminate, when the drawing of water-breath ceases* (Hengstenberg, &c.)

7. *And the body*, &c. We are to remember the Creator, and strive to do his will before he summons us, through death, to the bar of judgment. The וְ in וְיָשֹׁב is not *causal*, assigning a reason for what has hitherto been said (Luther, &c.); nor is it *then*, introducing the *apodosis* (the Bishops' Bible, the Authorised Version, Stuart, &c); nor does it denote *or, or ever* (the Zurich Bible, Coverdale, Hodgson, Spohn, &c.); but it is the regular *copula* (the Septuagint, the Vulgate, the Geneva Bible, Knobel, De Wette, Noyes, &c.) Instead of the normal future יָשׁוּב, the apocopated form יָשֹׁב is used, to make it conform in vowel-points to וְיֵרֹץ in the preceding verse. Such instances of uniformity, being deemed an ornament in the style, were frequently effected at the expense of altering

the earth as it was, and the spirit goeth back to God who gave it.

regular forms (comp. מוֹבָא, *entrance,* instead of מָבוֹא, to correspond with מוֹצָא, Ezek. xliii. 11 ; צְאֶינָה instead of צֶאנָה, to correspond with רְאֶינָה, Song of Songs iii. 11 ; see also *infra,* verse 11, and Gesen. § 59, Rem. 3 ; Ewald, § 118, d). עָפָר, *dust,* is metonymically used for the *lifeless body,* because it is formed of dust, Gen. ii. 7, iii. 19 (comp. עָפָר הֲיוֹדְךָ, *shall the corpse praise thee ?* Ps. xxx. 10) ; hence the Chaldee has appropriately paraphrased it בִּסְרָךְ דְּאִתְבְּרִי מִן עַפְרָא, *thy flesh,* or *body, which was formed of dust.* Most commentators take עַל, again, as synonymous with אֶל, and appeal to the phrases שׁוּבְךָ אֶל־הָאֲדָמָה and וְאֶל־עָפָר תָּשׁוּב, in Gen. iii. 19 and Ps. civ. 29, to corroborate this explanation. But the very fact that Coheleth deviates here from the well-known phrases which he himself has used elsewhere (iii. 20), shews that he intends to convey thereby a different shade of meaning, which is here called forth by his speaking of the *spirit* as well as of the body ; whilst, in the passages alluded to, the *body only* is mentioned. As Coheleth tells us in the next clause that the spirit goes to God, ascending, as it were, on high (*vide* iii. 21), the body is beautifully contrasted therewith, by being described as *thrown upon* (עַל) *the earth.* The Septuagint (ἐπὶ . . . πρὸς), the Syriac, the Chaldee, &c., have therefore rightly distinguished between עַל and אֶל in this verse. כְּשֶׁהָיָה, *as it* (*i. e.,* the body) *was,* that is to say, prior to its animation ; the body shall go back to remain upon the earth in the state wherein it was before the soul occupied it, hence *lifeless.*

And the spirit, &c. Le Clerc tells us that by the returning of the spirit to God is meant *its reabsorption into God, the original principle from which it was torn off, just as the body turns into earth again, becomes amalgamated with the earth, the original*

element from which it was taken, ATQUI UT CORPUS REVERSUM IN TERRAM DESINIT ESSE CORPUS HUMANUM, ET DISSOLVITUR ; ITA SPIRITUS, REDIENS AD DEUM EAM PATI MUTATIONEM, CREDERE POTUIT SALOMO, QUA DESINEBAT ESSE SPIRITUS HUMANUS, thus making the passage to enunciate the doctrine of the theistical philosophers of Greece, who denied the future *personality* of the soul, and held the refusion of it into the τὸ ἕν, or the ANIMA MUNDI, *the world-soul ;* he quotes, in illustration of our verse, the parallel words of Epicharmus, Συνεκρίθη καὶ διεκρίθη, καὶ ἀπῆθην ὅθεν ἦνθε πάλιν γᾶ ἐς γᾶν, πνεῦμα δ' ἄνω, *they were huddled together, and they were separated, and they returned again to the place whence they came; the earth in earth, the spirit above;* and Euripides —

'Εάσατ' ἤδη γῆ καλυφθῆναι νεκρούς,
"Οθεν δ' ἕκαστον ἐς τὸ φῶς ἀφίκετο,
'Ενταῦθ' ἀπελθεῖν, πνεῦμα μὲν πρὸς αἰθέρα,
Τὸ σῶμα δ' ἐς γῆν· οὔτι γὰρ κεκτήμεθα
'Ημέτερον αὐτό, πλὴν ἐνοικῆσαι μόνον
Κἄπειτα τὴν θρέψασαν αὐτὸ δεῖ λαβεῖν.

Let the corpses be buried in the earth, Whence each part comes into existence; thither They return, the spirit to the ether, And the body to the earth. Not as our own Do we hold it, but only as a sojourner, and in fief. The mother which nourishes it must receive it back.   SUPPL. 529–534.

This interpretation is followed by Warburton (Divine Legation, lib. v. § 6), Knobel, Hitzig, Heiligstedt, Noyes, &c., who also quote Lucretius —

Cedit item retro, de terra quod fuit ante, In terras; et, quod missum est ex ætheris oris, Id rursum cœli relatum templa receptant.

" Thus all things rise, thus all again return: Earth takes what earth bestowed; and back to heaven Remount the ethereal dews from heaven that fell."— DE NAT. RER. ii. 998, &c.

But we submit that this doctrine is thoroughly heathenish, and, though largely believed by the Greeks and

Romans, is utterly at variance with the tenor of the Bible, as well as with the usage of the same language in other parts of this book. 1. The fact that God is uniformly described throughout the Bible as a *personal* and *super-mundane* Being, separated from, independent of, and infinitely above all matter — to the ignorance or denial of which, on the part of the Heathen philosophers, the emanation-theory in question is to be ascribed—is utterly subversive of the said absorption of the human spirit into the world-soul. 2. Nothing can be more plain than the description which the Bible gives of the radical and essential difference between the Creator and the creature, and which the sacred writer of this book repeatedly sets forth. To make therefore a Hebrew writer, who believes in this essential difference between the ontological natures of God and man, enunciate the amalgamation of the human spirit with the Godhead, is most unjustifiable. 3. The abhorrence of sin, and the approbation of holiness, manifested throughout the Scriptures, the curse denounced against the sinner (Deut. xxvii. 26), stamping the polluted soul with a *character indelibilis*, precludes the possibility of a Hebrew writer teaching that this awful distinction will at once and for ever be destroyed, as soon as man dies and the guilt-laden soul is absorbed in a holy Deity, who hates iniquity and sin. 4. We said that this explanation is also at variance with the same phraseology used by Coheleth elsewhere. It is admitted by all parties that the words רוּחַ עֹלָה לְמָעְלָה, *the spirit going upwards*, i. e., to heaven, in iii. 21, mean *immortality*, just as the contrary phrase רוּחַ יֹרֶדֶת לְמַטָּה לָאָרֶץ, *the spirit going downwards to the earth*, denotes *mortality;* and those especially who are anxious to shew that Coheleth denies the immortality of the soul triumphantly appeal to this

very phrase. Now we submit that the phrases *the spirit going upwards to heaven*, and *the spirit returning to God, i. e.*, to heaven, the habitation of God, are essentially the same; and, if the former means *immortality of the soul*, it is an outrage to the laws of language to deny the meaning to the latter. 5. Finally, this reabsorption-theory makes the sacred writer utter the greatest nonsense imaginable. Coheleth started with the problems and mysteries in the moral government of God, wherein the god-fearing are allowed to suffer and the godless to prosper, and the comfort he has now to give to these afflicted saints, as well as the admonition to all, is, " Remember thy Creator, fear the Lord, keep his commandments, begin it in early life, before decrepit old age sets in and deprives you of your powers, and before your spirit, in common with all other spirits, the sin-polluted and the pure, is merged in the world-soul!" What a solution of the grand problem! What a comfort to the afflicted saints! what a reason to fear God! what an inducement to do good! But how apposite, how solemn, how consoling is the obvious interpretation; we are to fear God in spite of the seeming incongruities in his present moral government; we are to keep his commandments, beginning in early life, whilst we are able to do it, before old age creeps upon us and impairs our faculties, and death summons our souls before the tribunal of the Creator, when it will be TOO LATE! Then every deed done in the body shall be judged, every mystery explained, and every wrong redressed. This, then, is the momentous and all-important conclusion to which Coheleth brings us, after having led us through the various perplexities and conflicts of this world to the sure and certain hope of victory in the world to come.

THE EPILOGUE.

CHAPTER XII. 8—14.

Thus all human efforts to obtain real happiness are vain (xii. 8); this is the experience of the wisest and most painstaking Coheleth (9, 10); the Sacred Writings alone are the way to it (11, 12); there is a righteous Judge who marks, and will, in the great day of judgment, judge, everything we do; we must therefore fear him, and keep his commandments (13, 14).

8, 9 Vanity of vanities, saith Coheleth; all is vanity! And

8. *Vanity of vanities*, &c. Having concluded his demonstration that all *human* efforts to adjust the destinies of man are vain, and that the righteous Judge will in the great day of judgment rectify all, by rewarding the righteous and punishing the wicked, Coheleth resumes, in this Epilogue, the scope of his argument, beginning with the very words of the Prologue. Ibn Ezra, Luther, the Zurich Bible, Coverdale, Spohn, De Wette, Knobel, Rosenmüller, Ewald, Herzfeld, Noyes, Hitzig, Heiligstedt, Stuart, Philippson, Elster, &c., connect this verse with the preceding section. But against this is to be urged — 1. That this formula is never used at the *end* of a sentence or section, as may be seen from the eighteen passages where the declaration of vanity is made; 2. That the only other place where this full formula occurs is at the *beginning of the prologue*, and it is therefore most natural that it should be also at the *beginning of the epilogue*; 3. That the doctrine of immortality and a future judgment, when all that is now conflicting shall be rectified, wherewith Coheleth concluded in the preceding verse, cannot be characterised as *utter vanity;* and 4. That the following verse, which begins with a *copula*, shews that this verse belongs to it. As to the assertion that verses 9-14 are not genuine, and have been added by a later hand

(Döderlein, Schmidt, Berthold, Umbreit, Knobel, &c.), it is most arbitrary, and to be repudiated. Nothing can be more weak than the arguments brought to support this allegation. We shall examine them in the same order as they are advanced by Knobel—

1. "The whole addition is superfluous, and altogether without an object in such a book as Coheleth. It is incomprehensible why the writer, who pursued a purely didactic tendency in the composition of this book, should have added this unimportant notice. He began simply with the theme of the whole (i. 2), he concludes simply therewith (xii. 8), after having worked it out. No one expects anything else which might disturb the winding up of the whole." But we submit that the words "All is utter vanity," do not contain the theme of the book, and that nothing can be more appropriate, after having led us through all the intricacies of the argument, than to set forth, in a striking and solemn manner in this epilogue, the grand solution, to correspond to the prologue, which contains the great problem. So striking a prologue, without a correspondingly striking epilogue, would have left the book unfinished.

2. "Coheleth speaks in the *third person* in this supplement, whilst in the book itself, and in places where

he simply referred to himself, he used the *first person*. Let this not be objected to on the score that in the book he addresses himself to others as teaching and admonishing, and therefore speaks of himself appropriately in the first person, for he also does the same in the epilogue (verse 12), without, however, speaking in the first person. This difference of treatment can only be satisfactorily explained on the assumption that it proceeds from different authors." But this very fact, so far from being against its genuineness, corroborates it, inasmuch as it shews that the prologue and the epilogue proceed from the same hand, for *both* are in the *third* person. The cause of this is simple and obvious. Coheleth is represented as belonging to the *past* (*vide* p. 247), and the description of his *bare* problem and solution must necessarily be given in the third person; whereas the narrative of the various futile efforts to satisfy the cravings of his soul in any other way would have materially diminished its power if it had also been in the third person. To render the scene life-like and effectual, Coheleth is most beautifully represented as living, moving, and having his being in the midst of us.

3. "It must also be noticed that the epilogist urges the fear of God and piety as the end of all wisdom (ver. 13); but this Coheleth could hardly predicate of his wise lessons. It is true that he, too, recommends the fear of God; but this is by no means the sum of his wisdom, it is not the end to which his doctrine is directed. His tendency, on the contrary, is to shew that all is vanity, that it is therefore best cheerfully to enjoy life." But this objection is based on a false view of the design of the book.

4. "The notion of a future judgment, to be held strictly by God, which the epilogist propounds (verse 14) as the view of Coheleth, is equally against its genuineness." Nothing can be more preposterous than

this objection. A comparison of the proposition contained in the prologue with the sentiments expressed in the epilogue, will shew that it is the very conclusion which Coheleth was driving at, and that he, as a *god-fearing* Jew — not an atheistic or pantheistic heathen philosopher — could come to no other, starting, as he does, with that solemn proposition. We submit that, if Knobel and his fellow objectors to the genuineness of this epilogue had rightly understood the import of the prologue, they would never have made these gratuitous objections. Besides, the seventh verse of this very chapter, which is admitted to be genuine, propounds the immortality of the soul.

5. "Finally, the remark that the making of many books has no end (verse 12), can hardly proceed from the mouth of Coheleth, who most probably lived in the time of the Persians." But this is purely imaginary, as neither Knobel nor any one else can adduce any solid reason why this allusion to the existence of many books does not tally with that period. We know from Diodorus (i. 49) and others, that large libraries existed in Egypt and elsewhere, and we cannot suppose that the Jewish mind, which was highly cultivated, as is evident from the sublime poetry of the Old Testament, would be less active than the heathen. Besides, the large wreck of Midrashic literature we still possess — for time has destroyed this prodigious work — shews beyond doubt that the Hebrews were actively prosecuting the sciences and arts of the day. We have given Knobel's arguments verbatim, believing that, by looking at them in full, the reader will better perceive their feebleness. This is the only instance where קֹהֶלֶת has the article, evidently to shew that *the* Coheleth who commenced the prologue with "Vanity of vanities!" is the identical one that concludes the epilogue with the same assertion, thus inseparably connecting the beginning with the end.

besides that Coheleth was a wise man, he also taught the
people wisdom, and carefully and studiously composed many
10 parables.   Coheleth sought to find words of comfort, and he

9. *And besides that*, &c.   To give
additional weight to the solemn doctrine repeated in this epilogue, Coheleth, in accordance with the custom
of Eastern authors, mentions his fit-
ness for undertaking this work, that
he was a sage, a public teacher, and
a profound author.   One possessing
such qualifications for investigation
and passing judgment on things,
ought therefore to elicit adequate
attention and obedience from the
reader (comp. i. 2).   As יוֹתֵר signifies
1. *That which remains* (1 Sam. xv. 15);
2. *Further;* 3. *More* (*vide supra*, ii.
15); and 4. *Besides* (Esth. vi. 6),
Ewald, Hitzig, Heiligstedt, Stuart,
Elster, Fürst, Hengstenberg, &c.
translate this clause *it remains* (*i. e.*,
to be said) *that Coheleth was a wise
man, moreover he taught*, &c., the
Vulgate, Luther, the Auth. Version,
Rosenmüller, Noyes, &c., *and moreover the Preacher was wise, he still
taught*, &c.; the Geneva Bible, Mendelssohn, Boothroyd, Preston, &c.,
*and the more wise the Preacher was,
the more he taught*, &c.; whilst Rashbam, Coverdale, Gesenius, Knobel,
De Wette, Vaihinger, Philippson, &c.,
render it *and besides that Coheleth
was wise, he also taught the people
knowledge;* the latter rendering is to
be preferred, because it needs not the
harsh ellipsis of the first; it does not
leave עֹד to clog the sentence as the
second does, and avoids the artificial
construction of the third.   The
Hagadic explanation of this clause,
as found in the Chaldee, וְיוֹחֵר מִן כָּל בְּנֵי
אֲנָשָׁא הֲוָה שְׁלֹמֹה דִי מִתְקְרֵי קֹהֶלֶת חַפִּים, *and
Solomon, who was called Coheleth, was
abundantly wise above all the children
of men*, construing the Hebrew וְשָׁקָה
קֹהֶלֶת חָכָם יֹתֵר מכל, will account for the
otherwise meaningless rendering of
the Septuagint, καὶ περισσὸν ὅτι ἐγένετο ὁ
ἐκκλησιαστὴς σοφός.   Commentators are
also divided as to the meaning of
אִזֵּן, some deriving it from אֹזֶן, *to hear*,

render the Piel *to give ear, to heed*
(Aquila, the Syriac, the Chaldee,
Rashbam, Luther, Coverdale, the
Auth. Version, Michaelis, Spohn,
Hengstenberg, &c.); or *he made hear,
he taught* (the Vulgate, Rashi, the
Geneva Bible, Le Clerc, &c.); whilst
others, deriving it from אָזַן, *to weigh*,
translate the Piel *to weigh well, to
consider* (Ibn Ganach, Gesenius,
Knobel, De Wette, Rosenmüller,
Herzfeld, Noyes, Heiligstedt, Hitzig,
Stuart, Elster, Vaihinger, Philippson,
&c.), which is more compatible with
the immediately following וְחִקֵּר.   The
meaningless rendering of the Sept.
καὶ οὖς ἐξιχνιάσεται κόσμον παραβολῶν, *and
the ear found out ordinary parables*,
taking אֹזֶן for אָזַן, is to be traced to
Hagadic influence (comp. Talmud,
Erubin, 21; Midrash Yalkut *in loco*).
Herzfeld rightly remarks, that as
וְאִזֵּן וְחִקֵּר have *no object*, and תִּקֵּן has *no
copula*, the two verbs are best taken
adverbially, as qualifying תִּקֵּן, which
is of frequent occurrence (*vide supra*,
viii. 8).   For the adverbial use of
הַרְבֵּה see i. 16.   The Septuagint connects it with the following verse.

10. *Coheleth sought*, &c.   The great
labour and care which he bestowed
upon the writing of the many parables
mentioned in the foregoing verse,
Coheleth tells us he did not diminish
in composing this book.   His supreme anxiety was to discover truth
which should comfort and cheer the
hearts of those who were perplexed
with the mysteries of God's moral
government and the destinies of man,
and he frankly wrote down the words
of truth.   דִּבְרֵי־חֵפֶץ, *words of comfort*,
does not stand in apposition to דִּבְרֵי
אֱמֶת, *words of truth*, the former referring to *gracefulness of diction*, and
the latter to *propriety of sentiments*
(Mendelssohn, Michaelis, Holden,
Rosenmüller, Umbreit, Herzfeld,
Noyes, Hitzig, Heiligstedt, Stuart,
Philippson, Elster, &c.), as a graceful

11 wrote down frankly the words of truth.　The words of the

style would be *unworthy of such
research and mentioning* (בֶּקֶשׁ לְמִצֹא) in
so solemn a description, and would
not be placed *before* the all-important
object of the book; but is *identical*
with דִּבְרֵי אֱמֶת, *words of truth*, according to the general rule of parallelisms
in this book, and is therefore designated as words of delight (comp. Ps.
xix. 10; Prov. viii. 6 – 10).　Ibn
Ezra's explanation of it by *analogy*
is preposterous. כָּתוּב, the *participle
passive*, like the infinitive, being preceded by a finite verb, has the
distinction of that verb implied
(comp. viii. 9); hence Aquila, the
Vulgate, and the Syriac rightly render
it *he wrote*, which led some erroneously to think that they read וְכָתַב or
וַיִּכְהֹב.　Hitzig's alteration of it into
כָּתוּב, which is followed by Stuart, is
simply arbitrary.　The abstract יֹשֶׁר,
uprightness, frankness, like וְרָבָה, *will-
ingness* (Hos. xiv. 5), and other nouns,
is used *adverbially* for *uprightly,
frankly* (compare Ewald, § 279, c);
the clause is well rendered by the

Syriac ﻮﻛﻟﺎ ﺣﻘﺎ, and
Luther unb er ſchrieb recht bie Worte
ber Wahrheit.　The rendering of the
Septuagint γεγραμμένον εὐθύτητος, which
is followed by Coverdale, the Bishops'
Bible (*right scripture*), the Geneva
Bible (*upright writing*), &c., making
it depend upon בֶּקֶשׁ לְמִצֹא, is contrary
to the word כָּתוּב, which never means
a writing ; this is expressed by כְּתָב.
The Vulgate, SERMONES RECTISSIMOS
AC VERITATE PLENOS, *words most
right and full of truth*, is utterly at
variance with the words of the text ;
Rashbam's construction, דִּבְרֵי יֹשֶׁר וֶאֱמֶת,
words of uprightness and truth, arbitrarily transposes יֹשֶׁר and אֱמֶת, and
supplies the copula before the latter.
Ibn Ezra's strange opinion that
כָּתוּב יֹשֶׁר is the name of a book, *Catub
Jasher*, a *commentary* upon the *book
of Jasher*, which is no more extant
(הוא פירוש וכמוהו על הספר הישר ואיננו אצלנו)
is only equalled by his explanation
of the former clause.　The Autho-

rised Version, *and that which was
written was upright, even words of
truth*, besides supplying most unwarrantably so many words, is extremely
awkward.　Desvœux's translation,
*and one that could well write down
this true discourse*, which he explains,
" Solomon took pains, not only to
compose well, but likewise to have a
good copyist" (pp. 231. 486), is most
preposterous.　It only remains to be
added that the Syriac, though leaving
הַרְבֵּה at the end of the foregoing
verse, like the Septuagint, also begins
this verse with הַרְבֵּה.

11. *The words of the wise*, &c.
From his general abilities and productions (verse 9), and the labour
bestowed upon this work especially
(10), Coheleth, as is to be expected,
passes on to the great object and
original source of this treatise.　And
as this work is one of a large collection, all composed by different people,
all having the same great end in
view, though striking out various
ways to reach it, and all being derived from the same fountain-head,
the sacred writer shews, by a metaphor from pastoral life, how the
employment of apparently opposite
methods by the different writers of
the sacred volume harmonises with
the fact that they all derive their
knowledge from *one* source, to effect
one great result, viz., the happiness
of man.　Just as the goad and the
stake, apparently opposite in their
tendencies, the one *driving onward*
to fresh pastures, the other *keeping
back* to the old ones, are employed
by the same shepherd to subserve
one great object ; so the words of
the wise, which lead onward, propounding new things, and the words
of the masters of the assemblies,
which *keep back* to, and establish in
the old things, proceed from one
source, and have one common object
in view.　That Coheleth is comprised
among (חֲכָמִים), *the wise* here mentioned, whose words drive onward
like goads, is evident from the fact

wise are like goads, and those of the masters of the assemblies are like fixed stakes, given by the same shepherd.

that he is characterised as (חָכָם) a
wise man in verse 9. דָּרְבָן, *i. q.*, דָּרְבֹן,
1 Sam. xiii. 21, like שִׁרְיוֹן and שִׁרְיָן, is
from דָּרַב, *to prick*, with Dagesh line
omitted (comp. קַרְנָן אָבְרָן, Esth. viii.
6; Ezek. xl. 43; Gesen. § 21, 2, c;
Ewald, § 163, d), and denotes a *goad*,
commonly used by shepherds in the
East to stimulate cattle to go on
quickly, and hence is a striking
metaphor to express what *urges forward*, and tends to the opening of
new spheres. The figure is well explained by Ibn Ezra יש בדברי הקדמונים
דברים שהם כדרבונות לבהמה שמיסרים ומפקחים
הנפש, *among the words of the ancients
there are some which are like goads
to cattle, correcting and opening new
things to the mind;* so also Herzfeld, and substantially the same the
Chaldee, Rashi, Rashbam, Holden,
Knobel, Noyes, Vaihinger, Ewald,
&c., who, however, fail by confining
themselves exclusively to the idea of
teaching, and ignoring that the principal object of the goad is *to drive onward.* The explanation of Gesenius,
*aculeorum instar alte descendunt in
pectora hominum iisque manent infixa*
(Thesaurus, *s. v.*), taking the point
of comparison to be the pricking,
the *vivid impression,* which is followed by Hitzig, Heiligstedt, Stuart,
Elster, &c., is totally at variance
with the use of the goad, which is
not to prick but *to drive forward,*
the pricking being made subservient
to this primary object.

And those of the masters, &c. The
stakes here referred to play a most
important part in nomadic life, inasmuch as they are the supporters and
keepers of the shepherds' abodes.
To them, when driven into the
ground, is the tent fastened, to enable
the workmen to spread it, and to
them, also, are the cords tied by
which the tent is extended. Hence
a stake became a metaphor for one
upon whom the care and maintenance of the state depended (Zech.

x. 4), and *a firmly fixed stake* is used
for an immovably established position of such a state supporter (Isa.
xxii. 23). It is therefore obvious,
that when Coheleth compares the
teachings of the masters of the assemblies to fixed stakes he thereby means
that they propound *firmly established
notions ;* these masters are, as it
were, *conservatives,* whilst the wise
men are *liberals.* מַשְׂמֵר, *i. q.*, מַסְמֵר,
the שׂ and the ס, as frequently, being
interchanged, is from סָמַר, *to stand
erect, to be pointed, to be sharp,* and
hence signifies *a nail, a spike, a stake*
to fasten tents (comp. 2 Chron. iii. 9;
Jer. x. 4), and, like its synonym יָתֵד,
is of *common gender,* which accounts
for its being construed with the
masculine נְטוּעִים. It is moreover to
be remarked that the *feminine* termination וֹת‒ is here designedly used
instead of the *masculine* יִם‒, to correspond with דָּרְבֹנוֹת (comp. verse 7).
That מַשְׂמֵר here is not *a nail driven
into the wall,* as some will have it,
is evident from דָּרְבָן, by which it is
preceded, and רֹעֶה, which follows it,
shewing that the whole is a pastoral
scene occupied by *tents,* which have
no *walls* to drive nails in. נְטַע, *to
stick in,* is also used in Dan. xi. 45
for driving in *tent-spikes.* The subject דִּבְרֵי, which, according to a well-
known omission, is not repeated,
must be supplied before the *genitive*
בַּעֲלֵי, from the first clause. For an
exactly parallel case, see x. 12, 13.

The Syriac ܡܪ̈ܝ ܐܣܩܘܦ̈ܬܐ, *master
of the thresholds,* has evidently arisen
from the carelessness of the transcriber, who has inadvertently inserted a ܒ after the ܡ.

Given by the same, &c. Though
these teachings are apparently opposite in their tendencies, yet they are
communicated by the same shepherd
to his different servants, and conduce
to one great object. נִתְּנוּ refers both

12 And beyond these, my son, beware! to make many books

to דְּבָרִים, *the words*, and to זָרְבָן and מַשְׂמֵר, the *goad* and *stake*, and is followed by מִן, which is not unfrequently taken by *the efficient cause* after a passive verb (comp. Gen. ix. 11; Job xxiv. 1; Song of Songs iii. 10; Gesen. § 143, 2; Ewald, § 295, c). רֹעֶה, *shepherd, i.e.,* God, who alone imparts these different lessons of heavenly wisdom to his inspired servants. Very significant and emphatic is the expression אֶחָד, *the same* (*vide* ii. 14), shewing the *unity* of the fountain-head from which all these *various streams* derive their existence. With this simple explanation, which leaves to every word its natural meaning, and violates no points or accents, we shall give some of the multifarious renderings, leaving the reader to decide which is the preferable translation. The Septuagint, the Vulgate, and the Syriac translate it, "the words of the wise are as goads and as nails firmly fixed, which have been given by those of the counsel from one shepherd;" Luther renders it, diefe Worte der Weifen find Spieße und Nägel, gefchrieben durch die Meifter der Verfammlungen, und von Einem Hirten gegeben, *these words of the wise are spears and nails written by the masters of assemblies, and given by one shepherd;* the Zurich Bible has dann weyfer lüten wort find als ftacke mit benen man fttupffet, vnnb nagel die bnrchtringend, mit benenn [die menfchen] zemen gehalten werdend, bann fy werdend vonn einem einigen hirtenn gegeben, which is literally adopted by Coverdale, "for the words of the wise are like pricks and nails that go through, wherewith men are kept together; for they are given of one shepherd only;" the Bishops' Bible again has, "for the words of the wise are like pricks and nails that go through, of the authors of gatherings, [which] are given of one shepherd," remarking, in the margin, "authors of gatherings he calleth wise men," because they

gather the sayings of the wiser sort of men in their books." The Geneva Bible, which is followed by the Auth. Version, renders it, "the words of the wise are like goads and like nails fastened by the masters of the assemblies, which are given by one pastor;" according to Broughton it means, "the words of the wise, as goads and as nails fastened in the sheepfolds, being given from one shepherd;" according to Lightfoot (Works, ii. 575), it ought to be, "the words of the wise are as goads, and as nails fastened by those that gather the flock into the fold, which are furnished by the chief shepherd;" and, according to Desvoeux, it means, "one shepherd gave the words of the wise like goads, and appointed the masters of collections, like planted repositories." Hodgson, again, with equal certainty, tells us that it means, "like goads or like points that pierce, are the sayings of the wise; the persons employed to collect them were appointed by none but the teacher;" whilst Mendelssohn, Friedländer, and Preston assure us that it ought to be rendered, "the words of the wise are like points of goads, and the sayings of the gatherers cleave to the soul like nails implanted, agreeing together as if they proceeded from one thinking mind."

12. *And beyond these,* &c. Having adverted, in the foregoing verse, to the variety and sufficiency of the teachings in the sacred writings, and to the Divine source from which they emanate, Coheleth now warns his readers against seeking satisfaction in profane books, the making and perusal of which will only yield endless trouble and pain; just as he found it by experience, when acquiring knowledge in order to fathom the mysteries of Providence, and to find repose for his soul (*vide supra*, i. 18). The importance of this caution, not to seek peace of mind in the multitude of books, will be more obvious if we bear in mind the arrogant

there is no end, and much study is a weariness of the flesh.

pretensions of some of the ancient writings, and that the library at Thebes had the inscription ψυχῆς Ιατρεῖον, *pharmacy of the soul* (comp. Diodorus, i. 49). Hence also the similar advice of Horace to " listen to the words of the wise " —

Inter cuncta leges et percontabere doctos,
Qua ratione queas traducere leniter ævum."

" Consult with care the learned page,
Inquire of every scienced sage,
How you may glide with gentle ease
A down the current of your days.
Epist. lib. i. epist. xviii. 96, 97.

The Vulgate, the Chaldee, Rashi, Rashbam, Luther, the Zurich Bible, Coverdale, the Bishops' Bible, the Geneva Bible, Grotius, Michaelis, Mendelssohn, Gesenius, De Wette, Philippson, &c., rightly construe יֹתֵר with מִן, *more than, beyond, besides*, as is evident from מִמֶּנִּי, *more than, or besides me*, in Esth. vi. 6, and from the usage of this phrase in post-biblical Hebrew. The construction מֵהֵמָּה with הִזָּהֵר, *by these be admonished*, which is adopted by the Authorised Version, Desvoeux, Hodgson, Holden, Knobel, Noyes, Hitzig, Heiligstedt, Stuart, Elster, Vaihinger, Hengstenberg, &c., is both contrary to the usage of יֹתֵר מִן, and is contradicted by Ps. xix. 2, where it is evident that הַזָּהֵר is construed with בְּ, and not with מִ. The pronoun הֵמָּה refers to the immediate antecedent, *i. e.*, the words of the wise and of the masters of assemblies, by which the whole of the sacred Scriptures was characterised in the foregoing verse. בְּנִי, *my son*, is not *Rehoboam*, who is here prophetically or otherwise cautioned (Gill, Preston, &c.), but is an affectionate term by which teachers generally addressed their disciples or readers (comp. Prov. i. 8. 10. 15; ii. 1; iii. 1; iv. 1, &c.), because teachers and disciples are regarded as sustaining the relationship of spiritual parents and children (comp. Judges xvii. 10; 1 Sam. x. 12; 2 Kings ii. 15, v. 13). For הִזָּהֵר, *to be warned, to take care*, which Ibn Ezra rightly

explains by הִשָּׁמֵר, see iv. 13. Preston's objection to this rendering, that " the expression of so illiberal a sentiment cannot have been intended by Solomon," is obviated by the fact that Coheleth does not caution against using profane books *absolutely*, but warns us not to attempt to find in them that satisfaction for the cravings of our immortal souls which the sacred Scriptures alone can yield. Equally untenable is the objection of Vaihinger, that *this rendering anticipates the next clause, wherein is contained the caution against other books*, inasmuch as this clause does not give the warning, but *the reason for it*. Rashbam's explanation, ויתר ממה שהחכמים מזהירים אותך שהרי אין קץ ויכולת לעשות ספרים הרבה לכתוב כל כחכמות בתוכם, *and more than these wise men can teach thee, teach thyself, because it would be endless trouble to make the many books required for writing down all the necessary wisdom*, which is followed by Herzfeld, who accordingly fills out the sentence וְיֹתֵר מֵאֲשֶׁר יוּכְלוּ הֵמָּה לְהַזְהִירְךָ בְּנִי הַזָּהֵר, *but more than these can teach thee, my son, teach thyself;* and Philippson, who, without supplying the supposed ellipsis, renders it aber mehr als diese, mein Sohn, belehre dich selbst, will not be entertained by any one who believes the inspired writings to contain the best lessons, and to be able, above all other teachings, to make men wise unto salvation. Still more unnatural is the *fresh* conclusion at which Ewald has arrived in his Jahrbücher (iii. 124), that the meaning of this is und was aus ihnen (den Sprüchen) erübrigt (d. i. was aus ihnen folgt, sich ergibt) davon laß dich warnen! (dem folge nach), *and what remains of them* (i. e., *that which results from these maxims, which they teach) thereby be admonished (follow it)*. Hitzig's translation of עֲשׂות סְפָרִים וְגו״ by *to make many books, without end, and much exertion of mind, are a weariness of the flesh*, which is followed by Stuart, regarding אֵין קֵץ as synony-

13 In conclusion, everything is noticed; fear God, and keep

mous with מָאֹד, and as added to הַרְבֵּה for the sake of intensity, thus making this clause and וְלַהַג הַרְבֵּה *two subjects* or nominatives of the sentence—proceeds from the Chaldee paraphrase, and is contrary to the rhythm and evenness of the construction, inasmuch as it assigns to עֲשׂוֹת סְפָרִים too many adjuncts, and leaves לַהַג with the solitary הַרְבֵּה. Besides, the close relationship between קֵץ אֵין, *endless task*, and יְגִעַת בָּשָׂר, *weariness of the flesh*, shews that they are *both predicates*. For the omission of the ל before the infinitive עֲשׂוֹת, see iii. 4.

13. *In conclusion, &c.* The epilogue, like the treatise (*vide* verse 7), concludes with the awful but consoling doctrine of a final retribution. The fate of the godly and ungodly, which is now so perplexing (*vide supra*, i. 11), will not be the same. There is a righteous Judge who takes cognizance of everything we do; we must therefore fear him and keep his commandments, this being the duty of every man. סוֹף דָּבָר, literally *the end of the matter*, though occurring nowhere else in the Hebrew Bible, is frequently employed by post-biblical writers for *in conclusion, finally.* The phrase הַכֹּל נִשְׁמָע exactly corresponds in construction to הַכֹּל נִשְׁבָּח in ii. 16, and must therefore be translated *everything is heard* or *noticed;* the passive הַכֹּל נִשְׁמָע, *everything is noticed*, is used instead of the active הַכֹּל שֹׁמֵעַ הָאֱלֹהִים, *God noticeth everything*, because of the immediately following אֶת־הָאֱלֹהִים יְרָא, *fear God*, which precludes the latter mode of expression. This explanation is moreover corroborated by the words עַל כָּל־נֶעְלָם, *concerning every secret thing*, in the following verse, which is simply an explanation of הַכֹּל נִשְׁמָע, shewing, beyond doubt, that the latter refers to *God*, who notices *all* our doings, and hence will judge even our *secret deeds.* That this plain sense of the words should have been overlooked, and such a variety of forced explanations

should have been resorted to, as is to be found in the ancient versions and modern commentaries, is most remarkable. Thus the Septuagint (τέλος λόγου τὸ πᾶν ἄκουε, *the end of the discourse the whole hear*) takes הַכֹּל as *apposition* to or epexegetical of סוֹף דָּבָר, and altering נִשְׁמָע into שְׁמַע, the *imperative*. This *construction*, not the alteration, is followed by Knobel, Herzfeld, De Wette, Ewald, Hitzig, Heiligstedt, Stuart, Philippson, Vaihinger, Hengstenberg, &c.; some of these, however, differ in their renderings, as, for instance, " the sum of the discourse, the whole, let us hear" (Knobel and De Wette); " let us listen to the end of the thing, or rather the whole" (Herzfeld); "the end of the discourse, of the whole, has been heard" (Ewald), &c. But this explanation — 1. Unnecessarily violates the accents; 2. Assigns to the words a very unnatural construction; and 3. Would, to say the least, require דָּבָר to have the *article*. Still more forced are the Vulgate, FINEM LOQUENDI PARITER OMNES AUDIAMUS, *the conclusion of the discourse let us all hear together*, taking הַכֹּל for *all unitedly;* and the Syriac, ܐܢܶܫܡܰܥ ܣܘܦܳܐ ܕܡܶܠܬܳܐ ܟܽܠܳܗ̇, *the end of the discourse, in total is hear all*, doubly translating הַכֹּל, viz., *in total* and *all;* and likewise the Septuagint, altering נִשְׁמָע into שְׁמַע. Whilst Luther (laſſet uns die Hauptſumme aller Lehre hören), who is followed by Coverdale (" let us hear the conclusion of all things"); the Geneva Bible (" let us hear the end of all "); Authorised Version (" let us hear the conclusion of the whole matter"); Desvoeux, Hodgson, Noyes, &c., mistake דָּבָר, the *absolute*, for the construct. כָּל־הָאָדָם is not *the whole of man, i. e.*, the sum and substance, the end of man's existence (the Vulg., Rashbam, Ibn Ezra, the Geneva Bible, the Authorised Version, Hodg-

14 his commandments, for this every man should do; for God

son, Ewald, Herzfeld, Heiligstedt, Preston, Elster, Philippson, &c.), inasmuch as this phrase uniformly denotes *all men, every man,* nor *since for this are all men,* the ל being supplied before זֶה (Rashi); nor *this belongeth to, is for, every man,* supplying ל before כָל (Geier, Le Clerc, Holden, &c.), which requires too hard and unwarrantable an ellipsis, but *this every man should do;* יַעֲשׂוֹ is to be taken over to it, in accordance with a well-established fact, that when the same verb, though of a different tense, gender, or number, is to be employed in two or more clauses of the verse, it is not unfrequently omitted in one clause, and must be supplied from the other (*vide supra,* x. 12).

The Syriac, ܟܳܠܗܘܢ ܕܗ̄ܢܳܐ ܐܶܬܺܝܗ̄ܒ ܡܶܢ ܐ̱ܠܳܗܳܐ ܒ̇ܚ̣ܕ, *for this is given to all men by one master,* is evidently a corruption; ܡܶܢ ܐ̱ܠܳܗܳܐ ܒ̇ܚ̣ܕ ܕܗ̄ܢܳܐ was undoubtedly a marginal gloss upon נְתְּנוּ מֵרֹעֶה אֶחָד in verse 11, and has here been inserted by mistake.

14. *For God will bring,* &c. The admonition to fear God and to keep his commandments, which was enforced in the foregoing verse, by the declaration that he takes cognisance of everything (הַכֹּל נִשְׁמָע), is here further urged by the fact, that this observing of everything is not all; that there is a future judgment appointed over all the secrets of men, when God shall bring before his tribunal every human action which he has noticed, whether good or bad. The declaration that *every deed* will be brought into judgment, which cannot possibly refer to an earthly tribunal (comp. v. 7), and the fact that this judgment is to be over *every secret thing, i.e.,* is to extend over every action of ours, which is concealed from our fellow-creatures, and can therefore not take place in

ordinary courts of justice, shew incontestably that Coheleth speaks of a future judgment, when God, the righteous Judge, shall reward every man according to his deeds, whether they be good or evil. So plain and convincing are the words of the text, that even Knobel, who labours to prove that Coheleth denies the immortality of the soul, is constrained to say, betrachtet man die Stelle unbefangen, so muß man den Gedanken an ein förmliches Gericht, wie man es sich als nach dem Tode eintreten denkt, darin anerkennen. Darauf führt 1) schon der Ausdruk, daß Gott jede That in das Gericht d. h. vor seinen Richterstuhl zur richterlichen Beurtheilung bringen werde, sowie 2) der Ausdruf, daß dieses Gericht über alles Verborgene werde abgehalten werden. Die letzte Formel wird immer da gebraucht, wo von einem förmlichen Gerichte z. B. dem nach dem Tode die Rede ist; vergl., Rom. ii. 16; 1 Cor. iv. 5; 1 Tim. v. 24, 25, *if one considers this passage impartially, he must admit that it speaks of a formal judgment, which, as is believed, will take place after death. This is evident* — 1. *From the expression, God will bring* EVERY WORK *into judgment, i. e., will bring it before his judgment-seat for judicial examination; and* 2. *From the statement that this judgment will be over* EVERY SECRET THING. *The latter phrase is always used when a formal judgment, a judgment after death, is spoken of* (comp. Rom. ii. 16; 1 Cor. iv. 5; 1 Tim. v. 24, 25). The absence of the article in בְמִשְׁפָּט shews that it belongs to עַל כָּל־נֶעְלָם, *i. e., the judgment over* or *concerning every secret thing, the judgment extending over* or *appointed respecting every secret thing;* so that עַל marks the *object* of the judgment (*vide supra,* ii. 20, iii. 18). The Septuagint's rendering of it by *with,* which is followed by the Geneva Bible, Authorised Version, Noyes, &c., and which has given rise to the rendering *as well as, and* (the Zurich

will bring every work to the judgment appointed over every
secret thing, whether it be good or evil.

Bible, Coverdale, the Bishops' Bible,
Hodgson, &c.), is therefore inadmissible. The Vulgate, ET CUNCTA, QUÆ
FIUNT, ADDUCET DEUS IN JUDICIUM
PRO OMNI ERRATO, *God will bring
into judgment all things that are done
for every error*, is a tame paraphrase.
The Syriac ܟܠ ܠܐ ܕܟܣܐ ܘ ܠܝܬ,
*respecting all things secret and re-
vealed*, adds וְנִגְלָה after נֶעְלָם. Ibn
Ezra's explanation of עַל by כִּי, *i. e.*,
כפי כונת הלב אם טוב ואם רע, *according to
the intention of the heart, whether it
be good or evil*, which is followed by
many modern commentators, is precluded by כָּל before נֶעְלָם; Luther's
version entirely ignores the word עַל.
The Massorites repeat verse 13 after
verse 14, because of the word רָע,

evil, being anxious that the inspired
book should not terminate with so
harsh an expression, and that the
reader should leave off with words
of comfort. For this reason the last
verse but one is also repeated at the
end of Isaiah, Malachi, and Lamentations. To shew, however, that the
verse thus repeated does not belong
to the text, the Massorites have
not pointed it, and added in each of
these books סִימָן יח״קק, *mark It-Kak*,
i. e., note that this is one of the four
books indicated by the initials יח״קק,
the י standing for ישעיה, *Isaiah ;* the
ח for תרי עשר, *twelve Minor Prophets*,
of which Malachi is the last; the
first ק for קינה, *Lamentations*, and the
second ק for *Coheleth* — which have
the penultimate verse εὐφημίας χάριν
repeated.

THE

WORDS OF COHELETH,

SON OF DAVID, KING IN JERUSALEM.

———

2 Vanity of vanities, saith Coheleth, vanity of vanities, all is
3 vanity: man hath no advantage from all his toil where
4 with he toileth under the sun; for generation passeth
away and generation cometh on; while the earth abideth
5 for ever. The sun also riseth and the sun setteth, and,
though it pantingly goeth to its place, it riseth there again.
6 The wind goeth to the south, and turneth to the north; it
goeth round and round, yet the wind returneth to its course.
7 All the streams run into the sea, and the sea doth not
overflow; the place where the streams go to, thence they
8 return again. All words are feeble. Men could never utter,
the eye could never be satisfied with seeing, and the ear
9 could never be filled with hearing all. What hath been still is,
and what hath been done is still done, and there is nothing
10 new under the sun. If there be anything of which it
is said, Behold this is new! it hath been long ago, in
11 the time of old, which was before us. But there is no
remembrance of former men, nor will there be any remembrance of future men among those who will live
hereafter.
12, 13   I, Coheleth, was king over Israel in Jerusalem. And
I gave my heart to enquire diligently into wisdom
respecting all that is done under heaven; this is a grievous

business which God hath given to the children of men
14 to busy themselves therewith. I considered all the
works that are done under the sun, and behold they are all
15 vanity and striving after the wind; for the desponding
cannot be set right, since he that is gone cannot be num-
16 bered again. I therefore spake to my heart, saying, "I, lo!
I have acquired far greater wisdom than any one who was
before me over Jerusalem — my heart having seen much
17 wisdom and knowledge, for I have given my heart to
know wisdom and knowledge — I know that even this is
18 striving after the wind. For, in much wisdom is much
sadness, and multiplying knowledge is multiplying sorrow
ii. I then spake to my heart, Come, now, let me try thee
with mirth, and thou shalt see pleasure! And, lo! this
2 too is vanity. To mirth I said, Thou actest foolishly!
3 and to pleasure, What doeth she? I resolved with my
heart to entice my body with pleasure, my mind guiding
with wisdom, and to lay hold on folly, till I should see
what is good for the sons of men which they should do
4 under heaven, the numbered days of their lives; I therefore
increased my possessions, I builded me houses, I planted
5 me vineyards, I made me gardens and pleasure-grounds,
6 and I planted in them trees of all sorts of fruit. I made
me pools of water, to water therefrom the grove yielding
7 trees; I bought me men-servants and maid-servants,
and had house-born servants; I had also many herds of
oxen and sheep, above all who were before me in Jeru
8 salem; I amassed me also silver and gold, and the treasures
of kings and kingdoms; I got me men-singers and women-
singers, and the delight of men—a large number of wives;
9 so that I greatly increased above all that were before me in
10 Jerusalem, my wisdom also aiding me therein; and nothing
that my eyes desired did I withhold from them; I did not
keep back my heart from any pleasure, as my heart was to
receive happiness from all my toil; and this was to be my

11 portion from all my toil. But when I looked at all my
works which my hands worked, and at the toil wherewith
I toiled to accomplish them, behold, all was vanity and striving after the wind, since there is no advantage under the
12 sun. I then turned to consider wisdom, and madness, and
folly;—for what is the man that will succeed the king, who
13 was made king long ago?—and I saw that there is an advantage to wisdom over folly, as is the advantage of light over
14 darkness. As for the wise man, his eyes are in his head,
while the fool walketh in blindness; and yet I knew that the
15 same fate will meet both. I therefore spake with my
heart, A fate like that of the fool must also meet me, even
me, and why am I then wiser? and I said to my heart
16 that this too is vanity; since there is no remembrance of
the wise man as of the fool for ever, for, as in time
past, both will be forgotten in days to come. And, alas! how
17 like the fool dieth the wise man! Therefore I hated life,
for the work which is worked under the sun pressed heavily
upon me, as all is vanity and striving after the wind;
18 and I hated all my gain which I gained under the sun,
as I must leave it to the man who shall come after me, and
19 no one knoweth whether he will be a wise man or a fool,
and yet he shall have power over all my gain which I have
20 wisely gained under the sun; this, too, is vanity. Thus I
turned to cause my heart to despair of all the gain which I
21 gained under the sun; for here is a man who hath laboured
wisely, and prudently, and skilfully, and must leave it
as a portion to a man who hath not worked at it at all;
22 this, too, is vanity and a great evil. For man hath nothing
from all his labour and the striving of his heart that he
23 laboureth under the sun, since his business grieveth and
irritateth him all his days, and his mind doth not rest even
24 at night; this also is vanity. There is nothing better for
man than to eat and drink, and let his soul enjoy pleasure
25 in his labour; even this I saw cometh from God: for who

should eat, and who should hasten thereunto, except I?

26 For to the man who is good before Him He giveth wisdom, and knowledge, and joy; but to the sinner He giveth the business to gather and to amass, that he may give it to him who is good before God. This, too, is vanity, and striving after the wind.

iii. There is a fixed time for all things, and an appointed
2 season for all undertakings under heaven; a time to be born, and a time to die; a time to plant, and a time to pluck
3 up that which is planted; a time to kill, and a time to save;
4 a time to break down, and a time to build up houses; a time to weep, and a time to laugh; a time to mourn, and a time
5 to rejoice; a time to cast away stones, and a time to gather up stones; a time to embrace, and a time to refrain from
6 embracing; a time to seek, and a time to lose; a time to
7 keep, and a time to cast away; a time to rend garments, and a time to sew them together; a time to be silent, and a time
8 to speak; a time to love, and a time to hate; a time of war,
9 and a time of peace. He who laboureth hath therefore no
10 advantage from that wherein he laboureth. I have considered the business which God hath given to the sons of men to
11 busy themselves therewith; he hath made it all beautiful in its season; he hath also put eternity into their heart, only that man understandeth not the work which God hath made
12 from beginning to end. I knew, then, that there was no good for them but to rejoice and do themselves good all
13 their life; and also that if a man eat and drink, and enjoy
14 pleasure in all his labour, it is a gift of God. I knew that whatever God hath made, the same continueth for ever; to it nothing can be added, and from it nothing can be taken; and God hath so done it that men may fear
15 before him. What hath been was long ago, and what is
16 to be was long ago, for God recalleth what is past. And, moreover, I saw under the sun, that in the place of justice there was iniquity, and in the place of equity there was

17 iniquity. I said to my heart, God will judge the righteous
   and the wicked, for there is a time of judgment with Him,
18 for every thing and deed.   Yet I said to my heart respecting
   the children of men, God hath chosen them to shew that
19 they, even they, are like beasts.   For man is mere chance,
   and the beast is mere chance, and they are both subject to
   the same chance; as is the death of one, so is the death of
   the other, and both have the same spirit; and the advantage
20 of man over the beast is nothing, for both are vanity : both
   go to the same place, both were made of dust, and both turn
21 into dust again : no one knoweth whether the spirit of man
   goeth upward, and whether the spirit of the beast goeth down-
22 ward to the earth.   Wherefore I saw that there is nothing
   better for man than to rejoice in his labours, for this is his
   portion, since no one can bring him to see what will be here-
iv. after.   Then I saw again all the oppressed who are suffering
   under the sun, and beheld the tears of the oppressed, and
   they had no comforter, and with their oppressors there was
2 violence, and they had no comforter; and I esteemed the dead
   happy who have died long ago, more than the living who
3 are still alive; and happier than both, him who hath not
   been born, who hath not seen these evil doings which are
4 done under the sun.   Then I saw that all the toil, and
   all the skill in work, are from jealousy of one toward
   the other, this also is vanity and striving after the wind ·
5 the sluggard foldeth his hands and yet eateth his meat ;
6 better a handful of enjoyment than two handsful of labour
7 and striving after the wind.   And again I saw a vanity under
8 the sun ; here is one who hath no one with him, hath not
   even a son or a brother, and yet there is no end to all his
   labour; even his eyes are not satisfied with riches ; and for
   whom do I labour and deny my soul any of my riches ? this,
9 too, is vanity, and a grievous business.   Happier are two than
10 one, because they have a good reward for their labour; for if
   one fall, the other will lift up his fellow; but woe to the

solitary one who falleth and hath no fellow to help him up.
11 Moreover, if two sleep together they are warm; but a solitary
12 one, how can he be warm? And if an enemy overpower the
solitary one, two surely will withstand him, and a threefold
13 cord is not easily broken. Happier is a poor and wise youth
than an old and foolish king who knoweth no one to counsel
14 him. For a prisoner may go from prison to a throne,
whilst a king may become a beggar in his own kingdom.
15 I see all the living who walk under the sun, associating
16 with the youth who succeedeth him; there is no end to
all the people, to all over whom he ruleth. Yet those who
will live afterwards shall not rejoice in him, for even this
17 is vanity and striving after the wind. Keep thy feet when
thou goest to the house of God, for to obey is a nearer way
to Him than to offer the sacrifice of the disobedient, as
v. they who obey know not to do evil. Do not hasten thy
mouth, and do not urge thy heart to utter words before God,
for God is in heaven and thou art upon earth, therefore let
2 thy words be few; moreover, dreaming cometh through the
multitude of things, and foolish talk through the multitude
3 of words. When thou vowest a vow to God, hesitate not to
pay it, for fools have no fixed will; pay that which thou hast
4 vowed. Better that thou shouldst not vow than that thou
5 shouldst vow and not pay. Do not suffer thy mouth to
cause thy flesh to sin, and do not say before the angel that it
was an error: why should God be angry on account of thy idle
6 talk, and destroy the work of thine hands? For all this is
through the multitude of idle thoughts, and vanities, and
7 much talking; but fear thou the Lord. If thou seest oppression of the poor, and perverting of justice and equity in the
land, be not alarmed at the matter; for there is a superior
8 watching the superior, and superiors again over them; and
the advantage for the people is, that it extendeth to all; even
9 the king himself is subject to the field. Whoso loveth money
is never satisfied with money, nor he who loveth riches

10 with what they yield; this, too, is vanity. For when riches
    increase, those that consume them increase; what advantage,
    therefore, hath the owner thereof, except the looking thereon
11 with his eyes? Sweet is the sleep of the husbandman,
    whether he eat little or much; whilst abundance doth not
12 suffer the rich to sleep. There is a sore evil which I have
    seen under the sun — riches hath been hoarded up by the
13 rich for the owner thereof to his hurt. For the riches
    perish in some unfortunate business, and he begetteth a
14 son when he hath nothing in his possession. As he cometh
    forth from the womb of his mother, even as he cometh
    naked, he returneth again, and taketh nothing from his work
15 which he may carry away as his possession. And even this
    is a sore evil, just as he cometh so must he go, and what
16 advantage hath he who laboureth for the wind? Yet he
    eateth all his days in darkness, and is much disturbed, and
17 hath grief and vexation. Behold, that which I have seen is
    good, that it is well for man to eat and to drink, and to
    enjoy the good in all his labours which he laboureth under
    the sun, the numbered days of his life which God hath
18 given him; for this is his portion; and also, that if a man
    to whom God hath given riches and wealth is enabled
    to eat thereof, and to take his portion, and to rejoice in
19 his labour, this is a gift of God. He should remember that
    the days of his life are not many, that God causeth him to
    work for the enjoyment of his heart.
vi.   There is an evil which I have seen under the sun, and it
 2 weigheth heavily upon man. Here is a man to whom God
    hath given riches, and wealth, and abundance, so that his
    soul lacketh nothing of all that it desireth, and God hath
    not given him the power to eat thereof, but a stranger eateth
 3 it; this is vanity, and a sore evil. Though one beget a
    hundred children, and live many years, yea, numerous as
    may be the days of his years, yet if his soul is not satisfied
    with good, and even if the grave did not wait for him, I say,

4 Better than he is an untimely birth; for this cometh in
nothingness and goeth in darkness, and with darkness is its
5 memory covered; it doth not even see, and doth not know
6 the sun; it hath more rest than he. And if he live twice a
thousand years and see no good, do not both go to the same
7 place? All the labour of this man is for his mouth, and yet
8 the soul cannot be satisfied; for what advantage hath the
wise man over the fool? what the poor man over him who
9 knoweth to walk before the living? Better, indeed, is that
which is seen by the eyes, than that which is pursued by the
soul; yet this, too, is vanity and striving after the wind.
10 What hath been was long ago called by name; moreover, it
is known that he is a man, and cannot contend with Him
who is mightier than he; what advantage then hath man?
11 Moreover, there are many things which increase vanity;
12 and who knoweth what is good for man in life, the numbered
days of his vain life, which he spendeth as a shadow? and
who can tell man what shall be after him under the sun?
vii. A good name is better than sweet perfume, and the day of
2 death than the day of his birth. It is better to go to the
house of mourning than to go to the house of feasting,
because this is the end of all men, and the living will lay it
3 to heart. Better is thoughtful sadness than wanton mirth,
4 for by a serious countenance the heart is improved. The
heart of the wise, therefore, is in the house of mourning, and
5 the heart of fools in the house of mirth. It is better for a
man to listen to the reproof of a wise man, than to hear the
6 song of fools; for as the crackling of thorns is under the pot,
7 so is the laughter of a fool; this, also, is vanity; for extortion maketh the wise man foolish, and bribery corrupteth the
8 heart. The end of a reproof is better than its beginning,
9 forbearance is better than haughtiness. Do not, therefore,
hasten on thy spirit to be angry, for anger is cherished in
10 the bosom of fools. Do not say why was it that former
days were better than these; for thou wouldst not, from

11 wisdom, ask after them. Wisdom is as good as riches, and
   moreover hath an advantage over them for those who see the
12 sun. For to be in the shelter of wisdom is to be under the
   shelter of riches, and the advantage of wisdom is, that
13 wisdom enliveneth the possessor thereof. Consider, moreover, the work of God, since no man can straighten that
14 which he hath made crooked. In the day of prosperity live
   therefore as in prosperity, and in the day of adversity consider
   that God hath also made this as well as that, to the end that
   man should not discover anything which will be after him.
15 I have seen in my fleeting days, both the righteous die in
   his righteousness, and the wicked live long in his wickedness.
16 Be not therefore very righteous, and make not thyself too
17 wise, for thou wilt only make thyself to be forsaken. Be not
   very wicked, and be not foolish, lest thou die before thy
18 time. It is better that thou shouldst lay hold of this, and
   also not let go thy hand from that, for whoso feareth God
19 will make his way with both. Wisdom alone is greater
   strength to the wise, than many mighty men who have been
20 in the city; for there is not a righteous man upon earth who
21 doeth good and sinneth not. Moreover, give not thy heart
   to all the words which are uttered, lest thou hear thy servant
22 speak evil against thee; for thy heart knoweth that oftentimes
23 thou also hast spoken evil of others. All this have I tried
   by wisdom; I wished to be wiser, but it was far from me.
24 Far remaineth what was far, and deep, deep! who can find
25 it out? I and my heart turned to know and diligently to
   examine practical wisdom, in order to know the cause of
26 wickedness, vice, and mad folly, and I found woman more
   bitter than death; she is a net, her heart a snare, and her
   hands are chains; whoso is good before God shall escape from
27 her; but the sinner shall be caught by her. Behold what I
   have found, saith Coheleth — taking one thing after another
28 to find the result — and what my soul is still seeking, and I
   have not found; one man among a thousand I have found,

29 but a woman among all that number I have not found : only
behold this have I found, that God made man upright, but
viii. 1 they seek out many devices. Who is like the wise
man? and who like him that understandeth the meaning of
the thing? The wisdom of this man enlighteneth his
2 countenance, and his stern visage is changed. I say, then,
obey the king's command, and especially because of the oath
3 of God. Do not go away hastily from his presence, do not
even stand up because of an evil word, for he doth whatsoever
4 pleaseth him; inasmuch as the word of a king is powerful,
5 and who shall say unto him, What doest thou? Whoso
keepeth the commandment knoweth not an evil word. Moreover the heart of the wise man knoweth a time of judgment;
6 for there is a time of judgment for everything, when the
7 tyranny of a man is heavy upon him. Because he knoweth
not what will be, and because no one can tell him when it
8 will be. No man is ruler over his spirit to retain the spirit,
and there is no power over the day of death ; and there is no
furlough in this battle, and no cunning will save the wicked ;
9 all this I have seen, having given my heart to all the doing
that is done under the sun. There is a time when a man
10 ruleth over men to their injury ; and thus I have seen wicked
men buried and come again, and those who did right depart
from the place of the holy, and be forgotten in the city ;
11 also this is vanity. Because sentence is not forthwith
executed for evil work, the heart of the sons of men is full
12 in them to do evil, and because a sinner doeth evil a hundred
years and is perpetuated. But I also knew that it shall be
well with those who fear God, who truly fear before Him ;
13 and it shall not be well to the wicked, and, like a shadow,
he shall not prolong his existence, because he doth not fear
14 before God. Still there is this vanity happening upon the
earth, that there are righteous men who have wages like
that of the wicked, and there are wicked who have wages
like that of the righteous ; I said that this, too, is vanity.

15 And I praised mirth, because there is nothing better for
    man under the sun than to eat, and drink, and rejoice, and
    this will follow him in his work during the days of his life
    which God giveth him under the sun.

16   As I gave my heart to know wisdom, and to see the work
    which is done under the sun, how that one doth not see
17 sleep with his eyes by day and by night, I then saw that
    man cannot find out all the doing of God which is done
    under the sun; wherefore man laboureth to search it, and
    cannot find it out; and even if the wise man saith he under-
ix. 1 standeth it, he cannot find it out. For all this have I taken
    to heart, and proved all this, that the righteous and the wise,
    and their labours, are in the hand of God; these men know
    2 neither love nor hatred, both are before them, both just as
    before all others; the same fate happeneth to the righteous
    and the wicked; to the good and pure and to the impure;
    to him who sacrificeth and to him who doth not sacrifice; as
    is the good so is the sinner, he that sweareth as he who
    3 feareth an oath.   This is the greatest evil of all that is done
    under the sun, that there is the same fate for all, and that,
    although the heart of the sons of men is full of evil, and
    madness is in their hearts during their life, yet, after it, they
    4 go to the dead; for who is excepted?   To all the living there
    5 is hope, for a living dog is better than a dead lion; since the
    living know that they shall die, but the dead know not
    anything; and there is no more any advantage to them, for
    6 their memory ceaseth to be; also their love as well as their
    hatred and their zeal have long perished, and there is no
    more any portion for them for ever in all that is done under
    7 the sun. Go, then, eat with gladness thy bread, and drink
    thy wine with cheerful heart, as God hath long since been
    8 pleased with thy works; let thy garments be white at all
    9 times, and let no perfume be lacking upon thy head; enjoy
    life with the woman whom thou lovest, all the days of thy
    vain life which He giveth thee under the sun, all thy vain

days, for this is thy portion in life, and in the labour where-
10 with thou labourest under the sun: whatever thine hand
findeth to do, whilst thou art able, do it; for there is no
work, nor device, nor knowledge, nor wisdom in Hades,
11 whereunto thou art going. Then again I saw under the
sun, that the race is not to the swift, nor the battle to the
strong, nor yet bread to the wise, nor riches to the intelligent,
nor favour to the learned; that the time of misfortune cometh
12 upon all, and that man doth not even know his time; like fish
which are taken in a destructive net, and like sparrows which
are caught in a snare, like these are the sons of men ensnared
in the time of misfortune, when it suddenly cometh upon them.
13 Even this wisdom have I seen, and it seemed great to me:
14 There was a little city, and few men in it; and a powerful
king came against it, and besieged it, and built great towers
15 over it. And there was found in it a poor wise man, and he
saved the city by his wisdom; and yet no one remembered
16 that poor man. Therefore I say, wisdom is indeed better
than force, yet the wisdom of the poor is despised, and his
17 words are not listened to. Though the words of the wise
are listened to with greater pleasure than the shouting of a
18 foolish ruler, and wisdom is better than instruments of war,
x. 1 yet one fool destroyeth much good; a dead fly maketh sweet
ointment stinkingly to ferment; a little folly is more mighty
2 than honourable wisdom. Still the mind of the wise man
3 is at his right hand, but the mind of the fool at his left; and
even when the fool walketh on the road he lacketh his mind,
4 and yet he saith of every one, He is a fool! If the anger of
the ruler is kindled against thee, quit not thy place, for
5 gentleness preventeth greater outrages. There is an evil
which I have seen under the sun — an outrage as that which
6 proceedeth from a ruler; a great fool is placed in many high
7 positions, and the noble sit in degradation: I have seen
servants upon horses, and masters walking on the ground
8 as servants. Yet he who diggeth a pit shall fall into it,

9 and whoso breaketh down a wall a serpent shall bite him;
he who breaketh up stones shall be hurt therewith; whoso
10 cleaveth wood shall be cut thereby. If the axe be blunt,
and he do not sharpen it beforehand, he shall only increase
the army; but the advantage of repairing hath wisdom.
11 if the serpent bite without enchantment, there is no advan-
12 tage to the charmer. The words from the mouth of the
wise man gain him favour, but those from the lips of the
13 fool destroy him; the beginning of the words of his mouth
is folly, and the end of the words of his mouth is mischievous
14 madness. The fool also speaketh much, though no man
knoweth what shall be here nor what shall be hereafter;
15 who can tell him it? The work of a fool wearieth him
16 because he knoweth not how to go to the city. Woe to thee,
O land, when thy king is childish, and thy princes feast
17 in the morning! Happy thou, O land, when thy king is
noble, and thy princes eat in proper time, for strength and
18 not for feasting! Through slothful hands the roof falleth
19 in, and through lazy hands the house leaketh. They turn
bread and wine, which cheereth life, into revelry, and the
20 money of —— is made to supply both. Still do not
revile the king even in thy thoughts, and do not revile the
prince even in thy bed-chamber, for the bird of the air
conveyeth the report, and the winged creature telleth the
xi. 1 story. Cast thy bread upon the surface of the water, for in
2 the process of time thou mayest find the profit of it; give a
portion thereof to seven and even to eight, for thou knowest
3 not what misfortune there may be upon the earth. When
the clouds are full of rain they empty it upon the earth,
and when the tree falleth in the south or north, in the
4 place where the tree falleth there it lieth; whoso therefore
watcheth the wind shall not sow, and he who looketh at the
5 clouds shall not reap. As thou knowest as little the course
of the wind as the formation in the womb of the pregnant,
so thou knowest not the work of God who worketh all

6 things. Sow, then, thy seed in the morning, and withhold not thine hand therefrom in the evening, since thou knowest not which shall prosper, this or that, or whether both shall
7 be alike good ; and the light shall be sweet, and it shall be
8 cheering to the eyes to see the sun. For even if a man should live many years, he ought to rejoice in them all, and to remember that there will be many dark days, that all
9 which is coming is vanity ! Rejoice, O young man, in thy youth, and let thy heart cheer thee in thy youthful days, and pursue the ways of thine heart, and the things which are seen by the eyes, and know that, respecting all these,
10 God will bring thee into judgment. Banish, therefore, sorrow from thy mind, and put away sadness from thy body,
xii. 1 for youth and manhood are vanity; and remember thy Creator in the days of thy youth, before the days of evil come, and the years arrive of which thou shalt say, I have
2 no pleasure in them : before the sun becometh dark, and the light, and the moon, and the stars, and the clouds
3 return after the rain; when the keepers of the house shall quake, and the men of power writhe, and the grinding-maids shall stop because they have greatly diminished, and the women who look out of the windows shall be shrouded
4 in darkness; and the doors shall be closed in the street: when the noise of the mill shall grow faint, and the swallow shall rise to shriek, and all the singing birds shall retire ;
5 yea the people shall be frightened at that which is coming from on high, and at the terrors which are on their way; and the almond shall be despised, and the locust shall be loathed, and the caper-berry shall be powerless; for man goeth to his eternal home, and the mourners walk about the street:
6 before the silver cord goeth asunder, and the golden bowl escapeth, or the bucket breaketh upon the fountain, and the
7 wheel is shattered at the well, and the body returneth to the earth as it was, and the spirit goeth back to God who gave it.

8   Vanity of vanities, saith Coheleth; all is vanity!
9 And besides that Coheleth was a wise man, he also taught
   the people wisdom, and carefully and studiously. composed
10 many parables.   Coheleth sought to find words of comfort,
11 and he wrote down frankly the words of truth.   The words
   of the wise are like goads, and those of the masters of the
   assemblies are like fixed stakes, given by the same shepherd.
12 And beyond these, my son, beware! to make many books
   there is no end, and much study is a weariness of the flesh.
13 In conclusion, everything is noticed; fear God, and keep
14 his commandments, for this every man should do; for God
   will bring every work to the judgment appointed over every
   secret thing, whether it be good or evil.

APPENDICES.

I.

ANCIENT VERSIONS.

The comparison of the ancient versions with the original, instituted throughout the Commentary, has shewn us that there are considerable discrepancies between them and the Hebrew. Many and various have been the attempts made by critics to account for these divergences. Some have supposed that the translators had a different text to what we now have; others that they had a meagre knowledge of the Hebrew, and misunderstood its meaning; some have maintained that they have designedly deviated from the original, and that no heed is to be paid to their false renderings; whilst others, again, have assured us that the Jews have since wilfully corrupted the text, that the unadulterated readings are to be found in the ancient versions, and that the Hebrew text must be corrected by them. These extreme opinions, however, proceed from the erroneous supposition that the ancient translators had the scientific and well-defined rules of exegesis, as well as the critical apparatus, which we now possess, and that the genius of the Greek and Latin languages admits of a literal and verbatim translation of the Hebrew; so that by turning the Greek or Latin version again into Hebrew, we obtain the words, the gender, number, and tense of the original. Thus, we are gravely assured, by eminent critics, that the Septuagint's rendering of קֹהֶלֶת אָמְרָה by εἶπεν ὁ ἐκκλησιαστής shews the incorrect separation of the words in the Hebrew; ὁ ἐκκλησιαστής being a masculine noun *in Greek*, the Hebrew word קֹהֶלֶת, for which it stands, must also be masculine, and hence cannot be construed with אָמְרָה, a *feminine* verb (*vide supra*, p. 388). The folly of this mode of proceeding will appear all the more glaring when we bear in mind that, apart from the difference of idioms, which frequently necessitated the addition or omission of words or the solution of tropes, and the inadvertences, inconsistencies, and mistakes which are to be found in all human productions, the translators, having been Jews, or impregnated with Jewish opinions, followed the Hagadic mode of interpretation, and frequently explained the text according to the rules described in the Introduction (p. 30), thus giving us rather the views of others *about the meaning of passages* than that which the words themselves signify.

Every repetition of a word or sentence in the Scriptures, every figure of speech, parallelism, and synonymous expression, word, syllable, letter — nay, the very shape and ornaments, or titles, the similarity of appearance or sound of one letter or word to another Hebrew or *foreign* letter or word, are regarded by the Hagadic interpreters as furnishing a clue to unlock the recondite and mysterious treasure concealed in the Bible. Hence the various senses assigned to the same word or phrase when repeated; hence the alteration of letters or words according to the exigencies of the place; hence the interchange of assonances, or of letters and expressions resembling each other; hence the different separations of the same word; hence the reduction of letters and words to their numerical value, and their explanation by other letters and words of the same quantity, and many other modes of dealing with the text, most of which have been pointed out in the Commentary as having been practised by the ancient translators. The extent, however, of the Hagadic influence on the ancient versions can only be ascertained by a careful comparison of these versions with the Midrashim, the Talmud, and the Chaldee paraphrases. It will then be seen that many of the discrepancies between the ancient versions and the Hebrew text are neither owing to ignorance on the part of the translators, nor to different readings, nor to a wilful corruption of the text, but are simply the result of the application of one or other of the Hagadic rules of interpretation, examples of which have been given in p. 30, &c., and throughout the Commentary. All that remains to be done now, is to classify some of the deviations of those versions. The Septuagint, being the oldest version, claims our attention first.

A. The Septuagint.

The Hagadic influence on this version manifests itself in various ways, and accounts for, as well as explains, many renderings which are otherwise inexplicable and unintelligible. Thus —

1. The particle את, the sign of the accusative, which occurs as such seventy-one times in Coheleth, is in forty-two instances — i. 13; ii. 3. 10. 12. 14. 20. 24; iii. 11. 15; iv. 3. 5. (twice) 8. 10; v. 3. 5. (thrice) 18. 19; vii. 7. 13. (twice) 14. 18. (twice) 21; viii. 8. 9. 16. (twice); ix. 7. 11. 12. 15; x. 20; xi. 5. 6. 8; xii. 1. 13. (twice) — regarded as *the accusative;* whereas in the other twenty-nine instances — i. 14; ii. 17. 18; iii. 10. 11. (twice) 17. (twice); iv. 1. 2. 3. 4. (twice) 15; v. 6; vii. 15. 26; viii. 8. 9. 15. 17. (twice); ix. 1. (twice) 15; x. 19; xi. 7; xii. 9. 14 — it is rendered by σὺν = *with.* Commentators have been perplexed to account for this barbarism and violation of grammatical propriety; but a reference to the Hagadic exegesis will shew that this Hebrew particle was looked up to as having a mystical significance, because the two letters, א and ת, of which it is composed, are the alpha and omega of the Hebrew alphabet (comp. Midrash Rabba, Yalkut, and Rashi, on Numb. vi. 13.). Hence the anxiety of the translator to indicate this particle in Greek, when a passage appeared to him to be fraught with special mysteries.

2. The Hagadic influence is still more evident in the peculiar renderings and paraphrases of ii. 12. 17; iii. 15; iv. 17; v. 1; vi. 8; vii. 6. 12. 21; viii. 1; x. 17. 19; xi. 9; xii. 9, where whole phrases and sentiments of the Hagada have been introduced into the Greek version, as has been shewn in the Commentary, many of which can only be understood by comparing them with the Midrashim or Chaldee paraphrase.

3. As the object of this mode of interpretation is more to shew the recondite and spiritual meaning of every detached verse and clause than to elucidate the design of the inspired book, such sentences as apparently savoured of heterodoxy are made orthodox by adding or explaining away some words (comp. ii. 15. 17; xi. 9).

4. Changing letters or words for those which are similar in appearance or sound, is one of the rules whereby the many meanings of the text are obtained (comp. i. 18; ii. 3; v. 16. 17; vii. 22; viii. 6. 9. 12; ix. 2, with Introduction, p. 31).

5. Such exegesis can have no regard for the recurrence of some phrases;

and hence the same sentences are rendered according to the will of the translator (comp. i. 9 with iii. 15), who frequently adds words (i. 1; vii. 2; x. 19), or alters them (vii. 18; viii. 10; x. 10), or changes them (i. 13; ii. 3; viii. 18), when it is deemed necessary to obtain a particular sense.

6. When the translator has no recondite meaning to evolve, and adheres to the text, his renderings sometimes follow the very order of the words in the Hebrew and are exceedingly obscure (comp. viii. 11.), but sometimes are happy, and are a valuable contribution to modern criticism, e.g. v. 15; viii. 5. 9. 15; ix. 17, and many other passages duly noticed in the Commentary.

B. AQUILA.

The disrepute into which the Septuagint had fallen among the Jews induced Aquila, a Jewish proselyte who flourished about A D. 150, to undertake a new translation, which he executed with slavish literality, as is evident from the surviving portion of it. He, too, translated the mysterious particle אֶת by σύν.[1] The Talmud speaks in high terms of this version.[2] And though it is to be greatly regretted that the fragments of it which have escaped destruction are too small to shew us what sense the translator attached to the difficult portions of Coheleth, yet they frequently indicate the old readings of the text.

C. THEODOTION.

Whether it was the servile, and at times unintelligible, version of Aquila, or some other cause, which made it necessary that another translation of the Hebrew verity should be made, it is now difficult to say; all that we know is, that Theodotion, also a Jewish proselyte, a native of Ephesus and a contemporary of Aquila, published a fresh translation shortly after the former appeared. The fragments which have come down to us of his version of Coheleth are too insignificant to enable us to judge what mode he adopted in translating this difficult book. It appears, however, from his translation of this (comp. i. 13; iii. 19; viii. 6), and other portions of Scripture. that he made both the Septuagint and Aquila the basis of his translation, and that he followed the Hagadic exegesis, as is evident from Gen. iv. 4., where he translates וַיִּשַׁע יְהֹוָה by καὶ ἐνεπύρισεν ὁ Θεός, and God set on fire, of which St. Jerome highly approves, and remarks, unde scire poterat Cain, quod fratris munera suscepisset Deus et sua repudiasset, nisi illa interpretatio vera esset, quam Theodotion posuit: Et inflammavit Dominus super Abel, et super sacrificium ejus, &c. Ignem autem ad sacrificium devorandum solitum venire de cælo.[3] Rashi, who gives us the Hagadic explanations, says, ירדה אש ולחכה מנחתו, a fire descended and consumed his sacrifice. Theodotion also renders וַהֲמִשִּׁים עָלוּ בְנֵי־יִשְׂרָאֵל מֵאֶרֶץ מִצְרַיִם by πεμπταίζοντες δὲ ἀνέβησαν οἱ υἱοὶ Ἰσραὴλ ἐκ τῆς γῆς

---

[1] Aquila autem proselytus et contentiosus interpres, qui non solum verba, sed etymologias quoque verborum transferre conatus est, jure projicitur a nobis. Quis enim pro frumento, et vino, et oleo possit, vel legere vel intelligere, χεῦμα, ἀπωρισμὸν, στιλπνότητα (Deut. vii. 13.), quod nos possumus dicere fusionem pomationemque et splendentiam. Aut quia Hebraei non solum habent ἄρθρα, sed et πρόαρθρα; ille κακοζήλως et syllabas interpretatur et litteras, dicitque σὺν τὸν οὐρανὸν καὶ σὺν τὴν γῆν, quod Græca et Latina Lingua omnino non recipit.—Hieronym. Ep. ad Pammach. de opt. gen. interpretandi. Comp. Henry Owen, An Enquiry into the present state of the Septuagint version of the Old Testament, p. 102; Davidson, Biblical Criticism, p. 216.
[2] Sabbath, 8, b; Yoma, 41, a.; Megilla, 73, b.
[3] Hieronym. quæstion. Heb. in Genesin ad h. versum.

Αἰγύπτου, *and one of five did the children of Israel go out of the land of Egypt* (Exod. xiii. 18) ; according to the Midrash (*in loco*), which explains וַחֲמֻשִׁים by אחר מחמשה יצאו, which is also mentioned by Rashi, who remarks, החומשים, that דבר אחר חמושי׳ אחד מחמש מחומשי׳ יצאו וארבעה חלקים מתו בשלשת ימי אפלה is also explained by *one of five*, i.e., *one from five went out, and four portions died during the three days of darkness*. It is also owing to Hagadic influence that Theodotion frequently retains Hebrew words without translating them (comp. Exod. xii. 11 ; Levit. xiii. 6. 19), fearing lest he might not succeed in giving the correct equivalent in Greek.

D. SYMMACHUS.

Shortly after the appearance of the above two versions, Symmachus, who is represented by Eusebius and St. Jerome as an Ebionite, published a third translation, which is greatly superior to its predecessors, and has been justly held in high estimation by the most judicious of the Fathers. The fragments which remain of this shew that Symmachus aimed more at giving the sense of the Hebrew in intelligent, perspicuous, and elegant Greek, than at being slavishly literal (comp. i. 13 ; ii. 25 ; vi. 21). He was master of the Hebrew and Greek, and has given us some happy renderings (comp. i. 13 ; iii. 1 ; iv. 1. 12 ; ix. 4 ; x. 3. 9 ; xii. 1) ; yet he also sometimes follows the Septuagint (v. 8 ; ix. 2 ; x. 9), even in its Hagadic interpretations (iii. 15) ; he also mistook words (v. 2), and adopted the mistakes of Aquila and Theodotion (viii. 12).

E. THE SYRIAC VERSION.

The best version that antiquity has produced is the Syriac. This precious relic, which has been preserved to us entire, is of inestimable value for the criticism and interpretation of the Old Testament; the Syriac being a cognate language, the translator has frequently been able to give in the version the very roots of the original, and to follow the very order of the words and construction of the Hebrew. That this version was made direct from the Hebrew is evident —

1. From the several mistakes into which the translator has fallen. Thus, for instance, he mistook ברם and בראם (iii. 18), כי בראם האלהים for לברם האלהים having the same pronunciation in Hebrew, which could only be done by the translator having the Hebrew before him. The same is the case with his mistaking נחלה, *an inheritance*, for נחילה, *an instrument* (vii. 11) ; חילים, *the army*, for הללים, *the slain* (x. 10) ; and changing עלם into עמל, by a transposition of the second and third radicals, which is effected directly from the Hebrew.

2. From the translation following the very order of the words in the original, *e. g.*

ידעתי	כי כל אשר יעשה	האלהים	הוא יהיה לעולם	עליו אין להוסיף	וממנו אין לגרוע
ידעת	דכל דעבד	מריא	הו נהוא לעלם	עלוהי לית למוספו	ומנה לית למבצר

chap. iii. 14.

והאלהים עשה	שייראו מלפניו
ומריא עבד	דנדחלון מנה

מתוקה שנת העבד	אם מעט ואם הרבה יאכל	והשבע לעשיר	איננו מניח לו לישון
חליא שנתא דפלחא	אן זעור אן סגי אכל	וסבעא לעתירא	לא שבק לה למדמך

chap. v. 11.

ובכן ראיתי רשעים קברים ובאו	וממקום קדוש יהלכו וישתכחו בעיר	אשר כן עשו
והידין חזית רשיעא דקבירין ואתין	ומן אתרא דקודשא אזלו ואתטעו במדינתא	דהננא עבדו

chap. viii. 10.

The parallels require no comment, and are an irrefragable proof that the Syriac version was made directly from the Hebrew. As this invaluable translation has been greatly neglected, I have collated it with the Hebrew, the result of which may be seen in the following columns: —

THE SYRIAC.		THE HEBREW.
ספר קהלת היא שלמה בן דוד מלך ישראל		
לא ישבע איש	i. 8	לא יוכל איש
מה יעל	ii. 2	מהולל
וסבתי אני ליאש את לבי	3	
קניתי לי עבדים	7	קניתי עבדים
ובני בית הרבה		ובני בית
עשיתי לי שדה ושדות	8	שדה ושדות
ובכל יטל	11	ונעמל
בדין עם שעשהו	12	את אשר כבר עשוהו
כי הסכל דבר הרבה	16	
ממנו	25	ממני
שמש	iii. 1	שמים
עת לאבד ועת לבקש	6	עת לבקש ועת לאבד
בחייהון	12	בחיו
לרדוף את הנדף	15	את הנדף
כי בראם האלהים	18	לברם האלהים
יניע להם	19	כי
יקרה את כלם		להם
טוב בהם	22	טוב
בכל שיהיה		במה שיהיה
טוב מתת	iv. 17	מתת
לעשות טוב		לעשות רע
תדר	v. 3	תדר נדר
אלהים	5	מלאך
הרבה התעה	6	הרבה
ומשפט	7	משפט וצדק
לבעל הטובה	10	לבעליה
מה יתרון בכל	15	מה יתרון לו
וקצף וחלי ואבל כעס	16	וחליו וקצף כעס
ראיתי אני קהלת	17	ראיתי אני
מענה לו	19	מענה
יאכלנו אחריו	vi. 2	יאכלנו
וחלי הוא		וחלי רע הוא
כי יש יתרון לחכם מן הכסיל מה [היתרון] כי העני וגו'	8	כי מה יותר לחכם מן הכסיל מה לעני וגו'
שם טוב	vii. 1	שם
ויום המות טוב		ויום המות
יתן טוב אל לבו	2	יתן אל בו
מכלי קרב	11	עם חכמה
כצל	12	בצל
ראה נפשך	14	ראה
אל תרשע הרבה למה ישנא הרבה	17	אל תרשע הרבה
אשר ירברו רשעים אל תתן לבך לא תשמע	21	אשר ידברו אל תתן לבך אשר לא תשמע
יותר מן שהיה רחוק	24	רחוק מה שהיה
אשר בקשה	28	אשר עוד בקשה
פי מלך שמר	viii. 2	אני פי מלך שמר
כאשר	4	באשר

THE SYRIAC.		THE HEBREW.
כי אין שיודע למה שהיה ומה שיהיה לו אחריו מי	viii. 7	כי איננו ידע מה שיהיה כי כאשר יהיה מי
ביום מלחמה	8	במלחמה
וידע אני	12	כי גם יודע אני
על כן	16	כאשר
ולבי ראה את כל זה	ix. 1	ולבור את כל זה
כל לפניהם הבל		הכל לפניהם
לטוב ולרע לטהיר ולטמא	2	לטוב ולטהור ולטמא
והוללות רע בלבבם	3	והוללות בלבבם
כי רצה האלהים	7	כי כבר רצה האלהים
		כל ימי חיי הבלך אשר נתן לך תחת השמש כל
כל ימי חיי הבלך	9	ימי הבלך
מצודים	14	מצודים גדולים
ומלט הוא המסכן	15	ומלט הוא
מכבוד הרבה	x. 1	מכבוד
והוא פנים	10	והוא לא פנים
וחללים יגבר		וחילים יגבר
עמלי הכסילים	15	עמל הכסילים
ללכת אל המדינה		ללכת אל עיר
לחם יין ושמן	19	לחם ויין
והכסף יענה ויטעה אותם בכל		והכסף יענה את הכל
יולך את קלך	20	יוליך את הקול
יגיד דבריך		יגיד דבר
תן חלק לשבעה אף לשמונה כי לא תדע מה רעה יהיה על הארץ	xi. 1	שלח לחמך על פני המים כי ברב הימים תמצאנו
שלח לחמך על פני המים כי ברב הימים תמצאנו	2	תן חלק לשבעה וגו׳
בארץ צפון	3	בצפון
אשר	5	כאשר
כל בקר זרע	6	בבקר זרע ּ
וטוב לעינים ויותר לראי השמש	7	וטוב לעינים לראות את השמש
ייטיבך לבך	9	ייטיבך לבך בימי בחורותיך
ולא דעת	10	והשחרות
ואור הירח	xii. 2	והאור והירח
וינץ עליו השקד וינוץ השקד	5	וינאץ השקד
ותפרה האביונה ותפר האביונה		ותפר האביונה
בית עמלו		בית עלמו
שלמד	6	עוד למד
הרבה בקש קהלת		בקש קהלת
בעלי ספות	11	בעלי אספות
כל שמע	13	הכל נשמע
כי זה מרצח אחד נתן לכל אדם		כי זה כל האדם
על כל נעלם ונגלה	14	על כל נעלם

Now a careful analysis of these variations between the Syriac and the
Hebrew will shew that they may be traced to the following sources : —

1. Hagadic influence (ii. 12. 15. 16; iii. 15. 19; iv. 17; v. 1; vi. 8; vii.
   21; x. 19; xii. 5).
2. Carelessness of transcribers (iii. 6; xi. 1. 2; xii. 11. 13); mistaking
   letters that resemble one another (vii. 12; viii. 4).
3. Later additions, e. g., the superscription, &c.
4. A desire to have the same verb as a similar phrase in the corresponding clauses of the verses i. 8; ii. 2.

5. Glaring mistakes, which arose from inadvertency (ii. 7 ; viii. 8) ; from marginal glosses (viii. 17 ; x. 19 ; xii. 5) ; from joining clauses (ii. 7 ; vii. 2).
6. The translator mistook the roots (iii. 18 ; vii. 11 ; x. 10).
7. Bad renderings on the part of the translator (vii. 24 ; viii. 7. 16 ; xi. 7 ; xii. 2) ; or made by another hand (xi. 10 ; xii. 6. 13).
8. Omissions (v. 3. 7 ; vi. 12 ; vii. 28 ; viii. 2. 12 ; ix. 7. 9. 14 ; x. 10 ; xi. 9).
9. Additions by way of explanation, some good (v. 3. 10. 15. 17 ; vi. 12 ; vii. 1. 3 ; ix. 15 ; x. 1. 15 ; xi. 3. 6 ; xii. 14) ; some bad (v. 6. 16. 19 ; vii. 4 ; ix. 2 ; x. 19).
10. Better readings than the Hebrew (ii. 7. 11 ; viii. 8).

It must also be added that a comparison of i. 10. 13 ; ii. 3. 15 ; v. 6. 16 ; vii. 2. 21 ; viii. 4 ; ix. 1. 2. 9 ; x. 19 ; xi. 10. 13, with the Septuagint's renderings of these passages, will convince the most cursory reader that a later and unskilful hand has been tampering with the Syriac, trying to make it agree with the Septuagint. Chapter xi. 10, where the barbarous and non-Syriac ܠܐܟܠܐ ܗܘ is put in for the Hebrew וְהַשַּׁחֲרוּת, to answer to the Septuagint's ἡ ἄνοια, shews that the masterly Syrian who translated Coheleth had nothing to do with it.

F. The Old Italic.

The Old Italic Version forms the basis of the one on which St. Jerome wrote the *Commentarium ad Paulam et Eustochium*. St. Jerome indeed declares, in the preface to this commentary, " I followed nobody's authority; but though I translated from the Hebrew, I at the same time adapted my translation to the manner of the Septuagint in such things as did not differ much from the Hebrew ; " yet a careful analysis of it will shew that the words of the Father must not be interpreted strictly, and that his version is a patchwork of the Hebrew, the Septuagint, the Old Italic, Aquila, Theodotion, Symmachus, and the Midrash. That it is largely made up of Jewish traditions, we have seen in the Introduction (p. 3, &c.), and throughout the Commentary. A few instances will suffice to shew how St. Jerome drew upon the Greek versions, whether they were right or wrong. הוֹלֵלוֹת (i. 17) is rendered by Aquila πλάνας, by St. Jerome *errores ;* נָחַת (iv. 6), Symmachus μετὰ ἀναπαύσεως, St. Jerome *cum requie ;* וְהַשָּׁבָה לְעָשִׂיר אֵינֶנּוּ מַנִּיחַ לוֹ לִישׁוֹן (v. 11), Symmachus ἡ δὲ πλησμονὴ τοῦ πλουσίου οὐκ ἐᾷ καθεύδειν, St. Jerome *et saturitas divitis non sinit eum dormire ;* וְכָתוּב יֹשֶׁר (xii. 10), Aquila and Symmachus συνέγραψεν ὀρθῶς, St. Jerome *scriberet recte.* The fact, however, that St. Jerome has thoroughly espoused the Hagadic mode of interpretation, and incorporated in his commentary so many of the Hagadic expositions, renders his writings important for *historical* purposes, inasmuch as the Jewish traditions preserved by him frequently furnish us with the clue to the sources whence the Septuagint derived its renderings.

G. The Vulgate.

Three years after the publication of the above commentary, St. Jerome finished the translation of Coheleth contained in the Vulgate. When we add to what has already been said about his approving the Hagadic explanations and drawing upon the different Greek versions, that he only took *three days* to translate *the three* reputed books of Solomon. viz., Proverbs,

Coheleth, and the Song of Songs, as he informs Bishops Chromatius and Heliodorus,[1] we shall not wonder that the Vulgate on Coheleth —

1. Has largely copied the Hagadic explanations (i. 15 ; ii. 12. 17 ; iv. 1 ; vi. 8 ; vii. 3. 6. 12. 14 ; ix. 3. 6 ; x. 17. 19 ; xi. 8) ; and also taken words in a double sense (viii. 18 ; x. 10), according to the same mode of interpretation.

. Misunderstood the usage of phrases (i. 16, 17).

3. Altered words and whole sentences (i. 10 ; ii. 12 ; viii. 10 ; x. 10. 18), sometimes to avoid apparent discrepancies (viii. 13), and sometimes omitting them altogether (i. 5 ; ii. 12 ; iv. 2 ; viii. 4).

4. Abounds in inconsistencies (i. 9 with iii. 15 ; iv. 7), and loose and unaccountable paraphrases (ii. 3. 16 ; iii. 9 ; vii. 12).

5' Has largely copied Symmachus, whose version St. Jerome greatly admired. Comp. אֵירָה טוֹב . . . וְלִבִּי נֹהֵג בַּחָכְמָה . . . תַּרְתִּי בְלִבִּי(ii. 3) Symmachus καὶ ἐνοήθην ἐν τῇ καρδίᾳ μου . . . ἵνα τὴν καρδίαν μου μεταγάγω εἰς σοφίαν . . . ποῖον τὸ σύμφορον, the Vulgate *cogitavi in corde meo* . . . *. ut animum meum transferrem ad sapientiam . . . quid esset utile ;* הֶה אֲשֶׁר־רָאִיתִי אָנִי (v. 17), Symmachus ἐμοὶ οὖν ἐφάνη, the Vulgate *hoc itaque visum est mihi ;* וְלַשֵּׂאת אֶת־חֶלְקוֹ (v. 18), Symmachus καὶ ἀπολαῦσαι τῆς μερίδος αὐτῶν, the Vulgate *et fruatur parte sua ;* יְהוֹלֵל חָכָם (vii. 7), Symmachus θορυβήσει σοφόν, the Vulgate *conturbat sapientem ;* לֹא יָדַע (viii. 5), Symmachus οὐ πειραθήσεται, the Vulgate *non 'experietur ;* עַל־כֵּן מָלֵא לֵב (viii. 11), Symmachus ἀφόβω καρδία, the Vulgate *absque timore.* It will be seen that all these are instances of departure from the literal meaning of the text, and that there is, therefore, no other way of accounting for this extraordinary agreement in the loose renderings, than that the later paraphrast copied the earlier one. St. Jerome has also adopted many of Symmachus' good renderings. Comp. מְקַלֶּלְךָ (vii. 21), Symmachus ποιδοροῦντός σε, the Vulgate *maledicentem tibi ;* אֲשֶׁר כֶּן־עָשׂוּ (viii. 10), Symmachus ὡς δίκαια πράξαντες, the Vulgate *quasi justorum operum.*

For further strictures upon the Vulgate we must refer to the Commentary, where its peculiarities have been noticed in their respective places. We would only add, that too much stress cannot be laid upon the necessity of tracing the sources of the Vulgate, and of forming a true estimate of its merits and demerits, inasmuch as the Reformers, in their translations, have drawn largely upon this version.

H. The Chaldee Paraphrase.

The importance of this paraphrase to historical exegesis is incalculable, inasmuch as it contains the Hagadic interpretation of Coheleth, and gives us the sources of all the preceding versions. Through it, many of the obscure passages in the Septuagint, Aquila, Theodotion, Symmachus, the Vulgate, the Syriac, &c., become intelligible, as has been shewn in different parts of the Commentary. Convinced that a more extensive comparison of it with the ancient versions than the limits of our Commentary have permitted us to institute, will greatly contribute to the criticism of these versions, we subjoin a literal translation of the whole Chaldee paraphrase, and only wish that we could also give a translation of the Midrashim on

---

[1] *Itaque ægrotatione fractus, ne penitus hoc anno reticerem, et apud vos mutus essem, tridui* opus nomini vestro consecravi, interpretationem videlicet trium Salominis voluminum, *Masloth . . . Cohelet . . . Sirhassirim.* Præf. in libb. Salomonis.

Coheleth, which would have shewn to a still greater extent how much the old translations and the modern versions which follow them are indebted to the Hagada —

i. 1 THE words of prophecy which Coheleth, that is, the son of David the
2 King, who was in Jerusalem, prophesied. When Solomon the King of Israel foresaw, by the spirit of prophecy, the kingdom of Rehoboam his son, which will be divided with Jeroboam the son of Nebat, and that Jerusalem and the holy temple will be destroyed, and that the people of Israel will be led into captivity, he said by the divine word, Vanity of vanities is this world! vanity of vanities is all which I and my father David have laboured
3 for, all of it is vanity! What advantage is there to a man, after his death, from all his labour which he laboured under the sun in this world, except he studied the word of God, in order to receive a good reward in the
4 world to come from before the Lord of the world? King Solomon said, by the spirit of prophecy, The good generation of the righteous departs from the world because of the sins of the wicked generation that is to follow them, but the earth abides for ever and ever, to reserve the punishment which is to come upon the world, on account of the sins of
5 the children of men. And the sun rises in the day from the east, and the sun goes down in the west by night, and hastens to its place, and goes through the path under the sea, and rises the following day from
6 the place where it rested yesterday; it goes all the side of the south in the day, and goes round to the side of the north by night, through the path under the sea; it turns round and round to the wind of the south corner in the revolution of Nisan and Tamuz, and returns on its circuits to the wind of the north corner in the revolution of Tishri and Tebeth; it comes through the windows of the east in the morning, and
7 goes into the windows of the west in the evening. All the rivers and streams of water go and flow into the waters of the ocean which surround the world like a ring, and the ocean is not full, and to the place where the streams go and flow there they go again through the channels of the
8 sea. The ancient prophets have exerted themselves in all the things which will take place in the world, and they could not find out their end; therefore, a man has no power to declare what will be after him, neither can the eye see all that is to be in the world, nor can the ear be filled with hearing all the words of the inhabitants of the
9 earth. What was aforetime, the same will be afterwards again, and what was done aforetime the same will be done again to the end of all generations, and there is no new thing in the world under the sun.
10 There may be something of which a man says, Behold, this is a new thing, but it has been long ago, in the generations which were before us.
11 There is no remembrance of former generations, and also of the coming ones that will be, there will be no remembrance of them among the
12 generations which will be in the days of the King Messiah. When King Solomon was sitting upon the throne of his kingdom, his heart became very proud of his riches, and he transgressed the word of God, and he gathered many horses, and chariots, and riders, and he amassed much gold and silver, and he married from foreign nations, whereupon the anger of the Lord was kindled against him, and he sent to him Ashmoda the king of the demons, who drove him from the throne of his kingdom, and took away the ring from his hand, in order that he should roam and wander about in the world to reprove it; and he went about in the provincial towns and the cities of the land of Israel, weeping and lamenting, and saying, I am Coheleth, whose name was formerly called Solomon,
13 who was king over Israel in Jerusalem: and I gave my heart to ask

instruction from God at the time when he appeared unto me in Gibeon, to try me, and to ask me what I desire of him, and I asked nothing of him except wisdom, to know the difference between good and evil, and knowledge of whatsoever was done under the sun in this world, and I saw all the works of the wicked children of men,—a bad business which

14 God gave to the children of men to be afflicted by it: I saw all the works of the children of men which were done under the sun in this

15 world; behold, all is vanity and breaking of the spirit. A man whose ways are perverted in this world, and who dies therein and does not repent, has no power to become right after his death; and whoso departs from the law and the precepts in his life, has no power to be

16 numbered with the righteous in paradise after his death. I spake with the thoughts of my heart, saying: I, behold! I have increased and multiplied wisdom above all the wise who were before me in Jerusalem,

17 and my heart has seen much wisdom and knowledge; and I gave my heart to know wisdom, and the fear of the Kingdom, and knowledge and discretion, I know it by experience that even this is a breaking of the

18 spirit to the man who is employed to find them out. Because a man who increases his knowledge when he is guilty, and does not repent, increases the anger of God; and he who accumulates wisdom and dies in his youth, increases the sadness of heart to his relations.

ii. 1 I said in my heart, I will go now and try mirth, and behold the good of this world; and when pain and affliction befell me, I said by the divine

2 word, Also this is vanity. To laughter I said, in time of affliction, It is mockery; and to mirth, What profit is it to the man who indulges in it?

3 I tried in my heart to enrapture my flesh in the house of the feast of wine, and my heart conducted with wisdom, and to seize the folly of youth, until I examined and saw which of them was good for the children of men, that they may do while they abide in this world under the heavens, the num-

4 ber of the days of their life. I multiplied good works in Jerusalem. I built houses, viz., the temple, to make atonement for Israel, and a royal palace, and the conclave, and the porch, and a house of judgment of hewn stones, where the wise men sit, and the judges, to give judgment; I made a throne of ivory for the sitting of royalty; I planted vineyards in Jabne, that I and the Rabbis of the Sanhedrin might drink wine, and

5 also to make libations of wine, new and old, upon the altar; I made watered gardens and parks, and I sowed there all kinds of herbs, some for food, some for drink, and some for medicine, and all kinds of aromatics; I planted therein sterile trees, and aromatic trees, which the spectres and evil spirits brought me from India, and all kinds of fruit-bearing trees; and its boundary was from the wall of the city of Jeru-

6 salem to the margin of the river Siloah; I made receptacles of water, whence to water the trees and the herbs; I made pools of water, to water

7 from them even the thicket which produces fine wood; I bought bond-men and bond-women from the children of Ham, and other foreign nations; and I had officers placed over the eatables of my house, to provide for me and the people of my house food twelve months of the year, and one to provide for me during the leap-year; I had also cattle

8 and sheep more than all generations before me in Jerusalem; I gathered also treasures of silver and gold; even right weights and measures I made from good gold; and the treasures of kings and provinces were given to me as tribute; I made for the temple musical instruments, that the Levites might play them at the sacrifices, and citherns and flutes that the male and female singers might play them in the wine house, and the delights of the children of men; and warm springs, and baths,

channels pouring out cold water, and channels pouring out warm water;
9 and I multiplied goods and increased riches more than all generations
before me in Jerusalem, because my wisdom stood with me and assisted
10 me; and whatsoever the Rabbis of the Sanhedrin asked of me respecting
pure and impure, innocent and guilty, I did not withhold from them any
explanation of these things; and I did not keep my heart from the joy of
the law, because I had the inclination of heart to enjoy the wisdom given
me by God more than any man, and rejoiced in it more than in all my
labour; and this was my good portion which was assigned to me, so that
I might receive for it a good reward in the world to come, more than for
11 all my labour. And I considered all my works which my hands had
worked, and my labours which I had laboured to do, and behold! it was
all vanity and breaking of spirit; and there is no profit in them under
the sun in this world; but I shall have full reward for good work in the
12 world to come. And I gave attention to consider wisdom, and the fear
of the kingdom and understanding, because what use is there to a
man to pray after the decree of the King, and after retribution? behold!
13 it is then already decreed about him and executed on him. And I saw
by the spirit of prophecy that there is an advantage to wisdom over folly,
above the advantage of the light of the day over the darkness of
14 night. The wise man reflects in the beginning what there will be at
last, and prays and averts the evil decree from the world; while the fool
walks in darkness; and I also know that if the wise man does not pray,
and avert the evil decree from the world, when retribution shall come
15 upon the world, the same destiny shall befall them all. And I said in
my heart, a destiny like that of Saul, the son of Kish, the king, who
turned aside, and did not keep the commandment given to him about
Amalek, and the kingdom was taken from him, will also befall me; and
why then am I wiser than he? And I said in my heart, that also this
16 is vanity, and there is nothing except the decree of the Lord. For the
remembrance of the wise man is not with the fool in the world to come,
for after the death of a man, that which happened long ago in his lifetime, when the days come which are to follow him after his death, everything will be disclosed; and why, then, say the children of men that the
17 end of the righteous is like that of the wicked? And I hated all evil life,
because the evil work which is done against the children of men under
the sun in this world displeased me, for it is all vanity, and breaking of
18 spirit. And I hated all my labour which I laboured under the sun in
this world, for I must leave it to Rehoboam my son, who comes after me,
and Jeroboam his servant will come and take away out of his hands ten
19 tribes, and will possess half of the kingdom. And who knows whether
wise or foolish will be the king who is to be after me, and reign over all
my labour which I laboured in this world, and over all which I accomplish in my wisdom under the sun in this world? and I was confounded
20 in my heart, and again said: This, too, is vanity. And I turned about
to despair respecting all my labour which I laboured to acquire, and
21 was wise to accomplish under the sun in this world. Because there is
a man whose labour is in wisdom, reason, and justice, and he dies without issue; and to a man who did not labour for it, he is to give it, that
22 it may be his portion; also this is vanity, and a great evil. For what
pleasure has this man for all his labour and breaking of his heart,
23 wherewith he laboured under the sun in this world? For all his days
are sorrowful, and his business kindles his anger, even in the night he
sleeps not on account of the thoughts of his heart; this too is vanity.
24 There is nothing comely for a man but that he eat, drink, and make his

3 T

soul see good before the sons of men, in order to do the commandments, to walk in the straight path before him, so that it may be well with him from his labour; also this I saw, that if a man prospers in this world, it
25 is from the hand of the Lord, who decrees it so for him. For who is occupied with the words of the law, and who is the man that has anxiety
26 about the great day of judgment which is to come, besides me? For to the man whose works are straight before God, he gave wisdom and knowledge in this world, and joy with the righteous in the world to come; and to the wicked he gave all evil employment, to gather money and to heap up much wealth, to be taken away from him, and to be given to him who pleases the Lord; this, too, is vanity for the wicked, and breaking of spirit.
iii. 1 To every man comes a time, and to every thing an opportune
2 season under the sun. There is a special time to beget sons and daughters, and a special time for killing disobedient and perverse children, to kill them with stones according to the decree of the judges; and an opportune time for planting a tree, and an opportune time
3 for rooting up a planted tree: an opportune time for killing in war, and an opportune time for healing the sick; an opportune time to
4 destroy a building, and an opportune time to build up a ruin: a time to beweep the dead, and an opportune time to be joyful with laughter; an opportune time to mourn over the slain, and an opportune time to
5 dance at nuptials: an opportune time to throw away a heap of stones, and an opportune time to gather stones for a building; an opportune time to embrace a wife, and an opportune time to abstain from embrac-
6 ing her, in the seven days of mourning: an opportune time to wish for riches, and an opportune time to lose riches; an opportune time to keep merchandise, and an opportune time to throw merchandise into
7 the sea, during a great storm: an opportune time to tear the garment for the dead, and an opportune time to sew together the torn pieces: an opportune time to be silent and not to rebuke, and an opportune
8 time to speak words of reproof: an opportune time to love each other, and an opportune time to hate the wicked: an opportune time to make
9 war, and an opportune time to restore peace. What advantage has the toiling man, who labours to make treasures, and to gather mammon,
10 unless he is helped by Providence from above? I saw the painful business and punishment which the Lord gave to the children of men
11 who are wicked, to afflict them therewith. King Solomon said by the spirit of prophecy, God made everything beautiful in its time; for it was opportune that there should be the strife which was in the days of Jero-boam, son of Neboth; it was to have been in the days of Sheba, son of Bichri, and it was delayed, and came to pass in the days of Jeroboam, son of Nebat; for if it had been in the days of Sheba, son of Bichri, the temple would not have been built, because of the golden calves which the wicked Jeroboam made, and placed one in Beth-el and one in Dan, and put watches on the road, and they stopped the pilgrims to the feasts; and therefore it was delayed up to the time when the temple was built, in order not to hinder Israel to build it. He concealed from them also the great Name written and expressed on the foundation-stone, the evil inclinations in their hearts being known to Him; for if it had been delivered into the hands of men, they would have used it, and found by it what will come to pass in the latter days, world without end: and He also hid from them the day of death, in order that it should not be known to man from the beginning what will come to pass at the end.
12 King Solomon said by the spirit of prophecy, I know that there is

nothing good among the children of men, but that they rejoice in the
13 joy of the Law, and do good in the days of their life. And also that if any
man eats and drinks and sees good in his days, and causes his children
to inherit all his labour in the time of his death, this is a gift given to
14 him from the Lord. I know by the spirit of prophecy, that every thing
which the Lord does in the world, whether good or evil, whatsoever is
decreed from His mouth, will be for ever; to it man has no power to add,
nor has any one power to take from it; and at the same time, when
punishment comes into the world, it is the Lord who does it, that the
15 children of man may fear before Him. - What has been from the beginning has come to pass; and what will be at the end of days has already
happened; and at the great day of judgment the Lord will demand the
poor and the needy from the hands of the wicked who persecuted him.
16 And further, I saw under the sun in this world, the place of judgment,
in which false judges condemn the innocent, in his judgment, in order
to acquit the guilty; and the place where the innocent is found, there the
guilty is to tyrannise over him, because of the guilt of the wicked gene-
17 ration. I said in my heart, that God will judge in the great day of
judgment the righteous and the guilty, because a time is appointed for
every thing, and for every work done in this world they will be judged
18 there. I said in my heart concerning the children of men, as to the
chastisements and evil events which come upon them, God sends these to
try and to prove them, to see whether they will return in repentance and
be forgiven and healed; but the wicked who are like beasts do not repent,
19 therefore they are reproved thereby to their own condemnation. For as to
the destiny of the wicked, and the destiny of the unclean beast, it is one
destiny for both of them; and as the unclean beast dies, so he dies who
does not return in repentance before his death; and the breath of life of
both is judged alike in every manner, and the advantage of a sinner over
20 the unclean beast is nothing but the burial place; for all is vanity. All
go to one place; all the inhabitants of the earth are made of dust, and
21 when they die, all return to the dust. Who is wise to know the breathing spirit of the children of men, whether it goes upward to heaven, and
22 the breathing spirit of cattle, whether it goes down to the earth? I saw,
therefore, that there is no good in this world, but that man should rejoice
in his good works, and eat and drink, and do good to his heart; because
this is his good part in this world, to acquire thereby the world to come,
so that no man should say in his heart, " Why am I distributing money
to do charity? I had better leave it to my son after me, or be nursed for
it in my old age ;" because who can bring him to see what will be after
him?

iv. 1 And I turned and saw all the oppressions which are done to
the righteous in this world under the sun, from the hand of their
oppressors; and there is none that should speak consolation to them ;
and there is none to deliver them from the hand of their oppressors with
2 strong hand and power, and none comforts them. And I praised the
dead who have long since died, and do not see the punishment which
comes into the world after their death, more than the living, who live in
3 this world in so much misery, till now. And better than both of them
is he who has not lived till now, and has not been created, who does not
4 see the bad doings which are done in this world under the sun. And I
saw all the trouble and every good work which the children of men do, to
be nothing but jealousy, man emulating his neighbour, to do like him ;
he who emulates his neighbour to do good like him, the word of heaven
will do him good; and if he emulate him in evil, to do like his badness,

the word of heaven will do him evil; and also these things are vanity for
5 the wicked, and breaking of spirit. The fool goes and folds his hands in
summer, and will not labour; and in winter eats all he has, even the
6 garment from the skin of his flesh. Better for a man one handful of
food with comfort of soul, and without rapine and violence, than two
handsful of eating with rapine and violence, which in future will be
7 requited in the judgment in labour and breaking of spirit. And I
turned and saw the vanity which is destined to be in this world under
8 the sun. There is a solitary man, and no second besides him, he has
even no son nor brother to inherit his property, and there is no end to
all his labour, and even his eye cannot be satisfied with his riches, and
he does not say to his heart, "Why am I labouring and restraining my
soul from good? I will arise now, and will do charity therefrom, and
will be joyful in this world with the children of men, and with the
righteous in the world to come;" this, too, is vanity, and an evil work.
9 Better two righteous in a generation than one, and it is they who lead
successfully, and cause their words to be heard; they have a good
reward in the world to come for their labours which they laboured to
10 sustain their generation. For if one of them falls upon the bed and lies
sick, the other will cause his friend to rise by his prayer; but if there is
only one innocent man in a generation, if he falls upon the bed and lies
sick, he has no companion in his generation to pray for him, yet shall he
11 rise by his own merit from his sickness. Also if two sleep together—a man
and his wife, they will be warm in the winter; but one, how can he be
12 warm? And if a wicked and strong man rises in a generation, and his
works are injurious, and cause punishments to come in the world, two
righteous shall stand up against him, and abolish the punishment by
their merits; and how much more useful are three righteous who are in
a generation, and peace is among them, like a chain that is woven of
13 three-fold cords, which does not easily break. Better, *i. e.*, Abraham—
who is the poor youth, and in whom was the spirit of prophecy from the
Lord, and to whom the Lord was known when three years old, and
who would not worship an idol—than the wicked Nimrod, who was an old
and foolish king. And because Abraham would not worship an idol, he
threw him into the burning furnace, and a miracle was performed for
him from the Lord of the world, and he delivered him from it; and even
after this, Nimrod had no sense to be admonished not to worship the idol
14 which he worshipped before. For Abraham went out from the family of
idolaters, and reigned over the land of Canaan, for even in the reign of
15 Abraham, Nimrod became poor in the world. King Solomon said, By
the spirit of prophecy from the Lord, I foresaw all the living who walk
in their folly rebel against Rehoboam, my son, under heaven, and
divide his kingdom to give it to Jeroboam, son of Nebat — except the
tribes of Benjamin and Judah, whose heart was faithful with the boy,
that is, Rehoboam my son, who, second in my kingdom, is to rise and
16 reign in Jerusalem, the place of his inheritance. There was no end to
all the house of Israel, to all the righteous before whom he ruled; but
they advised him in their wisdom to lighten their yoke, and he in his
folly went and took counsel with the youth, and they in their folly,
advised him to make heavier the yoke of his kingdom upon the people
of the house of Israel, and he left the advice of the aged, and followed
the advice of the latter; but these latter ones were afterwards confounded
and displeased with him, and they caused him to flee, so that the ten
tribes should separate from him; and the wicked Jeroboam ruled over
them; I said this too is vanity for Rehoboam my son, and breaking of

17 spirit to him. Thou son of man, guard thy feet when thou goest to the sanctuary of the Lord to pray, so that thou goest not there full of sin before thou has repented, and incline thine ear to receive the teaching of the Law from the priests and sages, and be not like fools, who bring sacrifices for their sins, and do not leave off their evil works which they hold in their hands, and they have no acceptance, for they know not whether they do good or evil therewith.

v. 1 Do not hurry on thy language so as to make a mistake in the words of thy mouth, and let not thy heart make a vow, resolving to do something at the time when thou prayest before the Lord, for the Lord rules over all the world, and sits upon the throne of glory in the high heavens, and thou sittest on earth, therefore let the words 2 of thy mouth be few. For as a dream comes through the thoughts of the heart engaged in a multitude of business, so the noise of 3 the fool through the multitude of empty words. When thou vowest a vow before the Lord, do not defer to pay it, for the Lord hath no pleasure in fools, because they defer their vows and do not pay, but 4 thou, whatsoever thou vowest, pay. It is better for thee that thou 5 vowest not, than that thou vowest and pay not. Do not degrade the words of thy mouth to cause judgments of Gehenna upon thy flesh; and in the day of the great judgment thou wilt not be able to say before the avenging angel who exercises dominion over thee, that it is an error; why then shall the anger of the Lord be kindled against the voice of thy 6 shamefully uttered language, and destroy the works of thine hand? For in the multitude of the dreams of the false prophets, and in the vanities of sorcerers, and in the many words of the wicked, believe not, but serve the wise and the just; from them seek instruction, and fear before the 7 Lord. When thou seest the oppression of the poor, robbery, and justice in the city, be not astonished in thy heart, saying, How can the will of the Lord be with all this? for the mighty God from on high watches the works of the children of men, whether good or evil, and from his presence are sent forth proud and powerful men to rule over the wicked, and to be 8 appointed masters over them. And the great advantage of cultivating the land is above all, for when the subjects of a country revolt, and the king flies from them into the country, if he has no more to eat, this very 9 king becomes subject to a labourer in the field. A merchant who loves to acquire money, and men of business, shall not be satisfied in amassing money; and he who loves to heap up great mammon, has no praise in the world to come, unless he has done charity with it, because he has not 10 deserved to eat fruit; this, too, is vanity. When good is multiplied in the world, the children of men who eat it are also multiplied; and what advantage is there to the owner who gathers it unless he does good with it, that he may see in the world to come the reward given with his eyes. 11 Sweet is the sleep of a man who serves the Lord of the world with all his heart; and he has rest in his grave, whether he lives few years or many years: after having served the Lord of the world in this world, he will inherit in the world to come a reward for the works of his hand. And the wisdom of the Law of God belongs to the man who is rich in wisdom; in the same manner as he occupies himself with it in this world, and exerts himself in learning, so will it rest with him in the grave, and not leave him alone; just as a woman does not leave her husband to 12 sleep alone. There is a sore evil which I saw in this world under the sun, and there is no remedy for it; a man who gathers riches and does no good with them, and at the end of days these riches are kept for him for 13 his condemnation in the world to come. And the riches, which he leaves

to his son after his death, shall perish, because he got them in an evil employment, and they shall not abide in the hand of the son whom he has
14 begotten, and nothing whatever shall remain in his hand. As he came
out of his mother's womb naked, without a covering, and without any
good, so shall he return to his grave, void of merit, just as he came into
this world; and he shall receive no good reward whatever for his labour,
to carry with him into the world whither he goes, to be a merit in his hand.
15 And this also is a sore evil, and there is no remedy for it, as he came
into this world void of merit, so he shall depart into that world; and
16 what advantage has he that he laboured for his spirit? Also all his days
he dwells in darkness, that he may eat his bread alone, and he sees in
17 much indignation, and his life is in sickness and vexation. And behold
that which I have seen good for the children of men, and that which is
comely for them to do in this world, that they eat and drink from their
labours, in order not to put forth the hand to oppression and rapine, and
to keep the words of the law, and to have compassion on the poor, so
that they may see good in all their labours wherewith they labour in this
world under the sun, the number of the days of a man's life, which God
in his providence gives to him; for this is his portion, and none's beside
18 him. Also every man to whom the Lord has given riches and wealth, and
if the Lord gave him power to eat of it in this world, and to do good with
it, and to receive a full reward in the world to come, and to rejoice in his
work with the righteous, behold! this is a gift which is given to him in
19 providence, it is from the Lord. For not many are the days of man's
life; who tries to find out the days of his life, how many of them will be
good, and how many of them will be evil? because it is not in the power
of the children of men; but it is fixed about him from the Lord, how
many days he shall suffer, and how many days he shall be in the joy of
his heart.
vi. 1   There is an evil which I saw in this world under the sun, and it
2 is great upon the children of man. A man to whom God gave in his
providence riches, honour, and wealth, and his soul lacks nothing of
all which he desires, and the Lord has not given him power, on account
of his sins, to enjoy it; but he dies without issue, and his kinsman would
not take possession of his inheritance, wherefore his wife will be married
to a stranger, and he will take away the inheritance and consume it; all
this his sins have brought upon him, because he did therewith no good
whatever, and his riches turned out to be to him vanity and a sore evil.
3 If a man should beget a hundred children, and live many years, and be
in power and dominion all the days of his life, and his soul has not
enjoyed the good which he has, because he loved his riches, and has not
acquired therewith a good name, nor even prepared himself a grave, I say
by the divine word, better than he an untimely birth, which has not seen
4 this world. For in vanity he came into this world, and departs in darkness into that world; and in darkness is his name covered, because he
has no merit, and has not acquired a good name worthy of remembrance.
And even the light of the sun he saw not, and did not know good from
5 evil, to discern between this world and the world to come. And if the
days of the life of this man were two thousand years, and he had not
studied the Law, and had not done judgment and justice by the oath
of the word of the Lord, in the day of his death his soul will go to
7 Gehenna, to the same place whither all sinners go. As for all the
labours of man, he labours for the food of his mouth; and by the word
of the mouth of the Lord he is sustained, and even the soul of man is not
8 satisfied with eating and drinking. For what advantage has the wise

man in this world over the fool, because of the wicked generation by
which he is not accepted; and what is this poor man to do but to study
the law of the Lord, that he may know how he will have to walk in the
9 presence of the righteous in paradise. It is better for a man to rejoice
about the world to come, and to do righteousness, and to see a good
reward for his labours in the day of the great judgment, than to go into
that world with an afflicted soul; for this is vanity, and a breaking of
10 spirit to a guilty man. That which has been in the world, behold! its
name has long been called, and has been made known to the children of
men from the day that the first Adam existed, and all is the decree of the
Lord; and men cannot stand in judgment with the Lord of the world,
11 who is stronger than he. For there are many things which multiply
vanity in the world, what advantage has the man who is occupied with
12 them? For who is he that knows what will do men good in this world,
but to study the Law, which is the life of the world; and all the number
of the days of his vain life which he lives, are in the time of his death
considered like a shadow; for who is he that can tell man what there is
before him in this world under the sun?

vii. 1 Better the good name which the righteous acquire in this world,
than the anointing oil which was poured upon the heads of kings and
priests; and the day wherein a man dies and departs to the grave
with a good name and merits, than the day wherein the wicked is
2 born into the world. It is better to go to a mourning man to comfort him, than to go to the house of a feast of wine of the scorners;
for into the house of mourning thither is the end of all men to go,
for upon all is decreed the decree of death, and by going into the
house of mourning the righteous man sits down and takes to heart
the words of death; and if there be any evil in his hand he will leave it,
3 and return in repentance before the Lord of the world. Better is the
anger wherewith the Lord of the world is angry with the righteous in
this world, than the laughter wherewith he laughs at the wicked; for by
the displeasure of the face of the Shechinah come famine and punishment into the world to improve the heart of the righteous, and they pray
4 before the Lord of the world, who has mercy upon them. The heart of
the wise mourns over the destruction of the temple, and grieves over the
captivity of the house of Israel; and the heart of fools is in the joy of
the house of their scoffings; they eat and drink and fare sumptuously,
5 and do not take to heart the affliction of their brethren. Better to sit at
the teaching of the house of instruction, and to hear the reproof of the
wise in the Law, than for a man to go to hear the sound of a musical
6 instrument of a fool. For as the sound of the crackling of thorns which
burn under a pot, so is the noisy laughter of the fool; this also is vanity.
7 For the robber mocks at the wise man because he goes not in his way,
and destroys with his evil speech the prudent heart of the wise, which
8 was given to him as a gift from heaven. Better the end of a thing than
the beginning thereof, for in its beginning man knows not what its end
will be, but the end of a good thing is known to a good man; and better
before the Lord is a man who rules over his spirit and subdues his
9 carnal thoughts, than a man who walks in the pride of his spirit. And
when chastisements from heaven come upon thee, do not hasten thy
heart to anger, and to utter words of rebellion against heaven, for if
thou bearest them patiently, they will depart from thee; and if thou art
rebellious and angry, know that anger rests in the lap of fools till it has
10 destroyed them. In the time of oppression, say not what was before
now was good in the world; for the former days were better, and the

men of that generation had better doings than these, therefore good came
11 to them; and thou askest not according to wisdom about this. Good is
the wisdom of the law, along with the inheritance of money, and better
still for a man to humbly conduct himself with men, the dwellers of the
12 earth, who see good and evil under the sun in this world. For as a man
is sheltered under the shadow of wisdom, so he is sheltered under the
shadow of money, when he does alms with it; and the advantage of
knowing the wisdom of the law is that it raises its possessor from the
13 grave for the world to come. Consider the work of the Lord, and his
strength, who made the blind, the hunchback, and the lame, to be
wonders in the world; for who is he that can make straight one of these,
14 but the Lord of the world who made him crooked? In the day when
the Lord is doing good, be thou also happy and do good to all the world;
that the evil day may not come upon thee, see and behold! and also
God has made this against that to reprove the men of the world, so that
15 man should not find after him any evil in the world to come. All this
I saw in the days of my vanity, that from the Lord are decreed good and
evil to be in the world, according to the planets under which the children
of men are created; for there is a righteous man perishing in his righteousness in this world, and his merit is kept for him for the world to
come; and there is a wicked man who prolongs his days in his guilt, and
the account of his evil doings is kept for him for the world to come, to be
16 requited for it in the day of the great judgment. Be not over-righteous
when the guilty is found guilty of death in thy court of judgment, so as
to have compassion on him and not to kill him; and do not thus become
over-wise with the wisdom of the wicked who stand in the way, and do
17 not learn their ways; why, then, wilt thou destroy thy way? Go not
after the thought of thy heart to sin much, and do not make thy way far
from the teaching of the law of God to become a fool; why shouldst
thou cause death to thy soul, and the years of thy life be shortened to
18 die, before thy time comes to die? It is good thou shouldst combine
the affairs of this world, namely, to do good to thyself in the way of
merchants, and also that thou hold fast thy portion in the Book of the
19 Law, for a man fearing before the Lord performs the duty of both. And
the wisdom of Joseph, son of Jacob, helped him to make him wise before
his ten righteous brethren, who ruled in the fear of the Lord; and the
evil spirit did not rule in them when they were in the metropolis of
Egypt, and did not kill their brother Joseph who annoyed them at that
20 time with the voice of his words. For there is no righteous man in the
land, who does good all his days, and sins not before the Lord; but the
man who sins before the Lord, it behoves him to return in repentance
21 before he dies. Moreover give not thy heart to accept all the words
which the wicked speak to thee, that the days may not come when thou
shalt hear thy servant curse thee, and thou hast not the power to be
22 delivered from his hands. Then see to it, adjudicate thy cause when a
man curses thee who is not like thyself; for also many times thy heart
23 knows that thou too hast cursed other men. All that I said I have
tried by wisdom: I said by my word, I shall also be wise in all the
24 wisdom of the Law, but it was far from me. Behold, long has it been far
from the children of men to know all that has been from the days of old;
and who is he that will find out by his wisdom the secret of the day of
death, and the secret of the day when the King Messiah will come?
25 I turned to think in my heart, and to know and to examine and to seek
wisdom, and the estimate of the reward of the works of the righteous,
and to know the punishment of the guilt of the fool, and the understand-

26 ing of the fear of the Kingdom. And I found a thing more bitter to man than the bitterness of the day of death, namely, a woman who causes much tribulation to her husband, and entangles him; in whose heart are snares, and whose hands are bound that she might not work with them; the righteous before God is the man who gets rid of her by a bill of divorcement, and relieves himself of her; but the guilty before God is the man
27 who abides with her, and is ensnared with her adultery. Behold, this is the work which I have found, said Coheleth, who is called Solomon, King of Israel, I have examined the planets one in connection with the other, to find out the account of the children of men, what will be in their end.
28 There is another thing which my soul is still seeking, and I have not found, namely, a perfect and just man, without any corruption, as Abraham; from the days of the first Adam till the righteous Abraham was born, who was found faithful and just among the thousand kings that gathered together to build the tower of Babel? and a woman, as Sarah,
29 among all the wives of those kings, I have not found. Only, behold! this I found, that God made the first Adam upright before him and just; and the serpent and Eve seduced him to eat of the fruit of the tree, because those who eat its fruit would be wise to discern between good and evil, and they brought upon him and all the inhabitants of the earth the day of death; and they sought to find many accounts in order to bring terror upon the inhabitants of the earth.
viii. 1 Who is as a wise man, that he can stand before the wisdom of the Lord, and know the interpretations of his words, like the prophets? The wisdom of a wise man enlightens the brightness of his face among the righteous, and as for the impudent, all his ways are changed from
2 good to bad. Guard thy mouth about the commands of the King to keep whatsoever he commands, and be also on thy guard about the matter of an oath of the Lord, that thou swear not by the name of
3 his word in vain. And in the time of the anger of the Lord do not cease to pray before him, tremble before him, go and pray and seek mercy from him, because thou canst not stand in an evil matter; for
4 the Lord of all worlds, the Lord, will do what he pleases. In the place where the word of the King who rules over all the world is gone forth, it is done immediately, and who is the man that would
5 restrain his hand, and say unto him, What doest thou? The man who keeps the commandments of the Lord shall not know any evil in the world to come; and the time of prayer, and judgment, and truth,
6 is known in the heart of the wise. For to every business there is a good and an evil time, and by a true judgment is the whole world judged; and when it is decreed from the Lord that punishment should be in the world, it is because of the guilt of evil doers which is heavy
7 upon them. For no wise man knows what will be with him at the end, for when it shall be the pleasure before the Lord to afflict him, who is he
8 that will tell him it? There is no man who has power over his breathing soul to retain the soul of life, that it should not depart from the human body; and there is no power in the day of death for a man to save his companion, and no instruments of war to help in the battle, and guilt
9 will not save its master in the great day of judgment. All this I saw which has happened in this world, and I gave my heart to know all the work which is worked in this world under the sun, at the time when
10 man rules over man to afflict him. And indeed I have seen sinners who are buried and blotted out of the world, from the holy place where the righteous dwell, and went to be burned in Gehenna, and are forgotten from among the inhabitants of the city, and as they have done to others,

11 so it is done to them; also this is vanity. And because the evil thing, the punishment of the wicked, is not quickly executed upon their evil works, therefore the heart of the children of men is full in them to do
12 evil in this world. And when a sinner does evil a hundred years, and space is given him from the Lord in order that he may repent, yet is it revealed to him by the Holy Spirit, and I know that it will be well in the world to come with those that fear the Lord, that fear before him,
13 and do his will; and that it shall not be well with the wicked, and there shall be no space for him in the world to come; and in this world the days of his life shall be cut off, they shall fly and pass away like a
14 shadow, because he feared not before the Lord. There is a vanity that is decreed to be done upon the face of the earth; there are righteous to whom evil happens as if they had done like the deeds of the wicked, and there are wicked to whom it happens as if they had done like the works of the righteous; and I saw by the Holy Spirit that the evil which happens to the righteous in this world is not for their guilt, but to free them from a slight transgression, that their reward may be perfect in the world to come; and the good that comes to the sinners in this world is not for their merits, but to render them a reward for their small merit they have acquired, so that they may eat their reward in this world, and to destroy their portion in the world to come; I said, by my word, this
15 also is vanity. And I praised the joy of the Law, since there is no good for man in this world under the sun, but to eat and drink and rejoice in his labour and in his portion, which is given to him from heaven, and not stretch out his hands in violence and rapine; and this will lead him to peace in that world, and he shall receive a perfect reward for his labours wherewith he sincerely laboured all the days of his life, which
16 the Lord gave him in this world under the sun. As I gave my heart to know the wisdom of the Law, and to see the business which is done upon the earth, for even the wise who desires to be occupied with the Law and to find wisdom must toil, since he has no rest in the day, and sees no
17 sleep with his eyes in the night. And I saw every mighty work of the Lord, for it is awful; and man cannot find out the mighty work of the Lord which is done in this world under the sun; when man labours to seek what will be, he shall not find it; and even if a wise man says by his word, that he will know what will be at the end of days, he cannot find it.
ix. 1 For all this I have taken to heart, and to examine all this that the righteous and the wise, and their disciples who are under them, studying the law, are in the hand of the Lord, whatsoever will take place in the world in their day is decreed by him; the love wherewith a man loves, and the hatred wherewith he hates, there is no prophet in the world who knows it; whatever happens to man has been decreed before-
2 hand, according to the planet, to take place. Everything depends upon the planets, whatever happens to anyone is fixed in heaven; the same destiny is to the innocent and to the guilty, to him who amends his ways and purifies his soul, and to him who defiles his soul, to him who brings a holy sacrifice, and to him who does not bring holy sacrifices, alike to the righteous and the sinner, to the man who perjures himself, and the
3 man who fears an oath. This is a great misfortune in all the world, which occurs under the sun, some one fate is for all, for every inhabitant of the earth; and also the heart of the children of men is full of evil on account of it, and fear is in their hearts all the days of their lives, and after the end of man it is reserved for him to be reproved with the dead
4 in the judgment of the guilty. For who is the man that adheres to all

the words of the law, and has hope to acquire the life of the world to
5 come? for a living dog is better than a dead lion. For the righteous
know that if they sin, they shall be regarded as dead men in the world
to come, therefore they keep their ways and sin not; and if they sin they
return in repentance; but the wicked do not know any good, for they
do not make good their works in their life, and do not know any good
in the world to come, and they have no good reward after their death,
6 for their remembrances are forgotten from among the 'righteous. After
the death of the wicked they are useless; their love, as well as their
hatred and jealousy, behold, they have perished long ago from the
world! and they have no more a good part with the righteous in the
world to come, and they have no enjoyment from all that is done in this
7 world under the sun. Solomon said, by the spirit of prophecy from the
Lord, The Lord of the world will say to all the righteous in their face, go
eat with joy the bread which has been laid up for thee for the bread
which thou hast given to the poor and needy that were hungry, and
drink with a good heart the wine which has been preserved for thee in
paradise for the wine which thou has mingled to the poor and needy that
were thirsty; for behold, thy good work has long been acceptable before
8 the Lord. At all times let thy garment be white from all pollution of
sin, and acquire a good name, which is likened to anointing oil, for the
which a blessing will come down upon thy head, and thy goodness will
9 not fail. See good life with the wife thou lovest, all the days of thy vain
life, which the Lord, through destiny, has given thee in this world
under the sun, for this is thy portion in life, and in the labour wherewith
10 thou labourest in this world under the sun. Whatever good and charity
thy hand finds to do, do it with all thy power, for after death there is no
work for man, nor account, knowledge, or wisdom, in the grave whither
thou goest; and nothing will help thee except good works and alms
11 alone. King Solomon said, When I sat upon the throne of my kingdom,
I considered and saw in this world under the sun that men who are
swift as eagles are not helped by running to escape from death in battle,
and that the mighty are not helped by carrying on war in their strength,
nor are the wise helped by their wisdom to find bread in the time of
famine, nor are the intelligent helped by their intelligence to gather
riches, nor are the prudent helped by their prudence to find favour in
the eyes of a king, for time and fate befall all according to their planets.
12 For man knows not his time; whether that which will be in the world
and come upon him will be good or evil; like fish of the sea which are
caught in a net, and birds of heaven which are caught in a snare, so are
the children of men taken in an evil time, which is appointed to fall
13 upon them in a moment from heaven. Also this I saw, which is wisdom
14 in this world under the sun, and it is great to me. The body of a man,
which is like a small town; and in it are a few mighty men, just as the
merits in the heart of man are few; and the evil spirit, who is like a
great and powerful king, enters into the body to seduce it, and besieges
the body to seduce it, and builds around it a place to lie in wait, because
he wishes to cause him to depart from the way which is straight before
the Lord, to catch him in the great snares of Gehenna, in order to burn
15 him seven times for his sins. And there is found in the body a good
spirit, humble and wise, and he prevails over him, and subdues him by
his wisdom, saves the body from the judgment of Gehenna by his power
and wisdom, like a man who makes war and delivers the inhabitants of
the city by the wisdom of his heart; and man does not remember afterwards the good spirit who saved him, but says in his heart, I am

innocent; just as the inhabitants of that town do not remember the poor
16 man who delivered them. And I said by my word, Better the wisdom
of the righteous, than the force of the strength of the wicked; for the
wisdom of the righteous and his merit save both him and the men of his
generation; whilst the power of the wicked who persists in the stubborn-
ness of his heart not to return in repentance, only destroys himself
alone; and the wisdom of the righteous poor is despised in the ages of
the wicked of his generation; and when he reproves them for their evil
17 works, they do not receive his words of reproof. The words of prayer of
the wise, offered in silence, are accepted before the Lord of the world,
above the exclamations of the wicked who rules over fools, that speak
18 much, and are not accepted. Better is the wisdom of the wise in time
of oppression, than instruments of war in the time of waging war,
and one sinner in a generation causes much good to perish from the
world.
x.1 And the evil spirit which dwells at the gate of the heart is as a fly,
causing death in the world by betraying the wise when he sins, and
destroying the good name which was before like anointing oil, perfumed
with aromatics; and how much more beautiful and precious than the
wisdom of the wise and the riches of the rich is the man whose folly is
2 slight and insignificant? The heart of the wise is to acquire the Law
which was given by the hand of the Lord, and the heart of the fool is to
3 acquire riches of silver and gold. And also when the fool walks in an
offensive way, his heart lacks wisdom, and he does things which are not
4 right to do, and all say that he is a fool. If the evil spirit rules over
thee, and strives to overcome thee, leave not the good place wherein
thou usest to stand, for the words of the law were made to be remedies
in the world, to remit and blot out great sins from before the Lord.
5 There is an evil which I saw in this world under the sun, and what
injury is it in the world! just as an error hastily uttered against a man,'
6 and that by a ruler! The Lord from the high heavens makes the
wicked and foolish king to be strong in his good star, and to minister
prosperously, and his armies to be excellent and numerous; whilst thy
people, the house of Israel, are subject to him in exile; and because of
the multitude of their sins the rich in goods became poor, and dwelt in
7 humiliation among the nations. King Solomon said by the spirit of
prophecy, I saw nations who were before subject to the people of the
house of Israel, now prosperous, and riding on horses like princes,
whilst the people of the house of Israel and their nobles walk on the
8 ground like slaves. Justice answered and said thus: They brought all
this upon themselves; as a man who digs a pit upon the high road falls
into it, so the people which transgresses the decrees of the word of
the Lord, and destroys the fences of the world, falls into the hand of a
9 wicked king, who bites them like a serpent. King Solomon the prophet
said, It is revealed to me that Manasseh, the son of Hezekiah, will sin
and worship idols of stone, wherefore he will be delivered into the hand
of the King of Assyria, and he will fasten him with halters; because he
made void the words of the law which are written on the tables of stone
from the beginning, therefore he will suffer for it; and Rabshakeh, his
brother, will worship an image of wood and forsake the words of the Law
which are laid in the ark of shittim wood: therefore he shall be burned
10 in a fire by the angel of the Lord. And when the people of the house
of Israel sin, and the heavens are made strong as iron to keep back the
rain, and that generation does not pray before the Lord, all the
world is afflicted with famine on their account; and when the multitude

gather themselves together and overcome their evil spirit, and appoint
their superiors to ask mercy from the Lord of heaven, there is acceptance
11 for them, because of the abundance of their true wisdom. When the
fiery serpents are roused to devour and to injure the world, it is because
of the sins of the house of Israel, for not having been occupied with the
words of the Law in quietness; and there will also be no advantage to
the slanderer who talks with a threefold tongue, because he will be
12 burned in the fire of Gehenna. The words of the mouth of a wise man
that is found in a generation pray when punishment comes upon the
world, and he removes the punishment and finds mercy before the Lord;
but the lips of the fool are full of reproach, and therefore all the world
13 is destroyed. The beginning of the words of his mouth is folly, and the
14 end of the word of his mouth is evil agitation. And the fool multiplies
empty words wherein there is no use, so much so that no man knows
what will be in his days; and what will become of him at the end, who
15 can tell him? The labour of a fool who labours in folly wearies him,
because he will not learn to go to the city where the wise dwell to seek
16 instruction. Woe to thee, O land of Israel! when wicked Jeroboam
shall reign over thee, and remove from thee the morning sacrifices, and
thy princes shall eat bread before offering the daily morning sacrifice.
17 Hail thee, O land of Israel, when Hezekiah son of Ahaz, from the family
of the house of David, King of Israel, who is mighty in the law, shall
reign over thee, and shall perform the obligations of the commandments;
and thy nobles, after having brought thee daily sacrifice, shall eat bread
at four [i.e., ten o'clock in the morning,] from the work of their hands in
18 the strength of the Law, and not in weakness and blindness of eyes. By
weakness of the study of the Law and the commandments, man becomes
poor in children, and by despising the commandment which commands
the woman to observe the time of uncleanness of blood and she did not
19 observe it, she is always in a menstrual state in her house. The
righteous joyfully make bread to nourish the hungry poor; and the
wine which they mix for the thirsty will be pleasure to them in the
world to come; and the redemption money will proclaim their merit in
20 the world to come in the face of all. Even in thy mind, in the innermost recesses of thy heart, curse not the king, and in thy bed-chamber
revile not a wise man, for the angel Raziel proclaims every day from
heaven upon Mount Horeb, and the sound thereof goes into all the
world, and Elijah the high priest continually hovers in the air like an
angel, the king of the winged tribe, and discloses the things that are
done in secret to all the inhabitants of the earth.
xi. 1 Give thy nourishing bread to the poor who go in ships upon the
surface of the water, for after a period of many days thou wilt find
2 its reward in the world to come. Give a good portion of the seed
to thy field in Tishri, and do not cease from sowing even in Kislev,
for thou knowest not what evil will be upon the earth, whether the
3 early or latter will succeed. If the clouds are full of rain, they will
pour the water upon the earth, because of the merit of the righteous;
and if there is no merit in that generation, they will pour it into
the sea and desert, so that the children of men should not enjoy it;
and if it is once decreed from heaven that the king should fall and
be removed from his dominion, it is by the word of heaven; or that
plenty or famine is to be in the south or north, in the place where
4 this counsel has been decreed there it will certainly be. A man who
regards sorcerers and charmers will never do good, and he who watches
the planets will not reap a reward, for sorcerers are like the wind, not to

be seized by human hands; and planets are like the clouds of heaven,
5 which pass away and do not return. As thou knowest not how the spirit
of the breath of life goes into the body of an infant which rests in the
womb of its pregnant mother, and as thou knowest not whether it is a
male or female until it is born, so thou understandest not the work of
6 the Lord, who made all in wisdom. In the days of thy youth take a wife
to beget children, and in the time of thy old age do not leave the wife of
thy portion so as not to bear children, for thou knowest not which
of them is destined to be good, one or the other, or whether both will be
7 alike good. And sweet is the light of the Law, and fitted to enlighten
the dark eyes to behold the glorious face of the Shechinah, which will
brighten from her splendour the face of the righteous, that their beauty
8 may be like the sun. For if the life of man is many days, it becomes
him to rejoice in all of them, and to study the Law of the Lord; let him
remember the days of the darkness of death, and not sin, for many are
the days wherein he shall lie dead in the grave to receive the judgment
from heaven for the life he loved, all the time punishment comes upon
9 him for the vanity he has done. Rejoice, O young man, in the days of
thy youth, and let thy heart be cheerful in the days of thy childhood,
and walk in meekness with the ways of thy heart, and be careful as to
the seeing of thy eyes, and do not look upon evil, and know that for all
10 this the Lord will bring thee into judgment. And put away anger from
thy heart, and bring no evil upon thy flesh, for youth and the days of
black hair are vanity.
xii. 1 And remember thy Creator to honour him in the days of thy youth,
before the evil days draw nigh to thee, and the years come upon thee
2 when thou wilt say, I have no pleasure in them. Before the glorious
brightness which is like the sun be changed, and before the light
of thy eyes be darkened, and before the comeliness of thy cheeks
becomes black, and before the apples of thy eyes, which are like stars,
3 be dim, thy eyelids drop down tears like clouds after rain. In the
day when thy knees tremble, and thy arms shake, and the grinders of
thy mouth cease till they cannot chew food, and thy eyes which look
4 through the openings of thy head darken, and thy feet be fettered from
going into the street, and the appetite for food shall depart from thee,
and thou shalt awake from thy sleep at the sound of a bird, as at thieves
that go about during the night, and thy lips shall relax from saying a
5 song. Thou shalt even be afraid to remember the works which have
been before now, and a little rising will be in the face of thy soul, like a
great mountain when thou walkest on the road; and the top of thy hip-
bone shall come out from leanness like the almond, and the ancles of
thy feet shall be swelled, and thou shalt be hindered from rest, for man
tarries to go to the place of his burial; and the angels that seek thy
judgment walk about like mourners, walking about the street, to write
6 the account of the judgment. Before thy tongue is dumb from speaking,
and the skull of thy head dashed in pieces, and thy gall at the liver
7 broken, and thy body hastens into the grave, and thy flesh which is
created of dust will return again into the earth as it was before, and thy
breathing spirit will return to stand in judgment before the Lord who
8 gave it thee. When Solomon, king of Israel, reflected upon the vanity
of this world, and upon the vanities which the children of men do,
9 Coheleth said by his word, All is vanity. And Solomon, who was called
Coheleth, was abundantly wise above all the children of men, and
further, he taught the people of the house of Israel wisdom; and he
attended to the voice of the wise, and searched the books of wisdom, and

by the spirit of prophecy from the Lord composed many wise books, and
10 very many prudential maxims. King Solomon, who was called Coheleth, desired by his wisdom to pronounce judgment upon the thoughts of the heart of man without witnesses, therefore he was told by the spirit of prophecy from the Lord, Behold, it has long been written in the Book of the Law through Moses, rabbi of Israel, right and faithful words, that by
11 the word of witnesses shall every thing be established. The words of the wise are like inciting goads and forks, which incite those who are destitute of knowledge to learn wisdom, as the goad teaches the ox; and so are the words of the rabbins of the Sanhedrin, the masters of the Halachas and Midrashim which were given through Moses the prophet, who alone fed the people of the house of Israel in the wilderness with
12 manna and delicacies. And more than these, my son, take care, to make many books of wisdom without an end; to study much the words
13 of the Law, and to consider the weariness of the flesh. In the end, a thing which was done in this world in secret will altogether be made manifest, and known to all the children of men; therefore fear the word of the Lord, and keep his commandments, that thou sin not in secret; and if thou sinnest, be admonished to repent; for behold, this ought to be
14 the way of every man. For the Lord will bring every work before the great day of judgment, and make public the thing which is hid from the children of men, whether good or evil.

II.

VERSIONS OF THE REFORMERS.

A. LUTHER'S VERSION.

As soon as the Reformation began in Germany, Luther felt that its extension and maintenance could only be accomplished by enabling the people at large to possess and read the Bible in their vernacular language, which he at once determined to do. Considering that up to that time the knowledge of Hebrew was hardly ever cultivated to any great extent among Christians, and that they had no scientific grammars and lexicons, except those written in Hebrew, to assist them in the acquisition of this language, it will be obvious that Luther could not have made his translation of the Old Testament without the aid of the Vulgate, which he had diligently studied prior to the commencement of the Reformation. How much Luther's Version is indebted to the Vulgate, may be seen from the following comparison:

THE VULGATE.		LUTHER.
Quid est quod fuit? Ipsum quod futurum est? Quid est quod factum est? Ipsum quod faciendum est.	i. 9	Was ist es, das geschehen ist? Eben das hernach geschehen wird. Was ist es, das man gethan hat? Eben das man hernach wieder thun wird.
Investigare sapienter.	13	Zu forschen weislich.
Magnus effectus sum . . . et mens mea contemplata est multa sapienter et didici.	16	Ich bin herrlich geworden . . . und mein Herz hat viel gelernet und erfahren.
Et qui addit sientiam, addit et laborem.	18	Und wer viel lehren muß, der muß viel leiden.

THE VULGATE.		LUTHER.

THE VULGATE.

Cogitavi in corde meo abstra-here a vino carnem meam, ut animum meum transferrem ad sapientiam devitaremque stulti-tiam.

Possedi servos et ancillas, mul-tamque familiam habui.

Omits לִי עֲשָׂוֹת.

Et futura tempora oblivione cuncta pariter operient.

Cum requie . . . cum labore et affiictione animi.

Et appropinqua ut audias.

Mutas curas sequuntur somnia, et in multis sermonibus inveni-entur stultitia.

Ubi multa sunt somnia, plu-rimæ sunt vanitates et sermones innumeri.

Fructum non capiet ex eis.

Pereunt enim in afflictione pessima ; generavit filium, qui in summa egestate erit.

Et in curis multis, et in ærumna atque tristitia.

Non enim satis recordabitur dierum vitæ suæ, eo quod Deus occupet deliciis cor ejus.

Et quidem frequens apud ho-mines.

De hoc ego pronuncio, quod.

Sicut enim protegit sapientia, sic protegit pecunia; hoc autem plus habet eruditio et sapientia, quod vitam tribuunt possessori suo.

Ego os regis observo, et præ-cepta juramenti Dei.

Renders the *future* מַה־שֶּׁיִּהְיֶה præterita.

Et quanto plus laboraverit ad quærendum, tanto minus inveniat.

Multo labore exacuetur.

Si mordeat serpens in silentio, nihil eo minus habet qui occulte detrahit.

Renders the *future* מַה־שֶּׁיִּהְיֶה quid ante se fuerit.

Et in bono sit cor tuum.

LUTHER.

ii. 3 Da dachte ich in meinem Herzen, meinen Leib vom Wein zu ziehen, und mein Herz zur Weisheit zu ziehen, daß ich ergriffe, was Thorheit ist.

7 Ich hatte Knechte und Mägde, und Gesinde.

11 *The same.*

16 Und die künftigen Tage ver-gessen alles.

iv. 6 Mit Ruhe . . . mit Mühe und Jammer.

17 Und komme daß du hörest.

v. 2 Denn wo viel Sorge ist, da kommen Träume; und wo viele Worte sind, da hört man den Narren.

6 Wo viele Träume sind, da ist Eitelkeit und viele Worte.

9 Wird keinen Nutzen davon haben.

13 Denn der Reichthum kommt um mit großem Jammer; und so er einen Sohn erzeuget hat, dem bleibt nichts in der Hand.

16 Und in grossem Grämen und Krankheit und Traurigkeit.

19 Denn er denkt nicht viel an das elende Leben, weil Gott sein Herz erfreuet.

vi. 1 Und ist gemein bei den Menschen.

3 Von dem spreche ich, daß.

vii. 12 Denn die Weisheit beschirmet, so beschirmet Geld auch, aber die Weisheit gibt das Leben dem, der sie hat.

viii. 2 Ich halte das Wort des Königs, und den Eid Gottes.

7 *The same,* was gewesen ist.

17 Und je mehr der Mensch arbeitet zu suchen, je weniger er findet.

x. 10 Muß man es mit Macht wieder schärfen.

11 Ein Wäscher ist nichts besser denn eine Schlange, die unbschworen sticht.

14 *The same,* was gewesen ist.

xi. 9 Und laß dein Herz guter Dinge sein.

In all the examples where Luther agrees with the Vulgate, be it remembered, the Vulgate deviates from the Hebrew. The following, i. 11 ; iii. 9. 10. 11. 15. 18. 19 ; iv. 1. 9. 16 ; v. 5. 8. 14. 18 ; vi. 5. 6. 7. 8. 10. 11. 12; vii. 7. 12. 14. 24. 25. 26 ; ix. 11. 15. 17 ; x. 1. 3, 5 ; xi. 1 ; xii. 3, are instances of Luther's own loose paraphrases and deviations from the original. We dwell upon this subject more particularly, because Luther's version, as we shall see, has been made the basis of some of our English translations ; and it is only by forming a right estimate of the former that we can judge of the latter.

B. THE SWISS, OR ZURICH VERSION.

Stimulated by the example of Luther, the ministers of the Church at Zurich undertook to render the Scriptures into the Swiss dialect. After elaborately descanting upon the propriety of translating the Bible into the vernacular languages of the people, the translators tell us in the Preface that they have adopted Luther's version of the Pentateuch, Joshua, Judges, Kings, and Chronicles, which had been printed previously in this dialect, altering it, however, so as to make it both more in accordance with their dialect and more literal ; and that they had made an original translation from the Hebrew of the Prophets, Job, the Psalms, Proverbs, Ecclesiastes, and the Song of Songs. How they could obtain from the Hebrew that which they frequently make Coheleth say, will, I believe, puzzle the reader quite as much as it puzzles me, when he shall have perused the extracts given under Coverdale. The first edition of the Bible was published at Zurich in 1531, by the famous Christopher Froschover, who received many of the English Reformers who were exiled in the reign of Queen Mary.[1] Mine is the second edition, published in 1536 ; it is a splendid folio, printed upon excellent paper; the title-page is richly decorated with woodcuts representing the creation of man, his temptation, fall, redemption, &c., printed with red and black ink ; woodcuts as well as ornamental letters are profusely introduced throughout the book, and the illustrations in the Apocalypse are after Holbein ; the execution of the whole would be an honour to any printing establishment in England. It is greatly to be regretted that this important edition is so extremely rare.

C. COVERDALE'S VERSION.

The first published English version of Coheleth, made, *as is generally asserted*, from the Hebrew, is that of Myles Coverdale, who published the first English translation of the entire Bible. Coverdale himself, so far from claiming to have made it from the original, distinctly tells us in the very title-page that he has "faithfully and truly translated out of Douche and Latyn in to Englishe," and again honourably acknowledges, in the Prologue to the Christian Reader, "I haue had sundrye translacions, not only in Latyn, but also of the Douche interpreters, whom, because of theyr syngular gyftes and speciall diligence in the Bible, I haue bene the more glad to follow for the most parte, accordynge as I was requyred." How closely Coverdale has followed these Douche = Deutsche, *i. e.*, German or German-Swiss interpreters, of " singular gifts and special diligence in the Bible," may be seen from the following parallel columns, where he has not

[1] Comp. Strype, Memor. iii. i. 232; The Zurich Letters, 1558 – 1570, the Parker Society's ed. p. 11.

only literally translated the Swiss Version, but even inserted its *parenthetical marks* : —

THE ZURICH or SWISS BIBLE		COVERDALE'S BIBLE.
Es ist nüts dañ eptelkeit (spricht der Prediger) ja eptelkeit alles.	i. 2	All is but vanitie (saieth the Preacher), all is but playne vanitie.
Dañ wz bleybt dem mēschen über von aller seiner arbeyt.	3	For what els hath a mā, of all the laboure.
Der wind durchwäyet mittag . . . kumpt er wider in sich selbst.	6	The wynde goeth towarde the south . . . turneth in to himself agayne.
Dann da die flüß hinlauffend, dannen här kommend sy auch wider.	7	For loke vnto what place the waters runne, thence they come agayne.
Die ding die gewesen sind, die werdend wider; vnnd die ding die geschehen sind geschehend wider.	9	The thinge that hath bene done, cōmeth to passe agayne; and the thinge that hath bene done, is done agayne.
Ich der Prediger ein Künig Israels vnnd Jerusalem, hab fleyß angewendt wie ich erfüre vnd durchgründte das wüssen aller dingen die vnder dem himmel geworden sind.	12	I myself the Preacher, beynge Kynge of Israel and Jerusalē, applyed my mynde to seke out and search for the knowledge of all thīges that are done vnder heauē.
Sóliche müy vnd arbeit hat Gott den menschen geben, das sy darinn gefestiget wurdind.	13	Such trouayle and laboure hath God geuē vnto the childrē of mē, to exercyse thē selues therī.
Dann wo vil weyßheit ist, da ist auch vil angst vnnd sorg.	18	For where moch wyszdome is there is also greate trouayle and disquietnes.
Also, das ich znm gelächter sprach.	ii. 2	In so moch that I sayde vnto laughter.
Ich bauwet herrliche schöne werke.	4	I made gorgious fayre workes.
Böum allerley früchten.	5	Trees of all manner frutes.

It will be seen that in the last two instances Coverdale has even followed the Swiss *construction*, at the expense of the English idiom, making "manner" an adjective, to imitate allerley früchten by *all manner frutes*. We cannot institute this comparison any further, as we should have to give by far the greater portion of the book, the instances in which Coverdale follows the Vulgate and Luther being comparatively few. The above examples are most decisive, inasmuch as they shew that Coverdale agrees with the Swiss Bible where the Swiss Bible deviates from the Hebrew. If, however, any one should still be so credulous as to believe that Coverdale, in translating from the Hebrew, hit exactly upon the same loose paraphrases and errors as the Swiss Bible, his credulity will vanish when he reads through the headings of the chapters, which we subjoin entire —

THE ZURICH or SWISS BIBLE.		COVERDALE'S VERSION.
Alle ding wie sy ermißt vnd betrachtet, sind sy eptel, vnder allen dingen nichts aber schwechers vnnd vnstäters dann der mensch.	i.	All thinges (yf a mā wyl cōsidre them wel) are but vanite. Neuertheles amōge them all there is nothīge weaker and more vnstedfast, then man him self.

THE ZURICH or SWISS BIBLE.

COVERDALE'S VERSION.

ii.

Er bildet in difem capitel vnd anderen offt an die red vnd fitten die die gottlofen treybend, damit er befter fomlicher zü verfchmächt aller creaturē, den menfchē allein vff Gott füre.

In this chapter (and in the other also) he maketh oft tymes mēsion of the wordes and conuersaciō of the vngodly ; that by this meanes he maye the better cause men to despyse all creatures, in respecte of the only euerlastinge God.

iii.

Leert das alle ding jr gelägne zeyt habend; kummer vnnd müy der in allenn dingen ift, gibt Gott dem menfchen zur übung. Was der menfch von feiner arbeit neüßt, ift ein gaab Gottes, dienet darzü das wir jn vor augen habind.

Euery thinge hath a tyme. There is no thīge, but God hath put tedyousnesse and trauayle in it, to exercise men withall. What so euer a man enioyeth of his laboure, the same is a gift of God, geuen to the intent that men shulde feare him.

iv.

Mangerley dingenn trachtung. Item das nichts fo hoch fey, verachtet es fein pflicht vnnd ampt, fo wirdt es auch verachtet.

A cōsideracion of diuerse thinges. There is nothinge so excellent and hye, but yf it do not the deuty and office where vnto it is ordered, it shalbe brought lowe.

v.

Wider die torechten vn kräffen glübd. Man fol fich nit verwun deren das vil vnbills gefchicht, dann der fchälcken find vil. Wider die reychen vnd reychtagen.

Agaynst foolish and temerarious vowes. Let no man maruayle that so moch euell is done, for the wicked are many. Agaynst the riche and agaynst riches.

vi.

Wider die reychen die jr reychtagen nit nieffen gethörend, wie torecht fy fpginb.

Agaynst those riche mē that darre not enioye their riches : how mad and foolish they be.

vii.

Niman weißß was güt vnnd fünfftig fey, wie foftlich ein güter nam fey. Von nußbarkeit der weyßheit.

No man knoweth what is for to come. How worthy a thīge is to haue a good name. The profit of wyszdome.

·viii.

Von gehorfame die man Gott vnd feinen oberen pflichtig ift. Von eyds pflicht: wie man die buldmüt Gottes nit verachten fol: das es vnmüglich fey dem menfchen die werck die in der welt find zü erburen.

Of the obediēce which men owe vnto God and to their heades. The lōge sufferaunce of God is not to be despised. It is not possible for eny mā to cōprehende the workes that be in the worlde.

ix.

Das es allen menfchen gleych gange, beßhalb der menfch mit fröuben vn danckbarkeit nieffen fol die gaaben Gottes: weyßheit übertriffst alle ding.

Like thinges happen vnto all men : therfore with myrth and thankfulnesse shulde men enioye the giftes of God. Wyszdome passeth all thinges

x., xi.

Hieriñ find vil weyfer fprüchen vnd nußbarer leeren, deß gleychen im eylfften.

In these two chapters are many wyse and profitable sentences, wel worthy to be considered of euery man.

xii.

In difem capitel zeiget der Prediger fein meinung gruntlich an, als wölte er fprechen, wie ich ioch von allen dinge die vnter der

In this chapter the preacher sheweth his whole meanynge, as though he wolde saye: As for all the thinges that be vnder the

THE ZURICH or SWISS BIBLE.   COVERDALE'S VERSION.

Sonnen find erfaren, betrachtet, xii. Sonne (wher of I haue spoken), I
vnd gerebt hab, fo ift doch das der   haue cõsidered them, and proued
befchlufß, Das nichts ftepff vñ veft   them metely wel by experience.
ift dañ Gott, vnb fein gericht von   And this is the conclucion, that
jugent auf vnb allweg vor angen   there is nothynge stedfast and
haben.   durable but God himself, whõ
                                         men ought to feare, and to haue
                                         his cõmanndements before their
                                         eyes euen from their youth vp.

With these facts before us, we are amazed at the ignorance prevalent
upon the sources of our first published English Bible, which has been made
the basis of succeeding versions, and that the editor of the reprint of
Coverdale's Bible should characterise it as " a faithful version of the
original Scriptures,"[1] and assert that the mention of its being translated
"out of the Douche and Latyn," which Coverdale was in conscience bound
to make, " was no doubt a bookselling artifice of the time, to make the
work circulate better, as being intimately connected with the Reformed
doctrines, which were then equally well known by the term German or
Dutch doctrines . . . that Coverdale did not follow Luther's version, it only
requires a very slight comparison of the text to prove ; but he no doubt
availed himself, *where there occurred any difficult reading*, of all the different
means of assistance within his power."[2]   More unpardonable is Anderson's
ignorance upon this version. He who would taunt Bishop Marsh with
having committed blunders respecting the sources of Tyndal's translation,
and with very bad taste triumphantly assert, " it is singular enough that no
English prelate should have ever made himself acquainted with the history,
character, and acquirements of William Tyndale,[3]" ought, in writing such
bulky volumes upon the Annals of the English Bible, to have been better
acquainted with the origin and merits of Coverdale's version than to assert,
with reference to " Coverdale's qualifications as a translator from the
original, there can be little or rather no question, after what Mr. Whittaker
has so ably written respecting his acquaintance with Hebrew, — though, at
the same time, his *leaning* to the Vulgate and German versions has been
made equally apparent by Professor Walter ; "—or to assure us, in a foot-note,
that " the interpreters themselves cannot now be positively fixed," and then
confidently to tell us that Coverdale " certainly does not appear to have
venerated ' these interpreters ' as *authority ;* he regarded their translations
with ' gladness,' and therefore could not, upon all occasions, be free from
some degree of bias."[4]   Had Anderson compared a single chapter in
Coverdale's Bible with the Swiss Version, he would not have committed
such egregious blunders. It is to be regretted that Mr. Pearson, the
editor of "Remains of Myles Coverdale," should have so positively declared,
in his biographical notice, that Coverdale's Version " throughout bears
marks of a close attention to the Original,"[5] and that Mr. Bastow should

[1] The Holy Scriptures Faithfully and Truly Translated, by Myles Coverdale,
Bishop of Exeter, 1535 ; reprinted by Samuel Bagster, 1838 ; Preface, p. iv.
[2] *Ibid.*, Bibliographical Description.
[3] The Annals of the English Bible, by Christopher Anderson, London, 1845,
vol. i. p. 285.
[4] The Annals of the English Bible, vol. i. p. 564.
[5] Remains of Myles Coverdale, edited for the Parker Society, by the Rev.
George Pearson, B. D., Rector of Castle Camps, p. xvi.

have implicitly copied these blunders in his very excellent and useful Bible Dictionary.[1]

As the Appendices are already larger than I anticipated, I must reserve the examination of the remaining English translations, including the Authorised Version, for the next volume, when it will be shewn that they are all more or less based upon the versions of antiquity.

III.

ADDENDA ET CORRIGENDA.

PAGE 58.

We have said, in the Introduction (p. 58), that Mr. Preston's mistranslation of Maimonides' vindication of Coheleth (i. 4), against the imputation that it propounds the eternity of the world, obliged us to make a new translation, which we subjoin, together with Mr. Preston's version, and the original.

הרבה מאנשי תורתינו חשבו כי שלמה ע״ה יאמין הקדמות ׳ וזה סלא איך ידמו בארם שהוא מאנשי
תורת מרע״ה שיאמין בקדמות ׳ ואם יחשוב אדם שזה נטיה ממנו מדיעות התורה ויציאה מעקרי הדת ׳
וחלילה לאלהים ׳ איך קבלוהו ממנו רב הנביאים והחכמים ולא חלקו עליו בו ולא גנזהו לאחר מותו ׳ כמו
שנמצא שחיבוחהו בנשים נכריות וזולתם ׳ ואמנם הביא אם להשיוב זה עליו ׳ מאמר ההכמי׳ בקשו לגנוז ספר
קהלת מפני שדבריו נוטים לדברי מינות ׳ וכן הוא העניין בלא ספק ׳ ר״ל שבפשושו של ספר ההוא ענייני׳
נוטים לצד דעות זרות מדעות התורה יצטרכו לפירוש ׳ ואין הקדמות מכללם ׳ ואין לו פסוק יורה על
הקדמות ולא ימצא לו בשום פנים פסוק מבואר בקדמות העולם ׳ אמנם יש לו פסוקים מורים על נצחותו
והוא אמת ׳ וכאשר ראו כתובים מורים על נצחותו השבו שהוא מאמין שהוא בלתי מחודש ואין הענין
כן ׳ אמנם לשונו בנצחות הוא אמרו ׳ והארץ לעולם עומדת ׳ עד שהוצרך מי שלא שיר בזה ההרוש
שיאמר הזמן המשותף לה ׳ יכן יאמרו באמרו יתצלה ׳ עוד כל ימי הארץ ׳ שהוא כל ימי הנגזרים לה ׳ ואני
תמיה מה יאמרו במאמר דוד ׳ יסד ארץ על מכוניה בל תמוט עולם ועד ׳ ואם יהיה ג״כ אמרו עולם ועד
לא יחייב הנצחות ׳ יהיה האל יתצלה א״כ יש לו מדת זמן אחת כי הכתוב אמר בנצהותי יתצלה ׳ ה׳ מלך
עולם ועד ׳ ואשר הרעהו שהעולם לא יחייב הנצחות אלא כשיחובר בו עד ׳ אם אחריו באמרו עולם ועד ׳
לפניו באמרו עד עולם ׳ א״כ מאמר שלמה ׳ לעולם עומדת ׳ למשה ממאמר דוד ׳ בל תמוט עולם ועד ׳
וכבר באר דוד עליו השלום וגלה נצחות השמי׳ והתמרת חקיהם וכל מה שבהם על עניין לא ישהנה לעולם
ואמרו ׳ הללו את יי׳ מן השמים וכו׳ כי הוא צוה ונבראו ויעמידם לעד לעולם חק נתן ולא יעבור ׳ רצוני
לומ׳ שאלו החקים אשר חקקם לא ישתנו לנצח ׳ כי זה החק רמז לחקות שמים וארץ הקודם זכרם ׳ אלא
שהוא כיאר שהם נבראים ואמר כי הוא צוה ונבראו ׳ ואמר ירמיה ע״ה נותן שמש שמש ואור יומם הקות ירח
וככבים לאור לילה אם ימושו החקים האלה מלפני נאם י׳ גם זרע ישראל ישבתו מהיות גוי ׳ כבר גלה ג״כ
שהם אצ״פי שהיו נבראים רצוני לומר אלו החקים הם לא ימושו ׳ וכטיבוקש זה ימצא בזולת דברי שלמה
ע״ה ׳ וכבר זכר ג״כ שלמה שאלו מיעשי האל ר״ל העולם ומה שבו עומדים על טבעם לנצח ואצ״פ שהם
עשויים ׳ אמר כי כל אשר יעשה האלהים הוא יהיה לעולם עליו אין להוסיף וממנו אין לגרוע ׳ הנה כבר
הגיד בזה הפסוק שהטעולם ממעשה האל ושהוא נצחי ׳ ונתן העלה גם כן בנצחותו והוא אמרו ׳ עליו
אין להוסיף וממנו אין לגרוע ׳ שזהו עלה להיותו לעולם ׳ כאלו אמר כי הרבר אשר ישתנה אמנם ישתנה
מפני חסרון כיס שיש בו וישולם ׳ או תוספת בו אין צורך אליה ותחסר התוספת ההיא ׳ אמנם פעולת
הש״י אחר שהם בתכלית השלמות ואי״א התוספת בהם ולא החסרון מהם ׳ אם כן הם יעמדו כפי מה
שהם עליו בהכרח שא״א הכצא דבר מבוא לשנויים ׳

MR. PRESTON'S TRANSLATION.

MANY men who hold our law think that Solomon believed in the existence of our world from all eternity. But it is wonderful that any one holding the law of Moses should believe in this doctrine. And if it had come into the mind of one who did not believe the statements of our law, it would not be wonderful; but God has shown that this cannot have been the case with Solomon, because all the prophets and wise men received his writings *as canonical,* and never called them in question, nor even after his death spoke at all disparagingly of him on this ground, as we find that they did with respect to certain "strange women," and several other matters; but what has led men to think so is the fact, that "our wise men sought to hide the book of Ecclesiastes, because of the apparent inconsistencies of many of its expressions;" and there can be no doubt that that book, taken in its obvious sense, contains expressions apparently repugnant to belief in the law. But as to the existence of the world from eternity, there is no passage to indicate that such was his belief, though there is one, it is true, which shows that *he believed that* the world will not perish, but last for ever. Because, then, they saw that there was a verse proving the stability of the world, they thought erroneously that he believed that the world was not created. Now the verse which speaks of the future eternal duration of the world is this: "The earth abides for ever." Some have interpreted the expression לְעוֹלָם as signifying only for a "definite" time. But I should like to know what they will make of the passage which we find in David, (Psalm x. 4, 5.) "He has founded the earth on its basis, that it should not be removed for ever and ever," עוֹלָם וָעֶד. But if you should say that the expression עוֹלָם וָעֶד does not demonstrate its eternal duration, but only its duration for a definite time, you will necessarily say at the same time,

NEW TRANSLATION.

MANY who adhere to our law thought that Solomon, peace be upon him, believed in the eternity of the world; but this is very strange.* How could they suppose that one who adheres to the law of Moses, peace be upon him, can at the same time believe in the eternity of the world? But if one should think that in this Solomon deviated from the teachings of the law, and departed from the articles of our religion, and God forbid this, how could the great prophets and sages receive this from him without contradicting or blaming him after his death, just as we find that they have condemned him for his strange women, and for some other things? This suspicion, however, arose from the fact that our sages wanted to make Coheleth apocryphal, because its sentiments incline to heresy. And indeed it is true that the obvious sense of the book inclines to doctrines foreign to our law, and requires explanation, but the eternity of the world is not amongst them; and there is not a single passage either propounding the eternity of the world, or even touching this subject, though there are passages in it setting forth its perpetuity, which forsooth is true. And when they saw that there were verses which show its perpetuity, they concluded that he also believed in its non-creation, which is not true. The passage which speaks of perpetuity is "the earth abideth for ever," (Coheleth i. 4.) and there are some even who, not being able to find in it the subject in question, take these words to denote a limited period, just as, they say, the words of the Most High, "while the earth remaineth." (Genesis vii. 18.) But I wonder what these persons will say to the declaration of David, "He has fixed the earth upon her foundations, she shall not be moved, (עוֹלָם וָעֶד) for ever and ever." (Psalm civ. 5.) If the phrase עוֹלָם וָעֶד does not denote *perpetuity,* then must the existence of the most high God himself have

MR. PRESTON'S TRANSLATION.

that the Creator will only reign for a definite time, as we find in Psalm x. 16: "The Lord is King עוֹלָם וָעֶד for evér and ever." Now it is generally allowed that עוֹלָם does not denote eternity of duration except when joined with עֶד. Solomon, therefore, speaks less strongly than David; but David furthermore, in the 148th Psalm, assures us that the heavens and all things they contain will last for ever, and will suffer no change; where he says, "Praise the Lord in the heavens, &c." to where he says, "he hath established them for ever and ever," וַיַּעֲמִידֵם לָעַד לְעוֹלָם and he adds, חָק נָתַן וְלֹא יַעֲבוֹר, i. e., "because the precepts which he has given will not be changed;" where by "precepts" he intends "the laws of nature," i. e., "the laws of the constitution of heaven and earth ordained before they were created." But that they were created, is clear from what he says, "he commanded, and they were created." Jeremiah also says, "Thus saith the Lord, who maketh the sun for a light by day, and the ordinances of the moon and the starsfor a light by night; if those ordinances depart from before me, saith the Lord, then the seed of Israel also shall cease from being a nation before me for ever." Here he informs us that those laws are never to be abrogated, though they were at first put into operation by supreme power. Solomon says, too, that "All things which God has made," (viz., the world and all things in it) "are stable in their nature, although all are created things;" for he has these words, "all things which God has made shall be for ever; no one can diminish from them or add to them;"

NEW TRANSLATION.

a definite period, since we find that the Scripture describes the perpetuity of the Most High by, "the Lord is King (עוֹלָם וָעֶד) for ever and ever." (Ps. x. 16.) And what thou shouldst know is that the word עוֹלָם does not denote perpetuity, except when עֶד is added to it, either after it as in the passage עוֹלָם וָעֶד or before it, as in the phrase עֶד עוֹלָם. This being the case, the phrase of Solomon, לְעוֹלָם עוֹמָדֶת, abideth for ever, (Coheleth i. 3.) is not even so strong as that of David, בַּל תִּמּוֹט עוֹלָם וָעֶד (Psalm civ. 5.) shall not be moved for ever AND EVER. Now David, peace be upon him, has already declared that the heavens and their ordinances will last for ever, and undergo no change, when he says, "Praise the Lord from the heavens, ... for he commanded and they were created, he hath also established them for ever and ever, he hath made a decree which shall not pass;" (Psalm cxlviii. 1 - 6.) i e., the ordinances which he has established will never be changed, for the word חֹק here denotes the ordinances of heaven and earth described in the preceding part of the psalm, although he declares that they were created, when he says "he commanded and they were created." (Ib. v. 5). So also Jeremiah, in the passage, "thus saith the Lord which giveth the sun for a light by day, and the ordinances of the moon and of the stars for a light by night, ... if those ordinances depart from before me, saith the Lord, then the seed of Israel shall also cease from being a nation before me for ever," (xxxi. 35, 36.) has already declared that the ordinances, though created, will never be abrogated. And if thou wilt examine it, thou wilt find the same in other passages of Solomon, peace be upon him; inasmuch as Solomon also affirms that these works of God, i. e., the world and all things therein, are perpetual in their nature, though they were created, since he says, "all things which God hath made shall exist for ever, nothing can be added

MR. PRESTON'S TRANSLATION.	NEW TRANSLATION.
and he thus at the same time states that the work of God, and all that is in it is the work of God, and assigns the reason of their eternal duration in the words, " There is no adding to them or diminishing from them ;" as if he had said, " everything which suffers change, suffers it either in consequence of some defect in it, where there is a want of perfection, or of some superabundance of something not necessary to its perfection ; but since the works of the Creator are absolutely perfect, and no addition or diminution can be made in them, they will necessarily remain as they are, because there is nothing to induce change in them."	to them, nor can anything be taken away from them ;" (Coheleth iii. 14.) thus declaring here that the world is created by God, and yet is perpetual. He moreover gives the cause of its perpetual duration, when he says, " nothing can be added to it or taken away from it," (Ibid.) and herein lies the cause of its perpetual existence ; as if he had said, Every thing which suffers change, suffers it either because it has some defect, and hence must be perfected, or because it has something redundant and useless, and this must be removed! But since the works of the blessed God are absolutely perfect, as it is impossible that they should have anything redundant, or be defective, therefore they must necessarily remain as they are, because it is impossible that any thing could be found to induce a change.

PAGE 11.

בן זונין is to be rendered the *son of Zonin*, or *ben Zonin.*

PAGE 66.

The point in which they are all alike is that they were all obliged to alter the literal sense of the book into palatable sentiments, and none of them gave a plausible reason how he could draw wholesome food, or elicit sweetness from this rock, is a more correct rendering of Aramah's words, הצד השוה שבהם שכלם נדחקים לשנות את טעמו בדברי' מתוקים ולא אחד בהם נתן בו טעם לשבח בטעמים מספיקים מן הסלע נוציא מאכל בריאה ומעו יצא ממתקים.

PAGE 293, CHAP. ii. 16.

It is not Ibn Ezra himself, but one quoted by him, who takes בשכבר in the sense of כשכבר, *as in time past.* The passage quoted (p. 293) is to be translated *one of the interpreters said that* בשכבר *denotes* TIME PAST, *but when he saw that the words* הימים הבאים *stood in his way, he said it ought to be* כשכבר.

PRINTED BY DAVID MARPLES, LORD STREET, LIVERPOOL.

Lightning Source UK Ltd.
Milton Keynes UK
UKOW06f2325130416

272213UK00018B/378/P